SUSAN B. ANTHONY

BY KATHARINE ANTHONY

SUSAN B. ANTHONY:

HER PERSONAL HISTORY
AND HER ERA

Doubleday & Company, Inc.

GARDEN CITY, NEW YORK, 1954

LIBRARY OF CONGRESS CATALOG CARD NUMBER 54-8919

PREFACE & ACKNOWLEDGMENTS

◦§ Though Susan B. Anthony has often been called the greatest woman this country has produced, she has not been a great favorite with its biographical writers. In many ways her fame has been memorably preserved; by monuments such as the big California tree named for her, the Susan B. Anthony Memorial House in Rochester, the statue in the National Capitol and the bust in the Hall of Fame, the numerous documentary collections in the public libraries, and—more than all else—by the final triumph of her lifetime strivings, the Susan B. Anthony amendment. But aside from her first biography, written partly during her life and completed after her death, and two chronicles of later date, one of them a juvenile work, her life has not made its due mark on the literary field. Considering that almost fifty years have elapsed since her death, this is a small harvest.

Her memory has survived mainly by tradition; by newspaper clippings, anniversary papers, memorial addresses, and commemorative pamphlets. Through this medium she has come down to us as the symbol of her cause, as the official representative of the fifty-odd years of its history with which she was identified. In this somewhat less than human form, the legend has long preserved her. The organization that she fostered so well that it still persists under new aims and designations has always kept her name on the masthead. But behind the name the personality of the woman has continued rather vague and to some extent even distorted.

The purpose of this biography is to restore the woman behind the name as nearly as possible from the existing documentary materials. It is not a history of the woman suffrage movement but the history of a woman's life. At the same time the movement, which was as much a part of her as her own arms and legs, forms the foreground of her picture. Also essential to her portrait are the many historical persons and events with whom and with which she was vitally connected. But the main effort has been to depict her as a human being with arms and legs, impulses and emotions, experiences and reactions; not as the figurehead of the feminist cause.

The girl who sprang from a small nest of Quakers in the northern Berkshires and became in adult life one of the leading reformers of her age challenges some curiosity. Susan remained a Quaker all her life. On her eightieth birthday she wrote to a group of Quakers in Virginia, "I still retain my membership in the Hicksite Friends of Rochester." Without disturbing her original roots she grew and branched out as an effective public character and a highly matured personality: "one of the most wonderfully balanced women of the world," as someone aptly called her in an obituary tribute. The cause she led has been described by some historians as the most important of the century. In a list of American social reformers of the past included in the World Almanac, fourteen out of the twenty persons named were famous as workers for woman suffrage. The importance of her reform measures the great distance she traveled. All this she accomplished in an age when a woman was handicapped by sex at every turn and proceeded at her own risk with every untried step. With each advance, she carried, as it were, the whole of American womanhood with her. She always insisted that *they* carried *her*, but it was she who stood at the front and took the brickbats and the epithets.

Susan did not enter the suffrage movement early. She was thirty when Mrs. Stanton and her husband introduced her to the principles of Jeffersonian democracy. Henceforth the die was cast. With the zeal of a convert she embraced the new faith. Since democracy obviously meant that women should vote, she saw this as the first requirement for democracy's fulfillment. To the end of her life she remained a passionate democrat, seeing the vote as the symbol of women's emancipation and independence as well as the indispensable condition of a true republican government. The pursuit of the ballot brought many incidental benefits and privileges in its wake. In her old age, still voteless, she conceded, "The world has never witnessed a greater revolution than in the status of woman during this past half-century." But she knew full well that all these things would never have come about except as the result of raising a higher and more radical standard.

Could Susan B. Anthony return to the scene of her activities, she would probably be disappointed with the fruits of the victory she gave her life to win. The relatively small part played by women in practical politics, the many invidious state laws that stand on the books, the small proportion of women in the highest centers of learning—such survivals would probably affront her as much as they ever did.

More than all else would she deplore the continuing low level of women's incomes. Next to the vote for her sex, she pioneered for economic independence. She summed up the matter by saying, "A condition of dependence, pecuniary or political, can not bring about the best development of any individual or any class." In her long crusade for suffrage she often paused to complain about the poverty of her sex. Of her spiritual successors, only Virginia Woolf has been more outspoken on the subject. That the millions of women holding jobs in the U.S.A. still earn less than half of the men's wages would be shocking intelligence for Susan. Perhaps it is just as well for those who have inherited her mission that, as she once told her friend, Annie Besant, very firmly, she had no intention of returning to this troubled planet once she had left it.

Susan lived her life almost entirely without beauty. Her excursions into the aesthetic were enjoyable but rare and unnecessary. She cared little about music or poetry or art. Novels were judged by their ethical or philosophical content. She enjoyed nature but was more interested in its scientific implications than in its other aspects. She had a real allergy for romance. When her followers began calling her "Joan of Arc" she stopped that very quickly. A reporter who once asked her, "What thanks did you receive for the stand you made?" obtained the simple answer: "I had my own thanks for retaining my self-respect." Always bluntly honest, she reached out for nothing in her career or environment that she did not inwardly desire, and she had little craving for the artistic embellishments of life. She herself was perfectly aware of this. She had a fine ear and eye for the beauty of ethical conduct, and that was all she asked for aesthetic enjoyment.

This biography owes a special debt to Ida Husted Harper's three-volume work on the Life of Susan B. Anthony, published in 1897 and 1908. Its comprehensive survey of her public career, year by year, has furnished, as it was intended to do, a guidebook to that side of her life. For the personal aspects of her history, I am indebted to the many relatives and friends of Miss Anthony who have generously loaned letters, diaries, and reminiscences, and have patiently answered questions by correspondence. To Ann Anthony Bacon, Susan B. Anthony's niece, who loaned me her aunt's diaries and many of her letters; to Martha Taylor Howard, of the Rochester Memorial House; and to Percy E. Clapp of the Records Committee, Society of Friends, my acknowledgments are due for encouragement and help extending over a long period. Among the many others whose kindness I have drawn upon are: Emma Swift and Marion Mosher, of the Rochester Public Library; Florence Mosher, Rochester; the late Emma B. Sweet, Rochester; Dr. David Rhys Williams, Rochester; Mary S. Baum, Adams (Mass.) Free Library; the late William B. Browne, North Adams; Mrs. Grant Tefft, of the Greenwich (N.Y.) *Journal*; Oren B. Wilbur, Society of Friends, Easton, N.Y.; Luther B. Anthony, Raubsville, Pa.; Thomas K. Baker, Kansas City, Mo.; Mrs. Henry A. Baker, Reno, Nev.; Mary Mosher Winchell, Severna Park, Md.; Una R. Winter, Upland, Cal.; Dorothy G. Harris, Swarthmore, Pa.; Anna B. Hewitt, Haverford, Pa.; Amy Ver Nooy, Poughkeepsie, N.Y.; Anne Stanton Burchard, New York; and Edna Yost, New York. This is by no means a complete list, as many others have informally, and even inadvertently, helped me in the course of my research.

I should state here explicitly that none of these kind persons is in any way responsible for the faults or merits of this book. For the development and interpretation of the facts which they and other accredited sources have given me, I am alone responsible. Any impressions or ideas which are conveyed or expressed in the attempted unfolding of Susan B. Anthony's life are entirely my own.

CONTENTS

x   *Contents*

ILLUSTRATIONS

SUSAN B. ANTHONY

"I WAS BORN A QUAKER"

‌🙢 I   There is no famous character in American history who can show a longer and more detailed ancestry than Susan B. Anthony. It was not a matter in which Susan B. herself took any great interest, being a woman who was primarily concerned with the doings of her own times; and, in her dictated biography, written near the end of her life, it receives but brief and passing attention. It is, however, so lengthy and documented as to be regarded as valuable Americana, interesting, for its own sake, to those who like to probe into the origins of American culture, and furthermore interesting as the specific background of the individual, character, and personality known as Susan B. Anthony. The mysterious confluence and combination of ancestral influences and tendencies which helped in her case to shape a human destiny are certainly something to be pondered upon.

The reason for our detailed knowledge lies mainly in the long line of Quaker forebears—six generations of them—who preceded her and in the meticulous care with which the Quakers recorded their births, deaths, and marriages, and partly in the five generations of English ancestors who preceded the American Quakers and who were important enough to leave their names on record. Originating the five English generations was the first recorded ancestor, William Anthony, who, until 1515, had lived in Cologne, Germany. The said William Anthony, presumably a German, was the impasse beyond which the family genealogist did not dare to go.

Not being a genealogist, we may embark on a theory. A little knowledge of the history of Cologne informs us that it was founded by the Emperor Claudius at the request of his wife, whose name was Agrippina, on a spot on the Rhine where she was born. He planted a colony of Romans there which was called Colonia Agrippina, to be eventually changed to Cologne. It was a thriving Italian colony for more than three hundred years, when the Germans took it over. William Anthony of Cologne bore a surname which is unknown in the German language but is familiar enough in Italian. It is probable that he inherited his name and lineage from some early Roman or Italian colonist. At the age of twenty he was a skillful goldsmith—a trade that suggests Italian rather than German extraction. The goldsmith trade achieved its climax in Italy during the lifetime of William Anthony in the work of Benvenuto Cellini, almost an exact contemporary.

Arriving in London in 1515, William Anthony in time became chief mint engraver to the court of Edward VI, settling down and occupying this office during the reign of Edward, Mary, and a part of the reign of Elizabeth. He was a man for whom one migration was apparently enough. We assume that he was a Protestant. A little further knowledge of the history of Cologne suggests that he may have been driven out of the city by the excessive Protestant-baiting which characterized its government around 1515, the year of his departure.

The goldsmith's descendants in England became physicians. His grandson, Dr. Francis Anthony, achieved his alphabetical place in the *Biographia Britannica*, and after a long and contumacious life was buried in the church of St. Bartholomew the Great, where a handsome tablet celebrates his memory. Two sons of Dr. Francis also became physicians. Dr. John Anthony, the elder, lived in Hampstead, where his son John—occupation unknown—was born. This particular scion, in the spring of 1634, sailed from Hampstead for America on the good ship *Hercules*. When he left his native land he had reached the mature age of twenty-seven.

We may assume that he was a Puritan. Also, he chose a good time for his departure. The battle between Charles I and his Parliament was on, the persecution of the Puritans by Bishop Laud with the King's connivance was at its height, and the Puritans were leaving for the New World in droves. John Anthony's choice of destination was singular but favorable. He landed in Portsmouth, Rhode Island, when the province was still a wilderness belonging to the Indians. Roger Williams and the Providence Plantation were still two years off in the future. Rhode Island was then, and continued under Roger Williams to be, free of all religious controls, the refuge of the various dissenters and recusants who had had to flee first from England's and latterly from Massachusetts' bigotry and intolerance. John Anthony took up land, which was lying around everywhere "for free," and married one Susanna Potter. His descendants remained quiescent in Portsmouth and its vicinity for the following one hundred and thirty-six years.

II   But not completely quiescent. A further and more intense religious adventure awaited them. Mary Dyer introduced Quakerism into Rhode Island in 1657, and one of the first converts to the Quaker faith was Abraham Anthony, the son of the first settler. With Abraham Anthony and his wife, Alice Wodell, begins the long list of marriages, births, and deaths marking the progress of four generations of John Anthony's descendants through the Friends' records of Portsmouth and Dartmouth.

They were reasonably quiescent, inasmuch as none of them, so far as we know, defied the Massachusetts authorities by entering the forbidden state. Quakers from Rhode Island who did so came home with their ears cut off, the marks of flogging on their backs, or the effects of a long jail sentence upon them. Sometimes they came not home at all, for the final penalty for entering Massachusetts was hanging. Four of Abraham Anthony's fellow citizens in Portsmouth thus attained martyrdom. One of them was the dauntless Mary Dyer, who was hanged on the Boston Common in 1660 for this capital offense. The early Anthonys, having entered the country by way of Rhode Island and having no connections with Boston, apparently stayed clear of the fatal city.

Abraham Anthony and his descendants continued steadfast in the Quaker belief, confirmed and strengthened therein by the visit of George Fox, the English founder, to Rhode Island in 1671. Quaker married Quaker, and the resulting Quaker families lived together in isolated groups, since their religious code demanded a simplicity of living which distinctly set them apart from ordinary or "worldly" men. The Anthonys followed the Quaker rules in all respects and were duly listed in the successive monthly and yearly records. Abraham, the first Quaker, was followed by William, Jr., who was followed by David. William, Jr., lived in a settlement of Friends in Dartmouth, Massachusetts, just across the border. Apparently Quakers in Dartmouth, so close to Rhode Island, were not molested by the Massachusetts authorities. Here David Anthony was born, reared, and duly married to Judith Hicks, "6th 3 mo. (called Mar.), 1747, O.S." Two sons were born in Dartmouth, Elihu and Humphrey, the latter on "February 2, 1770, N.S."

In the same year David Anthony and his wife joined with other Dartmouth Quakers in a migratory project. Religion does not seem to have had much to do with it, beyond the customary desire of the Friends to live in a restricted community. Some Quakers from Smithfield, Rhode Island, had set forth for the promised land in northwestern Massachusetts in 1769; in 1770 a Dartmouth group of families—including David Anthony, his wife, and his two sons—accomplished the long and perilous journey into the Berkshire wilderness.

◄§ III In a faraway corner of the northern Berkshires lay an irregularly shaped valley known as East Hoosac. The ownership of the district had formerly been a subject of dispute between Massachusetts and New York. Drained by the Hoosac River, which flowed north and emptied into the Hudson, and separated from the southerly Berkshires by the Pittsfield watershed, the district's natural outlet was the Hudson River and the cities along its banks. But after some argument with "sundry gentlemen from Albany," the Massachusetts Legislature had captured the valley for that state. In due time it became the background of Williamstown, Adams, and Cheshire—all Massachusetts towns.

On this lonely Berkshire region the Quakers of Dartmouth and Smithfield had fixed their attention and built their hopes. It was not unlike a neglected strip to the south, between Connecticut and the Hudson, into which Quakers from New York had already filtered and where they had already built villages. Whatever happened to any of the Quakers was soon known to all the others in the intensive social relationships they cultivated. The Quakers from

Rhode Island followed the example of the Dutchess County Quakers by taking over the neglected valley to the north. They continued to invade it for two years, after which the stream apparently began to slacken. The Hoosac acres were not unlimited like those of the true American West, which, incidentally, the settlers of 1770 thought they had just about reached. The Quakers soon owned most of the farms in the vicinity.

Almost at once they organized the East Hoosac Friends' Meeting and within a few years they built the meeting house, which still stands as the chief historical ornament of the town of Adams.

Other farmers, not Quakers, took charge of local political affairs, including the incorporation of East Hoosac into a town called Adams. (The Quakers held to East Hoosac.) The political complexion of Adams may be judged from the fact that the town was named for Samuel, not John, Adams. Of the two patriots, the more fiery stood godfather to the Berkshire settlement. The local sentiment, excluding the Quakers, who naturally took no part in the war, was highly revolutionary.

How little Massachusetts has changed during the course of years can be seen from the following episode. In September 1950 the North Adams *Transcript* came out with a highly indignant editorial denouncing a Cape Cod publication which had printed a paragraph decrying the Berkshires. The Cape Codder stated that in its own vicinity there were "no dark pockets in the hills such as one finds in the western part of the state where isolation and ignorance have brought about conditions quite appalling." The *Transcript* demanded a full apology, which was handsomely made, and the feud of 1950 was ended. But it shows how persistently the idea of the remoteness and wildness of the Berkshire settlements has lingered in the more populated regions of the East.

◄§ IV   When David and Judith Anthony arrived in East Hoosac, they acquired a large farm on the slope of Mount Greylock. Like all the other settlers who had come from a seaboard community, David Anthony had to adapt himself to a wholly new mode of life. Surrounded by steeps and hills, the settlers turned to cattle raising and cheese producing, which they carried on famously, until soon the name of Berkshire cheese became a household word. In spite of the great distance, they drove their cattle and carried their cheese to Boston, the only great market they had ever known. David Anthony and his son Humphrey after him faithfully adhered to the practice. All his life Humphrey Anthony drove his cattle through the difficult passes of the Berkshires and all the way across the state to find a market for them.

David and Judith Anthony prospered on their farm and added six children in Adams to the two they had brought from Dartmouth. They became an important family, only slightly less important than the Lapham family, who had pioneered from Smithfield in the same year and who owned a large tract of land on the so-called Intervale, a bench at the foot of the Green Mountains. It was eminently suitable that a son of the Anthonys should marry a daughter of the Laphams. Humphrey Anthony, aged twenty-three, and Hannah Lapham, aged twenty, were married in the Quaker meeting house on March 21, 1793.

Humphrey and Hannah Anthony lived on the Lapham farm, in a home Hannah's father built for them. The homestead was eventually bequeathed to Hannah by her father and entailed upon her children. Of these she had nine. Her oldest son was already begetting offspring before she ceased bearing hers. Such an overlapping was not unusual for the time when eight, nine, or ten children formed the average family.

◄§ V   Hannah Lapham Anthony was a handsome brunette with very dark eyes. She became an elder of the Quaker Meeting, as her mother had been before her, but neither mother nor daughter had the true gift of speaking. They were none the less revered and honored. Hannah Anthony, however, manifested one indulgence: she ordered her silken Quaker bonnets from New York, and the rest of her attire, though in Quaker style, was correspondingly elegant. Her husband, Humphrey Anthony, had blue eyes, was an excellent farmer and mechanic, and was content with the simplest Quaker rating. His wife and his mother-in-law attained the High Seat.

Their eldest son, Daniel, came into the world on January 26, 1794, with the black eyes of his mother. He was soon followed by two sisters, Susannah and Hannah, and, after an interval, by a brother, John; and then by brothers and sisters until Humphrey, Jr., the ninth child, was reached. A schoolhouse was built beside the road and a teacher employed by the parents for the education of their own and the neighbors' children. In this school, which must have been pretty good, Daniel and his sisters showed early promise. Daniel continued alternately working for his father and attending school until he was eighteen.

About this time Hannah Lapham Anthony, who ordered her bonnets from New York, manifested other ambitious ideas. She was more aware of the world outside than the average East Hoosac Quaker. For instance, by the year of her son Daniel's birth, she had observed the establishment of Williams College at the foot of Mount Greylock, about ten miles from her home. Although Williams College from the first had no specific religious connection, it was, from the Quaker point of view, a worldly institution and promoted a worldly education which Quakers could not endorse. To Hannah Lapham Anthony, this college, almost under her nose, suggested the idea of higher education, unsuitable though it was for the young Quakers of Adams.

Three years after Williams came the establishment of a Quaker boarding school in Dutchess County, New York. It was called the Nine Partners' School from the name of the district in which it was located and the name of the Quaker Meeting with which it was associated. The Nine Partners' School represented a much-heralded enterprise of the New York Yearly Meeting, brought about by the persistent and year-long efforts of a group of progressive members. From the time of its establishment its fame spread far and wide, and Quakers from as far away as Boston sent their children there to be educated. Its early teachers were specialists in their subjects; some published textbooks with a wide reputation and used in worldly schools.

The fame of Nine Partners' penetrated to Hannah Anthony's attention and became the goal of her ambition for her children. Why she waited so long to send her son Daniel there is a question. Her husband, Humphrey Anthony, had to be persuaded, and the year of Daniel's entrance, 1812, is suggestive of another reason. In that year, the first of the renewed war with England, Williams College was all but decimated by the call for recruits—Williams was, in fact, almost wiped out by the ensuing three years of war. Humphrey

Anthony, a true Quaker at heart, though not of the High Seat, could not conscientiously support a war. Most likely the war crisis induced him to yield to his wife's insistence that Daniel, who had reached the ripe age for enlistment, should be quietly immured in the Quaker school at Nine Partners'. It was in line with his Quaker principles that the girls should share the same advantage. So Daniel's two sisters, aged seventeen and fifteen, were sent along with him. They did not return home, even for a visit, for over two years. By that time the War of 1812 was about finished.

An unexpected hitch occurred at the end. Daniel, who had become an assistant teacher at the age of nineteen, wished to remain in that capacity instead of returning to the farm. Humphrey's indignation and disgust knew no bounds. Daniel came home eventually, provided with flattering testimonials from his co-workers, which he carefully preserved throughout a lifetime. Reluctantly he resumed his duties on the farm.

Humphrey had seen enough. When his fourth child, John, stimulated by his mother, asked for his turn at Nine Partners', Humphrey bought him off with one hundred dollars. Hannah Lapham Anthony's ambitious designs were therewith arrested for all time. The rest of the children were forced to get along with such education as the parental school afforded. This was considerably improved by the teaching ability of young Daniel, which Humphrey was willing he should employ in the home school when farm work allowed it.

The two Anthony girls likewise showed the effects of their schooling in being less satisfied than formerly with the simple ways of East Hoosac life. However, they were soon married and Humphrey was relieved of their guidance. Susannah married Thomas Brownell, a Quaker, and Hannah married Isaac Upton Hoxie, a non-Quaker of Adams. After one year of marriage, Susannah Brownell died, childless. Hannah Hoxie, after her one misstep in marrying out of unity, began to show the good effects of her Nine Partners' training. Though married to the worldly Hoxie, she adhered faithfully to Quaker ways and soon showed signs of possessing the true gift of speaking. She outstripped her mother and grandmother by becoming a minister and a well-known Quaker preacher, speaking at quarterly and yearly meetings from Adams to New York, always with great acclaim. She became the chief ornament

of the East Hoosac congregation and one of the most creditable
and distinguished graduates of the Nine Partners' School.

◆§ VI In Cheshire, lying just to the south of Adams and drained
by the upper Hoosac, a rival though friendly community of Baptists
had been set up shortly before the Quakers arrived in Adams. The
first Baptists came from Rhode Island, and Cheshire was first called
the New Providence Plantation. Their first thought was to secure
a proper spiritual leader and pastor. This was achieved in the person
of Elder Werden, who came to Cheshire from Providence in 1770
and served the congregation till 1791, when he was succeeded by
Elder John Leland. Elder Leland attained fame as the donor of the
mammoth cheese made by the women of Cheshire and presented
to President Thomas Jefferson in Washington in 1801. The donation is significant, as evidence of the thriving dairy industry uniting
Cheshire and Adams and of the political atmosphere prevailing in
both towns. The two historic gestures of these towns pertained to
Samuel Adams and Thomas Jefferson. The worldly population of
Adams and the Baptists of Cheshire were evidently Republicans in
the classic sense of the word.

The Baptists flocked into Cheshire for a few years. With them,
as with the Quakers, it seems that religion had little to do with
their migration. The persecution of the Baptists, who, like the
Quakers, had been whipped at the cart's tail in Massachusetts, had
been relaxed. Still, the sect, perhaps fearing a recurrence, was restless. Jonathan Richardson's family left prosperity and comfort in
Scituate, Massachusetts, to join the Baptist settlers in the Berkshire wilderness. They stood high in the fold, Richardson being the
clerk of the Cheshire congregation. Another pioneer family, the
Reads from Rehoboth, Massachusetts, likewise sat under Elder
Werden, the American patriot. Within a few years the daughter
and the son of these pioneer families, Susannah Richardson and
Daniel Read, were married.

It was shortly after this that the Revolutionary War began. The
Baptists of Cheshire, having no pacifist scruples, were at once involved. Elder Werden called for enlistments from the pulpit.
Daniel Read, just married, was the first to stand up. In his subsequent army career he saw most of the important actions in New

England. He fought under Ethan Allen at Ticonderoga, under
Arnold at Quebec, under Stafford at Bennington, and under John
Brown at Stone Arabia. He served with honor everywhere but did
not achieve the rank of officer. Apparently reluctant to leave the
army, he came home some time after peace was declared, having
spent all in all about ten years in the service.

That his wife Susannah had learned to manage very nicely without him goes without saying. Still, he settled down to the business
of farming and family-breeding with such grace as he could muster.
Six children were added to the one he had left behind him, and
with the help of his upstanding wife his farming business prospered.
Around 1800 he bought a farm of a hundred acres lying at the
junction of Cheshire and Adams in a nook called then, and still so
called, Bowen's Corners. Samuel Bowen kept a tavern there, and a
main-traveled road, the Savoy Road, leading eastward through the
Berkshires, ran past it.

Besides Sam Bowen, the ex-soldier's nearest neighbor was
Humphrey Anthony, whose considerable acreage adjoined his own
comparatively modest domain. Humphrey Anthony, the Quaker,
and Daniel Read, the Baptist, had besides their differing religions
little else in common. Between Read and Sam Bowen, on the other
hand, there sprang up at once a strong friendship. Presumably
Bowen, like Read, had seen army service. At any rate, the two men
found a great deal to talk about, so that Read spent more time in
the tavern than on his farm. But his wife ran the farm and so little
harm was done.

Read used some of his spare time to dabble in politics. He was
elected to a few local offices and in 1814 sat in the Massachusetts
Legislature. Mrs. Ida Husted Harper's biography of Susan B. Anthony says that her grandfather, Daniel Read, was a Whig in politics. This seems unlikely, since there was no Whig party at the time
(at least in this country) and the Whig party which arose later
was an outgrowth of the Federalist group. That Read, coming from
the Berkshires and uniting this with a rebellious temperament,
could have been a Federalist seems most improbable. It seems
much more likely that he was a Republican of the Jefferson-Madi-
son vintage. He survived only one year in the Massachusetts Legislature, which was dominated by the commercial and shipping interests of the East. That a Berkshire townsman should have
survived long among these interests is not likely.

Daniel Read's chief claim to fame rested on his leaving the Baptist Church to become a Universalist. How this ultra-radical belief ever penetrated to his sequestered life is not recorded, but we might recall that Read, in his prolonged army years, had gone places and seen things. He might have met a Universalist missionary on his wide tours. Furthermore, Samuel Bowen, his great friend, had embraced the same religion. The two men were regarded as a public scandal, inasmuch as they refused to acknowledge the existence of a literal hell. It was plain that they were such great sinners they could not admit the certainty of their doom. Had they been quiet about their beliefs they would have been less notorious; but from their stronghold in Bowen's Tavern they preached their heresies and made ceaseless propaganda for Free Salvation.

The handful of Universalists left a strong mark on the town. About twenty years later a young man named Nathaniel Hawthorne visited Adams on one of his adventurous tours. He recorded his impressions in a journal which was ultimately reprinted in his *American Note-Books*. One entry reads:

Aug. 18, 1838. In the evening there was a strange fellow in the bar-room . . . a cattle drover, who had stopped there for a night with two cows and a Durham bull. All of his talk turned upon religion. A group of Universalists and no-religionists sat around him, making him their butt and holding wild arguments with him. . . . While this fellow was enumerating Universalists in neighboring towns, who had turned from their errors on their deathbeds, some one exclaimed, "John Hodges? Why, he isn't dead. He's alive and well." Whereat a roar of laughter.

It is not to strain the point to suggest that John Hodges could have been Daniel Read; Hawthorne would naturally have altered the name. Read had removed from the vicinity several years previously and was living with his daughter in New York State. For all that his former neighbors knew, he was "alive and well"; but as a matter of fact he had just died in his daughter's home. In one respect his defenders were faithful to the spirit if not the fact of his end. He never retreated from his convictions and died at a ripe old age strong in the Universalist faith.

Susannah Read remained strong in the Baptist belief. She prayed unceasingly for her husband and bore her lifelong grief at his defection as best she could. She is said to have worn "the skin off her knees" petitioning for him. But the work of running the farm and caring for seven children left her little time for grieving. Daniel's neglect of business is ascribed by family tradition to a general impairment of his health brought on by his long war service. He lived to the age of eighty-four without any major illness of any kind. As for his idleness, it is a common observation that a long war service does not prepare a man well for the everyday business of life. He left a respectable estate, accumulated by the industry and thrift of his wife.

≈§ VII   Of the children of this pair we have to concern ourselves with but two, both of them daughters. The little girl who was left in embryo when her father went away to war was given the name of Avis. Avis was six or seven years old when she first saw her father, but she grew up to be amazingly like him. In Susan B. Anthony's personal reminiscences she says of this aunt of hers:

There was but one woman in the country who knew anything about politics,—knew about Andrew Jackson and Thomas Jefferson and everything that was going on in the world outside. She was Aunt Avis Read, Daniel's daughter. . . . This woman was beyond the ordinary. She was a democrat; something of an invalid; smoked her pipe, sat in a corner, and read the papers. People used to come from miles around to hear her talk politics; men, of course. Women thought her strange and queer. What she had to say at an election or a campaign was of vital interest to the voters, because she was informed, and information in those days was gained by concentrated attention on whatever news was available. There were no daily papers, only a few monthly papers or magazines, and these were considered a great advance in civilization.

A second daughter of the Reads was born after her father's return from the Revolutionary War, on December 2, 1793, and was called Lucy. She was as different from Avis as could be; pretty, playful, and feminine. Lucy was about seven when her parents brought her to Bowen's Corners, adjoining Humphrey Anthony's farm in Adams. She attended the local school, learned to spin, bake, and sew, and grew into the docile child of her strong-minded female parent. She showed her father's influence in only one respect: when she had reached the age of twenty-three, she was still uninitiated into the Baptist Church. In still another respect her father's influence prevailed: she was allowed to dance.

~§ VIII   In 1815 the war was over. Even faraway Adams felt the general lightening of the pressure and took up life again with a renewed sense of ease. The Quaker farmers improved their holdings, expanded their pastures, and built new roads. Williams College, which had all but passed out, drew a new breath of life. The young veterans came home in numbers, for in spite of the state's official opposition the young men of the Berkshires had enlisted heavily. There was much marrying and giving in marriage. Within a short space of time Humphrey Anthony's three oldest children were married to local partners.

Daniel Anthony, freshly returned from distant parts and fabulously educated, was running the school on his father's premises. Although Lucy Read was pretty tall to be a pupil, her parents thought it wise to send her to the fount of culture just opened down the road. At the cost of only a few dollars she could benefit at second hand from the culture of Nine Partners'. Less intellectual than her sister Avis, she had a taste for reading and was not unintelligent.

So the blue-eyed Lucy Read became one of the advanced pupils in the school of Friend Daniel Anthony. Her teacher taught her to memorize lines of Cowper's *Task* and Young's *Night Thoughts*, the standard literary course at Nine Partners'. His own best subjects were mathematics and mechanics, but these were not suitable for a pupil who, both by sex and taste, was inclined to the more graceful faculties. Of the same age, teacher and pupil were quickly aware of the differences of sex, and the inevitable soon happened. As if the Anthonys and Reads had planned it, which they certainly had not, Daniel and Lucy fell in love.

They were married on July 13, 1817, aged twenty-three. Lucy Read, of the romantic turn, always remembered the season and described it to her children as the time "when strawberries were ripe in East Hoosac." The courtship and marriage, with a ceremony by the justice of the peace, were very quiet. Neither family was much pleased, though signs of active opposition are lacking.

It was the first marriage of an Anthony outside of the Society of Friends for many generations (though Daniel's sister Hannah soon afterward followed his example). One can imagine the influences to which Friend Humphrey attributed these deviations of his children and the untenable position in which they placed his good wife. It was a fact (which Humphrey perhaps did not know) that the local magnate of Nine Partners' village, one Thomas Hart, was a Baptist who had married a Quaker and that this happy and prosperous couple maintained their separate religions in marriage. But for this insidious example, it is indeed possible that Daniel would never have married outside the fold.

Lucy Read herself had some qualms about marriage with a strict young Quaker. Susan B. Anthony, her daughter, reflecting back upon it in after years, concluded that it was "a pretty adventurous romance." In anticipation of the quiet life she would lead with her Quaker husband, Lucy stipulated that she was to have one last dancing party before the final act. Daniel agreed and accompanied her to the farewell gala. He sat against the wall, stolidly upright in his broad-brimmed hat, watching, while Lucy danced with one partner after the other until four o'clock in the morning. If in all her life she ever again asserted herself to the same extent there is positively no record of it.

The young couple had departed on their honeymoon trip before the news got well around. The wedding journey was Daniel's idea, a splurge, carried out in style. In a light one-horse wagon, a buggy, they took off across New York State and covered an incredible distance over the poor roads of the time. They did not turn back until they reached Rochester, New York, which in 1817 was a thriving village founded by a Maryland colonel of that name. Neither Daniel nor Lucy dreamed at that time that Rochester held any promise in the future for them. Daniel may have met some Quakers there, for it was in that same year that the Quaker pioneers began coming in.

Not to overestimate their adventurousness, it might be noted that they had been preceded by some individuals from Lucy's family and Daniel's Lapham connections. These long-lost relations Daniel and Lucy discovered and visited along the way. But Daniel's journey, unlike theirs, was a round trip and ended in Adams.

By the time the couple reached home, safe and sound, their

families were reconciled—disciplined, no doubt, by Daniel's tremendous trip. Their families had not expected to see them return
alive from what was still regarded as "the Indian country." The
Read family took them in and gave them a piece of land, while
Daniel's father gave him the lumber to build a house. Considering
that the house is still firmly standing, it seems remarkable that so
short a space of time was consumed in its construction. In no time
at all the young people were living there and Daniel had opened
a small store in the front corner room. *Nota bene:* something besides farming was immediately added.

The foregoing is the family chronicle. The Quaker dates (and
there is no quarreling with Quaker dates) fail in some details to
bear it out. For instance, on July 31, 1817, less than three weeks
after the marriage, the East Hoosac Monthly Meeting went on
record as follows:

This Meeting is informed by way of the Preparative Meeting
that Daniel Anthony has for a length of time been in the practice
of dealing in spirituous liquors and has also married out of the unity
of Friends. Sam'l Wells, Robert Nisbet, and Benjamin Briggs are
appointed to visit him on said accounts and report their sense with
respect to the state of his mind.

Things could scarcely have moved as fast as this unless the house
was built before the marriage or the liquor selling began before the
house was built. Be the solution what it may, on July 31, 1817,
Daniel's name was up before the Quaker overseers on two counts
of misconduct.

His case dragged on until the September meeting, when the committee reported that they had "visited him to a good degree of
satisfaction and according to their sense he appeared in disposition
to make Friends satisfaction—he having forwarded to this Meeting
an acknowledgment of his misconduct."

But the Quakers, always deliberate, held the matter over until
the next meeting. The note of October 4, 1817, reads:

Two of the committee in the case of Daniel Anthony report attention another opportunity with him and did not find anything
different from what they reported at last Meeting and claiming
the attention of this Meeting think it best to accept his acknowledgment and continue him a member of our Society and Samuel

Wells and Stephen Hoxie are appointed to inform him of the con-
clusions of this Meeting and report.

The prolonged hearings must have been an ordeal for a young
man who had never before been disciplined; who, on the contrary,
had received high testimonials for his probity of conduct. However,
he had come through it successfully and was retained as a member
of the Society.

In future years Susan B. Anthony was inclined to think that the
combined prominence and influence of the Anthony and Lapham
families had something to do with the leniency shown in her
father's case. This was doubtless true but probably not the whole
story. Daniel had fallen into error, be it noted, on two separate
counts. The Quakers had already begun to condone marriage with
an outsider in certain cases. Their second charge against him, liquor
selling, was one which they could not condone; and neither did
Daniel, in his heart.

He had evidently strayed into it by accident, through opening
a general store such as usually purveyed liquor in that region.
Brought face to face with his error, he saw and acknowledged it.
He would sell no more liquor, and the question of his marriage out
of the unity of Friends was to be dropped. In the sequel it was
dropped, and so was the liquor selling. Daniel was ever a shrewd
bargainer.

There were many times and occasions in Daniel's future life when
he demonstrated his sincere conversion to the cause of temperance.
He never went back on the promise he had made to the overseers
not to sell liquor. He did more than that: he became an active
temperance worker, achieving considerable local fame for his successful work.

His wife sometimes teased him about his interviews with the
committee, from which she had of course been excluded, accusing him of having told them he was sorry he had married her.
Daniel always replied with dignity that he had told them he was
sorry he had been obliged to violate a Quaker rule in order to
marry the woman he loved; which, as far as it went, was probably
actually what he said. He did not add that in return for the favor
he had promised to give up liquor selling forever. Lucy Anthony
herself did not become a Quaker, but she allowed her husband full
sway in bringing up the children in orthodox Quaker ways.

CHAPTER TWO

HOUSE ON THE SAVOY ROAD

◄§ I The town founded by Quakers and named for Samuel Adams lends some excuse for ill-natured critics to call it a "dark pocket." As much can be seen from Hawthorne's description, written in 1838: "These hills, surrounding the town on all sides, give it a snug and insulated air; and viewed from certain points, it would be difficult to tell how to get out without climbing over the mountain ridges; but the roads wind away and accomplish the passage without ascending very high." A snug and insulated valley is something quite different from a dark pocket, and the somber young Hawthorne found its aspect generally attractive, noting with pleasure the unusually brilliant cloud effects that flitted high over the valley. But the note of isolation was certainly present and suggests the romantic quality which attracted Hawthorne to the place.

The natives, however, worked hard to overcome the handicap. Humphrey Anthony gave the land for a road which ran along the boundary of his property and turned eastward to Savoy. Known as the Savoy Road, it was a gateway through the Berkshires and thus to Boston. In Humphrey's limited vision of the world there was practically no other city. Most of his fellow settlers shared the same view, and the Savoy Road became the busy outlet from the Green Mountains to the eastern lowlands from which they had all come.

The tract which Daniel Read gave to his son-in-law, Daniel Anthony, lay on this road. Exactly opposite stood Sam Bowen's tavern, where travelers often paused for refreshment. Daniel Anthony built his house close to the road in order that his store might be directly on the highway. His home and the tavern, also close to the road, were vis-à-vis neighbors. When the Anthony children came along, the two oldest girls would sit on their doorstep while "Uncle Sam Bowen" would sit on his, and they would spell the words he called to them across the road. He could seldom stump them and he regarded them as unusually "smart." When Uncle Sam was not available for this pastime, they understood that he was in the barroom talking Free Salvation with their grandfather. The girls were also at times not available for the game, as they often played in the attic with their rag dolls.

It was a comfortable and commodious house, even with the shop taken out. The parents' bedroom formed the other front corner room, in which from time to time Lucy Anthony was brought to bed of her successive children. They came fast and there were eight in all (the first five were born on the Savoy Road). All but one, stillborn, were handsome, healthy babies.

⊸§ II   The eldest, born July 1, 1818, was a girl. Daniel showed his loyalty to the Quaker faith by naming her for the wife of William Penn, whose name was Gulielma, soon shortened for this little girl into Guelma. In Mrs. Harper's life of Susan B. Anthony it is stated that "William Penn married a member of the Anthony family." The statement is not accurate, since William Penn's two wives are well known and neither was a member of the Anthony family. The correct original statement stands in Susan B. Anthony's *Reminiscences* and conveys that her "father's ancestors came from England and were somehow related to William Penn." This is easily possible and probably true. The early Anthony generations seem to have known a great deal about their English forebears. Had Guelma been a boy, the proud Quaker father would doubtless have called the child William Penn. She became Guelma Penn, familiarly referred to as "G.P."

The second child, born February 15, 1820, was a girl. She was named Susan Brownell for Daniel's sister Susannah, who had accompanied him to Nine Partners' and who had recently married the Quaker, Thomas Brownell. She died, without issue, one year after her namesake was born; and Thomas Brownell passed forever out of the Anthony chronicle, leaving as the one solitary memento of himself the name bestowed on his wife's niece. As Susan Brownell Anthony grew up, she abandoned her middle name in favor of the initial "B." and stuck to it consistently. The name had no associations for her except the legend of an early death in her father's family, and a second memory, more painful to her personally, later on added to it.

After Susan came Hannah, born September 15, 1821, and named for Daniel's other sister who had gone to Nine Partners'. The stillborn child followed. Susan thought she could remember its burial, though she must have been only between two and three at the time. Her recollection bears the mark of childish authenticity, not hearsay: "I can remember . . . walking across a stubble field with grandfather, barefoot; grandfather's lifting me up and carrying me . . . so that I saw the little box put into the ground." This seems to betoken a retentive early memory.

After the three closely knit little girls came the long-awaited son, born August 22, 1824, and named Daniel Read for father and grandfather. He was the last to be born on the Savoy Road. The three who came later, when the family had moved into another world, were Mary Stafford, born April 2, 1827; Eliza Tefft (Tefft for a neighbor in the new world), born April 22, 1832; and Jacob Merritt (Merritt from a Nine Partners' associate), born April 19, 1834.

Little Eliza Tefft did not survive long. She died of scarlet fever at the age of two, leaving the usual legend of brightness and beauty belonging especially to children who die very young. When Susan B. was an old lady she still recalled the little Eliza's bright sayings and actions and claimed she was the "cunningest" child ever known.

The rest of Daniel Anthony's children were destined for long-lived careers and a bond of family union which lasted throughout. They were a Quaker family acting out their heritage, bound more strongly than usual by the all-pervasive and catalytic personality of a very unusual father.

&§ III Lucy Anthony, the mother of Susan B. Anthony, was a silent woman. As a bride she was probably overwhelmed by the

superiority of her husband's talents and education; and if with time
she overcame this, the habit was already too profoundly established
ever to be changed. Her personality remains shrouded in a mist, or
rather transubstantiated into a ceaseless round of domestic tasks
of which she seemed the embodiment but not the originator.

Her life was the typical life of the housewife of Adams. The
winters were long and the summers were short: the first frost on
the doorstep came in September, the last in May. The spinning,
weaving, cooking, and sewing for her family were done by her own
hands. The water came from a spring at the foot of the pasture,
carried in pails by herself until smaller hands and feet could be
called into service. The children crowded along, three children in
three years, but they were taught to help as soon as they could
wipe a dish. The production of every item of food, clothing, and
warmth for a growing family, as well as the production of the family itself, depended on the woman at the center. Lucy Anthony
gave up singing to her children because her husband's religion disapproved of singing; then she also gave up talking to them, which
was a far greater loss.

Susan B. Anthony told her first biographer this story of her
mother's exceeding reticence. Before the birth of each child, Lucy
shut herself off from public gaze and declined to speak of her condition even to her own mother. This extraordinary behavior was
less unusual in those days than it would be in ours. In fact, the
taboo against speaking openly of pregnancy prevailed until comparatively recent times. Lucy Anthony bears comparison with Mrs.
Robert Elsmere, who was endowed by her creator, Mrs. Humphry
Ward, with a similar shyness as late as 1888. Catherine Elsmere
"flushed delicately" when her husband came home from a short
absence and asked her "how she was feeling." The popular heroine
of 1888, who was "within a few weeks of motherhood," was still
blushing after nine months of pregnancy at the mention of it.
Mrs. Daniel Anthony's behavior paid tribute, perhaps in an exaggerated form, to the same taboo. Still, her silence toward her own
mother seems to overdo the social taboo. Evidently she was an
unusually repressed character.

Susan, looking backward, regarded her mother's early married
years, as well as her whole life, as a supreme ordeal of hardship.
Susan's grandmother helped a great deal. She wove and dyed the

woolen dresses of the little girls and made the small garments for each new baby, laying them in a drawer and saying nothing about them. She did all this in addition to running the farm for a shiftless husband and caring for her own children. On the other side of the family, Grandmother Anthony demonstrated an equal ability. She had raised nine children, enjoyed a fine reputation as cook and housekeeper, and made the cheese which her husband sold in Boston for two cents the pound more than any other Berkshire cheese. She also cared for the bees, which were cultivated in such numbers that the Anthony homestead was familiarly known as "The Bee Hive." To these activities she added the duties of an elder in the East Hoosac Meeting.

These two grandmothers of Susan B. Anthony appear in no wise as drudges. They appear not as the victims of their order but movers and originators. That it never occurred to Susan to compare her mother with her grandmothers seems strange, but it never did. The trials, hardships, and anxieties of Lucy Anthony impressed her daughter as far beyond what was fair, just, and normal. She assimilated to the pattern her idea of the lives of most married women. Perhaps she was right—for her period. The generation before that, however, seems more like the married women of our day, whose heads are neither bloody nor bowed as they cope with the conditions of a changing order.

◦§ IV   Daniel Anthony was the young man of the hour in Adams. He worked his land, of which he had not too much, and promoted his store, *without liquor*. Like his mother, who had done the unheard-of thing by sending her children to Quaker boarding school, Daniel was given to ideas. What he had seen of the background of Nine Partners', Hart's Village, had made a lasting impression. Not only Thomas Hart's Quaker-Baptist marriage but also Hart's mills, Hart's prosperity, Hart's enterprise had enlarged his personal horizon. Rather than expand his farm, as his father would have done, Daniel dreamed of owning a mill. Mills were an unheard-of thing in the district of those days, though the town of Adams in these days consists of practically nothing else. The hitch in Daniel's dream was that Hart's enterprises had practically all been gristmills, for Dutchess County had blossomed into wheat fields with great

harvests. The Swiss-like contours of East Hoosac were never intended for grain cultivation, and gristmills in the district were out
of the question.

Nevertheless, Daniel brooded on plans for a mill. His instructor
in arithmetic and mechanics at Nine Partners' had been Jacob
Willetts, outstanding master in his field. Daniel had also seen the
practical application of textbook principles in the construction of
Hart's mills. The grandeur of machinery had dawned upon his
mind and he was able to build a mill on paper—but for what?

At this point came news from eastern Massachusetts which gave
substance to his dream. The Waltham mills near Boston, which
had begun to turn out cotton cloth in 1815, had so profited by
Madison's embargo on English imports that they had grown into
a multiple enterprise. They were now branching out into a series
of associated mills. The eastern factories were obtaining cotton
from the South by sea, but Daniel could just as easily obtain it by
way of New York and the Hudson.

Daniel's mill at once took shape. He created it in the year 1822,
two years after Susan was born. A small stream on his father-in-law's
property, called Tophet Brook, was to be utilized for water power.
He made a businesslike contract with Read, whereby "D. Read
agreed to let D. Anthony have as much water from the brook on
his farm as will run through a hole six inches in diameter."

Tophet Brook must have dried up mightily since Daniel's time,
as its present-day contents would never fill a six-inch hole. Even
then the scoffers were plentiful and circulated a story to the effect
that one day his mill stopped and investigation revealed that his
wife was washing clothes in the brook! The story serves a double
purpose: it casts a side light on Daniel's optimism and indicates
further how astoundingly new a cloth mill was. Whatever topo-
graphical changes may have come about meantime, the Tophet
carried enough water to make Daniel's mill a going concern.

It occupied thirty by forty feet of ground space and was three
and a half stories high. A huge overshot wheel, twenty-six feet in
diameter, reached to the level of the third floor. Within the tall
narrow structure were from twenty to twenty-six power-driven
looms. The strong building, its amazing water wheel, the power-
driven looms, hitherto unknown in Adams, were all the work of
Daniel Anthony's own brain and hands. He doubtless had aid

with the rougher parts of the building, but the refinements and precision work were his. When the great wheel began to turn and the many looms to weave as one, Daniel's pride must have been hard to contain. It was the dazzling fulfillment of an ambitious dream.

Susan B. Anthony says in her *Reminiscences* that her father's cotton mill was the first of its kind in South Adams. One other factory, she says, spun yarn but did no weaving. The farmers picked up the yarn and the women wove it on their looms at home. Daniel Anthony's looms on Tophet Brook were the first power-driven looms in the South Adams district. An uncle of his on his father's side, David Anthony, constructed a cloth mill in South Adams on the Hoosac four years after Daniel had constructed his. This uncle is usually given credit for introducing textile manufacturing in Adams. But Daniel's mill had definitely preceded his and furnished him with a practical example.

It was Daniel Anthony who took the first step in the conversion of Adams into the conglomerate mass of factories which it ultimately became. The managers, labor organizers, and working people who throng its streets today, the unbelievable quantity and variety of the fabrics turned out, are all the outgrowth of Daniel Anthony's ingenuity and enterprise. The log mill which his neighbors thought ridiculous set the pattern for all this industrial development.

When Daniel eventually left this mill, he turned it over in good condition to Isaac Hoxie, who continued to operate it for eight years. The building was then removed (perhaps because of the failing water power, which was also doubtless seasonal) to another location, where when last heard from (in the Anthony genealogy of 1904) it was still standing in a good state of preservation. No trace of the busy mill can now be found on the spot where it stood. It was hard for Daniel's younger children, born elsewhere, to realize, when they visited the spot, that such a mill had even existed. It seems to have been correspondingly hard for local historians to credit its existence. But Susan, as one of the older children, remembered it definitely in its prime and so described it in her *Reminiscences*.

The first product of Daniel's factory went to his wife. "Cotton cloth," says Susan, "just coming into use, was considered a luxury.

Mother had sheets and pillow-cases half-cotton, half-linen. She was thought to be very fortunate to have such beautiful cloth." Daniel was soon ready for the market, however. He induced the Green Mountain girls to come down from their fastnesses by the lure of hard cash, and he soon had as many hands as he had looms. They boarded with his wife and his sister Hannah Hoxie—about equally divided. He started the concern with no capital at all, though he may have had some manual help from his brother-in-law Hoxie, who seems to have had some interest in the enterprise.

For a picture of the mill girls who surrounded Susan Anthony's childhood we can do no better than turn again to Hawthorne's *Note-Books*. It was twelve years later when Hawthorne arrived, and cotton weaving had grown fast in that time. "Along our road," says Hawthorne, "we passed villages and factories, the machinery whizzing, and the girls looking out of windows at the stage, with heads averted from their tasks, but still busy. These factories have two, three or more boarding-houses near them . . . often with bean vines running up round the doors." He observed that a man with a Caravan of Animals had come to town, preferring to stop there rather than in a farming district because the mill girls had money to spend. The selectmen had hesitated whether to permit this diversion but had yielded. Hawthorne further noted "an affair of stealing" in a boardinghouse. "A woman of forty or upwards was accused of stealing a needle-case and other trifles from a factory girl. . . . She had come here to take passage on a stage, not knowing one could not travel in Vermont on Sundays. I heard Eliza telling another girl about it under my window, and she seemed to think the poor woman's reluctance to be searched arose from the poorness of her wardrobe and contents of her hand-box." The mill girls were a prosperous class by comparison with the poor farm women. They could buy needle cases and patronize a show of wild animals.

§ V   Though Susan lived under the same roof with a crowd of mill girls, she records no individual memories of them. As they went to work at 6 A.M. and worked until 6 P.M., sometimes even longer, and holidays, except Sundays, were practically unknown, she could not have seen them around very much. Like the travelers who stopped at Bowen's Tavern and enlivened the Savoy Road, they made no great conscious impression. At this time her conscious life was bound up with that of her sisters.

Her childish memories concerned her immediate family. The main picture is that of three little girls, born eighteen months apart, always together, playing in the attic or helping in the kitchen. When they started to school they attended the same district school their mother had attended. Grandfather Anthony's school, maintained for his younger children, was presumably too advanced for small beginners.

Susan's two grandmothers, active, strong characters, with their well-run households, stood at the top of their respective hierarchies. The Anthony children were fed and cosseted by both grandmothers. To the end of her life Susan would relate detailed memories of the boiled dinners of the one and the hasty puddings of the other; the maple sugar, apples, doughnuts, and cookies indiscriminately dispensed by both sides of her family tree. Her *Reminiscences* suggest that all her life Susan had a special palate for good food; a poor cook and housekeeper were always anathema to her.

Of the two grandmothers, Grandmother Read was manifestly her favorite. Perhaps Susannah Read was the more human, having a good deal to put up with in the ways of her husband, the town heretic, who was also somewhat given to drink. Except for her praying, she did not otherwise interfere with him. She must have had a most tolerant character.

Hannah Lapham Anthony was the more awesome of the two. Her superior circumstances contributed to the impression; her linen and her pewter porringers and her silk bonnets from New York were signs of her social position. Susan describes one night the children spent in her house: "In the morning we sat around her great round table, and grandmother, with her black eyes and black hair, moved around from place to place feeding us." Thus she usually seemed to view this grandmother, as if slightly from a distance.

Toward her own mother Susan as a child was surprisingly critical. Once when her mother chided the children for stopping after school at Grandmother Read's to eat the same dinner they could have had at home, Susan saucily replied, "Why, Grandma's potato peelings are better than your boiled dinners." This story has no sequel to show that she was properly punished for her pertness. On the contrary, its preservation by the family suggests that she was looked upon as "smart." (The story does not appear in Susan's *Reminiscences*, though she must have told it to Mrs. Harper, her biographer, who preserved it. Could it be that Susan was personally somewhat ashamed of it?)

On another occasion Susan's criticism lingered in her memory long enough to appear in her *Reminiscences*: "All our little woolen dresses were dyed by Grandmother Read. One of my greatest grievances . . . was that mother loaned our three little Sunday-go-to-meeting dresses to some poor children whose mother died. I thought it was very cruel, and that we should have loaned the old ones and worn the best ones to the funeral ourselves." The child's resentment may be accepted as natural, but why the memory of it should last so long is still a question. There was not much understanding between this child and her mother.

When Susan was three, she and her older sister Guelma were sent to Grandmother Anthony's to stay during the birth of the fourth child. They stayed six weeks, during which they had whooping cough and learned to read. Susan's memories of the visit centered around Rhoda Brownell, the teacher in her grandfather's school, who "also made Quaker bonnets for the women all around." The millinery art had no appeal for Susan, but Miss Brownell's skill as a teacher was rewarded by an eager pupil. She taught the two little girls to read. "We just loved those books and we pored over them too much," says Susan.

When she went home, expecting to be praised for her newly acquired skill—"The first thing mother noticed was that my eyes both turned toward my nose." The dire tragedy was attributed to the effects of the whooping cough on the eyes of a child just learning to read. "Mother was awfully distressed about it. She thought I had the prettiest eyes of any child she ever saw." Still suffering from grief and shock over her stillborn infant, Lucy Anthony could not accept this newest cause for unhappiness. The thought of curbing her demonstrations for Susan's sake seems not to have occurred to her. The child who had expected only praise for her progress was met as if she had suddenly acquired a stigma.

The mother must have been correct in her observation that Susan's eyes had not been crossed previously. If so, they probably needed only rest and quiet to become normal again. In fact, as Susan says, "the left eye gradually straightened itself." But even with time, according to her, the right eye never did. From this moment she was marked with the penalty of her overambitiousness and destined to carry the penalty throughout her life. Logically, the experience should have killed all ambition within her. The logic of the emotions, however, follows its own laws, and in Susan's case it did not follow those of Aristotle. It was as if she said, "With a great sum obtained I this freedom"—and her freedom was to be just as ambitious as ever she cared to be.

With all her anguish, Susan was not through with the crisis. It was to return again at a later time of life, indeed more than once, to torment and try her. One might think she was a vain child to have suffered so much. That may be true. But her state also reflected the pride and vanity of the grownups, primarily of her mother, operating upon her.

The teacher who had unwittingly brought so much misery upon her bore the name of Brownell. This was probably a further reason for wishing to forget the name. It was associated with a traumatic experience of her childhood.

◌§ VI   Susan's memories of the Quaker meeting house at Adams are few. Her father went to First Day and monthly meetings and belonged to the inner Quaker circle, for he had in no way lost his standing. Lucy and the children went with him. They had to drive there. When the business session began, Lucy and the children would have to go out. If the weather was fine, they walked about in the graveyard outside. "There were no stones or slabs of any kind to mark the graves. People were buried right along in rows as they came." (This was in Susan's childhood; later the Quakers were allowed to erect simple tombstones.) If the weather was bad, Uncle Isaac Hoxie would take Lucy in his wagon "to wherever she or father were going to visit" and Daniel would bring along Aunt Hannah Hoxie later.

The Quaker practice of "visiting" was as regular if not quite as sacred as that of attendance at meeting. No meeting day without its accompanying visit, a custom in which the Anthonys on the Savoy Road took their proper turn. Their visits were chiefly limited

to the numerous Anthony-Lapham connections who had for more
that three generations been spreading through the hills and now
formed the background of Daniel's social relationships. Only by his
marriage outside the "unity of Friends" had he in any way deviated from the inherited round of Quaker customs.

Building, dominating, creating, Daniel soon became a successful businessman and the responsible head of a family. His household
had all the necessities and some of the comforts of life. Another
baby had come and this time it was a son. His wife, whose ceaseless,
backbreaking drudgery her daughter Susan never ceased to lament,
had the help of a thirteen-year-old servant girl in the house. How
this was managed when all of her compeers were in the factory is
not to be explained, unless she was paid wages equal to theirs. To
employ a servant bordered almost on luxury in that simple community. Daniel had achieved prosperity beyond the usual in his
environment.

His business activities included periodic trips to New York,
where he went to sell his cotton cloth. The drive with his loaded
wagon to Troy, the long boat trip down the Hudson, his deals in
the city were as nothing to him. His repeated disappearances from
the home, when his over-all, pervasive, and activating influence was
withdrawn, meant much to the children, especially Susan. If the
travelers on the Savoy Road failed to inspire her with wonder—
where they came from, where they were going—it was because they
were strangers. When an intimate part of herself, her dear father,
took to the road, she followed him in her imagination through the
long journey to its mysterious end in the city. His almost rhythmi-
cal arrivals and departures lingered in her mind to form one of her
lifelong patterns of behavior.

CHAPTER THREE

THE GREAT MIGRATION

▪§ I   News traveled fast along the Savoy Road and still faster along the Hoosac and the Hudson. Strangers came to Adams to wonder and admire at the sight of a textile mill in the Berkshires. Daniel Anthony's reputation as a genius spread rapidly. It reached the attentive ears of Judge John McLean (perhaps only a justice of the peace), who lived in Battenville, New York, about forty-four miles northwest of Adams. Judge McLean came down to see with his own eyes the miracle at Bowen's Corners.

By this time Daniel was ready to expand but, hampered by his limited water power, found himself unable to do so. To acquire a location on the Hoosac was the obvious next step, but he had no capital. His forefathers had been thoughtless enough to take up land on the hills (dairying being their object), and Daniel had no means of approach to the river. The judge, who had come to feel out "the state of his mind," found that it was open to suggestions.

McLean was the owner of an abandoned mill of some kind in Battenville, located on the banks of the swiftly flowing Batten Kill. It was not the equal of the Hoosac, but it was vastly better than Tophet Brook. His well-timed suggestion was that Daniel should take over this mill, convert it into a cloth factory, and become his partner. McLean was to supply the capital and Daniel the skill and the labor. Aspiring to a larger field of activity, Daniel was soon persuaded, and McLean's proposition was accepted.

The wails of his wife and their respective families, who looked on Battenville as a faraway western locality, had no effect upon him. With his usual headlong energy he prepared for the great migration. The mill, still running, was turned over to Isaac Hoxie, and his household goods were hastily packed. Whatever he was to realize from his Adams property was to be invested in Battenville. McLean was as eager as Daniel for the transfer. He sent his son, the fourteen-year-old Aaron McLean, with a good team of horses and a fine green wagon to transport the family to their new home. In this style they made the journey to New York in one day, with their goods following in humbler wagons.

McLean's eagerness and haste had allowed no time to find a dwelling for them. They were housed in his own home, a stately old New England-type dwelling with multitudinous rooms and innumerable windows. Susan was overawed by the handsome parlor and very curious about the Negro slaves, a fine-looking mulatto woman and "little black Sue," who were the property of McLean. This was Susan's introduction to the colored race; Quakers were not allowed to own slaves and there had been none in Adams. Her small sister Hannah was frightened at the sight of "little black Sue" and cried woefully, but Susan liked her and played with her and in after years remembered her as the prototype of Topsy when that memorable character came into the world.

◂§ II   The village of Battenville did not present too much that was new and strange to Daniel's family. The local scenery, with sloping hills converging on a rushing stream, was rather similar to East Hoosac. There was no peak like Greylock, whose shining summit and long shadow had been so familiar; no level Intervale like that which Grandfather Anthony had ruled over; but otherwise Battenville presented much the same kind of sidehill world.

Life continued in about the same terms as the life they had left. Daniel's family soon moved into a house of their own, where they remained for six years. The children continued to come; Mary and Eliza Tefft were born. Daniel continued the work of constructing mills, bridges, houses, though on a larger scale than in Adams. These were strenuous but successful years for him, dominated by high hopes.

His first task, of course, was to reconstruct the old mill and set up the machinery. This was followed by a brick building, combining a store and a machine shop for repairs. The factory was weaving. Lucy Anthony, even in their first small house, was obliged to board the mill girls, though girls from local families were also beginning to be hired. Daniel was certainly expanding. It was not long before he decided that he must build a proper home for himself. His idea of a proper home was ambitious and took a long time to be realized. The local legend runs that he was six years in building his house. But Susan's *Reminiscences* record that he began burning the bricks early in 1832 and that they moved into the house at the end of 1833.

Daniel Anthony, trained by the Quaker Jacob Willetts, must have been a very good construction engineer. His dwelling house is still standing, sturdy and solid and architecturally beautiful. Even the hastily built frame house at Bowen's Corners is still in existence, well preserved as a family residence. Even his log mill survived removal to a different site. The mill which he constructed at Battenville is still in use as a paper mill.

Daniel intended to have the finest house in the vicinity. It would have been easy to imitate the New England house of John McLean, lumber from the Green Mountains being so handy and plentiful. But he chose brick. The bricks had to be burned on the premises. He erected a kiln and employed ten or twelve men to run it. Susan's mother cooked for these men; or rather, her mother being ill, Susan and her sisters did the cooking. She long remembered the boiled dinners and pies they prepared for these heavy consumers. At the same time she was still such a child that she would go with her sisters to the brick kiln after hours and play, "piling up the bricks and then letting them slide down."

When finished, the house had two tall stories and a commodious garret. Four spacious fireplaces, two at each end, provided for considerable heat. A curving stairway and handrail in the entrance hall added an air of grandeur and dignity. Later on Daniel conceded the addition of a two-storied ell made of clapboards, to be used as a woodshed below and as a schoolroom above. It was a very handsome house, standing above the road and facing the hill, overlooking the mill and the river in the valley.

Almost the first event of importance to take place in the new house was the birth of Lucy Anthony's eighth and last child, Jacob Merritt, in 1834. Forty-nine years later Susan wrote in her diary: "This is Brother J. Merritt's 49th birthday. How well I can remember dear Mother's sad face on that morning of his birth in the new brick house at Battenville." Why should Lucy Anthony, with six healthy children, with the finest home in Battenville, with a devoted and successful husband, have worn a sad face on this particular morning? Was it thus that she welcomed all her children? It is not surprising that Susan had a fixed idea that her mother's lot in life, between drudgery and childbearing, had been excessively hard. The impression, early communicated and ineradicable, formed her chief bequest from this silent woman.

The relatives from Adams came to admire, to see and behold Daniel's prosperity in the new world. The aged Reads, Susan's grandfather and grandmother, sold their farm and arrived to spend their declining years in their son-in-law's comfortable home. Ten years of uninterrupted prosperity as a cotton manufacturer followed, establishing Daniel as a figure of importance in Battenville. He could look back on Hart's Mill of Nine Partners' as a goal that he had far outstripped.

◂§ III   Through all, he remained a Quaker. He was obligated by the rules of his Society to play a humane role in life as an employer and as a citizen. Unless Susan's memory exaggerates, he was a model employer by the most advanced standards of his time. "There was an evening school," says Susan, "for a great many of the grown-up boys and girls had never had an opportunity for education. School was from eight to nine o'clock, and it was unpopular not to attend. Half the employees of the factory were there, learning to read and write or spell. Father would do the teaching himself. . . . He regarded his employees as his family and his duty to give them mental culture. When we had a teacher for our private school, she would also teach the evening school. He kept a school on Sunday for the factory hands who wanted to go. . . . Every employee had a little garden around his house for vegetables and flowers in connection with his one-and-a-half-story tenement that father built."

Robert Riegel, in Young America, tells us that in the 1830s "no reform movement was better advertised than temperance." The movement was well organized throughout the East. One of its most active leaders was the Reverend John Pierpont, grandfather of the famous American financier J. Pierpont Morgan. His poem, *Dash the Bowl to the Ground*, became a classic of the movement. Temperance moved forward in the 1830s even ahead of abolition, though as a rule the two reforms went hand in hand.

In Battenville, Daniel Anthony threw himself heart and soul into the temperance movement. The village was greatly afflicted with drunkenness. Daniel set his face firmly against the evil from the start. He would sell no liquor in the company store and he refused to "treat" the men who came for the "raising" of the company houses. John McLean warned him that the effect would be disastrous, but Daniel's will prevailed and McLean's apprehensions were not realized.

His greatest success was seen in his handling of individual drunkards. He refused to employ anyone in the factory who got drunk. A foreman named Elijah Hyatt, with whom he had labored for some time, finally had to be discharged. Hyatt's widowed mother and his two maiden sisters, with all the earnestness they could muster, appealed to Daniel to give the culprit one more chance. Daniel consented. To the great surprise of his family and the entire village, Hyatt reformed his ways. He became secretary of the temperance society and lived and died at a ripe old age, a sober man.

Daniel waged a steady campaign against the liquor shops of the town and county. He was instrumental in getting a Temperance House built, whose double-deck piazza with spindle rails was an admired feature of the town for many years. Long after Daniel's time it was taken down to make apartments for mill hands. His success as a reformer brought his name and fame into the foreground of a great temperance rally held in the capitol at Albany. "The Assembly Chambers rang with his [the delegate's] praise of Daniel Anthony's temperance work in Battenville, only one place being left there of many where rum was sold."

Daniel spent little of his energy on politics. He did not vote. As a Quaker who did not believe in war, he refused to pay taxes to a government which did. But this required a subterfuge. As was the practice of many Quakers, he would lay his purse before the collector, saying, "I shall not voluntarily pay these taxes; if thee wants to rifle my pocket-book, thee can do so." Another problem that troubled his Quaker conscience was the use of cotton, product of slave labor, in his factory. He made every effort to obtain cotton from other sources than the American South, but it was practically impossible.

◄§ IV   One may be sure that, in removing his family from Adams, Daniel had taken care that they were not removed from Quaker influences. Judge McLean's family and most of the villagers were Scotch Presbyterians. But only ten miles away as the crow flies lay Easton, New York, a thriving community of Friends. Daniel knew the Easton Meeting well. His parents sometimes drove to the Easton "Quarterly," a favorite meeting place for Quakers from Vermont, Massachusetts, and New York. For some reason the Easton Meeting had greater vitality than most. As other meetings have been from time to time "laid down" for purposes of worship, including even that of Daniel's native Adams, the Easton Meeting has continued to survive. To this day its notices of worship appear regularly in the local newspaper.

Almost simultaneously with Daniel's removal from Adams came the historical separation of the Quakers into the Hicksites and the Orthodox. In the great division both the Adams and the Easton Friends declared themselves in favor of Elias Hicks. There was a period of some excitement as Hicks went up and down the land preaching the authority of the Inner Light, while English "missionaries" followed him preaching the authority of the Scriptures. In the ensuing division few families went unscathed. Humphrey Anthony's oldest brother Elihu departed from the Adams group, taking with him his aged pioneer father David to join the Orthodox group in Saratoga, New York. This left a deep wound in the Anthony clan spread out solidly through the Berkshire hills.

The majority of the American Quakers declared themselves as Hicksites. In the end it was largely a division between the American and the English branches of the Society. The Americans responded not only to the inspired leadership of Elias Hicks but also to a doctrine more congenial to the American temperament.

The transfer of Daniel Anthony's membership from Adams to Easton was a simple matter. Both meetings by this time were

Hicksite. The Easton records show that his certificate of removal from Adams, dated "11th mo. 29 da. 1827," was duly received and accepted by the Easton Meeting. At that date he was the only actual member of the Friends' Society in his family.

Five years later, October 13, 1832, the Easton Meeting accepted the Anthony children into membership. "Daniel Anthony and his wife Lucy informed this Meeting they were desirous that their children Guelma, Susan, Hannah, Daniel R., Mary, and Eliza should be received under the care of Friends." A committee of men and another of women were appointed to visit the family and report "their sense of the case." The committees made their visits and reported at two successive monthly meetings. After a month the men's committee was ready to grant the request, but the women's committee requested another month for deliberation. Finally, on January 17, 1833, the six Anthony children were enrolled as members of the Society of Friends.

Susan remembered the occasion vividly, as she played a prominent part in it—at least in her own version. On a particularly cold First Day, she alone attended meeting with her father. Her mother protested, but her father took her anyhow. When the business session began, she had to go out in the cold. Susan tried to avoid this by hiding herself behind the stove, "curled up as quiet as a mouse." But an observant lady elder "stepped down from the High Seat" and, after questioning her about her membership, which was not yet accomplished, ushered her out. The child then decided to go to a neighbor's house, where an unusually fierce dog set upon her and "caught her right in the cape of her new cloak." Clothes were then and always a vulnerable point with Susan, and when her mother saw the torn coat collar she was also much upset.

There was a great deal of talk about it. Mother declared that I should never go again, or any of us. This was the reason we children became Friends. Father made a request that all of his children should be taken into the Society. We were accepted, even sister Mary, who was a mere baby. If both father and mother had been members, we should have been birthright Quakers; as mother was not a Quaker, he had to make the request, or wait until we were grown-up to make our own request. Father's request was based entirely upon the desire to have us at Meeting without being turned out in the sleet and snow.

This version of the episode, written sixty-five years later, still carried the marks of Susan's childish self-importance. The step was taken by her parents mainly on her account. That her father's request was based entirely on his desire not to have his children turned out in the sleet and snow seems hardly credible of this serious Quaker. That Daniel had long been contemplating such a step seems more probable. Guelma was fourteen; Susan, twelve; Hannah, eleven; and Daniel R., eight. The time for action had come. It was also essential (as Susan did not appear to know) that Daniel's wife, a non-Quaker, should join in his request. Perhaps the accident of the torn coat collar was needed to bring Lucy Anthony to this point. At any rate, the elders of the meeting took up the matter with the utmost seriousness, debating it long and carefully before accepting the children, and there is no reason to suppose that Daniel's seriousness was any less than theirs.

Daniel's religious enterprises were still not concluded. Within a year he was again before the Easton Meeting with a request that he, with his children and some other Friends living in Battenville, should be allowed to hold meetings for worship in the schoolroom of his house. The request was readily granted. Long afterward a lady who had once attended the services in the Anthony home wrote to Susan: "I distinctly remember . . . the Quaker Meeting held in the school-room on First Days. Your father's meditative face casting a spell of solemnity over the little audience, when the utterance of some one's spirit throbbings was heard or a long silence ensued." As long as the Anthony family remained in the Battenville home, the Quaker services continued to be held under their roof.

≪§ V   On first arriving in Battenville, Susan and her sisters went to the district school. "I remember," she says, "I studied arithmetic and wanted to learn long division. The teacher didn't know enough to teach me. At last I went to a great farmer boy, who helped me." Susan must have been nine or ten, quite old enough to learn long division. But girls were not supposed to learn long division. The deciding factor, however, was that the district schoolteacher did not know enough to teach it. As soon as the brick store was finished, Daniel decided to employ a competent teacher for his children. Battenville children who could pay the small fee attended. The school was later moved into the ell of the house, especially built for the purpose. In this home school maintained by her father, Susan had her lessons until she reached what would now be regarded as high school age.

Her teachers were Sarah Perrine, an indifferent scholar recruited from the district school; Mary Perkins, graduate of an elite girls' boarding school north of Boston; Sarah Anthony, a cousin and a graduate of a Quaker boarding school; and Nancy Howe, another well-educated cousin. Daniel's standards were high and grew higher as his girls grew up. Mary Perkins, who was not a Quaker, introduced the children to poems and "school books with pictures" and she would have introduced them to singing had their father's Quaker principles allowed it.

Still, Susan's schoolroom was not a gloomy place. Nancy Howe long afterward wrote to Susan: "The year I spent at your father's was the happiest of my whole long life. . . . It had never been my fortune before to live in a household with an educated man at its head, and I felt a little shy of your father but soon found there was no occasion. . . . He seemed to have an eye for everything, his business, the school, and every good work." One of the paying pupils similarly wrote many years later: "Your letter . . . brings vividly to mind the Battenville school where I learned ideal and practical lessons of life. Sarah Anthony's precise methods and Mr. Wright's striking personality with Cousin Daniel's quick solution of problems in mathematics I distinctly remember, as also the bevy of dear companions that met daily in the school-room. . . . Cousin Hannah's rich store of mirth, R.D.'s sarcasm and drollery,—how like a flood these things rush before the mirror of by-gones!"

Along with Susan's school tasks ran the uninterrupted flow of housework. The Battenville house contained a large household. Besides the family, there were Grandfather and Grandmother, the schoolteacher, and some mill girls. Some of Daniel's hands still came from the Green Mountains. Besides helping with the cooking and cleaning for this large number, the Anthony girls were supposed to sew, to knit, to weave—to excel in all kinds of fine needlework. Susan excelled in fine sewing. During an attack of illness at the age of eleven she produced a "sampler" of a most superior quality. With their housework and schoolwork, the girls in Daniel's home were scarcely less busy than the girls in the factory down by the river.

There was one big difference—wages. Susan B. Anthony told her biographer that her father paid the mill girls $1.50 a week. The Lowell mills of that period paid the girls about $3.00 a week, but their board money, $1.25 a week, was first taken out. Daniel's girls probably received $1.50 and their board. To Susan and her sisters $1.50 was a fortune.

It happened one day that Sally Ann Hyatt, who lived in the village, was ill and unable to work. On their father's remarking the fact, both Susan and Hannah set up a clamor to be allowed to work in her place. Daniel saw no objection, but he needed only one. He had the girls draw straws, with the understanding that the winner should divide her wages with the loser. Susan won and went into her father's mill for two weeks, to work as a spooler, and came out with $3.00 in her hand. Hannah spent her share on a pretty green beaded bag. Susan spent hers on half a dozen blue china cups and saucers as a present to her mother. An aged resident of Battenville recently said to the writer: "She has told me this many times and never failed to say that Battenville was where she earned her first dollar."

Where she really started work was not in the factory but in the schoolroom. At fifteen she began to teach in the summer when only the little ones attended. She then branched out by going to Easton to teach in a Quaker family for $1.00 a week and board. Next she taught in a district school for $1.50 a week and board. In each step she took she had been preceded by her sister Guelma and expected to be followed the next year by Hannah. This was her father's system for the three girls.

In Battenville, where Daniel figured as one of the two local magnates, his course was criticized. His business was prosperous and he was regarded as a rising man. McLean's daughters did not go into the factory nor hire out as teachers; nor did their friends. But Daniel had his own ideas about his daughters' education and as usual went his own way. He began this course well before he saw the handwriting on the wall, while he still believed that the economic future of his family was assured. He wanted his daughters to be independent.

◦§ VI   It was customary for girls of the "better" families of Battenville to be sent away to boarding school after they had finished with the local opportunities. The McLean girls and the Mosher girls, both of non-Quaker families, were sent to boarding schools. Daniel planned that Guelma, Susan, and Hannah should have the same advantage. As an honor graduate of Nine Partners', he knew there was more to education than his small home school provided. For some reason, his thoughts did not turn back to Nine Partners', which had survived the great division and was functioning as well as ever. His own girls were not a mere farmer's daughters, as his sisters had been, but the daughters of a prosperous manufacturer. His thoughts turned to Philadelphia, the center of Quaker culture.

On Guelma's reaching seventeen, Daniel received the following circular:

DEBORAH MOULSON, having obtained an agreeable location in the pleasant village of Hamilton, in the vicinity of Philadelphia, intends, with the assistance of competent teachers, to open immediately a Seminary for Females. . . .
Terms, $125 per annum, for boarding and tuition. . . .

The circular proceeded to state the high aims of the seminary and outlined an ambitious course of study. Deborah Moulson, it was stated, believed it her duty to promote the education of girls, "according to moral discipline in simplicity of speech, behavior, and apparel; endeavoring to unite an useful literary education with that tuition of the understanding, which will induce them, on reasoning principles, to depart from that kind of dress and address which leads the youthful mind so far from the path of propriety. . . . The course of study will include the following branches of English Education: Orthography, Reading, Writing, Arithmetic, Grammar, Geography, with the use of maps and globes, the elements of Astronomy, Natural Philosophy and Chemistry, History and Composition."

This formidable announcement did not in any way alienate Daniel's interest. He had himself kept a school in which basic Quaker principles were adhered to and in which the pupils had nevertheless been happy. Miss Moulson's circular was in fact no

more severe and stern in tone than those of many girls' schools of
the time, which strove thus to inspire confidence in prospective
parents and patrons.

Deborah Moulson's previous history suggests that Daniel may
already have had some knowledge of her. Deborah sprang from a
Virginia Quaker family. Her mother, a widow with two children,
moved to Philadelphia in order to earn a living. On reaching
maturity, Deborah began to move about, as her "certificates of removal" show, in pursuit of the profession of teaching. Reputed to
be a talented water-color painter, at thirty she gave it up, her
Quaker conscience telling her it was too frivolous. Prior to opening
her Philadelphia school she had taught at Rensselaerville, New
York, in the Quaker school attended by Sarah Anthony, Susan's
cousin. At Rensselaerville she could have made the acquaintance
of Daniel Anthony at some quarterly meeting or other. At any
rate, he was one of the first to receive her circular and among the
first to respond to it.

Guelma entered Miss Moulson's Seminary when it opened in
1836. Her sister Susan followed her in 1837. In the meantime
Susan lived at home, except for two short absences at teaching, and
enjoyed the prestige of being the eldest daughter. She had many
friends and among the closest were the young McLeans, children
of her father's partner in business. Though the McLeans were not
Quakers, circumstances drew her closer to them than to some of
her companions who were. It was a pleasant year. There were
some rumblings of trouble in business, but even the elders looked
on this as symptoms that would pass. Susan apprehended nothing
and looked forward to the great adventure of going away to school
when her turn should come.

CHAPTER FOUR

BOARDING SCHOOL

≈§ I   It was a snowy day in November when Susan set forth on her journey to school. She wore a plain drab dress and bonnet, and her father, who accompanied her, wore a black suit and broad-brimmed hat. Daniel and his daughter were Quakers, and anyone who saw them could perceive the fact. Father and daughter were on their way to Deborah Moulson's Seminary in Philadelphia.

They left Battenville in a small uncovered wagon drawn by the family horse, with only blankets to protect them from the falling snow. At Easton, ten miles away, they were obliged to turn in at Elder Wilbur's to escape the storm and they remained there over-night. The next day they pushed on through the steadily falling whiteness to Albany, where, says Susan's diary, the poor horse was as glad to find shelter as themselves.

Susan and Daniel boarded the Hudson steamboat *The Swallow* for New York. Arriving on First Day, they attended Quaker wor-ship in Brooklyn. They then took another boat for South Amboy, changed to "the cars" for Bordentown, and in still another boat proceeded down the Delaware to Philadelphia. An omnibus carried them to a wayside tavern stop, whence they walked to Hamilton.

All this travel was familiar to Daniel, who often went to Phila-delphia to sell his cotton cloth. For Susan it was an epoch-making revelation. Before reaching Hamilton she experienced every variety of transport in common use at the time and arrived an enlightened traveler. She had been initiated into her father's world—a world unsuspected by her homekeeping mother and hitherto seen by Susan only in her imagination. She realized the importance of the experience and immediately recorded all its details in her diary.

Susan and Daniel found the school empty. They had not been expected, and "Guelma with most of the scholars had gone on a visit to the Fairmount Waterworks" (our first glimpse of Miss Moulson's rather modern way of educating young ladies). Daniel bespoke a holiday for Guelma on the morrow and returned to his Philadelphia lodgings. The next day he took Susan and Guelma on a sight-seeing tour of Philadelphia, visiting Independence Hall, William Penn's residence, the harbor, and the streets. They finished with dinner at a city tavern. Daniel was a man who did nothing by halves.

All of Susan's pleasure evaporated when at nine o'clock that evening her father prepared to leave her. "Oh, what pangs were felt, it seemed impossible for me to part with him. I could not speak to him to bid him farewell," she wrote, and added, "A week from this time the thought of the parting arose and I felt as if I could not contain myself." Though her father had tried to make his girls independent, Susan was bound by an emotional tie unusually strong for a girl of seventeen. If her affection had been distributed more equally at home, including some clinging to the older sister who remained with her, she would scarcely have suffered such severe pangs. But she would not then have been so much her father's daughter, the chief inheritor of his drives, his "ideas," his genius, and his dreams. Her pangs of the moment were quite real.

II Deborah Moulson's curriculum, as stated in her circular, seems rather oddly chosen for young ladies of the time. The emphasis placed on science, "Geography with the use of maps and globes, the elements of Astronomy, Natural Philosophy and Chemistry," must have indicated her own taste rather than the popular demand. According to Susan's diary, the lessons on science were no empty boast; she listened to many lectures on the nature of carbon and chlorine, on the constellations, and on the metamorphosis of insects.

How this Quaker schoolmistress had become interested in science is not known, but her taste accidentally concurred with

Susan's, which could have stood some broadening. The basic idea of Miss Moulson's school, however, was the close relationship between morality and literature—Deborah holding that no pupil could achieve excellence in literature without equivalent excellence in morality. Susan's many self-castigations for her lapses in morality were made doubly bitter for their supposed inhibitory effect on her progress in literature.

As to literature, it was represented by orthography and composition and readings in the New Testament. The first two were taught by the practice of letter writing. The girls wrote their home letters in the schoolroom on slates; they were then corrected by the teacher, copied, and sent out. Susan's letters were essays in moral sentiment, which must have been extremely gratifying to her parents as evidence of the high plane on which she lived. The only literary works studied were Young's *Night Thoughts* and Cowper's *Task*. These poems, which had been studied by Daniel Anthony and Lucretia Mott at Nine Partners' twenty-five and thirty years earlier, were still Deborah's only concession to imaginative literature. She held strictly to the Quaker taboo on everything approaching the fine arts. Taking her pupils to the Academy of Arts and Sciences in Philadelphia, she led them quickly past all other exhibitions and directed their attention to the "numerous specimens of minerals, animals, and the shell tribes." Susan did not miss the arts and was enthralled by her glimpses into natural history. "I was ready to exclaim, 'Oh, Miracle of Miracles,' with the celebrated Naturalist in speaking of the metamorphosis of insects," she said. She spelled *metamorphosis* correctly.

⚜ III   In her relations with Miss Moulson, Susan apparently met severity and injustice from the first. Impressed by Deborah's solemnity and strictness, she tried hard to please her, but failed. Her sister Guelma, on the other hand, easily won Deborah's praise. One day in a burst of anger Susan charged the schoolmistress with favoritism. "Thy sister Guelma," answered Deborah, "does the best she is capable of. Thou hast greater abilities and I demand of thee the best of thy capacity." The truth was that Susan was trying so hard she was failing; while Guelma, by just taking it easy, earned the teacher's approval. Susan's miseries at Hamilton were not unlike those of Jane Eyre at Lowood, and they proceeded largely from the same cause—the natural response of a bullying and self-righteous character to the immediate presence of a sensitive and defenseless victim. As told in her diary at the time, the experiences of Susan's school life at Hamilton are both touching and exasperating.

She had written a composition of which she felt rather proud.

D. came down in the afternoon and came to the desk where I sat and examined some of our writing-books. . . . I, thinking I had improved very much, offered mine for her to examine. She took it and pointed out some of the best written words as those which were not well written. She then showed me the dot of an *I* and asked me the rule for dotting the *I*. I acknowledged I did not know. She then said it was no wonder she had undergone so much distress in both mind and body, and that her time had been devoted to us in vain. This was like an Electrical shock to me. . . . When school was out, I first went to the privy to give vent to my tears, and then back to the house and upstairs, where without restraint I indulged in tears. . . . And we had a new scholar to witness all this. . . . I feel as if I could not go in Deborah's sight.

Soon after this Susan wrote a secret letter to a girl friend in Battenville. Some of the girls did this and dispatched their missives successfully. But Susan's caught the Argus eye.

2. mo. 22.—I anticipated that my letter to S. F. Brown had been sent to the Post Office. At noon D. sent for me. I being in the attick went down with cheerfulness, but what was my surprise on beholding the said letter and the expression of her countenance. She said she could not suffer such writing and such composition to go from her school . . . and besides I had broken the rules of the school in copying it without her seeing it and correcting it. She gave me the letter and said if I would write it on my slate again she would correct it. But I do not feel that I have time to write another. Phebe Miller wrote one yesterday without its being corrected. If I am the worst of all sinners, O may I be conscious of it.

She brooded over the affair to the neglect of her diary for some time. Resuming her entries at last, she wrote:

3. mo. 4.—I cannot say that I have recovered from the shock I then received. I have not yet written to S. F. Brown and do not know that I shall while in Hamilton. I feel continually as if S.F.

would think me neglectful of the friendship which once existed between us.

Nothing more was said about the letter by Deborah until near the end of the term. All the girls were making preparations for going home. Guelma had given up her position as assistant, and the two sisters were anxiously expecting their father to come and take them away. Deborah then suddenly called Susan to her room and asked her about the letter. Susan miserably admitted she had not rewritten it. "She laughed and said I was a naughty girl, then requested me to write it again." The easily reconciled Susan went through the process of writing it all over on a slate again, having it corrected, and then copying it for the post. Deborah had apparently decided that she must close on friendly terms with the daughter of a man of some consequence in Quaker circles.

The worst of Susan's crimes was the accidental breaking of Deborah's desk. The great, tall, gangling girl, in an access of "trying hard," decided one day to sweep down the cobwebs in the schoolroom, of which she had heard Deborah complain.

3 mo. 11.—Accordingly, I took off my shoes, took the broom and mounted the desks for that purpose, little thinking of the mortification and tears it was to occasion. After going around the room, I stepped on D.'s desk that I might sweep in that part, thoughtlessly, and strained the lock, bent the hinges, and how much more damage I do not know. . . . Then when D. came down I said, "Deborah, see what I have done. I have broken your desk." She appeared not to notice what I had said, walked to the desk, looked at it, and asked who broke it. Someone answered, "Susan Anthony." "What," says she, "Susan Anthony step on my desk!" She said she would not have thought of setting a child on it, and much more. I thought I couldn't contain myself. She asked me how I came to step upon it but I was too full to answer and rushed from the room in tears. That evening, after we read in the Testament, she said that where there was no desire for Moral improvement there would be no improvement in Reading. There was one by the side of her who had not desired Moral improvement and had made no advancement in Literature. Never will this be forgotten.

≈§ IV Deborah's theory was a double-bitted ax which was wielded with especial effect on the conscientious and ambitious

Susan. If one side did not strike her down, the other did. Deborah also had a way of making a mystery of the pupils' offenses, using such expressions as "There is one by my side who . . ." and "There are those present who . . ." Whatever the moral offense that followed, it seemed to Susan directly attributed to her. For at this age and under this treatment she felt that she was capable of all sins. "O, the happiness of an innocent mind," she exclaimed in her diary. "Would that I could say mine was so, but it is too far from it."

Susan's deep training in Quaker doctrine made her especially vulnerable to Deborah's methods. "If I am the worst of all sinners, O may I be conscious of it. . . . O that I could say to Deborah that if I am the cause of this lasting Obstruction I wish her to inform me." To be an "Obstruction" in the Friends' sense of the word was to be a vile sinner, so lost as to create a barrier between the Spirit and the whole congregation. It was one of the worst things a Quaker could be, inasmuch as it wrought harm to the whole meeting. The fear that she might be such an obstacle to the good life of her fellows caused Susan hours of secret torment. But she could never muster the courage to speak to Deborah about it. The only person who gave her any help was Lydia Mott, an assistant teacher slightly older than herself. To Lydia, Susan once on impulse confided her state of mind. "I told her I sometimes felt as if I were the worst of all beings. She said it was right to think so sometimes, but not to give up to discouragement." On this one slight encouraging note Susan was buoyed for a time into regions of peace and hope.

✍§ V Yet she was not wholly unhappy. While she floundered in the depths of conscience and doctrine, she remained at heart still a child, delighting in the large snowflakes on the porch, the ringing of the bells in Philadelphia, the joy of an occasional short sleigh ride. She records this in her diary: "Cordelia E. Marple has a little juniper bird which she found on the snow where a sportsman had been and had wounded it, but not so much that it can sit on a bush and eat juniper berries. It is now on the window forward of my seat." Most of all she enjoyed the companionship of her fellows and joined in their "levity and mirthfulness and nonsensical conversation." Though she sometimes rebuked herself for it, she forgot her good resolutions and fell again and again. After one of Deborah's moral lectures she confessed to her diary: "She seemed to think there were those who countenanced others in their faults by smiling at them instead of kindly reproving them. I am too well aware that it is too much the case with me."

Susan and her sister became friends with the two Miller girls, about their own age. Susan went so far in her diary as to describe them as "lovely innocent girls"; but then she thought better of it and crossed out *innocent*.

In line with her age—she had her eighteenth birthday while at school—she liked boys. John Moulson, Deborah's brother, was the only boy about the place. Susan was on friendly, joking terms with John. He brought the mail and sometimes teased her by withholding her letters from home. Susan never lacked for speech with John as she did with his sister. She maintained a similar give-and-take relationship with Aaron McLean in Battenville, with whom she corresponded. When Aaron wrote in midwinter that the Hudson River was navigable, she noted archly in her diary: "Aaron was quite kind in informing us that we could go home now as well as in the spring, but I think for one that I will not accept the invitation, as I would rather remain and endeavor to improve in both Morality and Literature."

A letter from Aaron brought news of a wedding in Battenville. Susan's comment reflected strong views on marriage and concluded with a rather naïve concept of the matrimonial tie. She said in her diary:

I cannot express my surprise with as much force as he did. The reason is, I suppose, that I cannot realize the fact. Sometimes I am ready to say, it cannot be so, and think it a piece of stuff A[aron] has invented to astonish us. But when reason returns I can quickly discover it to be impossible for him to have invented. But they are married and we cannot render them otherwise, as I say. I think any female would rather live and die an old maid. Is it possible that Harriet Stout is married to Moses S. Hartwell and his five children?

⋑§ VI What Susan learned at Miss Moulson's was valuable if not broadening. Considering the time she wasted in moral agoniz-

ing, it is surprising that she learned anything. But in later life she
gave signs of having gained some idea of science, which, though
superficial, nourished a native tendency. Deborah's training in
orthography, down to the dotting of an *i* correctly, did a great deal
for her level of performance in that field, which remained always
high. The total lack of literary and art appreciation continued an
abiding loss, which Susan shared, however, with many other distinguished graduates of Quaker institutions.

Deborah's attitude toward Susan contains one extenuating factor.
Deborah was an invalid, slowly succumbing to a fatal disease—con-
sumption. After long years of teaching she had only just succeeded
in establishing her own school when this disease attacked her. During her first year, when Guelma was a student, she managed very
well. In the second year, when Susan appeared, her illness had
gained upon her. Fighting for her life, missing classes sometimes
for days and even weeks, the stricken woman tried bravely to deny
her condition. She would not admit her illness, and her self-decep-
tion in this respect enhanced a lack of sincerity apparently native
to her. Absent from class through illness, she declared the class
suspended as a punishment for this or that. Or else she owned up
to her illness and ascribed it to the worry and anxiety occasioned
by her pupils' behavior. Her frequent absences therefore cast a
mantle of gloom and guilt over the entire school. It was an atmosphere in which a sensitive girl like Susan was bound to suffer
greatly.

Realizing that her school was running down, Deborah engaged
an assistant from Philadelphia, Mr. Joshua Coffin. She had to have
a man to teach the peculiar subjects of her curriculum. Mr. Coffin
introduced Susan to the idea of algebra, which he was teaching to
Lydia Mott. Susan became so avid about the subject that she continued to pursue it, and eventually, a few years later, succeeded in
finding a teacher. She had a factual mind, and every step of her
education, at home and at school, helped to confirm her tendency.
Nothing was ever aimed at awakening the imagination; everything
steadily aimed at stamping it out.

Mr. Coffin also introduced to the school the idea of phrenology,
a pseudo science just then attracting much notice and within the
next few years attaining wide vogue and popularity. Coffin brought
out a phrenologist from Philadelphia who "examined the girls'

heads." In Susan's case, as she recorded, "He began with the good organs and said nothing of the bad ones. I should like to know the whole." She was not satisfied with his favorable report; it certainly did not agree with that of Miss Moulson. Her interest in the subject continued. When her father came to take her home he must needs also submit his head to the phrenologist. "He said everything the Phrenologist said was the truth and nothing but the truth, and Father concluded there must be something in it."

⋖§ VII   Daniel took his daughters to Philadelphia to the yearly meeting. Yearly meetings were the high note of every Quaker's life, and the Philadelphia Yearly Meeting was a great event for rural folk like the Anthonys. Daniel wished his daughters to have the experience and they spent two nights in a Philadelphia hotel for that purpose. On the way home they stopped in Brooklyn to visit relatives and to shop. In spite of his mounting business troubles, Daniel could not forgo the chance of giving the girls one last fling in the big world as he knew it.

They reached home on a fine May day. Susan had been absent six months, but it seemed like a year. Spring softened the outline of the Battenville hills and the birds nested and sang in the budding trees, putting one little "juniper bird" to shame. Susan had left home in the bitter snow, and the world had been remade in her absence. It was benign and beautiful.

But the atmosphere at home was not keyed to the harmony. She had been forewarned by her father's letters of a great change impending. He had written he might have to give up the Battenville house and move somewhere else. Aaron McLean had also uttered some bleak warnings. But they had not been repeated, and Daniel had showed no signs of economy during their homeward journey. The stark facts dawned upon Susan when she first reached Battenville. Apprehension had become reality and the dreadful details of her father's crisis stared her in the face. The date for Daniel's assignment of his property was at hand; there was nothing left but to prepare the legal papers and deliver them to the court.

Aunt Hannah Hoxie, on a visit to the family, gave them poor comfort. "She sympathized with us on account of losing our property," said Susan, "saying it would be hard for us to give up going in the company we have become accustomed to. But"—she added with spirit—"I do not think loss of property will cause us to mingle in low company." Aunt Hannah did nothing to help Susan bear the shock, though as a Quaker preacher she might have been expected to administer some comfort.

Susan's distress concerned itself, characteristically, with her father's condition. On reaching home, the buoyant Daniel seemed to give up utterly. He had not the courage to take the legal papers to the court himself but sent them by Aaron McLean. He shut himself up on First Day and did not attend the meeting in the schoolroom, a more serious symptom than Susan realized. But she realized a lot. "The great depression . . . has worn hard on my dear Father's mind. O, that he may have the courage to pass through all the trying scenes of life," she wrote.

But Daniel soon revived and again became able to act for himself. When the papers had been filed, together with an inventory of everything he owned—mill, house, furniture, the clothes of his wife and daughters, everything to the last trifling possession—he moved to obtain a stay of execution. He was accordingly permitted to stay undisturbed in his house for a year. His native optimism revived and his flow of "ideas" became normal again.

Meanwhile Susan had been offered a position as teacher in Union Village (now Greenwich). In the days when she had taught without needing to do so, she had never hesitated; but now when she had no choice, she entertained qualms. In teaching this school she would have to lay aside "the singular language," which, in Deborah Moulson's category, constituted one of the worst of all sins. She still lingered in a definite fear of doing anything that might displease Deborah. To her surprise, Guelma had dropped her Quaker speech unhesitatingly on reaching home. Susan could not understand this. She considered and decided that she would maintain the Quaker style at home at all costs, while using the worldly language in the schoolroom.

Before the end of May she was established in Union Village and writing gloomily in her diary: "I again left my home to mingle with strangers, which seems to be my sad lot. Separation was rendered the more trying on account of the embarrassing condition of our business affairs." She was unhappy and confused and continued to be so. Of this sad time she writes in her *Reminiscences:*

I was boarding at a house on the main road. I sat looking out of the window one morning before going to school, and saw a big two-horse wagon passing. It was Uncle Read. I jumped up and rushed out. I knew he was going to Battenville to see Father, and this made me weak with home sickness. But I couldn't make him hear, and I had to teach all day feeling sad and unhappy. Just as soon as school was out I started for home. I hoped for a pick-up ride; but no one came along, so I walked all the way. I had on a pair of buckskin shoes that blistered my feet.

But on Monday she was back in school performing her duties. Her weakness had passed and she was able to go through the routine of a familiar task. She taught all of that summer and into the fall. Her diary fell silent for the rest of that year—a sure sign with Susan that her interest in life was at a low ebb.

◄§ VIII· When Guelma Anthony returned home from school she had been away for two years. This was the term of higher education which Daniel considered suitable for his daughters, and Susan would have had the same had the financial crash not intervened. Guelma had been able to stay on the full term.

Guelma had changed. In the midst of the excitement and concern, Aaron McLean, aged twenty-six, was instantly aware of the change. Aaron had known Guelma and Susan since they were eight and six respectively. The three had grown up together. A kindly-disposed youth, he took on the part of big brother to the girls, as their own brother, "D.R.," was too young for the part. Aaron wrote often to Guelma and Susan at Hamilton and apparently to both equally. Sometimes he sent newspapers, which were as welcome as letters in those days of scarce newsprint. Susan said in her diary that no one was as thoughtful and as kind as Aaron about sending news.

The change in the relations of the trio could have brought nothing less than a shock to Susan. She found herself left out while the other two sought opportunities for tête-à-têtes. She noticed the fact in her diary without comment. "Sarah Jane Hyatt was here, went home and told that G[uelma] and A[aron] were in the dining-room alone."

Susan was immature in some ways though by no means in all. She should have realized, and probably did, that Guelma, nearly two years her senior, had the first claim on a playmate who had turned into a young man. She had long been accustomed to Guelma's first claims as the elder and no doubt she sometimes resented them. While at school she wrote in her diary: "I dreamed last night of going home, meeting them all, and kissing them, but had left G.P. at Hamilton." Her actual return was nothing like the dream.

Susan's diary gives no hint of any hurt at the time. At first she did not understand. "G.P. had dropped the singular language." (Aaron was not a Quaker.) But Susan did not understand why. She then went away to teach while Guelma, though teaching also, stayed at home with the family, really to be near her lover. Susan seems to have taken a very dull-minded view of what was going on.

⌔ IX   In his hour of trouble Daniel Anthony's thoughts turned back to Nine Partners'. If he had only remained there as a teacher, how different his life might have been! From brooding he evoked another idea. He still had his Battenville home and would have it at least for a year. He would turn it into a boarding school for boys.

Somewhat doubtful of his own abilities and having, as usual, other irons in the fire, he decided to engage a headmaster. Daniel could be trusted to engage no second-rate teacher, and in Daniel Wright he secured a very superior scholar. By this plan he could give most of his time to the one small mill he still owned and which might be developed into a paying concern. He sent out notices and soon had eight boarding scholars assembled under his roof. To these were added his own three younger children and day pupils from the neighborhood. Only Daniel could have moved so fast. In June he and Daniel Wright were ready to start, and they ran the school with reasonable success for a year.

These were hard times for everybody. Aaron and Guelma could not think of marrying. McLean's fortunes were involved almost as deeply as Daniel's. He had not lost his home, built long before the golden age of credit arrived, but he had lost his mills; and his son had to go out seeking for employment. Susan had to teach in Union Village, which was a real grievance to her, when a scholar like Daniel Wright was dispensing wisdom and learning in her own home. "Out of the whole time I have attended three months," she said at the end of the year. "I shall probably never attend school again." In January, Grandmother Read died, and her body was laid out in the fine entrance hall with the graceful banister. Daniel had preserved his house just long enough for his wife's aged parents to die within its shelter. As the year went by, the small profit from the school and the lesser profit from the mill pointed more and more to the final abandonment of the Battenville home.

Near the end of the term the school suffered a serious setback. The boys lived and slept in the attic, which had been converted into a dormitory. The hillside behind the house was on a level with this story. Some member of the family, walking on the hillside, glanced through the windows and observed the boys, who should have been studying, engaged in cardplaying. The school was instantly in a tumult. "There was no school yesterday, there was not much study among us," says Susan's diary. "In the evening . . . Father told 4 of the boys, who were in the kitchen washing, they might pack up for Easton (first stop on the way home)." It was a terrible loss for Daniel's small register, so near the end, too. But rather than countenance a vice like cardplaying Daniel would have closed the whole school instantly.

Daniel Wright restored order and finished the term with something of a flourish. The middle of March was graduation day. "There were considerably many collected here. . . ." wrote Susan. "We were examined a very short time in each study and read our compositions and the gentlemen declaimed. My composition was most miserably read; on account of my agitation a blurr came over my eyes, so that I did but scarcely get through with it. . . . All the rest got through comfortably and when my turn came, I, one whom all thought the most courageous and least liable to feel any of those horrid feelings——" She did not finish. Her agitation and the grammar problem were too much for her.

Susan felt a special sadness because this day represented the end of her school life. "All the advancement which I here-after make must be by my own exertion and desire to gain useful knowledge." What did she expect? As a matter of fact, she had had far more education than the average American girl of her times could boast of. In her future relations with the public there was far too little appreciation of the quality and thoroughness of her early training, limited though it was in some directions by Quaker prejudice. Her preparation for a career was as good as or better than that of most of her associates, and remained so until the day when college graduates flocked into the lists.

In the spring of 1839, just a year after Susan left Hamilton, her father received from the school an announcement of Deborah Moulson's death. Susan learned from Lydia Mott the details of the teacher's last illness. "D. was confined to her bed for the last two months, and her sufferings were great." The news helps to extenuate the capricious behavior of the schoolmistress during Susan's year at her school. But Susan could not think this out. "How well I can remember her advices and reproofs," she wrote in her diary. "It might be said in truth she was too good to remain on Earth, her sun has set in glory." With this noble tribute she tried to bury her sense of injury, not out of pity for Deborah, who had been sick and suffering, but because in her nineteen-year-old philosophy death wiped out all wrongs. Thus her sense of injury persisted underneath for many years.

CHAPTER FIVE

DANIEL'S BANKRUPTCY

◦§ I   By this time it was apparent that McLean's noble foray
into the Tophet Valley, promising to supply capital if Daniel
Anthony would supply skill and labor, was based on false pre-
tenses. Not that McLean so viewed it. Most businessmen of his
inflated times would have considered his offer as made in good
faith. One congressman of the day put the situation in a nutshell
by proclaiming: "What is the cause which makes us, above all
others, a happy, great, and prosperous people? Sir, it is contained
in two words: it is our Credit System." What the judge planned
to supply was not capital but credit. His standing with the local
banks was unfortunately excellent. At first the mills prospered and
the so-called owners were happy, great, and prosperous. Then the
benign credit system collapsed.

The financial policies of Andrew Jackson had undermined it,
and the election of Martin Van Buren, committed to the same
program, pulled out the last prop. The late Charles Beard, commenting on the debacle, says: "The fact was that one of the
periodic cycles of capitalism was at hand and the party in power
. . . could offer no effective remedy, if any there were." McLean
and Daniel had assumed that the day of accounting was a long way
off if it ever actually came. When the panic of 1837 overtook them
they were still cheerfully "expanding" their enterprise and debts.

An isolated industry like theirs stood not a chance. The cotton
mills around Boston, buttressed by a complex combination of

mills, insurance companies, warehouses, and even railroads, seriously felt the shock. They suspended dividends for a while. Still, though they wobbled, they floated, owing to their swollen and interlocking background. Nothing that Daniel and McLean could do would save their investment.

In September 1837, Daniel went from city to city trying to sell his cloth. From New York he wrote to his brother John, still a farmer in Adams:

Such times in everything that pertains to business never were known in this land before. Today I have passed through Pine street and have not seen a single box or bale of goods of any kind whatever. Last year at this time a person could hardly go through the street without clambering over goods of all descriptions. A truck cart loaded with merchandise is now a rare object. A bale of goods can not be sold at any price. The countenances of all our best business men are stretched out in perpendicular direction and when the time will let them come back into human shape not even the wisest pretend to guess. Those that are out of all speculative and ever-changing business consider themselves in a Paradismal state.

He pushed on to Washington, where the President had called a special session of Congress, trying to espy through their deliberations some ray of hope for the small businessman. He reported his experiences in a letter to his wife:

Washington, Sept. 11, 1837.—I arrived last evening—came in R. Road cars from Baltimore, 39 miles, in two hours, over a barren and almost uncultivated country. The public buildings and one street called Pennsylvania Avenue are all that are worth mention in this place. . . . As a specimen of some of the big finery in the town, I will name one room in Martin's house, 90 ft. by 42, the furniture of which cost $22,000. . . . Our Congressmen are some like other folks, they look out first for themselves. They have spent most of this day in debating whether *they* shall be paid in *specie.*

If Daniel looked back with regret to his little mill in Adams before the serpent of high finance entered his Eden, he was too robust to dwell on it. He looked forward to the next step, and at first events seemed to reward him. A false dawn of recovery followed the early panic. It was then that he sent Susan to the Hamilton school for the winter. Later, when his notes fell due, he obtained another year of grace for paying them. He struggled on with the small mill that he owned and with his boarding school until, at the end of the year, the day of reckoning came at last. In March 1839 all was irretrievably lost.

The furniture of the house was removed to the company store for sale at public auction. Every article in the place was inventoried: Lucy's beautiful cotton sheets, her silver spoons, the groceries in the pantry, the family Bible, the daughters' clothes. Susan, who had been teaching for most of the year, noted in her diary: "I purchased things to the amount of 11 dollars." The money she had earned was used to buy back the belongings of her family. Fortunately she was not the only one with cash on hand. Lucy Anthony's brother Joshua Read had come all the way from Palatine Bridge, New York, to attend the sale and bid for the main part of his sister's household belongings. Without Uncle Joshua's timely aid the family would have been stripped to the last pot and pan.

To Susan it brought a startling and unforgettable revelation: the house and everything in it, down to the needles and pins of the wife, belonged to the man of the family. Her mother's things, given her by her own parents, had been seized to pay her father's debts. She would not soon forget the lesson.

The furniture salvaged by Uncle Joshua was taken to a house three miles away which Daniel had rented. The family had already repaired thither, devoid of clothes and baggage. Their refuge was an abandoned tavern in Hardscrabble (then so called), standing on the bank of the rushing Batten Kill. It had been much used formerly when logging down the Green Mountains was a more lively trade. Some travelers still came that way, and when they turned up Lucy Anthony took them in, which added a trifle to her income.

The inn was a large frame house with a wide hall, great high-ceilinged rooms, and the unfailing mark of its kind in those days— a double-deck piazza with spindle railings. The third floor had been built and used in the tavern's heyday for a dance hall.

On each side of the house stood a small mill, one for grist and

another for satinette. Mortgaged, to be sure, they were Daniel's
to use for the next few years. By operating them he hoped to redeem the mortgage and to get on his feet once more as a manufacturer. The family spent freezing winters in the vast rooms and
earned a bare living by entertaining travelers.

These were hard years for the Anthonys, as they were for almost
everybody else. Daniel's hopes for redeeming the mortgage proved
footless; he took to logging; he broke his leg. The only real earners
were the older daughters, who were steadily teaching for $2.50 a
week and giving every cent they earned to their father to pay the
interest on the mortgage. Daniel, demoted from businessman to
day laborer, toiled endlessly without getting ahead. As a small contribution to respectability, he got the name Hardscrabble changed
to Centre Falls and managed to have himself appointed as postmaster. This meant the family could send and receive letters without having to pay postage. It was their only luxury.

The odd thing is that under these conditions the family appears
to have been more than ordinarily happy. Lucy Anthony declared
in her old age that these had been the happiest years of her life.
Quite contrary to Aunt Hoxie's dismal prophecy, Susan and her
sisters mingled more than formerly with the young people of Battenville and the vicinity. They shared in parties, buggy rides, and
picnics. There was no change whatever in their social status, and
the girls had grown old enough to enjoy society.

◄§ II   Susan enjoyed the change from school tasks to the activities of settling in a new home. "I once more resume and hold communion with my little record," she wrote. "Did a large washing
today. . . . Spent today at the spinning-wheel. . . . Baked 21
loaves of bread. . . . Have our carpet in the loom, I have been
weaving for several days past; yesterday and today wove 3 yds. . . .
The saw-mill was raised sixth and seventh days; 20 men took tea
with us on sixth day and 12 on seventh day." All this was like the
old happy time in East Hoosac.

It was spring in Centre Falls and Susan was nineteen. She observed the boys around her and compared their looks. "Moses Vail
arrived here seventh day on a visit. . . . I think Moses is a very

clever fellow, though not so handsome as some." [Why did she cross out the last six words? Did she have some particular handsome fellow in mind?] She took especial notice of Job Whipple and William P. Norton. They called frequently, Whipple directing his attentions to Susan and Norton his to Hannah. Susan spent some thought upon Whipple. She attended a party rendered noteworthy by his absence. "J Whipple was not there on account of a swollen face, caused by having some front teeth out and taking cold." When Whipple's attentions strayed, as they sometimes did, she was not happy about it. "J[ob] is a most noble-hearted fellow, kind and courteous in his manners, friendly and obliging to all. I have respected him highly since our first acquaintance. J[ob] is at M[aria] Wilson's this evening. May he know that he has found in me a spirit congenial to his own and not suffer the glare of beauty to attract both eye and heart." Susan thought herself to be totally devoid of the glare of beauty, but she believed that a woman could have other attractions.

Whipple and Norton continued to call all through the spring. Susan's diary records: "J. Whipple and W. Norton from the Village called here last night and made quite a little visit. I had very good times and so did all the rest, I guess. I awoke this morning a little after midnight, arose and went to the window and saw the constellation Libra and some others, which so filled my mind with the beauty of the stars that I could not get to sleep again. I lay some time, and then got up, found it about 15 minutes past four. The morning was splendid indeed." In some way or other the previous evening had left her too excited for sleep.

In May the friendship was interrupted. Susan again went away from home to teach in New Rochelle.

&§ III Eunice Kenyon, the daughter of a family of the Easton Meeting, conducted a Quaker school for girls in New Rochelle. The offer of the position came through the meeting, to which the Anthonys also belonged. Susan lost no time in accepting it. Within a few days she was on her way, making her second journey down the Hudson on a crowded steamboat.

Daniel put her on the boat at Troy, and from there on she was escorted by Eunice's brother Christopher. On the boat she listened to a discussion of slavery and saw with her own eyes some living and breathing slave-owners. The Southerners were engaged in an argument with those around them, and Susan listened with wide-eyed horror to their incredible statements about slavery.

Arriving in Brooklyn, she attended yearly meeting, where a second revelation of the world's wickedness awaited her. A Quaker preacher, Rachel Barker, addressed the congregation on the subject of prostitution and houses of ill fame. It seems a strange subject to be discussed at a general meeting where children of all ages were often brought along. But so it happened, and Susan, understandably, received a shock. "She called the houses of ill-fame 'the abomination of desolation'; truly is she exercised for the licentious part of the community. O may the language of her heart sink deep into their hearts who are guilty and prove a safe-guard to those who have never yet entered those wretched abodes." The rest of the program, which she described as "very good," included a long religious homily by her own aunt Hannah Hoxie from Adams. But Aunt Hannah's high discourse could not erase from her mind the revelations she had received from Rachel Barker's talk.

At New Rochelle she resumed the stilted tone of the letters she had written from Deborah Moulson's school. The moral compositions she had produced when Deborah looked over her shoulder were reproduced, and Deborah, had she been alive, would surely have praised them. She then proceeded to put the world around her to rights. Slavery, intemperance, prostitution, and Martin Van Buren were all mixed up in her mind as sources of evil. Wherever they lifted their heads, Susan would stamp them out. She was no longer the girl who had smiled at the faults of her companions instead of correcting them.

There was neither man nor boy at Miss Kenyon's school to joke with her as John Moulson had joked at Hamilton. But Job Whipple and William Norton still tried to keep on jolly terms with her, with the following sad result:

I received three papers yesterday afternoon, was much surprised to find one from J. Whipple and one from R. Wilson and the third from W. Norton. What they sent them for I cannot imagine. They were mailed the same day and all the same day's paper. They were the Washington Co. *Sentinel* and the contents were none of the

most polite, a piece of poetry on love, and a piece entitled "Ridin'
on a Rail" and numerous little stories and things equally as bad.
What they mean I can not tell, but silence will prove the best
rebuke. Dreamed last night of being at home and thinking much
about this curious incident. Maybe when I grow older and wiser
I can unravel this mysterious affair.

If Whipple and Norton were again heard from that summer, the
diary does not mention it. Silence had probably administered the
desired rebuke. Susan had certainly changed a good deal since her
gay evening with the same boys, which had so uplifted her feelings
that she communed with the stars. In her first boarding-school
teaching she naturally tended to follow Deborah Moulson's example. To this something had been added: the startling revelations
of the eloquent Rachel Barker. Venial sins were associated with
utter corruption, for did they not lead to the worst? She could not
write to her young sister Mary without preaching to her. She could
not send Mary a simple present without imposing a penance. "I
also send a fine grass linen pocket handkerchief to be yours when
you have corrected that fault; then tell G.P. if she will mark your
name nicely on it and then call it your own. Mother had better
be the judge."

In her access of self-righteousness Susan decided that she must
reform Aunt Eliza Dickinson's husband, though Uncle Albert was
old enough to be her father. The Dickinsons had been at Brooklyn
Yearly Meeting with her and had boarded at the same place. At
table Susan had observed Uncle Albert drinking cider and ale. Accordingly she took her pen in hand, and as her diary says, "lectured
him severely." Uncle Albert replied promptly:

Thy aunt Ann Eliza says to tell thee we are temperate drinkers
and hope to remain so. We should think from the shape of thy letter that thou thyself hadst had a good horn from the contents of
the cider barrel, a part being written one side up and a part the
other way, and it would need someone in nearly the same predicament to keep track of it. We hope thy cranium will get straightened when the answer to this is penned, so that we may follow the
varied thoughts with less trouble. A little advice perhaps would be
good on both sides, and they that give should be willing to receive.
See to it that thou payest me down for this.

This letter seems to have been just what Susan needed. She said in a letter to Aaron McLean:

I have just received a letter from Uncle A. F. Dickinson and such a dressing down as he has given me for talking to him about wine and cider can't be beat by anybody, the quantity of blackguard can't be measured, but hardly. But I guess it is tit for tat with us. . . . I do sincerely hope our folks will not by and by begin to think wine is harmless and therefore they can offer it to travellers. But why have I written that, for are they not stronger and firmer in the truth than myself?

On the question of slavery, Susan found New Rochelle wanting. This was surprising and confusing to her. She had not known that Quakers could err on a question in which they were plainly directed by their religion. Three colored girls, visiting in the neighborhood, brought the local opinion to light. "They have been in the habit of attending Friends' Meeting where they have lived," wrote Susan, "but here they are not allowed to sit even on the back seat. One long-faced elder dusted off a seat in the gallery and told them to sit there." Incensed at this treatment, Susan took every occasion to be friendly with the girls, visiting them and inviting them to her school for tea. "They are indeed fine *ladies*," she wrote indignantly. "To show this kind of people respect in this heathen land affords me double pleasure."

In the late summer Martin Van Buren passed through the village. Susan refused to look out of the window at him, while most of the school stayed away to see the President. With great disgust she learned later that Aaron McLean and her parents had driven to Saratoga to see Van Buren on his tour. Aaron reported: "I saw him drink no wine, although there was plenty about him, nor did your father and mother, who saw him dine at the United States Hotel." But Susan could accept no alibis for Matt, as she disrespectfully called him. He not only drank wine but also frequented the theater, that resort of sin for all good Quakers. The truth was that she felt Van Buren was responsible for the financial panic that had wrecked her father's life, and she could not forgive him. Even her father's tolerance could not penetrate the hard shell she had taken on.

Susan was fast retreating into a corner where she must live alone. In New Rochelle she was lonely; and the more lonely she grew, the more determined she seemed to push others away from her. The school provided her with no companionship; the headmistress, Eunice Kenyon, being away most of the time. One sympathetic Quaker family lived nearby, but Susan saw very little of them.

She brooded over Rachel Barker, a young woman who spoke with so much self-possession before a great audience. She wrote to Aaron, with whom she had evidently argued the question, about women's preaching: "If you could hear *her* preach once, you would (after it) believe in women's preaching. What an absurd notion that women have not intellectual and moral faculties sufficient for anything but domestic concerns!" There was a new note in her relations with Aaron since her Hamilton days. They were always arguing.

⋙ IV   To admit that she was jealous of Guelma's happy engagement was impossible for Susan. It would have been equivalent to admitting that she was an abandoned woman. There are signs, however, that in the most simple and natural way this was the case. Soon after reaching New Rochelle she recorded this dream:

6-10-1839   Second day.—I dreamed of being married last night, queerly enough too. I imagined myself in New York and Father with me. It seemed as if I had married a Presbyterian priest that I had never seen before that day. Thought I repented thoroughly before one day had passed. It appeared to me that I had acted rashly; my mind was much troubled.

Aaron McLean was a Presbyterian and a very pious one, about as pious as his brother, who was a Presbyterian minister (all ministers were "priests" in the Quaker vernacular).

Aaron continued as thoughtful and attentive as he had always been, sending her copies of the *Rural Respository*, a dignified publication which contained no poems on love and "other things equally bad." But in between his kindnesses he lapsed more and more into faultfinding. "I entreat you to be prudent in your remarks," he wrote, "and not attempt to 'niggerize' the good old Friends about you. Above all, let them know that you are about the only Abolitionist in *this* vicinity." (This was not true; Susan's father and the Easton Quakers were Abolitionists.) Susan was taking private lessons in algebra; Aaron produced the standard objection that algebra was not in woman's sphere. His criticisms were constant, but Susan's newly adopted attitudes often presented the challenge. Still, Aaron remained the one with whom she discussed her deepest interests.

One particular letter to him began: "I do not wish you to say I am foolish before you read all I have to say. "This was followed by several pages describing a plan for growing silkworms in Centre Falls. It seems that Eunice Kenyon and some of her neighbors had gone heavily into the silkworm craze of the time. By Susan's account, they had made money out of it, at the slightest possible cost in time and expense. It was all pure profit. Susan proposed that she and Hannah should conduct a school in the Centre Falls house and raise silkworms on the side, as Eunice did. It required practically no time to care for them—the children could collect the leaves—the only essential was plenty of mulberry trees. She urged the family to scout for mulberries in the neighborhood; she herself remembered where there was at least one tree. She had no idea of the number of such trees at home and still less idea of how Eunice had obtained a market for her cocoons. It was a beautiful dream. Susan was endowed with some of her father's imagination, and nothing showed it more clearly than her great caterpillar fantasy.

≥§ V   Eunice Kenyon's school, unlike Deborah Moulson's, had a pleasant, wholesome atmosphere. Susan wrote to her parents: "I think the school is a good one, though not managed as Deborah's was. E[unice] is cheerful and communicative with her scholars. She has black hair, a large and very dark face; but I believe a good heart and a charitable spirit are enclosed within. She dresses about as plain as Sarah Burtis did the first time she taught school at our house." Eunice was a woman of solid virtues and plain clothes. There was less excitement in her environment than in Deborah's, and there were also fewer mysteries.

The pupils were young children. The teaching was easy. They were allowed simple pleasures, like cultivating their own flower beds around the house, keeping their own collections of shells, and going sea-bathing at a neighbor's who had a "bathing-house." "We had fine times," said Susan, "though it required much patience and care with those little girls. They dropped some of their things in the water." Susan enjoyed the long walks to the beach and the glimpses of sailing vessels and steamboats on the Sound. All this was peaceful and relaxing but not stimulating as the world around Daniel always managed to be.

After a couple of months Eunice went home for a holiday and left Susan in charge. It is enlightening to know that she was paid for her services at the rate of two dollars a week. All went well in Eunice's absence except for a slight mishap. A mother and grandmother of one of the pupils dropped in for a day's visit. "I am happy I do not have city folks to wait on every day," said Susan. "They however seemed interested in nothing but their own Darling children." All went agreeably until it came out that Susan had sent one of their Darlings to bed as a punishment. The mother became angry and insisted that Susan, as a mere assistant, had exceeded her authority. She finally left, promising to complain to Eunice. "I hope they will," wrote Susan. "I hope she will not be such a fool as I was to cry, but hold to her rights; and I know she will, as she possesses and feels more independence than I fear I ever shall."

Eunice's return to school brought no relief, but the contrary. She fell ill, and Susan had to nurse her in addition to teaching the school. Eunice's sickness, though apparently not serious, alarmed Susan more than was necessary. Deborah Moulson's recent demise had lodged the idea of death in her mind. Susan had never before seen a typical doctor of the times at work. "The doctor came and gave her a dose of calomel and bled her freely, telling me not to faint as I held the bowl. Her arm commenced bleeding in the night and she lost so much blood she fainted. Next day the doctor came . . . and gave her another dose of calomel." The final effect was good; Eunice recovered; but the treatment gave Susan a lifelong horror of bleeding and calomel, and she kept as far away from these remedies as she could.

❧ VI   Susan had been vaguely promised an engagement of ten months, but her stay was abruptly terminated at the end of the summer. She went home to attend Guelma's and Aaron's wedding, which took place on September 19, 1839.

She had had some correspondence with Aaron, referring indirectly to the approaching nuptials. In one letter she wrote: "You, who have been exposed to this fever [an epidemic of romance, she charged, was sweeping the village] ought to be very careful. Remember the old saying, 'that an ounce of prevention is worth a pound of cure.' " A jesting reference which suggests that she did not know how far things had gone between Aaron and Guelma. She followed this by another letter, still more mystifying:

Aaron:— . . . As regards these extra happenings and going to New Rochelle, I don't think and don't know. I do not wish to hear any more of them in this offish way. If you have anything to say, say it, or if you wish anything, express it in plain English, that I may no longer be left in uncertainty with respect to matters and things. . . .

It was after this that Guelma and Aaron got down to serious business and stated in plain English that they wished to fix the date for their wedding and that it depended in part on Susan's plans for coming home. Susan debated the matter in her diary. She wished so much to go home for her sister's marriage, "a solemn occasion," she added, "for such I esteem it." It was easier on her conscience to go home for a solemn occasion than for a joyous one. She needed an excuse for breaking her engagement with Eunice.

◆§ VII   At Centre Falls, Susan took the first school at hand, the local district school. It was in this position that she demonstrated her power to command by thrashing a big boy, the bully of the class, into complete submission. Her first biographer, Mrs. Harper, describes the incident as an example of the young teacher's courage. In her own Reminiscences of the time Susan does not mention it. Only two months before, she had shed tears over being reprimanded by the mother of a pupil. Her weeping and her violence might be symptoms of an upset state of mind.

She took up her social life in the village where she had left it off. Picnics, outings, excursions to the neighboring villages and even as far as Saratoga were common occurrences. Long tête-à-tête buggy rides were the most common engagements. Susan did not lack for these. She had her preferences among the local swains, but she had no skill in attracting those she preferred.

In the course of a long drive to Saratoga she received a proposal of marriage. The young man was not one of her favorites. (Her favorite had been borne off by another girl.) Yet she was amiable enough with her second choice to cause him to offer her his hand and heart. She was not one of the girls who stayed at home without an escort when the other girls went out. She was no wallflower in Centre Falls.

VIII   Shortly after Guelma's marriage she came to grips with her secret problem. Since childhood she had suffered from a sense of inferiority owing to the strabismus of one eye. In all the years of her growing up she had endured it silently. Nothing could reassure her about her looks, not even the attentions of the boys nor a proposal of marriage. Since the day when her mother had deplored and bewailed the affliction, nothing could ever reassure her. She had reached the age of twenty with the fixed idea that her defective right eye had permanently destroyed her looks.

Then for the first time she heard that there was an operation for cross-eye. There was even a doctor in Union Village, a few miles away, who performed it. The ever-devoted Daniel immediately came to her aid. He drove her over to Union Village, remained with her during the operation, and paid the doctor who performed it. Susan recalled the experience as a much more serious affair than it actually could have been. Because of her deep emotional investment she remembered it as major surgery. The result was profoundly tragic. When the bandages were taken off, she says, "We found he had cut the muscle too much, and that threw the eye the other way." She had waited twenty years for the miracle, and when it came it failed her.

Susan says she "used to put on her mother's spectacles and run off out of sight." She thought she could see better through those glasses, though her mother was forty-seven and she was twenty. The malpractitioner continued his services by advising that "if she could find anything to see through let her put them on." So Susan continued wearing her mother's spectacles all through her youth. She must have had an exceedingly good pair of eyes to stand so much abuse. To the end of her life she possessed excellent vision and unusually serviceable eyes.

It is hard to reconcile this story with Susan's various photographs. The strabismus must have been very slight; it is not perceptible in the daguerreotypes taken at the ages of thirty-two and thirty-six and reproduced in the Harper biography. It was not until the age of forty-eight that she got the idea of being photographed in profile so as to conceal her defect. She followed this plan afterward, with very few exceptions.

The testimony of those who knew her leads us to think that she exaggerated the condition. Her cousin and secretary for twelve years, Mrs. Emma Sweet, told the present writer: "She had a sort of cast in one eye. I guess you would say crossed." At the same moment, hanging on the wall behind Mrs. Sweet was a treasured full-face photograph of Susan showing nothing at all peculiar about the eyes. This might be explained by the statement of Mrs. Harriet Taylor Upton, Susan's close friend for fifteen years: "Asked to explain more fully the defect in one of Miss Anthony's eyes, Mrs. Upton said one eye was crossed—either turned in or out—but when she looked straight at you, one did not notice it. Also she wore glasses a large part of her life—this helped to hide the defect."

From the first it was never as noticeable as Susan imagined. Mrs. Upton, who knew her well, could not say whether the eye turned "in or out." If Susan could have been more unconscious of it, others might have been the same. Furthermore, she believed that on account of the defect she possessed an impaired vision. As she grew older this idea seems to have vanished, and she put more and more strain on her eyes as the years went on. But, by contrast, her sensitivity about its effect on her looks seemed to increase. Very curiously, as an old lady she was more concerned about it than she had been as a girl.

§ IX   Removal to Centre Falls had interrupted the religious services in Daniel's Battenville home. But the ten-mile drive to the Easton service was considered no great hardship in those days. Many of the Friends had to drive much greater distances.

Daniel's relations with the Society had continued good. To be sure, a slight flurry had once arisen when, during one of his trips to New York, he had bought a camel's-hair cloak with a wide cape and a colored kerchief to wear around his neck. Some of the Friends objected to the wide cape and brightly colored kerchief as "out of plainness," but Daniel had continued to wear them and was not disciplined.

The tavern he occupied in Centre Falls led to a graver misdemeanor. The young people of the neighborhood asked for the use of the dancehall on the top floor. They approached Daniel with a strong argument: in his house they would not drink, while dancing at the public tavern would tempt them to do so. Lucy Anthony, who had once loved to dance, saw no harm in granting the request. But what about his daughters, Quakers like himself? It was finally settled that the dance hall could be used. The girls could even go up and watch the dancing but not take part in it. "We didn't dance," says Susan's diary, "but Guelma and Hannah wanted to, awfully."

Daniel, who had not hesitated to dismiss boys from his school for cardplaying, temporized on the question of dancing, though the latter was equally forbidden by the rules of the Society. His enthusiasm for temperance, a crusade he had carried on with much success in the neighborhood, influenced his decision. He permitted the dance hall to be used, and the young people danced there happily in full soberness. He had broken the Quaker rules by marrying "out of unity" and by wearing a cape "out of plainness," and had done so with impunity; but he had now to learn there was a limit beyond which he could not go.

There ensued long discussions between Daniel and the Quaker overseers. This time he did not show a "state of mind" satisfactory to the committee. He had got into a complex situation by espousing a social reform. The Quakers had always discouraged tavern keeping as an occupation for their members, and Daniel's case was further proof that it led to difficulties.

In the records of the Easton Meeting, one can read in faded ink the story of Daniel Anthony's trial:

23 da. 2 mo. [1843]—The Committee to visit Daniel Anthony on account of his deviation report they have made him a visit and he acknowledged the justice of the charge but did not evince a disposition to condemn the offense, or to [make] Friends satisfaction. After a time of consideration it is concluded to refer the subject another month under the care of the Committee.

16 da. 3 mo. [1843]—The Committee continued in the case of Daniel Anthony inform they have made him another visit but find nothing different from their former report. After a time of consideration the Meeting concluded to disown him from being any longer a member of our Society. Dorus Delavergne and Rob't Baker are appointed to inform him he stands disowned and furnish him with a copy of the complaint against him if required, and, acquaint him with his privilege of appealing.

Reuben Baker, one of the overseers, summed up the case: "It is with great sorrow we have to disown Friend Anthony, for he has been one of the most exemplary members of the Society, but we can not condone such an offense as allowing a dancing-school in his house." Daniel was certainly out of alignment. He knew what he had to do. When he had married a non-Quaker wife he had produced "the state of mind" necessary to retain him in the meeting. At that time, of course, his family on both sides had been prominent and influential Quakers. Daniel himself had been a prominent and influential local citizen until recently. Perhaps he was also being disciplined for his failure in business, though the dance hall was the deciding issue. Quakers were encouraged to go into small businesses but were strictly forbidden to speculate. One regular query of the monthly meeting was: "Are Friends careful to keep their business within the line of propriety so as not to jeopardize the happiness of their family and not get into debt?" Daniel had certainly violated this rule egregiously. Only by making over his entire property to his creditors had he been able to retain his standing as an honest man. Had he not tried to pay his debts, the Quakers would instantly have disowned him. Even as it was, he had been exposed as a speculator. On top of this, he was running a dance hall.

Daniel accepted his disownment with philosophy. He made no appeal. "Father felt very badly," says Susan, "but he said that it was the very best act of his life—saved more young men to the good life than any other one act of his life—that he was turned out of the very best Society in the world for doing it." He could, and still did, attend meeting, though not the business sessions; and his children were in no wise affected by his disownment. Still, this was a severe blow for a birthright Quaker, and Daniel must have felt it to be so. His mother, the High Seat Quaker, had been dead for two years and was spared the knowledge of her son's downfall. But his father, still actively farming the old homestead, had to hear the sad news, in addition to all the other bad news recently heard from his son. Humphrey probably regarded it as the end of the road that had begun with the Nine Partners' school.

◁§ X   Daniel's disownment by the Easton Meeting took place at the mid-point of his toilsome reconstruction course. He had spent five years buffeting the hard conditions of Centre Falls. They could not have been so bad. He continued to exert himself for the education of his children. He sent his daughter Hannah for two winters to Canajoharie, to attend the Young Ladies' Academy. She stayed with Uncle Joshua Read of that town. He also sent his son Daniel R. to the academy at Union Village, which must have been an even greater financial strain. Having thus sent the four oldest away to school, he left the two youngest to be educated by their older brother and sisters, who took the responsibility seriously.

While Hannah was away at school, Susan was also away from home. She taught in the home of an Albany merchant who had retired and bought a house at Fort Edward. The Taylors were cultivated people, not Quakers, who kept a school for their own and the neighbors' children. Here Susan had some broadening experiences. The Taylors often had visitors from Albany, among them "the beautiful Abigail Mott, a Friend and thoroughgoing Abolitionist." Mr. Taylor took Susan and some guests to a Whig convention in a very stylish turnout—a green wagon drawn by a team of white horses. Susan enjoyed the outing and the speeches very much. It was the first time she had ever heard political speeches, and these delegates who loudly deplored the effects of the Jacksonian policies found her an eager and sympathetic listener.

Despite its cultural advantages, the teaching in Mr. Taylor's home yielded only the standard $2.50 a week. Hannah and Susan came home, and both resumed teaching in the local schools. This was the time when Susan discovered that the men teachers of the district were paid $10 a week, four times as much as the women teachers. With money so scarce in her family, this gave her something to think about.

Hannah's sojourn in Canajoharie, like Guelma's in Philadelphia, had turned her into a young lady. Returning to the home town, she soon settled down to one young man. Eugene Mosher was the young man, the brother of several elder doting sisters who, like the Anthony girls, had been sent away to school. The Moshers were an Easton family, intelligent beyond the average, but not Quakers. It soon became evident that Hannah, like Guelma, was about to marry out of unity.

In the spring of 1845 Susan found herself once more helping with preparations for a wedding. Weaving and spinning, sewing and knitting, dressmaking and cooking kept her busy at home. Hannah was married in September, six years almost to the day after her sister Guelma's marriage.

On the same date Daniel Anthony's last struggling mill was taken over by his creditors. His lumbering and logging, his wife's boarders, his daughters' constant teaching had not paid the mortgage. In the midst of his second financial crash his daughter Hannah was married, as in the midst of the first his daughter Guelma had been. The young men of the vicinity were not mercenary; poverty was no bar to romance. Two of Daniel's daughters were married off after he became practically penniless.

CHAPTER SIX

THE ERIE CANAL

❧ I Daniel Anthony's second great migration was not the high-hearted venture his first had been. For five years he had labored unsuccessfully to reconstruct his fortunes. If the logging, the milling, or even the tavern keeping had paid moderately, he might have remained in the Batten Kill Valley. He did not own a farm with which to feed and clothe his family. His last mill was gone and he owned nothing.

He was practically forced to seek a "new location," though it cannot be denied that the idea was congenial to his nature. In imagination he ranged over the entire country and in his actual travels he covered a vast deal of ground. Writing from Fort Edward when she taught there in 1844, Susan said, "My mind . . . muses on the absence of that dear Father and seems to fly far hence and mingle with his spirit, while he is wandering o'er the lonely wilds of old Virginia. . . . O that he may make no change of land but for the better! To do what will be for the better is no easy task, unless frail man were allowed to draw aside the veil of futurity and know the exact state of things and events to come." She was worried about her father and had good reason to be. Her dreams were troubled. "Yes, even here," she continued, "where we hope to be refreshed by that sweet sister sleep, we are often tried with the most unhappy imagery." Beneath her rhetoric lay a real fear with a real basis. Her father's Battenville move, which had ended so disastrously, gave her no feeling of security about his next move.

From the wilds of Virginia he proceeded to roam the wilds of Michigan. But something drew him back again to the state of New York; probably Uncle Joshua, who did not fancy sending his sister so far away. On his way home Daniel stopped at Rochester. He might have gone straight to Rochester in the first place, for there were many reasons for heading there. But then he would have missed a great deal of travel and lost a fine opportunity of seeing the country.

He had seen Rochester briefly in 1817, when he and Lucy made their wedding journey. It was a realizable place for Lucy, though the years had brought great changes. One of the changes had moved Rochester much nearer to Adams than it had been when it was reachable only by wagon roads.

This was the miraculous Erie Canal, opened to traffic in 1825. The canal had been the biggest and most talked-of event in New York State for many years. While it was under construction the towns along the banks plotted great futures and competed for development. A Waterloo resident of today told the writer: "My grandfather had a choice between Waterloo and Rochester. He chose Waterloo as then the most promising." Not all of them lost like Waterloo; it was amazing how many of the would-be cities had their dreams fulfilled. Rochester was converted almost overnight by the famous waterway into a large city.

The Erie Canal became one of the great historical influences of the times. Settlers flocked into the growing towns and the surrounding wheat country, while still bolder settlers, headed for the Great Lakes region, created a steady flow of through-way traffic. Rochester profited by the traffic and the farming business. The center of the wheat-growing district, it soon boasted of its flour mills, storage houses, stores, and banks. From a small village, founded only a few years before Daniel first visited it, it had developed into a prosperous city.

Daniel was looking for a farm. That he had money to buy a farm needs explanation. The money belonged to Lucy, his wife, who still had her share of her late parents' estate. This was due to the shrewdness and foresight of Joshua Read, the brother who had rescued her silver, sheets, and other household belongings from auction at Battenville. Uncle Joshua had claimed the entire inheritance as his own. By this method he had saved his sister's share from the claims of her husband's creditors. He still held the money, claimed as his own, and was prepared to yield it up only for the purchase of a farm. In his opinion, the only salvation for Daniel was to return to the occupation he had forsaken in his youth. Rochester appealed to Uncle Joshua as the center of good farming land.

The city was teeming with farm agencies on the watch for new settlers. Mary Livermore, another suffragist of Susan's era, tells in her memoirs of how one of these fast-working agencies got hold of her father and sold him a wretched farm. His wife considered it awful, rebelled, and his family returned after two years to Boston. Daniel was fortunate in having better-advised cousins already on the scene. He looked up Louis Burtis, who had married Sarah Anthony, the former teacher of Daniel's children in Battenville. Burtis knew of just the right place, thirty-two acres, with a good dwelling, only four miles from Rochester, and for the right price. Daniel's decision was quickly made. The farm passed into the ownership of Joshua Read, in whose titular possession it remained for a number of years. Daniel still had creditors back in Battenville who would have snatched the farm right out from under him if his wife had owned it. But Uncle Joshua was too shrewd for them. He held onto the place until, by the change of law, Lucy Anthony could hold it, inviolate, in her own name.

꧁ II The purchase was made in the spring, but removal was postponed until fall. Hannah's approaching marriage and Guelma's expected baby were the reasons for the delay. These events, when they came, united the family more than ever with the old home and made leaving it all the harder. But it was a cheerful summer filled with happy preparations for a new and promising life.

Susan's hopes were the same as her parents'. She was twenty-five, already wearing glasses. With every reason for doing so, she seems not to have realized that spinsterhood was upon her. Her brother Daniel R., almost five years younger than herself, was already keeping company with a Battenville girl, proposing marriage to her. Susan went serenely on, making a wonderful quilt for her sister Hannah and acting as though her chances were simply unlimited. She said nothing in her diary *against* marriage.

In the atmosphere of an engagement—there is something contagious in the air surrounding a bride-to-be—Susan received her second serious proposal. A Quaker elder from Vermont stopped over at Centre Falls on his way to the Easton Quarterly. While staying there, he asked Susan to marry him. The circumstances were romantic. Asking for a fresh drink of water from the well, the elder followed Susan and her pitcher to the font and there popped the question. It was a lovely summer day; they were isolated from the others; the elder had asked for an innocent drink of water (many of the Quaker elders took stronger drink). Susan could not have wished for circumstances more propitious. The man was suitable, a widower with a fine home and a prosperous farm not so far away. He made a sincere plea, saying, among other things, that Susan reminded him of his first wife. Susan, who had no intention whatever of accepting him anyway, found it convenient to resent the comparison. In telling the story afterward she would say with a laugh that she told him she "did not intend to be a second." One of her girlhood friends, still living, said to the writer, "I can hear her laugh now as she told it." Evidently she was pleased with the proposal even though she did not accept it.

The elder was in earnest. When Susan said no, he insisted that she should think it over while he was absent at Easton; on his return he would stop by again to receive her answer. Susan then told him positively not to return; she had definitely decided that she did not want to marry and that she was going out to western New York to share her parents' fortunes. The elder had at least surprised her into a clear knowledge of her intentions.

Susan had no conscious plan of rejecting marriage. In Centre Falls she belonged, without any singularity, in the marriageable circle of girls. The eye defect, which she inwardly so deplored, made no difference. Her father's poor circumstances, as her sisters' marriages showed, made no difference. She was getting a little over-age, so that a widower dared to approach her; but there were plenty of widowers. In the future she would never again be on the same equal, easy terms with the people around her, and proposals of marriage would be fewer. She was unconsciously forming a habit.

III   Early in November the émigrés started. Daniel and his wife, Susan, Mary, and Merritt made up the party. Daniel R. had found work in a store in Lenox, Massachusetts, and remained behind. Traveling by stage and accompanied by their own horse and wagon, they reached Troy. Here furniture, horse, and wagon were loaded on a barge known as a "line boat." They then took a train for Palatine Bridge to visit Uncle Joshua until the line boat overtook them. At Palatine Bridge they boarded the barge and lived on it, camping, as it were, for a week, cooking with their own pots and pans and sleeping in their own bedclothes.

They reached Rochester on November 14, 1845. Susan would never forget it. The line boat pulled into one of the city landings especially provided for canalboats. The "packets," usually chosen by passengers, had special landings. It was late afternoon when they stepped from the barge into the mud of Fitzhugh Street. There was no possibility of staying all night at a hotel, for Daniel had just ten dollars left in his pocket. His horse and wagon were fortunately at hand, however, and there was a home awaiting them. Unloading only a few necessities for the night, they set forth on the four-mile drive to their house. Through Fitzhugh Street, past the Quaker meeting house, then westward along the Buffalo Road, they drove as fast as old Gray could carry them. In the gathering darkness they could just barely make out the house on a low hill when the horse finally came to a stop.

Daniel had tarried overlong for this journey. He had indeed made the canal trip well ahead of the ice, but taking over a farm in November showed bad judgment. The first night was frosty and cold. Lucy Anthony had brought meal and found milk in the house, so she managed to stir up a kettle of mush for supper. The hungry family thought they had never eaten anything that tasted so good. Afterward Daniel and Lucy went to bed in the one bed and the others slept on blankets on the floor. Daniel's cheerful conversation kept everybody's spirits up. Susan did not mind sleeping on hard boards; she was immune to physical discomforts. But the arrival at the dark, cold, lonely home always remained in her memory as one of her most forlorn experiences. It was nothing like the warm old Bee Hive at Adams.

This was but the beginning. They had to survive on their reserves until spring. The family chronicles are extremely reticent about the winter. Daniel found employment teaching the district school near the Rapids. It was too much to hope that Susan could also get a

school. The family had to live on Daniel's ten dollars a week. It
would have been worse if they had had to live on Susan's two dollars. In the spring Daniel R. came on and took over the school,
while his father fell to work with might and main on the farm.

In the meantime, poor as they were, they had entertained visitors. Another Read uncle, long since settled in Cayuga County,
could not wait to see his long-lost sister and came with his daughter in midwinter for a stay. They were snowed in for a week. It was
during that week that Daniel relaxed his Quaker rule against singing, and the younger ones sang as much and as loud as ever they
wished. Daniel no doubt figured it was better to sing than be
hungry.

Uncle John must have passed the word on to Uncle Joshua in
Palatine Bridge. Came spring and Uncle Joshua was all prepared
with another big rescue. By this time the need was less stringent,
though the farm had not yet begun to produce anything. But
Daniel had saved the family from starvation by teaching and had
established himself with his Quaker neighbors as an intellectual
and competent citizen.

✍§ IV The winter would have been worse but for the Quakers.
When Daniel visited Rochester in 1817 he might have seen
Quakers already in the village. They started a meeting in Riga,
an outlying settlement, in 1818; settlements quickly followed in
Chili, Wheatland (near Daniel's farm), and several other centers.
When Colonel Rochester's outfit built an Episcopal church in
Fitzhugh Street, the various Quaker groups were ready, by uniting,
to erect a simple frame meeting house in the same street. From
Rochester's early beginnings, the courthouse, the Episcopal church,
the Quaker meeting house were prominent sights of the town.

When the canal came through, the Quakers in Rochester and
Monroe County were said to be about six hundred in number.
Three years later the historic separation threatened their existence.
But the main body joined the Hicksite persuasion and remained
in possession of the Fitzhugh Street building. From this time on
they continued to strengthen their organization and became important factors in Rochester's religious and business life.

Among the most prominent Quaker citizens were Isaac and Amy

Post (Post was the owner of a prosperous drug firm); Elias and Rhoda de Garmo (nearest neighbors of Daniel's farm); William and Mary Hallowell; Samuel and Susan Porter. These families were from the first Daniel's friends in Rochester and he was therefore not without backing in his efforts to get on. They continued to be his friends and his daughter Susan's friends for all the years to come.

With this group Daniel found himself spiritually very much at home. He had long been interested in temperance, which had indirectly led to his ousting by the Easton Quakers. These Rochester Friends, like Daniel, were earnest workers in the temperance cause. They were also, like himself, uncompromising advocates of antislavery. The Anthonys, the Posts, the De Garmos, and the Hallowells jointly subscribed to Garrison's paper, *The Liberator*, and it was read religiously by all four families. Garrison's fiery principles were a part of their lives. Daniel had emerged at fifty-two into a congenial climate of the mind. The Erie Canal had opened up a new intellectual world for him.

CHAPTER SEVEN

THE HEADMISTRESS

⊷§ I   Passing through Palatine Bridge on their way to Rochester, Daniel and Susan Anthony had scarcely had time to observe how important Uncle Joshua was as a citizen. A shrewd businessman, he had anticipated Horace Greeley's advice, gone west, and grown up with the country. In the towns of Palatine Bridge and Canajoharie—joint towns like Budapest and Walla Walla—his investments and interests had ramified in all directions. He was a director of the bank, one of the owners of the toll bridge, the turnpike, the stage line, and the hotel. A substantial citizen, he was also one of the trustees of the Canajoharie Academy. By a fortunate coincidence, in the spring of 1846 the headmistress-ship of the academy's Female Department fell vacant. It was a position made to order for Joshua's well-qualified niece, Susan Anthony of Rochester.

On April 25, 1846, Susan's father, returning from the post office, handed her the following formal communication:

To Miss Susan Anthony,
    Rochester, N.Y.
    At a meeting of the Trustees of the Canajoharie Academy held this day, it was unanimously Resolved to offer you the Female Department upon the terms which have heretofore been offered to the teachers of that department, viz: the tuition money of the Female Department less 12 ½ percent., the teachers collecting their tuition bills. Should these terms meet your views, please favor

us with an answer by return mail. The next term commences on the first Monday of May proximo.

We are Very Respectfully Yours,

JOSHUA READ, LIVINGSTON SPRAKER, GEORGE G. JOHNSON

This formal announcement was accompanied by a note from her cousin, who told her that she had received twelve votes and "the next lady" seven, after which the board had decided to make it unanimous.

The all-powerful hand of Uncle Joshua was again at work on the family fortunes. The letter was like the dove descending on the ark with the olive branch in its mouth. Susan's preparations were simple. She wrote from Canajoharie later, "I have now got my wardrobe pretty well replaced, no, *placed* for the first time." She returned to Canajoharie in style on the "packet"; there was no time for the line boat. On Saturday before school began she stood in Uncle Joshua's presence.

Her benefactor was in bed, very ill, but he mustered strength to give Susan his best advice. She was entering an important period of her life, he said, and her success would depend largely upon her thinking that she knew it all. He added kindly that she would board with his married daughter in Canajoharie as a more youthful home and a more convenient location than his own in Palatine Bridge. Susan took time to notice that the doctor was treating her uncle with "calomel and morphine" and, remembering Eunice Kenyon, was gloomily impressed. But despite her forebodings, Uncle Joshua recovered quickly. Susan was warmly welcomed in her cousin Eleanor's home across the river.

Susan was indeed all that she had been represented to be—an experienced and well-qualified schoolmistress. This was just as well, for the academy, whose large bell dominated the town by ringing out the hour of nine every morning—and still does to this day— ranked as a reputable and widely known institution. It was not coeducational; the boys were taught on the first floor, the girls on the second. On exhibition days and similar occasions the departments co-operated. The headmaster was intelligent and able and, if not liberal in his social ideas, was kindly by disposition. Susan taught under his direction without the least sense of friction.

❧ II   It was this academy that Susan's sister Hannah had attended while the family lived at Centre Falls. The pupils ranged from young ladies down to little girls. Susan started with twenty-five pupils of mixed ages, and as far as we know the number did not increase. With the tuition at $5.00 a year, she received a yearly salary of $125, of which one eighth, or $15, was to be paid to the trustees. This left her with a balance of $110, out of which, according to a letter she wrote to her father, she paid $45 a year for board. She had earned as much as this in the Battenville district school. The Canajoharie Academy added only distinction and a supposedly better social environment.

For the first time in her life she spent all she earned on herself. Her father was provided with a farm; Mary had begun to teach at home; Merritt did a man's work on the farm. Besides, Joshua Read would never have approved of her sending money to her father. With the past hard winter still in her mind, she felt herself in clover. Of the hardships of that winter, she said in her *Reminiscences* that lonesomeness was the worst. In Canajoharie she had the companionship of her married cousins and the comfort and ease of their homes. Her feeling of indebtedness to Uncle Joshua was measured accordingly.

Canajoharie, on the canal, had been passed over by the Quakers in their westward march. The original settlers were Dutch Reformers, Baptists, and Germans. Such names as "Palatine Bridge" and "Rueff's Tavern" survive as birthmarks of its origin. The dominant group was a solid combination of practical, hardheaded Protestants of Dutch, German, and English descent. Stirred by the approach of the canal, they founded the Canajoharie Academy in 1824. It was the pride of the town, the only great achievement stimulated by the canal boom. To Susan's country-bred eyes, Canajoharie presented the aspects of a small city.

Susan's first biographer remarks that when she went to Canajoharie she ceased to be a Quaker. This was certainly true as far as the outward and visible marks of Quakerism were concerned. In her letters home she dropped the Quaker dating "3 da. 2 mo." and abandoned the "thee and thou" completely. More strikingly, she gave up the Quaker mode of dress. She dressed like her cousins, who, it may be added, dressed like the young ladies of the academy. Quaker plainness would have been wholly unsuited to her position. Yet she turned to worldly dress with more enthusiasm than the circumstances really demanded. *Godey's Lady's Book* took the place in her cousin's home that had been occupied by the *Liberator* in her own.

She must have pored over the *Lady's Book* to good purpose. She wrote home: "I have a new pearl straw gypsy hat, trimmed in white ribbon with a fringe on one edge and a pink satin stripe on the other, with a few white roses and green leaves for inside trimming." In short, she became a lady of fashion. "Your daughter and sister Susan cuts an important swell. You would scarce imagine it to be the same young lady who once made a brown cambric calash with no ruffle in front, because she was so conscientious, to carry to Rensselaerville." About Hannah she added, "I suppose she feels rather sad that she is married and can no longer have nice clothes." Guelma had had one merino dress when she married and was probably still wearing it. Susan, the spinster sister, was the only one of the three who could afford to dress well. Her satisfaction over this was a bit transparent.

The shops of Canajoharie presented a temptation she had never experienced. She had seen a few shops in her travels through Philadelphia and New York, but she had bought nothing in them. She probably looked the other way. With her cousins she visited the Canajoharie shops often, if only for recreation. She became a patron. She bought a broché shawl for $22.50, a fox muff for $8.00, a hat for $5.50, and a merino dress for $16. This would have wiped out half a year's salary. She added a mantilla that cost $30. She learned to be a judge of materials—delaine, barège, merino, lawn, and silk—and she had dresses made of all. She did not go so wild as to buy jewelry, but she borrowed the ornaments of her amiable cousins and wore them.

Suddenly released from drabness, she did what many Quaker girls did. She went to the other extreme. Under the pretext that she had to keep up with her cousins, she indulged in many extravagances. One is reminded by all this that Susan was the daughter of a man who had almost been turned out of meeting for wearing a brightly colored scarf and a wide cape on his coat and who had gone on wearing them in spite of Quaker disapproval. Even the Quaker men sometimes rebelled against their drabness.

On her first examination day Susan was as much excited over her costume as over her professional success. She wrote:

> *Canajoharie, Aug. 12, 1846*
>
> Dear Friends at the Cottage:
> It is now noon of that awful day, that day of days. Do I not carry a pretty steady hand, considering? Well, I have examined four classes before Mr. Hagar and Trustees. . . . Succeeded far better than I had even hoped. Mr. Caldwell says this noon, "Well, Schoolmarm, you have got on a little too much paint this time." . . .
>
> I got up as soon as it was light, washed as Lewis [Dio; temperance leader] says all over, put on some new shoes Mr. Caldwell got me in Albany, patent leather heels and toes, and blue prunella half-gaiters. . . . After breakfast combed my hair down in the old-fashioned way, not over my ears, braided it in four braids, then went down and Eleanor sewed them together and put in the shell-comb. Then I put on my new gown which is plaid—white, blue, purple, and brown—has two puffs around the skirt, cuffs to the sleeves, with puffs and buttons where they end and puffs at the wrist, sleeves cut up like Mr. Cashmere and undersleeves. I have made out of my linen wristlets and some linen of Mr. Caldwell's ruffled shirts a new collaret about my neck. Mag's gold pencil with a pen in it and Susan's watch and black chain—that makes up the costume. In fine all say the school marm looks beautiful and I heard some of the scholars expressing fears lest some one might be smitten and they be deprived of their new teacher.

Susan's reference to Dio Lewis of temperance fame shows that she had not forgotten all serious things. She wrote the home folks to send her Comstock's *Chemistry* and Abercrombie's *Intellectual Faculties*, with which to pursue her own education. She was also seriously interested in teaching and she urged her brother Daniel R., who was now teaching near Rochester, to write and discuss school problems with her. Her own proficiency as a teacher was soon established in the town. This was not accomplished without a great deal of hard work at school, while the elaborate gowns in which she took so much delight had to be sewed entirely by hand. She had no idle hours.

It was in Canajoharie that she had her first daguerreotype made.

She is wearing the marvelous plaid of purple, white, blue, and brown, with a mantilla—evidently *the* mantilla—around her shoulders. She is *not* wearing spectacles, and there is apparently nothing wrong with her eyes. In fact, nothing is heard of either spectacles or eye trouble in Canajoharie. The Read girls, who delighted in dressing up their country cousin, knew nothing about the trouble or at least took no stock in it. Susan seems to have forgotten all about it herself.

She had beaux and escorts to accompany her to parties and take her on long drives. Among them were several widowers, who are apt to have serious intentions. But all passed in succession without leaving an impression. Among other things, she seems to have learned to dance. A little discouragement in this field attended her efforts. "I certainly shall not attend another dance," she wrote, "unless I can have a total abstinence man to accompany me, and not one whose highest delight is to make a fool of himself." She explained further to Mary: "I felt streaked, though I can assure you not much that I was at a dance as that I was a witness to brandy-sipping." She had accepted dancing but not drinking.

❧§ III   Susan's family in Rochester did not see her for two years. Meanwhile Daniel developed the farm laboriously and, more than that, successfully. He planted hundreds of fruit trees, grew wheat and rye, kept cows and raised pigs. In the rear of the house, beside the barn, he built a small blacksmith shop. On a small scale he reproduced the activities of his father's large farm in Adams. Lucy planted flowers in abundance. "The walk was lined from gate to front door with pinks. It was a beautiful country residence," says Susan in her *Reminiscences*.

Then, after all, Daniel declared the place too small to provide his family with a decent living. Remembering his father's vast acres, he called it "a six-penny farm." He had enlarged his acquaintance with Rochester businessmen and soon came in touch with a rising occupation, one in which his age was no handicap. The New York Life Insurance Company, just sprouting into existence, needed a man in the Rochester district. "Agents were recruited in the most hit-or-miss fashion," says the *History* of the New York Life. "Anyone could sell life insurance." Daniel Anthony was recruited in

1847. In the same year a young man in Indiana by the name of
Lew Wallace was engaged by the New York Life in the same
capacity. "I'll have to 'puff' here considerably," wrote young Wallace to his New York headquarters. "Two other companies have
agencies of older date. . . . I'll have to work up with them, as it
were, 'hand over hand.'" Wallace did not do so well and turned
his hand to literature—with the eventual achievement of *Ben Hur*.
Daniel Anthony got off to a better business start. In a short time
he was doing so well that, as he put it, he could "afford the luxury
of keeping a farm." When at home he still put in long hours of
work on the farm and at the forge. But most of the time he was
on the road with his horse and buggy, combing the ground for
new customers. He had once more, this time for good, escaped the
steady servitude of the farm.

The life insurance business flourished, though naturally with ups
and downs. Daniel grew up with the business. In the 1850s he
induced his son-in-law, Aaron McLean, to leave Battenville for
Rochester, to become, like himself, an agent of the New York Life.
His own sons were too much like himself to settle down to the
prosaic business of selling life insurance. But Daniel was no longer
young, he no longer dreamed of getting rich, and there was much
satisfaction in handling two different occupations at the same time.
There was no monotony in his life.

IV For the first time since his school days he had companions
who fostered his idealism. The Hicksite group of Quakers were the
backbone of liberal thought and action in Rochester. They promoted temperance, anti-slavery, and free religion. They subscribed
to the *Liberator* and the *Anti-Slavery Standard*, viewing them as
necessities like shoes or bread. They had created a local sentiment
which induced Frederick Douglass to settle there and to issue his
paper, the *North Star*, with the Rochester imprint. Douglass became one of Daniel Anthony's closest friends. Living nearby in
Syracuse was Samuel J. May, minister of the Unitarian church and
one of the famous reformers of the day. He was also an intimate
friend of Daniel, who sold life insurance in Syracuse.

It was natural that the woman's rights movement of 1848 should
find a welcome with the Hicksite group. The convention called by

Elizabeth Cady Stanton, Lucretia Mott, Martha Wright, and Mary Ann McClintock in Seneca Falls on July 19 and 20, 1848, moved on to Rochester by invitation two weeks later. In going, it took another forward step. At Seneca Falls the meeting had been presided over by a man, James Mott; but in Rochester it was presided over by a woman, Abigail Bush. Two Quaker women, Rhoda de Garmo and Amy Post, insisted upon this, and Lucretia Mott and Mrs. Stanton both protested at first. After Abigail Bush presided, with professional skill and authority, Mrs. Mott and Mrs. Stanton admitted that they had been wrong.

The Posts, De Garmos, Hallowells, Willises, and Anthonys of the Rochester Quakers were present in full force. All signed the Declaration of Woman's Rights framed by the Seneca Falls convention. The right of the elective franchise was included, on Elizabeth Cady Stanton's insistence, among the other rights demanded. With the Seneca Falls and Rochester conventions the national woman suffrage movement was born. Daniel Anthony, his wife, and his daughter Mary were charter members of the movement.

Susan Anthony, in Canajoharie, reveling in silks and barèges, knew little of the excitement that had stirred her family and friends. She saw the accounts in the newspapers and laughed at some of the gibes of the reporters. At the moment the great event of her life was attending the circus. "Joshua came up to bring an invitation from his Pa for me to go to the circus this P.M.," she wrote her brother; "I believe I will accept, as I have never attended a circus. I might see something to amuse my young mind." So she went to see Messrs. Sands, Lent, and Co.'s Greatest Show on Earth and had a fine time. She wore the blue lawn and the gypsy hat with pink roses under the brim.

Her communication with her family up to this time had been at a minimum. She had corresponded with and visited her married sisters in Easton and Battenville instead. She paid her first visit home in 1848, and her father's first visit to her in Canajoharie came that same summer. By this time the change in her was most obvious. She bought two new expensive dresses for her visit home. She stayed only a week and was accompanied by her cousin Margaret and Margaret's small children. The home folks could not fail to notice the change. It was soon after this that her father came down to visit her.

◄§ V One social reform only was popular in Canajoharie. In many parts of the state temperance had become the pet cause of the wealthy and respectable. Julia Ward Howe says that no alcoholic stimulant ever appeared on her father's table, though the Wards were a fashionable New York City family. The prosperous Langdons of Elmira, who later were to demur at Mark Twain for a son-in-law, were also temperance people. Many solid citizens of Canajoharie stood for temperance. Susan stuck to her temperance principles, which were quite reconcilable with elegant clothes. In 1848 she stepped out actively for the cause, adding to the role of schoolmistress that of a ladylike reformer. On March 1, 1849, the Daughters of Temperance, of whom Susan was now the president, gave a large fair and supper to raise money. Susan managed the affair.

It turned into an occasion in honor of Susan. Her description of the party runs: "I was escorted into the hall by the Committee where were assembled about 200 people. The room was beautifully festooned with cedar and red flannel. On the south side was printed in large capitals of evergreen the name of 'Susan B. Anthony.' I hardly knew how to conduct myself amidst so much kindly regard. They had an elegant supper. On the top of one pyramid loaf cake was a beautiful bouquet, which was handed to the gentleman who escorted me (Charlie Webster) and by him presented to me." Her three years in the town had made her a person of influence and popularity. She had furthered the cause of temperance in a ladylike way, and her vision of social reform went no farther than this.

She made her first speech in public at the Temperance Fair. It was read from a copybook manuscript which is still preserved in the Library of Congress. Her sentiments, neither hesitating nor timid, followed the accepted trend of the day, her warnings being chiefly addressed to the drinking sons of well-to-do families. Her school examinations had prepared her for this great appearance. Steadying her voice, she began:

"Welcome, Gentlemen and Ladies, to this, our Hall of Temperance. We feel that the cause we have espoused is a common cause, in which you, with us, are deeply interested. We would that some means were devised, by which our Brothers and Sons shall no

longer be allured from the *right* by the corrupting influence of the
fashionable sippings of wine and brandy, those sure destroyers of
Mental and Moral Worth, and by which our Sisters and Daughters
shall no longer be exposed to the vile arts of the gentlemanly-
appearing, gallant, but really half-inebriated seducer. Our motive
is to ask of you counsel in the formation and co-operation in the
carrying-out of plans which may produce a radical change in our
Moral Atmosphere. . . .

"How is this great change to be wrought, who are to urge on
this vast work of reform? Shall it not be women, who are most
aggrieved by the foul destroyer's inroads? Most certainly. Then
arises the question, how are we to accomplish the end desired? I
answer, not by confining our influence to our own home circle,
not by centering all our benevolent feelings upon our own kindred,
not by caring naught for the culture of any minds, save those of
our own darlings. No, no; the gratification of the *selfish* impulses
alone, can never produce a desirable change in the Moral aspect
of Society. . . .

"It is generally conceded that it is our sex that fashions the Social
and Moral State of Society. We do not presume that females possess unbounded power in abolishing the evil customs of the day;
but we do believe that were they en masse to discountenance the
use of wine and brandy as beverages at both their private and public
parties, not one of the opposite Sex, who has any claim to the title
of gentleman, would so insult them as to come into their presence
after having quaffed of that foul destroyer of all true delicacy and
refinement. . . .

"Ladies! there is no Neutral position for us to assume. If we
sustain not this noble enterprise, both by precept and example,
then is our influence on the side of Intemperance. If we say we
love the Cause, and then sit down at our ease, surely does our
action speak the lie. And now permit me once more to beg of you
to lend your aid to this great Cause, the Cause of God and all
Mankind."

Susan addressed the upper classes, but she introduced a new idea
to them. They should act for the benefit of those outside as well
as inside the family circle; and, above all, they should act. In her
first public speech on any occasion she spoke for deeds instead of
words. At the same time, she made a public speech and was praised
for it. In the outside world women were being excoriated for speaking in public, as Angelina Grimké, Lucy Stone, and Antoinette

Brown already well knew. But Canajoharie was shut off from the world and saw nothing extraordinary about Susan's performance except its amazing "smartness" for a woman.

◄§ VI The year 1848 brought a legal change in woman's status in New York State. In April of that year the married woman's property law was passed by the Legislature, permitting a wife who inherited property from her own parents to hold it in her own name. Uncle Joshua Read now saw fit to transfer the title of the Rochester farm to Lucy Anthony, protected as it was by this new law against her husband's creditors. It meant a great deal to the family—to Daniel, who had developed the farm; to Lucy, who felt the pride of ownership; and to the sons and daughters, who had put so much hard work into it. The general effect was to release the strangle hold of Uncle Joshua's guardianship and benevolence.

In August, Susan paid a brief visit to her home. Cousin Margaret, who accompanied her, brought back glowing accounts of comfort and plenty on Daniel's farm. Things had changed greatly since that first dismal winter. Soon afterward Susan's father came to Canajoharie for a brief visit. While there he brought up the subject of abolition at Uncle Joshua's dinner table. "I had to laugh to hear Father talk to Uncle on the subject of American slavery," wrote Susan. "Uncle's Old Hunker to the back bone. . . . Father kept very cool, never talked but in his accustomed key. . . . I was really glad to have Father express his sentiments with regard to reform. Though the good folks call us crazy fanatics now, the day will come when they must acknowledge their stupidity."

After Daniel had gone, Susan had a passage with George Caldwell, her cousin Eleanor's husband. "You think my Father a little crazy on the subject of slavery." "No," he said, "not a little but a good deal. I never saw a man so wrapped up in a Nigger as your Father is in Douglass." While there was temperance sentiment in Canajoharie, abolition sentiment was taboo. Daniel had introduced a bone of contention between Susan and her cousins. The beautiful harmony that had previously existed was painfully disturbed.

Daniel had been pouring out his Abolitionist principles to Susan for some time on paper. Susan had not paid much heed until she saw her father so openly and bravely challenging the opposition.

She now turned to the subject with a new light in her eyes. There was no doubt about her father's stand on slavery. He wrote:

Dear S.:

Your mother, myself, and Merritt went this morning to Friends' Meeting which is now held in No. 3 School House on Corn Hill.

. . .

Had I but the mind and tongue of a Douglass or of many others of the Nigger race I would have preached to them myself. For in these days of—I was about to say light and knowledge—it seems too bad to go to Meeting where people profess to gather for the purpose of good and not hear a single (good) word spoken. . . . By this I do not mean to carry the idea that any more good is done in the Churches where long sermons, prayers, and heavenly music are each in systematic order dealt out . . . in accordance with the most popular notions of the American Church . . .

Step a few miles South, and tomorrow our beloved Brethren of the same Church will be found engaged—lawfully, honestly, and very religiously engaged—in the brotherly and humane acts of riveting iron fetters and handcuffs upon the Brethren and Sisters of the self-same Church of God;—that the said Brothers and Sisters may with the greatest security . . . be transported to a far distant land, where both body and soul are to be dealt with in accordance with the customs and usages . . . sanctioned by both the Civil and Religious Institutions of this Republican and Christianized land.

Of what use is preaching and all this pretended and blind devotion so long as this horrible business of trafficking in the bodies of men, women, and children is sanctioned and actually carried on by those making the highest pretensions to goodness. . . . A good Presbyterian, a thief, a stealer of the members of his own Church! A good Baptist, buying and selling the full impress of the image of God! A noble, magnanimous Episcopalian, even Henry Clay himself, a thief, a man-stealer worse than a Pirate on the seas, but much talked of for the highest office in this Republic! And when we take a peep at our goodly Methodists . . . the rulers of this same Church even in these Northern States are such that forbid their ministers from even discussing the subject of slavery. . . .

I can truly say that I am happy in the thought that I am a member of that Society which has for its territory no less space than all creation and for its members every rational creature under Heaven.

In a letter that followed, Daniel informed his daughter that the Rochester Quakers had split up on the subject of slavery. Daniel and his group—about half, he said—had withdrawn and started a new meeting. "That portion of the Society," he said, "who are not exactly satisfied to confine their operations for ameliorating the conditions of man within the compass of an old shriveled-up nutshell and who are of the opinion that each individual should have the right to think as well as act for himself . . . in rolling on the wheel of reform, has left the more Orthodox, wise, and self-righteous part of the Society to attend to nothing but matters of pure and undefiled religion. This latter portion of Friends not wishing to have their holy and almost devout meditations any longer disturbed by the intercessions of the friends of the bondman."

Daniel's violent letters acted like a bombshell on Susan's Canajoharie quiet. He came into her bland circle of cousins like a lion let loose in the streets. After his argument with Uncle Joshua, things were not the same again. In her first letter after his departure Susan began to agitate the question of returning home. "Father left on the afternoon packet," she wrote. "I heard the horn and opened the north blind, waved my handkerchief and he shook his umbrella in return. The briny waters would come in spite of me. I can endure no part with friends going in any direction save towards my home." And then she added: "If my life is spared till the close of the present school year, I will never again place myself where I may not now and then . . . visit my Mother and at least spend Sundays under the parental roof." The solution was simple. She would leave Canajoharie and get a teaching position much closer to Rochester.

In the following winter the school principal, Mr. Hagar, resigned and a young man from Alabama, the son of a slaveholder, took his place. Susan had other reasons for disliking him; she thought him too rigid and severe. This made her all the more determined to leave.

Next the California gold fever invaded Canajoharie. The quiet town surrendered wholly as to an epidemic. Nothing else was talked about. "There are 25 young men going to leave for the gold fields this spring; they are going round the Cape," Susan wrote. Her cousin Margaret's husband was among them. "I take my pen in hand," she wrote to Aaron, "to inform you that I am likely to have plenty of company [lone wives left behind]. Even those who have

long basked in matrimony must in these times that try men's pluck
be left to live a lone life."

Susan did not approve of Margaret's husband's going. Margaret,
with three small children, was expecting another baby in the spring.
Yet here was Joseph planning to be absent for two years. All during
her pregnancy Margaret opposed her husband's plans with might
and main. She clung to Susan, begging her to stay with her in case
of the worst. Susan, who had grown to love her cousin like a sister,
suffered much on her account. But there was nothing she could do.
"I hope he will yet change his mind, but when he says it, it is said."

In her heart Susan secretly wished that she too could go. Though
she called the adventure a "bubble," her imagination was fired by
it. She was free and foot-loose and longing for a change. The California dream fell into the vacuum. "Oh, if I were but a man so that
I could go!" she wrote. Women would soon be going to Oregon
and California in numbers, but most of them were married or going
to be married as soon as they got there. Incorrigible spinsters were
not wanted on the Western Coast. Susan's interest in California
was the emptiest of dreams.

⪦§ VII   Her real adventure that spring was destined to be a
tragedy. Margaret's baby was born in March. Margaret's husband
had remained at home, after all. Susan wrote her mother:

Canajoharie, March 7th, 1849

Dear Mother:

I now take my pen in hand to inform you that we have a sweet
little girl, and that I have assisted in the performance of the various
duties. Margaret has been anxiously waiting since one week yesterday. The baby was born yesterday (Tuesday) A.M. at 2½ o'clock.
Margaret had a pretty hard time. I was with her through the whole,
had Dr. White, Eleanor, and a Mrs. Snyder. It's rather a tough
business, is it not, Mother?

Oh, I am so glad she is through with it. I never slept a wink, went
to school the next A.M. Every time one of the girls would speak, I
imagined it was Margaret's groan. It was a nervous forenoon. In the
P.M. I staid home and went to bed. . . . Aunt Mary [Margaret's
mother] was not invited to the party. She does not like it very
much, but all thought that her presence would only make herself
sick and Margaret worse.

As soon as her cousin's baby came, Susan's mind reverted to her plans for going home. A few days later she wrote: "I have written my resignation. The people begin to believe I am in earnest and well they may, for I am off."

A month went by in which Cousin Margaret showed improvement and the baby throve. Susan had heavy duties with her school-work and with her nursing and domestic tasks in the house. Margaret's husband had built a new house. Susan planned to help them move into their new home and then to leave. Her sturdy constitution enabled her to stand up well under all this strain. In one of her letters to her mother, written late at night when she was almost asleep, came an irrelevant sentence: "They say I grow handsome."

Then, when all seemed to be going well, Margaret suffered a relapse. Her doctor and another whom Joseph summoned from Syracuse said that it was prostration of the nervous system. She wasted away for three weeks under Susan's loving eyes and tireless, devoted nursing. She would put her arms around Susan's neck to rise and would take only such nourishment as Susan gave her. Without a word of suffering she drifted farther and farther away from them, until one night at the midnight hour she died. It seemed to Susan and some of those around her as if she no longer wanted to live.

Susan stayed on through the funeral and the sad parceling out of the children. She took the new baby to its grandmother's home and stayed there herself until her school term ended. She then went to Battenville for the summer, to recuperate in her sisters' company from the soreness of heart that afflicted her.

In the fall she headed once more for Rochester via the Erie Canal. Four years had passed since her first migration with the family to their Rochester home. The migration had not "taken" with her, as she had returned to Canajoharie, which was more within the purlieus of the old life than of the new. Rochester, which was to be the home of her future, was practically unknown to her when she took up her residence there in the fall of 1849.

Susan's departure from Canajoharie has been misinterpreted so often that it deserves a word. Her first biographer inadvertently gives the impression that she left because of her cousin's death and as the result of the shock and horror produced by that experience. Nothing could be more untrue or remote from the facts. She did not leave Canajoharie suddenly but in accordance with a long-adopted plan. She tended her cousin through her confinement and all that followed with the devotion of a mother, and she accepted through tears all the circumstances of her death with complete realism. Her grief over the final tragedy was the most natural grief in the world. Her diary and her letters show there was nothing resembling shock or horror in her experience. On the contrary, they show nothing but sympathy, tenderness, and courage—and all these, considering her reticent nature, surprisingly freely expressed.

Susan B. Anthony at the age of 28, from a daguerreotype.

CHAPTER EIGHT

DISCIPLE OF WOMAN'S RIGHTS

❧ I   When Susan came home to live on the farm, the Hicksites had reached a high degree of upset and confusion. They had broken with Fitzhugh Street on the slavery issue, and the Unitarian church, to which they had retreated, had accidentally acquired a secessionist minister. The situation was typical of the confusion of the times. But Daniel's group were staunch Garrisonians, adhering to the principle of "immediate and unconditional emancipation," which gave them an inner bond of union regardless of institutional ties. Though wanderers, they maintained themselves as a firm coterie.

This was Daniel Anthony's opportunity. Instinctively a leader, though never an orator, he quietly attracted the group of homeless reformers to his farm in the country. Their meeting place was his dinner table on Sundays, where as many of them as would forgathered around his hospitable board. Fine old Quaker or Abolitionist names like De Garmo, Post, Hallowell, Willis, Porter, Wilder, and Frederick Douglass were frequently represented. Any Abolitionist speaker who visited Rochester was entertained as well. When Garrison and Wendell Phillips came to town, they were entertained at Daniel Anthony's farm.

In 1850, Susan's first year at home, the Fugitive Slave Law was passed, cementing the anti-slavery group more firmly than ever. The business of forwarding runaway slaves to Canada, always active in Rochester, one of the main doorways to freedom, became more lively than ever. The many underground railway stations represented at Daniel's table not even the guests could tell, so secretly were they operated. It was generally known that Frederick Douglass, assisted by contributions from England, offered a kind of Mecca for the runaways. Almost as well known for her defiance of the law was Amy Post, the wife of Isaac Post, the prosperous Quaker druggist. Daniel's contribution to the group was the unlimited hospitality of his farm.

These informal meetings went on for several years and were interrupted only when William Henry Channing, the famous Unitarian and Abolitionist from Boston, came to take charge of the Unitarian church. The wandering Quakers, including Daniel Anthony and his family, quickly returned to the Unitarian fold. Daniel's daughters were surprised to see how the once rigid Quaker accepted the Unitarian services. "My father," wrote Mary, "for the first time felt that he could conscientiously listen to what the Society of Friends called 'hireling ministry.' . . . The liberal preaching of William Henry Channing in 1852 proved so satisfactory that it was not long before this was our accepted church home." For Susan the climax came when her father, having once begun with a "hireling priest" and congregational singing, finally broke down completely and consented to pay pew rent. Not all of Channing's parishioners were as enthusiastic as Daniel, however, for the church continued to be split over the slavery issue. After a couple of years Channing left Rochester to take charge of a church in Washington, and from there went to England. But the church remained sufficiently Abolitionist to retain the Anthonys.

Susan left Canajoharie with exactly three hundred dollars saved up out of fifteen years of schoolteaching. By previous agreement with her father, she spent her first year at home helping to run the farm while he spent most of that year in Syracuse enlarging his business. Occasionally she went back to teaching, substituting for absent teachers in the Rochester public schools. She usually mentioned 1850 as the year when she finally gave up teaching, but she really hung on for another two years, not knowing what else to do with herself.

She had passed her thirtieth birthday and felt the need of a change, some new content for her life. While her father still looked forward to her ultimate marriage, Susan herself did not foresee this step as giving the new content she desired. She spent two or three years casting about, without compass or anchor, waiting for destiny to show its hand. She could count on her father's co-operation, for Daniel himself would have liked to step out in the public arena. But time and misfortune had made him cautious and he encouraged his daughter to do so instead. If she married, well and good. Quaker women were not handicapped by marital status.

Looking back on the situation in her *Reminiscences,* Susan seems somewhat surprised at the small attention she paid to finances. "I never thought of the bread-and-butter end of it," she wrote. "Father would always bring home bolts of dress material; so I had enough clothes to wear. . . . Father encouraged my public work from the start." Daniel, who had risen from ruin and defeat, felt he could now afford to give his daughter's services to social reform. Writing from Canajoharie, Susan had said, "Reform needs to be the watchword! And some one must preach it who does not depend on the popular nod for his dinner." Daniel had reassured her that she could depend on him for help.

Susan's introduction to her father's group was on a humble plane. She cooked and served the dinners for the Sunday guests and, like many a woman in the same situation, was torn between her eagerness to hear what was said and her desire to sustain her reputation as hostess and cook. She managed to hear a great deal, enough to make her realize the difference between the pro-slavery sentiments of Canajoharie and the radical and aggressive attitude of the Rochester resistants. There was not the least question in her mind about where she stood. She stood foursquare with her father, the rabid Abolitionist.

❧ II   Her first steps in the outside world were noticeably cautious. She joined the Daughters of Temperance, the only organized body of women in Rochester, and started them at once on a program of practical action. Under her direction they organized and held fairs, festivals, and suppers to raise money for the cause. With her Canajoharie experience, it was easy for her to run these affairs and thus seemingly to create money out of the air for the slender temperance purse. The Daughters were surprised and delighted and happily elected Susan as their delegate to the various temperance conventions, which in those days were crowded public gatherings.

Returning from such a gathering, Susan passed through Seneca Falls, where William Lloyd Garrison and George Thompson from England, the most distinguished Abolitionists of the day, were scheduled to give addresses. Her Seneca Falls hostess was Mrs. Amelia Bloomer, editor and publisher of a paper called the *Lily*, officially described as "Devoted to the Interests of Women." Its primary interest was temperance, the cause which had brought Susan and Mrs. Bloomer together. The *Lily* did not advocate woman suffrage. Temperance was a conservative reform, while woman suffrage was considered *ultra* (Lucretia Mott's name for it). Mrs. Bloomer avoided Elizabeth Cady Stanton, who also lived in Seneca Falls, because she was known to be, like Lucretia Mott, one of the *ultras*. Mrs. Stanton sneaked her contributions into the *Lily* under an assumed name. Later on she had the satisfaction of counting Mrs. Bloomer on her side and of seeing the *Lily* develop into an organ of woman's rights.

But when Mrs. Stanton met Mrs. Bloomer on the street in 1851, accompanied by Miss Anthony, the two merely exchanged greetings and passed by. Mrs. Stanton describes the meeting in her *Reminiscences:* "Walking home with the speakers [Garrison and Thompson] who were my guests [also her husband's], we met Mrs. Bloomer with Miss Anthony on the corner of the street waiting to greet us. There she stood with her good earnest face and genial smile, dressed in gray delaine, hat and all the same color relieved with pale-blue ribbons, the perfection of neatness and sobriety. I liked her thoroughly from the beginning." But Mrs. Stanton did not invite Susan to her house. She assumed that Miss Anthony was of the same conservative type as Mrs. Bloomer at the time. Susan had been dying to meet Mrs. Stanton.

She digested her disappointment as best she could. She had heard much at home about the woman's rights convention and Mrs. Stanton's aggressive stand to have the franchise included in the resolutions. Her statement read: "Resolved, that it is the duty of the women in this country to secure to themselves their sacred right to the elective franchise." At the time, members of the convention, including Lucretia Mott and Mrs. Stanton's husband, Henry B. Stanton, had thought this was going too far. But Mrs. Stanton stood out firmly and was loyally supported by Frederick Douglass in the debate. The convention finally adopted it by a narrow majority. Daniel Anthony and the others who signed the declaration had therefore signed the franchise clause along with all the rest. Susan's eagerness to meet the doughty little champion arose from discussions and opinions heard in her own home. Her family was on Mrs. Stanton's side.

A few weeks later—in the summer of 1851—Susan had the pleasure of seeing Mrs. Stanton plain. Eagerly pursuing her campaign for woman's rights, Mrs. Stanton invited Susan and Lucy Stone to meet Horace Greeley at her house to join in a coeducational discussion. In her all-inclusive program of emancipation she thought she saw in the late Canajoharie headmistress a lady well cast for the part of promoting coeducation. Nothing came of the coeducational project; Horace Greeley headed it off with a compromise. But the meeting of Susan B. Anthony and Elizabeth Cady Stanton became a historic event.

On the strength of what passed, Lucy Stone afterward always claimed that it was she who had converted Susan B. Anthony to the cause of woman suffrage. It was true that Lucy Stone, as well as Mrs. Stanton, was already known as an ardent suffragist. Lucy Stone had first voiced the claim in a lecture she gave in her brother's church in 1847. However, the first organized demand for the vote came through Mrs. Stanton and was made by the woman's rights convention of 1848. It was from this convention that Susan's father had received the gospel, and it was her father who in turn passed it on to Susan. What there was left for Lucy Stone to do is hard to imagine. It is possible that some Quaker-like reluctance to the general idea of voting—for *both* men and women—still lingered on in Susan's mind. Some chance word of Lucy Stone might have helped her over this hurdle into an openly declared position. It is interesting that neither Susan nor Mrs. Stanton ever said a word in contradiction of Lucy Stone's claim that she had converted Susan.

At all events, the important result of the meeting of the three was the lifelong friendship then and there established between Susan and Mrs. Stanton. Mrs. Stanton fulfilled the ideal that Susan had previously conceived of her, and Susan's true character revealed itself once for all to Mrs. Stanton. They needed but one meeting to recognize their affinity—something that the Transcendentalists of New England had popularized in theory and was to be practically demonstrated in Susan's and Mrs. Stanton's future lifelong relationship.

≈§ III   Still, Susan stuck to her last. In the cause of temperance, for which she had been trained from childhood, she felt that she could not go astray. She did not know that a woman who has once stepped out of line in any form of public work would find one door after another opening to her. In January 1852 the Sons of Temperance held a mass meeting in Albany. Susan attended as a delegate from the Rochester Daughters, along with a number of women from other Daughters' societies. Supported by the presence of so many women, Susan rose to speak to a motion. She was promptly confronted by a ruling that women delegates were not allowed the privilege of the floor. It was explained that "the Sisters were not invited there to speak but to listen and learn." Without a moment's hesitation Susan walked out of the hall, followed by a few other women. The majority, however, remained, whispering their disapproval.

Gathering her handful of rebels, she repaired to the home of her old friend Lydia Mott, a Quakeress shirtmaker in Maiden Lane. With Lydia's help she organized a meeting for women, secured a basement room in a Hudson Street church, and inserted a notice of the meeting in Thurlow Weed's *Evening Journal*—accomplishing all this before nightfall. When the time came, her band was ready, strengthened by the addition of the Reverend Samuel J. May from Syracuse, David Wright from Auburn, and Lydia F. Fowler from New York, all of whom happened to be in Albany on business and responded to Susan's newspaper notice. These were all public speakers, who readily joined in the program and contributed to the evening's success.

It was a bitter cold night, and the church basement was not in the best of repair. Midway in the program the stovepipe fell down, filling the room with smoke, while the freezing air, pouring through the opened windows, mingled with the smoke to make the audience cough and sneeze. Once the gentlemen had restored the stovepipe, the sturdy meeting resumed business and organized itself into a Woman's State Temperance Society. It was decided to call a convention to be held in Rochester in the spring.

Susan had the aid of her father, William Hallowell, and other Rochester Friends in sponsoring the call for this April convention. She alone carried on the heavy preliminaries, while Horace Greeley came through nobly with private advice and public notices in the New York *Tribune*. Elizabeth Cady Stanton promised to attend and make the principal address. Susan engaged Corinthian Hall. The convention took place as planned and continued through six sessions, over all of which she presided with skill and self-assurance. It was her first successful public appearance.

How Susan, a Quaker, came to be so familiar with parliamentary usages she has never told us. All early Americans seem to have been born with the knowledge, and apparently even the Quakers, including female Quakers, were not immune. Susan carried the convention through smoothly. The only rifts in the harmony came when Mrs. Stanton demanded that drunkenness should be made a legitimate cause for divorce and when she suggested that women should give less money to foreign missions and more to social improvements at home. Susan managed, however, to carry her through the ensuing shock and rejection and, in the final roundup, to have her elected president. The society was nothing if not modern in its organization; they elected nine vice-presidents. Susan contented herself with the humble drudgery of secretary. Their positions represented her idea of the relative merits of herself and Mrs. Stanton—her fixed and unchanging regard for her friend's superior talents and aptitudes. In her eyes Mrs. Stanton came very close to being perfection.

For the first time there was a Woman's State Temperance Society in New York, headed for all practical purposes by Susan B. Anthony. The Men's State Temperance Society had to face the fact when they called a convention in Syracuse. They issued a noncommittal invitation, which after some hesitation Susan and Mrs. Bloomer decided to accept. The Reverend Samuel J. May of Syracuse, Daniel's personal friend, acted as their intermediary with the gentlemen of the society. Mr. May could get nothing decisive from them, so Susan and Mrs. Bloomer, armed with their credentials, entered the hall and sat down with a group of obedient sisters. Their appearance was the signal for an excited debate, in which the whole question of woman's rights was opened up, angrily discussed, and violently denounced. Mr. May tried to speak for the women, but no one would listen. Susan tried to put in a word but was ruled out of order. So the women once more withdrew to hold a meeting of their own in a neighboring church. This time Susan delivered the principal address.

The promotion of temperance, which she had chosen as the safest and sanest outlet for her reforming impulses, continued to be stormy. In January 1853 a general temperance rally took place in Albany, where the men and women held separate meetings and no trouble ensued. Then came a so-called World's Convention, held in New York, at which turmoil and hysteria broke out and again sent the women flying to a convention of their own. The point was that it was not decent for a woman to speak in public on any subject whatsoever, even on a moral issue. The clergymen and churchmen who controlled the temperance movement almost unanimously maintained this point of view. The New York newspapers, excepting only Greeley's *Tribune*, supported the reverend gentlemen editorially and even outdid them in abusive eloquence.

§ IV   At the height of the temperance crusade the cause acquired an unexpected but logical champion. The manufacturer of sarsaparilla, one wealthy Mr. Townsend, offered Susan and her friends his services and backing. Susan, Mrs. Bloomer, and the Reverend Antoinette Brown decided to accept the offer. They addressed temperance meetings in three of the largest halls of New York City with crowded audiences and with Mr. Townsend magnanimously paying all expenses. Encouraged by their success, the women made an upstate tour on their own through a dozen cities, charging admission fees and paying their own expenses.

During this tour Susan's father wrote her as follows:

I see notices of your meetings in multitudes of papers, all, with a few exceptions, in a rejoicing mood that woman at last has taken hold in earnest to aid in the reformation of the mighty evils of the day. Yet with all this "rejoicing" probably not one of these papers would advocate placing the ballot in the hands of woman as the easiest, quickest, and most efficient way of enabling her to secure not only this but other reforms. They are willing that she should talk and pray and "flock by herself" in conventions and tramp up and down the State, footsore and weary, gathering petitions to be spurned by legislatures, but not willing to invest her with the only power that would do speedy and efficient work.

It is evident that Daniel Anthony was a thorough convert to votes for women as early as 1853. A Quaker who had never cast a vote in his life, he had reached the conclusion that the ballot for women was the first step toward temperance as well as all other reforms. Mrs. Stanton's influence on Daniel had been reinforced, if not indeed preceded, by that of his good friend, Samuel J. May, of Syracuse, known as one of the earliest champions of the franchise for women. May had published a pamphlet, *Rights and Condition of Women*, in 1846, which was widely read and circulated and which expressly demanded for women the right to vote.

Susan's work for temperance was soon destined to end completely. In June 1853 the second convention of the Woman's State Temperance Society was held in Rochester. Elizabeth Cady Stanton, in her president's address, did some necessary explaining. "We have been obliged to preach Woman's Rights," she said, "because many, instead of listening to what we had to say on Temperance, have questioned the right of women to speak on any subject." Again she insisted on repeating her demand that drunkenness should be admitted as a cause for divorce.

As the meeting went on, a widespread unease with Mrs. Stanton developed. It had never occurred to the temperance women to exclude men from membership—some of their best friends had been Hallowell, May, Douglass, and Daniel Anthony. In their second convention the men had become more numerous and insisted on holding the floor most of the time. Susan was distraught; losing all of her finesse, she made an indignant speech accusing the men of trying to drive the women from their own society. The conservative element—men *and* women—coalesced with one object in mind: the ousting of Mrs. Stanton as president. They wished to purify the temperance cause from any taint of woman's rights, especially the right to divorce.

When Mrs. Stanton failed of re-election as president, Susan promptly resigned as secretary, although she had been unanimously re-elected. She now saw the two causes nearest her heart, temperance and woman's rights, as one and inseparable, and she had run her course as an adjunct of the clergymen's movement for temperance. Her resignation put an end to women's work for temperance in New York State, where it remained quiescent for twenty years, until Frances E. Willard came along and revived it.

◄§ V   Meantime, Susan had attended her first woman's rights convention. It will be noted that the movement had made considerable headway before Susan officially joined up. But in working for temperance with Mrs. Stanton she had been in training for the suffrage cause. She was no tyro when she came to her first suffrage convention.

This meeting was called the Third National Woman's Rights Convention. The Seneca Falls convention of 1848 was not called "national." The first so-called National Woman's Rights Convention was held in Worcester, Massachusetts, in October 1850. The moving spirit of this convention was Paulina Wright Davis of Providence, Rhode Island. Mrs. Davis had the support of Garrison and Phillips, Lucretia Mott, Lucy Stone, Antoinette Brown, two of the Blackwell sisters, and many other famous reformers who attended and made speeches. The convention was called "national" because the delegates came from nine states. It received widespread notice and publicity, including a favorable article by the wife of John Stuart Mill in the *Westminster Review* in England.

Mrs. Davis then proceeded with her second national convention, held in the same place the following year. It was equally well reported and was again distinguished by the presence and support of such reforming spirits as Garrison, Phillips, and Channing. Mrs. Stanton did not attend either of these conventions, but she sent letters to both. The third national convention was called at Syracuse, New York, in 1852.

At Syracuse, Susan for the first time saw action. She was put on the nominating committee and at once began to register. Paulina Wright Davis wished to retire as president and suggested as her successor Elizabeth Oakes Smith, a popular fiction writer of Boston. Lucretia Mott also favored Mrs. Smith, whose literary fame, now gone with the wind, was so great in those days that Lucretia thought it might help to popularize the cause. Lucretia told her husband, who was on the nominating committee, to push Mrs. Smith. It was no use.

Mrs. Smith had come to Syracuse garbed in the latest and most

extreme modes of the day. Susan knew the type from her Canajoharie experience; she knew the kinds of ideas that went with
those clothes. "When I was at Canajoharie I was under the most
conservative influence," she confessed in her *Reminiscences*. She
had long since returned to plain semi-Quaker attire. Quite flatly she
told the committee that a woman who dressed like Mrs. Smith
"could not represent the earnest, solid, hard-working women of the
country." James Mott, himself a Quaker, argued that all women did
not need to dress as plainly as Quakers; but Susan's arguments prevailed, and Mrs. Smith was not nominated. Incidentally, Susan was
mistaken about Mrs. Smith. She was a firm believer in woman's
rights and followed Susan's banner in the years to come without ever
showing the least resentment for this early snub. Susan's candidate
was elected—the beautiful, gracious, noble Lucretia Mott, garbed
as always in faultless Quaker dress but endowed with the utmost
worldly shrewdness and ability.

Susan's next contribution was eminently practical. After strain-
ing her ears to hear what was said by some of the delegates, she rose
and said, "Mrs. President, I move that hereafter the papers shall
be given to some one to read who can be heard. It is an imposition
on the audience to have to sit quietly through a long speech of
which they cannot hear a word. We do not stand up here to be seen
but to be heard." It was plain to all that the new recruit was of the
sensible, not the flowery, kind; that she would make a good hewer
of wood and a drawer of water for those of more grace, tact, and
eloquence. It was also plain that on her own ground she was fearless. They rewarded her by making her secretary.

A glowing feature of the convention for Susan was the presence
of those two rebel spinsters, Lucy Stone and Antoinette Brown.
Lucy Stone, agent of the Massachusetts anti-slavery society, and
Antoinette Brown, ordained minister of a regular church, were mature professional women. Susan admired them for their gift of
oratory, Lucy Stone especially, whose eloquence was most rare and
moving. They stood out among the others, showing her that she
had been so right in choosing spinsterhood. She joined herself to
them in spirit, working ardently for woman's rights, to which the
three of them were wholly dedicated. It recalled a memory of her
childhood, when three little sisters played together in the attic,
with only one aim and one object among them. Susan saw herself

with Lucy Stone and Antoinette Brown as a new and beautiful and emancipated sisterhood.

◆§ VI   Some of the newspapers, commenting facetiously on the Syracuse convention, dubbed it the "bloomer" gathering. Bloomers had in fact made their first public appearance on its platform. The costume was not originated by Mrs. Amelia Bloomer, to whom history gives the credit, but by that "glass of fashion and mould of form," Mrs. Elizabeth Smith Miller, daughter of the wealthy reformer, Gerrit Smith. Mrs. Miller designed it in imitation of the garment used in the standard water cures. It consisted of long full pantaloons reaching to the ankles, over which a short skirt reaching a little below the knees was drawn. The style was known to the public as the "bloomer"; to those who wore it, as "the short dress."

It is impossible now to imagine the outcry over this invention. Mrs. Miller, who designed it, wore it constantly. Her father, Gerrit Smith, thought the whole movement for woman's rights was bound up in it; so did her husband, Charles Dudley Miller, who escorted his bloomer-clad wife into the most expensive and exclusive New York and Washington hotels without an iota of embarrassment. Mrs. Miller defended it as practical.

In the spring of 1851, Mrs. Miller came to Seneca Falls to visit her adored first cousin, Mrs. Stanton, wearing her newly designed costume. Mrs. Stanton and Mrs. Bloomer were at once intrigued, as women are prone to be on seeing the latest model worn by a usually well-dressed friend. When the editor of the Lily, having a certain celebrity of her own, appeared on the streets of Seneca Falls thus attired, the name of the costume was settled. "Bloomer" it became and "bloomer" it was to remain, down to the present day. Unfortunately few pictures of the costume have been preserved to enlighten us as to the general effect. The one surviving memento of Elizabeth Cady Stanton attired in the famous raiment is not a photograph but a drawing, and not a good one. Except for the old-fashioned wide-brimmed hat and the dolman-like outer robe, she would pass unnoticed on any of our streets today. In her day the apparition appears to have caused a shock.

Mrs. Miller was serious about her mission. It was Mrs. Stanton, however, who took over the propaganda. The Lily also helped considerably, and the editor had the satisfaction of seeing her circulation rising by leaps and bounds. In no time at all Mrs. Stanton had Lucy Stone and many of her adherents in bloomers. It was Lucy Stone who appeared in bloomers at the Syracuse convention in 1852, where Susan first saw the costume publicly demonstrated.

After this convention Susan finally gave in. Mrs. Stanton had been working on her since spring, but it was not until December that she had the satisfaction of seeing her Quaker friend accoutered and arrayed in the new fashion. "Well, at last I am in short skirt and trousers," wrote Susan to Lucy Stone from Mrs. Stanton's house, where the transformation had been effected. As Susan did nothing by halves, she had her long brown hair cut short at the same time. Lucy Stone also wore her hair short.

Susan was wearing the short dress and trousers, with short hair, all through the temperance campaign sponsored by Mr. Townsend. In the New York halls and the upstate cities Susan and Mrs. Bloomer talked temperance to large audiences which, one suspects, came out mainly to see their apparel. At the World's Temperance Convention in New York, Susan and Lucy Stone made their appearance in the famous garb. At the last temperance convention in Rochester, where they decided to abandon the cause, Susan and Mrs. Stanton presided over the meeting clad in their bloomer costumes. In view of the popular reaction—which was just about one hundred per cent negative—it seems odd that they were permitted to hold their meetings in peace.

It was not the newspapers but the small boys and loafers on the street who tortured the wearers most. Although the vogue spread and was seen everywhere, it was never really domesticated. Characteristically, Mrs. Stanton was the first to give it up. Susan, as she would have said, "having put her hand to the plough," was slow to retreat. She passed a second cold January in trousers in Albany. Mrs. Stanton, already wearing conventional skirts, met her there for urgent suffrage business. A letter from Lucy Stone, indicating that she was about to follow Mrs. Stanton's example, reached Susan in Albany. Her anguished reply ran as follows:

Your letter caused a bursting of the floods, long pent up, and after a good cry, I went straight to Mrs. Stanton and read it to her. She has had a most bitter experience in the short dress, and says she now feels a mental freedom among her friends that she has not known for two years past. If Lucy Stone, with all her power of eloquence, her loveliness of character, who wins all that hear the sound of her voice, can not bear the martyrdom of the dress, who can? Mrs. Stanton's parting words were: "Let the hem out of your dress today, before to-morrow night's meeting." I have not obeyed her but have been in the streets and printing-offices all day long, had rude, vulgar men stare me out of countenance and heard them say as I opened the door: "There comes my Bloomer!" O, hated name! I have been compelled to attend to all the business here, as at Rochester. There every one knew me, knew my father and brother, and treated me accordingly, but here I am known only as one of the women who ape men—coarse, brutal men! Oh, I can not, can not bear it any longer.

Within a month, however, Susan followed Mrs. Stanton's advice, let out her hem, and began to let her hair grow. Mrs. Miller and Mrs. Bloomer continued to wear the dress for several years, apparently suffering but little annoyance and nonchalantly taking that which came. Finally, even Mrs. Miller laid it aside and, like Gertrude Ederle, who swam the Channel, she promptly forgot all about her feat. None of them seemed to realize that they had headed a lasting innovation, one that would henceforth never completely die out.

The anguish that Susan and Lucy Stone suffered in laying the dress aside was very real. Mrs. Stanton, feeling her responsibility, tried to console them. "I wish to write to Lucy Stone," she told Susan. "I know what she has suffered and what she must suffer in consenting to bow again to the tyranny of fashion. I hope, Susan, you have let down a dress and petticoat. The cup of ridicule is greater than you can bear." This from the woman who could calmly face in public the most insulting and abusive opposition is, to say the least, interesting. Susan, also, who could have faced a raging lion, exhibited the same unworthy cringing about the clothes on her back. Was it because they felt they were renegades to the cause of woman's rights? Of course they did. They all cried; with Susan it was a "bursting of the floods." Afterward she felt better. In the years to come she never harked back to the experiment with any expressed signs of regret. With her it was history that had been outlived.

Still the bloomer, while it lasted, represented a sincere revolt on the part of the women. The evidence is apparent in how quickly and widely it spread. Bloomer-clad women were seen on the streets of Cincinnati as well as in New York. It was the supreme symbol of their rebellion against convention. One cannot help recalling, by its similarity, the historical tragedy of Joan of Arc, who, after all her consenting, recanting, and acceptance of the Church, could not at the last moment bring herself to the act which would have saved her—the sacrifice of her male attire. What it meant to her, nobody knows, except that she said: "I would rather die than revoke what God has made me do."

With Susan and Mrs. Stanton the motive was not deeply religious. Woman's rights, though a precious ideal, operated on a less mystical plane. Moreover, neither of them had the constitution of martyrs, for the simple reason that deep in their hearts they felt that they were going to win. They withdrew from this skirmish, only to start another. As far as Mrs. Stanton was concerned, this was virtually the only battle of her life in which she yielded to the enemy outright. As for Susan, she compensated for the loss of the bloomer battle in many less spectacular but even more aggressive ways. Neither of them carried a guilty conscience out of their defeat. They felt that they had freed themselves for the pursuit of a much higher goal.

৵§ VII   Susan was knocking on a door that she half dreaded to see opened. To demand that women be allowed to speak in public required of her the purest courage, for she was no speaker. Most of her associates were natural-born or well-trained orators; Mrs. Stanton, Lucy Stone, Antoinette Brown, Lucretia Mott, the Grimkés, and many more were but seeking a chance to exercise their talents. Susan had to learn the art of public speaking step by step and with great effort. It may be remembered that the true gift of speaking had not descended upon Daniel Anthony. The spirit had chosen his sister Hannah instead as a mouthpiece. Though Daniel expressed his sentiments fluently in writing, he remained silent in Quaker meeting. Silence would get Susan nowhere in the field of woman's rights.

She made up her mind to try her luck at a teachers' convention, where at least she would be at home with her subject. She attended the Elmira convention, where three fourths of the audience were dumb and silent women, without getting up her courage to say anything. The next year, 1853, when the convention met in Rochester, Susan resolved to take the plunge. Wearing her bloomer dress, she waited for her opportunity. It came with the discussion of the subject: "Why the profession of teacher is not respected as that of lawyer, doctor, or minister." Susan rose in her place and addressed the chair in easily heard tones (she had warned herself to speak loudly): "Mr. President." The presiding officer happened to be a professor of mathematics at West Point, who, in the full-dress uniform of the Academy, added a touch of military authority to his already impressive person. "What will the lady have?" he asked benignly. "I wish to speak to the question under discussion," replied Susan in a clearly audible voice. The president would entertain a motion to that effect, he said, and one gentleman in the audience made it. The debate about whether she should be allowed to speak lasted half an hour, while Susan remained standing, fearful she might lose her chance if she sat down. The vote turned in her favor by a small margin.

She mustered all her courage and began: "It seems to me you fail to comprehend the cause of the disrespect of which you complain. Do you not see that so long as society says woman has not brains enough to be a doctor, lawyer, or minister, but has plenty to be a teacher, every man of you who condescends to teach tacitly admits before all Israel and the sun that he has no more brains than a woman?" She had intended to add some other thoughts, but after this contribution her courage failed her and she sat down. At least she had opened the forbidden door.

She continued to attend the teachers' conventions and to express her opinions from the floor. A few years later she offered a resolution in favor of coeducation. The same West Point professor was present and stoutly led the opposition. "These resolutions . . . ," he said, "are the first step in that school which seeks to abolish marriage, and behind the picture presented by them, I see a monster of deformity." On this occasion Susan wore conventional skirts, but the West Point professor was not deceived by her disguise. He knew her as one of those horrid unsexed women who would begin with coeducation and end with the sterilization of human society.

◆§ VIII   The Quakers of Rochester seem to have taken a calm attitude toward Susan's bloomer experiment. It was while wearing the short dress that she and her brother Daniel R. applied for admission into the Rochester Society of Friends. They were attending Dr. Channing's church, but that did not make any difference. Most of their father's group did the same, while retaining their membership in the Society. Susan and Daniel R. decided they wished to be enrolled with the other Quakers of Rochester and took steps to that end in 1853.

Susan probably initiated them. In 1847, while the family lived on the farm and Susan in Canajoharie, Daniel R. and Mary had applied to Easton for their certificates of removal. The Easton Meeting had duly forwarded the documents in proper form, but for some reason they had never been presented. When Susan returned to the farm none of Daniel Anthony's children was an enrolled member of the local Quaker meeting. Daniel himself, of course, was not entitled to full membership.

Susan apparently decided to rectify this. She and her brother wrote to Easton for their certificates, but Mary did not join them. She had evidently chosen to let her membership lapse, which it did at this time and was never afterward renewed. There are indications that Mary, her mother's child, had chafed more than the others at Quaker restrictions. Susan and Daniel R., however, secured the proper credentials from Easton in May 1853. The papers, announcing that Susan B. and Daniel R. Anthony had "settled to satisfaction their temporal affairs in Easton" and were "recommended to the Christian care of the Rochester Meeting," were duly received and promptly presented.

The following entries in the Rochester book of records reports the proceeding:

Rochester Monthly Meeting of Women Friends held at Mendon, 29th of 7th mo., 1853.

Received a certificate of removal in favor of Susan B. Anthony from the Easton Monthly Meeting, which on reflection this meeting is united in appointing Rhoda Ewer and Phebe Frost to take the necessary care in her case and report to the Monthly Meeting.

Rochester Monthly Meeting of Women Friends held at Rochester, 26th of 8th mo., 1853.

The committee appointed to take the necessary care in regard to receiving the certificate of Susan B. Anthony report they have attended to their appointment, and she expressed a wish that friends should dispose of her certificate as they thought best. After a time of reflection this meeting is united in receiving it, men friends concurring therewith.

Received a certificate of removal in favor of Daniel R. Anthony from Easton Monthly Meeting held 12th of 5th mo., 1853, which is accepted.

There is nothing unusual in this phraseology, except the item that Susan wished "friends should dispose of her certificate as they thought best." Her personality was such that the most rigid of Quaker formulas could not prevent it from coming through. When Friend Rhoda Ewer and Friend Phebe Frost "attended to their appointment," they were received by Susan in bloomer dress, which at the time she expected to be wearing indefinitely. By her remark, she probably intimated that the Friends must take her in bloomer dress or not at all. The record shows that they were willing to do so and that the men Friends concurred. That was the end of it. The liberality of the Rochester Quakers was fully demonstrated. This made it all the harder for Susan to lay aside the bloomer dress when the time came for her to do so. It was always easier for her to fight the opposition than to disappoint the generosity of friends.

CHAPTER NINE

FRIEND OF ELIZABETH CADY STANTON

◄§ I   When Susan first met Mrs. Stanton, the latter had all the advantages that age, experience, and social position can give to a woman—provided that a mere woman can have any advantages whatever, which Elizabeth Cady Stanton was not prepared to admit. A matron of thirty-six, already wearing the insignia of maturity—lace caps—married to a man of some consequence, the mother of four children, and the author of a Woman's Declaration of Rights, she had every reason to expect from Susan a certain amount of respect. Susan paid it with the appellation of "Mrs. Stanton," from which she never deviated during a lifetime of close friendship. To Elizabeth Cady Stanton from the first she was "Susan." Despite an alliance both mutual and equal, they remained "Mrs. Stanton" and "Susan" to the end. Susan was Telemachus to Mrs. Stanton's Mentor, and the passage of time could not change the relationship.

By comparison with Susan, Mrs. Stanton had accumulated a varied and extensive education. As a child she had been allowed the run of her father's office—her father being district judge in Johnstown, New York. At home she had been tutored not only in the ordinary subjects but in Greek and Latin. As a teen-age girl she had been sent to Emma Willard's Seminary in Troy, a school that ranked as fashionable and also as thorough. A somewhat prolonged maidenhood, enlivened by the companionship of two congenial sisters, was terminated at twenty-five by her marriage to Henry B. Stanton, ten years her elder. Her father, Judge Cady,

made much troublesome opposition to this marriage, since the
aspiring son-in-law had neither a business nor a profession. After
some ups and downs, occasioned partly by her father's opposition
and partly by Elizabeth Cady's unsureness of her own heart at
times, the marriage finally took place.

Henry Stanton was considerably overshadowed by his brilliant
and irrepressible wife. This was true during his lifetime but still
more true when history took over and decided to celebrate the
wife and quietly forget the husband. Stanton was nevertheless a
man of parts. If he was impecunious when his wife met him, it
was because, like Garrison, he had dedicated his life to the cause
of anti-slavery instead of promoting his own career. Stanton was
the hero of the famous incident at Lane Seminary in Cincinnati,
when Dr. Lyman Beecher announced there was to be no discussion
of slavery within its walls. Henry B. Stanton and a friend, Augustus
Wattles, walked out of the school at this point, though Stanton,
for one, had made the most extreme sacrifices to attend Dr. Beecher's famous college.

Henceforth Stanton worked as agent for the American Anti-
Slavery Society. For seven years he was derided, stoned, and driven
out of towns, while churches where he had spoken were burned
in his wake. On many of his tours he was accompanied by John G.
Whittier, the Quaker shoemaker, poet, and anti-slavery agitator.
The two worked well together. Stanton was a fluent orator, and
Whittier no orator at all. But Whittier who abounded in shrewdness and finesse was often able to get a hearing for Stanton when
Stanton could not have managed it. It was in the role of anti-slavery
agitator and orator that Stanton was introduced to Elizabeth Cady
at Gerrit Smith's house, where both were guests. On the basis of
his meager salary from the Anti-Slavery Society he proposed marriage to Miss Cady. Her father said no, and after some reconsideration Elizabeth sadly acquiesced to her father's wishes.

But Stanton's oratorical talent was yet to win his bride. In the
following year, because of this talent, he was named as a delegate
to the World Anti-Slavery Convention in London, with all of his
expenses paid. The chance to accompany him abroad disposed of
Elizabeth Cady's last doubts. After a hasty marriage they sailed
for London and the convention, where the Americans were due
to make their mark. The American women delegates, including

Elizabeth Cady Stanton and Lucretia Mott, were excluded from the floor and assigned to sit in a gallery, while William Lloyd Garrison, in protest against the ruling, insisted on sitting with the women. Mrs. Stanton and Mrs. Mott rebelled against their treatment and then and there decided on some kind of formal protest. Their decision was eventually carried out in the Seneca Falls convention of 1848.

The impression made by the American delegate, Henry B. Stanton, was extremely fine. His wife thought him at his best when he espoused the cause of the rejected women sitting in the gallery, but the English anti-slavery society estimated all his efforts highly and invited him to remain and make speeches throughout the British Isles. The Stantons enjoyed almost a year of foreign travel, which both of them utilized to the full, absorbing culture and knowledge on every hand. Their contacts with leaders in the rising English Liberal movement of the '40s enlarged their political horizon.

This was the end of Stanton's anti-slavery work. He entered his father-in-law's office in Johnstown and studied law for a year. He then chose Boston, rather too ambitiously perhaps, for the practice of his newly gained profession. As a lifetime Democrat and a well-known anti-slavery man, he found the cards stacked against him. Boston was uphill all the way. When he handled a suit against Abbott Lawrence and his brothers (which, surprisingly enough, he won), he found himself shut out from all business with the ruling clique of the city. He survived precariously for five years, after which, on his father-in-law's advice, he decided to exchange Boston for Seneca Falls in New York. He and Elizabeth moved into a nice large house (handsomely shingled now, though it must have been clapboarded in their time), shaded by tall trees and two miles distant across the Seneca River from the business part of the town.

Here it was that Susan B. Anthony, four years later, first saw Mrs. Stanton walking with Garrison and Thompson, her famous guests, along a Seneca Falls street. Though Mrs. Stanton, in describing the episode, failed to mention they were her husband's guests also, they very definitely were. At the time Mr. Stanton was still the head of his family.

◄§ II Mrs. Stanton was quite lonely in Seneca Falls. After a year of broadening experience in England and five years of association with Boston's intellectuals, she found little stimulus in the provincial town. She turned to the Quakers in the vicinity, the McClintocks and the Hunts, for congenial companionship. When Susan Anthony, another Quaker, appeared on the horizon she was prepared to welcome her. As a foot-loose creature, free to come and go, Susan appealed strongly to Mrs. Stanton, tied down by many children. She had three when she came to Seneca Falls, and four more were born there. Susan could go to Seneca Falls though Seneca Falls could not go to her. She became Mrs. Stanton's legs and Mrs. Stanton became her pen. Mrs. Stanton wrote Susan's ideas into speeches, and Susan went to the front and delivered them. Sometimes Mrs. Stanton wrote her own ideas into speeches, and Susan delivered those also. That was how their collaboration began.

Their close friendship became a cause of prolific comment. Many people tried to break it down, partly out of self-defense, for together they were really formidable; partly out of jealousy and envy, for it was evident that the two, while pursuing a serious cause, were having an extremely good time doing it. Mrs. Stanton's children testified to the happiness of the arrangement. Her son Gerrit wrote to his brother: "Little did we think, in our younger days, when we beheld, at the old ranch in Seneca, mother and Susan scratching away at speeches, petitions, resolutions, what big guns they were to be." Her daughter, Harriot Stanton Blatch, said years later, "They had such a good time. There was so much happiness in their union. Aunt Susan used to take care of us children while mother wrote a speech. Father and Aunt Susan's father were friends. It was all so intimate and warm, so different from the bleak, ill-natured legend about them." The children did not realize that their mother and Susan were putting on a serious show, but they did know they were enjoying it. As they grew older, they were more enlightened, and two of them, Harriot and Theodore, became their mother's staunch supporters in the suffrage movement.

Susan and Mrs. Stanton themselves scarcely knew how their collaboration was managed. In an early letter to her friend Susan used a phrase that attained wide circulation and was frequently quoted. The saying, "Mrs. Stanton makes the bullets and Miss Anthony fires them," was attributed to this one and that one; but the one who originally used it was Susan. She wrote:

Rochester, June [   ], 1856
Dear Friend: . . . Not a word written on that Address for Teachers' Convention . . . and the Mercy knows when I can get a moment, and what is worse, as the Lord knows full well, is, that if I get all the time the world has—I can't get up a decent document. So for the love of me and for the saving of the reputation of womankind, I beg you with one baby on your knee and another at your feet and four boys whistling, buzzing, hullooing Ma Ma set yourself about the work—it is of small moment who writes the Address, but of vast moment that it be well done. I promise you to work hard, oh, how hard, and pay you whatever you say for your time and brains—but ah! Mrs. Stanton don't say no, nor don't delay it a moment, for I must have it all done and almost commit it to memory.

Now let me tell you, Do you write all you think of ready to copy, and then you come out here, or I will come to you and copy.

The Teachers' Convention comes the 5th and 6th of August. The Saratoga Woman's Rights Convention, the 13th and 14th, and probably the Newport [convention] the 20th and 21st.

During July I want to speak certainly twice at Avon, Clifton and Sharon and Ballston Springs and Lake George—— Now will you load my gun, leaving me only to pull the trigger and let fly the powder and ball [italics added]—— Don't delay one mail to tell me what you will do—for I must not and will not allow those school masters to say—See, these women can't or won't do anything when we do give them a chance—— No they shan't say that, even if I have to get a man to write it—but no man can write from my stand point, nor no woman but you—for all, all would base their strongest argument on the unlikeness of the sexes. . . .

Will give you every thought I have scared up on another slip—— Now do I pray you to give heed to my prayer—those of you who have the talent to do honor to poor, oh how poor womanhood, have all given yourselves over to baby making, and left poor brainless me to battle alone. . . .

If the spirits would only just make me a trance medium and put the right words into my mouth—you can't think how earnestly I have prayed to be made a speaking medium for a whole week—if they would only come to me thus, I'd give them a hearty welcome. . . .

Do get all on fire and be as cross as you please. . . . You remember Mr. Stanton told how cross you always get over a speech?

From this distraught letter one gains a picture of how greatly Susan depended on Mrs. Stanton in those early years. They were like Jefferson and Madison, ambling on horseback through the forest and planning the destruction of the enemy. Also like Jefferson and Madison, they were dealing with a stock of ideas for which neither claimed originality, for the simple reason that they regarded them as everlasting truths. There is a hint in this letter that Susan sometimes paid Mrs. Stanton for her assistance, but there are no other references to bear this out. It could have happened occasionally.

Mrs. Stanton wrote in her *Reminiscences* a summing up of their partnership:

Whenever I saw that stately Quaker girl coming across my lawn, I knew that some happy convocation of the sons of Adam was to be set by the ears, by one of our appeals or resolutions. . . . Then we would get out our pens and write articles for papers, or a petition to the legislature; indite letters to the faithful, here and there; stir up the women in Ohio, Pennsylvania, or Massachusetts; call on the *Lily*, the *Una*, the *Liberator*, the [*Anti-Slavery*] *Standard* to remember our wrongs. We never met without issuing a pronunciamento on some question. In thought and sympathy we were one, and in the division of labor we exactly complemented each other. I am the better writer, she the better critic. She supplied facts and statistics, I the philosophy and rhetoric, and, together, we have made arguments that have stood unshaken through the storms of long years; arguments that no one has answered.

So entirely one are we that, in all our associations, ever side by side on the platform, not one feeling of envy or jealousy has ever shadowed our lives. We have indulged freely in criticism of each other when alone, and hotly contended when we have differed, but in our friendship of years there has never been the break of one hour. To the world we have always seemed to agree and uniformly reflect each other. Like husband and wife, each has the feeling that we must have no differences in public. Thus united, at an early day we began to survey the state and nation, the future field of our labors. . . .

So closely interwoven have been our lives, our purposes, and experiences that, separated, we have a feeling of incompleteness—united, such strength of self-assertion that no ordinary obstacles, difficulties, or dangers ever appear to us insurmountable.

Susan could never forget what she owed to Mrs. Stanton for buttressing her self-confidence in the early days of her stewardship. In the field of public speaking she especially needed encouragement. Mrs. Stanton wrote: "I have no doubt a little practice will make you an admirable speaker. Dress loosely, take a great deal of exercise, be particular about your diet and sleep enough. The body has great influence upon the mind. In your meetings, if attacked, be cool and good-natured, for if you are simple and truth-loving no sophistry can confound you." Some of this physical advice was more needed by the giver than by the receiver, but it was Susan who practiced it.

From Lucy Stone, also, Susan received encouraging council: "Why do you say the people won't listen to you, when you know you never made a speech that was not attentively heard? All you need is to cultivate your power of expression. Subjects are so clear to you that you can soon make them as clear to others." Finally, Antoinette Brown joined the others in urging her onward: "Don't hesitate [to speak] but in the name of everything noble go forward and you shall have our warmest sympathy." To go forward in any situation, however difficult and complex, was exactly what Susan's constitution inclined her to do. Antoinette Brown's advice was easy to follow.

Susan struggled with herself and tried, then tried again, and at last triumphed. She became an excellent platform speaker. Judging from the many newspaper reports quoted in her first biography, her style was much favored by her audiences—many people preferring her factual flow to the more florid trend of some orators. In simplicity and sincerity she was never to be surpassed.

III However strongly attracted to Lucy Stone and Antoinette Brown—they were her guiding stars for a time—Susan forged a bond with Mrs. Stanton more fundamental and lasting. For this strong and enduring tie one is inclined to look for some emotional foundation aside from the social and intellectual interests that united them. Human beings are seldom held together for a life-time by common social and political views, no matter how identi-cal. Some deeper basis of sympathy can usually be predicated of such a close and long-lasting friendship.

What basis of sympathy could be assumed between a happily married woman, the mother of seven children, like Mrs. Stanton and a firmly established spinster like Susan? For many years there has been no slightest clue to anything in their private lives that might explain their emotional tie. In fact, they were unusually successful in presenting themselves to the public as practically without private lives. The only glimpses into their backgrounds were those concerned with housekeeping and cooking and Mrs. Stanton's methods of caring for her children. Beyond this their personal lives remained dark and hermetically sealed.

A recent biography of Mrs. Stanton sheds a little more light on the subject. The author, Miss Alma Lutz, received the story from the late Harriot Stanton Blatch, who had evidently decided that enough time had passed to reveal a harmless secret in her mother's life.

The story, as told in Miss Lutz's *Created Equal*, suggests that Mrs. Stanton was not quite so happily married as she allowed the world to believe. The disturbance in her affection began far back in her girlhood when she was attracted by a law student in her father's office. Edward Bayard was ten years older than herself and, while Mrs. Stanton was still in her teens, married her older sister. When Elizabeth Cady, a charming ingenue just out of the Emma Willard school, visited her sister's home (which happened to be in Seneca Falls), the young husband fell in love with her and de-clared his feelings. The sympathetic biographer supposes that he was caught off guard. Much older than Elizabeth and married to her sister, he appears to have exhibited far too little self-control. The young girl responded with her whole maidenly heart and was at once involved in a secret and hopeless love affair.

Edward Bayard did nothing to alleviate her problem. On the contrary, he sought out every opportunity to see her, clandestine and otherwise, and finally went so far as to propose an elopement. Elizabeth's sense of decency and loyalty would not permit her to go this far, though it had not prevented her from forming a decep-tive alliance with her sister's husband. She assumed that as long as the affair was conducted on a wholly platonic basis she had not betrayed Triphena.

The romance went on for years. Elizabeth struggled to free herself but apparently without co-operation from Edward. In one of her periods of self-conquest she met Henry Stanton, the famous orator, wearing among the Abolitionists surrounding him the aura of a hero. Stanton fell in love with Elizabeth and Elizabeth fell in love with the orator. When her father interposed delay by objecting to the marriage, Edward Bayard once more appeared upon the scene and (incredibly!) upbraided her for faithlessness. But for the sudden and irresistible lure of the London trip and the accompanying necessity for speedy action, Elizabeth Cady might never have married Henry Stanton. She probably would never have married.

Mrs. Stanton might at least have thanked her husband in her mature years, as Jane Welsh Carlyle did, for having rescued her from a life of sterile spinsterhood. Apparently spinsterhood was what her fond lover expected of her. But like Jane Carlyle, Elizabeth Stanton was never wholly satisfied with the husband she secured, though Jane Carlyle had the grace to be thankful for her status. It never occurred to the high-spirited Elizabeth Stanton to be humbly thankful for anything. Instead she nursed the fleeting ideal of Edward Bayard through many years to come, while he assisted in various ways in prolonging the old romance. For instance, he would not trust himself to be left alone in the same room with her, though it must have sometimes seemed awkward and inexplicable for an in-law to behave so. The continued experience of reality appears not to have shattered the dream.

Mrs. Stanton's biographer considers this romance as the source of Mrs. Stanton's long crusade for free divorce. From the beginning she insisted on forcing the issue into the foreground of woman's rights, often against the wishes of her most radical colleagues. She continued to do so all the rest of her life. This is considered by Miss Lutz as the result of her continuing enslavement to the image of her early love. Mrs. Stanton was a woman with a powerful mind which enabled her to do many great and noble things in her time but apparently failed her in solving her own primary problem. The phenomenon is not unusual.

Susan B. Anthony would have known her friend's story from

herself. Susan was her confidential companion, her more than sister, for the greater part of her life. If Susan knew the story, she was in no wise alienated by it, but on the contrary drawn closer to her friend. Susan also nursed, though perhaps in lesser degree, a similar vain dream. A reading of her early diaries shows that from her girlhood days her thoughts and feelings were much occupied with the young man who married her older sister. The young man in her case could scarcely be suspected of having encouraged her affections. Her involvement was a young girl's natural fancy for the prince of the village, by far the handsomest young man in the town. But withal it was a fancy that did not evaporate easily, especially in a character so marked by fidelity as was hers.

Susan's good sense told her that to dissipate a dream one must take action. She grappled with her problems in her own practical way. She adopted Aaron into her affections as a real older brother and resolved to fill her life with interests and activities. She strove to compensate for her imagined lack of beauty by action in the field of social reform. She realized that an old maid had to keep busy, busier even than the typically overworked and hard-driven wife and mother, if she did not want to sink into a nonentity. Finally, she felt that the only recourse of a girl without beauty was to demonstrate brains.

Both Susan and Mrs. Stanton saw themselves in a certain sense as deprived of love. Mrs. Stanton might have learned, had she chosen to do so, to love her husband, who was so much more worthy in all respects than the ghostly lover of her fantasy. But as the years went on she grew less and less pleased with him. Susan became more and more fixed in the habit of refusing marriage. This sympathy and understanding for each other took the place of the love both thought they had missed and accordingly removed loneliness from their lives. As one, they survived battles which they could not have survived alone. "Such pine knots as you and I are no standard for judging ordinary women," wrote Mrs. Stanton proudly to Susan. They were a pair of happy warriors.

§ IV The year 1854 brought a big victory in New York State for woman's rights. It was not won by a single bound but by a long and arduous preparation. Susan had found in her temperance work an object lesson on women's poverty. If she organized a temperance group in a town, she returned the next year to find it dissipated. The members, wives and housekeepers, would explain they had no money of their own to keep it going. "I never before took in so fully the grand idea of pecuniary independence," said Susan. "Woman must have a purse of her own, and how can this be so long as the law denies to the wife all right to both the individual and the joint earnings?" She drew up, with William Channing's and Samuel May's help, a triple-barreled petition for the rights of women in regard to wages, to the guardianship of their children, and to the exercise of suffrage. This petition she launched at a woman's rights convention in Rochester, then circulated it widely through volunteer workers throughout the state.

She focused her attention in 1854 on the property rights aspect of the bill. The law of 1848, which had allowed her mother to possess her own farm, was limited specifically to real estate inherited from a parent. A married woman could not control her own wages nor possess any other property independent of her husband. The petition to correct this, for which ten thousand signatures had been obtained, she had ready to present to the State Legislature in February.

The occasion was a great day for Susan and Mrs. Stanton; Susan had gathered the petitions and Mrs. Stanton was to address a joint session of the two chambers. Even Judge Cady was impressed by his daughter's appearance before the august Legislature. The women were in evidence early—Susan in bloomers, Mrs. Stanton in skirts—and the press was not more critical of the one than of the other. When Mrs. Stanton had spoken, they felt they had crossed a Rubicon. The bill was not passed, of course, but it was given a respectful hearing and would again be presented.

Once more the faithful went forth, piling up leg work under their constitutional right to "petition the Government for a redress of grievances." The early suffragists deserve laurels for their incredible physical effort for the cause. When transportation was scarce and primitive, they tramped from door to door, even from village to village, exhausting themselves in the use of their only constitutional privilege. Fortified by the precedent of John Quincy Adams, who had constantly defended the right of petition from the floor of the House, the women exploited their constitutional right to trudge to the fullest extent. Susan attended to the printing, the mailing, and the collection of the forms.

After the Albany hearing, Susan turned toward the South with Ernestine Rose. Mrs. Rose was a Polish lady of Jewish birth and unusual eloquence, who had developed radical views in Europe and had come to America to lecture about them. Always ready to do battle for anti-slavery, women's rights, and free religion, Mrs. Rose was cordially welcomed in American reform circles. Susan and Mrs. Rose decided to carry the gospel of liberalism to the city of Washington, with Susan to arrange meetings and Mrs. Rose to do the speaking. Susan had laid aside her bloomers and was allowing her hair to grow. Mrs. Rose was to be scrupulously careful not to mention the subject of slavery. Yet they drew very small audiences. "Washington people seem to gratify their love of speech-hearing by attendance at the Capitol," Susan observed.

The trip had some advantages for Susan. It was her first sight of Washington, Capitol Hill, the White House, Mount Vernon, the original documents of the Constitution and the Declaration of Independence. The historical monuments meant a great deal to a Quaker whose training in patriotism had been rather desultory up to the present. Her new friends, Elizabeth Cady and Henry B. Stanton, had both started life as fiery patriots. By comparison with them, she had a great deal of historical background to make up and she made up quite a lot on this trip. She loved Washington at first sight.

The city gave her her first real sight of slavery, of which her father had written several years before: "There are Black Folks in abundance here, but they don't act as if they were even under the pressure of hard times and much less the cruelties that we hear of slaves having to bear." According to Susan's diary, their demeanor had not altered much since her father's visit. Amiable and nonchalant, incredibly numerous, they produced an atmosphere that caused Susan to exclaim with horror, "I am getting accustomed to slavery!" But a little investigation brought the true facts to light. The maid in the hotel was revealed as a slave, hired out to the hotelkeeper by her master for eight dollars a month, "not a penny of which went to the girl." Her master was only required to keep her in clothes, which an obliging maid in a hotel seldom needed to buy. It was literally true that Sarah belonged to her master, and Susan had the satisfaction of feeling her hackles rise. She was *not* getting accustomed to slavery.

Mrs. Rose took Susan to call on a lady whom she described as "the living curiosity of Washington." The curiosity turned out to be Anne Royall, the eighty-five-year-old publisher, living with her dog and cat in a tumble-down office on Capitol Hill. They found her working on her editorial for next week's *Huntress*. Susan was appalled at the filthiness of Mrs. Royall's person and environment, little considering that Mrs. Royall, on the last lap of her earthly pilgrimage, reserved what energy she had to write and publish her adored paper. Susan was among the last visitors who saw her in her pitiably neglected old age. She said to Mrs. Royall, "What a wonderful woman you are!" and Mrs. Royall answered calmly, "I know it." Of what use is it to pretend when you have one foot in the grave?

While Mrs. Rose lectured, Susan sat silently by in the wings. In the following winter, starting on Christmas Day, Susan embarked on her first lecture tour. Armed with petitions, making her own dates, charging and collecting the fees, and doing all the speaking, she canvassed fifty-four counties out of the sixty in New York State. The traveling alone, by any and every conveyance, in the coldest winter months, through the bleakest, loneliest parts of the state, was in itself a heroic feat. But she rejoiced to break even in her finances. Her father wrote her on her route: "Would it not be wise to preserve the many and amusing observations by the different papers, that years hence, in your more solitary moments, you and maybe your children can look over the views of both the friends and the opponents of the cause?" This was the beginning of Susan's famous clippings and the scrapbooks she kept all her life and left on her death to the Library of Congress.

⊷§ V   In that winter the question of marriage once more obtruded itself upon her life. "You and maybe your children," her father had written, evidently regarding his daughter as still marriageable. Nothing was farther from Susan's thoughts. Struggling onward by wagon or sleigh through sleet and snow, from village to village, haranguing her audiences on women's property and guardianship rights, she was not exactly a figure to attract a romance. Yet a suitor suddenly materialized out of the frozen waste.

A Quaker gentleman whom she had met in Albany appeared as if by accident in the character of a fellow passenger. At Lake George he took charge of Susan's comfort, had a plank heated for her feet, and managed her various problems. When her meeting was over he reappeared out in front with an elegant sleigh and a pair of fine horses, prepared to drive Susan to his home for Sunday. After a pleasant visit with his sister, who presided over his house, Susan proceeded on her way through the frozen Schroon Lake country. But now she was driven over the snow-covered roads by her attentive friend in a fine sleigh with every possible comfort. As soon as the inevitable proposal came and the inevitable refusal followed, his attentions terminated and Susan was left to plow her way through the frozen drifts alone.

Susan visited almost every town short of Canada. She had resolved to canvass the whole state. By the time she reached her friends' homes, Martha Wright's in Auburn and Mrs. Stanton's in Seneca Falls, spring was on the way. The winter she had chosen for her state-wide tour was one of the bitterest in history.

May brought distressing news; at least it was distressing to Susan. Lost in the frozen North, she had heard nothing of the preparations for the two weddings, which she now first learned of as prominent events. Lucy Stone (without changing her name) had married Henry B. Blackwell, and Antoinette Brown was about to marry his brother Samuel. The bridegrooms were well known as woman's rights advocates and as brothers of the independent and talented Blackwell sisters. That Lucy Stone had married *without* changing her name and that both she and Antoinette Brown had acquired partners dedicated to the suffrage cause gave small comfort to Susan. Apparently she had believed that Lucy and Antoinette were devoted to a life of spinsterhood like herself. In her dismay and resentment (had she not just refused a good husband for the sake of the cause?) Susan wrote reproachful and indignant letters to her friends. Her letters had no effect upon the happy brides, but they survived to give Susan the reputation of being an avowed enemy of marriage. The whole effect was to drive her more firmly than ever into the alliance with Elizabeth Cady Stanton, who she knew by experience would always be true to the cause no matter how many babies or households she might have to distract her. What the two others might do in the future she had yet to learn.

Susan was either greatly exhausted by her winter's campaign or painfully let down by the desertion of her friends, or perhaps depressed by both. For the first time in her life she had to call in a doctor. She suffered from a severe and persistent backache, for which the doctor's remedies seemed to bring no relief. She finally decided to try the popular water cure at Worcester, Massachusetts, conducted by Dr. Seth Rogers, a cousin of her mother.

Susan's belief in the water cure was enthusiastic. Her inherent suspicion of all drugs was such that she welcomed any course that dispensed with them. The ritual of wet packs, shower baths, dressing and undressing, and exercising kept her so busy that she "did not have time to put two thoughts together." The personality of Dr. Rogers had much to do with her cure: he conversed with her in a leisurely fashion, took her for long drives, and placed his library at her disposal. Stretched on a lounge in the sunshine, she read *Sartor Resartus, Consuelo, Villette, Corinne,* Frances Wright's *A Few Days in Athens,* and many other books she had never expected to have time to read.

While at the cure she paid a visit to Boston, where she was entertained by Garrison's family. They took her to the theater to see *Hamlet.* In Boston she saw Lucy Stone and Antoinette Brown for the first time since her return from the North, and all differences were buried. She attended anti-slavery rallies with Dr. Rogers and became more and more immersed in the Abolitionist cause, which was gathering momentum all the time under Garrison and Phillips.

She returned to Rochester in November with her health entirely restored. She had enjoyed a real vacation, received the intellectual stimulus for which she had long been starved, and made friends with the brilliant Abolitionist circle of Boston. She took out an insurance policy in her father's company, the New York Life, and received a first-class rating as a risk from the company doctor. Her backaches were completely forgotten.

At one point in her winter sweep of 1855, Susan paused overnight in her native town of Adams. While she was holding forth manfully in the Baptist church on woman's rights, she saw her aged grandfather, Humphrey Anthony, entering the door. Stunned for a moment into silence at the sight of her Quaker ancestor entering a Baptist church, Susan stood and watched him while he deliberately advanced up the aisle and seated himself on the pulpit steps. With a proud gesture she stepped forward and assisted him to a seat on the platform. Leaning forward, the old man appeared to listen with the deepest interest to his grandchild's discourse on woman's rights. At the close he said, "Well, Susan, that is a smart talk thee has given us tonight." There was little in it that the Quaker-indoctrinated old man did not understand. Susan had not traveled as far away from the home base as he had feared.

CHAPTER TEN

THE FIGHTING ABOLITIONIST

⊷§ I From the beginning the Abolitionists welcomed women into the fighting ranks. Among the earliest leaders were Angelina and Sarah Grimké, who had freed their slaves and left their South Carolina home to preach the gospel of emancipation in the North. The women of Boston, led by Maria Chapman, Lydia Maria Child, and Elizabeth Peabody, wrote for the press, held fairs to raise money, and spoke in public for the cause. Abby Kelley, the Quaker schoolmistress, abandoned teaching to become one of the first missionaries of the American Anti-Slavery Society. As a testimonial to the women's efforts, Garrison had chosen to sit out the World Anti-Slavery Convention in the woman's gallery when they were banished from the floor.

Abby Kelley, who married her co-worker, Stephen S. Foster, was among the first women speakers who came under Susan B. Anthony's ken. Susan had just returned home from Canajoharie when the Fosters arrived in Rochester for a week's campaign in the neighborhood. Susan accompanied Abby Foster on her round of meetings. Abby still had some of the old Quaker "ranting" in her style of oratory, and this was in no wise diminished by the opposition she encountered on this early tour.

Susan was greatly impressed by Abby Foster, whose fiery periods awakened echoes in her own ancestral Quaker blood. She did not join the Abolitionist forces at once, though urged by Abby Foster to do so. But for the next five years, while working for temperance and woman's rights, she was moving toward her ideal of "the sublime height where now stand Garrison, Phillips and all that small but noble band whose motto is 'No union with slaveholders.'" She saw the Abolitionists as the elite of all the reformers of the hour, partly because of the genius of their leaders and partly because of the unstinted support they gave to the woman's rights cause.

In September 1855, while invalided at Dr. Rogers' Water Cure, she met the leading lights of Garrison's society and was seen and noted by them. As a result she became an agent of the American Anti-Slavery Society, holding a position on a par with that formerly held by Henry B. Stanton. On January 1, 1856, she received a formal letter from the secretary of the Anti-Slavery Society offering her a position, to begin at once and continue until May. Susan had already arranged a tour of lectures for the woman's property rights bill, and the dates were fixed. She could not accept at once. The offer was postponed and renewed in October 1856, just before Buchanan's election and his administration, which forced the antislavery issue into a fighting cause.

She was again faced by a hard winter. The political climate was also against her. The opposition of both parties—the Democrats and the newly formed Republicans—was strong. Garrison's group demanded nothing less than immediate and unconditional emancipation, and no political party in the country stood for it. Susan also faced a hard life as an organizer. Her speakers developed chills, fevers, and domestic emergencies, so that she herself, engaged up to the hilt, had to replace them. The secretary of the society wrote her: "We sympathize in all your trials and hope that fairer skies will be over your head before long. Garrison says, 'Give my love to Susan, and tell her I will do for her what I would hardly do for anybody else' . . . You must be dictator to all the agents in New York; when you say, 'Go,' they must go, or 'Come,' they must come, or 'Do this,' they must do it. I see no other way of getting along, and I am sure that to your gentle and wholesome rule they will cheerfully defer." Many of Susan's speakers had served on the Abolitionist platform longer than she and had no intention of deferring to her or to anyone else. Still, she managed. She had her reward when the secretary wrote her in the spring, "We have made the following a committee of arrangements for the annual meeting:

Garrison, Phillips, Edmund Quincy, Johnson, and Susan B. Anthony." To sit on the national committee with these famous Abolitionist leaders was an honor which Susan up to now would never have dreamed of.

Her anti-slavery work had brought her recognition and had introduced other changes in her life. For the first time since leaving schoolteaching she had achieved a regularly paid salary. This amounted to ten dollars a week and her expenses. She could manage on this because she still wore her old Canajoharie dresses, toned down, turned, dyed, made over, and matched for worn spots. Ten dollars a week was more than she had ever received as a teacher, and it gave her a renewed feeling of financial independence.

When Florence Nightingale, Susan's contemporary in England, was endowed at a similar age with an independent income by her father, it represented a great turning point in her life. Susan, with her salary, and Miss Nightingale, with her allowance, both felt they had achieved financial independence and the self-determination that this brings. Though the income was not adequate for their needs, it was an epoch-making experience in both their lives. In those days, when financial independence was rare for a single woman, the psychological effect of money she could call her own was nothing less than liberation. In their middle thirties, Susan and Florence Nightingale, thus emancipated, became conscious of great aims.

A short while later Susan wrote: "I cannot bear to make myself dependent upon relatives for the food I eat and the clothes I wear; I have never done it and hope I may never have to," and still later she declared: "No genuine equality, no real freedom, no true manhood or womanhood can exist on any foundation save that of pecuniary independence." Susan was only comparatively independent but apparently unconscious of it when the slack was taken up by her devoted and dedicated Abolitionist father. In fact, as far as the farm was concerned, Susan probably paid her way in those days when woman's labor was at a premium. She always put in her time at home working as hard as a hired servant.

The second epoch-making change wrought by her anti-slavery work concerned her public speaking. In 1857 she threw away her manuscript and learned to speak from notes. She felt so strongly about human slavery that she could not bear to be tied down in speaking of the evil. As might be expected, she took her pattern from Abby Kelley Foster and declaimed rather violently. But it got her away from depending on her manuscript.

The Abolitionists were like the colonial rebels in one respect: it was easier to see King George as a tyrant because he lived in a faraway country; the Southern slaveholders were likewise tyrants far removed from sight. The Abolitionists did not care in the least if the South wanted to fly off by itself and stay there. Garrison thought it might be a good idea. When Susan inveighed against slavery she was lashing a country that was not her own. In after years she became extremely national-minded, but never in her whole lifetime did she learn to see the South as a part of the nation to which she belonged.

Once at a Quaker meeting in Easton she encountered a Virginia Quaker who undertook to apologize for slavery in his state. "Christ was no agitator, but a peace-maker," he said; "George Fox was no agitator; the Friends at the South followed these examples and are never disturbed by fanaticism." Susan was horrified to hear such words proceeding from another Quaker. She was instantly on her feet and she heard herself saying: " 'I came into this world not to bring peace but a sword. . . . Woe unto you, scribes and Pharisees, hypocrites that devour widows' houses!' Read the New Testament, and say if Christ was not an agitator! Who is this among us crying, 'Peace, peace, when there is no peace'?"

Only one written speech survives from the hundreds she made during her Abolitionist crusade. This sets down in black and white the passionate words that were usually extemporaneous—scathing attacks upon "the arrogant usurpers of the South," "the bloated self-conceit of traitors and rebels," and the "Hydra-Monster which sucks its life-blood from the unpaid and unpitied toil of the slaves." In the midst of her tirades she would suddenly become Susan again —the Susan to whom common sense was always the last and greatest refuge. Here is a passage from the one preserved manuscript:

But if you emancipate the slaves, What will you do with them? What will the black man do with himself, is the question for him to answer. I am yet to learn that the Saxon man is the great reservoir of human rights to be doled out at his discretion to the nations of the earth.

Do with the Negroes? What arrogance in us to put the question!

What shall we do with a race of men and women who have fed, clothed, and supported both themselves and their oppressors for centuries. Do for the slaves? Why, allow them to do for us what they are now doing for Jeff Davis. . . .

When her Abolitionist work ended and she returned to woman's rights, she seldom flamed with the same fierce indignation. But also she never returned to her former dependence on the pedestrian manuscript. Though speaking with a lesser heat, she could forge her sentences from a naked mind, standing in front of a listening crowd.

II Susan was one with her family in the fight for the slaves. The Anthonys belonged to the small fearless band who operated in underground ways from the vantage point of Rochester. John Brown of Osawatomie often visited the city and stayed at the home of Frederick Douglass. He came there from Kansas, where he had organized guerrilla forces to fight the pro-slavery interests of the state. Merritt Anthony, Susan's brother, aged twenty-two, caught the Kansas enthusiasm from John Brown in person and left the farm to enlist in his band. Susan's older brother, Daniel R., followed Merritt to Kansas the next year—the same year in which Susan enlisted as an Abolitionist speaker. Standing behind them all, fighting for emancipation, was Daniel Anthony, unwavering in his moral and financial support and considering no sacrifice too great to stamp out the evil.

Susan's brother Merritt was with John Brown in the raid on Osawatomie, which gave Brown his title. Merritt was quite ill with fever (probably malaria) at the time of the raid and Brown was spending the night in his cabin. In the early morning the shooting began. John Brown rushed forth at once, telling the youth on no account to leave the house. No sooner was he out of sight than Merritt seized his gun and followed him into the thick of the fray. He seems to have exhausted himself in getting there and spent the hours of conflict lying, with his gun ready, on the bank of the creek. He barely had strength to crawl back to his cabin, where he lay for weeks, untended and uncared for, until the fever abated. Owing to his illness, no news of him came to his family for some time after the battle. The first dependable report was brought by a man who had taken part in the battle and had since traveled from Osawatomie to Rochester. The anxiety of the family was not relieved till then. Susan wrote him at once:

Rochester, September 18, 1856

Dear Brother Merritt:

How much rather would I have you at my side tonight than to think of you daring and enduring greater hardships than our Revolutionary heroes. Words can not tell how often we think of you or how sadly we feel that the terrible crime of this nation against humanity is being avenged on the heads of our sons and brothers. . . . Wednesday night, Mr. Mowry, who was in the battle, arrived in town. Like wild fire the news flew, D.R. was in pursuit of him when father reached his office. He thought you were not hurt. Mother said that night, "I can sleep now there is hope that Merritt still lives"; but father said: "I suppose I shall sleep when nature is tired out, but the hope that my son has survived brings little solace to my soul while the cause of all this terrible wrong remains untouched." . . .

Your fish pole never caught so luscious a basketful as it did this afternoon. I made a march through the peach orchard with pole in hand to fish down the soft Early Crawfords that had escaped even the keen eyes of father and mother when they made their last detour. As the pole reached to the topmost bough and down dropped the big, fat, golden, red-cheeked Crawfords, thoughts went away to the owner of the rod, how he in days gone by planted these little trees, pruned them and nursed them and now we were enjoying the fruits of his labor, while he, the dear boy, was away in the prairie wilds of Kansas. I thought of many things as I walked between the rows to spy out every ambushed, not enemy, but friend of the palate. With the haul made I filled the china fruit dish and then hallooed for Mary L. and Ann Eliza to see what I had found, and down they came for a feast. I shall send Aaron and Guelma the nicest ones and how I wish my dearest brother could have some to cool his fevered throat.

Evening.—Father brings the Democrat giving the list of killed, wounded and missing, and the name of our Merritt is not therein; but oh! the slain are sons, brothers and husbands of others as dearly loved and sadly mourned.

Later.—Your letter is in to-day's Democrat, and the Evening Advertiser says there is "another letter from our dear brother in this morning's Shrieker for Freedom." The tirade is headed "Bleeding Kansas." The Advertiser, Union, and American all ridicule the reports from Kansas, and even say your letters are gotten up in the *Democrat* office for political effect. I tell you, Merritt, we have "border ruffians" here at home—a little more refined in their ways of outraging and torturing the lovers of freedom, but no less fiend-ish.

Daniel Anthony's sacrifice of his sons was not regarded as tem-porary, even from the start. Daniel R. and Merritt had not gone to Kansas merely to enlist for the duration but to become citizens and ensure freedom for the future state. Clarina Howard Nichols writes in the *History of Woman Suffrage* a vivid account of how she and her sons left a comfortable home in Vermont to join the Free State immigrants. They formed a considerable migration. Susan's brothers were directly enlisted by John Brown, and the decision was made as an act of high idealism and great self-sacrifice on the part of the whole family.

It fell to Susan's share to help out on the farm. Her father em-ployed a hired man and Susan worked beside him. She got the idea that if women spent more time in gardening and less time in the kitchen the world would benefit. In this mood she decided to raise raspberries for the market and persuaded Daniel to spend two hun-dred dollars on a raspberry patch, from which she expected to reap a profit. Her Abolitionist lectures interfered with her farm duties and, with respect to the raspberry patch, they interfered destruc-tively. She left for the winter's tour without instructing Simon, the hired man, to prepare the young plants for the cold. The bitter winter took its toll and the raspberry investment proved a total loss.

The newspapers somehow got hold of the story and used it for a moral homily on woman-out-of-her-sphere. Susan's family also showed her no sympathy (the loss of two hundred dollars in the frugal clan was not a light matter). Her sister Mary wrote, an-nouncing the calamity: "I hope, Susan, when you get a husband and children, you will treat them better than you did your raspberry plants, and not leave them to their fate at the beginning of winter." Her brother-in-law Aaron McLean added this sermon: "As to your raspberry 'spec,' I regret to tell you it has gone up. The poor, little, helpless things expired of a bad cold about two weeks ago. Do you remember that text of Scripture, which says, 'She who by the plow would thrive, herself must either hold or drive'? It has cost you $200 to learn the truth of it."

Aaron McLean's sermon from Rochester needs explanation. Since 1856 the McLean family had been established nearby—in the city, not on the farm. That was why McLean was now on hand to lecture Susan in a brotherly way about her raspberry fiasco.

◄§ III   Susan began the year 1859 by attending the anti-slavery convention in Albany. She stayed with her friend, Lydia Mott, in Maiden Lane. All the great men of the convention—Garrison, Phillips, Pillsbury—dined at Lydia Mott's table and relaxed in her home to an unusual degree. For some reason or other the convention was characterized by a holiday spirit, in which Susan participated, although the year 1859 lay ominously close to the irrepressible climax. Apparently the Abolitionists thought it a year like any other.

Susan remained with Lydia Mott six weeks to work on the State Legislature for the women's property bill. "Well, I am a member of the lobby," she wrote, "but lacking the two most essential requisites, for I neither accept money nor have I any to pay out." She had good advice, however, from Thurlow Weed at the *Evening Journal* office, where she called frequently. Weed, originally a Rochester newspaperman, had been Susan's patron and chief adviser since her outburst against the temperance clergy in 1854. Susan and the hard-boiled politician appear to have got on well together.

When the Anti-Slavery Society met in New York in May, the event came off quietly. It was all too quiet for John Brown, who attended the sessions, hoping for some vigorous action. He had made the long trip from Kansas, where men were fighting and dying for freedom, to be met with flowing periods and graceful oratory on the part of his Eastern allies. He went away, says Charles Beard in his *Civilization*, feeling that there was too much talk and too little life in the movement. Judging by Susan's account of the recent Albany meeting, Brown's criticism was justified. The Abolitionists were momentarily resting on their oars. But for the frontiersman there was no such rest. A war was going on in Kansas, and these people in the East were apparently content that it should be contained there.

Brown spent that summer in secret preparations. Little is known of them except that money was sent to him from Boston and that it went through the hands of A. Bronson Alcott, Louisa May Alcott's father. A shipment of pike staves was sent from an ax factory in Collinsville, Connecticut. In August, Brown wrote to Frederick Douglass, asking Douglass to meet him in a Pennsylvania town and to bring Shields Green with him. Green was an escaped slave who had stopped on in Rochester and ran a small business. Douglass did not go, but Shields Green did, and was afterward taken with Brown and hanged at Harpers Ferry.

The news of John Brown's raid on Harpers Ferry and his subsequent capture and execution brought a shock to the entire country. To the Abolitionist circles in Rochester it meant more than shock; it rang an alarm bell. Frederick Douglass departed for Canada by the same route over which he had expedited so many slaves, little thinking he would someday need to take it himself. From Canada he went on to England, where he remained for a whole year.

Gerrit Smith of Peterboro, who had given John Brown a farm and cared for it in his absence, sustained the shock less firmly than any other member of this Abolitionist group. The effect on him was traumatic. He was taken to the State Asylum for the Insane at Utica and stayed there under treatment for several months. His very sensible wife paid him frequent visits, comported herself affectionately and steadily, and her behavior, combined with the hospital treatment, restored him eventually.

Susan Anthony and her father, connected by close ties with all of these unfortunates, went their way silently in their own home As well-known Abolitionist agitators, relatives of one of Brown's guerrillas, and intimate friends of Frederick Douglass, they might well have been suspected or accused of complicity. But Susan showed no signs of fear for herself. When the word came that December 2, 1859, had been set for Brown's execution, she emerged at once into the foreground of public affairs. Supported by a few Abolitionists and Quakers, she decided to do all that was left to be done for John Brown—hold a memorial meeting on the date of his execution. She engaged Corinthian Hall and appealed to Parker Pillsbury, editor of the *Liberator*, to make the memorial address. Pillsbury consented and wrote, ironically enough, advising her to get some "Republican or Gerrit Smith follower" to preside over the meeting. Most of the people so described were in miserable hiding.

Susan trudged the streets of Rochester, canvassing the liberals of the city, but none of them would consent to preside.

She herself presided over the meeting. She collected fifty cents as admission fee from an audience of three hundred persons, having been thus advised by a Quaker friend, Samuel D. Porter. He said this would tend to keep out the possible disturbers. Pillsbury made an eloquent speech and everything went off quietly. Susan locked the door, paid for the hall, and sent the rest of the admission money to John Brown's family. Brown had lost one son in Kansas, had two more killed at Harpers Ferry, and had himself been hanged. The widows and orphans of the Brown family were indeed numerous and in dire need of help.

Susan had acted promptly in an emergency. She did not think of her act as requiring great courage. It was merely one of the things that could not be left undone and, above all, it was action instead of repining—the rule she had learned to live by.

~§ IV   Woman's rights began to look up financially. It had been one of the poorest of all the reforms that appealed to the public's attention. Aside from a few generous fathers and husbands, men were slow to support it with money. It struggled along on twenty-five-cent admission fees and the firm determination of the women to make themselves seen and heard. Susan had followed the example of William Lloyd Garrison, who started his anti-slavery drive as a hard-working printer without any outside support. Garrison set out to free the slaves, scarcely knowing how he would support his own family. He had nevertheless organized a powerful movement. Like him, Susan believed in the magical power of the truth to conquer and survive all obstacles.

Through an Abolitionist friend, woman's rights had it first windfall. In December 1858, Susan received the following letter from Wendell Phillips:

Dear Susan:—I have had given me $5,000 for the Woman's Rights cause; to procure tracts on that subject, publish and circulate them, pay for lectures and secure such other agitation of the question as we deem fit and best to obtain equal civil and political position for women. The name of the giver of this generous fund I am not allowed to tell you. The only condition of the gift is that it is to remain in my keeping. You, Lucy Stone, and myself are a committee to spend it wisely and efficiently. . . .

It was the first financial gift made exclusively for woman's rights as separated from the Abolitionist cause. Francis Jackson, the donor, belonged to the second generation of the Jacksons, who were associated with the Appletons, Lowells, and Abbotts in founding and promoting the great textile mills of Massachusetts. This powerful combination had ridden out the depression which had wrecked Daniel Anthony's enterprise, and had continued to prosper and lay up fortunes for the families of the original investors. It seemed just and appropriate that a part of the profits which had been amassed from the labor of New England mill girls should be diverted to the cause of woman's rights. Unconsciously Mr. Jackson was performing an act of social justice.

His motives, however, were purely personal. An unworthy son-in-law, one Mr. James Eddy, had taken advantage of the Massachusetts guardianship laws to remove his children from the home of their mother. At that particular time Susan and Mrs. Stanton were engaged in the effort to reform the guardianship laws of New York, to give to the mother equal rights with the father over their children. Mr. Jackson felt a personal concern in their success.

With the help of Mr. Jackson's money Susan renewed her campaign most energetically, sending out speakers at twelve dollars a night and piling up petitions with speed and impressiveness. The reputation of having a financial backer did not hurt their cause with the legislators. Other influences came to their aid, among them Horace Greeley, who wrote to an Assembly member commending the women's bill. Susan and her friends began to take hope.

From the inner circle of Boston Abolitionists again came largess. Mr. Charles F. Hovey died in the following spring and left a fortune of $50,000 to be expended for several reforms—primarily for anti-slavery and woman's rights. Hovey stated in his will that he believed primarily in two principles: "No union with slave-holders" and "The natural rights of men and women are equal." He added that he wished no prayers said over his body, because, "The priesthood are an order of men, as I believe, falsely assuming to be reverend and divine, pretending to be called of God; the great body of them in all countries have been on the side of power and oppression; the world has too long been cheated by them; the sooner they are unmasked, the better for humanity." This blast against the priesthood appealed strongly to Elizabeth Cady Stanton, who, while working for woman's rights, also did what she could to unmask the priesthood. Susan always felt too grateful to the obscure Methodists and Baptists who opened their doors to her to join with Mrs. Stanton and Mr. Hovey in a general denunciation of the Church.

Like Mr. Jackson, Mr. Hovey left his gift in the care of "Wendell Phillips and his associates." There was a firm opinion in Boston that only those who had money knew how to take care of money. In this belief Mr. Hovey allowed great discretion to Phillips and the other custodians in the allocation of the funds among the respective reforms. This provision was to lead later on to some differences between Susan and Phillips, as chief custodian.

V In the summer of 1859, without any obvious reason, Susan plunged into the depths of a profound depression. The old back complaint reasserted itself, and she called in the doctor again. He told her to rest. She decided she would read and improve her "literary culture," perusing among other things Mrs. Gaskell's recently published *Life of Charlotte Brontë*. She began to write a lecture entitled "The True Woman" and worked on it for three unhappy months. For Susan to philosophize meant that Susan was lost. As long as she dealt in facts her philosophy flowed underneath, easily, smoothly, concurrently, but when she handled the delicate fiber of analysis directly in the foreground, her mind worked like a fish out of water. She at last finished "The True Woman," but there is no evidence that she ever used it as a public lecture.

Susan had seen little of Mrs. Stanton that year. Expecting her sixth child, Mrs. Stanton had been unusually ill during her pregnancy; had even failed to fulfill her woman's rights engagements as formerly. In late March she wrote to Susan:

Dear Susan:

I have a great boy, now three weeks old. He weighed at his birth without a particle of clothing 12¼ pounds. I never suffered so much before. I was sick all the time before he was born, and I have been very weak ever since. He seemed to take up every particle of my vitality, soul and body. Thank Heaven! I am through the siege once more. But, oh! Susan, what have I not suffered for the past year? It seems to me like a painful dream.

Write soon.

Yours as ever,
E. CADY STANTON

One might think that this letter would have partially consoled Susan for her spinsterhood, if spinsterhood was what worried her. For it does appear that she was having a brief period of worry about this matter. She had developed some purely social contacts with her environment, involving her in "moon-light rides" with masculine companions. It meant a temporary return to the sentimental atmosphere of her girlhood. If some particular suitor and a downright proposal emerged, it cannot be clearly discovered. "Mr. Blank walked home with me," says the diary; "marvellously attentive. What a pity such powers of intellect should lack the moral spine." Evidently she found it necessary to fortify herself against Mr. Blank. Restless, discontented, weighing marriage not only in the abstract but in relation to the eligible men around her, Susan became ever more deeply perplexed.

Her best friends—Mrs. Stanton, Mrs. Blackwell, Mrs. Stone— were all married. Her only intimate spinster friend was Lydia Mott in Albany. She entered in an argument with Lydia by correspondence:

I am not complaining or despairing, but facts are stern realities. The twain become one flesh, the woman, "we"; henceforth she has no separate work, and how soon the last remaining monuments (yourself and myself, Lydia), will lay down the individual "shovel and de hoe" and with proper zeal and spirit grasp those of some masculine hand, the mercies and the spirits only know. I declare to you that I distrust the power of any woman, even of myself, to withstand the mighty matrimonial maelstrom! . . .

In the depths of my soul there is a continual denial of the self-annihilating spiritual or legal union of two human beings. Such union, in the very nature of things, must bring an end to the free action of one or the other, and it matters not to the individual whose freedom has thus departed whether it be the gentle rule of love or the iron hand of law which blotted out from the immortal being the individual soul-stamp of the Good Father.

Lydia Mott replied sensibly that the woman who lost her individuality in marriage probably had not possessed any before. But this does not seem to have convinced Susan or raised her spirits. Where were the social ideals in which her soul usually expanded? Abolitionism was at a low ebb. Woman's rights, though now stimulated by paid speakers, was a pedestrian affair. "Oh, if we could but make our meetings ring," she said, "like those of the Anti-Slavery people, wouldn't the world hear us?" But even the antislavery people no longer rang as once. "For the past five years," she wrote, "I have gone through this routine and something within keeps praying to be spared from more of it. There has been such a surfeit of lecturing the people are tired of it." The people were not tired; but Susan was tired—very tired and very lonely. Her final complaint was perhaps the real one. "Then I never was so poor in purse and I fear to end another campaign with a heavy debt to still further encroach upon my small savings." Susan was thirty-nine. How would she ever achieve financial independence working at reform on a salary of ten dollars a week?

In this mood of depression she wrote to her friend:

Dear Mrs. Stanton:
How I do long to be with you this very minute—to have one look into your very soul and one sound of your soul-stirring voice. . . . Mrs. Stanton, I have very weak moments—and long to lay my weary head somewhere and nestle my full soul close to that of another in full sympathy. I sometimes fear that, I too, shall faint by the wayside—and drop out of the ranks of the faithful few. . . . Oh, Mrs. Stanton, how my soul longs to see you in the great Battlefield. When will the time come? You say in two or three years. God and the Angels keep you safe from all hindrance. . . . If you come not to the rescue, who shall! Mrs. Stanton, do write me a good long letter. . . . Don't fail to write me. . . .

As one survives the woes of adolescence eventually, so, it seems, does one also survive their periodic recurrences. Slowly Susan's habits of activity asserted themselves. The mental therapy of floor scrubbing and carpet weaving, provided at so much expense for patients nowadays, was available in her case "for free." Susan even scrubbed the window shutters on the house. There was a minimum of posing in her disposition; she fancied herself neither as an invalid nor as a heroine, nor as a combination of the two. Thus she was

saved from the kind of hysterical illness which afflicted the more
delicately bred Florence Nightingale for years. A well-balanced
realist, Susan did not play with her emotions. She was capable of
profound despondency but not of the play-acting that would super-
ficially relieve it. No one in the world was less of a sentimentalist.
The habit of facing the truth, confirmed by long practice, came to
her aid and the bondage to depression passed.

Susan had never declared her intention of being an old maid. But
it is pretty clear that she now saw this condition awaiting her and
that she took a long stride in her mind toward its acceptance during
that summer. In those days no woman past forty could expect to be
married, and Susan was fast entering the bourn where only as an
old maid could she survive. Henceforth she seems to have been
pretty well settled in her mind about marriage.

The year 1859 had been a year of bereavement as well as sickness
for Mrs. Stanton. Judge Daniel Cady died, but in the end he had
failed to disinherit his daughter as he had so often threatened. The
ambivalent relationship had closed on the positive side. In fact, life
had been preparing Mrs. Stanton for the great "Battlefield" and she
was now ready for the fray—much readier than Susan had dared to
hope. The beginning of 1860 found them both armed, equipped,
and battle-ready for the Albany arena. One would never have recognized in them the repining spinster and the complaining mother of
scarce three months before. They had something to do and they
did it with energy and spirit.

Susan, attending as usual the woman's rights convention in
Albany and plodding her accustomed round, learned that the
women's property and guardianship bill would come up before the
Legislature in the next session. She rushed back to Seneca Falls,
helped Mrs. Stanton to write her speech for the Legislature, and
returned with her friend in tow, prepared to the last word, look,
and gesture for the critical hearing.

It was a triumphant day for both of them. Mrs. Stanton, somewhat more portly but just as handsome as when she had appeared
six years before, stood at the Speaker's desk and addressed the joint
session. The chamber was packed. She spoke for two hours, while
the audience, many of whom were standing, maintained an unbroken stillness, anxious to hear every word. The speech, preserved
in the *History of Woman Suffrage*, is indeed one of Mrs. Stanton's

finest. She dealt with the point at issue, property rights, guardianship, etc., only in passing, for her whole speech was a manifesto of woman's rights such as only Mrs. Stanton and Susan could produce. Once they had started, it was hard to confine them to one particular wrong. After the bill had passed, Mr. Colvin, its sponsor in the House, approached Mrs. Stanton and Susan and apologized because it did not include woman suffrage.

The law, which formed an amendment to the property law of 1848, provided that women should not only control inherited property but should also *own and control their own earnings* [italics added]. A married woman could make contracts and go into business. A married woman could sue or be sued, and any money so recovered should be her own property. And, finally, "Every married woman shall be joint guardian of her children with her husband, with equal powers, etc., etc., regarding them."

Considering the law that it replaced, it was indeed a revolutionary step. Susan had done more to create a background of public opinion in its favor than any other living person. Since her earliest temperance work she had been striving to put money into women's pockets, and the property law was one way of accomplishing it. In its final draft of the law, the Judiciary Committee conferred with Susan as to some of its terms and adopted some of her suggestions. Thanks to its provisions, New York State would be a much better state than Massachusetts, for instance, for a married woman to live in. Susan's soul glowed in the knowledge of what this new area of freedom would mean for the future woman.

CHAPTER ELEVEN

THE CIVIL WAR

✑ I As the Civil War approached, Susan and Mrs. Stanton had to choose one of two courses. They could join forces with the newly organized Republican party, based on no further extension of slavery, or stick with the Abolitionists, who called for immediate and total emancipation. The menfolk of their respective families joined the new party. Henry B. Stanton was one of its founders, played an important part in its early struggle for existence. Susan's brother Daniel R. was one of its early recruits. Coming home from Kansas, Daniel R. made his first political speech as a Saratoga meeting of the Eastern Free Soilers. Susan was present and felt very proud of her thirty-six-year-old brother. Her pride, however, did not influence her in the choice of her own course.

Susan and Mrs. Stanton cast their lot with the non-political crowd of simon-pure Abolitionists. At one point Mrs. Stanton, living in sequestration before her last child was born, appears to have wavered slightly. "You Garrisonians," she wrote to Susan, apropos of a small Fabian victory, "are such a crotchety set that generally, when all other men see cause for rejoicing, you howl the more grievously. How is it now? I desire to know, for as I am one of you, I wish to do what is most becoming to one of the order." Presumably Susan got her friend into line in a minimum of time. As women, they had an inherent distrust of political leaders and partisan politics equaled only by that of Garrison himself. Throughout Buchanan's administration and throughout the Civil War, they stuck to his banner. They stayed as long as Garrison stayed.

Up to the Republican National Convention of 1860, it appeared that the candidate of the thriving new party would be William H. Seward of Auburn, New York. So confident of victory were Seward and his friends that Auburn decked itself out in festal array and eager well-wishers crowded his lawn when the incredible news of Lincoln's nomination came through. Such a hasty removal of bunting and trappings was not again to be seen in New York until Mr. Dewey's supporters demonstrated it in November 1948. For the Abolitionists the exchange of Seward for Lincoln did not mean an improvement. The platform of the Republican party was their main target, the candidate their secondary foe. The election of Lincoln on this compromise platform—the exclusion of slavery from the Western territories—only added fuel to their flame.

The Abolitionists went all out in a great campaign to convince the new party that they meant business. Having profited from the labors of women in New England—women like Maria Weston Chapman, Lydia Maria Child, Abby Kelley Foster, the Grimkés, Prudence Crandall, and Lucy Stone, they naturally turned to New York women for help in their state. This was all the more necessary since so many of their male supporters had accepted the half a loaf offered by the Lincoln party. Susan Anthony, long their representative in New York, was directed to organize the work in that region. She immediately called Mrs. Stanton to her side and raised the Garrison standard: "No compromise with Slaveholders. Immediate and Unconditional Emancipation." Mrs. Stanton responded, while her husband went off with the Lincoln organization. Subsequently joined by Samuel J. May, Beriah Green, Aaron M. Powell, and Stephen S. Foster—all veteran Abolitionists—Susan planned a revival tour to cross the whole of New York.

It was a task for the tried and true only. New York was divided between Democrats and Republicans, and both parties were determined to put down the Abolitionists. Susan's group of agitators moved as a body; to separate would have been disastrous. They spoke only in cities and towns, hoping thereby to reach greater crowds; but, by the same token, they encountered a greater organized opposition.

Susan presided over all the meetings. On this tour she learned to meet and deal with mobs. In every city the crowd was ready, and the police, whether under a Democratic or Republican mayor, played the part of indifferent bystanders. In Buffalo, where the tour began, the speakers were not allowed to be heard at all. For two days the mob held high carnival, invaded the platform, and turned off the lights. Through it all Susan managed to keep her place on the stage. In Rochester the same performance was repeated; not a speaker could be heard; bedlam reigned. The chief of police mounted the platform and declared the meeting adjourned. The next day being Sunday, a colored congregation of the city invited the Abolitionists to use its church. Here three successful though quiet meetings were held, giving everybody a chance to be heard.

The riots continued on schedule, the disturbers resorting to various methods of enforcing their will. At Port Byron, cayenne pepper in quantities was thrown on the stove. At Utica the hall was locked and barred against them, although Susan had paid sixty dollars in advance for its use. At Syracuse, the home of Samuel J. May, the mob, well organized by leaders, took possession of the hall. Not a speaker was allowed to speak. Rotten eggs were thrown, benches broken, and knives and pistols gleamed in the crowd. The rioters climbed upon the stage and forced Susan and her group to leave the hall. That evening two hideous mannikins, the one labeled "Samuel J. May" and the other "Susan B. Anthony," were dragged through the streets of Syracuse and were finally burned, to the accompaniment of wild yelling and leaping, in the main public square.

The meeting in Rome was thus described by Susan:

Last evening there was a furious organized mob. I stood at the foot of the stairs to take the admission fee. Some thirty or forty had properly paid and passed up when a great uproar in the street told of times coming. It proved to be a closely packed gang of forty or fifty rowdies, who stamped and yelled and never halted for me. I said, "Ten cents, sir," to the leader, but he brushed me aside, big cloak, furs, and all, as if I had been a mosquito, and cried, "Come on, boys!" They rushed to the platform . . . seated themselves at the table, drew out packs of cards, sang the Star Spangled Banner and hurrahed and hooted. After some thirty or forty minutes, Mr. Foster and Aaron Powell came down and I accompanied them back to Stanwix Hotel, where the gang made desperate efforts to get through the entrance room in pursuit of the "damned Abolitionists." The Republican paper called us pestiferous fanatics and infidels, and advised every decent man to stay away. . . . And yet a hundred unmolested conventions would not have made us a tithe of the sympathizers this one diabolical mob has done.

The first city where they were given any hearing was Albany, their last stop. The mayor of Albany happened to be a gentleman of some determination—a gentleman, moreover, who was somewhat handy with the trigger. Imbuing the policemen with his own determination, he planted them thickly throughout the hall. He then seated himself on the platform with his revolver laid across his knees and ordered Miss Anthony to open the meeting.

She did so; and the eloquent periods of Mrs. Stanton and the other speakers rang out for the first time since the tour began with never an offensive interruption. Three sessions, morning, afternoon, and evening, were held in this way. At the close of the evening session, however, the mayor thought it would be foolish to strain his luck any further. Putting his pistol back into its holster, he approached Susan with a humble request. "It would be a personal favor," he said, "if you would call off the meetings scheduled for tomorrow." Susan complied, and he added hastily, "I will still protect you if you insist." Susan, persuaded to let well enough alone, made an announcement that the meetings were over. She had less reason to regret this when she found, later, a mob gathered outside waiting to follow the speakers to the Delavan Hotel. But the mayor and police were chaperoning them and the mob maintained a polite distance.

At Albany the party separated. It had been a dangerous pilgrimage, rough stuff. At several points just a little more riot might have spelled tragedy. Only Abolitionists who were true to the bone could have stood it. Yet Susan and Mrs. Stanton never flinched; nor did Daniel Anthony, following his daughter's progress in the daily newspapers; nor did Henry Stanton, who, though he had left the Abolitionists, could recall similar experiences of his own early years, when, as he said proudly in his memoirs, "I was mobbed in every state from Indiana to Maine!" Susan and Mrs. Stanton remained in Albany long enough to attend the woman's rights convention, which immediately followed. So imminent now was the great war that this woman's rights convention proved the last of their gatherings for the next five years.

Those were brave days for Susan Anthony and have been far too little appreciated in her own and our national history. The Abolitionist headquarters in Boston esteemed her highly, not merely for her intrepid leadership but also for her sentiments. Susan was both presiding officer and speaker on this tour. Abby Foster sent her a letter of commendation on her speech:

It is a timely, noble, clear-sighted and fearless vindication of our platform. I want to say how delighted both Stephen and myself are to see that you, though much younger than some others in the anti-slavery school, have been able to appreciate so entirely the genius of our enterprise.

During the dangerous period up to and during the war, Susan gave her whole time and strength to the Abolitionist cause. She toured the state like an avenging angel, shouting out passionate and inflammatory speeches—speeches which reflected less of her own personality than the spirit of the cause with which she identified herself. Her speeches were usually delivered from notes, but one of them is still preserved and gives an idea of her rousing style.

"Hundreds of men [she declared] who never thought of emancipation a year ago, talk of it freely, and are ready to vote for it and fight for it now. Can such ever go back to the times of Fugitive Slave Laws, when the right of free speech on this whole question was denied, and Northern freemen were the slave-hounds of the South? . . .

"Think you the people of the North can ever settle back into their old inglorious peace, after declaring, by an overwhelming majority, that slavery shall not plant its foot in one inch of the 14,000,000 acres of free territory? After rising like one man to defend their votes at the point of the bayonet, from every branch of industry and art, from the forum, the pulpit, and the professor's chair? After giving up home and ease and the hard-earned wealth of years, can they, after sacrifices such as these, baptized in the blood of their bravest sons, consent to submit to the rule of the slave-holding oligarchy?

"Would Northern men . . . listen in our Senate Chambers to the bloated self-conceit of traitors and rebels, who in their barbarous warfare, their cruelty to our dead and dying, and prisoners of war, had violated all and every law of civilized nations?

"No, no, there can be no reconstruction on the old basis, but by the humiliation of the North! Recognition of the Independence of the Southern Confederacy would be far less degrading and ruinous.

"Abolitionists, for thirty years, have been trying to beat this simple gospel logic into the head and heart of the North—they have piled facts on facts to demonstrate it, but the people turned a deaf ear and cried, 'Why are you come to torment us before our time?' . . .

"For months we have stood in battle array against the arrogant usurpers of the South, our national existence even in imminent peril, and yet we will not stab to the heart the Hydra monster that glares us in the face, his fiery eye-balls looking insolent defiance, as he contemplates all our boastful military preparations for his defeat. It is only when the still small voice of *freedom to the slaves* floats along the lines, that he begins to tremble. He knows his one vulnerable part and shields it from attack. May we soon see it and come to know that, however much we may harass and cripple him, however often and totally overthrown his hosts, the monster though crushed to earth will surely rise again. He sucks his life-blood from the unpaid and unpitied toil of the slaves and can only die when those bleeding backs and breaking hearts are wrested from his gory lips."

Never in her whole career as a suffragist did Susan make a speech like this. Never in her whole career as a woman's rights campaigner, though challenged by countless insults and rebuffs, did she rise to such heights of denunciation and rhetoric. She had patterned her style after Garrison, her own and her father's hero, who was a master of invective. The aggressive strain in her Quaker ancestry came out in her anti-slavery work. Her only thought was to rebuke the world for sin and call it to repentance. Parrington said of Garrison, "He was an agitator after the ancient Hebraic pattern." Susan's attitude placed her in the same niche with Garrison.

Yet in the course of years and in the records of the Anti-Slavery Society, Susan's name has been almost forgotten. This is perhaps explained by the fact that the standard biography of William Lloyd Garrison, written by two of his sons, gives little credit to Susan for her great and loyal contribution. Mrs. Stanton receives the same scant notice. Susan is mentioned in Garrison's biography once as a passing guest in the Garrison home and once again in the explanation of Garrison's eventual break with her and Mrs. Stanton, after the emancipation for which these women had worked so heroically had been accomplished. Apparently the eventual break obscured Susan's former record and deprived her of her proper place in the history of the Abolitionist movement.

The only recognition which Susan and Mrs. Stanton received for their anti-slavery work came from the pen of Mrs. Stanton's husband, Henry B. Stanton, who said in his *Random Recollections* (unfortunately not widely read):

Emancipation in this country and Great Britain owes much to women . . . [names the earliest pioneers] The celebrity in this country and Europe of two women in another department [suffrage] has thrown somewhat into the shade the distinguished service they rendered to the slave in the four stormy years preceding the war and in the four years while the sanguinary conflict was waged in the field. I refer to Elizabeth Cady Stanton and Susan B. Anthony.

As a contemporary comment on the national scene, Mr. Stanton's tribute merits close attention. He was not himself involved with the Abolitionists at the time, but no one knew better than he how much they owed to the efforts of his wife and Susan. He paid them their only historical and just recognition on record.

◄§ II   During the year prior to the war a slight rift had occurred between the woman's rights leaders and their Abolitionist allies. No one paid much attention to it at the time, and the outbreak of the war brought them all solidly together again in the one camp.

The year 1860 started off triumphantly for woman's rights with the adoption of the property and guardianship law by the New York Legislature. This was immediately followed by a public statement by Henry Ward Beecher in favor of woman suffrage. Beecher was the great man of the day, and the women counted his accession to their cause as an important public victory. Out of their limited treasury they paid Beecher a hundred dollars for his speech and spent fifty dollars more on reprints for free distribution. Though groaning at the cost, they considered that the money was well spent. Susan and Mrs. Stanton approached the May anniversary of Seneca Falls in New York in a jubilant—perhaps overjubilant—frame of mind.

In her opening address Susan recounted the recent gains of woman's rights in a highly optimistic statement. Among other gains, she mentioned "Mass-meetings to sympathize with the 'strikers' of Massachusetts [which] are being called in this metropolis by women." Susan's slip was passed over partly because the labor movement was so newly born that the audience did not recognize its existence and partly because Mrs. Stanton's error which followed was so much more egregious.

Mrs. Stanton was scheduled to repeat the speech she had made before the Albany Legislature. Susan's enthusiasm for the document required that it be further broadcast to the world. But Mrs. Stanton, seldom content to let well enough alone, felt that she must needs add something to her claims. This she did in the form of a set of resolutions in favor of more liberal divorce laws. She backed them up by an address displaying more than her usual emotion and eloquence. She was riding her old hobby, which in 1853 had broken up and dissipated for all time Susan's carefully built and well-organized State Temperance Society. She would again have pulled down the walls—had the walls been less strong. She had not confided her plan for this speech to Susan beforehand, but she had discussed it with Lucy Stone, who had replied in a letter, "That is a great, grand question, may God touch your lips." Mrs. Stanton presented her theme with eloquence, but Lucy Stone was not present to hear her. As usual, it fell to Susan to handle the difficult consequences.

After waiting a moment to allow the emotions which Mrs. Stanton had aroused to subside, Wendell Phillips got to his feet. He sincerely regretted that the subject had been brought up; pointed out that divorce concerned men and women alike and did not belong to the woman's rights question; proposed that no vote on the resolutions should be taken; and finally that the resolutions themselves be expunged from the record.

Wendell Phillips's influence over this group was profound and unquestioned. Susan herself had never questioned his decisions. Horrified to find herself placed between Phillips and Mrs. Stanton, she hesitated not for a moment. Susan was still Mrs. Stanton's ally. Her instincts and her principles were all on the side of free speech. The idea that Mrs. Stanton's resolutions should be expunged from the record was to her intolerable. Gaining the floor, the Susan who had once trembled at addressing a teachers' meeting dared to oppose the great Phillips.

"I hope [she said] Mr. Phillips will withdraw his motion that these resolutions shall not appear in the records of the Convention.

I am very sure that it would be contrary to all parliamentary usage. . . . And as to the point that this question does not belong to this platform,—from that I totally dissent. Marriage has ever been a one-sided matter, resting most unequally upon the sexes. By it, man gains all—woman loses all; tyrant law and lust reign supreme with him—meek submission and ready obedience alone befit her. Woman has never been consulted; her wish has never been taken into consideration as regards the terms of the marriage contract. . . . She must accept marriage as man proffers it, or not at all.

"And then again, on Mr. Phillips's own ground, the discussion is perfectly in order, since nearly all the wrongs of which we complain grow out of the inequality, the injustice of the marriage laws, that rob the wife of the right to herself and her children—that make her the slave of the man she marries.

"I hope, therefore, the resolutions will be allowed to go out to the public, that there may be a fair report of the ideas which have actually been presented here, and that they may not be left to the mercy of the secular press. I trust the Convention will not vote to forbid the publication of the resolutions with the proceedings."

Susan was fortunate in having Garrison, who was present, second her point of view. He likewise saw the danger to free speech inherent in Phillips's motion and saw no reason why divorce should not be discussed at a woman's rights meeting. He did not favor the resolutions but he favored a full and complete report of them. And thus it was decided. The convention voted with Susan and Garrison and against Phillips. Mrs. Stanton's speech, complete with resolutions, was published in the report of the convention.

Susan and Mrs. Stanton, however, were greatly disturbed because they had displeased Phillips. To them he stood for all that was great and noble in public life. To find themselves set apart from him was a heavy trial. They sturdily sought to console each other. "I find my only comfort in the glorious thought of Theodore Parker," wrote Susan. " 'All this is but the noise and dust of the wagon bringing the harvest home.' These things must be, and happy are they who see clearly to the end." To this Mrs. Stanton replied: "We are right. My reason, my experience, my soul proclaim it. Our religion, laws, customs, are all founded on the idea that woman was made for man. . . . The men know we have struck a blow at their greatest stronghold. Come what will, my whole soul rejoices in the truth I have uttered."

Phillips was a good loser. When Susan later applied for money from the Hovey fund to publish the report which he had opposed, he sent it to her promptly, accompanied by a cordial letter.

Somewhat later in the same year Susan again came in conflict with her Abolitionist sponsors, again to her great but unavoidable grief. Characteristically, she was not involved for anything she said but for something she did. She interfered quite boldly, though secretly, in a family affair originating under the Massachusetts marriage laws.

One evening while she was staying with Lydia Mott in Albany, a certain Mrs. Phelps (a stranger to them both) came to the door with her little daughter and asked for refuge. Mrs. Phelps's husband, it developed, had separated from her and removed her children from her custody. Having obtained permission for her daughter to visit her, Mrs. Phelps took the child and fled to Albany. Knowing nothing of Lydia Mott except that she was a Quaker, she came to this lady's door for help. She explained that at home she could get no help because everyone feared to offend her husband, a member of the Massachusetts Senate. Even her brothers, the one a United States senator and the other a Boston attorney, refused to do aught to offend the law. Mrs. Phelps correctly judged that the person least intimidated by the law would be a Quaker, and so she knocked at the little shop door of Lydia Mott.

It was the beginning of a very complicated conspiracy for Susan. She qualified very well as a conspirator, owing to her experience with the underground railway in Rochester. After she and Miss Mott had arrayed the mother and child in dilapidated garments, she boarded the train with them for New York. The trio arrived at ten o'clock. Susan herself was not too well acquainted with the city in 1860. She had heard that women "unaccompanied by a gentleman" would not be admitted to a hotel at that hour and found it to be true. Having tried several hostelries, she said to the next clerk who alleged that he had no room: "You can give us a place to sleep or we will sit in this office all night." The clerk murmured something about the police and Susan replied, "Very well, we will stay here till they come and take us to the station." Baffled by her display of stubbornness, the clerk decided that he had a room after all if they were not too particular.

Susan had to tramp the streets next day to find a permanent

refuge for her charges. She left them at last, footsore and weary, with Abby Hopper Gibbons, the daughter of Isaac Hopper, the Quaker philanthropist. From Mrs. Gibbons's home the exiles passed to that of Mrs. Elizabeth Ellet, the author of the once-popular *Women of the Revolution*. Among various friends Mrs. Phelps and her daughter were supplied with a home and Mrs. Phelps did sewing to help in their support. One of her brothers unbent and sent her money secretly through Lydia Mott.

It was soon known to the Phelps connection who had spirited Mrs. Phelps away, though not where the lady had been concealed. Her husband threatened Susan and Lydia Mott with arrest and suit. Susan was constantly pursued by letters threatening to have her arrested on the lecture platform. It was natural that Garrison and Phillips should be disturbed by this threat to one of their Aboli-tionist speakers. Aside from this, there were probably other points of connection between themselves and the Massachusetts politi-cians involved. Soon both Garrison and Phillips were writing to Susan and Lydia, advising them to retire from the perilous adven-ture.

"Let us urge you, therefore," wrote Phillips, "at once to advise and insist on this woman's returning to her relatives. Garrison con-curs with me fully and earnestly in this opinion, thinking that our movement's repute for good sense should not be compromised by any such mistake." Garrison wrote to Susan directly: "Our identi-fication with the woman's rights movement and the anti-slavery cause is such that we ought not unnecessarily involve them in any hasty and ill-judged, no matter how well-meant, efforts of our own. We at least owe to them this—that if for any act of ours we are dragged before courts we ought to be able to show that we acted discreetly as well as with good intentions."

Garrison and Phillips evidently feared that Mrs. Phelps's relatives would make good their threats to hale Susan and Lydia Mott be-fore a criminal court. Susan's father also thought that a legal action was entirely possible and warned his daughter to be prepared for it. "My child," he wrote, "I think you have done absolutely right, but don't put a word on paper or make a statement to any one that you are not prepared to face in court. Legally you are wrong, but mor-ally you are right, and I will stand by you."

Susan wrote very briefly and positively to Garrison and Phillips:

I can not give you a satisfactory statement on paper, but I feel the strongest assurance that all I have done is wholly right. Had I turned my back on her, I should have scorned myself. . . . That I should stop to ask if my act would injure the reputation of any movement never crossed my mind, nor will I now allow such a fear to stifle my sympathies or tempt me to expose her to the cruel, inhuman treatment of her own household. Trust me that as I ignore all law to help the slave, so will I ignore it all to protect an enslaved woman.

The end of the story can be easily foreseen. The only surprising thing is that it dragged on so long. The well-protected Mrs. Phelps lived quietly with her daughter in New York, in comparative peace and security, for a whole year. A little skillful detective work might have revealed her whereabouts much sooner, but the offended relatives wasted time in hounding Susan and Lydia Mott, unable to believe that they would not soon break down and restore the missing persons to their legal guardians. As last, foreseeing no such chance, they fell back upon the time-honored method, traced the woman and child to their dwelling, and seized the daughter as she was on her way alone to Sunday school.

Susan was greatly cast down by the disapproval of Phillips and Garrison during the episode. She wrote in her diary: "Only to think that in this great trial I should be hounded by the two men whom I adore and reverence above all others!" But her injured feelings did not forewarn that there would be other aspects of woman's rights in which she and her Abolitionist friends would not always see eye to eye.

✑§ III   The disaster that overwhelmed the country, the fall of Fort Sumter on April 12, 1861, put an end to all differences between male and female Abolitionists. It put an end to some of the differences between the Abolitionists and the government, though by no means to all. Phillips came out for the war but not for Lincoln; Mrs. Stanton, likewise, for the war but not for Lincoln. Garrison, the non-resistant, at first adopted a policy of watchful waiting. But all were to be affected by the rising war hysteria, by the awful amalgam of fear and hatred generated by the presence of danger.

Trained in a deep abhorrence of war, Susan at first floundered in the great confusion. Look where she would, she could see no consistency. "All our reformers seem suddenly to have grown politic," she wrote to Lydia Mott. "All alike say, 'Have no conventions at this crisis!' Garrison, Phillips, Mrs. Mott, Mrs. Wright, Mrs. Stanton, etc., say, 'Wait till the war excitement abates.'" As it is with every war, so it was with this great and long-awaited conflict: the people could not believe that it would last very long. Susan's father, a lifelong conscientious objector, having accepted the enlistment of his sons in the Kansas guerrillas, now accepted their enlistment in the Lincoln forces. The Rochester Friends quietly but steadfastly refused to discipline any young man who enlisted in the Union Army. Dismayed and confused in her innermost soul, Susan was slow to find her place in the swiftly unfolding history around her.

In May 1861 she sat at home, idle and spiritless, while the women of the North were rushing into the fray with amazing zeal and capacity. Dorothea Dix and Clara Barton lost no time in inaugurating the nursing services with which their names were afterward associated. Dr. Elizabeth Blackwell was organizing the Women's Sanitary Commission. Josephine Griffing was on her way toward creating the Freedman's Bureau, on which she was to spend the energies of her remaining life. Anna E. Dickinson was taking her first steps in a meteoric career as orator for the war party. Lucy Stone, like thousands of women, was scraping lint and making shirts for the Union soldiers. Even timid Louisa May Alcott was fired by the general fervor to enlist as a nurse in a Washington hospital. Anna Howard Shaw, aged fourteen, was driving the plow in the place of her father and brothers, who had walked out of the fields at the first call for recruits. Myriads of women in the Northwest were following Anna Shaw's example. Mary Livermore, passing through Illinois, reported seeing "Women in the fields everywhere, driving the reapers, binding and shocking, and loading the grain. . . ."

Mary Livermore was one of the most active of the war heroines of the age. She nursed in hospitals from Cairo to New Orleans and knew the Mississippi River as Mark Twain knew it, from St. Louis to the delta. Mrs. Livermore met Lincoln scores of times and conferred with Grant over and over. A leader of the Sanitary Commission, she organized a soldiers' fair in Chicago which raised a hundred thousand dollars. A still greater heroine, whose name, though less known, should outshine them all, was Anna Ella Carroll. Miss Carroll devised the military plan which General Grant followed in his Tennessee River campaign—the strategy which enabled the North for the first time to gain the upper hand and ultimately to win the victory. Only Lincoln and his cabinet knew that Anna Carroll was the author of Grant's winning strategy, but they kept the secret so as to spare the self-love of a great general. They kept it so well that history is still uninformed on the subject.

It is doubtful whether these women would have stepped out so promptly or would have been so competent if the school of woman's rights had not already prepared them. The workers were ready. Yet the two leaders who had been the heart and soul of the woman movement had not yet found their places in the vast war organization. Committed as they were to total emancipation, they could not rush into a war which, at the beginning, asked for so much less. Again Susan and Mrs. Stanton found themselves in close agreement with Garrison, a very gratifying reunion for all of them.

Susan's first solution coincided with the general trend for women. She returned to farming. Daniel's roaming instinct, long quiescent, was aroused to action by the public crisis. Life insurance was badly hit by the war. Both Daniel and McLean felt the shock of hard times. A letter of Aaron's to the company in 1861 is preserved in its records: "If we are to make reports promptly on the first of each month, it will cause a mighty crushing of bones in our business. We think it not too large an estimate to say that our remittances would be reduced to one-half." These conditions were a terrible set-back for Daniel, who believed that he had found in life insurance a commercial haven for the rest of his days. Given Daniel's temperament, it is not inconceivable that he considered following his two sons to the Kansas frontier and starting a new life once again in his old age. But at first he merely proposed to gratify a long-delayed wish to visit his sons and said he considered the moment propitious. Within a month after war was declared he was on his way to Kansas.

Susan had a real summer at farming. Though her work was not as primitive as Anna Shaw's in Michigan, it was of the same nature. She planted the crops, cultivated them, harvested them, and sold them. For homework she wove twenty yards of rag carpet, pieced a silk bedspread, and quilted coverlets and petticoats. With all this, she found time to read more than usual. She read *Adam Bede* and *Casa Guidi Windows*—"a grand poem and so fitting to our terrible struggle." But when, after a session of reading, she was unexpectedly called to address a public meeting and did not, as she thought, do her best, she felt extremely guilty about the reading. Her mission in life was to make reform speeches and not to gather personal culture. She could go straight from farm work to a good rousing Abolitionist talk. She could read Buckle's *History* and Darwin's *Origin of Species*, and did read them, without endangering her mission, but a good novel threw her out of her stride. Untrained in her Quaker youth to read works of imagination, she remained all her life naïve and overimpressionable where such works were concerned. To her, *Adam Bede* was such an experience.

Daniel returned home in September 1861. The farm had been well managed. The life insurance business of his particular company had picked up. This was due to the fact that the New York Life continued to take risks on new policies, regardless of the war, when some other companies refused. In the second year of the war his company did more business than in any other year since its organization. Daniel found his farm and business both in good condition.

With affairs thus in good order, Susan ventured on a round of meetings on her own, using for her theme "Emancipation—The Duty of the Government." "I can not feel easy in my conscience to be dumb in an hour like this," she wrote to Lydia Mott. "I am speaking now extempore and more to my satisfaction than ever before. . . . I am entirely off the old anti-slavery grounds and on the new ones thrown up by the war." She continued the line she had taken before the war. The war excitement had not abated, as so many people had expected, and Lincoln still continued to profess the policies which the Abolistionists loathed. Susan visited Mrs. Stanton and together they attended anti-slavery conventions in Albany and New York. Susan could get no one to support her in her desire for a woman's rights convention and so she went over wholly to her anti-slavery work.

In 1862 Henry B. Stanton received an appointment as Surveyor of the Port of New York. Mr. Stanton had long been an applicant for the post and had been a staunch supporter for Lincoln as President. But Mrs. Stanton's public activities helped in no wise to promote her husband's political advancement. One of Lincoln's "spies" in New York reported thus adversely on Mrs. Stanton: "Elizabeth Cady Stanton [is] President of the American Woman's Rights Convention and author of violent Abolition tracts. She badly damaged her own cause (Woman's Rights) last spring by a speech in this city so very loose on the marriage relation as to call down severe reproof from Wendell Phillips and various female members of the Convention. . . . Those who know the Stanton know her un-'reliability.' " The useful informer further advised that Mrs. Stanton had a niece who was married to a well-known Southern sympathizer who "had $100,000 invested in a manufactory of arms rifles . . . in Massachusetts." Nevertheless, Mr. Stanton received the desired appointment, and his family prepared happily for their removal to New York.

Susan flew at once to Seneca Falls to help her friend. Her duty was to keep the four Stanton boys out of the way while the moving went on. She was no tyro at this, having often done as much while Mrs. Stanton wrote a woman's rights speech. She took the boys on ahead to New York and looked out for them until the rest of the family arrived at the new residence. They settled at first in Brooklyn but soon exchanged this for a house at 75 West Forty-fifth Street.

Leaving the Stantons to bask in their good fortune, Susan set forth anew on her Abolitionist rounds. Her hopes were rising, though Lincoln as yet had given no sign of yielding, and she spoke with a new animation. On this tour she also had the pleasure of taking with her her niece from Rochester, Ann Eliza McLean. Together they visited the old homestead in Adams.

Susan's grandfather, Humphrey Anthony, aged ninety-two, spent more time in his kitchen chair now and less in his fields. His granddaughter, the "smart" public speaker, was his only link with his oldest son, whom he had lost on that day when he sent him to Nine Partners'. He vaguely remembered that some war had had something to do with that. The handsome young girl at Susan's side was said to be his great-granddaughter, the child of Guelma, who had also gone out of his life, by way of this very same kitchen door, on a sorrowful spring day thirty-six years ago. The two women came to him from a remote outside world which was said to be again convulsed in a sinful war but from which he was now, as he had always been, mercifully removed. He could see the sun rise over the East Mountain and watch it set beyond Greylock, and in between lay the only world he had ever known. This was Susan's last visit to her grandfather.

⋙§ IV   On September 23, 1862, following the Union victory at Antietam, Lincoln issued the Emancipation Proclamation, which was to become effective January 1, 1863. The historic document, world-shaking though it was, was far from satisfactory to the Abolitionists. It may have been written with Lincoln's blood, but the Garrisonians were demanding blood, flesh, and bones. Garrison had begun by saying: "I will not equivocate, I will not excuse, I will not retreat a single inch," and on this note he continued to harass Lincoln to the end.

Susan was again lecturing for the Abolitionists, upholding the standards of Garrison, and incidentally spending much of her time at home. On a Sunday morning in November 1862, while she and her father were reading the *Liberator* and gravely discussing the deficiencies of the Proclamation, her father complained of feeling ill. It was an unheard-of thing in the family for Daniel to be ill. He was put to bed with some concern and from then onward developed a painful and mortal illness.

His life insurance record describes his death as due to a disease of the heart; but as nearly all the deaths on the antiquated page are attributed to the same cause, the diagnosis cannot be taken too literally. An accurate diagnosis was hard to obtain in those days, and most people die when the heart fails. The intense suffering of his illness was ascribed by his doctor to neuralgia of the stomach, because the agonizing pains which racked him for two weeks before the end were centered in that region. Susan stayed with him all during this time, striving helplessly with her mother and her sister to give the tortured invalid some measure of relief. His death took place November 25, 1862.

The funeral services must have been held at Daniel's own farm. The Unitarian church which he had formerly attended had been burned to the ground shortly after the services for John Brown. There was no Unitarian pastor in the city. The Quakers had no church home; they were meeting, by an old custom of theirs, in each other's houses. In any case, Daniel was not entitled to a Quaker burial, nor to have his end recorded in the Friends' book of births and deaths. It was not so done. The Reverend Samuel J. May came over from Syracuse to conduct the funeral services and Frederick Douglass, Daniel's long-time friend, delivered a eulogy. The Rochester newspapers reported the funeral but did not report the addresses of May and Douglass, though both were famous characters. There was a war on.

The next annual report of the New York Life Insurance Company noted Daniel Anthony's death, along with that of several other agents who died the preceding year. Of Daniel, the report stated briefly that "he had long been in the service of the Company." Concerning another agent, who had built up a business of a hundred thousand dollars a year in Virginia (owing partly to the practice of allowing planters to take out life insurance on their slaves), the company obituary grew more expansive, describing the deceased as "a highly educated man who had enriched his mind by extensive reading and foreign travel." Daniel's business had certainly been on no such scale as this, but it had been reasonably valuable to the company and very valuable to his dependents. Still active in business, still managing his farm, he continued to the last to be the mainstay of his family. Though he was sixty-eight, his conduct was that of a man in his prime. His life insurance policy amounted to one thousand dollars.

How much of his earnings had gone into the apprenticeship of Susan as a social reformer one does not know and it does not matter. For Daniel this represented a satisfying moral investment and one of the chief compensations of his own monotonous business life. Susan was now to be deprived for all time of his benign helping hand, not merely in her financial straits but in the whole field of her endeavor for a better life for human beings. Fortunately for her, his guidance had endured until her feet were well planted on the ground of the future and her vision of her place in life was definitely outlined.

CHAPTER TWELVE

WAR WORK IN NEW YORK

∞§ I   Susan's war work in New York, which consumed two years of her life, took the place of woman's rights for the duration. None of her friends, including Mrs. Stanton, thought it wise even to mention woman's rights. So Susan remained the same fighting Abolitionist throughout the Civil War that she had been before its outbreak.

After her father's death she spent only a brief period of mourning. She felt that she would be closer to him by returning to her usual labors. There seems to have been no urging on the part of the family that she take over the farming, though she was well qualified and this was the outstanding need of the moment. Her talents and fame were so well recognized by her family that they accepted public work as her real career. Her mother and Mary took over the farm and Susan was left free to roam.

After the Stantons were settled in New York their thoughts turned toward Susan, especially after her bereavement. In January 1863, the month in which the Emancipation Proclamation went into effect, they moved from Brooklyn to the larger house in New York. Wendell Phillips, who happened to be in New York, expressed his disappointment in the Proclamation to Theodore Tilton, Mrs. Stanton's new friend, and referred incidentally in the highest terms to Susan Anthony. Tilton conveyed this good opinion to Mrs. Stanton, who passed it on to Susan. In the same letter she urged Susan to come to the city and offered her a room in her house.

At about the same time Henry B. Stanton, who happened to be in Washington, wrote to her as follows:

Washington, January 16 [*1863*]

My dear Friend:

I date from the federal capital. Since I arrived here I have been more gloomy than ever. The country is rapidly going to destruction. The army is almost in a state of mutiny for want of its pay and for lack of a leader. Nothing can carry the North through but the Southern negroes, and nobody can marshall them into the struggle except the Abolitionists. The country was never so badly off as at this moment. . . . You have no idea how dark the cloud is which hangs over us. . . . We must not lay the flattering unction to our souls that the Proclamation will be of any use if we are beaten and have a dissolution of the Union. Here then is work for you, Susan, put on your armor and go forth!

All this urging had the effect of detaching Susan quickly from the farm. She arrived in New York, as usual, ready for action. From long practice she and Mrs. Stanton wasted no time in drawing up the blueprint for a women's organization. It was more than a blueprint, for the flow of thought and the opulent style of Mrs. E. C. Stanton were never hampered by useless brevity.

Their first step, an "Appeal," published in the *Tribune*, was promptly followed by a "Call" for a national women's convention, signed by Mrs. Stanton and Susan and distributed by mail far and wide. One can picture, in passing, the effect of these lucubrations when they arrived on the desk of Mr. Lincoln. The President had once said, "If the Abolitionists want me to lead, let them get out of the way and let me lead." But here were two Abolitionist characters out in front again, and naturally bent on forcing his hand.

Mrs. Stanton's "Appeal," addressed to women, showed the cloven hoof at once. She invited her sex not only to participate in the charity work of the war but to take a hand in its policies. She wrote:

When our leading journals, orators, and brave men from the battle-field, complain that Northern women feel no enthusiasm for the war, the time has come for us to pledge ourselves loyal to freedom and our country. Thus far, there has been no united expression from the women of the North as to the policy of the War. Here and there one has spoken or written nobly. Many have vied with each other in acts of generosity and self-sacrifice for the sick and wounded in camp and hospital. But we have, as yet, no means of judging where the majority of Northern women stand.

If it be true that at this hour the women of the South are more devoted to their cause than we are to ours, the fact lies here. They see and feel the horrors of the war; the foe is at their fire-sides; while we, in peace and plenty, live as heretofore. There is an inspiration, too, in a definite purpose, be it good or bad. The women of the South know what their sons are fighting for. The women of the North do not. They appreciate the blessings of slavery; we, not the blessings of liberty. We have never yet realized the glory of those institutions in whose defense it is the privilege of our sons to bleed and die. . . .

Let every woman understand that this war involves the same principles that have convulsed the nations of the earth from Pharaoh to Lincoln . . . and choose this day, whether our republican institutions shall be placed on an enduring basis, and an eternal peace secured to our children, or whether we shall leap back through generations of light and experience, and meekly bow again to chains and slavery. . . .

To counsel grim-visaged war seems hard to come from women's lips; but better far that the bones of our sires and sons whiten every Southern plain, that we do their rough work at home, than that liberty, struck dumb in the Capital of our Republic, should plead no more for man. Every woman who appreciates the grand problem of national life must say war, pestilence, famine, anything but an ignoble peace. . . .

Shall a priceless heritage like [ours] be wrested now from us by Southern tyrants, and Northern women look on unmoved, or basely bid our freemen sue for peace? No! No! The vacant places at our fire-sides, the void in every heart says No!! Such sacrifices must not be in vain!! The cloud that hangs o'er all our Northern homes is gilded with the hope that through these present sufferings the nation shall be redeemed.

The foregoing was certainly patriotic enough. In the "Call" that followed, however, certain qualifying phrases cropped up which suggested the Abolitionist hand beneath. It ran, in part:

At this hour, the best word and work of every man and woman are imperatively demanded. To man, by common consent, is assigned the forum, camp, and field. What is woman's legitimate work, and how she may best accomplish it, is worthy our earnest

counsel one with another. We have heard many complaints of the
lack of enthusiasm among Northern women; but when a mother
lays her son on the altar of her country, she asks an object equal to
the sacrifice. In nursing the sick and wounded, knitting socks,
scraping lint, and making jellies, the bravest and best may weary if
the thoughts mount not in faith to something beyond and above it
all. . . .

A grand idea, such as freedom or justice, is needful to kindle and
sustain the fires of a high enthusiasm.

The Women's National Loyal League, by these words called into
being, held its first session in the Church of the Puritans on May
14, 1863. It was the date of the annual meeting for woman's rights
—a meeting that had not taken place for three years. Susan presided
and made the main speech of the day, a strong plea for universal
emancipation. She urged the women to "forget conventionalisms;
forget what the world will say, whether you are in your place or out
of it," and, looking only to their own consciences for approval, to
get out and work for justice and the right. Besides Mrs. Stanton,
she had her old comrades, Lucy Stone, Antoinette Blackwell, and
Ernestine Rose on the platform with her. In spite of everything, she
had managed to have a woman's rights meeting. Mrs. Stanton was
elected president and Susan secretary of the new Loyal League.

All of the suggested resolutions were adopted, including one that
asked equal rights for women as well as Negroes. Some of the
women objected to this resolution as out of place in the present
national crisis. Susan had to exert herself to get it carried, but succeeded. It was, however, left in abeyance in the subsequent program of the league. She had to content herself with the fact that
it was in the record. Another resolution, in which Susan concurred,
expressed approval of the draft. The main resolution was adopted
only after the final clause had been added. It ran:

We, loyal women of the nation, assembled in convention this
14th of May, 1863, hereby pledge ourselves one to another in a
Loyal League, to give support to the government in so far as it
makes a war for freedom.

The Abolitionist-tinged convention at once formulated a petition, addressed to Congress, asking for the unconditional emancipation of all the slaves in the Union. The rest of its program consisted

of collecting a mere item of one million signatures for the petition,
which in their enthusiasm they had promised. From long experience the women, especially Susan, knew what this entailed.

With Mrs. Stanton to supply the propaganda—consistently hard-
pedaling the "Loyal" note—and Susan to handle the petition work,
the league sprang at once into prominence. Senator Sumner from
Massachusetts, who stood for emancipation by congressional action,
became its most logical and effective collaborator. Sumner often
wrote: "Send on the petitions; they give me an opportunity for a
speech." . . . "I am grateful to your Association for what you have
done to arouse the country to insist on the extinction of slavery."
Susan redoubled her efforts to roll up signatures, to devise ways and
means of sending the petition out through the country, to enlist
volunteers for the work, and to collect the results in her office as
speedily as possible.

On February 9, 1864, she had the first installment of 100,000
signatures ready for Congress. Sumner presented the mountainous
pile with one of his historical speeches. The league continued until
August 1864, when the number of signatures had reached almost
400,000. By this time public opinion had crystallized, partly
through military events, partly through political developments, and
partly perhaps through the tireless propaganda effort put forth by
the Women's National Loyal League. The Thirteenth Amendment
was well on its way.

❧§ II   By this long and arduous duty Susan accumulated office
experience. She lived as an office worker in New York for two years.
She knew at first hand the problems of the working girl who had
to survive on twelve dollars a week. By boarding with Mrs. Stanton
at a reduced price and by lunching on less than fifteen cents a day,
she managed. "I go to a restaurant near by for lunch every noon,"
she wrote. "I always take strawberries and two tea rusks. Today I
said, 'All this lacks is a glass of milk from my mother's cellar,' and
the girl replied, 'We have very nice Westchester County milk.' So
tomorrow I shall add that to my bill of fare. My lunch costs, berries,
five cents, rusks five, and tomorrow the milk will be three." Still,
though mostly confined to office work, Susan had to get about, to
go places. There was no allowance for transportation in her budget.

Her sturdy history as a walker was considerably increased by her mileage on foot in New York.

The twelve dollars a week that she received as salary came through Phillips from the Hovey fund. This merely ensured her existence. The expenses of the Loyal League—rent, clerk hire, postage, printing—had to be met somehow, and Susan had to raise the necessary money. By planning a course of lectures at Cooper Institute she realized a small fund. Henry Ward Beecher donated one Sunday's collection in his church—a magnificent $200. The pennywise Susan then hit upon her most paying expedient. She charged everyone who signed the petition one cent for the privilege. Believe it or not, she realized $3,000 from this incredibly tedious device. As the total expenses of the league came to $5,000, it may be seen that her picayune financing saved the day. She closed her office in August 1864, with an outstanding indebtedness of $4.72, which she personally paid. The league had supported itself all the way. The work the women had accomplished, under the lash of Susan's drive and urgency, was something that could not be measured in terms of cold cash.

Susan started the league in a corner of the New York anti-slavery headquarters. She soon moved to a small office of her own in Cooper Union. Bare of furniture but for a couple of borrowed chairs, her office did not at first even boast of a desk. Robert Dale Owen, whom Lincoln had sent to take charge of the New York Freedman's Bureau, came to the rescue by presenting her with a small but businesslike desk. Susan treasured this desk. On closing the Cooper Institute office, she sent it to her brother in Kansas. In time the relic made its way back to the Susan B. Anthony Memorial house in Rochester, where it may still be seen among the other relics of the reformer's career.

✎§ III   The draft act was passed on the day of Susan's arrival in New York, March 3, 1863. On the following July 11 the drawing began. That night the riots broke out, lasting until July 17. It was estimated that twelve hundred people were killed. The Negroes were hanged on trees and left hanging there. Official buildings were burned. One military officer was killed and his body dragged through the streets. Brooks clothing store was looted. Everywhere, in the worst disorders, women took a prominent part.

Susan and Mrs. Stanton had seen mobs before, had dealt at first hand with them, but they had never encountered any like this one. Mrs. Stanton's oldest son was seized by a gang in front of her house and carried off by them before her eyes. He saved himself by offering to treat as he was dragged past a saloon, and the lynching party resolved itself into a drinking bout. His fate was not known to his mother until many hours later.

The fury of the mob was directed against the Negroes as the prime cause of the trouble, against the three-hundred-dollar men (the draft provided that a man could purchase a substitute for this sum) and the Abolitionists. But in the sequel, it was due to the cowardice of the mob that only the Negroes, as the most defenseless, were seized and subjected to the final penalty.

Susan and Mrs. Stanton naturally considered themselves in the direct line of attack. Mrs. Stanton departed with her brood as quickly as possible for upstate New York, whence she wrote to Mrs. Gerrit Smith:

Johnstown, July 20, 1863

Dear Cousin Nancy:—Last Thursday I escaped from the horrors of the most brutal mob I ever witnessed, and brought my children here for safety. The riot raged in our neighborhood for the first two days of the trouble largely because the colored orphan asylum on Fifth Avenue was only two blocks away from us. I saw all those little children marched off two by two. A double portion of martyrdom has been meted out to our poor blacks, and I am led to ask if there is no justice in heaven or on earth that this should be permitted through the centuries. But it was not only the negroes who feared for their lives. Greeley was at Dr. [Edward] Bayard's a day and a night for safety, and we all stayed there also a night, thinking that, as Henry, Susan, and I were so identified with reforms and reformers, we might at any moment be subjects of vengeance.

I was alone with the children, expecting every moment to hear the wretches thundering at the front door. What did I do? I sent the servants and the children to the fourth story, opened the skylight and told them, in case of attack, to run out on the roof into some neighboring house. I then prepared a speech, determined, if necessary, to go down at once, open the door and make an appeal to them as Americans and citizens of a republic. But a squad of police and two companies of soldiers soon came up and a bloody fray took place near us which quieted the neighborhood.

Susan described her experience in the following letter to her mother and sister written on July 15, the fifth day of the riot:

These are terrible times. The Colored Orphan Asylum which was burned was but one block from Mrs. Stanton's and all of us left the house on Monday night. Yesterday when I started for Cooper Institute I found the cars and stages had been stopped by the mob and I could not get to the office. I took the ferry and went to Flushing to stay with my cousin, but found it in force there. We all arose and dressed in the middle of the night; but it was finally gotten under control.

On the date of this letter, signs of abatement had appeared, but the riot lasted out another two days. Stoic and Quaker as usual, Susan was back in her office as soon as revived transportation could get her there. The riot was but another demonstration of the need for the Abolitionists to work.

◄§ IV Susan had never before been so completely separated from her family. This was partly because her father (who had written her so faithfully) was no longer there, and also because of the barrier raised by the war. As with so many others, the Civil War had broken her home ties. She might as well have been at the front, as in a sense she was. The family accepted her absence as complete and proceeded on various readjustments to life from which she was left out.

The year after her father's death Hannah Mosher's family moved to Rochester. Eugene Mosher sold his home and business in Easton, New York, to gratify his wife's wish to be near her family. The clannishness of the Anthonys was something hard to resist. The move did not prove as successful as he had hoped. Mosher became a traveling salesman, work which he did not like after the comparative independence of his own small business but which he clung to for his family's sake. Thus Guelma and Hannah were reunited while Susan remained in New York.

A second epoch-making event was the marriage of Susan's oldest brother in January 1864. Daniel R. had reached the age of forty before embracing matrimony. A certain young lady of Battenville boasted many years later that she might have been Susan B. Anthony's sister-in-law if she could have endured the "Anthony nose." If Daniel R. really so lost his head in early youth, he recovered manfully and held on afterward to his bacherlorhood. He had not only the family nose but the ambition and determination that went with it. He left schoolteaching in Rochester to stake out a claim in Kansas and, having once "gone West," remained to achieve a prosperous career in Leavenworth. Now, approaching forty, he was the owner of the Leavenworth *Times*, the Leavenworth postmaster, and also the recently elected mayor of the town. Not till then did he take time off to get married. He married for love. Miss Anna Osborne of Edgartown, Martha's Vineyard, was a beautiful, charming, and cultured young lady, but withal ready to go West with her Lochinvar. She was also not without financial prospects.

Susan's mother, widowed and reduced in fortune as she was, could not dispense with an infare for the bride of her oldest son. The farm, though gay and pretty with fruit trees and garden pinks in the summer, was brown and snow-flecked in January. The house needed all hands to make it cheerful. Susan rushed home at her mother's behest and joined her three sisters in providing the infare, which, in the days when refreshments to the last crumb came out of the family kitchen, was very much of a task. She saw her beatfied brother, his charming young bride, her sisters, her mother, and the same friends she had seen last at her father's funeral. The few days at home passed like a dream, and reality seemed to return only when, seated once more in her Cooper Institute office, she drove her pen steadily to make up for lost time.

Her visit was further saddened by the thought that it might be her last look at the farm. Her mother and sister Mary had already written her of their resolve to sell the place. Her mother was seventy-one and Mary was teaching in Rochester. Mary's long, lonely drives to and from the city were extremely wearing, especially in the winter storms. It was clearly unwise for the two women to keep up the farm. "I know I ought to get rid of this care, and Mary and I should not try to live here alone," wrote Lucy Anthony to Susan. Her mother had decided the matter without consulting her, and Susan accepted the omission as just and right. She wrote: "Your letter sent a pang to my very heart's core that the dear old home, so full of the memory of our father, must be given up. I wish it could be best to keep it . . ." But she offered no protest.

At some time in 1863, in the first year of the Loyal League, Susan was surprised by a serious offer of marriage. It came in a letter from Ohio, indited by a prominent politician of the state. The writer, a widower, who had known her in her girlhood (he must have been one of her many Battenville beaux), earnestly proposed that Susan should become his second wife. That he had preserved her memory through so many intervening years was, to say the least, a flattering tribute. Since her diary for this year is lacking, we have no way of knowing her reaction to the episode. There are objective reasons for assuming that by the time of the Civil War Susan had philosophically adjusted herself to a single life. The last time she had shown signs of wrestling with her soul on the subject of marriage was in 1859. Busy as she was with national affairs in 1863, she must have found it comparatively easy to decline this proposal.

◆§ V   In August 1864, Susan's Abolitionist work approached a standstill. She prepared to close the Cooper Institute office and return to Rochester. The work of the Women's Loyal League had been successfully completed. Her political outlook had grown perceptibly in the course of the work. She had become more national-minded in her way of thinking. Mrs. Stanton had been ahead of her in historical perspective, having started from a Revolutionary ancestry and with a broader education and tradition. She had become a "little nation" follower of Garrison under protest. Quaker-bred and Quaker-educated, Susan had been more accustomed to think of people in smaller units—an attitude required by the Quaker system of discipline. The war had broadened her vision. Working even indirectly for the Union had widened her concept of the state. Living with the Stantons, where the war was discussed on a high level of political understanding, had enlarged her political horizon. She came out of it with a new sense of the nation, a higher estimate of the Federal Union, and a lower estimate of states' rights.

All this she had learned under Lincoln, without being aware of his guidance. She still resisted him. Both she and Mrs. Stanton came out for Frémont for President because they did not trust Lincoln. They were backed up by Wendell Phillips and most of the die-hard Abolitionists, who regarded Lincoln's re-election as a set-back for full emancipation. Many years afterward Mrs. Stanton looked back on this period with sincere regret. As a very old lady she wrote in her diary: "I see now the wisdom of his course, leading public opinion slowly but surely to the final blow for freedom. . . . My conscience pricks me now when I recall how I worked and prayed in 1864 for the defeat of Lincoln's re-election." But if Susan ever revised her attitude in her late years, she did not place it on record.

She left New York in August and took a leisurely journey home. At Auburn she stopped for a wedding. The son of William Lloyd Garrison married the daughter of Martha Coffin Wright; it was the happy joining of two celebrated Abolitionist families. From this joyous celebration, she proceeded onward to Rochester, unaware, it seems, that the threat of death was hanging over one of her own family. Ann Eliza McLean, the beloved niece whom she had taken with her on her last pilgrimage to the old Berkshire homestead, had been suddenly taken ill. She died soon after Susan's arrival. She was twenty-three. This was the first of the deaths among the young of her family that Susan had to face. She had left her home in one phase of mourning; she returned to it in another.

Her mother was still on the farm. Like most such dreaded projects, its execution had been postponed. But now a purchaser had been found and Lucy and Mary Anthony were packing up to leave the farm for good in December. It was decided that they would board with Aaron and Guelma, the cruelly desolated parents, until they could find a home of their own. No one in the Rochester family circle seems to have thought of what was to become of Susan.

Susan was a free woman. She could do what she liked with her life. Of what did her life consist? She had no job; she had no home; and she had no savings. She would soon be forty-five. The career of being a spinster is sometimes quite as heroic as tradition makes it out to be. She helped in the sad business of packing up and sorting the family belongings, watched the garden pinks fade under the first touch of frost, and swept the first fallen leaves away from the house. Like so many thousands of other women and men who had given their lives to the war, she was at loose ends, not knowing which way to turn.

⊷§ VI   In New York things not strictly in the line of war work
had happened to Susan. The general war fever, acting almost inevitably upon the instincts and emotions of every individual's life,
had made no exception in her case. It was under these circumstances that she first met Anna Dickinson, the precocious orator
and one of the most famous women of the Civil War era. Such
is fame—the fame of Anna Dickinson, at any rate, whose name
soared into the empyrean and floated down with deadly accuracy
into oblivion. Susan's attachment to Anna Dickinson became the
most passionate affection of her life.

At first she was only one of the crowd who responded to Anna's
magic eloquence and her dramatic story. A birthright Quaker whose
father, a small businessman in Philadelphia, had early enlisted in
the anti-slavery crusade, the girl had a strong appeal for Susan.
Anna's father had been well known to James and Lucretia Mott,
who spoke well in retrospect of his talents, describing him as one
of the most impassioned orators they had ever known. He suddenly fell dead at the conclusion of an anti-slavery speech in 1846.

The widow, Mary Dickinson, had five children to support and
educate, the youngest of whom, Anna, was four years old. By
taking in sewing and keeping boarders, Mary Dickinson brought
them along until Anna was fifteen. Anna had been sent on a
Friends' scholarship to a local boarding school for five years. Her
achievements at school must have been solid, judging by her display of scholarship in public life; but she achieved no fame during
her school years. Her reputation for precocity began with her first
public address, made at the age of seventeen. She had grown up
under conditions of the direst poverty and for the two years previous to this speech had been teaching school for a pittance. Even
that pittance was a godsend to her family.

The subject of her first speech was "The Rights and Wrongs
of Women." This attracted the attention of Dr. Hannah Longshore, pioneer in woman's rights, who invited Anna to her house
and made a protégée of her. Soon afterward she made another speech
at the Anti-Slavery Society anniversary. James and Lucretia Mott
were present. Lucretia Mott and Hannah Longshore now got to-

gether and planned a public lecture for Anna, engaging a hall and selling eight hundred tickets. The lecture, again on woman's rights, was a complete success. But Lucretia Mott still thought it would be wise for Anna to lecture only occasionally in and around Philadelphia until she matured. Anna did not agree; but while her sponsors lingered, she secured a job in the Philadelphia Mint. She earned twenty-eight dollars a month and, though the youngest in the family, was its chief financial prop.

In May 1861 she spoke again at the anti-slavery convention. With flaming phrases she castigated McClellan for his military failures and described them as "treason." When she got back to the United States Mint, she found that she had lost her job. But William Lloyd Garrison, who heard the speech, liked it and invited her to bring her talents to New England. He did not, however, offer her a salary, and Anna worked for a time in a millinery shop.

Early the next spring she decided to write to Garrison and offer her services as a lecturer on woman's rights and anti-slavery. She was now nineteen. Garrison engaged her for a short tour around Boston and for one important appearance in Music Hall. The Music Hall audiences were ordinarily addressed by speakers like Emerson and Wendell Phillips. Anna's contribution was considered a sensational success. Wendell Phillips, who heard it, was by his own description scarcely less than enraptured. While Anna remained in Boston he became her devoted friend. "I see him almost every day," wrote Anna to her sister.

Anna Dickinson was very beautiful. Her picture in the *History of Woman Suffrage* is by all odds the most pulchritudinous of the whole gallery. For some reason Henry B. Stanton did not acknowledge Anna's personal beauty. He said this picture did her more than justice. The public did not agree with him. Her looks and her youth, combined with her daemonic-like eloquence, made her from the first the idol of the press. Speaking freely from only a handful of scribbled notes, she could hold her audience spellbound for as much as two hours. She gave the impression of being under some magical control, inspired by a spirit outside and beyond herself.

Susan must have seen Anna Dickinson for the first time in New York on the first of May 1862. On that date she was in New York,

having preceded the Stantons to their new home. She was immediately taken captive, fully as enthralled and enraptured as Wendell
Phillips himself. Anna spoke on woman's rights and abolition with
equal fluency and conviction. Susan was seized by a vision of what
Anna Dickinson might become in the future, and the vision possessed her mind for many years to come. Anna Dickinson would
be her own personal fulfillment.

The girl was the right age to be Susan's daughter. Quaker-bred,
as she was, adhering to the same "thee" and "thou," wearing the
same Quaker garb (as Anna still did at the time), she vividly
recalled, by contrast, the awkward, gangling, unformed girl who
had gone to Philadelphia to study under Miss Moulson. How different from that gawky school girl was this fearless, flaming spirit
who had already burst upon the world as a finished orator! Susan's
deepest feelings were stirred as she identified herself with a startling
apparition.

Anna had the habit of responding to older women with spontaneous warmth, as, for instance, she responded to Dr. Longshore
and to Mrs. Isabella Hooker, whom she usually addressed as
"Marmee." Anna had a perfectly good mother of her own, but
apparently one mother was not enough for her exuberant affections. Her attitude, added to Susan's upwelling maternal instincts,
started the intimate friendship which quickly developed between
them.

The following letter from Anna to Susan dates from the beginning of their acquaintance in 1862:

The sunniest of sunny mornings to you, how are you today? Well
and happy, I hope. To tell the truth I want to see you very much
indeed, to hold your hand in mine, to hear your voice, in a word,
I want you—I can't have you? Well, I will at least put down a
little fragment of my foolish self and send it to look up at you.
. . . I work closely and happily at my preparations for next winter
—no, for the future—nine hours a day, generally; but I never felt
better, exercise morning and evening, and never touch book and
paper after gaslight this warm weather; so all those talks of yours
were not thrown away upon me.

What think you of the "signs of the times?" I am sad always,
under all my folly;—this cruel tide of war, sweeping off the fresh,
young, brave life to be dashed out utterly or thrown back shattered

and ruined! I know we all have been implicated in the "great wrong," yet I think the comparatively innocent suffer today more than the guilty. And the result—will the people save the country they love so well, or will the rulers dig the nation's grave?

Will you not write to me, please, soon? I want to see a touch of you very much.

Very affectionately yours,

ANNA E. DICKINSON

✑§ VII   When Susan first went to New York to start the Loyal League, Anna was in New England, engaged in the greatest of her compaign exploits. The state of New Hampshire, lukewarm toward the war, was holding elections. The Republican committee, as a last resort, called Anna Dickinson into the campaign. Her speeches turned the tide and the Republicans swept the state. Connecticut elections followed, with a similar problem at the start, which was, however, completely solved by the entrance of Anna upon the scene. Her genius for campaign speaking, always remaining cool, handling hecklers successfully, always speaking to the issue, astonished the older hands at the business. Her reputation grew by leaps and bounds, and the New England Republicans had the grace and chivalry to pay her a good deal of money.

When Anna reached New York in May, a vast meeting was arranged for her in Cooper Institute. Five thousand people crammed the hall. Henry Ward Beecher introduced her. The young oracle was almost crushed by the enthusiasm of her audience when the meeting broke up. At the close of her speech Henry Ward Beecher said, "Let no man open his lips here tonight. Music is the only fitting accompaniment to the eloquent utterances we have heard." It was said that Anna was paid one thousand dollars for her Cooper Institute speech.

Susan was not in the least put off by Anna's complete immersion in Republican partisan politics. Nor did Anna's first response to the possession of money seem to her like the straw in the wind that it really represented. With a little money in hand, Anna began to overspend herself. She wrote to her family from New England to rent a larger and a better house, a request her family all too willingly fulfilled. The address, 1710 Locust Street, became well known in after days as the frequent resort of Theodore Tilton, Garrison, Phillips, Congressman William D. Kelley, Whitelaw Reid, and Susan B. Anthony. Yet Susan overlooked the rising signs of self-importance in her protégée, who after all was only twenty years of age. Her vision of Anna as the destined leader of woman's rights, returning to the fold when the war years were over, refused to waver.

Anna's address before Congress on January 16, 1864, was considered the grand climax of her career. The invitation was arranged by Congressman William D. Kelley from Philadelphia, who had originally discovered the swan in Philadelphia's back yard and adopted her as a daughter. Anna usually addressed him in her notes as "Papa." In those early formal days of society, all of Anna's friends, including Kelley, Phillips, Susan, and many others, appear to have relished their escape into Anna's informality. Kelley's fellow congressmen were curious to hear the prodigy and willingly co-operated in the idea. They invited her to use their own Capitol chamber, the House of Representatives, and charged themselves admission for the privilege of hearing her. The proceeds were to be turned over to the Freedman's Bureau.

Up to this time Anna had been following the Abolitionist line, attacking the policies of the Administration. Yet with the President, whom she was accustomed to lash so freely, sitting in the audience before her, Anna hesitated. She ended her talk by calling for the re-election of Lincoln, to the great surprise of her Abolitionist friends. Anna could give no explanation for her sudden about-face. She was probably as much surprised as everyone else to hear herself endorsing the President. At the same time one might recall in this connection that Congressman Kelley, the sponsor of the great occasion, was a strong Lincoln supporter.

Susan was engaged at the time in co-operating with Sumner, who represented the utmost non-co-operation with the President. Like most of the Abolitionists, she ignored Anna's momentary apostasy in the House of Representatives. Her thoughts remained fixed on the nurture of this girl into a future woman's rights leader.

Her first act on starting the Women's Loyal League had been to solicit Anna Dickinson's aid. In April 1863 she wrote her: "Our Woman's Rights Central Committee [has] resolved to call a 'Meeting of the Loyal Women of the Country' . . . I hasten to write you before the day is definitely fixed to invite you to be one of the speakers. . . . The aim . . . is that we, who have so many years demanded a place in the civil and political management of the nation, shall express our thoughts of the work for this crisis, especially the work for women. . . . I see what wonders you are doing in slaying the Copperheads. Well, go ahead; it is a glorious work."

Anna did not speak for the Loyal League. A little later Susan had a hasty note from her, dated from Mrs. Hooker's home in Hartford. The note asked Susan to send Mrs. Hooker pamphlets, etc., on woman's rights—whatever she had to send. Mrs. Hooker afterward recorded that Anna Dickinson had converted her to woman's rights at this time and had given her her first true view of Susan B. Anthony, "a fearless defender of true liberty and woman's right of public speech." Susan took hope from this passage that Anna, however deeply engrossed in party politics, was not forgetful of her real mission.

In the summer of 1863 Susan saw a great deal of her young friend. She made frequent trips to Philadelphia to see her, and even to see her family during Anna's absence. In the fall came the Pennsylvania elections and the enlistment of Anna Dickinson in the state campaign. The Republican State Committee engaged her for twelve days of speaking at one thousand dollars a day. Congressman Kelley and Whitelaw Reid must have been behind this munificent offer, and it was Kelley who persuaded her to accept it.

Anna's acceptance was not wholly mercenary. She accepted it for patriotic reasons and for the challenge it offered her. The miners of Pennsylvania did not support the war or the draft and threatened a revolt to the Democrats. The Republican State Committee hit upon the expedient of sending a woman into the field. They reasoned that the miners would not attack a woman. They were mistaken. Anna Dickinson was shot at in a public meeting and narrowly escaped being killed. Her bravery under attack turned popular opinion in her favor and she finished the campaign in a whirl of success. She was given credit for helping the Republicans to carry the state. But she was not paid the twelve thousand dollars for her twelve days of speaking. She was not paid anything.

On July 1, 1864, Susan was in Rochester. (How she got there on that date is a mystery to the writer, when she was supposed to be at her busiest in her New York office. A curious fact, but of

no importance.) From Aaron McLean's house in the city she wrote
the following letter to Anna:

> Rochester, N.Y.
> 69 North St.
> July 1,/64

My dear Anna:

In the midst of this mad phrenzy for "Old Abe" and bitter persecution of Frémont—my thought has so often turned to you that
now my pen is scribbling.

Do you, can you, stand alone through this terrible whirlwind?
Do you not all the time feel that God is *not* in it—but now as of
old in the "still small voice?" It seems to me that *Liberator* and
Standard are gone "stark mad" in their echo of the politicians'
cry—"Save the Union." We read no more of the good old doctrine, "Of two evils choose neither."—"Do the right and trust the
consequences with God." . . . And what compensation is there
now, when, as it seems to me it surely will, some other than the
goal they crave comes of all their cry for Union and Union men—
alias Lincoln and Lincoln men. I don't know but Frémont is a
corrupt man. But I don't believe that he is; be that as it may it
is safe only to speak and act the truth—and to profess confidence
in Lincoln would be a lie in me.

Good, somehow, will come uppermost though in getting there
all men are constantly getting the lesson, if they could but see and
hear it, that it is not through any trick or desire of politicians but
in spite of all such.

Anna, I heard of your good word at Kennett Square [Abolitionist
meeting] through Mrs. Hurn of Philadelphia. I never felt so sure
of you and so proud of you as in your last Cooper Institute speech
in New York. Your life, your power, like so many, like all true lives,
lies in speaking the absolute truth, not in echoing the popular cry of
the multitude. And so long as you look *within* for guidance in the
spirit and letter of your utterances, you are safe. To speak as will
please the people is always failure.

Anna, tell me about yourself—how is that throat—and the cough?
Are you resting? Where do you rusticate this summer? Do you see
your position as to the Presidential struggle? Would you join in a
series of mass meetings through the principal cities of the North,
provided we can get Mr. Phillips to enlist. It seems to me that if
we had a grand series of mass meetings, with Phillips and you and
perhaps F. Douglass as the bright particular stars, the people could
be roused to the demand of entire freedom and perhaps equality

of civil and political rights for the black man . . . The few Abolitionists who still believe in struggling against the popular evil current must cry aloud and spare not . . .

Anna, my best love goes out to you, and my most earnest hope that you may keep close to the "still small voice" that has thus far safely led you on—truth, that will never err, however hard its promptings seem sometimes.—So good bye and some times remember and write to

Your affectionate Friend
SUSAN B. ANTHONY

It was impossible that Susan did not know that Anna had already come out for Lincoln in her Washington speech earlier in the year. The news had been heralded far and wide by the National Republican Committee, so highly did they regard the support of this twenty-one-year-old girl. Apparently Susan was trying, by appealing to old Quaker principles, to draw Anna back into the Abolitionist fold. She could not bear the thought of losing her personally.

After the windup of her Loyalist League work, Susan saw nothing of Anna Dickinson for more than a year. They had no communication with each other. Susan was occupied with family affairs, and Anna, at the close of the war, without a moment's loss of time, entered the lyceum field. Her extraordinary success as a lyceum feature made her headline news in the papers, and only through these could Susan keep up with her.

CHAPTER THIRTEEN

CHAMPION OF WOMAN'S RIGHTS

◁§ I Susan's situation at the end of the war must have appeared to Daniel R., the good brother, as a bit forlorn. Married for a year and anxious to carry the responsibility he had inherited as head of the family, he sent her an urgent invitation to share his home in Kansas. D.R. acted in accord with the mores of the time: the married brother must spread a sheltering wing, the wife never questioning, over the solitary life of a maiden sister. Family loyalty was strong in Daniel R. Susan might have made her home with her brother for the rest of her life had she been that kind of woman.

To do him justice, Daniel R. did not picture Susan's role as that of houseworker and helper in bringing up the children. She was to be his assistant rather than his wife's. Daniel R. had amassed a number of growing interests as newspaper publisher, postmaster, mayor, and investor. He had so many irons in the fire that he could well afford a smart woman as assistant in his office. For one thing, Susan could relieve him of considerable editorial work, and he could see her functioning in that capacity for their mutual benefit.

Susan's trip to Kansas, undertaken in the dead of winter, was rather rough. The Mississippi was frozen over. "I paid a dollar for a ride across the Mississippi on the ice," she wrote. In Missouri she boarded an immigrant train packed with large families heading for Kansas and Nebraska settlements. The train and the wayside country were in a state of dilapidation. The engine broke down from time to time and the overpacked car became what Susan denominated "a pig-sty." At one place where the train stalled, she observed that the men of the party were resorting to a hovel near the siding for the purpose of washing their hands and faces. In an upsurge of equal rights she followed them to the lavatory and enjoyed the luxury of a wash-up herself. She negotiated the purchase of a cup of coffee with the woman in charge, who said on handing it to her, "This is no rye; it is real coffee." And so it was, to Susan's astonishment; in the midst of the dirt and dilapidation, a real symptom of peace was observed.

When she had been in Leavenworth for two weeks, she wrote to Mrs. Stanton:

> Leavenworth, Kansas
> Tuesday, Feb. 14,/65

My dear Mrs. Stanton:

Your letter of January 23rd found me in the above city and State and in my brother D.R.'s home, with his little pet wife, he being absent in Washington, D.C.

I arrived here Jan. 31st. About two weeks previous there came invitations too solid to be resisted by way of R.R. Tickets and bank check. So I waited only to have my tip-top Rochester dressmaker make the new five-dollar silk of last winter—you remember—stopped a few days in Chicago—but did not call on the League women—weather cold.

I like Leavenworth much better than I expected and thus far the pet wife is all that she promised at first sight. She has a splendid black (stallion) horse, "Bill," and a nice carriage and drives *herself* every day. Last week she took me out every P.M. . . .

Brother Dan has a neat little snow-white cottage, with green blinds, the very same he told you you might have. . . . Brother Dan owns a paper which he wants me to help to edit. He wants to make it the most radical mouth-piece of Kansas—but you know I can't get off anything when I know it is to go into print. I wish I could talk through you the things I'd like to say to the young martyr state.

I hear you say, how long are you going to be in Kansas? and I can't tell you—6 months or a year, if I like it—6 weeks or less if I don't—nothing fixed. . . . Mother has broken up housekeeping and she and Mary are boarding at brother McLean's. . . . Then sister Hannah has moved into a neat, new brick house next door— so all are together. . . . This arrangement left me "free to roam." Hence I am in Kansas as a beginning. . . .

Susan enjoyed the ease and comfort of her new position at first. "I am afraid I shall get into the business of being comfortable," she wrote to her family. But she had been cautious about committing herself as to the length of her stay. Two months later she wrote again to Mrs. Stanton, registering some change in the trend of her satisfaction.

Even the Stantons, who had once considered themselves settled for life in New York, had been cast adrift by the outbreak of peace. Daniel R., while in the East, had suggested to Henry B. Stanton that he might do better with his profession in Kansas than in New York. Mrs. Stanton followed this up by writing to Susan, asking her to cast about for an opening for her husband. After two months in Leavenworth, Susan wrote, discouraging the plan. She wrote feelingly, saying that she yearned to work with Mrs. Stanton again; that if they had money they could start something together *anywhere*, but that without money they could start nothing *anywhere*, and this included Kansas.

She had quickly found out that her brother's idea of a radical newspaper did not tally with her own. He would not allow her to write editorials favoring suffrage for women or for the Negroes. Originally a Free Soil Republican, Daniel R. was having his own troubles adjusting to the swiftly changing policies of the post-war Republican regime. As he intended to adjust, he could not allow Susan's social reforms to complicate his problem.

◈§ II   Susan's duties at the office became very dull. As she could write nothing that verged on politics, she was reduced to clipping and rewriting items from the numerous exchanges. When she went out occasionally with her sister-in-law, she did not know how to make conversation. It was an event when she met a certain congenial Mrs. Johnson. "Mrs. J. is the first and only woman I've met," says the diary, "who speaks of any question, public or private, political or religious, save the frivolities of 'Society.'" Clearly Susan was a round peg in a square hole. At the same time, she proved of great assistance in making baby clothes, for she was an excellent seamstress and fine sewer. When the baby came, she was again in high favor, having had considerable nursing experience with her

sisters and cousins in similar emergencies. Afterward she relapsed
into comparative uselessness.

There was no lack of excitement in the family scene. Her sister-
in-law's drives with her spirited horse furnished some of it. "Rode
out with Annie in the A.M. Ran into a big wagon on Delaware
Street. D.R. right there." Next came a telegram announcing that
Brother Merritt, still in the Army, would pass through Leavenworth with his wife and children on the way to his next post.
Susan got on the steamboat at Leavenworth and journeyed with
them as far as St. Joseph. She was deeply moved to find that Merritt, who had left home a mere boy, had turned into a gaunt and
"weather-worn" old soldier. Greatly concerned about his unsettled
state and his waif-like family following him around, she could still
do nothing about it. Merritt was mustered out soon afterward and
settled comfortably at Fort Scott with his family. Susan saw his
situation at its worst.

Later that same spring Daniel R. ran into one of those shooting
affairs in which the editors of newspapers were likely to be em-
broiled in those days. To be the editor of a newspaper was to ply
a dangerous trade. Henry B. Stanton tells in his memoirs about a
friend in Connecticut, a teacher, who always wore a pistol, "though
he had no use for it there," and adds, "When he went to Cincinnati, and took up the editorial pen, the pistol came into play."
Similarly, Susan's brother, as an editor, sometimes found his pistol
coming into play.

Daniel R.'s paper had criticized a citizen named Stone, who
first attacked him on the street with an umbrella and then
ganged up with his friends to lie in wait for him. D.R.'s friends
ganged up in their turn. Both sides were armed as a matter of
course.

Susan's diary records the fray with her usual brevity:

May 13, 1865.—Col. J. R. Jennison [a friend of Stone's] attacked brother D.R. at 5½ P.M. Shooting occurred. Jennison hit
in the leg.

May 14, 1865.—The fears of brother D.R.'s friends are very great.

May 27, 1865.—Col. Jennison able to ride out. He threatened to
shoot D.R. still.

The skirmish ended with only one man shot in the leg. But blood had been drawn and the affair was considered liquidated. Susan stood by, not stunned so much as uncomprehending, like a Martian who had dropped in on a human scene. She had watched the quarrel develop with the inevitability of masculine logic, which had allowed no consideration whatever for a "little pet wife" and a newborn child. Kansas was a man's world, a world of continuing war. Susan could only record the facts in which her brother was involved and refrain from all comment.

She spent much of her time in Leavenworth trying to help the Negroes, who were pouring into Kansas in miserable droves and for whom there was little organized assistance. She persuaded her brother to employ a Negro printer, but the other printers threw him out. She kept on trying to get work for him at his own trade but was unsuccessful. He became a laborer. On Sundays she addressed the Negroes in their schools and churches and urged them to strive for the vote.

But Kansas was not entirely indifferent to her reputation. When July 4, 1865, came around Susan was invited to address the crowd at the patriotic celebration. She and a Kansas congressman were the chosen orators of the day. She enjoyed the stage ride to Ottawa, most of it over unbroken prairie, and was glad to be on the platform again, though it was anguish as usual to prepare her speech. She spoke for an hour, attacking the policies that Johnson had inherited from Lincoln, and finally putting in a good word for woman suffrage. The Republicans declared themselves well pleased with her effort and proposed to print her talk for circulation. But the congressman came to dinner and suggested that she leave out the paragraph about woman suffrage. Susan insisted on retaining it but trod softly. "I showed him I had done so only by way of illustrating the point that *no class* can be trusted to legislate for another," she said. It was her first clear warning that the Republican party was going to do nothing about woman's rights.

◄§ III When Susan had left for Kansas, she shared the general expectation that the Anti-Slavery Society would disband. This was Garrison's idea. Garrison had created the society and considered that with the adoption of the Thirteenth Amendment its work was completed. Scarcely had Susan reached Kansas, however, when her correspondents in the East reported that a lively disagreement had arisen. Phillips insisted that the society should continue for the purpose of obtaining votes for the freedmen. Garrison resigned as president and Wendell Phillips was elected in his place. Henceforth the Anti-Slavery Society existed for the promotion of Negro enfranchisement, to be achieved by the enactment of a further Federal amendment.

Susan was kept informed of these developments by the faithful pen of Mrs. Stanton. It was easy for them to side with Phillips, believing as they did in the superlative power of the vote. As soon as Susan learned of the dissension, she wrote to Phillips, approving his stand. He replied: "Thank you for your kind note. I see you understand the lay of the land and no words are necessary between you and me. If Garrison should resign, we incline to Purvis for president for many, many reasons. We [the Hovey Committee] shall aid in keeping our standard floating till the enemy comes down." Though satisfactory to Susan, Phillips's note was somewhat less than ingenuous. He must have known that the sedate and retiring Purvis had not the slightest chance of becoming the society's president.

From long experience with her public work, Phillips wanted Susan on his side. No one knew better than he how great had been her services to the Abolitionist cause. On July 18, 1865, Susan wrote in her diary: "Got a letter from Mrs. Stanton from Johnstown. Sent one from Phillips to her. He says 'Tell Susan to come East; there is work for her to do.' "

This was followed by letters from Lydia Mott and Parker Pillsbury, urging her return, while from Mrs. Stanton came the last, irresistible plea:

I hope in a short time to be comfortably located in a new house where we will have a room ready for you when you come East. I long to put my arms around you once more and hear you scold me for my sins and short-comings. Your abuse is sweeter to me than anybody else's praise for, in spite of your severity, your faith and confidence shine through all. O, Susan, you are very dear to me. I should miss you more than any other living being from this earth. You are intertwined with much of my happy and eventful past, and all my future plans are based on you as a coadjutor. Yes, our work is one, we are one in aim and sympathy and we should be together. Come home.

This might have moved a harder heart than Susan pretended to possess, even had it not been supplemented by a news item which immediately followed. One day in August, Susan was sitting in her brother's office, reading and snipping the exchanges as usual, when a paragraph from Washington caught her eye. It dealt with the recently proposed Fourteenth Amendment.

The purpose of the amendment was twofold: to give the right of the franchise to the emancipated slaves and to withhold the same right from the ex-rebels of the South. In a lengthy introduction designed to effect both objects, the word "male" was introduced to qualify and disqualify the voters. The word "male" had never before been used in the Constitution, as Susan well knew, and its introduction at this juncture instantly aroused her alarm. She began to lay plans for returning to the East. Her life as an old maid in her brother's household was at an end.

She quickly concluded arrangements with the *Anti-Slavery Standard* to work her way eastward by making public speeches and collecting subscriptions for the *Standard*. Daniel R. had paid her way out to Kansas, but she had to get herself back again under her own power (though her brother did hand her a couple of passes). Thus she spent a month on the homeward journey, paying her fare out of her share of the subscription money, but reaching home at one o'clock in the morning without money to pay for a carriage. "Walked up to Aaron's house," says the diary. "Policeman escorted me."

Still alarmed by the introduction of the word "male" in the Constitution, she started on her way through Auburn, New York, Philadelphia, and Boston, like Paul Revere riding to spread the alarm. She called on the old colleagues to wake up and take note of what was happening. Most of them were indeed asleep. They had not had a national convention since 1860, and it was now the end of '65. But she found the old guard, Mrs. Stanton, Lucy Stone, Antoinette Blackwell, Lucretia Mott, like herself, primed and ready for action. Mrs. Stanton set to work drafting woman suffrage petitions, and Susan secured five hundred dollars from the Hovey Committee to print and circulate them. Before the end of the current session they had ten thousand signatures ready for Congress.

Susan went to the anti-slavery convention in Boston in fine spirits. She thought she had discovered a simple solution for the problem. She had talked it over with her New York friends, Henry Ward Beecher and Theodore Tilton, and they heartily approved. Her plan was to amalgamate the Anti-Slavery and the Woman's Rights societies into one organization—the National Equal Rights Association—which should strive for universal suffrage, enfranchising women and Negroes alike. Susan laid her idea before the anti-slavery convention. But when it came to a formal vote, Phillips announced that it required three months' notice for the society to change its name. The convention formally deputized the secretary to send out such a notice in order that the plan could be proposed at the ensuing May convention. Susan saw that a corresponding notice went out to the Woman's Rights Society and returned home happily convinced that her plan would work.

§ IV In due course the two societies met in New York. As the membership of the two organizations was practically identical, the one meeting followed immediately upon the other. The anti-slavery convention took place first. When Susan brought up the question of amalgamation, Phillips declared it out of order, as no notice regarding the proposed change of name had been sent out. He had countermanded the order of his own society. He then proceeded for the first time to make his position clear: he was definitely not in favor of the coalition. His followers in the Anti-Slavery Society thereupon voted it down.

At the woman's rights meeting which followed, Phillips made a long and eloquent speech on theoretical woman suffrage, but implying that the cause was not an immediate issue. Susan rose and made her speech, presenting the resolution as planned—to change the Woman's Rights Society to the American Equal Rights Association—and sat down. Without the co-operation of the Anti-Slavery Society, the women's society was converted into an organization for human rights, asking votes for women and Negroes alike. There was nothing else that she could do.

The next day Susan met Phillips by accident in the *Standard* office. Mrs. Stanton and Tilton were also present. Phillips took the

Susan B. Anthony at the age of 48.

bull by the horns and unfolded to the others his entire view of the matter. The time was ripe for Negro suffrage, he said, but not for woman suffrage, and he used many beautiful words in explaining himself and convincing the others. Presently Susan heard Tilton, who had so recently commended her plan, falling into line with Phillips's views. To her still greater surprise, she heard Mrs. Stanton chiming in with the two. It took Susan just one moment to shatter the harmonious atmosphere: she suddenly blurted out that she would sooner cut her right hand off than ask suffrage for the Negroes and not for women. Phillips left right after this, and Susan was obliged by an appointment to leave also. As she went out, she heard Tilton say to Mrs. Stanton, "What does ail Susan?" and Mrs. Stanton reply, "I can not imagine; I never before saw her so unreasonable and absolutely rude."

Such was the magnetic influence of Phillips that after all his evasions and his indirect handling of Susan's plan Mrs. Stanton could still see nothing to do but trust him. After she went home and thought the matter over, she saw it more clearly. Susan, coming in that night, found her walking up and down and wringing her hands. "I never was so glad to see you," she cried. "Do tell me what is the matter with me. I feel as if I had been scourged from the crown of my head to the soles of my feet!" She who deemed herself emancipated had been subdued by the age-old tactics of man's devious way with woman. Phillips had treated them at first like children, countermanding parliamentary action behind their backs, and then, unabashed by the discovery, coming out against them frankly in public. Mrs. Stanton resented this with all the fury of her excitable temperament, and resented it all the more because she had for a moment succumbed.

Mrs. Harper, Susan's biographer, explains the slip by saying that Mrs. Stanton was "psychologized" by Phillips. The word does as well as any other to express the subtle emanations by which the famous Bostonian won friends and influenced people. Not the least of his emanations was the aura of high caste which invariably went with him and to which only very rare persons can claim to be immune. Mrs. Stanton, with her background and upbringing, was more vulnerable to his aura than Susan, who, with her Quaker origin and upbringing, was one of the said rare persons. She admired Phillips extravagantly for his intellect, eloquence, and spirit, but the awe which he inspired by being the best blood of Boston was foreign to her bone-deep Quaker simplicity.

In extenuation of Phillips's deception—there is nothing else to call it—we might remind ourselves that the end of the war had forced him, like many others, to make sudden and crucial decisions. He had been obliged to break with Garrison, which must have been very painful. He wished to retain the assistance of such women as Susan and Mrs. Stanton and he wished above all to prevent any further breaks in his following. His mistake lay in thinking that, because they were women, he could finagle them; whereas, at least as far as Susan was concerned, this was impossible. For Susan now saw her road ahead as plainly as Phillips saw his. She was dedicated to the cause of securing suffrage for women as firmly as he was dedicated to securing it for Negroes. Beginning as united Abolitionists, they had struck into different paths.

⌁§ V   Susan and Mrs. Stanton sent their petitions broadcast. Busily circulating their document, they soon found that Phillips was not the only one who had deserted them. Their firm friends of other days, Senators Sumner and Wilson, refused to sign the petition. The former allies, Garrison, Greeley, Curtis, Tilton, Higginson, Fred Douglass, Gerrit Smith, refused to sign it. In the excitement someone coined the phrase: "This is the NEGRO'S HOUR." Seized upon by the deserters from woman suffrage as the last refuge, it attained a currency that supplanted all argument. Woman suffrage was temporarily demolished by it.

Susan and Mrs. Stanton continued to register their protest. Mrs. Stanton addressed a vigorous letter to the *Anti-Slavery Standard:*

It is all very well for the privileged order to look down complacently and tell us, "This is the Negro's hour . . . do not embarrass the Republican party with any new issue . . . the Negro once safe, the woman comes next." . . . But the disfranchised all make the same demand, and the same logic and justice that secures suffrage to one class gives it to all.

The struggle of the last thirty years has not been merely on the black man as such, but on the broader ground of his humanity. Our Fathers, at the end of the first revolution . . . in order to present to Great Britain . . . a united front, accepted the compromise urged on them by South Carolina, and a century of wrong, ending in another revolution, has been the result of their action. . . . The nation is ready for a long step in the right direction; party lines are obliterated, and all men are thinking for themselves. If our rulers have the justice to give the black man suffrage, woman should avail herself of that new-born virtue to secure her rights; if not, she should begin with renewed earnestness to educate the people into the idea of universal suffrage.

The American Equal Rights Association fought on. They sent a petition to Congress headed by the name of their most revered and sainted member, Lydia Maria Child. Sumner presented it apologetically, remarking that it was "most inopportune." He little realized that liberals like himself, as well as the women, were soon also to be purged as "inopportune." Lucretia Mott, another of the most revered and sainted leaders, invited Phillips to her house along with Susan. Lucretia and Susan together labored with him for an hour. But all was in vain. Phillips had taken his stand, and for once he was on the side of the dominant party.

The Republicans had taken over the country. With an overwhelming majority in both houses, they could *schalten und walten* like a many-headed dictator. The Fourteenth Amendment, creating more voters for the present incumbents, was pushed through as a party measure; and the Fifteenth Amendment, designed to buttress it, soon followed. The word "male" was engraved in the United States Constitution.

VI   Susan and Mrs. Stanton felt very bitter about their wholesale betrayal by the men whom they had most trusted. Susan was conscious of her age, forty-six (more conscious of it than when much older). Mrs. Stanton was five years farther along. If it was necessary, as Mrs. Stanton admitted, for women to begin all over again "with renewed earnestness to educate the people into the idea of universal suffrage," a long and tedious road lay ahead. Susan saw clearly now that they could not rely upon men to carry the banner for them. They needed women in vast numbers and they needed a standard-bearer who was much younger than Mrs. Stanton and herself.

She had long turned in her thoughts to Anna Dickinson for

the role, and she turned to her now with the force of desperation. She could not divest herself of the belief that Anna would eventually leave party politics and become the invincible leader of the woman suffrage movement. Anna's career as a lyceum lecturer offered no hindrance to the plan. On the contrary, it formed an asset. Anna had become the most popular platform figure in the country, outstripping the great Brahmins who came out of the East. The simple Quaker girl (no longer so simple in dress, however) was known to receive larger fees than some of the most famous men. To divert that golden voice to the women's cause became Susan's obsessive desire of the post-war years.

She resumed her correspondence with Anna immediately after her return from Kansas. Despite her urgent invitations, Anna was not present at either of the first two woman's rights meetings that followed the war. She wrote thus to Susan:

My very dear Susan Anthony:
. . . I'm a great deal of a Quaker—I don't like to take up any work till I feel called to it. My personal interest is perhaps stronger in that of which thee writes than in any other, but my hands are so full now. . . . Wait for me a little—forbear, and I honestly believe I'll do thee some good and faithful service; I don't mean wait for me, but be patient with me. I write this out of my large love for and confidence in thee. I will talk to thee more of it by the end of the month when I see thee in Boston and put my mite in thy hands; till then, believe me, dear friend,
Affectionately and truly thine,
ANNA E. DICKINSON

True to her promise, Anna attended the Boston convention and made one of her very best speeches. The "mite" which she had promised turned out to be one hundred dollars, a generous donation when measured by suffragist standards. Susan was transported. We have no way of knowing what the oracle said, owing to her habit of extemporaneous speaking. But it was life-giving for Susan that Anna spoke out in favor of woman suffrage when other Abolitionist friends were fast deserting the standard. Her hopes rose accordingly and she ardently pursued her purpose of trying to enlist Anna as a leader of the cause.

Anna was hard to reach, as her lyceum engagements kept her constantly on the move. Susan wrote at this time:

464 West 34th St.
New York, June 15, /66

My dear Annie:

I am obliged to stop over Sunday, so shall bring Mrs. Stanton
to the St. Denis to see you Monday evening at 7 or 8 o'clock, unless
I learn that you are otherwise engaged. Don't lose any good thing
for us, because we can see you Tuesday sometime. . . .

Susan was working hard to bring Mrs. Stanton and Anna Dickinson closer together. The St. Denis meeting did not take place.
She next persuaded Mrs. Stanton to go with her to Philadelphia
to pay a visit to Anna, but it proved to be a visit to the Dickinson
family only, as Anna was away lecturing. Then Susan got the Gerrit
Smiths to invite Anna to Peterboro in company with Mrs. Stanton.
But even this well-meant device failed, for Anna was not available.
It is just a little saddening to observe the veteran Susan paying
court to a young lady of less than half her age. It is even more
saddening to find her depreciating Mrs. Stanton's oratory in one
of her letters to Anna. She mentioned that Mrs. Stanton was doing
very well in public speaking and deserved much praise, "when you
remember how little practice she has had." Only those who know
of Anna Dickinson's superlative fame at that time (who nowadays
are few) can understand and excuse such a remark from Susan.
The inference remains that Anna and Mrs. Stanton were still far
apart.

Susan went on besieging the girl with letters. One gathers from
them that Anna, when in Susan's presence, responded to her enthusiasm and thus continually refreshed the hope that was in her
heart. In the fall Susan wrote:

Rochester, N.Y.
September 1, /66

Darling Anna E.:

I wish these Pennsylvania Politicians had held their pens till
another week, and yet I am glad to have you in Phila. next week,
and would run there too, but for the ifs in the way. I do so want
to see you and listen to your summing up of a Swampscott summer. . . .

The real truth seems to be that the miserable President with the
miserable Congress have thrown us back precisely to the point of
difference at which we began the war. And by doing so, make it

seem impossible to do more than fan the patient with the mere
hope to keep the breath of life in him—so you and I and all who
would see the Nation live are tempted again to rush into the thick
of the battle, at the beck of a party that does not, dares not, pro-
claims that it fights for man, for a' that and a' that; but bids us
in private, trust them; that if we'll help them to power again, they'll
then make laws and constitutions for Man, black. And to us
women, whom they fear they can not enlist without [it], they in
private add for women too.

I am sick to death of the arrant cowards and cut-throats, too,
for by their cowardice and failure to declare a man a man, we have
had Memphis and New Orleans. And I hope you, my dear Anna,
will tell them it is they, Congress, who are the guilty.

I hope you won't wear yourself out in the fall campaign, for
there is a higher, grander work for you, and you must save yourself
for it. Have you yet clutched the splendid speech, The New Republic, the tail end of which you caught sight of one of those
delightful nights at 1710 last June? I hope so, for it is destined
to be only woman who shall declare the new gospel, the risen
Savior. No man yet seems to see that it is the Nation's duty to
lay anew its foundations; they only propose to readjust the old ones
with a little chiselling of the black corner-stone. . . .

There is an advance step, one that the people will hail with
gladness, one that will sink present Republicanism to the lower
deeps of present Democracy. All that is wanting is a voice that
has the public ear to take the lead. Would that voice might be
the one and only woman the Nation now deigns to hear. Would
that you, darling Anna, might be the evangel. But you can not
until you receive the new baptism and so when the blessed hour
comes I know you will right joyously proclaim the salvation. . . .

Susan closed her exalted appeal on a practical note. She proposed
a series of lectures on woman suffrage across the state, in anticipation of the Constitutional Convention, and she wanted Anna to
deliver one of the series. She offered "to pay her precisely as much
as she got from other associations." And she would have raised the
money, too, had Anna consented.

A whole year passed without Anna's appearance on the suffrage
platform. Susan's friendship with her was not affected, however.
Having taken refuge in a Quaker rule which Susan also acknowledged, the girl was still waiting for inner guidance. Susan continued to urge her but always apologized for doing so. Meantime

Anna expressed the strongest pro-suffragist views in her personal letters. There was one particular letter of which Susan wrote: "I have read it and re-read it and every time been on the point of sending it to the press—but then I hardly dared to take the liberty." Anna had become her generous and warmhearted friend, and for the time being she let it remain at that.

At one point in this history, rather late at that, Mrs. Stanton interposed in her friend's pursuit of Anna. She warned Susan that the girl was not strong enough to be the leader of a cause, and she cautioned Susan against pushing her too far. Susan replied that Mrs. Stanton had no idea of the inner strength—superhuman almost—of the heroic maiden. At that particular moment Susan was exerting her last effort to persuade Anna to make the keynote speech at the coming suffragist convention. "If you can and will do it," she wrote, "not a Joan of Arc ever matched it—just the fire that will demolish the old fort and leave not a stone of it. But Mrs. Stanton says you can't do it. You'll surely break down. I tell her she judges your power by her own lack of it." Having done this much to satisfy her conscience, apparently in vain, Mrs. Stanton retreated from the situation. She would allow nothing to interfere with her loyalty to Susan.

In the fall of '66 Susan made this cryptic reference to a counter-influence: "I know the pressure to keep you from doing in the one direction. Still I mean always to keep beckoning you upward and onward till you speak right out in words the deep, rich, earnest love for your own sex that I know lies in the inner courts of your being." The influence to which she referred could only have been that of Anna's great friend, Wendell Phillips. Having failed to bring Susan and Mrs. Stanton over to his side, Phillips was determined to hold onto Anna Dickinson. Like everyone else in those days, he looked on Anna as an important political alliance.

His friendship with Anna was of long standing, dating back to her debut in Boston in 1863, when she had seen him "almost every day." In 1866 he cultivated the friendship more warmly than ever. There is no doubt that he aimed to alienate Anna from Susan's and Mrs. Stanton's cause and took some trouble to do so. Above all, he was human, as Susan also was human, and, like Susan, he was captivated by Anna's personal charm. They were competing for the possession of her soul.

Susan's anger with Phillips flared up from time to time and she took no pains to conceal it from Anna. She wrote:

> American Equal Rights Association
> No. 37 Park Row,
> New York, June 11, /67

Darling Anna Dick:

. . . Lucy Stone went to Boston last week. . . . Saw Col. T. W. Higginson, S. E. Sewell, and the Grand Mogul. And the latter told her, though he would not have the question of woman suffrage on the A[nti] S[lavery] platform, his speech the coming winter, was to be on that question.

So, Chicky Dicky, you must get the start by making the great speech in advance . . . and have the world and yourself know that Anna Dick didn't fall into line after the said great Oracle, but that she had led the way. . . .

Later in her letter Susan returned again to the subject of Lucy Stone's recent visit with Phillips in Boston.

. . . Said while she was sitting there in her plain, worn, gray Kansas travelling dress, the young, innocent, pretty little Mrs. Rockwood, robed in silk, with dainty gloves and jaunty hat, made her appearance. Lucy asked her if she would go to Kansas. She was too tired with much speaking, and Ma said she must lecture no more this summer. Whereupon the Divine W.P. said—"Perhaps you could go in the autumn, it would be a good thing for you to go." Lucy says the Look—— I have forgotten what I was going to say Lucy was going to say—it is so long since the above was commenced. . . .

A letter from Wendell Phillips to Anna of about the same date gives a glimpse of the rivalry that was going on:

> Aug. 13, /67

My dear Friend:

"There," as the boy cried who had trod on the tail of his aunt's cat, "I've gone and done it." That pesky Jamestown. I mislaid your letter, was sure you told me to respond to Preston, and now I find it was Bishop I ought to have believed in! Will you consent to believe me, stupidest of mortals, and so forgive me. . . . Teach me the way and I will walk therein. . . .

I don't see you in New England, or rarely. The quality, I suppose, of interviews must make up for quantity. I did once get rain-soaked in your presence, and I well remember one very pleasant minute of an interview, just before surrendering you to S.B.A. on the cars. This rainy season will easily enable me to repeat the first; perhaps some good fortune may duplicate the other some time.

Should you so far forgive my clumsiness as ever to address me— remember my address is always Boston.

W.P.

Anna apparently found no trouble in being on both sides at once. While she loved her own sex with the warm devotion with which Susan credited her, she loved the opposite sex just as warmly; and the attentions of the latter were essential to her well-being and more tangibly demonstrated. The Republican politicians paid her large fees, or at least promised to pay them, and Anna was always in need of money. The Dickinson family, shamelessly dependent upon her as their sole support, were constantly appealing to her for more funds, and Anna had developed expensive habits of her own. Even her steady lyceum income and her occasional high political fees could scarcely enable her to bear the heavy burden. She was regularly living beyond her means.

If Susan knew of this sinister problem in Anna's life, she overlooked it. The amazing maturity of the girl's talents blinded her to the fact that she was barely twenty. Susan expected of her the love and understanding of a woman of her own age, and the precocious girl was, surprisingly enough, qualified to give it. Susan was more confidential in her letters to Anna than she was to her diary. At the same time, her heart responded to the eternal miracle of youth. There was nothing that Anna could do in the form of impulsiveness which her doting friend could not find a way to excuse.

All this resulted in Anna's being able to maintain a continued silence on woman suffrage, very favorable to Phillips and the Republican party, while Susan could go on dreaming that she would one day inherit the leadership of the women's cause and marshal it to victory.

◀§ VII Presently Susan found herself returning to Kansas, but this time on public business. Kansas, next to the youngest state in the Union, brashly submitted the two most controversial issues of the hour to a popular vote. Two constitutional amendments were proposed; one would give the franchise to Negroes, the other to women. The state was ready for neither. The boldness of the procedure consisted in the fact that such unlikely propositions could be brought forth, discussed, and voted upon by the public. Though Susan had just spent a most disillusioning year in Kansas, her native optimism arose. Here was the opportunity that she and Mrs. Stanton had been praying for, and she proposed to exploit it to the fullest extent.

She persuaded Lucy Stone and Henry B. Blackwell to go out to Kansas and canvass the state for two months. Lucy had been in retirement so long that she refused to undertake the journey without her husband's company. By consenting to go along Blackwell initiated a long career for himself as a woman suffrage campaigner. Susan and Mrs. Stanton arranged to follow them at the end of the summer and wind up the campaign. The expenses of the Blackwells' tour were paid by the Francis Jackson fund, of which Phillips, Lucy Stone, and Susan were the trustees. Phillips did not wholly approve of the outlay, but Susan and Lucy Stone were in the majority. He had the satisfaction later on of telling Susan and Mrs. Stanton, when they were ready to follow, that the Jackson fund was exhausted. The Hovey fund, which he still controlled, had arbitrarily stopped all allowances for woman suffrage, although this was one of the causes specifically mentioned by the testator as continuously eligible. Susan was obliged to raise the money for her own and Mrs. Stanton's trip to Kansas. She did it by the old and oft-repeated method of house-to-house begging—very hard on her shoe leather.

In Kansas she established headquarters in Lawrence, the capital, and managed affairs from an extemporized office. She scattered tracts and pamphlets far and wide, a little extra item of two thousand dollars, which she also had to raise. She continued to the eleventh hour in her efforts to get Anna Dickinson into the Kansas field. Senator Pomeroy, inspired by Susan, showered Anna with telegrams offering free railroad transportation and generous fees for ten nights of speaking. Anna was pleased with Pomeroy's telegrams—pleased enough to keep the old yellow Western Union forms among the souvenirs of her life. But she did not accept his invitation.

Phillips, who did not wish to see Anna committed publicly

to the suffrage cause, was guarding his protégée very closely. He wrote:

Sept. 13, /67

Dear Friend:

You should not yourself write such perfect notes, if you wish other folks to write you. Who'd attempt to talk in De Stael's presence, lecture in Emerson's or orate (horrid word!) in front of Demosthenes. By the way, I doubt whether your little Quaker self ever saw a statue of Demosthenes, your great, great, great, great, great grandfather! Did you now? . . .

Now confess I showed the trust I had in your belief in my real friendship in the off-hand, unceremonious, cold, Yankee (there that's the climax) way I got rid of you the other day. If I had not believed that you believed in me enough to allow it, I'd have been polite as to any mere acquaintance. Old Hannah Adams, the first Yankee-blue-stocking . . . said, "No two were really intimate till they could sit together reading, hours, without feeling it necessary to talk." I add, "and till they can part uncivilly and still believe in each other." Good-bye. Take care of your health.

W.P.

Meantime Susan and Mrs. Stanton campaigned in Kansas, covering the prairie hinterland. Mrs. Stanton was driven over the state by the friendly ex-governor in a carriage drawn by a pair of strong mules. The Reverend Olympia Brown from New Haven was escorted in a similar equipage by an ex-army captain—the same man who afterward rowed Susan across the Missouri in a skiff late at night to enable her to keep an appointment. Susan was driven along prairie trails by some "Honorable" or other, otherwise unnamed. They left Lawrence at the end of September, going in different directions, to meet again in Leavenworth on November 4, the night before the election. The discomforts of the trip can well be imagined in a state where good roads did not yet exist. Mrs. Stanton's mules broke down and had to be replaced by a team of good horses. Susan's equipage got stuck in the mud and could be pulled out only by the supreme efforts of her masculine escort. Still they traveled on schedule and reached Leavenworth on the appointed day.

When the campaign began, the Republican State Committee had come out for Negro suffrage, taking no stand on the woman

question. The Democrats opposed both propositions. The Republicans then decided to oppose woman suffrage outright as a means
of bringing the German non-temperance vote into their count. In
the general confusion of the dominant party, both amendments
advanced toward defeat. Susan and her band had little hope toward
the end, but they kept on campaigning valiantly until the last vote
was cast. Susan's brother Daniel R. and his newspaper steered clear
of the women's cause during the campaign. But on the night of the
suffragist rally before the election D.R. sat on the platform with
his sister and cheered the suffrage speakers to the echo. The gal-
lantry of his sister and her Eastern friends in the face of discouragement was something to be proud of.

On November 5, 1867, the state of Kansas cast nine thousand
votes for woman suffrage and ten thousand for Negro suffrage out
of a total of thirty thousand votes. That the vote for the women so
nearly approached that for the Negroes was viewed by the women
as a triumph. It was the first time in the nation's history that the
question of woman suffrage had been submitted to a popular vote.
That nine thousand citizens of a single state had voted for it was
now a fact for the record, a milestone on the road where no marker
had before existed. Susan and Mrs. Stanton could still afford to
rejoice over a comparative victory.

❧ VIII   The Kansas campaign furnished their second political
adventure of the summer. Their own state of New York, where a
Constitutional Convention had taken place in June, had been the
scene of their first. Susan and Mrs. Stanton had spent months in
preparation and arrived at the convention heavily ballasted with
documentary and petitionary material. It was on this occasion that
they staged their well-known skirmish with Horace Greeley—
a skirmish which cost them the *Tribune's* support for their
cause.

After Mrs. Stanton had finished her formal address, the hearing
was given over to a question-and-answer period. Horace Greeley,
chairman of the suffrage committee, said to Susan: "Miss Anthony,
you know the ballot and the bullet go together. If you vote, are
you ready to fight?" (Greeley knew very well that Susan was a
Quaker as well as a woman, and he thought he saw a chance doubly

to challenge her.) "Yes, Mr. Greeley, just as you fought in the late war—at the point of a goose-quill," Susan replied. Greeley, the former friend of woman suffrage, had lately deserted to the post-war opposition. She realized that she had little to lose.

This was not all. Her second offense was far more serious. Susan and Mrs. Stanton had retained in the fast diminishing list of their masculine friends George William Curtis, the editor of *Harper's Weekly* and a delegate to the convention. They assigned their most important petition to Curtis to read, with instructions to read it at the last, just before Greeley, as chairman, rose to speak. The petition had been circulated by Mrs. Horace Greeley in Westchester County, and her name headed a list of three hundred petitioners. Mrs. Horace Greeley, the friend and pupil of Margaret Fuller, could not be alienated from woman suffrage by connubial or any other ties.

Curtis read his petition in orotund tones immediately before Greeley rose to give his adverse report. Placed in the position of denying his wife's petition, Greeley struggled visibly with his embarrassment, while the sound of subdued laughter ran through the chamber. Susan and Mrs. Stanton had not intended to hurt Greeley as deeply as this. His newspaper was constantly twanging on the theme, *The women do not want to vote*, and it was in the hope of answering this hackneyed argument that Susan and Mrs. Stanton had featured his wife's name. They had not considered that the existing differences between Greeley and his wife, known only to their personal friends, were thus painfully revealed to the public view. Greeley reacted to the exposure as might have been expected.

A noble, creative, and in public affairs very shrewd character, Greeley remained to the end of his days totally devoid of *savoir-faire* in trivial matters. He could not laugh things off. Meeting his two tormentors at a reception in Phoebe Cary's house, he declined to shake hands. Turning angrily upon Mrs. Stanton, he sputtered: "You are so tenacious of your own name, Elizabeth Cady Stanton, why did you not inscribe my wife's name, Mary Cheney Greeley, on her petition?" Mrs. Stanton, seldom conciliatory anyway, could only retort in kind. "Well," continued Greeley triumphantly, "I have given instructions that no praise shall ever again be awarded you in the *Tribune*, and that if your name is unavoidably to be mentioned, it shall be as Mrs. Henry B. Stanton." We have Mrs.

Stanton's word for it that this threat was afterward carried out to the letter.

The helpful results of the Constitutional Convention amounted to little. As one of the damaging results, Susan and Mrs. Stanton lost the support of a powerful New York newspaper. The Boston Abolitionists had long since deserted them. The Anti-Slavery Society continued to agitate for votes for Negroes alone, thus indirectly opposing the woman suffragists. The latter had made new friends in New York, men like George William Curtis, Henry Ward Beecher, Robert Dale Owen, who had no Abolitionist commitments and who continued to stand by them. But they were not the dedicated souls that the cause required. The women were thrown back on their own resources, which on the whole proved to be considerable. The outstanding leaders had never for a moment deviated; they had stuck together through everything. Lucretia Mott, Ernestine Rose, Lucy Stone, Elizabeth Cady Stanton, Antoinette Blackwell, Martha Wright, Susan Anthony formed a strong bridgehead ready for wholehearted action. But the clock had been turned back to the point of Seneca Falls, and it was necessary to start the movement all over again.

CHAPTER FOURTEEN

THE "REVOLUTION"

❧§ I   Susan's return from Leavenworth in the fall of 1865 settled one thing for her family. They were pleased with the prospect of having her in the East permanently and, as they hoped, more often at home than formerly. In this they reckoned without Susan.

Her situation probably had something to do with Lucy Anthony's next move, which was to purchase a home in Rochester. Two convenient houses, standing side by side, Nos. 7 and 9 (later 17 and 19), on Madison Street, were up for sale. Substantially built of red brick by one Dr. Wanzer, a dentist, who had lived in one of them, the houses were simultaneously placed on the market. They appealed to Lucy Anthony and her daughters because the brick structures recalled the old Battenville homestead (though architecturally they could not measure up to it) and because the adjoining locations kept the family together. Lucy Anthony decided to buy the larger house, while Eugene Mosher, Hannah's husband, decided to buy the other.

The deeds were signed on March 31, 1866. Lucy Anthony paid thirty-five hundred dollars for her house, and Mosher paid twenty-five hundred for his. Lucy had the money she had received for the farm, and the new home, like the farm, was held in her name. It was a two-story structure with ten or twelve fair-sized rooms, which, though lacking the grace and beauty of the old Battenville chambers, were comfortable and adequate. Lucy bought it as a home for herself and her single daughters but also as a home for her daughter

Guelma's family. By Lucy's standards a family of three was scarcely
a family at all. The McLeans with their two children became Lucy
Anthony's tenants, as she had formerly been theirs. The principal
change was that there was room for Susan, with her comings and
goings, in the new Madison Street house.

Susan, too, was made happy by the arrangement. She showed it
by having Mrs. Stanton as her guest soon after they had settled into
the place. But she was really too busy taking the woman's rights
movement out of moth balls to pay much attention to her new
home. Mrs. Stanton had offered her a home if she would return
from Kansas, and Susan found it more convenient to conduct her
various enterprises from Mrs. Stanton's New York house. Thus it
came about that, in the first few years of the family's occupancy of
No. 17 Madison Street, Susan did not spend much time in the
house.

II   In the final stages of their Kansas campaign Susan and
Mrs. Stanton had grown pretty desperate. They had exhausted their
financial and other resources and had another month to go. At this
point they had received and accepted an offer of aid from an unexpected quarter. On September 23 (before quite losing all sight
of hope) Susan had written to Anna Dickinson: "How funny that
Geo. Francis Train is coming into the State for a month to talk for
woman. What sort of a furor he will make!" Susan was aware that
Train's reputation as a Democrat and alleged "Copperhead" might
make him seem a dubious ally in Anna's eyes, as he seemed at the
moment in her own. But when a telegram came directly from Train
to her, offering help, she was by then ready to grasp at any straw.
She consulted her state committee, carefully communicating with
each one, and the consensus of opinion was that Train should be
invited.

Susan and Mrs. Stanton had grown so furious with the shifty
Republican committee that they were ready to welcome Beelzebub.
If they had realized Train's proneness to specialize in lost causes,
they might have been less elated. As it was, they took hope from
his promises and, later, from his bouncing presence. He spoke for
two weeks and changed the atmosphere of the campaign from the
beginning. He came like Don Quixote over the horizon, imbued

their tired spirits with new courage, and scampered like a schoolboy through the rest of the campaign.

Mr. Train really got votes for woman suffrage. Kansas was well populated with the Irish who had swarmed into the state to work on the Union Pacific Railway then under construction. The Irish laborers were uniformly Democratic. Many other Democrats had infiltrated from the South, Kansas being a border state. It was an unheard-of thing for a Democrat to mount the rostrum for woman suffrage, and Train's support excited interest by its novelty. He knew how to address his audience, using quips, jokes, and anecdotes instead of ponderous arguments. His own name for his tour was "The Great Epigram Campaign," the title under which he later published his speeches in pamphlet form. The voters laughed with him and went out and cast a ballot—still with him!—for woman suffrage. To his efforts could be credited most of the nine thousand votes eventually counted for woman suffrage.

Susan and Mrs. Stanton took equal shares in Train. But Train from the first preferred, and deferred to, Susan. This may have been due to a slight circumstance at the start of his tour. Susan, as commander in chief, had routed him through a series of small towns remote from the railroad. The city-bred Train was appalled by the trip expected of him and asked that it be changed. Susan explained that the dates and places had been announced and, rather than disappoint the country people, she would keep the dates herself. Train had no choice but to follow the original plan. Henceforth Susan had no trouble with him.

She accompanied him on most of his tour, attending to the routine chores connected with the meeting, while Train repaired to the nearest substitute for a hotel and prepared himself for his platform appearance. Susan fell into this the more naturally as she was accustomed to do it for Mrs. Stanton. Train was a neat gentleman who would not have appeared before a jungle audience without a change, shave, and cologne rinse to fortify him. Touring thus with Susan, who asked no favors for her sex, Train learned to understand her very well. As it happened, he neither drank nor smoked (Susan hated cigar smoke), and so it came about that they traveled as comfortably together as a pair of spinsters.

Susan afterward recalled with amusement some of their adventures in the backwoods. Among others was this story: "We found many people ill, and Mr. Train always prescribed not a drop of green tea, not a mouthful of pork, though that was the only meat they could get, plenty of fruit, though there was none to be had in Kansas, and a thorough bath every morning, although there was not enough water to wash the dishes."

Train's admiration and respect for Susan were rising every day. Near the end of their journey he asked her in the course of a conversation why the Equal Rights Society did not publish their own paper. Susan, who had dreamed of this for years, gave the obvious reply—they had no money. Train remarked quietly, "I will give you the money." That same night he announced from the platform that a woman suffrage paper would be published, with Elizabeth Cady Stanton and Susan B. Anthony in charge, as soon as these ladies returned to New York. Susan could not believe her ears. She was still racing about in a twosome with Train and had not seen Mrs. Stanton in weeks. She would have to be consulted, and quickly. With Train's driving genius at her elbow, time was of the essence.

She was due to meet Mrs. Stanton in Leavenworth on the night before the election. Meantime she had also become separated from her traveling companion. She felt she could not meet Mrs. Stanton without seeing Train beforehand and hearing him confirm with his own lips his amazing and impromptu offer. On the Sunday before Leavenworth, she was speaking in Atchison in the place of Train, who had been detained by a railway accident in St. Joseph. The broad Missouri River flowed between them. This was the night when she was rowed across the river in a light skiff (all the ferries having stopped) by a chivalrous ex-army captain to see Train. When she saw him, he not only confirmed the offer but proposed further that Susan and Mrs. Stanton should join him in a lecture tour on the way back East—with all arrangements and expenses to be taken care of by him.

Neither Susan nor Mrs. Stanton hesitated to accept these offers, newspaper and lecture tour alike. They were in no mood to look behind a proffered favor for motives, as long as the favor promoted woman suffrage. The meetings began in Omaha (where Train had large real estate interests) and continued through such large cities as Chicago, Springfield, St. Louis, Louisville, Cincinnati, Cleveland, Buffalo, Rochester, Syracuse, Albany, Springfield (Mass.), Worcester, Boston, Hartford, and New York. All the arrangements were made by telegraph, for which Mr. Train unshrinkingly paid one hundred dollars while Susan looked on aghast. The largest local halls were engaged for the meetings and the best hotels patronized for the ladies' accommodations. It seemed as if their host was trying to make up to them for their hard long weeks of traveling through rural Kansas. It must have taxed their speaking ability to the uttermost to address so many large audiences in such a short space of time—one month by the calendar. But they thought nothing of their own contribution by comparison with the three thousand dollars which Mr. Train paid out for the tour in cold cash. In her old age Susan remembered it as the most luxurious campaign trip she had ever taken in her whole life.

Under the influence of Train's informality Susan dashed off this note to Anna Dickinson, dated November 28, 1867:

On Cars Louisville to Cincinnati
Dear Anna:—The enclosed slips will indicate my alarm lest you, the Anna Dick, are off the track. . . . For I see your speech is not *The New Republic*, is not *Woman*, but only the black man. I tell you Anna, rats—that is, female rats—ought to know enough to leave a sinking ship. I just told this to Mr. Train. He says You ought to write that *stinking ship*. . . . The position of the Republican Party and all men who go only manhood suffrage . . . is terribly insulting to you and me and every woman of us—and to see you piping for it is sad, sad. But if you can't see—you can't—that's all. I hope to see you ere long, darling.

S.B.A.

When the singular trio arrived in New York the news of their tour had long preceded them. The first announcement had provoked an outburst of protest from the East. Friends had sent telegrams of disapproval to Susan and Mrs. Stanton in Kansas. As the tour progressed, expressions of displeasure still came in. As the publicity grew, the expressions became more intensified. Could it possibly be that the picture of these two woman suffragists, hitherto thought of almost as medicants, traveling in luxury, speaking in expensive halls, living in comfort, aroused a spark of envy? No. The horrified protest was based on principle, on the desire that a dignified reform like woman suffrage should be associated only with irreproachable public characters. George Francis Train could scarcely qualify for this category. He was a Democrat and an eccentric character. He was even reported to have said some disrespectful things about the Negro. To the Republican party, which used the Negro as a cover for every exploitative and grasping scheme that could be thought up, this made his name anathema. That Susan and Mrs. Stanton should associate themselves intimately with him was unthinkable. In the eyes of their former Abolitionist friends, degradation could go no farther. Garrison and Phillips at last had a real charge against them.

◄§ III   Susan and Mrs. Stanton were at first unaware of their official ostracism. They were living in a dream at last realized. They had great business on their hands. With Don Quixote in command, they were engaged in no less a task than starting a weekly newspaper.

Train had a remarkably creative mind. On the night when he had first announced the forthcoming publication, he had added: "Its name is to be the *Revolution*; its motto, 'Men, their rights, and nothing more; women, their rights, and nothing less.' This paper is to be a weekly, price $2.00 per year; its editors, Elizabeth Cady Stanton and Parker Pillsbury; its proprietor, Susan B. Anthony."

He had evidently got most of this out of Susan without her knowing it. It was her plan, in the main, half consciously, half unconsciously formulated. The question of having a woman suffrage paper had been talked about for years by Susan and her friends. She had discussed it many times with Lucy Stone and Antoinette Blackwell. They had all agreed that Mrs. Stanton should be the editor if the paper should ever come into being. "I am afraid it will be too late for her," Mrs. Blackwell had once written, "when we get it fairly established, which does not promise to be very soon." So Susan's discussions with the Blackwells and others had only amounted to preliminary imaginings, pipedreams recognized as such.

The most interesting detail was the title chosen for the paper: the *Revolution*. It was probably contributed indirectly by Mrs. Stanton. In her articles and speeches of the time she habitually referred to the Civil War and its consequences as the "second Revolution" through which the nation was passing. She saw clearly, even at the time, the full significance of passing events and gave the era its proper title, the second *Revolution* in American history. One

needs only to glance through her writings in the *History* to realize
how often she expressed the idea. Hence the *Revolution* was the
most likely name to be chosen by Susan, or by Train, for a timely
newspaper.

Train was a New Englander with a thoroughly conservative ancestry and background with which he had broken early in life. He
was thirty-eight when he first met Susan (she was forty-seven), a
striking-looking man with a dark complexion and very abundant
curly, almost grizzled black hair. He had a foreign, rather exotic
appearance, partly counteracted by the extreme carefulness with
which he groomed and valeted himself. His personal manners were
on a par with his dress—all of which formed a part of the correct,
outward Train. Inwardly he was without respect for persons or conventions unless they corresponded with his own instincts. For a
New Englander he was an oddity, not to be understood or explained by any existing standard or storied legend of the region.

By profession he was a financier. His business was money-making.
As little as it might appear from his beneficent relations with Susan
and Mrs. Stanton, profiteering was his dominant occupation. Had
he been single-minded in his aims and purposes he might have become one of the first millionaires of the country. He guided the
formation of the Crédit Mobilier, the corporation that financed the
Union Pacific Railway, the first railway to bridge the gap between
Omaha and Utah. He devised the corporation, but for some unknown reason was subsequently eased out—or squeezed out—from
the enterprise. This had some advantages, for when the Union
Pacific came under congressional investigation starting in 1867,
Train was in no way inculpated. His share in the enterprise was to
lay out "boom" towns and speculate in building lots along the railway. It netted him a fortune but no great one. Nobody was interested in buying homes; the vast crew of workers were interested
only in moving onward to California with the railroad. Rather
bored with the undertaking, he turned his back on it to go to the
rescue of some ladies he saw in distress.

While sojourning in the West, Train had acquired another unpopular cause besides woman suffrage. Lincoln's greenbacks, legal
tender since 1862, had become the beloved money of Western
farmers and laborers. Greenbackism had started as a movement. As
the post-war government prepared to retire them, the Westerners

became more heated in their defense. To the financial interests of the East, the bankers and bondholders, the paper money was maddening. But it would take a long time and a hard fight before they could abolish it.

Before that time came, the Greenbackers were destined to leave their mark on American history. In 1867 their long battle was only beginning, but the struggle was foreseen. The wizards of finance saw the first signs of the Greenback heresy wherever they appeared. Train, by embracing the cause and making lively speeches for it in the West, became an added advertisement and thereby an acute pain to the financial interests of Boston and New York.

Among the other more casual performances that shocked his Eastern critics was his announcement of his candidacy for the office of President. This was regarded by his more humorless enemies as proof that Train was insane. The announcement that called down this accusation on his head was made in one of his Kansas speeches. He had said, closing a suffrage speech:

"No, these women are no foreign emissaries. No, Mrs. Cady Stanton, Miss Susan B. Anthony, Mrs. Lucy Stone, and Miss Olympia Brown are the foreign emissaries that will alone have the credit of emancipating women in Kansas. Where is Wendell Phillips today? . . . Where is William Lloyd Garrison? . . . Where is Henry Ward Beecher? . . . Where is Theodore Tilton? . . . Where is George W. Curtis? . . . Not one of their old army generals at hand; nobody but the rank and file of the Democratic party, and that wonderful, eccentric, independent, extraordinary genius and political reformer of America, who is sweeping off all the politicians before him like a hurricane, your modest, diffident, unassuming friend, the future President of America, George Francis Train!"

With similar gaiety he announced in another speech made somewhat later:

"I intend to have all boys between 18 and 21 vote in 1872. Young men who could fire a Bullet for the Union should be allowed to throw a Ballot for their country."

Susan and Mrs. Stanton, grateful for his suffrage help, totally unversed in the technicalities of high finance, extended the right hand of fellowship to the irrepressible Train. Unwittingly they introduced to their fellow suffragists in the East, as their new comrade-in-arms, this serpent in the bankers' Eden.

✒️ IV Susan and Train were a fast team of workers. They had the first copy of the *Revolution* on the newsstands on January 8, 1868—less than a month after they came to New York. The first copy was as good in print and paper as those that followed it—a high standard which they maintained to the last. In materials and workmanship they used only the best, as one can see today by comparing the weekly with the yellowed and faded relics of its contemporaries. Elizabeth Cady Stanton and Parker Pillsbury appeared as editors, Susan B. Anthony as proprietor and manager. Their office was 37 Park Row, New York. The motto had been slightly changed: "Principle, not Policy; Justice, not Favors" was now on the masthead.

Parker Pillsbury came over to the *Revolution* directly from the *Anti-Slavery Standard*. He had disapproved of the Hovey Committee's action in withholding funds from the suffragists and resigned his position on the *Standard* in protest. Susan and Mrs. Stanton welcomed him to the *Revolution*. Pillsbury wrote the leaders, Mrs. Stanton the articles and items, and Susan's indomitable drive underlay and underwrote the expenses.

Train's name was not on the masthead. He appeared only as columnist. In a single short column he reported dealings on the Stock Exchange and other financial news, but not under his name. The cloven hoof appeared in the phrases with which he headed his department: "Gold, like our Cotton and Corn, for sale. Greenbacks for money: An American System of Finance." He had a partner in David M. Melliss, financial editor of the New York *World*, a name unknown to fame except through its brief association with the publishers of the *Revolution*. Melliss, like Train, put up money to support the paper. In Train's column he aired the unorthodox financial views which would have cost him his job on the *World*. While this feature formed a comparatively unimportant appendage in the eyes of Susan and Mrs. Stanton, it was not so viewed by the less innocent part of the public. Here, in the heart of New York, a stone's throw from Wall Street, the suffragists were issuing a paper that preached the heresy of Greenbackism.

The *Revolution* received scant welcome from the other papers of the city. Horace Greeley's *Tribune* ignored it; so did the *Anti-Slavery Standard*, which furthermore would not accept a paid advertisement of the paper for its columns. The *World* and the *Sun* acknowledged the entrance into the field of a spirited woman's rights weekly. Neither of them paid any attention to Train, so far ahead of him in fame were Susan and Mrs. Stanton. The primary heterodoxy of the *Revolution* appeared to be, as it was planned, the espousal of woman suffrage. The critics of the press focused their attention on the franchise issue. Henry J. Raymond of the New York *Times* disposed of the paper for his readers with a heavy-handed editorial entitled "The Ladies Militant":

It is out at last. If the women, as a body, have not succeeded in getting up a revolution, Susan B. Anthony, as their representative, has. Her *Revolution* was issued last Thursday as a sort of New York's gift to what she considered a yearning public, and it is said to be "charged to the muzzle with literary nitro-glycerine."

If Mrs. Stanton would attend a little more to her domestic duties and a little less to those of the great public, perhaps she would exalt her sex quite as much as she does by quixotically fighting wind-mills in their gratuitous behalf, and she might possibly set a notable example of domestic felicity. No married woman can convert herself into a feminine knight of the Rueful Visage and ride about the country attempting to redress imaginary wrongs, without leaving her own household in a neglected condition that must be an eloquent witness against her. As for the spinsters, we have often said that every woman has a natural and inalienable right to a good husband and a pretty baby. When, by proper "agitation," she has secured this right, she best honors herself and her sex by leaving public affairs behind her, and by endeavoring to show how happy she can make the little world of which she has just become the brilliant centre.

Only Theodore Tilton, editor of the *Independent*, gave the *Revolution* a real welcome and a sprightly Godspeed. But Tilton was known to be a good suffragist and a personal friend of Mrs. Stanton's.

Mrs. Stanton knew how to deal with critics like Henry J. Raymond. The conservative knight, burdened by his trappings, was easy prey for her lively pen, which darted here and there to pierce the weak points in his armor. Susan and Mrs. Stanton were rather enlivened by such attacks than otherwise. What saddened them were the formidable arrows directed at them by their old Abolitionist friends. Unlike the New York press, they did not overlook the column by Train.

In its fourth issue the *Revolution* published a letter from William Lloyd Garrison denouncing Train with remarkable energy:

Dear Miss Anthony:—In all friendliness and with the highest regard for the Woman's Rights movement, I can not refrain from expressing my regret and astonishment that you and Mrs. Stanton should have taken such leave of good sense, and departed so far from true self-respect, as to be travelling companions and associate lecturers with that crack-brained harlequin and semi-lunatic, George Francis Train! You may, if you choose, denounce Henry Ward Beecher and Wendell Phillips (the two ablest advocates of Woman's Rights on this side of the Atlantic), and swap them off for the nondescript Train; but, in thus doing, you will only subject yourselves to merited ridicule and condemnation, and turn the movement which you aim to promote into unnecessary contempt. The nomination of this ranting egotist and low blackguard for the Presidency, by your audiences, shows that he is regarded by those who listen to him as on a par with the poor demented Mellen, and "Daniel Pratt, the Great American Traveller." . . . He is as destitute of principle as he is of sense, and is in fact gravitating toward a lunatic asylum. He may be of use in drawing an audience; but so would a kangaroo, a gorilla, or a hippopotamus. . . .

Garrison rebuked the Greenbacker openly for holding unsound monetary views. He denounced him as a "mountebank and charlatan," considering his financial views as simply a part of his lunacy. Garrison was never much concerned about conditions in the financial world. As Parrington relates, he began life as "a village editor . . . with unconscious naïveté espousing the cause of Boston commercialism. . . . Up to the age of the early twenties he was going along with the crowd." Even when he changed into the fearless and flaming champion of freedom for the slaves, he was still going along with the commercial crowd. His great conversion left his politics and economics practically untouched. In conservative Boston, where he always lived, he found no reason to quarrel with the system around him. He was without imagination on a subject that intrigued a mind like Train's and he could not believe that the man sincerely held the beliefs that he avowed. To him "greenbacker" and "charlatan" were one and the same.

It was Susan's contradictory fate to be influenced both by Garrison's greatness and by his littleness. He induced her to enter the Abolitionist movement which occupied ten years of her life and to which she rendered so much noble service. Her association with Train, however, banished her forever from his good graces and cherished memories. To judge from Garrison's biography, as written by his sons, it blotted out for him forever the place she had earned in the history of his great cause. The same was true of Mrs. Stanton.

The militant pair were in natural course cast off by Wendell Phillips as well. Phillips sent no letter to be blandly exposed by the culprits in the pages of their journal. He rebuked them, however, with a gesture that was just as great a mistake. He snubbed Mrs. Stanton at a Boston reception. We take the story from an item in the Springfield *Republican*, as reported by its correspondent "Warrington," a lifetime friend of the suffragists:

Boston, Jan. 31, 1870.—Mrs. Stanton first appeared nearly a week ago, and excited the first alarm by appearing uninvited at . . . the Anti-Slavery festival. In a group of people, as the story goes, a niece of Wendell Phillips, seeing that he took no notice of Mrs. Stanton, said more than once, "Mr. Phillips, this is Mrs. Stanton,"—and then, as Mrs. Stanton came forward with her hand extended, Mr. Phillips put both hands behind him after the example of Dr. Johnson on a similar occasion, drew back and refused to speak to the lady.

How deeply all this hurt can be imagined. Susan and Mrs. Stanton put on a brave, even a fighting front, but they felt their disownment deeply. The men to whom they had looked so long for approval and inspiration had become their enemies. When Mrs. Stanton recalled how Phillips had espoused the women's cause in London in 1840 and how Garrison had sat a lone man in the women's gallery, she could not reconcile those days with what was now happening. When she and Susan together recalled the valorous days of the 1850s when they had stumped New York, braving mobs and defying rowdies, but upheld in their course by the same men who were now affronting them, they could not accept the present reality. The worst dagger thrust of all was the inevitable question, were they doing right?

Fortunately they were both protected from deep inner misery by their native optimism. Fortunately, also, there was the ceaseless activity of getting out every week sixteen pages of newspaper with an insufficient staff, insufficient funds, insufficient advertising, and insufficient subscribers. There was a high standard of contents to be achieved and sustained. No matter what their former friends said, did, or circulated, they had little time for grieving.

&§ V   The *Revolution* had its own domestic problems. The paper was scarcely launched when the first misfortune took place. The ever-active Train appeared in Susan's office one morning and announced casually that he was about to leave for England. Susan was appalled. She did not realize that her sponsor had just accomplished an enormous feat for her sake. He had spent a whole month on a single exclusive enterprise. The project was now launched; it was time for the introverts to take over and leave the extrovert to go about his proper business.

Train told Susan that Mr. Melliss would conduct his column and supply any needed funds in his absence, and that he was leaving her six hundred dollars in cash with which to carry on. With these few amenities Don Quixote sprang upon Rosinante and took off. Susan was left with a feeling that her foundations had suddenly collapsed. She wrote in her diary, "My heart sank within me; only our first number issued and our strongest helper and inspirer to leave us!" She had come to lean on Train not only for his financial support but for the priceless boon of his exuberant spirits. With her usual stoicism she concluded: "This is but another discipline to teach us that we must stand on our own feet."

Prominent in Train's repertoire of liberal causes was Fenianism, the Irish national movement. Fenianism, then at its peak in Ireland, was likewise extremely active in America and of course in England. In the same year, 1868, a Fenian riot occurred in Manchester, of which a ten-year-old girl named Emmeline Goulden was an interested spectator. Years later, as Emmeline Pankhurst, she recalled the affair, which ended with the hanging of three Fenian leaders, as one of the early influences that had turned her thoughts toward social injustices. Some event of the kind, possibly this very one, had induced Train to start pell-mell for England.

The British Government had heard of the American Train, who had recently spoken at a Fenian demonstration in Philadelphia. It had no intention of allowing such a subversive influence to land on British soil. Government agents met his ship at Queenstown and without a pretense of legality removed him from the ship and confined him in a Dublin jail. He was allowed to exchange the jail for a Dublin hotel, where he was kept for the next ten months under police surveillance. He had told Susan he was making a short trip, but he was gone for a year.

Handicapped as he was, Train did not forget his interest in the *Revolution*. He kept up a lively correspondence, narrating his experiences, in particular his arrest and imprisonment. This of course did nothing to improve the reputation of the *Revolution* among the more respectable and law-abiding. In his account of his arrest he insisted that sample copies of the *Revolution*, which he carried in his baggage, had contributed to his downfall. The government agents, he said, read the name of the paper and without further ado arrested him and confiscated the paper as incriminating evidence. Though interpreted as a specimen of Train's humor, the story could have been and probably was quite true.

He had expected to collect subscriptions and secure contributions in England, but his enforced stay under police supervision put an end to the thought. He could not send any money during the time, while Mr. Melliss gradually exhausted his resources.

On Susan's shoulders fell the burden of keeping the *Revolution* afloat. Neither Mrs. Stanton nor Pillsbury professed to have any knowledge of business. Susan's long experience at running the suffrage movement on a shoestring stood her in good stead. She kept the *Revolution* on the newsstands, though no one could see how she did it. In the effort to secure subscriptions and advertisements she encountered a solid phalanx of resistance around her. It was not only the expected resistance to a woman suffrage paper but, over and above this, the unexpected blockings and stallings of an unexplained character. But she kept plodding onward in the faith that she could one day break down obstacles that she did not fully understand.

⌁§ VI In due course Train returned to America and resumed his active connection with the *Revolution*. He continued his column and expanded his financial theories in some general articles. In one of these he represented Susan, who was as innocent of high finance as a newborn babe, as arguing the merits of Greenbackism with some senators in Washington (the *Revolution*, February 4, 1869). In another article, entitled "Miss Anthony among the Brokers," he portrayed her as calling on Jay Gould and Jim Fisk, the plotters and beneficiaries of the notorious Black Friday which was to shake the world four months later. Incidentally, Susan perceived no signs of the gold plot, for this was one secret of high diplomacy which Train's perspicacity had not penetrated at the time. In his sketch, which was semi-factual, Susan visited the magnates to request half-fare rates on the Erie Railroad for the delegates to the woman's rights convention. She received the concession, as she often did on such occasions. Train's version of the episode runs in part as follows:

An old building stands at the foot of Duane Street, facing the North River. . . . The building is the headquarters of the Erie Railway Company. The second story forms the royal apartments of Prince Erie. The edifice is a combination of the ancient donjon and the modern soap factory.

Some days ago, about 10 o'clock in the morning, a woman was seen rushing down Chambers Street. She was dressed in a neatly-fitted black silk, that had been "turned" but once. A modest-looking bonnet, plainly trimmed, surmounted her chignon, which was about the size of a turnip. A pair of spectacles spanned the bridge of her nose, and she carried a plain parasol of black silk. Her features were regular though angular, and a sharp pair of gray eyes flashed through her spectacles. Drawing her dress slightly above her feet, she dexterously avoided the greasy barrels of pork, mackerel, and hams lining the lower end of Chambers Street . . . and entered the iron grating at the entrance of the donjon.

At the foot of the stairs . . . she met an Italian, swathed in snowy napkins, with . . . three bottles containing borax, hair tonic, and bay rum in his hands. A small paper of gold powder peeped from his vest pocket.

"Is Mr. Jay Gould within?" asked the lady of the Italian. . . .

Here an Irishman, who was sitting on a rough bench near the door, cried out: "Beware, ma'am, of that man. He's only Prince Airy's barber, ma'am. A carriage from the Fith Avenue cum wid 'im!"

Without replying the lady mounted the stairs . . . and entered a small room, containing two mahogany desks and four chairs. Her feet melted into a rich green carpet, soft as thistledown. A dark-complexioned gentleman . . . occupied the desk to her left. He was dressed in exquisite taste, wore a silk tile, Mealio's make. . . . A gentleman in shirt-sleeves, velvet vest, and castor-colored pants was seated at the desk on her right. . . . A diamond, the size of a filbert, winked on his shirt bosom. He also wore a handsome tile.

Glancing at these two gentlemen, the lady drew a copy of the *Revolution* from her pocket and approached the dark-complex-ioned gentleman's desk. . . .

"I am one of the Editors of the *Revolution*. . . . The upholders of the Society for . . . Woman's Rights hold a Convention here this week. We know that you are the friend of every movement that tends to elevate and purify the morals of society. . . . I come to see if you would not reduce the rates of fare on the Erie road for those attending the Convention."

The gentleman in shirt-sleeves stopped his writing and looked as if he had heard the rumbling of an earthquake. Mr. Jay Gould began a lively conversation with Miss Susan B. Anthony, for the lady was none other than she. . . .

"So you are Miss Anthony of the *Revolution?*" inquired Mr. Gould.

"I am," replied Miss Anthony.

"Would it be ungallant of me to inquire who reports the Wall Street gossip for the *Revolution?*" continued Mr. Gould.

"I cannot tell you," answered Susan. "Our reports have created a great sensation. . . . I think you must acknowledge that the Wall Street reports of the *Revolution* are always accurate."

Mr. Gould made no reply. The gentleman in shirt-sleeves . . . arose to his feet, walked to Mr. Gould's desk, looked Susan in the eye for fourteen seconds, and then strode back to his desk. . . .

"I know," said Susan, "that it must worry you gentlemen might-ily to have the secrets of Wall Street laid bare in the *Revolution* every week, but . . . the jobbers are like a set of old women. They all tell stories about one another and the *Revolution* gets hold of these stories. But," she continued . . . "how about reducing the fares for the delegates to the Woman's Rights Convention? I know you have a noble heart, a kind disposition, and a generous——"

"Oh, certainly," interrupted Mr. Gould, "we will reduce the fares."

Here the shirt-sleeved gentleman again jumped to his feet . . . saying:

"Mr. Gould, I wish you would remember that the *Revolution* has done us more harm than have all the other New York journals put together."

Miss Anthony's gray eyes sought the mild blue ones.

"Is this Prince Erie?" she smilingly inquired.

"I am Mr. Fisk, at your service, Madam," replied the prince, gallantly lifting his hat. "Are you the queen of the strong-minded?"

Susan blushed, pulled a hair out of her chin, fastened her eyes on the diamond filbert, and answered: "I am the managing editor of the *Revolution*, with three private secretaries, and I am glad—I may say, I rejoice—to hear that it has done you so much injury. It is a sure indication that it can do the Erie road as much good, when that road is put on a sound basis."

The next number of the *Revolution* contained the glad announcement that those members of the Woman's Rights Convention coming to the city on the Erie road could procure return tickets free on application to Miss Anthony.

Soon after the publication of this sketch Train resigned from the *Revolution*. The hue and cry against the ladies led him to make this chivalrous gesture. The way in which he resigned, going right on contributing anonymously all through the rest of the year and in fact as long as the paper lasted, and the way in which the *Revolution* received his resignation eliminated any good effects that might have been expected from his action. "Our readers," said the *Revolution*, "will find Mr. Train's valedictory in another column. Now we shall look for a harvest of new subscribers as many have written and said to us again and again, if you will only drop Train we will send you subscribers by the hundreds. We hope the fact that Train *has dropped us* will not vitiate these promises." This was not conciliatory enough for the critics. They wanted Susan and Mrs. Stanton to renounce Train publicly and once for all.

&section; VII   There was inevitably some confusion among the women of the Equal Rights Association resulting from the Train alliance. The defection of the women hurt Susan most. For one dark moment at the start of the *Revolution* she and Mrs. Stanton felt they might have to stand alone.

Lucy Stone, who had so recently worked shoulder to shoulder with them in Kansas, was the first to denounce them. In a letter to Anna Dickinson, dated December 10, 1867, she exploded: "For this at least I am glad—that you are not compromised by the spectacle Miss Anthony is making of woman's cause by parading through the country with such a man as Train. It seems to me she can be scarcely less crazy than he is—she used our name to help her get up this most extraordinary lecturing tour *while we knew nothing of it.* The executive committee are very indignant, and justly so, while dear Lucretia Mott says, 'She cannot be President of a Society where such acts as this with Train are possible.' " Lucy Stone concluded her letter with this paradoxical statement: "You have done wisely for yourself by keeping away from us, I mean from our organization."

Mrs. Stone went further and published a card stating that the Equal Rights Association was not responsible for the cross-country lecture tour. Susan and Mrs. Stanton had gone to Kansas on their own responsibility; that is, Susan had raised the money. But they had certainly gone as authorized agents of the society as much as had Lucy Stone and her husband, who preceded them. They did not realize that in continuing their tour at Train's expense they had broken off the connection. They were startled and amazed that Lucy should think so.

In launching the *Revolution* afterward, they therefore took care to explain that they were acting on their own responsibility. Mrs. Stanton made their position perfectly clear. "The secret of all this furor is Republican spite. They want to stave off our question until after the Presidential campaign. They can keep all the women still but Susan and me. They can't control us, therefore the united effort of Republicans, Abolitionists, and certain women to crush us and our paper."

Caroline Dall, long-time suffragist of Boston, echoed Lucy Stone in a speech favorably reported in the Boston newspapers. There the opposition, so well started, began to fail. Lucretia Mott and Martha Wright, the dauntless Coffin sisters, after one stunned moment of surprise, decided to stand by Susan and Mrs. Stanton. "As regards the paper," wrote Martha Wright, "its vigorous pages are what we need. . . . Count on me, now and ever, as your true and unswerving friend." Lydia Maria Child, veteran Abolitionist of Boston, refused to obey the nod and continued friendly. Paulina Wright Davis of Providence, editor of the now defunct *Una*, came to the help of the new journal with a generous gift of money. Alice and Phoebe Cary of New York wrote for its columns and volunteered for office service. Anna Dickinson became a strong supporter of the paper, almost a collaborator.

In fact, the women rallied rather quickly from their first shock and the *Revolution* soon counted scores of important women among its friends. But as always the women themselves had no money. Mrs. Davis's gift of five hundred dollars was a monumental contribution. Susan struggled mightily with finances. Rent was a steady, relentless item. Paper and printing were a heavy expense, to be reduced only by a reduction in quality—an economy which Susan refused to permit. Rebuffed by the advertisers, she returned to lecturing in order to pay the current expenses, while Alice and Phoebe Cary substituted in the office for her. And still the *Revolution* steadily went into debt.

Women on the border line hesitated, were of two minds. Among them was Harriet Beecher Stowe, whom Susan and Mrs. Stanton eagerly desired as a contributor. Mrs. Hooker undertook to arouse Mrs. Stowe's interest and came back with a curious compromise. (Mrs. Hooker specialized in compromises.) She wrote to Susan: "We will give our names as corresponding editors for your paper and agree to furnish at least six articles apiece . . . during the year . . . without promised compensation . . . but on the condition that you will change the name of the paper to *The True Republic* or something equally satisfactory to us."

Susan submitted the proposal to Mrs. Stanton, who was absent on a lecture tour, and received the following reply:

St. Louis, December 28, 1869.—My dear Susan,—As to changing the name of the *Revolution*, I should consider it a great mistake. . . . You and I have not forgotten the conflict of the last twenty years—the ridicule, persecution, denunciation, detraction, the unmixed bitterness of our cup for the past two years, when even friends crucified us. A journal called the *Rosebud* might answer for those who come with kid gloves and perfumes to lay immortal wreaths on the monuments which in sweat and tears others have built; but for us and for that great blacksmith [Pillsbury] of ours who forges such red-hot thunderbolts for Pharisees, hypocrites, and sinners, there is no name like the *Revolution*. . . . But of course I stand by you to the end.

Mrs. Stowe remained firm, and so did the *Revolution*, continuing proudly to float its pennant without the prestige of publishing the most famous author in America. To make up for this and other losses, the editors reprinted serially Mary Wollstonecraft's *Vindication of the Rights of Women* and J. S. Mill's *Subjection of Women*. Still, the subscribers received their money's worth, for these works were not widely distributed and there were no free libraries.

◄§ VIII   Mrs. Stanton's scintillating pen and Pillsbury's trained journalism kept the contents of the paper at a high level. Short, witty paragraphs commenting on the news of the day were Mrs. Stanton's specialty; and while she must have annoyed the Philistines hugely, she must have made the intellectuals laugh heartily. Pillsbury's solid preachments nearby restored the paper's dignity. The editors were a well-balanced pair of collaborators. Absolutely one in principle, they were in personality as far apart as the poles.

The *Revolution* ventured into some unplowed fields. For instance, it devoted a great deal of space to workingwomen's problems. This derived from Susan's initiative and formed her department, though she had some help from Pillsbury, who possessed a slight acquaintance with men's trade unions. Women in the East, especially since the Civil War, were crowding into the labor market. In spite of their growing numbers, they were wholly unorganized, except for those who had long been employed in the New England textile mills. Susan had little knowledge of trade unions, but no one else had much either, including of course most of the workingwomen themselves.

It was Anna Dickinson who encouraged Susan to look into the workingwomen's problems, and she continued to stimulate her interest as time went on. Anna had once worked in the Mint and she possessed a keen eye for the social changes going on around her. She was in no position to guide, for she likewise knew little about the trade-union problem. Susan began boldly by organizing a

Working Women's Association and inviting the members to meet once a week in the *Revolution* office. She furthermore insisted that the printers who got out the *Revolution* should employ women typesetters for the job. This fact she proudly advertised in the pages of the journal. She opened the columns of the *Revolution* to the news of strikes.

In 1869 the *Revolution* published a letter from one Jennie Collins, the leader of a strike in Dover, New Hampshire. Miss Collins reported:

I have said . . . that two looms was a girl's work. Then they reduced their wages and added another loom. Again they cut down and added still another loom. . . . Now a girl's work is six and seven looms. . . . Formerly a piece of cloth measured thirty yards, now there are twelve more added to it . . . at the same price [wage].
There are forty-eight thousand factory girls in Massachusetts. They consume on the average six calico dresses a year, ten yards in the dress. From this you can see that the factory girls are the largest patrons of their employers. We working women will wear fig-leaf dresses before we will patronize the Cocheco Company.

Susan had some background of textile workers from her father's mill in Battenville, which she had known well at the age of eighteen. She was learning a little about labor problems, but she had to learn by experience. During a printers' walkout in New York she thought it would be a good time to advocate the admission of girls to the printer's trade. She attended an employers' meeting and suggested that they start a training school for girls—a suggestion not badly received by her particular audience. To her great surprise, she was promptly attacked by officials of the National Typographical Union, who abused her publicly and soundly. On second thought, she produced a retraction, which she published in the *Revolution*:

I did not mean to convey the impression that women, already good compositors, should work for a cent less per thousand ems than men, and I rejoice most heartily that Typographical Union No. 6 stands so nobly by the women's Typographical Union No. 1 . . . also that the women's Union No. 1 stands so nobly and generously by Typographical Union No. 6 in refusing most advantageous offers to defeat its demands. My advice to all women compositors of the city is now, as it has been since last autumn, to join the women's union, for in union alone there is strength, in union alone there is protection. Everyone should scorn to allow herself to be made a tool to undermine the just prices of men workers; and to avoid this union is necessary. Hence I say, girls, stand by each other and by the men, when they stand by you.

But this was not sufficient for the outraged labor leaders. When a few months later Susan attempted to attend a National Labor Union Congress, the convention with great pleasure voted down her credentials as delegate. The episode was hailed with glee by the anti-suffrage newspapers, which were equally anti-labor but joined for this once with the offended labor leaders. A short time after this a remonstrance against woman suffrage was presented to the Massachusetts Legislature signed by the officers of a working-men's union. The situation was complicated, and the more Susan learned about it, the more complicated it became.

⤙§ IX   The chief function of the *Revolution* was to hammer away at the Fourteenth and Fifteenth amendments, both of which were adopted while the paper was running its course. The amendments, which were drafted to enfranchise the Negroes, gave a sharp setback to woman suffrage by simply ignoring it. The qualification of all voters as "male" did the rest. These years formed the dismal years of woman suffrage. The *Revolution* counteracted their effect to a large extent. Instead of setting back the woman movement, as Garrison claimed it did, it helped to prevent the twilight from settling into darkness. As a visible and loud protest, it kept the suffrage question alive and in the foreground. At a time when organization was weak, the *Revolution* carried on the idea in a literary form, combining staunchness with expression when both were sorely needed.

The *Revolution* ran from January 1868 to May 1870. It ceased because it could not support itself. They were two of the happiest years of Susan's life. She never regretted the cost to her in money, labor, fatigue, and strain. Despite its almost desperate problems, she loved it. Since her childhood days in Adams and Battenville, newspapers rather than books had symbolized for her the nourishment of the intellectual life. Newspapers were in the Anthony blood. Susan's brother in Kansas founded a newspaper and clung to it throughout the rest of his life as his major interest. Susan did not want his kind of newspaper, but she would have preferred above all else in life to publish a sincere reform journal. And here, thanks to Train, she found herself actually doing it. When she arrived every morning at her Park Row office, she arrived on the wings of a dream.

To the end of her days she kept her bound copies of the *Revolution* near her and was frequently seen reading and re-reading the pages. This was not all sentiment and nostalgia, but well-placed appreciation. Even today the pages of the *Revolution* are astonishingly lively and readable.

CHAPTER FIFTEEN

THE SPLIT IN WOMAN'S RIGHTS

✑§ I   The Anthonys were from Massachusetts—from Dartmouth and Adams; they had always lived within its boundaries, first as a colony and then as a state. Susan was born in Massachusetts, in a town that was named for a Boston patriot. But she was never regarded by the Massachusetts suffragists as one of them, nor even as one who originally had sprung from Massachusetts stock.

The Anthonys were Quakers, everywhere an unpretentious people except in Philadelphia, where they had prospered commercially. Furthermore, they were farming people. Susan's grandfather was a farmer and her father continued to be a farmer even after he moved to Rochester. Susan was a farmer's daughter who had risen to the status of schoolteacher.

This was her simple background. When she began to defy convention, it was easy for her critics to attribute her conduct to her background. She was not a born lady. She neglected conventions because she had not been trained in them. It was not to be expected that one of Susan's independence would pay any attention to this attitude. But she was aware of it and showed her awareness on one or two occasions. Writing to her mother from Albany in 1867, she indulged in a little satire: "At the close [of the hearing] the cheerful face and cordial hand of our good Mr. Reynolds were presented to me. Mr. Ely also came up to be introduced, saying he knew my father and brother well, but had never had the pleasure of my acquaintance. Ah, when my 'wild heresies' become 'fashionable

orthodoxies,' won't my acquaintance be a pleasure to other Rochester people too? . . . It is always a great comfort to feel that we
have not distressed our *cultured friends*."

A loyal member of her clan, she was affected by whatever affected
the clan. Anyone who knew her at all knew this. In the summer of
1868, the first year of the *Revolution*, when more personal enmity
surrounded her than at any other time in her life, she suffered a
terrible shock from a crisis within her clan. It was no time for
domestic troubles to imperil her public position, already compromised, according to her enemies, by her ill-considered association with Train.

The crisis in question concerned her brother in Kansas. From
Susan's diary in 1865 we have seen what a tempestuous life Daniel
R. led as a frontier newspaper publisher. The men of Leavenworth
wore firearms and on occasion used them. When Anna Dickinson
visited Leavenworth on a lecture tour after the war, she wrote
scathingly of the place: "It will take one generation here to forget
the lessons of barbarism and another to learn those of civilization."
There was some truth in what she said as well as some exaggeration.

The pitcher that goes so often to the well is broken at last. Three
years after his shooting affray with Colonel Jennison, in which the
latter was shot in the leg, Colonel Anthony became involved in
another shooting episode with one Mr. Satterlee, of which the outcome was fatal. Mr. Satterlee was killed.

Whatever action may have been taken by the criminal court,
suffice it to say that Colonel Anthony was exonerated. This was
not sufficient for the Quaker Society of Rochester, of which Daniel
R. had been a member since 1853. His removal to Leavenworth had
not affected his membership, since no Kansas meeting existed to
which he could be transferred. The Rochester Friends regarded
him as still under their care—"care" being with them a literal and
serious word. Their responsibility reached as far as Leavenworth if
circumstances required it.

There was no avoiding an investigation of Colonel Anthony's
misdeed. The case went through the usual Quaker proceedings.
The preparative meeting formulated the complaint; then, upon
request for more investigation, reformulated it more specifically.
The charge was simply stated: Daniel R. Anthony had "resorted to
the use of a deadly weapon in a personal encounter with K. C. Sat-

terlee thereby causing the death of that individual." A committee was appointed to treat with the accused by the necessary correspondence.

In June the committee informed the meeting that "they had received a communication from [Daniel R. Anthony] in which he acknowledges the complaint to be true, says he does not believe it to be right to take life under any circumstances, it was done under the impulse of the moment to save his own life. That he had never justified the act but is sorry for it and now as ever fully believes in the principles so long maintained by the Society of Friends of which [he says] I am so unworthy a member."

At each of two subsequent monthly meetings the case was brought up for further discussion. In August "the Committee in the case of Daniel R. Anthony now produced a communication from him which was read." (Unfortunately the Quaker records do not quote the contents.) After reading D. R.'s letter the meeting "concluded to retain him as a member" and appointed a new and separate committee so to inform him. But this was not yet the end. The erring man's response to the decision had to be received and considered satisfactory before the decision became final. This fact was not recorded until November, whereas the first entry on the trial was dated in March. Owing to Quaker thoroughness, which regards time as unimportant, the investigation had occupied the greater part of a year. Furthermore, owing to a Quaker rule, no conclusion could be reached unless it was reached unanimously.

To Susan, who had shared in her brother's ordeal, the decision must have brought the greatest comfort. The outcome was one which certainly could not have been foreseen. It still stands as a rare if not unique chapter in Quaker discipline. What counted in the Quaker court was a man's attitude toward his misdeed, and Daniel R. had satisfactorily passed this test. The result rolled one heavy burden from Susan's heart at the end of a comfortless and otherwise much-troubled year.

The whole sorrowful story did nothing to enhance her position with her critics. The more conservative suffragists found cause to shake their heads and wonder if the movement was not in the hands of an unsafe person, rash in her own right and so sadly connected with rashness in her background. Pillsbury and Mrs. Stanton were privately labored with and besought to renounce in time one who seemed to be leading them on to destruction. When Mrs. Stanton and Pillsbury proved obdurate, it was seen that other methods of isolating Susan and the *Revolution* group (which still included Train) would have to be found. That Susan could ever rise above this accumulation of unfortunate associations was more than her enemies could believe.

❧ II   While the *Revolution* existed, the organization of the suffrage movement lagged behind. Susan and Mrs. Stanton had done all they could. The first woman's rights convention held after the war changed its name to the Equal Rights Association, in order to conciliate the Anti-Slavery Society. At the conclusion of this convention the women learned that the Anti-Slavery Society was not to be conciliated. Under the new name the suffragists committed themselves to work for universal suffrage. Henry Ward Beecher made a famous speech in which he upheld the combined issue, saying, "Now, when the red-hot ploughshare of war has opened a furrow in this nation, is the time to put in the seed. . . . Don't wait until quiet times come, until the public mind shuts up altogether. . . . I propose that you take expediency out of the way, and put a principle . . . in place of it—manhood and womanhood suffrage for all."

This was exactly the point of view of Susan and Mrs. Stanton, but the Boston Abolitionists did not share the view. The equal rights convention of May 1868 took place in a troubled atmosphere. T. W. Higginson of the Abolitionist faction said soothingly to Susan, "Now we want everything pleasant and peaceable here, do we not?" He meant just the opposite and showed it by trying, by an unparliamentary ruse, to put Lucy Stone in the chair left vacant by the absence of Lucretia Mott. Susan responded by simply shoving Mrs. Stanton, to whom as first vice-president the chair rightly belonged, along the platform and into her proper place. Higginson's move was followed by the painful experience of hearing her father's old friend Frederick Douglass advise women to subordinate their claims to those of the Negro; in other words, abandon their cause for an indefinite period.

At the next equal rights convention matters came to a head. At this convention, for which Susan had labored indefatigably, securing half fares for delegates and enlisting speakers for the program, the smoldering antagonism against her and her friend burst into flame. A Boston delegate rose and demanded that Susan and Mrs. Stanton resign from the Equal Rights Association, saying that they had repudiated its principles and "the Massachusetts Society could no longer cooperate with them." Frederick Douglass pushed his point further and proposed a resolution endorsing the Fifteenth Amendment. Susan opposed it on the ground that the amendment did not include women. The Equal Rights Association and the Anti-Slavery Society had hitherto been as one and the membership of both was composed largely of men—Abolitionists, of course. At this particular meeting they appear to have formed the majority. Douglass's resolution favoring the Fifteenth Amendment was passed. By the action of its own convention, the Equal Rights Association stood committed to support an amendment granting votes to Negroes and excluding woman suffrage.

Susan saw at last that the parting of the ways had come. It had come with a flash when Ernestine Rose, speaking from the floor, had said, "I suggest that the name of this society be changed from Equal Rights Association to Woman's Suffrage Association." Lucy Stone objected, saying she would not consent to this until the colored man had fully gained his rights. Mrs. Stanton objected, saying that a change of name required a month's notice. Susan heard them both and dismissed their objections: Mrs. Stone's because it defended the status quo which Susan now saw to be impossible, and Mrs. Stanton's because it represented parliamentary law which Susan respected but could also dispense with. Besides, she had no intention of merely changing the name of the old society. Her thoughts had leaped to the formation of a brand-new society.

She saw that there was little time to lose. If she was to rescue the woman suffrage movement from the anti-slavery group who had captured it, she had to act quickly. Very quietly she maneuvered the spontaneous gathering which followed. On Saturday evening, after the convention closed, a reception was held at the New York Woman's Bureau for about one hundred suffrage delegates remaining in the city. The guests came from a number of states, nineteen in all being represented. No woman came altogether unprepared, for the Woman's Bureau was also the office of the *Revolution*, and the *Revolution* had become the dividing line of the movement. At the reception an organization was quickly effected, to be known as the National Woman Suffrage Association; officers were elected, with Mrs. Stanton as president, and a constitution was adopted. The sole purpose of the new organization was to secure the franchise for women. To have prepared all this in one day Susan and Mrs. Stanton must have worked like Trojans.

They had simply bolted the Equal Rights Association and formed an organization of their own. The date was May 15, 1869. Two days later the *Revolution* formally announced the formation of the new organization, which aimed to work "distinctively for Woman Suffrage" and to favor a *sixteenth* amendment for that purpose. The small group must have felt very sad over this breaking of new ground and at the thought of the valuable friends they were leaving behind. But since these friends had completely failed them, there was no actual loss. They were cut down in numbers but regenerated in spirit, purpose, and integrity.

At first they were merely surprised over the smoothness of the transition. Their surprise was reflected in the pages of the *Revolution*, which cheerfully reported from week to week the progress of the new organization. Susan was highly elated when Anna Dickinson consented to inaugurate the new society by an address at Cooper Institute. Two weeks later she kept her promise, entrancing a large audience with one of her best discourses on woman's rights, entitled "Nothing Unreasonable." Susan's hopes for a rejuvenated suffrage movement, led by Anna's invincible young spirit, rose higher and higher.

✑§ III   Lucy Stone and Henry Blackwell were now living in Boston. Once after her marriage Lucy had written to Susan: "I am retiring from the field." Susan had never accepted this as final and had continued to urge Lucy into action during the years when the Blackwells lived in New Jersey. At last she consented, at Susan's insistence, to make the Kansas trip with her husband. The Kansas campaign restored her self-confidence and provided her husband with a congenial experience. He found that he liked speaking for woman suffrage. The following year they were invited to Boston and took a leading part in organizing the New England Suffrage Association.

Julia Ward Howe was persuaded by her friend T. W. Higginson to become its president. Higginson assured her that the organization would be "liberal and friendly, without bitterness or extravagance." Mrs. Howe had been selected for the prestige of her name, associated with a fine literary reputation and celebrated as the author of "The Battle Hymn of the Republic." Through her song she had become a national figure.

Mrs. Howe, a phenomenally cultivated woman, had previously conceived of herself as an ivory-tower character. She prided herself on her culture, which was real but had its odd symptoms. For instance, when she was taken to call on Lincoln right after the "Battle Hymn," she observed that he said, "I once heerd so-and-so tell a story." She noted this down at the time, and it became the chief memory she preserved of her visit to Lincoln. One may deduce from the importance attached to the slight episode how she also must have felt about Susan's homespun qualities, to say nothing of her recent and ill-judged aberrations. In all sincerity she joined up with those desiring to rescue a dignified social reform from those who were bringing odium upon it.

After the formation of the New England Suffrage Association, Lucy Stone and Henry Blackwell left New Jersey and adopted Boston as their permanent residence. Like many others, including Susan and the Stantons, the Blackwells had been unsettled and at loose ends at the close of the war. Blackwell had thought of moving to Chicago, had tried it, but had ended by moving to Boston instead. Whether he had received business inducements or whether the step was taken at the desire of his wife, one does not know. In any case, it had the effect of restoring Lucy to the region of her origin and of placing her in contact with the Abolitionist group. She became the logical standard-bearer and organizer of the Massachusetts suffragists.

In August 1869 Susan was astonished by the appearance of a public announcement. A convention would be held on November 24 and 25 in Cleveland, Ohio, for the purpose of organizing a National Woman Suffrage Association. It was signed by Lucy Stone, T. W. Higginson, Julia Ward Howe, Caroline Severance, and George A. Vibbert. This was immediately followed by a more impressive call with an imposing array of signatures from many states, including many of Susan's oldest and best friends. The call was directed to men and women alike and signed by both sexes.

Susan thought she had just organized a National Woman Suffrage Association, but apparently all she had done was to tip off the New England suffragists that something of the kind was needed. She had intended to leave only the Abolitionists behind, but in her haste and informality she had left the unsuspecting rank and file of suffragists throughout the country to be garnered in—as she said bitterly to Anna Dickinson—by "Lucy Stone and Co." The anger that had first flared up against the Kansas Republicans was again revived in her.

Susan never turned her back on an issue. She attended the American Woman Suffrage Convention in Cleveland. Her presence was noted. An item in the next week's *Revolution* reported: "Judge Bradwell of Chicago moved that Miss Susan B. Anthony, whom he had observed in the audience, be invited to take a seat on the platform. Mr. Higginson thought it was unnecessary as a general invitation had been extended to all desiring thus to identify themselves with the movement. Mr. Bradwell insisted; the resolution was put and carried. Miss Anthony walked to the stage and her appearance was greeted with much applause." Susan had many friends in the audience besides Judge Bradwell—friends who were for the first time becoming aware of what was going on.

Julia Ward Howe's presidential address was scholarly, beautiful, and well delivered, fully justifying her friends' highest expectations. The resolutions for organization were adopted by the meeting. In Lucy Stone's speeches she invariably referred to the organization as the National Woman Suffrage Association. But Henry Blackwell, who drew up the constitution, called it inadvertently the "American Association." So "American" it remained, abandoning the name "National" to the others, which Lucy Stone had not contemplated doing.

Susan's consternation at the *fait accompli* was overwhelming. Despite her occasional impatience with Lucy Stone, she had remained fundamentally loyal to her. Lucy's eloquence alone was enough to enchain her. Only a year before Susan had written to Anna Dickinson that Lucy's speech that day had "surpassed any other mortal woman speaker," adding that this included even the matchless Anna herself. She could never have believed that Lucy would join the outright opposition headed by Phillips and Garrison. But Lucy had done this, and the woman suffrage movement was rent in twain. Without Lucy to head them, the disgruntled Abolitionists would have got nowhere.

At their first convention the American group elected Henry Ward Beecher as president. Susan and Mrs. Stanton were by this time thoroughly disciplined. Beecher had recently stood with them against the policies of these same people whom he now consented to lead. Beecher merely said in explanation: "If there are two general associations for the same purpose, it is because we mean in this great work to do twice as much labor as one society could possibly do." But Susan and Mrs. Stanton knew better. Distressed and bewildered, they saw only the urgent necessity of healing the breach as quickly as possible.

Theodore Tilton, Mrs. Stanton's great friend, made sundry suggestions for reconciliation. Susan had little confidence in him and his remedies, but Mrs. Stanton had much. "What an iceberg is that Boston," Susan wrote to Anna Dickinson. "God help them to their live senses—nothing human can." She outlined Tilton's plan of action, declaring with expressions of the utmost agitation that she would have nothing to do with it. "No, no, I told him, self-respect, self-justice forbid it. I stand plaintiff, not defendant, before that woman and the Boston clique; and though you and Anna [sic] and every friend I love and loves me acknowledge me as having wronged her or them, I shan't, for it would be a lie, and if need be, I'll go alone to my grave with the truth on my lips." But however emotional and confused she waxed in private, in public she subscribed to Tilton's plans, having nothing better to offer in their place.

When the National Woman Suffrage Association met in May 1870, it changed its name meekly to the Union Woman Suffrage Society and elected a man, Theodore Tilton, as president. Tilton and Beecher, still the closest of friends in private life but heading for a sensational break to follow, thus became presidents of the rival organizations. The first action of the new Union Society was to send, through Tilton, a note of greeting and good will to the rival society, which was meeting simultaneously in New York with the intention, Susan said acidly, "of wiping up the Western friends here that week." Beecher replied to Tilton's note with another, equally gracious and complimentary. Nothing had been accomplished.

The Union Society then proceeded to draft a letter to the American Association, proposing that each appoint a committee of conference with the object of merging the two organizations into one. Why this letter was not drafted at once and sent in the place of the complimentary note is not clear. Had Susan been at the controls instead of Tilton, action would have been speedier. As a result, the proposition of the Union Society was not formally presented to the American Association until its next annual meeting. It was then rejected by a large majority vote. But earlier action might have met the same response.

Susan attended this convention, though no other member of the Union Society was present. Her only comment on the meeting reads: "Small audience, only fifty delegates. Poor show." But some unpleasantness had occurred, of which our only surviving account is that of Lucy Stone's daughter, written many years afterward and based on her mother's memories. Alice Stone Blackwell writes: "Miss Anthony made a speech warmly defending Mrs. Stanton's views on divorce, and in the excitement of the moment, she asserted that Mrs. Stone and Mr. Blackwell were not legally married. Col. Higginson, who was presiding, said . . . he himself had married them; and Miss Anthony immediately retracted and apologized."

Susan was alone among many whom she knew to be her detractors. The friendly overtures of her society had just been flatly rejected. In her eagerness to defend Mrs. Stanton, whom the Americans accused of bringing opprobrium on the movement by her espousal of divorce, she had probably pointed out that Mrs. Stone and Mr. Blackwell had also challenged convention by maintaining their separate names. She might even have referred to mistaken impressions that had resulted from this. But that she deliberately stated what she knew to be untrue is hard to believe. In her agitation she must have spoken confusedly, and what she did afterward must have been not to retract but explain—and apologize.

At this same convention Beecher resigned from the presidency, as he did not wish to be a party to what he now saw as a deleterious division in the suffrage ranks. This convention marked the end of all efforts at reconciliation between the National and the American Woman Suffrage associations. Henceforth the two organizations went their separate ways as divided entities. The National Woman Suffrage Association returned to its own name, restored Mrs. Stanton to the presidency, and made no more overtures. It required twenty years and the growth of a new generation to heal the breach that had been so quickly created.

✎§ IV Against the stormy background of the *Revolution* it was comparatively easy to raise money for a sedate woman's journal. If the women were so mad about a paper as the outbreak of the *Revolution* indicated, the Boston Abolitionists decided that they should have one—but on Boston's terms. One of the chief promoters of the idea had long been Lucy Stone. Lucy was a good organizer, a wonderful speaker, and a pioneer suffragist. There was no doubt that she would make a good director of a woman suffrage paper. By her removal to Boston she was made available for the purpose.

While the organization of the American Association was being developed, plans for the publication of a suffragist paper were also quietly being laid. At the Cleveland convention of 1869 a letter from William Lloyd Garrison, congratulating the association, said: "Its organ, should it have one, will not mistake rashness for courage, folly for smartness, cunning for sagacity, badinage for wit, unscrupulousness for fidelity, extravagance for devotion, effrontery for heroism, lunacy for genius, and an incongruous mélange for a simple palatable dish." The proprietor of the *Revolution* sat on the platform at Cleveland and listened. It was her first intimation and forewarning that a rival publication was on the way.

A stock company had been formed to finance the new paper. It was to be no fly-by-night enterprise, dependent on a temperamental "angel," but a real business concern conducted in the best Boston tradition—a tradition of trusteeships, annuity systems, family trusts, and sound funding. Negotiations with Mary A. Livermore of Chicago to become editor-in-chief, with Lucy Stone as assistant editor, were practically completed. Mrs. Livermore had had experience in editing a paper of her own, the *Agitator*, which she had published in Chicago. She was known as an able and facile writer. By another singular coincidence, Mr. Livermore, a Universalist minister, about that time obtained a church in the vicinity of Boston. All these favorable arrangements had been concluded in a remarkably short space of time, and the paper was about to be issued under the name of the *Woman's Journal*. Mrs. Livermore's *Agitator* would be merged and its lively name would pass into oblivion.

The first number appeared on January 8, 1870, two years to the day after the first appearance of the *Revolution*. Associated with Mrs. Livermore as chief editor were Lucy Stone, Julia Ward Howe, William L. Garrison, and T. W. Higginson; and, as business manager, Henry B. Blackwell. Mrs. Howe said in some fear and trepidation in the first number, "This first year of our Journal at least we are determined to live through." She was unduly timid. The *Journal* was locally well insured against failure. Organized by financial experts, the paper had every prospect to survive not only its trial years but many long years afterward. Besides its financial backing, a considerable body of advanced women, such as, for instance, the newly organized Sorosis in New York, were only waiting to support any nice woman's paper that might come along. It became the most long-lived suffrage paper in America, a family memorial of two generations of the Blackwell family. It ceased publication only in 1917, when it became merged with the *Woman Citizen* after almost half a century of individual existence.

෴ V   The effects of the new *Journal* were immediately felt in the *Revolution* office. It dropped the last straw on the overaccumulated burden of financial problems. Every possible economy had been adopted except those which Susan would not permit. No sign of retrenchment or deterioration appeared on the surface of the *Revolution* to its very end. As subscription seeker, loan getter, and general office executive, Susan had exhausted herself in preserving it. She resorted to lecturing, pouring her fees into the all-consuming hopper, and in this way contributed thirteen hundred dollars to the paper during the last two months of its life. Mrs. Stanton was no Maecenas after Susan's pattern. Mr. Stanton had not retained the surveyorship of the port and had returned to a poorly paid law practice and to still more poorly paid newspaper work. Mrs. Stanton had been obliged to resume her lyceum lecturing to pay for the education of her children. With the arrival of the *Woman's Journal* in the field, Mrs. Stanton saw financial ruin ahead and so she told Susan.

Susan's family, always her last resort, joined with Mrs. Stanton in urging retirement. Susan had already borrowed from her mother, and Mary had sacrificed her vacation to work in the *Revolution* office for love. Daniel R. wrote from Kansas: "I know how earnest you are, but you stand alone. . . . You have put in your all and all you can borrow, and all is swallowed up. You are making no provision for the future, and you wrong yourself by so doing. . . . Although you are now fifty years old and have worked like a slave all your life, you have not a dollar to show for it. This is not right. Do make a change." And Mary wrote, after returning home from her tour of duty in Susan's office: "You cannot begin to know how you have changed, and many times every day the tears would fill my eyes if I allowed myself a moment to reflect upon it. . . . We constantly fear that, in some of your hurried business transactions, your enemies will delight to pick you up and make you still more trouble." In some ways Mary was more worldly-wise than Susan.

Finally it was Theodore Tilton, the ever well-intentioned, who brought the matter to a climax. He persuaded Mrs. Laura Curtis Bullard, a wealthy suffragist who had a yearning for a paper and could support one, to purchase the *Revolution*, name and all, exclusive of its indebtedness. Tilton, an experienced editor, offered to help Mrs. Bullard, a tyro, with the editing if she would go ahead. Mrs. Bullard fluttered to the flame. She paid Susan exactly one dollar for the property, while Susan assumed sole responsibility for the paper's indebtedness, which by this time had climbed to ten thousand dollars.

It was a sad day for Susan when she gave up the paper. She had lunch with Tilton, Mrs. Bullard, and some of their friends and that night wrote briefly in her diary: "They decided to take the *Revolution* off my hands." She went straight from this luncheon to Hornellsville, New York, where she had a lecture engagement, and where she received a fee of $150, as much as Anna Dickinson was usually paid. The handwriting on the wall was plain: if she could not run a newspaper she could join the lyceum circuit. She came back to New York for the final obsequies. Signing the papers, she said in her diary, "was like signing my own death-warrant." And she said in a letter written at the same time, "I feel a great, calm sadness like that of a mother binding out a dear child that she could not support."

Late in life Susan told her biographer, Mrs. Harper, that she had "learned the business" and with a little more time she was sure she could have "made it go." This is very doubtful. Her paper had succumbed to the methods of a new regime in the business world which were fast proving their efficacy in disposing of rivals. But she believed her statement. It was many years before she gave up the dream of reviving the *Revolution*. Despite the load of debt that she carried on its account, her thoughts would constantly dwell on some miraculous way of bringing it to life again.

Mrs. Bullard's *Revolution*, which carried on for eighteen months, was never the same paper except in name. It became an inoffensive literary and social journal without winning any new subscribers or advertisers by the change. Mrs. Bullard began to repent her bargain and wrote to Susan, offering to return the paper to her. Susan's first reply was a firm refusal. Then, when the next day's mail brought a notice of a trustees' meeting (she had remained a trustee), she weakly decided to attend it. Her diary tells the story: "Got notice of Trustees' meeting of new *Revolution* for tomorrow at 3 P.M. Ordered carriage at door at 3:30 and walked up to dine at Mrs. Baker's. . . . Got back to 7 Madison Street, found note from Mrs. Stanton advising me to keep out of it. So gave up and sent off carriage."

Evidently she continued in the same state of conflict. A day or so later she took a carriage drive with a friend, and "in getting out of carriage on arriving home," her foot slipped from the stone and she fell "with head flat and hard on the side-walk. Pretty blue and black for a while, but no serious hurt." During the drive just completed they had passed by the family farm on Chili road where no doubt memories of the business failure which had sent her father thither had assailed her mind. Bearing, as they did, a close resemblance to her present predicament, such memories could have been most disturbing. People fall down every day and turn black and blue from their fall, but Susan was seldom one of them. She was unusually active and agile.

Outwardly, before the public, she gave no sign of her turmoil. Her valedictory published in the *Revolution* was matter-of-fact, even lighthearted in tone. It ran:

The public has already been informed (for the secret was stolen by the Paul Prys of the Daily Press before I had a chance to tell it) that Mrs. Laura Curtis Bullard, of Brooklyn, is about to become the chief editor of this journal. . . .

On the 1st of June next, I shall cease to be the *sole* proprietor of the *Revolution*, and shall be free to attend public meetings, wherever so plain and matter-of-fact an old worker as I am can secure a hearing. It gives me a throb of delight to say that this journal, which has always been the idol of my heart, holding the place in my affections which a fond mother gives to a pet child, is to be hereafter more sumptuously cared for, more advantageously brought up, and more elegantly settled in life, than I had ever dared to hope. . . .

This arrangement will be further evidence to my friends of the truth of the old proverb that "The *Revolution* never goes backward." Indeed so much good fortune is coming to me since my fiftieth birthday that some of my friends laughingly fear that I shall die young. But I am first resolved to see the Sixteenth Amendment inscribed on the pages of the Federal Constitution. . . .

Despite the optimism of her words, Susan realized that the true successor of the *Revolution* was the *Woman's Journal*, issuing regularly from Boston and advancing into the sixth month of successful publication. She realized that her initiative and sacrifice had paved the way for the *Journal*. Writing privately to a friend, she said, "None but the good Father can ever begin to know the terrible struggle of those years. I am not complaining, for mine is but the fate of almost every originator or pioneer who has ever opened up a way. I have the joy of knowing that I showed it to be possible to publish an out-and-out woman's paper, and taught other women to enter in and reap where I have sown."

But she was not generous enough to wish her paper turned over utterly to the Boston group. On hearing that Mrs. Bullard was finally abandoning the *Revolution*—after she had decided "to stay out of it"—misery and suspicion once more overwhelmed her. She wrote to Anna Dickinson: "T[heodore] T[ilton] is about to turn my Rev. over to Boston—thus putting in Lucy Stone's hands the prestige, the results of all my hardest 20 years. Well, all right! Such are the fates. So be it. For mercy's sake speak to me once more!!" This ultimate disaster did not happen. Tilton and Mrs. Bullard merely decided to suspend publication.

The division in the suffrage ranks, which culminated in the American Association and the *Woman's Journal*, was a major disaster. As Mrs. Stanton once astutely observed, "Divisions are always the most bitter where there is the least to differ about." Personal hostilities there certainly were, and rather bitter ones. The first break was that between Susan and Mrs. Stanton on the one hand and Wendell Phillips on the other. Mrs. Stanton handled Phillips severely in the pages of the *Revolution*. "Wendell Phillips should have passed," she wrote, "when slavery was abolished, from the *Abolitionist* to the *Statesman*, instead of falling back to the Republican platform." The accusation struck home. She also showed little mercy to Garrison. The secondary hostility was between Lucy Stone and Susan and Mrs. Stanton. Lucy's *amour propre* was hurt by the exclusiveness of their relationship. She had learned with time to tolerate this, when both of them combined to offend her sense of propriety. The question is, how far would the disunion and lack of sympathy have gone if the three had been left to their own feminine resources and devices?

When Mrs. Stanton's son Theodore and her daughter Mrs. Blatch were preparing a two-volume life of Elizabeth Cady Stanton in 1910, they tried to get beneath the surface of this part of their mother's history. They wrote to the only two surviving actors in the historic separation, Mr. Higginson and Mrs. Livermore, and asked them the same question: What was the fundamental cause of the split between the American and the National Woman Suffrage associations? Both responded in much the same way, almost in the same words, saying that papers and letters relating to the controversy had disappeared and along with them the controversy itself in the course of the years. They were not to be inveigled by historical research into the reconsideration of a subject regarded as dead and buried for all time.

The only piece of evidence deriving from the time is an entry in Susan's diary, dated December 18, 1870. The split between the suffrage camps was already an accomplished fact. Wendell Phillips had come to Rochester to speak in the Unitarian church. Susan's diary records: "Sunday.—Mary and self called at W. R. Hallowell's to see Wendell Phillips. Met me cordially, explained the W[oman] S[uffrage] political absorption of Massachusetts. . . . Geo. Claflin, S. E. Sewall, Frank Bird, Robinson and Slack all behind the

Woman's Journal, if the women wouldn't mention W[oman] S[uffrage]. Just as I said, *sold out to Republican party.*" Susan had named the leading Republicans of Massachusetts, who were all known to be theoretical friends of woman suffrage. Her statement of their condition must be taken to mean that the *Journal* was not to "mention" suffrage as an immediate and burning issue but as a desirable reform of the future. The difference was fundamental and it separated the two suffrage groups by an impassable barrier.

If the information given Susan was correct (there is no reason to doubt it), it is easy to see that there were other reasons for the split besides the personal hostilities among the women involved. Susan and Lucy Stone, though temperamentally estranged, might eventually have succeeded in arriving at some *modus vivendi*, working as bad yoke fellows, perhaps, but nevertheless as yoke fellows in the same cause. It was the entrance of outside influences, shrewdly making use of their division, that forced the separation into a deep-seated gulf. If the politicians had not gone into action, the catastrophic split might have been averted.

◁§ VI   While the Eastern suffragists were engrossed in their feud, an event of some importance to them was transpiring in the West. Quietly and at the very time when the split began, the Territory of Wyoming extended the full franchise to women. The principle for which they were waging such a complex war was vindicated by the government of a future state.

Co-operation between the men and the women turned the trick, producing results which surprised the promoters themselves. While male friends in the Territorial Legislature made political opinion, the women made moral propaganda. All hands were united in the chore of civilizing their Wyoming environment. The men were persuaded that the women's vote would help, and the pioneer women knew it would. The politicians of both parties, for their own reasons, promoted and adjusted to the reform. In 1869 the women of Wyoming began to vote.

The news was received by Susan and Mrs. Stanton with surprising calmness at the time. But Susan announced it at the next national suffrage convention in a speech in which she advised women "to emigrate to Wyoming and make a model State of it by sending a woman Senator to the National Capitol." Her own mission, she explained, was to remain in the States and work for a national amendment to enfranchise all women. She had leaped over the Fourteenth and Fifteenth amendments, once for all, to the idea of a sixteenth amendment which should enfranchise all women, as the Negroes had been enfranchised, by a single stroke. And to this idea she was to remain, except for one important divagation, henceforth forever faithful. Wyoming was a happy accident, but it did not go far enough.

Seeking a national amendment, Susan had no concept of the United States as a nation. A civil war had just divided the North from the South; the first transcontinental railway had barely been completed. Susan was still as provincial as were most people of her time. The Abolitionists, though they had obtained a Federal amendment, were equally provincial if not more so. Few reformers in any field had a picture of the country as a union. For most of them the "Union" stopped at Chicago. Susan was more enlightened than most, for her Union went at least as far as Kansas.

Meanwhile the variegated character of the country was such that the Wyoming suffragists voted at the polls while their Eastern counterparts struggled through years of disunion. Twenty years passed without change on either front. In 1890 Wyoming became a state and the women of Wyoming achieved national citizenship. In that same year the long-divided Easterners settled their differences and organized a reunion. It had taken them as long to heal their division as it had taken Wyoming to grow into a state.

⇜§ VII   Fortunately for Susan, she could not see the long road ahead, for she had reached the age of fifty. In those days fifty was regarded as an advanced, not exactly a hoary, age. Mrs. Stanton had yielded to popular opinion in this respect and had long since acknowledged herself to be old, but Susan did not look upon herself as aging in the least. She lived so ardently in the future that she forgot the passage of years. When her friends decided that she deserved the birthday tribute due her age and accomplishments, she was greatly surprised.

A little group of suffragists in New York, who had been close to Susan's life in the city, spontaneously started the affair. They thought that a cordial demonstration by her personal friends would reassure and console her for the troubles of the past year. From close contact they knew how magnificently she had confronted them. The celebration quickly outgrew its original intention. It became a demonstration of her real claim to fame. She had been recently included in an American book called *Eminent Women of the Age*, and her fiftieth birthday celebration went far to confirm her eminence.

Every newspaper in New York—the whole metropolitan press— contained an article on the occasion. Even the *Tribune* relaxed its taboo and produced a tribute to Susan, referring in due course to "Mrs. Henry B. Stanton" as her coadjutor. Greeley's assistant, Mr. Whitelaw Reid, wrote a letter intended to be cordial, saying that while he "deplored" her labors and her aims he wished to express "a hearty, cordial, admiring regard" for the "sincerity and unmistakably disinterested devotion" with which she had pursued them. His letter struck a note which was found in most of the papers. Reserving judgment upon her cause, they proceeded to pay the highest tribute to her personally as a public worker and social reformer.

Along with congratulatory letters, presents and gifts of money poured in. It was perfectly well known that Susan received no salary from her organization or from the *Revolution* and that she put what she earned from lecturing into both causes. Anna Dickinson sent her a gray silk gown and two hundred dollars. The Beechers, the Tiltons, her brother, her sister, and many friends sent checks for fifty dollars. In all, the birthday donations amounted to one thousand dollars. Though this did not even reimburse her for what she had sunk within the last two months in the *Revolution*, it was all voluntary and heart-warming. Susan had dedicated her life to a permanent deficit, and anything that reduced it floated her higher up in the current.

The reception was held at the Woman's Bureau, which had been tastefully furnished by one of the more prosperous sponsors of the suffrage cause. The bright gaslights and Victorian upholstery gave the rooms a tone of fashion and elegance. The only disappointment for Susan was Mrs. Stanton's absence; being ill, she did not appear. Perhaps she feared that from egregious old habit she would "steal the show" from her friend. Tall, amiable, smiling, gowned in a red and black dress of the popular "changeable" silk, wearing her usual fine white lace collar and cuffs, Susan reigned alone over the gay assembly. She did not look her age; no one could have guessed it if she had ever once in her whole truthful life thought of concealing it.

The Cary sisters, who specialized as party givers, added their social talents to those of the other hostesses. Phoebe Cary had composed a poem whose Victorian puns evoked many laughs and of which one stanza ran:

> She might have chosen an honored name,
>   And none had scorned or hissed it;
> Have written Mrs. Jones or Smith,
>   But, strange to say, she Missed it.

Susan tried to say a few words of appreciation in the vein of the evening, but before she was well started she launched into a suffrage talk urging all present to join her in working for a sixteenth amendment.

That night she wrote to her mother: "I can see the old home—the brick-makers—the dinner pails—the sick mother—the few years of more fear than hope in the new house, and the hard years since. And yet with it all, I know there was an undercurrent of joy and love which makes the summing-up vastly in their favor. How I wish that you and Mary and Hannah and Guelma could have been here—and yet it is nothing—and yet it is much." Then she turned to her diary and wrote: "Fiftieth birthday! One half-century done, one score of it hard labor for bettering humanity—temperance—emancipation—enfranchisement—oh, such a struggle! Terribly stormy night, but a goodly company and many, many splendid tributes to my work. Really, if I had been dead and these the last words, neither press nor friends could have been more generous and appreciative."

Many of her friends did indeed look on this occasion as a kind of finish. She had already put in twenty years of hard labor for the cause. In the mood of the moment she was inclined to agree with them.

CHAPTER SIXTEEN

GOOD TROUPER

‹§ I Even before the Boston contingent split off, Susan had conceived the idea of holding the annual suffragist conventions in Washington. The Boston contingent, wishing to form a national organization, proceeded to Cleveland, Ohio, ignoring the example set by the New York group. (From the time of President John Adams, it had been hard for Boston patriots to "see" Washington. For them it tended to remain Mr. Jefferson's capital.)

Susan and Mrs. Stanton were not alone responsible for the move to Washington. They were invited by Josephine S. Griffing, the founder of the Freedman's Bureau, who had organized a woman suffrage society in the capital. She was joined by Clara Barton, who had lately given her distinguished support to the suffrage movement. The call was signed by Josephine Griffing and her committee, and read: "All associations friendly to Woman's Rights are invited to send delegates from every state." This caught a few big fish from Kansas, Colorado, and Missouri, but the dominant figures, after the Washington group, came from New York and Philadelphia. Lucretia Mott took the chair, and the editors of the *Revolution* were much in evidence. A woman reporter from Philadelphia said at the end of her story: "To see the three chief figures of this great movement of Woman's Rights [Mrs. Mott, Mrs. Stanton, and Susan] sitting upon a stage in joint council, like the three Parcae or Fates of a new dispensation . . . is assurance that the women of our country . . . have advocates equal to the great demands of their cause." Her words, written in 1869, seem to foreshadow the monument, with the same three historic figures carved in marble, now exhibited in the national Capitol.

One immediate result of meeting in Washington was a closer working relationship with the members of Congress. Wade from Ohio, Julian from Indiana, Pomeroy from Kansas, Wilson from Massachusetts, all strong champions of the women's cause, became personally accessible. On March 15, 1869, immediately following the first national woman suffrage convention, George W. Julian of Indiana introduced a joint resolution in Congress proposing a sixteenth amendment for the enfranchisement of the women of the United States. Susan and Mrs. Stanton henceforth looked to these men as they had formerly looked to the Abolitionists for co-operation and help. The new alliance represented a long step forward in practical politics.

This meant more for the future than they could see at the moment. The present outlook was otherwise discouraging. The New York society, in the hands of caretaker Theodore Tilton, was languishing. In writing to an English correspondent Susan said it "seemed not less likely than the Cleveland movement to be under Republican man-power. You will neither see nor hear [she added] a word from suffrage society or paper which will be in the slightest out of line with the plan and policy of the dominant party. . . . Our movement is at a dead-lock."

If the political movement was dead, public opinion was very much alive, as Susan and Mrs. Stanton, lecturing up and down the country, could clearly perceive. They had only one subject— woman suffrage—and it paid amazingly. Before the end of 1870 Susan had paid sixteen hundred dollars on her *Revolution* debt. Her only problem was to make all the dates that were offered for her unvarying "Power of the Ballot." Mrs. Stanton was putting her children through college on her proceeds. All the people who came to see and hear them did not believe in woman suffrage, but the speakers seldom left an audience without making converts.

The lecture circuit was not an easy life. Mark Twain's letters of those years are full of groans and curses at the hardships he endured, which were certainly not worse and perhaps rather better than some that Susan and Mrs. Stanton endured with less complaint. Mrs. Stanton restricted her travels to eight months in the year, but Susan traversed the circuit for the whole year. She would interrupt her journey or cancel her engagements only if suffrage business arose. With her great proclivity for letter writing she kept sufficiently in touch with the "friends" to know where she was needed.

In October 1870 such a need arose and she rushed to the rescue of Paulina Wright Davis, who, though a New Englander, had stuck with the New York group. Mrs. Davis had planned a celebration in honor of the first national woman's rights convention ever held in the country. It would take place in New York, with Mrs. Davis, who was a woman of means, paying all the expenses. What she asked of the National Woman Suffrage Association was only interest, co-operation, and moral support. Susan, far out in the West, suspected that she would not receive much help from a society vegetating in the hands of Theodore Tilton. She rushed back to New York.

She was at once met by despairing appeals from "the friends" to call off the celebration. Her diary tells the story: "Mrs. Bullard took me in carriage to lunch with Mrs. Phelps. Mrs. Wilbour came. Each gave me $5.00 to go to Providence to get Mrs. Davis to throw up the Decade [celebration]." Susan left for Providence that evening and arrived at 4 A.M. "Took a carriage to Mrs. Davis," says the diary. "Woke her up. She came to the door. I got in bed with her, and not a wink did she or I sleep." By morning both Mrs. Davis and Susan had resolved that the meeting must go on. They telegraphed this decision to New York. The answer came back that it was too late; the notice of abandonment was already in the *Revolution*. "Mrs. Davis was frantic," says the diary. Susan was not. She boarded the first train for New York and after a series of changes reached Tilton's door the next morning. Mrs. Bullard's husband, a man of business and influence, was conscripted to "get countermand of abandonment in City exchange papers and an item in Associated Press of the error." The celebration was saved, and the three ladies who had set out to stop it were as pleased as everyone else.

They held a lively and successful convention. Mrs. Davis's history of the past twenty years of the movement proved a heartening antidote to the present gloomy outlook. Susan urged the suffragists to ally themselves with no political party until and except such a political party actively endorsed woman suffrage. There were letters from distinguished friends abroad and some foreign guests were present, including the indomitable Mrs. Wolstenholme Elmy from England, who would sanction with her aged presence a suffrage demonstration in London some thirty-five years hence.

۶۶ II At the close of 1870 Susan was summoned home by the illness of Thomas King McLean, her sister Guelma's only son. Five years before, the McLeans had lost a daughter, just blooming into womanhood; and now their only son, aged twenty-one, was doomed to follow her. He was due to graduate from Rochester University in the following year. When Susan arrived on the first of December his condition was critical. As was the case with her beloved niece she had come home just in time to see him die.

Stoical as her Quaker rule required, she went away on the night of his funeral to meet a lecture engagement. But she was intensely shocked by this second tragedy. A week or so later she was drawn back to her home to render what comfort she could to the bereaved parents. She found that her sister Guelma's health, already poor, had been further reduced by grief. For herself, she mourned the loss of the feeling of youth in the house. "Oh, how sad," she wrote in the diary; "what a vacancy, what a silence! No Thomas King to come in from college, to play the piano, and sing." But no matter what happened in those lecturing days there was no lingering for Susan. When she left home again it was for a long absence.

۶۶ III It was time for the third national suffrage convention in Washington. Mrs. Isabella Hooker thought that Susan and Mrs. Stanton had earned a holiday and for once they should be free to pursue their own careers. She offered to undertake the Washington convention to the last detail, including the raising of the money for necessary expenses. There was a hurried correspondence among the older leaders. Mrs. Stanton wrote to Mrs. Wright: "If Mrs. Hooker thinks she could manage the cause more discreetly and genteelly than we do, I am ready to rest and see the salvation of the Lord." Shrewd, Quaker-bred Mrs. Wright replied: "You

can imagine what success Mrs. Hooker will have with those wily
politicians. She thinks they will come serenely from their seats to
the lobby when she tries 'all the means known to an honest woman.'
I fear the means known to *the other sort* would meet a readier
response." Susan wrote to Mrs. Stanton:

Mrs. Hooker's attitude is not in the least surprising. She is precisely like every new convert in every reform. I have no doubt
but each of the Apostles in turn, as he came into the ranks, believed he could improve on Christ's methods. I know every new
one thought so of Garrison's and Phillips's. The only thing surprising in this case is that you, the pioneer, should say to each of
these converts: "Yes, you may manage. I grant your knowledge,
judgment, taste, culture, are all superior to mine. I resign the good
old craft to you altogether." To my mind there never was such
suicidal letting go as has been yours these last two years. But I
am now teetotally discouraged and shall make no more attempts
to hold you up to what I know is not only the best for our cause,
but equally so for yourself, from the moral standpoint, if not the
financial. . . . How you can excuse yourself is more than I can
understand.

Though Susan resigned all arrangements to Mrs. Hooker, she
canceled eight lecture engagements to be present at the convention. She arrived the day before it opened and found Mrs. Hooker,
for all her brave front, extremely glad to welcome her. In fact,
appalled at the difficulties she encountered, she had written to
Susan beseeching her to come on. Susan was already on her way.

On picking up the newspapers of her one preliminary day, Susan
was surprised to find the front pages carrying not the name of Mrs.
Hooker but that of Mrs. Victoria C. Woodhull. A lone eagle, un-
heralded, had swooped into the suffrage firmament. Solitary and
singlehanded, Victoria Woodhull had applied for and obtained a
hearing before the Judiciary Committee of the House of Representatives. The hearing would take place the next morning, at the
same hour when the national convention was scheduled to begin.
Mrs. Woodhull had not allowed a slight affair like the organized
woman suffrage movement to get in her way. She had not consulted
any one of its leaders. Hers was to be a solo flight.

Susan went out at once to find Mrs. Hooker, who had been a
house guest of Senator Pomeroy's for the past ten days, without

whiffing a sign of Mrs. Woodhull's impending foray. She had learned of it first, as Susan had, in the morning papers. Cast down by the news, she was inclined to ignore an occasion to which she had not been invited. Susan at once told her, however, that they should attend the hearing and find out what this Mrs. Woodhull intended. Senator Pomeroy supported Susan strongly, and together they persuaded Mrs. Hooker to postpone the opening of the convention. Paulina Wright Davis arrived from Providence in time to be added to the exploratory committee. Senator Pomeroy remained in the background but was well replaced by the Honorable A. J. Riddle, a friendly and able attorney of Washington. By the time their preparations were completed, Susan and Mrs. Hooker were almost under the impression that *they* had obtained a hearing before a congressional committee.

On reaching the committee room, Mrs. Woodhull, who had planned things quite otherwise, was much surprised to find that she was to have company. As if by prearranged plan, the solitary petitioner had expanded into a sizable group. The invaders listened with careful attention to Mrs. Woodhull's lengthy and legalistic "Memorial," the gist of which was to claim that she, as a woman, was already empowered by the terms of the Fourteenth Amendment to vote. When she had finished, Susan, Mrs. Hooker, and Mr. Riddle were allowed to make impromptu suffrage addresses.

Surrounded by her newly made friends, Mrs. Woodhull accepted their invitation to attend the opening of the national convention, which had been postponed on her account. She was given a seat of honor on the platform and invited to repeat for the audience the "Memorial" she had read in the morning. Embarrassed by her warm reception, Mrs. Woodhull was at first stiff and tongue-tied; but under Mrs. Hooker's bland encouragement she managed to repeat the "Memorial," though with less fire and fervor than before her morning's congressional and masculine audience.

By a coincidence Mrs. Woodhull traveled back to New York in Susan's company. They were on the same sleeping car. Susan observed her cautiously but saw nothing in her to criticize. On the contrary, she found much to approve. Her diary note on the journey closed with the remark: "Her husband, Col. J. H. Blood, met her on the Jersey side at 6 o'clock, Sunday, A.M." Mrs. Woodhull's domestic affairs seemed to be in order.

Susan had previously heard rumors to the contrary. Mrs. Woodhull and her sister Tennessee (later Tennie C. Claflin) figured as rather *outré* personalities in New York. They were seldom mentioned separately. Beginning their joint career in Ohio as professional spiritualists and healers, they had moved from place to place pursuing their profession. In Pittsburgh they met Cornelius ("Commodore") Vanderbilt, who was old and sick and resorted to them for treatment. On his advice they transferred their activities to New York, where they occupied a house in Great Jones Street in the district known as Greenwich Village. Under the patronage of Vanderbilt they entered the financial field and opened a brokerage business in Broad Street, with the name of Woodhull, Claflin, and Co.: Bankers and Brokers. They prospered and in time branched out again with a publication called *Woodhull and Claflin's Weekly*. At the time when Susan met Victoria in Washington, the *Weekly* had been running for several months and represented an achievement that commanded Susan's respect. She knew how hard it was to publish a paper in New York.

Tennie C. Claflin attracted some attention by her dress. She wore mannish (for that day) suits and a nobby little alpine hat, and she seldom changed her style. Her sister, Mrs. Woodhull, dressed conventionally and very elegantly, as, for instance, her appearance before the Washington committee pleasantly demonstrated. She presented other differences from her sister. She had been married twice. Tennie C. was said to have been once married, but she did not admit it. Mrs. Woodhull's present husband, Colonel J. H. Blood, whom Susan met at the Jersey ferry, performed, as may be seen, his marital duties faithfully. Her former divorced husband, Mr. Woodhull, whose name she continued to wear in public, preserved some kind of relation with the pair whereby he lived in the same Great Jones Street house with them. It was said that he was essential to the sisters' various enterprises. It was true that the text of the "Memorial" and *Woodhull and Claflin's Weekly* required more explanation than the education of the Claflin sisters was able to supply. However useful he may have been, the unconventional domestic situation attracted unfavorable mention and was morally condemned. It suggested a regime shudderingly called "free love" and was regarded as an affront to public decency.

Much of this story developed after Susan's Washington encounter with Mrs. Woodhull. Previous to this her acquaintance with the sisters had been limited to a visit to their brokerage firm. As soon as Woodhull and Claflin had opened business in Broad Street, Susan hastened down for an interview with these pioneer spirits. She found Tennie C. in the office, wrote her down in her notes as "Jennie C." and as "Jennie C." reproduced her in the *Revolution*. (Susan's record as a reporter would scarcely have qualified her for a job on the *Sun*.) Her story was chiefly interesting for its conclusion:

We could not help feeling a great throb of pleasure at meeting, as we passed out, a waiter from a restaurant, with a tray of hot luncheon on his head, and drawing from it an augury of better times to come for women, when they shall vote the right to put food in their mouths and money in their pockets, without asking men's leave.

But Susan did not make much impression on the Claflins. The sisters were absorbed in their own careers as businesswomen and active spiritualists. The *Weekly* was devoted to the promotion of spiritualism. Mrs. Woodhull, especially, was active in the cult, which had an organized following in those days. Ambitious in all respects, she claimed for her "control" no lesser spirit than Demosthenes.

None of this would have brought Mrs. Woodhull into Susan's path had not Mrs. Woodhull suddenly and out of the blue decided to become a suffragist, to head a suffrage movement consisting of herself alone. Susan was ready to welcome a spiritualist or any other kind of -ist who declared for woman suffrage. Furthermore, she was deeply impressed with the argument of Mrs. Woodhull's "Memorial," which had introduced a new gleam of hope into the suffragist line of reasoning.

The idea—that women were citizens of the United States whose privileges and immunities could not be abridged by the action of any state—was based on the Fourteenth Amendment. It was not entirely new when Mrs. Woodhull advanced it. Francis Minor, a St. Louis attorney, had first defended it in a long letter to the *Revolution*. Mr. Riddle, the Washington attorney, appears to have been familiar with it, perhaps through Minor's letter. Whoever wrote Mrs. Woodhull's plea must also have been familiar with it. Two members of the congressional committee which heard the "Memorial" signed a minority report in its favor: Loughridge of Iowa and Butler of Massachusetts. The idea had been slowly growing. What Mrs. Woodhull did for it was to dramatize it with her personality. As a result she presently found herself absorbed into the existing suffrage organization, which was not at all what she had planned. Still, it opened further opportunities.

Out on the lecture circuit Susan saw Mrs. Stanton briefly and reported the good services rendered by the (by now) notorious Mrs. Woodhull. They agreed to take on her defense. Mrs. Stanton had had some slight acquaintance with Victoria, probably through Tilton, who knew everybody both shady and select. She had written a joking note to her more than a year ago. "Dear Mrs. Woodhull: Will you ask Demosthenes if there is any new argument not yet made on the 14th or 15th Amendment that he will bring out through some of us at the coming convention?" A challenge to her "control" was no joke to Victoria, however much it may have seemed so to Mrs. Stanton. Demosthenes had not been ready for last year's convention but apparently had gone into action in time for this last one. Victoria's "Memorial" with its legalistic arguments and abstruse Latin phrases certainly bore the marks of long and ponderous study.

At the May anniversary which followed, Susan and Mrs. Stanton put Mrs. Woodhull on the platform. There was some murmuring in the ranks against this, so Mrs. Stanton had her seated between herself and Lucretia Mott, two bastions of respectability, she judged. Mrs. Woodhull was called on to speak and spoke well. But nothing helped her reputation. The New York newspapers had been alerted. They called the meeting "The Woodhull Convention" and described its purpose not as suffrage but as "free love." To make matters worse, a meeting of the American Woman Suffrage Association was being simultaneously held in the city. To set themselves as far apart as possible from the National gathering, they passed a resolution denouncing "free love." Susan's scorn of their action is seen in her diary: "American Woman Suffrage Meeting . . . passed resolutions saying they were not Free Lovers. Why not one saying that men are not thieves and murderers." Still, she was not entirely satisfied in her mind with the way things were going in her own camp. The next night she wrote a further note: "The great trouble allowing Mrs. Woodhull on our platform." She was slightly worried, but she was not to be stampeded into disowning a woman and a comrade by malicious newspaper attacks.

IV   In May 1871, immediately after the so-called "Woodhull" convention, Susan went to Tenafly. "Spent Sunday with Mrs. Stanton," says the diary, "and she decided to go to California with me. Hattie [later Mrs. Blatch] actually cried half the day, that her mother would go. Too mean—she said."

When Susan was twenty-nine she had longed to join the gold rush. She had said in her diary: "Oh, if I were but a man so that I could go!" The dream had never left her. It had lately been revived when Anna Dickinson accompanied the first trainload of congressmen to cross the continent in 1869. Even at that date Anna had been able to pay the expenses of her trip by lectures in California. After this example set by her paragon, Susan thought she and Mrs. Stanton might do as well in 1871.

In June the faithful companions turned their faces toward California, the fabulous land of the setting sun. They too were seeking gold in a less spectacular form. Hattie had still to finish college and the Revolution debt was far from paid.

From Chicago onward they were in a new world. After being buffeted, abused, and criticized, they seemed to have entered into a friendly haven. Instead of the carping Abolitionists, beaming wellwishers gathered around them. They traveled in luxury. "We have a drawing-room all to ourselves and here we are just as cozy and happy as lovers," wrote Susan. "We look at the prairie schooners slowly moving along with ox-teams, or notice the one cabin-light on the endless plains. . . . Ever since 4 o'clock this morning we have been moving over the soil that is really the land of the free and the home of the brave—Wyoming . . ." At Laramie City they stopped for a while. A crowd of women gathered at the station, and Mrs. Stanton addressed them from the platform of the train like a presidential candidate.

From Wyoming they moved into Utah, wide-eyed with curiosity about the Mormons and unconventionally open-minded about them. For some reason Susan was deeply moved by the atmosphere of the Mormon meetings. Was it because the primitive religious pioneers awakened memories of the Quaker band from which she had sprung? Her reactions, described in a letter to the *Revolution*, took a most exalted turn:

As they sang their songs of freedom, poured out their rejoicings . . . and told of the beatitudes of soul-to-soul communion with the All-Father, my heart was steeped in deepest sympathy with the women around me and, rising at an opportune pause, I asked if a woman and a stranger might be permitted to say a word. At once the entire circle of men on the platform rose and beckoned me forward; and, with a Quaker inspiration not to be repeated, much less put on paper, I asked those men, bubbling over with the divine spirit of freedom for themselves, if they had thought whether the women of their households were to-day rejoicing in like manner? I can not tell what I said—only this I know, that young and beautiful, old and wrinkled women alike wept, and men said, "I wanted to get out-of-doors where I could shout."

She pondered the women's side of it and decided that in the end women, whether as monogamous or as plural wives, had much the same problem to solve—the problem of economic dependence. "The saddest feature here," she wrote, "is that there really is nothing by which these women can earn an independent livelihood for themselves and their children, no manufacturing establishments, no free schools to teach. . . . Woman's work in monogamy and polygamy is one and the same—that of planting her feet on the ground of self-support."

As to polygamy itself, she concluded that the women were not as happy under the system as they were supposed to be. "Our afternoon meeting of women alone was a sad spectacle," she wrote. "There was scarcely a sunny, joyous countenance in the whole three hundred, but a vast number of deep-lined, care-worn, long-suffering faces—more so, even, than those of our own pioneer farmers' and settlers' wives, as I have many times looked into them. . . . Even the most devoted Mormon women say it takes a great deal of grace to accept the other wives."

She talked this over with the Mormon men. As some of them put it to her, was this not better than the system of "variety" which was so widely practiced in the Gentile world and which might confidently be expected to follow polygamy should polygamy be abolished? One man told her of a dream he had had picturing such a change and how the women in his dream did not care for it either. "Away with your man-visions!" Susan loftily replied. "Women propose to reject them all, and begin to dream dreams for themselves." She did not know exactly what she meant, but she knew that she was right.

That the Mormon women would soon vote under the territorial government was a fact that she barely noticed. For once the complexity of the woman problem seemed so great that she could not see the ballot as the sole answer needed. She formed several friendships with Mormon women and decided to regard them as she regarded her conventionally married friends. There were no obvious signs of difference between them and these intelligent Mormon ladies.

The state of California extended a welcoming hand as far as Salt Lake City. Ex-Governor Leland Stanford and Senator-elect Sargent (both with suffragist wives) telegraphed passes on the Union Pacific—passes to San Francisco and throughout the state. On July 9 Susan and Mrs. Stanton reached San Francisco and took lodgings in the Grand Hotel. Susan's dream of twenty years was at last fulfilled; she was in California.

◄§ V   Met by friendly greetings and gorgeous flowers, with passes everywhere, with the state open to her, Susan closed every door in her face with her first public appearance. It happened like this.

The night after their arrival Mrs. Stanton spoke in Platt Hall to an audience of a thousand. The papers gave her fine notices. The next night was Susan's turn. She also had a large audience and her lecture was her usually well-received "Power of the Ballot." She breezed along successfully until near the end, when she casually alluded to a crime of passion then causing much local excitement. A lady of doubtful virtue, named Laura Fair, had shot and killed a prominent citizen and lay in jail awaiting trial. In the development of her theme Susan declared that women needed the ballot for their protection; that the theory that men protected women was a fallacy, since they protected only their own wives and daughters. "If all men had protected all women as they would have their wives and daughters protected, you would have no Laura Fair in your jail tonight," she said. A storm of hisses broke out instantly. Susan waited and, when they stopped, repeated her statement. The hisses came again. Once more she waited, and once more she repeated her statement. The hisses came again, but this time they were mingled with applause and cheers from those who admired her for her courage.

"Every paper came out terrifically against me and my speech last night," says the diary; "never before got such a raking." If Susan had said something similar in New York, probably not too much attention would have been paid to it. The Western city had a certain local pride; Susan was a stranger, an interfering stranger. She was flatly accused of having defended the murderess, and the press showed her no mercy. She had stirred up a hornets' nest.

No one came to her rescue. The local suffrage committees of the state withdrew their requests for her to speak. She wondered miserably in her diary why Mrs. Stanton did not write something to the newspapers in her defense. But Mrs. Stanton was so busy filling lecture engagements up and down the state that she paid no attention to what was happening to Susan. Susan did not ask her help, and Mrs. Stanton most likely feared that with one word from her in her friend's defense *both* of them would go into exile.

The intrepid survivor of so many moral battles had been hit in a vulnerable place. She who had stood up so often and so firmly against public abuse succumbed almost tamely to this onslaught. Her warm reception all along the route from Colorado to Utah had not prepared her for punishment. Her casual discussions of the sex problem in Utah, which had perhaps misled her into committing the *faux pas*, had been no preparation for this California fierceness in defense of convention. "The shadow of the newspapers hangs over me," says the diary. "Some friends called but the clouds over me are so heavy I could not greet them as I would have liked. I never before was so cut down."

Susan's first aid in misfortune had always been nature. Though she often declared she had no poetry in her soul, she was always responsive to the wonder of the inanimate world. The little dabbling in science she had had at Miss Moulson's school had helped rather than hindered a native tendency. The girl who could feel awe at the miracle of a snowflake and at the collection of shells in a Philadelphia museum was open to other marvels of nature. The cure for her condition, therefore, lay close at hand. Though the people were unkind, the fabulous California scenery welcomed her.

Together with Mrs. Stanton she visited the Yosemite Valley, walked among the big trees, and climbed to the Donner and Tahoe lakes. The bloomers left over from their old-time crusade came in handy for horseback riding. She could bestride her man's saddle very featly and negotiate the steepest trails, while Mrs. Stanton, handicapped by her weight, was often obliged to proceed on foot. Susan wrote: "A more used-up mortal than I could not well exist, save poor Mrs. Stanton," who "at six arrived, pretty nearly jelly." After a few such experiences Mrs. Stanton left Susan to proceed by herself, which she did admirably. She would rub her aching muscles at night with spirits of camphor and order her horse for six o'clock the next morning.

She joined with the boldest exploring parties and visited the most inaccessible falls and lakes. Her most exciting experience seems to have been Mirror Lake:

Such a glory mortal never beheld else where. The lake was smooth as finest glass; the lofty granite peaks with their trees and shrubs were reflected more perfectly than costliest mirror ever sent back the face of most beautiful woman, and as the sun slowly emerged from behind a point of rock, the thinnest flakiest white clouds approached or hung round it, and the reflection shaded them with the most delicate, yet most perfect and richest hues of the rainbow. And while we watched and worshipped we trembled lest some rude fish or bubble should break our mirror and forever shadow the picture seemingly wrought for our special eyes that Sunday morning. . . . O, how nothing seemed man-made temples, creeds, and codes!

⊷§ VI Gradually her injured spirits recovered. When the date for her return came round it found her with restored courage but with meager earnings. Thanks to Stanford's passes and the many courtesies shown them, the travelers had enjoyed a maximum of sight-seeing at a minimum of expense. But Mrs. Stanton's profits, amounting to seven hundred dollars, were all they had *between them*. They had agreed to pool the earnings of the trip, and Mrs. Stanton bravely stuck to the bargain. This was another reason, no doubt, why she had failed to defend Susan, preferring to take half a loaf rather than lose all. The golden rewards to which both had looked forward had been cut in half by Susan's indiscretion.

Restored to her normal state of mind, Susan could not tolerate the thought of failure, financial or otherwise. She would go to the uttermost limits of the world before she would consent to that. Besides, during her enforced leisure she had made contact by correspondence with Abigail Scott Duniway, pioneer suffragist of Oregon. Mrs. Duniway had invited her to make a tour through Oregon and Washington.

So when Mrs. Stanton started East, Susan boarded a Pacific liner bound for Portland, Oregon. It was her first sea voyage and she ran into the roughest kind of weather. Aside from the terrible seasickness, she experienced all the terror of threatened shipwreck. "Could not sleep for the thought that every swell might end the ship's struggles." Reaching Portland after seven days, she then and there decided that when she returned to California it would be by overland stage.

Mrs. Duniway was to manage her tour for "one-half the gross proceeds." She met Susan with the assurance of two months of "profitable work." Susan was immensely cheered. Still the shadow of recent events hung over her, and she dreaded her first appearance in Portland. She wrote Mrs. Stanton: "I am awaiting my Wednesday night execution with fear and trembling." In her diary she wrote: "Never dreaded, trembled so, at the prospect before— fear of the press skinning me alive again, as did that of San Francisco." She was still unable to view her mishap objectively. As might have been expected, her talk was well received. The Portland *Oregonian* (which happened to be published by Mrs. Duniway's brother) gave her an excellent notice and introduced her to the state. But she did not need special favors. Her subject was a live one and she was known to be its very best exponent.

Through the roughest kind of travel, by river boat and stage-coach, by mud and corduroy roads, by arriving at 6 P.M. and starting off again at 2 A.M., she managed to keep all the appointments Mrs. Duniway had made for her. The hardships of travel did not irk her as long as the people were friendly. "We find the people everywhere enthusiastic and delighted," wrote Mrs. Duniway, who sometimes traveled with her. In Washington it was the same. Through Walla Walla, Olympia, and way stations Susan reached Seattle. Nothing could now prevent her from penetrating into "Queen Victoria's Kingdom." In Victoria she spoke several times to audiences composed entirely of men, as the English colonial ladies of 1871 did not attend public meetings.

Everywhere she spoke of woman suffrage, and woman suffrage only, and everywhere her talks were respectfully heard. But one Seattle editor penetrated her disguise. "She is a revolutionist [he wrote], aiming at nothing less than the breaking up of the very foundations of society. . . . Woman Suffrage . . . is but a pretext . . . by which to open Pandora's box and let loose . . . a pestilential brood to destroy all that is pure and beautiful in human nature."

Returning to Portland, she suffered a recurrence of her California fear and dread. Here she was almost struck dumb again. "It was the strangest and most unaccountable condition," she said. "The barest, baldest points and no thought beyond. . . . It was the most terrible experience of my life . . . of being compelled to speak when the spirit said nothing but No, No!" In some ways Susan's Quaker training handicapped her as a public speaker. But Mrs. Duniway found no fault with her speech; and Susan was further cheered by the opinion of Bethenia Owens, another Oregon pioneer like Abigail Duniway. The life stories of these women, as she learned them, were as inspiring as any she had ever heard.

Her return trip to California was accomplished wholly by stagecoach. She rode outside with the driver except when excessive rain or snow drove her inside. The November rains increased the mud, which was of incredible tenacity. "It is heavy clay," she wrote, "and rolls up on the wheels until rim, spokes and hub are one solid circle. The wheels cease to turn and . . . then driver and men passengers jump out and with chisels and shingles cut the clay off the wheels." Some of her travel was done by night. In this way she had a fine moonlight view of Mount Shasta, gladly forgoing all rest to gaze at the snow-capped peak. At a few places she stopped overnight and gave lectures—sometimes under the most trying conditions.

At one place they had forgotten to engage a hall; at another, the irate owner forbade its use at the last moment. As she neared San Francisco, her fears began to return, but at Sacramento a dove with an olive branch in its mouth approached her, announcing that the flood was over.

Miss Laura de Force Gordon and quite a number of suffragists had belatedly awakened to the idea that Susan had been unjustly treated by the San Francisco press. Perhaps the boldness of her dash into the far Northwest and the reports of her favorable reception there had helped them to revise their opinion. Californians knew that lecturing through that region required pioneer grit. The greatest influence in her favor was simply that of time. Susan had been away for three months and the public can forget in much less time than this. She found herself cordially welcomed where three months before she had been almost an outcast.

Miss Gordon had secured lecture engagements for her, which Susan filled without a return of the trepidation she had experienced in Portland. Just to show them that she had not changed, however, she gave a lecture on the Social Evil Bill then pending in the Legislature. Some of the California papers even sided with her. Her suffrage arguments were respectfully reported by most of the press. Susan could speak for an hour without once lapsing into flowery rhetoric, and many people seemed to like her the better for this.

On the night before her departure, friends, to the number of fifty, gave her a dinner and reception at the Grand Hotel, and the papers took complimentary notice of the affair. When she left San Francisco, she left as an honored guest. The memories of her former visit were apparently wiped out. Most important of all, they seemed to be wiped out in Susan's mind.

During her stay in the Northwest, Susan had learned from personal experience what the scarcity of women in that region meant. Though she was fifty-one, she looked much younger and, with her restored self-confidence, she gave more thought to her appearance. From Oregon she wrote to Mrs. Stanton: "I want to tell you that with my gray silk, I wore a pink bow at my throat and a narrow pink ribbon in my hair." The effect upon the starved males of the Northwest was all that could have been desired by a more designing woman. Her last letter from Portland to her mother and sister read:

What is more and most of all I received a letter from a gentleman, enclosing testimonials from half a dozen of the prominent men of the city, asking for an interview looking to marriage! I also received a serenade from a millionaire at Olympia. If any of the girls want a rich widower or an equally rich bachelor, here is decidedly the place to get an offer of one. But tell brother Aaron I expect to survive them all and reach home before the New Year, as single-handed and penniless as usual.

VII   Susan left San Francisco on December 15, 1871. She had been invited by Senator Sargent, who was on his way to Washington with his family, to share their accommodations.

They reached Laramie City all right. The next day, New Year's Day, 1872, they ran into a tremendous, magnificent, and world-engulfing snowfall. There they stuck, miles and miles from anywhere, on a steep upgrade at the highest point of the Rockies. Eventually the train moved on slowly and overtook another eastbound train, also engulfed in the drifts. The trains took five days to go from Laramie City to Cheyenne.

The Sargents had had the foresight to bring along extra food and a spirit lamp for making tea. The train supplied the passengers with dried fish and soda crackers and with melted-snow water to wash these down. Mrs. Sargent and Susan made tea and took it to the nursing mothers in the train. At Cheyenne young Georgie Sargent got out to explore, slipped on the snow, and broke his arm. Watching the impromptu and painful process of bonesetting, his mother fainted. It was after this accident that Susan insisted on getting out at Cheyenne to pay a call on Mrs. Amalia Post, one of the Wyoming pioneers who had brought woman suffrage to the territory in 1869. She paid her call and returned to the train without incident.

On New Year's Eve, while the train was speeding toward the blizzard, Susan repaired to a quiet spot aside from the Sargent family circle and meticulously cast up her accounts for the year. She had delivered sixty-three lectures in the East, twenty-six in California, and eighty-two in the Northwest—171 in all. Her receipts for the year amounted to $4,318; her expenses to $2,047. The balance, $2,271, would help pay the *Revolution* debt. At this rate it would take her more than four years to pay off the whole, when she had hoped to wipe it out in two or, at most, three years. California had not paid off, but Susan never wasted any time on empty regrets.

$\iff$ VIII In spite of the blizzard she reached Washington in time for the January convention. Hearing of her adventures, someone asked her if she were not tired. "Why should I be tired?" she replied; "I haven't been doing anything for two weeks." She found all in good order, with Mrs. Stanton and Paulina Wright Davis in charge.

By this time Susan was fully charged with the theory that women could vote under the Fourteenth and Fifteenth amendments. She had tried it out on her Western audiences and had discussed it with Senator Sargent during their long train journey. Sargent had not encouraged her, advising her rather to stick to the plan for a sixteenth amendment. But Susan refused to be thus guided. She launched her theory in the convention and urged it with all the enthusiasm at her command. There was no sign of Mrs. Woodhull, the alleged originator of the idea, at the convention, but Susan needed no help in putting it forth as her favorite scheme. Stirred by her enthusiasm, the convention sent out an urgent call to all women to exercise their right to vote at the coming presidential election.

Susan was obliged to rush back to her lecture assignments. In the spring she lectured through Kansas and Nebraska, making her headquarters at her brothers' homes in Leavenworth and Fort Scott. This meant that in addition to her lecturing she was much absorbed in family affairs. She left all plans and preparations for the May meeting in New York in the hands of Mrs. Stanton and Mrs. Hooker.

Early in March she was suddenly reminded of Mrs. Woodhull. Letters from Mrs. Stanton and Mrs. Hooker informed her that Victoria had suggested turning the National Woman Suffrage Association into a woman's political party and the calling of a meeting for that purpose. It was so well understood among the suffrage leaders that women without votes could not belong to a political party, either an existing party or one of their own, that Susan was surprised and annoyed with her colleagues for entertaining the proposition. She replied at once:

We have no element out of which to make a political party, because there is not a man who would vote a woman suffrage ticket . . . and all our time and words in that direction are simply thrown away. My name must not be used to call any such meeting. . . . Mrs. Woodhull has the advantage of us because she has the newspaper, and she persistently means to run our craft into her port and none other. If she were influenced by women spirits . . . in the direction she steers, I might consent to be a mere sail-hoister for her; but as it is, she is wholly owned and dominated by men spirits . . . reflected through her woman's tongue and pen as if they spoke directly for themselves.

This was certainly clear and definite enough. With the dispatch of her letter, Susan forgot Mrs. Woodhull again. She did not understand Victoria. With Susan an idea was a step toward possible action, but with Victoria an idea was merely a step toward another idea. While Susan was considering the practical application of her original theory, Mrs. Woodhull had been evolving another wholly new one. It came out in an April number of *Woodhull and Claflin's Weekly* in the form of an announcement. Briefly the paragraph stated that the National Woman Suffrage Association proposed the formation of a new People's party, to be organized at its forthcoming May convention, at which a platform would be adopted and candidates for President and Vice-President would be nominated. The names signed beneath were those of Mrs. Stanton, Mrs. Hooker, Mrs. Gage, and Susan B. Anthony.

Susan was sitting in a railroad station in Illinois, waiting for a train, when her eye first caught this notice. A man in the station had casually handed her a copy of *Woodhull and Claflin's Weekly* as something with which to pass the time. Susan's reaction could not have been greater had the kind gentleman handed her a bomb. Her habit of swift decision asserted itself. There was no question of delaying her response. A few telegrams, one of them positively withdrawing her name from the notice, the others canceling some profitable lecture engagements, cleared the deck and she was on her way to New York. She arrived three days ahead of time.

She strove to repair the damage in this short interval. Mrs. Stanton and Mrs. Hooker, caught red-handed, refused to admit their mistake, called her narrow-minded and domineering, and withdrew completely from the management of the convention. Susan was left to handle Mrs. Woodhull as best she could alone.

When the business committee met, as usual, before the convention, Mrs. Woodhull and a group of adherents appeared and announced they would hold a joint session with the suffragist group. Susan routed them with the information that the Convention Hall had been rented in her name and she would not allow its use by any but national suffragists. Mrs. Woodhull was forced to go forth and rent another hall. This was victory number one for Susan.

The next day Susan was presiding over a sadly demoralized convention. Mrs. Stanton had refused to act any longer as president. A most unwilling president, Susan was elected in her stead. Things were limping along badly enough, when Mrs. Woodhull again appeared in their midst and moved from the floor that the convention adjourn, to meet tomorrow with her convention in Apollo Hall. When Susan refused to put the motion, Mrs. Woodhull herself put it—and to Susan's surprise it was carried. Then Susan played her trump card. She declared the whole proceeding out of order since neither Mrs. Woodhull nor many of those voting for the motion were members of the National Woman Suffrage Association. Mrs. Woodhull had neglected to attend to this little matter. This was victory number two for Susan.

Susan then declared the convention adjourned, to meet in the same place the next day. But Mrs. Woodhull, having an audience apparently stacked with so many friends, was moved by her "control" to continue speaking and went on and on. Susan, as the lessee of the hall, ordered the janitor to turn off the lights. She alone had hired the lights as she had hired the hall.

Susan's diary reports the three-day duel as follows: "May 9th.—The Woodhull Co. bound to take possession of the Convention, but failed and left in disgust. . . . May 10th.—Small audience. The fiasco perfect, from calling People's Convention. Never did Mrs. Stanton do so foolish a thing. All came near being lost. . . . May 11th.—I never was so hurt with folly of Mrs. Stanton." And then on May 12, when the convention was over: "Sunday, pleasant day, but sad to me. Our movement as such is so demoralized by the letting go the helm to Woodhull. Though we rescued it, it was as by a hair-breadth escape."

Meanwhile, Mrs. Woodhull organized her "People's party" in Apollo Hall according to schedule. They proceeded to adopt a platform and to nominate Victoria C. Woodhull as a candidate for President of the United States. Mrs. Stanton and Mrs. Hooker began to wake up to the nature of the plot they had so light-mindedly facilitated. But it was too late for them to help Susan.

Susan's anguish was increased by the fact that Mrs. Duniway, at her urgent invitation, had journeyed all the way from Oregon to attend this convention. She was partly rescued by her ever-loyal friend, Dr. Clemence Lozier, who took Mrs. Duniway under her wing and offered her the hospitality of her home for as long as she would like to stay in New York. Susan tried to compensate with what was still in her eyes the choicest of all privileges; she took Mrs. Duniway out to Tenafly to visit Mrs. Stanton.

This was the end of all association between Susan and Victoria Woodhull. It is a curious fact that Mrs. Woodhull, a woman well able to bear a grudge, never afterward showed any grudge toward Susan. She uttered no criticism of her, either in her speeches or in her paper. Neither did she try to win her back, as she did Mrs. Hooker. Shortly after Susan's return home she wrote in the diary: "Letter from Hooker showing she is bound to throw herself into Woodhull's power again. So she will again need the Lord's special help to rescue her." One assumes that Susan stood ready to do the rescuing, should her forebodings be fulfilled, for she liked Mrs. Hooker in spite of her obvious failings. Besides, not only Mrs. Hooker but the tried and seasoned Mrs. Stanton had yielded to the siren's wiles.

Mrs. Woodhull's reaction—or rather her lack of reaction—to Susan's treatment was the expression of a real indifference. She was simply not interested in Susan's type. With her driving egotism, she saw in the woman's movement a chance to exploit her ego; but she quickly perceived, with the clairvoyance of the neurotic, that Susan was not so actuated. With this curious quality of selflessness, she could not attract Mrs. Woodhull. Victoria could not see in so characterless a person a being of much consequence.

CHAPTER SEVENTEEN

FIRST WOMAN VOTER

✒ I The presidential campaign of 1872 was one of the most exciting in American history. Grant's one term in office had earned him the title of the worst President the country had ever had. The Liberal Republicans organized and made a brave start to dispossess him. But they soon became discouraged, drifted away to Europe or otherwise disappeared, and left the nomination in the hands of a group of enterprising newspapermen. The result was the nomination of Horace Greeley, the New York editor. The Democrats stood not a chance. Emasculated by the Civil War, they could think of nothing better than to creep under the tent of the Liberals and adopt Greeley also as their candidate. The conservative Republicans were therefore opposed by only one important candidate, a newspaper editor without political experience. Though he put up a sturdy fight, they found it easy to mow him down and re-elect the standard-bearer.

Susan had her first experience of party conventions in this campaign. The veteran traveler appeared at every one of them. At Cincinnati, accompanied by Miss Gordon from California, and at Baltimore, accompanied by Mrs. Hooker, she buttonholed the delegates and demanded a woman suffrage plank in the platform. The most she achieved was a courteous treatment and skilled evasions. The Republican party in Philadelphia, however, which she attended with Sarah Pugh, surprised her by adopting the following resolution:

The Republican Party is mindful of its obligations to the loyal women of America for their noble devotion to the cause of freedom; their admission to wider fields of usefulness is received with satisfaction; and the honest demands of any class of citizens for equal rights should be treated with respectful consideration.

Henry B. Blackwell of the *Woman's Journal*, attending the same convention, was overjoyed by the resolution. Meeting Susan afterward at the Radical Club, he urged her to throw aside suspicion and rally the suffragists around the Republican candidate. Susan, inwardly more pleased than she was willing to show, especially to Blackwell, told him that women without votes could belong to no party but that the suffragists would always give aid and comfort to any party that declared itself outright for their cause. The Republicans, she told him in a subsequent letter, had not done this. Their platform "makes mention of woman, although faintly. It is 'the promise of things not seen,' hence I shall clutch it as the drowning man the floating straw . . . until something stronger and surer shall present itself." Meanwhile, she added, she might campaign for them.

Mrs. Stanton refused to share in even this limited optimism. "I do not feel jubilant over the situation," she wrote; "in fact, I never was so blue in my life. . . . I try to feel and to see that the 'Philadelphia splinter' is something. Between nothing and that, there is no choice, and we must accept it. . . . Dear Friend, you ask me what I see. I am under a cloud and see nothing." Still, she approved Susan's decision to take the stump for the Republican party; and, after Greeley's churlish refusal of the help some suffragist women offered him, she finally decided to go along with Susan and campaign for Grant.

Susan and Mrs. Stanton were rendered more amenable by the personality of Grant's running mate. Henry Wilson, nominee for Vice-President, had long been their outspoken friend in Congress, and he now lost no time in wooing their aid in the election of his chief. He pursued Susan, Mrs. Stanton, and Anna Dickinson with attentions and offers. Wilson did not pass through Philadelphia without stopping to take tea with Anna; and, according to a letter of Anna's to Susan, he offered her twenty thousand dollars for twenty speeches. Susan, who had voluntarily swung into line, was offered nothing resembling that sum. But she did receive five hundred dollars from the National Committee and another five hundred dollars from the State Committee to pay the expenses of meetings held in New York.

She engaged Mrs. Stanton, Olympia Brown, and Matilda Joslyn Gage to stump the state with her, starting with a Republican rally in her home city. She tried to induce Lucy Stone and Mary Livermore to speak at the Rochester meeting, but they positively declined, while Henry Blackwell at the same time wrote her, says the diary, "a long sermon on propriety." It is not clear what Susan had done this time, except to follow Blackwell's advice. Probably the aura of Mrs. Woodhull still hung over her. Proceeding by stages across the state, Susan's group campaigned lustily for the "Republican splinter," ignoring the other eighteen points of the platform. This did not entirely satisfy the committees, but they could not very well complain. The press of the state paid no attention to the speeches anyhow and featured the one impressive fact that Susan B. Anthony and Elizabeth Cady Stanton had come out for the reelection of President Grant. They wound up with a grand rally in Cooper Institute, where the dauntless women still talked the "Philadelphia splinter" to a vast audience which had come out to hear them eulogize the candidate. The next day Susan, with the thousand dollars all spent, as she considered, on the Republican cause, hastened back to Rochester.

A week later Anna Dickinson came into the campaign. She had turned down Wilson's offer of twenty thousand dollars to speak for Grant and accepted one of ten thousand dollars to speak for Greeley instead. Between Henry Wilson and Whitelaw Reid petitioning for rival candidates, Anna Dickinson had had a troubled summer. She had no single acid test like Susan's woman suffrage test to divide the sheep from the goats. She had too many interests. When the Republicans for whom she had campaigned so often in the past presented her with their candidate, she thought at first that she would simply remain absolutely silent. But neither Wilson nor Whitelaw Reid, especially Whitelaw Reid, would allow her to do this. Reid's stronger influence, combined with her profound repugnance for the Republican candidate, finally tipped the scales and sent her hurrying at the eleventh hour to speak out for Greeley. In one of her most famous speeches she said about the last word to be said about Grant's administration, and her words proved less of an argument for Greeley than an indictment against his opponent. Ten days after her masterly effort Whitelaw Reid's candidate went down to ignominious defeat. Anna was never paid the ten thousand dollars.

One of the casualties of the campaign was Susan's friendship with Anna. The break was not due to the divergence in their political paths. Susan understood perfectly why Anna came out for Greeley, and Anna understood perfectly why Susan *must* come out for Grant. Each of them respected the honest opinions of the other. Still, the political conflict played a part in loosening the tie.

Anna Dickinson's relation with Whitelaw Reid was reminiscent of her earlier relation with Wendell Phillips, when Phillips had tried to retain her for the Abolitionists against Susan's counter-urge toward woman suffrage. Both gentlemen considered Anna an ally to be actively courted and won. But the Whitelaw Reid of the moment added an attraction of his own: that which a handsome bachelor of thirty-five naturally offers to a charming unmarried lady of thirty. Their friendship was a matter of common observation; the newspapers sometimes had them engaged. Whatever their intentions were, they were known—if known at all—only to themselves. Reid was still a wary bachelor and Anna was still the most ambitious young woman of her generation. But the flirtation had gone very far and each of them did many things designed chiefly to please the other.

For instance, Reid had written a congratulatory letter to Anna's beloved Susan on the latter's fiftieth birthday, to match Anna's two hundred dollars and a gray silk gown. But two years later, when the campaign year rolled around, Reid began to see that Susan might not be such a harmless influence after all. As a mere vocal campaigner for woman suffrage—which he did not believe in anyhow—she had been negligible, even admirable in a way. But when she appeared at party conventions and campaigned for a party candidate, he realized that she might be the wrong friend for Anna.

At any rate, it was Susan's opinion that Anna's alienation was brought about by Whitelaw Reid. She had her first intimation of the estrangement when she met an old friend from Philadelphia on the street in New York. "Learned from him," says her diary, "that A.E.D. lets Susan [A.E.D.'s sister] tell him and others that I fabricated terrible charges against [illegible]."

A month later Susan was in Philadelphia and her diary for the day reads: "Sarah Pugh called with me at A.E.D.'s house. To my surprise found her home. Not the old-time greeting, but cold, cold. She charges me with betraying her confidence—Livermore and Hanaford. It is a plot of Whitelaw Reid's to break her off from me."

Susan's opinion was probably correct. Anna had lived at first hand through all the differences that separated Susan and Lucy Stone and had always remained loyal to Susan's side. It required some new dispensation, some fresh view of the old story, to make her change sides at this late date. Her sudden coldness toward Susan and her new defense of Lucy Stone's friends (Livermore and Hanaford) had to be accounted for. Susan ascribed it to Whitelaw Reid's influence.

Anna intimated at a later period of her life that she discovered at this time that all her former friends were too "old." The companionship of a young man nearer her own age doubtless helped her to this view. It may have been her own discovery. In any case, she acted impulsively, as she always did, to change the situation, for the instability that went along with her great talents permitted her no other course. Meanwhile, her alienation from Susan coincided with her switch to Greeley, which Whitelaw Reid had definitely been striving for.

⊷§ II   Susan's interest in party conventions and party campaigning were true indications of a new state of mind. If women really had the privilege of voting under the Fourteenth Amendment, as Woodhull, Riddle, and Minor maintained, what were they all now waiting for? At the beginning of 1872 she had told the delegates of the suffrage convention to go home and vote. For more than a year she had been talking up the Fourteenth Amendment to her audiences and had encountered no lively protest. It was time to put theory into action.

On November 1, 1872, the city of Rochester witnessed a surprising spectacle. Registration day at the polls found women, in pairs and small groups, to the number of fifty, wending their way to the registration headquarters. The public had been urgently summoned to do its civic duty by notices in the morning newspapers, which ran as follows:

Now register! To-day and to-morrow are the only remaining opportunities. If you were not permitted to vote, you *would fight for the right, undergo all privations for it, face death for it.* [Italics added.] You have it now at the cost of five minutes' time to be spent in seeking your place of registration, and having your name entered. And yet, on election day, less than a week hence, hundreds of you are likely to lose your votes because you have not thought it worth while to give the five minutes. To-day and to-morrow are your only opportunities. Register now!

There was nothing in the paragraph to show that it was addressed to the men only. In the registration office of the Eighth Ward, a shoemaker's shop on West Street, sixteen ladylike applicants presented themselves for enrollment. When they first appeared, headed by Susan, the inspectors hesitated; but not for long. Susan had brought along the Fourteenth Amendment and the state election law, which she read aloud to them, pointing out that nothing in the text expressly prohibited women from voting. She repeated her request to be registered as a voter. The inspectors obliged. One of them, a Democrat named Hall, observing the personnel of the group and remembering that their leader had been campaigning for the Republicans, registered a protest. But he was overruled by the other inspectors, and the names of the women were duly entered on the voting list. Several of them were Quakers and would not swear (Susan not among them; contrary to her usual custom, she took the oath on this occasion). But the law had made arrangements for Quakers and they were allowed to affirm. All of the sixteen were registered.

Their names were as follows: Miss Susan B. Anthony; Miss Mary S. Anthony; Mrs. Guelma Anthony McLean; Mrs. Hannah Anthony Mosher; Mrs. Rhoda de Garmo; Mrs. Sarah Truesdale; Mrs. Mary Pulver; Mrs. Mary S. Hebard; Mrs. Nancy M. Chapman; Mrs. Jane M. Coggswell; Mrs. Martha N. French; Mrs. Margaret Leyden; Mrs. Lottie Bolles Anthony; Mrs. Hannah Chatfield; Mrs. Susan M. Hough; Miss Ellen T. Baker. There were only three spinsters in the list—Susan, her sister, and Miss Baker. The rest were Rochester housewives to whom any idea of a sensational coup was as remote as the Pyramids. Like Susan, they were all terribly in earnest.

On election day, November 5, the same sixteen, without a single loss, repaired to the polls and, although some attempt was made to obstruct them, triumphantly succeeded in depositing their ballots. Nothing could now change the fact that they had voted and that their votes would be counted in the national election of that year. They had taken the bloom off the peach for all time. The many thousands who followed them in 1920, viewing themselves as the pioneers at the polls, had been irrevocably preceded by sixteen dauntless women in 1872.

Altogether there were fifty Rochester women who attempted to vote, but most of them did not get past their registration offices. Susan and her Eighth Ward neighbors were the only ones to make the whole journey successfully. Susan's spirit and courage, calling forth an element of recalcitrance in the old Rochester background, rendered the act possible. It was an example of great militancy carried out with complete unconsciousness of its defiance and daring.

The Rochester demonstration was unique. A few other women throughout the country attempted to vote, with varying degrees of success. Meanwhile, Susan anxiously hoped otherwise. She wrote to Mrs. Stanton at the end of election day: "I hope the morning's telegrams will tell of many women all over the country trying to vote. It is splendid that without any concert of action so many should have moved here." But she naïvely revealed in the same letter that an influence for concerted action had been at work: "I'm awful tired—for five days I have been on the constant run—but to splendid purpose—so all right."

In those days of slow communication only the Rochester newspapers had been alerted by the women's registration. The outside world did not hear of it until election day, after they had voted. As it was, the national political bosses and the press of the country were confronted by a *fait accompli*.

One Rochester daily paper of the Democratic persuasion had indeed issued a timely warning. The smart editor had dug out the enforcement act of the Fourteenth Amendment, which, boiled down to a minimum, stated: "Any person . . . who shall vote without having a legal right to vote; or do any unlawful act to

secure . . . an opportunity to vote, for himself or any other person
. . . shall be deemed guilty of a crime . . . and on conviction
thereof shall be punished by a fine not exceeding $500 or imprison-
ment not exceeding three years . . . or both at the discretion of
the Court."

When Susan read this paragraph the election was still three days
off. Her first thought was for the inspectors who, as persons who
secured the opportunity to vote for other persons, might unwittingly involve themselves. At dawn the next morning she was at the
registration office, assuring the young men that she would personally bear all the costs of any suit to which they might be subjected. Without financial resources of her own, she always knew she
could raise money for a just cause. The Eighth Ward inspectors
were surprisingly compliant in view of the published warning.
Those of the other wards were effectually terrorized and did not
allow the rest of the fifty women to cast their votes.

But Susan herself had been rendered more cautious. She had
fifteen women followers looking to her for guidance. She thought
she ought to see a lawyer. She spent the Saturday morning before
election day going from one law firm to another in search of advice.
But none of them would consider the case. She kept on climbing
stairs until she came to the office of Henry R. Selden, a prominent
attorney, formerly a judge in the Court of Appeals. Mr. Selden
listened thoughtfully while Susan unfolded her case. She had
brought with her the printed statements by Riddle, Butler, and
Minor, and these she laid before the lawyer. Selden was impressed.
He told Susan to leave her papers with him and he would think it
over until Monday morning.

On Monday morning he greeted Susan with the news that he
thought she had a right to vote under the Fourteenth Amendment,
and he added with old-fashioned courtesy, "I will protect you in
that right to the best of my ability." Susan hastened to spread the
news among her waiting band in time for them to act upon it the
next morning by casting their votes.

Susan was in high spirits over the outcome. She wrote Mrs.
Stanton:

Well, I have been & gone and done it! Positively voted the Republican ticket, straight, this A.M. at 7 o'clock; and swore my vote
in at that. . . . Fifteen other women followed suit in this ward; all

my three sisters voted—Rhoda De Garmo, too. Amy Post was rejected and she will immediately bring action against the registrars. . . . Hon. Henry R. Selden will be our Counsel. He has read up the law and all our arguments and is satisfied that we are right—and ditto Judge Samuel Selden, his elder brother. So we are in for a fine agitation in Rochester on the question.

In her recital of the details of the day she mentioned that "not a jeer, not a word, not a look disrespectful has met a single woman." The much-prophesied rudeness which women would encounter at the polls had failed to materialize. The man who would have been disrespectful to this dignified band of housewives would have been a boor indeed. But Susan was surprised and almost pathetically pleased over this minor victory. The long bullying she had received from the press had not prepared her for it.

✎§ III   Though foreseeing "a fine agitation," Susan had no idea of the form it would take. The Republican rulers, who had laid the trap for unreconstructed Southerners, were stunned by the capture of its first victims. Instead of a few miserable Ku-Kluxers, it had caught a respectable group of Northern housewives, voting the Republican ticket at that. There was no doubt that they were lawbreakers and must be promptly dealt with. If the sixteen got away, they would return a hundred strong the next time. The newspapers of the country, belatedly filled with excitement, began asking the government why it had allowed such a thing. Very shortly orders came through from Washington that the law should take its course. The ladies were charged with violating a Federal enactment.

If Rochester had been surprised to see women at the polls on November 5, it was even more surprised on November 28 to see perfect ladies being arrested. The date happened to be Thanksgiving Day, the holiday proclaimed by Lincoln nine years before. Perhaps Rochester did not yet take Thanksgiving Day seriously; anyhow, the local Federal authorities decided to move on this holiday. In the morning the deputy marshals went about ringing doorbells and handing out warrants to the ladies who answered.

Susan's doorbell was rung by Chief Marshal Keeney, dressed to the nines, with kid gloves and top hat. Keeney was embarrassed. After some remarks about the weather he produced a warrant for

Susan's arrest and similar warrants for her sisters. Susan, according to her statement, was taken by surprise. She had expected some kind of action but had not envisaged an actual arrest. She preserved a cool exterior, nevertheless. When the marshal politely suggested that the ladies could repair to the courtroom unattended, Susan declined the courtesy and insisted that he make the usual display of force. The marshal meekly escorted her to the court of justice. How her sisters reached the rendezvous she does not say.

In the dingy office of the commissioner of elections she found some of her fellow culprits already assembled. Susan sat with them and waited for the arrival of the rest. When all sixteen were present they still sat and waited. They looked about them at the same bleak, dirty courtroom in which the runaway slaves, under the Fugitive Slave Law, had been tried and returned to their masters. Some of the women present, including Susan, could remember the chamber of horrors from that day. Meantime, they had their first taste of what it meant to be a common criminal. They waited while the afternoon wore on and the twilight fell, and no one took any notice of their presence. At last the commissioner appeared and condescended to inform them that the district attorney, essential to the proceedings, had failed to put in an appearance. They could go home and come back the next morning.

By this time the commissioner and the district attorney were ready for action. While the other fifteen women sat by in silence, the officials focused their attention upon Susan. They were apparently much concerned about the part played by Selden in the women's demonstration. Susan must have sensed this, for she became immediately wary when he was mentioned. "Did Judge Selden give you an opinion?" they asked. "He was like the rest of you lawyers," she replied, "he had not studied the question." They persisted for some time along this line.

Question: Would you have made the same efforts to vote that you did, if you had not consulted with Judge Selden?
Ans.: Yes, sir.
Question: Were you influenced in the matter by his advice at all?
Ans.: No, sir.
Question: You went into this matter for the purpose of testing the question?
Ans.: Yes, sir; I had been resolved for three years to vote at the first election when I had been at home for thirty days before.

A second hearing took place before the commissioner. This was adjourned to a larger and cleaner chamber, for the women of the city had come out in crowds, braving the forbidden precincts out of friendship, fellow feeling, or curiosity. The atmosphere was refined. One newspaper described the defendants: "The majority of these law-breakers are elderly, matronly-looking women, with thoughtful faces, just the sort one would like to see in charge of one's sick room, considerate, patient, kindly." They were really no better off than the runaway slaves who had previously sat in their places. "The learned gentlemen who are conducting this movement," as Selden said of the prosecution, had just as little intention of letting them off. They all pleaded not guilty and were placed under a bail of five hundred dollars each. They were then ordered to appear before the Albany court in January.

Susan revolted at the idea of bail and asked for a writ of habeas corpus. Her petition was postponed to the Albany court, where it was heard, refused, and her bail raised to one thousand dollars. After leaving the Albany courtroom, Susan found that Judge Selden had gone her bail without consulting her. He could not be sure that she might not prefer jail. Susan reproached Selden for his cavalier action, but he only replied mildly: "I could not see a lady go to jail." Incidentally, Susan alone of the group had been obliged to go to Albany, as her case had been singled out as a test case.

She was next faced by a grand jury indictment. Twenty good and lawful men did present upon their oaths that "Susan B. Anthony of Rochester had knowingly, wrongfully, and unlawfully voted (the said Susan B. Anthony being then and there a person of the female sex) contrary to the form of the statute and against the peace of the United States of America and their dignity." Susan was bound over to the marshal for custody and her trial was set for the summer term of the Rochester court. She noted that Selden, who bore the legal burden, was getting better with every trial. "Judge Selden's argument vastly improved," she noted with approval after the Albany hearing.

§ IV In January, Susan attended the annual suffrage convention in Washington. At the railroad station she found Marshal Keeney walking up and down in some embarrassment. "Quite protested against my going," she notes briefly in the diary. Keeney continued to see her off at the station every time she had a lecture engagement, always protesting but never actually trying to prevent her going.

In Washington the suffragists were overjoyed to see her, as many of them had heard that she was in prison. The convention this year really centered around Susan. She made the opening address. "I stand here under indictment," she said, "for having exercised my right as a citizen to vote at the last election; and by a fiction of the law, I am now in custody and not a free person on this platform." She continued to advance the proposition that the Fourteenth Amendment, rightly interpreted, would settle the franchise question once for all. The other speakers fell into line and the convention adopted resolutions approving Susan's course and denouncing her prosecution as an "act of arbitrary and unconstitutional authority and a blow at the liberties of every citizen of this nation." When the ringing speeches, resounding resolutions, and vote of confidence were over, the women returned to their homes and left Susan to fight her legal battle alone. There was one exception, Matilda Joslyn Gage, who first emerged as Susan's supporter at this convention and who went away feeling that something more than words was expected of her.

Between the day of her arrest and the day of her Albany hearing two important messages had come to Susan from New York. On November 29 she wrote in her diary: "This evening at 7 o'clock my old friend Horace Greeley died. A giant intellect suddenly gone out!" Greeley had lost all in the campaign, even his own *Tribune*. The gibes, slurs, and ridicule which had been trumped up to destroy him had done their deadly work. Before the echoes of the campaign had subsided, Greeley was dead. Tears were shed for him, but they were tears of guilt rather than grief. Susan's grief was sincere. Suffrage had not had a kind word from Greeley for many years, but her thoughts went back to the days when they had truly been friends.

A month later there came another letter evocative of the past. In her diary for January 4, 1873, she wrote: "Letter from V. C. Woodhull offering her legal aid in my woman suffrage prosecution. One also from E. M. Davis [Lucretia Mott's son-in-law] asking if I am really in jail. Gave Davis full statement. No reply to Woodhull." It was only fitting for Mrs. Woodhull to offer her aid to Susan in a situation which she had done so much to bring about. But Susan had no intention of yielding to that siren voice again. She had turned out the lights on Victoria not for once but for all time.

At the same time she could have used some real help. The legal consequences of her voting bore down heavily. They demanded time and money, both of which she had expected to use for paying off the *Revolution* debt. She had no organization with funds or moral support to stand behind her. She alone must foot the bills, pay the piper, meet all the claims financially and morally arising from her act. A grand jury indictment is a burdensome reality. It stared her in the face whichever way she turned as a practical chore.

V All this while Susan's life at home had been growing more and more overcast by worry. For several years Guelma McLean's health had been a source of concern. Ever since the death of her son she had been visibly declining. Just before the election Susan had written in her diary: "Gula has serious lung difficulty, growing worse, of near three years' standing." But a few days after this entry, Guelma went to the polls twice over, to register and to vote. She attended the two hearings in the Rochester court, sitting out with the others the long and tedious afternoon when the district attorney did not appear. The next day she came again and when the case was continued went home, like the others, on bail. She did not appear at any of the subsequent hearings. This explains why the existing legends make such confusing statements about the number of Susan's adherents, varying from fourteen to fifteen. After Guelma's withdrawal there were only fourteen.

As the winter wore on, her condition grew worse. She was removed from her home to the house of a physician who wished to try a last desperate remedy. After a month of dire homesickness she returned without showing any improvement. The house in Madison Street became a house of illness, while the disease advanced implacably, reducing the beautiful Guelma to a skeleton of herself and striking her family down with heartsickness and grief.

In spite of her heartache, Susan met her legal engagements that winter with careful and conscientious preparation. In between she kept as many lecture dates as she could, for the pressure of debt left her no choice. Hard journeys and bad weather had never deterred her and she did not allow them to stop her this winter. She had always relied on a cast-iron constitution to carry her through all emergencies, and hitherto it had never failed her.

In February she was speaking nightly in a series of Indiana towns. Toward the last of the month, ten days after her birthday, she was scheduled to speak in Fort Wayne. Her hostess, Mrs. Williams, a prominent local suffragist, drove her to the lecture hall in the evening. Susan launched into her speech, which contained, as usual in those days, her arguments for voting under the Fourteenth Amendment. Halfway through her lecture, everything stopped for her. As she described it in her diary: "Became faint and full of pain when lecture was half done, and stopped; and was taken to Mrs. Williams's. Brandy and doctor. Seemed a total suppression of action." She did not admit that she had entirely lost consciousness, though the others knew that she had. But she added a detail to the picture by saying that she was "full of pain."

Her collapse was never fully explained. She believed it was caused by an open ventilator directly above her, through which a stream of cold air poured steadily down upon her head. She may have been right. It will be noted, however, that her fainting took place in the middle of making a speech—something that was always an ordeal for her, though she lectured continuously and made her living by doing so. It also took place at a time when her pressures without and anxieties at home had accumulated to an ominous load. But it did not occur to her that she could bend, even break, under a mental strain.

Her first thought on regaining consciousness was to stop the Associated Press. She told friends she feared that her aged mother might be stricken with shock. But she was too late. The next morning many newspapers reported her not only unconscious but dead. She decided the best thing to do was to show herself in public as quickly as possible. Three days later, still weak and trembling, but determined to go through it, she presented herself on the platform at Marion, Indiana. "A large house," she noted with satisfaction in her diary, saw her and heard her. The news went out that she was not dead. Fortunately for her, this was the last of her series of engagements.

Once at home, Susan forgot all about the warning she had received, which after all she regarded only as a warning to avoid bad ventilation. She found her sister Guelma pitiably weaker. "It is dreadful to see a loved one just sliding down, down, and no power to stay the disease," she wrote. From this it would seem that she had resolved to accept the truth. Perhaps with her collapse on the stage her last unconscious resistance to the cruel truth was gone.

She went briskly to work on practical matters. She called on Selden and his assistant, Van Voorhis; paid Selden $200 and Van Voorhis $15; after which the intrepid lady, known all over the country as a famous reformer, had just $3.45 left in the bank. She then called on the inspectors, who (like herself, free on bail and awaiting trial) had genially invited the former party of ladies to vote again in the forthcoming city elections. Susan tried to induce the ladies to accept, but most of them felt they had enough trouble and expense on their hands for the present. Still, Mrs. Mary Pulver and Mrs. Mary Hebard (wife of a Rochester editor) joined with her, and the three of them voted at the polls without incident or notice. "The gentlemen in charge of the movement" apparently also felt that one legal action at a time was enough.

On May 2, after her usual good-by to Marshal Keeney, Susan took the train for New York. The twenty-fifth anniversary of Seneca Falls was to be celebrated. The program was to be devoted to reminiscences by Lucretia Mott and Elizabeth Cady Stanton, the veterans of 1848. But the attraction of recent history got in the way, and the main subject was the arrest and impending trial of Susan B. Anthony for voting in Rochester. The women listened breathlessly while Susan recounted her adventures with the courts up to date. They declared by resolution that "not Susan B. Anthony but the government of the United States is on trial today." On this resounding note they again dispersed to their homes. No delegation, no committee, no member was appointed to attend Susan's trial, which at the time was only two weeks away.

CHAPTER EIGHTEEN

PRISONER AT THE BAR

◄§ I   In the summer of 1873 the lawmakers in Washington were confronted by a mass of reconstruction problems. The ruling party, the Republican, had all this to untangle, primarily in accordance with the party's own best interests. There was practically no opposition, except such as was offered by the Constitution. Still, this was subject to Supreme Court interpretation, which even in those days, as Mr. Dooley said later, tended to "follow the election returns." It was possible, though difficult, to solve the attendant problems for the benefit of the dominant party while still adhering to the letter of the law. But it took thought and application. The congressmen were kept busy, often burning the midnight oil.

That woman's rights should invade the foreground at this time was a distinct annoyance. Strange to say, the problem stood well out in front. Such idealism as had survived from the pre-war moral crusades had been harnessed by the women to their own vehicle of reform. The aggressive tactics of the Abolitionists had not been forgotten and were to some extent continued by the revived suffrage movement. The suffragists were going farther than they had ever gone before.

After declaring in its platform that the party was "mindful of its obligations to the loyal women of America, etc., etc.," the Republican party could not rudely brush them off. Susan B. Anthony and Elizabeth Cady Stanton had campaigned for the National Republican Committee, and so had many other suffragists throughout the country. After accepting their aid, the bigwigs could not about-face and declare that women did not belong in politics. They themselves had put them there.

The climax came, of course, when sixteen women in Rochester calmly walked to the polls and asserted their right to vote. It was a small but well-aimed bombshell into the heart of Washington. In the midst of more important business, the government had to take time off to do something about it. The situation demanded atten-tion from the top echelons. It even seemed serious enough for Roscoe Conkling, Grant's right-hand man and supreme boss of the New York Republicans, to take a hand in it. Conkling, the only senator who refused to do routine favors for his constituents be-cause he had no time for them, was obliged to use his valuable time to handle this revolt. After all, it was in his bailiwick.

Susan spent the spring of that year preparing for her trial, set for the May term of the Rochester court. She had on hand a carefully prepared argument, which she had been delivering for a year and which, contrary to her usual custom, she had fully written out. It was entitled "Is It a Crime for a United States Citizen to Vote?" In this she discussed citizenship in general and then launched into woman's rights. The speech ran in part:

"If we once establish the false principle, that United States citizenship does not carry with it the right to vote in every State in this Union, there is no end to the petty freaks and cunning devices that will be resorted to, to exclude one and another class of citizens from the right of suffrage. It will not always be men com-bining to disfranchise women; native-born men combining to abridge the rights of naturalized citizens, as in Rhode Island; it will not always be the rich and educated who may combine to cut off the poor and ignorant; but we may live to see the poor, hard-work-ing, uncultivated day-laborers, foreign and native-born, earning the power of the ballot and with their vast majority of numbers, com-bine and amend State constitutions so as to disfranchise the Van-derbilts and A. T. Stewarts, the Conklings and Fentons. It is a poor rule that won't work more ways than one."

She had learned to enliven the question of woman's rights by a fund of little stories, of which the following is a sample:

"A good farmer's wife near Earlville, Ill., who had all the rights she wanted, went to the dentist of the village, who made her a full set of false teeth, both upper and lower. The dentist pronounced them an admirable fit, and the wife declared they gave her fits to wear them; that she could neither chew nor talk with them in her mouth. The dentist sued the husband; his counsel brought the wife as witness; the judge ruled her off the stand saying: *A married woman can not be a witness in matters of joint interest between herself and her husband.* Think of it, ye good wives, the false teeth in your mouths a joint interest with your husbands, about which you are legally incompetent to speak!"

The speech had paid its way for some time, and in Monroe County, nearer home, it continued to do so.

Monroe County, of which Rochester is the county seat, had twenty-nine post office districts, all of which Susan proceeded to canvass, one by one. Announced by posters sent to the post offices, Susan delivered her speech twenty-nine times in twenty-nine halls in one month's time. The question of woman's rights was a live one, and Susan, an acknowledged authority, could always draw an audience.

The district attorney, hearing of her county tour, expressed some dissatisfaction. A local Democratic paper needled him with an editorial on "Susan B. Anthony as a Corruptionist." The district attorney informed Miss Anthony that he would move her trial out of the county if she kept on. Susan carefully and innocently replied that she was only reading and explaining the Constitution of the United States. This surely could not be described as an attempt to prejudice the jury. If her case was moved to another county, she added, she would straightway move in with an army of speakers. An army of speakers, indeed, when all the other suffragists were staying very quietly at home!

Her trial was scheduled for May 13. The district attorney, practicing familiar tactics, did not call the case until May 23. When after ten days of waiting the accused and counsel appeared, all ready and primed for action, the district attorney called for a change of venue and still further postponement. This irritated Judge Selden not a little, but Susan, having been forewarned, remained patient. The election inspectors, whose trial was attached to hers, continued absolutely silent. They had taken their cue once for all from Susan and quietly stayed in line.

The little town of Canandaigua, in Ontario County, had been

chosen for the trial, and June 17 as the date. About ten miles from Rochester, Canandaigua's spires could be seen from any Rochester height on a bright, cloudless day. But Ontario was another county and the district attorney's threat to Susan had been vindicated. The population of Ontario County had not been educated. Susan's diary for that night reads: "Made program to canvass County of Ontario and had bills printed."

But alas! Out of her "army of speakers" only one speaker materialized. Matilda Joslyn Gage, living in nearby Fayetteville, left her cookstove and her children and came to Susan's aid. Quite lacking in oratorical fanfare, Mrs. Gage possessed one of the best minds in the suffrage movement—past, present, or to come—and her intellectual grasp of the present emergency could hardly have been matched by anyone else in the movement. She could as ill afford the luxury of coming to Susan's aid as Susan herself could afford to do what she was doing. The suffragists of later years who wrought out of a full campaign chest could have no conception of the sacrifices made by these penniless dauntless women.

Mrs. Gage came and Mrs. Gage stayed. She and Susan covered the county of Ontario between them in less than a month. Susan spoke in twenty-one districts and Mrs. Gage in sixteen. Mrs. Gage's speech bore the provocative title: "The United States on Trial, not Susan B. Anthony." The last time she delivered it was before a Canandaigua audience on the night before the trial. By this time the district attorney had given up the unequal contest. The second marathon of speaking put on by Susan, assisted by Mrs. Gage, had reduced him to silence. And no doubt he had meantime been reassured that Washington would take care of everything.

◆§ II   It was a fine June day in Canandaigua when the trial was called. The courthouse always opened its sessions by tolling a large bell in the tower. Those who had business with the court dashed out of the hotels and the offices like students summoned to classes. It was not unlike the summons of the old Canajoharie Academy, calling Susan to a quiet teaching day under the benign Mr. Hagar. The day ahead, however, promised to be anything but quiet and its presiding genius to be anything but benign. But she settled into her seat with all the composure of a confident teacher. In fact, she seemed to regard the court and its minions as a group of rather difficult pupils.

Word must have gone forth to the elect that the trial would actually take place. There were notabilities in the courtroom who would not otherwise have been there. Ex-President Millard Fillmore had come over from Buffalo, where he still practiced law and politics. Judge Nathan Hall, who by rights should have tried the case but who for undisclosed reasons refused to do so, also sat in the courtroom. Hall was a severe judge but he was not good at taking orders, as he had once before showed by defying Washington. Several congressmen from neighboring districts of the state had turned up in Canandaigua to attend the trial.

Among those *not* present was the group of Rochester women who had voted along with Susan. They had probably reasoned that, after his previous roars, the district attorney would again refuse to accept a jury from Ontario County and again move a change of venue. Only Susan's sister Hannah Mosher accompanied her to the courtroom. (Her sister Guelma was of course too ill.) By the second day, however, the Rochester ladies had been alerted. Five of them, Hannah Mosher, Mary Pulver, Margaret Leyden, Mary Hebard, and Lottie Anthony took the train for Canadaigua and reported in the courtroom on the tolling of the bell. Susan listed the names of the five faithful ones in her diary that night.

Justice Ward Hunt, Associate Justice of the United States Supreme Court, had been somehow delegated to try this Circuit Court case. His replacement of the unreliable Hall was the first step in the preparations that had gone on behind the scenes. Mrs. Stanton pays her respects to Justice Hunt in these words: "A small-brained, pale-faced, prim-looking man, enveloped in a faultless suit of black broadcloth and a snowy white neck-tie." What was more to the point, Hunt had been newly appointed to his Supreme Court position by his friend and fellow townsman, Senator Roscoe Conkling. This was the first trial he had been called upon to preside over since his appointment. Hunt had long wished for a judgeship and had once tried for an elective position on the bench but had failed to get it. Now at last, through the patronage of the great New York senator, his wish had been fulfilled. He was naturally full of gratitude to his benefactor, whose only desire at the moment was to dispose of an embarrassing case.

Conkling's appointee, in all the splendor of black broadcloth and white tie, called the court to order. The district attorney opened with the usual routine. Judge Selden offered himself as a witness for his client, wishing to testify in open court that he had advised her course of action. Susan had tried to shield him from this responsibility by declaring that she had acted solely on her own initiative, but Selden was too chivalrous and truthful to allow this. He testified and then proposed to call Susan to the stand.

The district attorney declared she was not competent to testify in her own case, and the judge sustained him. Then, to Selden's great astonishment, the court proceeded to hear excerpts read from Susan's previous testimony. Selden's protests at this could not move the judge. Susan was to have no hearing in this court, regardless of any court rules to the contrary. Selden did his best to make up for her silence by delivering a three-hour argument for woman suffrage, such as Susan herself might have delivered if she had had the chance. She noted in her diary that night that it was "a masterly statement of the cause."

The next day brought forth still more extraordinary rulings from the bench. Selden had supposed that he was defending a client in a proper court of law, but the dogmatic judge converted the trial into an exasperating hodgepodge beyond all experience. The prosecution at last took the floor and summed up with much repetition but without much enthusiasm. He sensed, if he had not actually been told, that he did not have to strive for a verdict.

It was time for Judge Hunt himself to swing into action. He seemed anxious to get the last formalities over in a hurry. Putting on his spectacles, he drew a folded paper from his pocket from which he proceeded to read his charge to the jury. It was an exceedingly technical document, well packed with legal phraseology and precedents. No pains had been spared by the author of the production. Long afterward, in her memoirs, Susan stated categorically that Judge Hunt and Senator Conkling had had an interview just before her trial—just before, she said. When Hunt took his seat his black broadcloth probably still smelled of the perfume which the dapper senator affected. To have taken so much trouble, Conkling, an expert in law, must have thought that Susan had a case.

Hunt's concluding remarks were as follows:

"The question, gentlemen of the jury . . . is wholly a question . . . of law, and I have decided . . . in the first place that under the XIV Amendment, which Miss Anthony claims protects her, she was not protected in a right to vote. And I have decided also that her belief and the advice which she took do not protect her in the act which she committed. If I am right in this, the result must be a verdict on your part of guilty, and I therefore direct that you find a verdict of guilty."

The astonished Selden rose to his feet. "That is a direction no Court has power to make in a criminal case," he interjected. Turning a deaf ear, the judge added: "Take the verdict, Mr. Clerk." The clerk obediently intoned: "Gentlemen of the jury, hearken to your verdict as the Court has recorded it. You say you find the defendant guilty of the offense whereof she stands indicted, and so say you all." The jurymen sat stunned and silent. Selden made one more attempt. "Will the clerk poll the jury?" "No," snapped the judge. And without waiting another second he declared, "Gentlemen of the jury, you are discharged."

The well-established American respect for law and justice was outraged by Susan's trial. Newspapers that had no partiality for woman suffrage editorialized indignantly against Hunt's procedure. The New York *Sun* commented: "Judge Hunt might [thus] on his own *ipse dixit*, and without the intervention of a jury, fine, imprison or hang any man, woman or child in the United States." The *Sun* urged further that Hunt should "be impeached and removed." The Albany *Law Journal*, the trade journal of the state, thought it safer to ignore the subject. After a year had passed and Hunt had not been impeached or otherwise molested, the *Journal* ventured to make a comment. The editor admitted that Justice Hunt, though "a good and pure man," had made a "mistake" in gagging the jury—which, he added, would have found Miss Anthony guilty anyway. As for Miss Anthony—the *Journal* had a word of advice for her. If she did not like "our laws," she had better "emigrate."

Eight generations of Susan's ancestors, about as many as any American of her day could boast of, had helped to build up the country from which Susan was thus casually invited to emigrate. She would have been just as much entitled to her civil rights as a citizen without those eight generations, of course, but they made the editor's advice sound rather ridiculous. Mrs. Gage wrote one of her most vitriolic letters in answer to this attack, and it was given a prominent place in a Syracuse newspaper and copied by others. Except for the Albany *Law Journal*, the press generally was shocked by what happened at Canandaigua.

◆§ III   Up to the moment of her sentencing Susan was not allowed a word in court. She sat motionless in her place, directing her gaze through her spectacles at the various speakers. At one point, when the prosecution grew facetious, asking Selden if he conceded that on election day his client was a woman, Selden answered quietly, "Yes, now and ever, heart and soul, a woman." He put in a good word for a client who had thus far not been allowed to speak a single word for herself.

When the time came for the sentence, the courtroom was crowded. It was not often that the people could see a respectable lady being sentenced for a crime. Besides, there were plenty of people in the crowd who realized that this was a big issue and that Susan herself was a detail. The judge took his seat, evidently far more relaxed than he had been before he had obtained a conviction. Selden was slightly nervous, fully aware that the penalty—a fine up to five hundred dollars, or imprisonment up to three years, or both —might be severe. He had little reason to hope for consideration from this court. If any thought of the penalty crossed Susan's mind, she showed no sign of it, least of all when the black-clad figure on the bench leaned forward and, after ordering her to stand up, suddenly gave her a chance to speak. "Has the prisoner anything to say why sentence should not be pronounced?"

The prisoner had not been lecturing on woman suffrage for twenty years without having her facts in order, surprised though she may have been. The courtroom was as good as any other rostrum. Rising to her feet, Susan began:

"Yes, your Honor, I have many things to say; for in your ordered verdict of guilty, you have trampled under foot every vital principle of our government. My natural rights, my civil rights, my political rights are all alike ignored. Robbed of the fundamental privilege of citizenship, I am degraded from the status of a citizen to that of a subject; and not only myself individually but all of my sex are, by your Honor's verdict, doomed to political subjection under this so-called Republican government."

Hunt now saw his mistake. It would have been better to continue as he had begun. He broke in: "The Court can not listen to a re-hearsal of arguments the prisoner's counsel has already consumed three hours in presenting." Susan resumed:

"May it please your Honor, I am not arguing the question, but simply stating the reasons why sentence can not, in justice, be pro-nounced against me. Your denial of my citizen's right to vote is the denial of my right of consent as one of the governed, the denial of my right of representation as one of the taxed, the denial of my right to a trial by a jury of my peers as an offender against the law, the denial of my sacred rights to life, liberty, property, and—— [Hunt tried again to stop her.]

"But your Honor will not deny me this one and only poor privilege of protest against this high-handed outrage upon my citizen's rights. May it please the Court to remember that since the day of my arrest last November, this is the first time that either myself or any person of my disfranchised class has been allowed a word of defense before judge or jury——"

Hunt straightened up and said firmly, "The prisoner must sit down." Susan continued:

"All my prosecutors, from the 8th Ward corner grocery store politician, who entered the complaint, to the United States Mar-shal, Commissioner, District Attorney, District Judge, your Honor on the bench, not one is my peer, but each and all my political sovereigns; and had your Honor submitted my case to the jury, as was clearly your duty, even then I should have had just cause of protest, for not one of those men was my peer; but, native or for-eign, white or black, rich or poor, educated or ignorant, awake or asleep, sober or drunk, each and every man of them was my political superior; hence, in no sense, my peer.

"Even, under such circumstances, a commoner of England, tried before a jury of lords, would have had far less cause to complain than should I, a woman, tried before a jury of men. Even my coun-sel, the Hon. Henry R. Selden, who has argued my cause so ably, so earnestly, so unanswerably before your Honor, is my political sovereign. Precisely as no disfranchised person is entitled to sit upon a jury, and no woman is entitled to the franchise, so, none but a regularly admitted lawyer is allowed to practice in the courts, and no woman can gain admission to the bar—hence, jury, judge, counsel, must all be of the superior class."

Reduced to undignified self-defense, Hunt weakly retorted: "The prisoner had been tried according to the established forms of law." Susan allowed the error to pass.

"Yes, your Honor, but by forms of law all made by men, interpreted by men, administered by men, in favor of men, and against women; and hence your Honor's ordered verdict of guilty, against a United States citizen for the exercise of 'that citizen's right to vote,' simply because that citizen was a woman and not a man. But yesterday, the same man-made forms of law declared it a crime punishable with $1,000 fine and six months' imprisonment, for you, or me, or any of us, to give a cup of cold water, a crust of bread, or a night's shelter to a panting fugitive while he was tracking his way to Canada. And every man or woman in whose veins coursed a drop of human sympathy violated that wicked law, reckless of consequences, and was justified in so doing. As, then, the slaves who got their freedom must take it over, or under, or through the unjust forms of law, precisely so now must women, to get their right to a voice in this Government, take it; and I have taken mine, and mean to take it at every opportunity."

Hunt made his last effort. "The Court orders the prisoner to sit down."

"When I was brought before your Honor for trial, I hoped for a broad and liberal interpretation of the Constitution and its recent Amendments, that should declare all United States citizens under its protecting aegis—that should declare equality of rights the national guarantee to all persons born or naturalized in the United States. But failing to get this justice—failing, even, to get a trial by a jury not of my peers—I ask not leniency at your hands—but to take the full rigors of the law."

Here Susan sat down. The judge, who had already opened his mouth to bid her sit down, was obliged to change quickly to "The prisoner will stand up." Susan rose obediently and the judge chanted hastily: "The sentence of the Court is that you pay a fine of one hundred dollars and the costs of the prosecution."

Selden sighed with relief. Though he had been dared to do his worst, evidently Hunt was still following a prearranged plan. They had decided to go easy with the penalty once a conviction had been recorded. Susan exhibited no interest other than to remain standing and to say in low but clear tones:

"May it please your Honor, I shall never pay a dollar of your unjust penalty. All the stock in trade that I possess is a $10,000 debt, incurred by publishing my paper, the *Revolution*, four years ago, the sole object of which was to educate all women to do precisely as I have done, rebel against your man-made, unjust, unconstitutional forms of law, that tax, fine, imprison, and hang women, while they deny them the right of representation in the Government; and I shall work on with might and main to pay every dollar of that honest debt, but not a penny will go to this unjust claim. And I shall earnestly and persistently continue to urge all women to the practical recognition of the old revolutionary maxim, that 'Resistance to tyranny is obedience to God.' "

Susan's diary said that night: "Mrs. Gage went home and so did I." It is fortunate that the most exciting days of one's life can sometimes come to this commonplace end. Probably neither of them realized the possible extent of their defeat. In the opinion of some authorities Susan had come very near to capturing the vote. Selden's assistant in the trial, John Van Voorhis, stated this in after years as his considered opinion of the case: "There never before was a trial in the country of one-half the importance as this of Miss Anthony's. That of Andrew Johnson had no issue which could compare in value with the one here at stake. If Miss Anthony had won her case on the merits, it would have revolutionized the suffrage of the country and enfranchised every woman in the United States."

Susan was not sent to prison for refusing to pay her fine, because "Judge Hunt," explains Van Voorhis, "very adroitly, in . . . imposing a fine of $100, refused to add, what is usual in such cases, that she be imprisoned until the fine be paid. Had he done so, Miss Anthony would have gone to prison, and then taken her case directly to the Supreme Court of the United States by writ of habeas corpus. There she would have been discharged, because trial by jury had been denied her." Here, as in every step of the trial, the hand of the legal expert is seen in the court's misrule. To pervert the law so successfully, one must be indeed well acquainted with it. Hunt was only a simple provincial judge, but skilled enough to fol-

low to the letter the instructions of his superior, the senator from
New York.

◄§ IV   Susan was on hand for the inspectors' trial the next day,
as alive and alert as if she had not just been through three long
grueling days. The faithful Van Voorhis did his best for the inspectors, but without avail. It was just as necessary to convict them as
to convict the woman. The trial was a repetition of Susan's. The
irritable and dictatorial Hunt made his own rules and finally
charged the jury, in effect, to go out and find the men guilty. "Why
send them out?" asked Van Voorhis. "As a matter of form,"
snapped the judge. Even so, the jury could not agree on their first
retirement, and one man held out until the open bullying of the
judge broke his spirit.

Two of the inspectors made creditable speeches in their own defense. They were anything but public speakers, but they probably
felt they must not be outdone by a woman. Besides, they were
goaded into action by the unfairness of the judge. Each spoke at
some length in defense of his right to be tried by a jury. The judge
sentenced the three to a fine of twenty-five dollars each and payment of the costs.

Susan instantly advised them not to pay their fines but to go
about their business. She would take upon herself the payment of
the costs, as she had promised on registration day, but she urged
them on principle to ignore the penalty. The men agreed. The cases
of all the other women voters had been dropped, with the shibbo-
leth *nolle prosequi* against their names.

◄§ V   After the storm had blown over, friends in the outside
world began to wake up and take notice. When the news went
forth that Susan had been fined and ordered to pay costs, many
suffrage supporters showed deep concern. Letters of sympathy and
donations of money began to pour in. The sums amounted to more
than a thousand dollars, which seemed to Susan like a positive fortune and a timely endowment.

Except for the court costs, she surrendered none of this to the
government. She gave a lecture in Corinthian Hall which netted

her $180, and this she divided among the inspectors. Before the trial she had paid Selden and Van Voorhis $215. These gentlemen, who had given unstinted time and attention to the case, never sent her any further bill. Instead they gave her still further time and attention.

Susan's faith in the printed word, encouraged by the largess she had received, inspired her next undertaking. With the assistance of Selden and Van Voorhis, she prepared a full report of the trial and published it in pamphlet form. Three thousand copies were sent out to libraries and newspapers all over the country at a cost of seven hundred dollars. People read pamphlets in those days, and the report of Susan B. Anthony's trial for voting received much public attention. It is now a collector's item.

Her need to get back to the lecture platform was pressing. The *Revolution* debt, neglected for almost two years, hung heavy over her head. But the illness of her sister Guelma had reached its last stages, and Susan felt she could not bear to leave home on long journeys. Besides, she was needed for the nursing, as Mary was teaching and her mother, nearing eighty, an asthmatic invalid. It was not until Guelma's death released her in November that she returned to the lecture platform. She spent the rest of that winter filling as many engagements as she could hurriedly obtain. On February 25, 1874—a day when she happened to be at home—the three inspectors were arrested without warning and shut up in jail. As soon as Susan heard the news, she waded through the snow to the prison; and there they were, sure enough, behind bolts and bars.

At least two of them were. The elderly father of one had had enough of this nonsense and, without a word to his son, had paid his fine. The other two were still incarcerated and keeping up a cheerful countenance. It was dark when Susan arrived at the jail. She shuddered at their quarters and said in her diary that night "it was a dolorous place." She left them only to trudge onward through the darkness and snow to Judge Selden's house. Selden was not in town. She then stopped at a friendly newspaper office. She finally got home at ten o'clock, after four hours of plodding through the night, with nothing accomplished.

Early the next morning she sought out Van Voorhis, who was fortunately in town. He told her he could get the men bailed out "on the limits." With this assurance of their relief Susan left town

to fill a lecture appointment and returned three days later to find
that bail had not been granted. She went directly from the station
to the jail and arrived just in time to have breakfast with the
prisoners. They had now been locked up for five days and, aside
from their other inconveniences, had fared well as to food. Their
meals had been regularly prepared and sent in by the other fourteen
women voters. Still, one of them felt obliged to warn Susan that
his wife was raising a terrible row. Susan hastened again to Van
Voorhis. This time he was more successful, and before the irate
wife had time to put her threats into execution, her husband and
the other inspector were at home again. They had spent nearly a
week in the wretched Rochester prison.

Meanwhile, Susan had made connections with Washington. Her
Republican friends, Senator Sargent and Congressman Benjamin
Butler, wrote her to take it easy; they thought the men would be
pardoned. The Administration had no wish to persecute good Republicans beyond reason. Now that the dirty work had been done,
"Let us have peace," said Grant. On the day of the inspectors'
release on bail the President, over his own signature, ordered their
permanent discharge and a remission of their fines.

The voting ladies were not satisfied with this formal courtesy to
their sponsors. They wished to honor the men who had sat in jail
on their behalf in a more personal way. There was much baking
and whipping up of refreshments, and a reception in their honor
was held at Hannah Mosher's house. A terrible wind and snow-
storm swept the town that night, but fifty guests braved the elements and crowded the Mosher home. Susan and her sisters were
very gay at this party. "We had a delightful time," says Susan's
diary.

After a year and four months, the group who had crashed the
polls on November 5, 1872, were now free to go their own way. All
but Susan. She had a criminal judgment registered against her and
an unpaid fine. Nothing was done about it. When the inspectors
had been arrested, one Rochester paper had tried to incite a similar
treatment for Susan. "It is doubtful [said the editor] whether they
[the inspectors] had a right to refuse these votes. In any event their
offense is venial as compared with Miss Anthony's. . . . [It is] an
unseemly proceeding which persecutes these excellent young men
and hesitates to attack this woman. . . . Mr. District Attorney, it

is your duty to arrest Miss Anthony; to cross swords with an antagonist worthy of your steel." But the district attorney had no desire to demonstrate his valor, and Susan was not arrested. This was not due to chivalry, as the public generally assumed, but, as Van Voorhis has pointed out, to the shrewdest of legal foresight.

Looking back on Susan's monumental bout with the great political powers, one cannot help being surprised at the small support given her. Even Elizabeth Cady Stanton had no part or parcel in her great adventure. Susan did not hear a word from her either during the trial or for a long time afterward. She commented on this in her diary. As for the *Woman's Journal*, it could scarcely be expected to stand by her in such a crisis, and it did not. The *Journal* was all for waiting until the Constitution and the laws were changed so as to grant the franchise to women: "Then let Miss Anthony vote."

The group behind the *Journal* were busy at the time in taking up the slack that Susan's fearless forward drives had left behind her. They organized, under Julia Ward Howe's leadership, an Association for the Advancement of Women, in order that women might indeed advance but not too rapidly. They were raising a standard to which discontented women could repair without losing their social status. Though they did not include woman suffrage in their program, they attracted a certain number of suffragists. When these members, to their surprise, found that Susan B. Anthony had not been invited, they naturally raised the question why. The sponsors replied naïvely in a letter that "she could not be managed." When this was repeated to Susan, she laughed.

That same fall the *Woman's Journal* stepped out with an honor roll of the women who had worked wisely for woman suffrage within the year. The names of the two agitators, Elizabeth Cady Stanton and Susan B. Anthony, were conspicuously absent from the roll. However, as this happened to be the year that Susan had devoted entirely to woman suffrage, to the complete neglect of her own affairs, her absence from the list is all the more striking. She had impoverished herself, fought nobly, and suffered anguish and defeat in the cause of woman suffrage. Yet her sacrifices counted for nothing with the people who should have been the first to appreciate them. She had not worked wisely.

In striking contrast to this coldness was the warm support Susan received from men and women alike in her own city. The spirit which had fought the old Fugitive Slave Law was still alive in Rochester. Susan's fight for the vote was assimilated to that old memory, and a considerable element of the population respected and understood it. She became a prophet who was honored in her own country.

CHAPTER NINETEEN

A DEBT DISCHARGED

❧ I   At the close of her trial Susan's mind, released from pressure, turned to the sad condition of her sister at home. As if returning from an absence, she took stock anew of the inroads made by Guelma's mortal illness. She felt that she must stay at home as much as possible during the short time that remained.

The relation between the sisters had been unusually close. In their whole lives they had been but little separated. While Susan taught in Canajoharie, she spent her vacations in her sister's home at Battenville. Later Guelma's husband had been persuaded by her father to move to Rochester. When her mother sold the farm and bought the city home, Guelma's family had moved in with her. For eight years now Susan and her sister had lived under the same roof. Though Susan was frequently away, home was always home, and her sister's family were a part of it.

In their childhood Guelma had been the more beautiful and perhaps the brighter of the two sisters. A daguerreotype made of her near the end shows that, in spite of her emaciation, she was still beautiful. Her father had deemed no name good enough for his first-born but that of the wife of William Penn. He had sent her to school in William Penn's city. There Guelma had been the favorite of the headmistress, while Susan, following along, had become her scapegoat. The father's letters to Guelma showed great pride and confidence in her achievements at school, where she had been elevated to the post of teacher. Coming home, Guelma had married the prince of the village. He was a shipwrecked prince—but still a prince—and would always bear the marks of an unusually handsome countenance. He proved a reasonably good businessman, managing to survive the setbacks of the Civil War and doing much better afterward.

Life had dealt kindly with Susan's oldest sister until her three children were almost grown up. Then, in a breath, her oldest daughter was wiped out. Five years later her only son died. Then Guelma's own health began to fail. Susan seems not to have realized the danger at first, though she knew from the start that her sister's lungs were affected. People were already beginning to talk about Colorado air for the lungs. A man could sell life insurance in Colorado or even in California. Nothing was done. Guelma's family seemed to be hypnotized. Still there might have been time. Two years after the onset of her disease Guelma was still able to go to the polls with the other Rochester women and to sit through two long hearings in the Rochester courtroom.

On the day after her trial closed, Susan took over the main part of the nursing. For the rest of that summer and fall her diary recorded her sister's steady decline. "Sister Guelma is no better, but constantly losing ground, though so slowly as hardly to be perceptible from day to day. . . . Sister Gula looks very badly. It doesn't seem possible she can endure much longer. . . . Gula called for a glass to look at herself. She said, 'Death is stamped on my face.' In her agony of weakness, she cried, 'Oh, if I could only go to sleep and never wake again; but I must be patient to the end.' Then—'What will you do with me.' " Six days later the sufferer's wish was granted; on the morning of November 9, 1873, she died quietly in her sleep.

Susan had nursed the dying woman for four months. Her sisters Hannah and Mary had relieved her, but the brunt of the task had been hers. She was an excellent nurse, but that was a small part. She had attended the loved and the doomed one through the valley of the shadow, sustaining the failing spirit and courage up to the end, out of the depths of her own unfaltering strength. Susan accepted the end with the same fortitude. For her, Guelma had died on the night when she collapsed on the Fort Wayne platform.

Among those who came to the house to condole with her was

the aging Mr. Samuel D. Porter. Fourteen years before this date Susan and Porter had presided together over a meeting of mourning for the executed John Brown. Porter seemed to feel that Susan's bravery merited that he should come to stand beside her again as he had done then. Susan was deeply touched by his visit, all the more as her friends of the outside world were maintaining the silence brought on by her trial.

On Thanksgiving Day, one year after she had been arrested, a cousin, Anson Lapham, invited her to his home in Skaneateles. Susan went for the sake of the change. During the day Lapham called her into his study and handed her the notes for the sums she had borrowed from him for the *Revolution*. The notes amounted to four thousand dollars and they were all canceled. "In answer to my attempts to express gratitude," says the diary, "he said he felt the money well spent. By his manner he made me feel his respect and confidence in me. That is more to me than the wealth of the Indies." That Lapham did not regard the money spent on the *Revolution* as thrown away gave Susan the first lighthearted moment she had known for a long time.

✍§ II Three years had passed since Susan had voluntarily assumed the *Revolution* debt. For the first year and a half she had done fairly well with the payments. Then came her trial and Guelma's illness, when she could pay nothing. Early in 1874 some of her creditors began to show their teeth. What did she expect? Like the general run of debtors, she expected more time. Where and how could she raise immediate funds? She had spent the thousand dollars sent her after her trial on the printed record which she scattered broadcast. She had cleaned out her own savings as well, so that the year 1874 found her literally bankrupt.

She accepted the first lecture tour that came to hand. It took her through New England, where the gleanings were small. She had chosen a bad time to be out of funds. One of the periodic panics of the American system was then in progress, and creditors in general were nervous. Dashing from one small Connecticut town to another, Susan was pursued by threats from one Mr. J. W. Stillman of New York, who held her note for one thousand dollars.

Susan collected three hundred dollars to send him on account and telegraphed her friend Mrs. Phelps in New York to call on Mr. Stillman and beg for more time. The vouchers on her note were Mrs. Stanton, Anna Dickinson, and Paulina Wright Davis. Stillman was threatening to sue all of them, and Susan was desperate. Her only resource was to borrow again or ask her vouchers to borrow on her behalf. Anna Dickinson had definitely broken off her friendship with Susan. In fact, Anna's lawyer was also bombarding her with threats. Susan wrote Mrs. Stanton, frantically begging her to borrow on her behalf if possible. Mrs. Stanton replied by letter to Sister Mary, coolly saying that "Susan's family ought to pay it." This message, relayed to Susan at Willimantic, Connecticut, produced the dry comment: "My family don't see with her. They got none of the good from the *Revolution* and Mrs. Stanton got a great deal." She had nevertheless assumed the debt, and if Mrs. Stanton and the others held her to her bargain, she had no real right to complain.

She rushed home for aid. There she found another letter from Anna's lawyer laying it on the line. Meanwhile, Stillman *had* sued and had obtained judgment. Susan was liable for the principal, the interest, and the costs. As Mrs. Stanton had foreseen, it was Susan's family who finally met the crisis. Sister Mary came forward with her savings. "Loaned [borrowed] $500 from Sister Mary to pay it up." The rest she managed to squeeze out of her own earnings. The Stillman note, receipted and canceled, was sent to Anna Dickinson's lawyer. The whole episode was deeply painful to Susan on account of the part Anna had played in it. She did not know that the former lyceum queen had run into financial troubles of her own and was no longer the open-handed Anna of former days.

Mrs. Stanton had not overestimated the loyalty of Susan's family. After Mary had paid the Stillman note, Susan's mother came through handsomely. She too had sunk one thousand dollars in the *Revolution,* for which she held Susan's I O U. After obtaining the consent of her children, the old lady canceled the note, saying to Susan that she did it "in consideration of her staying at home through the illness of herself and Guelma during 1873–74."

In the summer Susan moved her lectures to New York State, where she did somewhat better financially. She was frequently at home, helping with the care of her invalid mother. In the fall a suffrage amendment was proposed in Michigan and she felt she must go to its aid. She proved a most popular speaker; but, alas! she could not charge an admission fee. "I could not have it said," she wrote Mary, "that I went to Michigan, at such a crisis, to make money for myself. . . . But," she continued, "I ought to go to work to earn money, for I need it if ever anybody did." The Michigan campaign at least showed that her audiences, by contrast with Anna Dickinson's, were not falling off. When a similar campaign followed in Iowa, Susan had grown more practical. She wrote that she would split the gate receipts with the state campaign committee, and her offer was gladly accepted. She cleared some money for herself.

She stayed on in the West, going the rounds in Wisconsin, Illinois, Kansas, and Missouri. It was a dreary life, as every lecturer of her time dolefully testified, except Susan. She was gradually picking up money—from time to time she sent sums home to be put in the bank—and all the while she was still campaigning for her beloved cause.

For a change she prepared a lecture on "Social Purity." While this brought her praise from an emancipated spirit like Bronson Alcott, who heard her deliver it in Chicago, it did not find favor with the general public. The West was not interested in social purity. Anna Dickinson had started her decline with a lecture on the "Social Evil," and for a moment it looked as if Susan was preparing to follow her example. But Susan quickly retrieved her mistake, returning to the theme that was expected of her.

A new lecture, entitled "Bread and the Ballot" and relieved of the hampering technicalities of the Fourteenth Amendment, was a fine discourse on simple democracy. Susan was now out for a sixteenth amendment and nothing else. Her style profited greatly by the simple exchange, and her audiences grew larger than ever. Returning to Chicago with "Bread and the Ballot" instead of "Social Purity," she celebrated a great triumph. "An immense audience," says her diary, "had hall packed, my speech was free, easy and happy, my audience quick to see and appreciate." There seemed to be no danger that her reputation was declining. It was her great good fortune to be a true believer in the principles she advocated and urged upon others. One would have thought that the West would prefer a more dramatic orator, but such was not the case. A St. Louis newspaper, commenting on the phenomenon, said:

No longer in the bloom of youth—if she ever had any bloom— hard-featured, guileless, cold as an icicle, fluent and philosophical, she wields today tenfold more influence than all the beautiful and brilliant female lecturers that ever flaunted upon the platform as preachers of social impossibilities.

The comparison referred without doubt to Anna Dickinson. It was true that Susan was no longer young. But in some ways she was younger than Anna, who had suffered from the harsh pangs of dis-illusionment. Friends might forsake Susan, justice might betray her, but disillusionment was not in her character. Her faith in humanity survived to keep her young.

Regardless of the cost in carfare, Susan could not skip the annual January convention in Washington. Mrs. Stanton, as usual, pro-tested, but Susan soon had her in Washington, and presiding. By that mysterious power which survived every crisis, she was still the stronger. While in New York, conscripting Mrs. Stanton, she called on the firm of printers to whom she owed two hundred dollars. The head of the firm met her with a receipted bill for the amount. She had scarcely recovered from this surprise when she encountered a second windfall. On her way back to Rochester she stopped to see Anson Lapham, who had already given her four thousand dollars. The old Quaker gentleman handed her a check for one thousand dollars, saying, "Susan, this is not for suffrage, but for thee, per-sonally." The check was quickly applied to reduce her *Revolution* debt.

She was doing very well with finances when another interruption came. Daniel R. Anthony had again become involved in a shooting affair, this time with nearly fatal consequences to himself. Susan dropped everything and went to his bedside. For two months his condition was critical and Susan nursed him all this while. The wounded man eventually recovered and Susan was given much credit by the newspapers for the favorable outcome. They published the story and enlarged eloquently upon the suffragist who had proved herself an expert nurse. No calculated publicity could have done half as much to raise Susan's stock with the public as did the story of her devotion to her brother. People who had dismissed her as an obsessed suffragist perceived that she was also a human being like themselves.

A friend who saw her a few months later commented on her "pale, sad face, so worn by lines of care and toil." She had good reason to look tired. But at least her goal was now in sight. She pressed toward it unceasingly. When the annual convention of 1876 came round she did an incredible thing for her. She decided not to attend it. She had learned her lesson from Stillman about clearing up outstanding notes. She was helped to her decision by the fact that Matilda Joslyn Gage would be presiding. Mrs. Gage, learned, steady, unflorid, would be in control and all would be safe.

Susan put on a big drive through the winter and the spring. It should be remembered that she averaged little more than thirty dollars for a lecture. Good weeks brought in as much as one hundred dollars, but they were sometimes followed by bad weeks with practically nothing. Only Susan's optimism could have sustained the gamble. All she cleared was sent to Mary for deposit in the bank. The great day came at last, just before the suffrage anniversary of 1876. On May 1 she wrote, "The day of Jubilee for me has come. I have paid the last dollar of the *Revolution* debt." When she later broke the news at the anniversary celebration, there was naturally a great jubilation.

It was national news. The papers of Chicago, Buffalo, Cincinnati, and New York reported her achievement and offered their congratulations. Once more the suffragist had scored in a moral victory. "She has paid her debts like a man," said one paper. "Like a man? Not so. Not one man in a thousand but would have . . . settled at ten or twenty cents on the dollar. . . . Miss Anthony is a very admirable person." The papers praised her financial integrity —"Whatever one may think of her political opinions," they usually added. Susan B. Anthony was fast growing to be the best argument for her cause, but this argument, as she well realized, was not good enough. She was a practical woman and knew there was hard work to be done.

⋙ III   After Mrs. Woodhull's unanswered offer of help in 1873, Susan had written Victoria off. That this woman could again upset her peace of mind, even indirectly, did not occur to her. She had no idea of the lengths to which the congenital mischief-maker will go to fulfill his or her destiny. Having utterly failed as a suffragist, Victoria looked about her for another road to power and fame. She found it in the Beecher-Tilton situation.

On the night before Susan had signed away her *Revolution* forever, she stayed at Theodore Tilton's house. Tilton was managing the transfer of her paper, and his wife was one of Susan's best friends. Susan's heart was as heavy as lead. Still, with her customary self-control, she could have slept well had Mrs. Tilton allowed her. Mrs. Tilton chose this night to pour her own sorrows into Susan's ear. Susan had the habit of letting her intimates get into bed with her and talk. This was apparently what Mrs. Tilton did, and she talked all night, regardless of the fact that her guest had a difficult appointment to keep next day.

After her wakeful night with Mrs. Tilton, Susan had to go through the business formalities of transferring her paper. That night she went to Hornellsville to lecture, returning to New York the next day. As soon as she found a chance to reach Mrs. Stanton's ear privately, she confided to her the story that Mrs. Tilton had told her. It did not occur to Susan to withhold it from Mrs. Stanton. Theodore Tilton was Mrs. Stanton's friend more than her own; through her Susan had become involved with the Tiltons. Like many emotionally unstable people, they were a very charming and engaging couple. "Theodore and Elizabeth Tilton," Susan wrote later, "were very friendly, loving to me and I to them. They seemed like beautiful children to me." It apparently did not strike her that as the parents of four children it was about time for the Tiltons to grow up. Mrs. Tilton's revelations shocked her into a sudden awareness that such beautiful childlikeness might have its dangerous side.

Mrs. Tilton's confidences, in brief, concerned her emotional relations with no less a person than the Reverend Henry Ward Beecher. Beecher, like Susan and many others, loved to drop in at the open house the Tiltons kept. But Beecher came oftener than most and stayed longer. After he bought his country estate at Peekskill, the Tilton residence became his "home from home." It was always filled with flowers from his country garden. He came every day. A romance developed between himself and his hostess. This was the story Susan confided to Mrs. Stanton.

Already the romance between Beecher and Mrs. Tilton was of old date. Early that year Beecher apparently had waked up from the dream and terminated the affair, which had been going on for about two years. About the same time, he resigned from the presidency of the American Woman Suffrage Association, which had placed him in an embarrassing public rivalry with Tilton, who was his friend and president of the National Suffrage Association. He was trying to put his house in order.

All might yet have been well, but Mrs. Tilton found it not so easy to forget. A mere wife and mother, associated closely with women much abler than herself, she had no claim to importance except that the great Beecher loved her. She clung fast to the shadow when the substance was past. She began to make revelations, thus keeping alive the vanishing romance. Incredible as it may seem, Susan, the rock-ribbed spinster, was her first choice as a confessor. This can be seen from the dates in Susan's diary. She spent no night at the Tiltons' except the one in May, before she retired from the *Revolution*. Immediately thereafter she went on a lecture tour in the West and did not return to New York until August. In the meantime, in the month of July, Mrs. Tilton had repeated her confessions to her husband.

The high-minded Tilton, since this was now old history, decided to forgive his wife. He decided, furthermore, to leave Beecher to his conscience, well aware of the secret torments his friend must be suffering. But Tilton, the poet, could not stick to his good intentions. His forgiveness was frail and he bickered with his wife unceasingly. Like her, he found it necessary to confide in someone else. The story was whispered, ramified through secret channels, and threatened to erupt at any moment.

Susan's night with Mrs. Tilton must have been much like the one Anna Dickinson spent with her two years later. Mrs. Tilton was still keeping her romance alive by reliving it. Anna was terribly upset, as this letter to her mother shows:

> *New Haven, Conn.*
> *Jan. 12, 1872*

Dear Marmee:—I do not know when I have felt as I have for the 48 hours; as though the top of my head was flying off.

I went over to Brooklyn, found Theodore gone and had Lizzie seize upon me and hold me fast. She would not let me go so I stayed with her through the night. And a terrible one it was. I would say she was heartbroken if she were not dead. She is very lovely and quiet and beautiful, but she is insane. A woeful melancholy insanity, and I do not wonder. I kept holding fast to myself, as she told me one thing after another, to be sure of my own identity and that I was really listening and heard aright.

The half has not been told. She sent her dear love to thee, asked about thee and returned to thee many times; and kissed me for thee when I said good-bye. I can't write about her; it is too much.

After confiding it to Mrs. Stanton, Susan had kept the story to herself for two years. What she did not know was that Mrs. Stanton, in May 1871, had told it to Victoria Woodhull. This was while Mrs. Woodhull was being cultivated as an addition to the suffrage movement. Victoria must have been something of a hypnotist along with her other clairvoyant arts, for some explanation seems to be needed for Mrs. Stanton's confidence in a woman whom she barely knew.

Thus Victoria was provided with materials for her second bid for publicity. Speaking before a national spiritualists' convention in Boston, she unveiled the Beecher-Tilton affair, not indeed as a scandal but as an instance of the state of spiritual broad-mindedness to which mankind was approaching. Such a *ménage à trois* would be accepted in a future and better world. To her disappointment, not a Boston or New York newspaper would report her story. She then turned to her own *Woodhull and Claflin's Weekly* and on November 2, 1872, reprinted her entire address.

The rest of the lurid history is well known: how Victoria and her sister were at once clapped in jail on the charge of "obscenity"; how George Francis Train rushed to their rescue and was himself incarcerated; how the Plymouth Church held a long trial, which ended by exonerating Beecher and expelling Mrs. Tilton; and how Tilton, not satisfied with all this, must needs bring court action against Beecher for alienation of his wife's affections. The court action ended in a hung jury.

It was unavoidable that Susan and Mrs. Stanton should be drawn into the sensational developments. By temperament and circumstances Mrs. Stanton was bound to play an active part. When Tilton brought his legal suit against Beecher, he tried to get her to testify. This she declined to do, but she could not have said more on the witness stand than she was already saying in the public press. She commented and wrote freely about the case to the newspapers, of course on Tilton's side. Her husband was gravely concerned—"very nervous," as Susan put it. He appealed to Susan—as if Susan could stop her! All Susan could say was, "Too bad, too bad!"

When public opinion turned toward a vindication of Beecher, Mrs. Stanton mounted her steed, armed cap-a-pie, bearing a lance for her protégé, Tilton. She hated the clergy, whom Beecher represented, and Tilton was personally very dear to her. She fought his battle valiantly. When all was over and he had been thoroughly routed, she still stood her ground, rendering first aid. At one time Tilton appears to have contemplated suicide; Mrs. Stanton was the one who dissuaded him. "After nature has showered so many gifts on a man as in your case," she wrote him, "the least he can do is to *live* and be grateful, and bless all good women with his love and friendship." Tilton changed his dismal plans and retreated to Paris, where he buried his gifts successfully in a placid café existence.

Susan came home from the West while the excitement was at its height. A Rochester pastor preached, "The law and the judgment are with God, not with man." "He had reference," said Susan, "to the Beecher-Tilton scandal . . . none *all* good, none *all* evil." The next day she went to the Hallowells' for tea. "Talked of the Beecher scandal. Everybody wants to be able to forgive him, even if he has been weak or wicked at some unguarded hour." At this time she was inclined to take the popular and lenient view of Beecher's conduct. She was to some degree even sympathetic. She philosophized, "It shows the value of having lived an open and above-board life—and yet there are many little incidents in my experiences that evilly construed might be so——" She never completed the sentence, probably unable to extract the least memento out of her whole life's experience worthy of a comparison.

It was the church trial that changed her attitude. When Mr. Beecher was exonerated and Mrs. Tilton expelled from the church, her sense of justice was outraged. It seemed to her perfectly possible for Beecher to tell the truth (the truth as she had heard it from Mrs. Tilton), but nothing of course seemed more impossible to the unhappy clergyman. He had taken his stand and he had to stick to it. But Susan, conscious of her own charity and that of others around her, was shocked at his assumption of total innocence.

She was not alone in her opinion. An active participant in the case was Mrs. Hooker, Beecher's sister, who urgently advised him to confess all and take the consequences. He paid no heed to her advice. Carefully refraining from writing to Mrs. Stanton, Susan committed the indiscretion of writing to Mrs. Hooker. It was her second misstep in the Beecher-Tilton scandal (her first was confiding in Mrs. Stanton) and, like her first, it registered. Mrs. Hooker "leaked" the letter, and it appeared in the Brooklyn *Argus*, to survive as the only public statement by Susan on the case.

The reply of your brother is not more startling, nor so open a falsehood, as that to Mr. Watters [a newspaper reporter]: "Of course, Mr. Beecher, this is a fraud from beginning to end?" "Entirely."

Wouldn't you think if God ever did strike anyone dead for telling a lie, He would have struck then?

For a cultivated man, at whose feet the whole world of men as well as of women sits in love and reverence, whose moral, intellectual, social resources are without limit—for such a man, so blest, so overflowing with *soul food*,—for him to ask or accept the *body* of one or a dozen of his reverent and revering devotees—*I tell you he is the sinner—if it be a sin—and who shall say it is not?*

Beecher's behavior in the crisis made Susan very sad. For an antidote she got out Hawthorne's *Scarlet Letter* and read it aloud to her family. In the story of Hester Prynne and Arthur Dimmesdale she found comfort, as Dimmesdale exemplified the nobility of character in which Beecher was so wanting.

It was promptly known in all the newspaper offices that Susan B. Anthony was in possession of Mrs. Tilton's story. There was a concerted rush to interview her, as there had been to interview Mrs. Stanton. She found reporters waiting for her at the stations and the hotels where she had lecture engagements. They used innumerable wiles to induce her to talk on the subject. Reporters who had been kind to the suffrage cause reminded her of this and pressed her for a return favor. It was said that one New York reporter followed her from place to place to pick up any chance word she might drop to friends. Her mail was heavy with admonitions from friends and strangers either to speak or not to speak.

Her diary contained such entries as: "A *Tribune* lady reporter, Mrs. Hague, was waiting [at the train] to interview me. What morbidity the newspapers do cater to." And: "Angerine, of the *Union*, called with the Brooklyn *Eagle* of Saturday, with 'Bessie' [the Tilton's maid] testimony in full, saying she had noticed intimacy of Tilton for a great many ladies, particularly Stanton and Anthony." But nothing could provoke Susan to talk with reporters. Getting nowhere with her, the newspapers began to divagate on Miss Anthony's reputation for truthfulness. The New York *Sun* declared: "Miss Anthony is a lady whose word will everywhere be believed by those who know anything of her character." A Rochester paper pronounced: "Whether she will make any definite revelations remains to be seen. . . . Her own character, known and honored by the country, will give importance to any utterances she may make." Susan's responsibility was great—and growing greater. If she had dropped an unconsidered word, the effect would have been thunderous.

It is worth noticing that neither Tilton's nor Beecher's lawyers called her as a witness in the court. Neither side dared risk the testimony of one who had such an awesome reputation for plain speaking and truthfulness. She would tell not only the truth but the whole truth. Neither of the principals in the suit was willing to risk anything of the kind. They left Susan to her silence as the greatest boon she could vouchsafe to them at the moment.

She drew some lessons from the scene that stand out as sound common sense. Her prescription for the woes of the Tiltons is still as good as ever. Writing to her brother in Leavenworth, she philosophized:

Whatever comes to those closely united by marriage or by blood, the one lesson from recent developments in Brooklyn is that none of the parties ever should take in an outside person as confidant. If the twain can not themselves restore their oneness, none other can. If parents and children, brothers and sisters, can not adjust their own differences among themselves, it is in vain they look to friends outside.

A whole year after the trial was concluded Susan saw Mr. Beecher unexpectedly in the Rochester railroad station. She was seeing her Kansas relations off on the train, when there in the waiting room near by she suddenly saw Beecher. "Rev. H. W. Beecher in the Depot," says the diary, "on his way to the Congregational Conference at Lockport. Could not catch his eye, nor did I see him look at me." She tried to catch his eye and evidently wished to greet him. But Beecher, remembering that letter in the Argus, regarded her as an enemy. That, certainly, Susan was not, however much the description would have applied to Mrs. Stanton.

CHAPTER TWENTY

THE PHILADELPHIA CENTENNIAL

⋙ I Most of Susan's troubles up to the age of fifty-three had
been public troubles, connected with the movement to which she
had given her heart and soul. From this age she ran into a sea of
private troubles, some of them imaginary and self-created and
others tragically real. They left deep wounds in her private life
which she had to heal as best she could without sympathy or
assistance.

After his wife's death, Susan's brother-in-law continued to live
with his deceased wife's family. Death had swept away everyone
who belonged to him except one surviving daughter, now married
and living in another part of the city. He had long been a fixture
in his mother-in-law's household and he remained a fixture. He
was not regarded as an "in-law" but as a true relation. In Susan's
diary he was always "brother Aaron" and never otherwise. A man
of unchanging habits, he seldom went farther than his downtown
business office, while Susan, by contrast, was forever dashing off
to distant parts of the country, as far as California. McLean's habits
contributed to the rocklike stability of Susan's home life—a stability as necessary to her sense of security as was her own freedom
to roam.

What could be more natural than that her sister's relict should
seek consolation in a second marriage? The dauntless Susan who
had faced a Federal judge and jury without a tremor found herself
cowering before the thought that such a change might be in store.

The common sense that she could bring to bear as a rule upon her troubles failed her utterly. The normally sensible and bravehearted woman was overcome by unreasoning anguish at the very thought.

With empty rooms in the house, the always frugal Mary had brought in one of her fellow teachers to board. Arriving home late one evening, Susan found that her brother-in-law had accompanied this young lady to a concert. Such a little thing to overwhelm her—but it did. "For the first time since the death of my dear sister Gula," says the diary, "there flashed over me the possibility of brother Aaron's marrying a young girl, the possibility that another woman's children might share dear Gula's portion." The thought, once harbored, refused to depart. The next day she wrote: "Staid home all day and like Banquo's ghost the one forbidden thought would not drop before my weary eyes. It may be small, it may be selfish, or it may be mean, but I can not bear to see another woman wedging herself into the place of my dear sister Gula. How can a man so stoop as to allow it. . . ." As for the young lady concerned, Susan could see little to admire in her— "nice, sweet, and pleasant, but too self-conscious to be acceptable." This did not sound in the least like the siren of Susan's imaginings.

Her self-torment went on for days. She rushed out (her words) to Mount Hope cemetery where she could weep alone. Her nights were haunted and sleepless. "Sleep seems fleeing from me. Heaven and the dear spirits help me to bear whatever is to come." What was to come? Probably nothing, but she had lost her sense of security and with it her grasp on reality. Meantime, she dwelt on her hurt as something felt on behalf of her deceased sister. That she had felt herself slighted, however, presently appeared in this entry: "Sister Hannah and self ran down to niece Maggie's . . . Brother Aaron there, came home with us. The first time he has walked with me or near me since Gula's death."

The school vacation, scattering the teachers to their homes, brought a welcome relief. But with September her problem became acute again, apparently with even less reality than before. There were two teachers staying with Mary now. McLean's rare attentions were directed to them both. Susan's diary registered a momentary compassion for the lonely man. "The thought of how happy dear Gula used to be as she walked off with him, and how happy and satisfied he was, and how alone he now must feel at every turn."

Elizabeth Cady Stanton, aged 60, and Susan B. Anthony, aged 55.

But her compassion was not deep enough to change her attitude. She next espoused the theory that a man, once married, was married forever. "To take a new wife seems admission that the former was not the true spiritual mate—else that polygamy is the true theory." She thought she had always believed this.

She had done nothing of the kind. In her lifetime Susan had received proposals of marriage from widowers and had seen nothing improper in them at the time. Only a few years before she had written home from Oregon, "If any of the girls want a rich widower or an equally rich bachelor, here is decidedly the place to get an offer of one." Her casual attitude toward widowers had vanished. She wrote to John Hooker, apropos of the cry of "free love" raised against the suffragists: "In my heart of hearts I hate the whole doctrine of 'variety' or 'promiscuity.' I am not even a believer in second marriages after one of the parties is dead, so sacred and binding do I consider the marriage relation." She had but recently evolved this doctrine, and, fortunately for her fame, she did not promulgate it further. Arising out of her own emotional needs, it passed with the circumstances which produced it.

Susan was not one to suffer in silence. She was also incorrigibly honest. She could not criticize McLean in her heart or behind his back without going to him directly. One day while she was helping him make some changes in his room she disclosed her secret concern. "I told him how we felt, and hoped he would not be caught in the net set for him by —— [her own blank]. He laughed at me. Said he only wanted to make it pleasant for the girls while they boarded with us." This did not wholly allay her concern, but she naturally felt much better after she had spoken out. About to leave on a lecture tour, she spent her last days in adding to the coziness and comfort of her brother-in-law's quarters. If by sheer physical comfort and convenience she could restrain him, she was determined that nothing in this line should be lacking. Her confidence had improved her relations with her brother-in-law, who accompanied her to the "Depot," as she said, "the first time since dear Gula's death."

The year had been a distressful one for Susan: in her own words, "one of untold and unexpected anxiety that weighs me down. God grant it is without cause save in my own fancy." She had made progress. She could now contemplate the idea that she had imagined the whole thing. After another whole year had passed she could even admit the existence of a mild flirtation, which, however, she could not condone. "Brother Aaron rounds out his 64th year today. And yet he is flirting with a school-marm 30 years his junior." As long as McLean did not remarry and shake the foundations of her home, she could accept, though somewhat grudgingly, his apparent means of preserving the status quo. The image was cracked, even broken somewhat, but she still had it in her hand.

What the existence of this fantasy meant to Susan is as much of a mystery to us as it must have been to her. A man who shared her ideals and aims not a whit, without intellectual kinship with her whatsoever, with a long, happy, and undisturbed married life in his past, he seems withal to have played a surprisingly important part in her life. There was only the bond of old habit, long association, and family affection between them, and these were not enough to account for Susan's volcanic explosion at the thought of losing him. What infinitesimal share had she ever possessed that she should so miserably despair at the thought of forgoing it? The only conclusion is that she was still influenced by her adolescent dream, which had survived all the chances and changes of her maturity.

Such anomalies in strong characters are not hard to find. Susan's friend Mrs. Stanton is revealed by her latest biographer, Alma Lutz, as a lifetime victim of an early foolish love. As we already know, Mrs. Stanton's girlish heart became fixed on the man who married her older sister. Miss Lutz thinks it was this lifelong romance which affected Mrs. Stanton's relations with her husband and furnished the basis of her ardent campaign for free divorce. Two of the stormiest natures in the world, Susan and Mrs. Stanton got along excellently together. Mrs. Stanton, being a most articulate woman, would naturally have confided her story to Susan. Susan, on the other hand, being one of the most repressed of all human beings, required a catastrophic event to turn her unconscious upside down, and even then she could not read it. But she must have confided to her bosom friend what she understood to be her situation. The filaments of sympathy and understanding which ran between them were strengthened by some unknown influence into indestructible bonds. It could have been the feeling of sharing a similar fate.

Susan showed a tendency, when hard pressed by life, to return to the region of her origin. At Christmas time, after her troubled year, she betook herself on a lecture tour through Battenville and Adams. "I went all through my Father's brick house," she wrote, "which was our home from '32 to '38. Many changes but still the old familiar place. I slept at McLean's in what used to be John C.'s [McLean's] parlor." She spoke at Centre Falls, where her two sisters had been married and she had been urged by the Quaker elder to follow their example. From there she went to Adams to her grandfather's house, now occupied by her youngest uncle, who, white-haired but "smart," received her cordially. In the morning she beheld old Greylock, covered with Christmas snow, rising unchanged before her as in her childhood days. In the evening she spoke in the town's largest hall. "Fine audience and much attention. Good collection." On this practical note she closed her sentimental journey.

No woman of her times or ours could travel faster or more casually than Susan. A couple of entries in her diary brought her to Washington, ready to hold the annual suffrage convention. Mrs. Stanton had warned her not to hold it because of the odium brought on the movement by the recent Beecher-Tilton scandal. But Susan consulted Lucretia Mott in Philadelphia and Mrs. Sargent in Washington and they advised her to go ahead. Outside of New York, it seemed, people had not succumbed so completely to the Beecher-Tilton hysteria. The newspapers of New York refused to print the advance notices of the convention but those of Washington and Philadelphia complied. The convention developed in Washington without untoward incident, and the Beecher-Tilton story was not once referred to. It is still like that. Travel a few hundred miles from New York and the legendary drama attracts no audience.

≈§ II Susan's imaginary troubles of the past year had vanished, crowded out by the arrival of real trouble at home. Her second sister, Hannah Mosher, had developed symptoms of the same disease that had carried off her elder one. Hannah, like Susan, had nursed the invalid devotedly. In those days little was known about sanitary precautions, and Hannah was possibly another of the many sacrifices to the general hygienic ignorance.

This time the family quickly reacted to the danger. The Colorado climate was quickly thought of as a resource. It was decided to ship Hannah off to Colorado as soon as possible. Her brother Daniel R., believing that the Kansas climate, being dry, would have the same curative effect, persuaded them to change her destination to Kansas. There she would, additionally, be under his personal care.

The terror that swept over Susan at this second visitation of the enemy can be imagined. She received the news early in January 1876, while on a tour through Iowa. She wrote to Mrs. Gage:

> Clarinda, Iowa
> Jan. 20, 1876

My dear Mrs. Gage:
Your postal via Fort Scott overtakes me here and I mail some envelopes. . . . My stock is nearly gone through. . . . I am getting up my own lectures now, at ⅔ of the gross receipts, and doing immensely better than at the $25. . . .

And now not only have I the awful drawing of the Washington Convention, every one of which I have always attended and fully meant to continue to do so to their end,—but the Doctors have pronounced my dear sister Hannah, Mrs. Mosher, fast following my dear sister, Mrs. McLean, and she is going off to *Denver alone*, and I feel that I must fly to her and try to help her to throw off the demon of disease.

But to help her to go I must work here and I am putting in every night and sending her the money. . . . It is too cruel to see her going down. I am dreadfully hampered—but am going to try to hold myself to the rack of work until I get my neck out of the yoke of the *Revolution* debt.

Now do you go straight to Mrs. Stanton and both of you sit down together and map out the work of the Washington Convention and the plans for the Philadelphia Centennial. Do say to the Committee for me how against my feelings it is to be absent for this first time—but that I know the Convention will not suffer half so much as I. . . . You are all strong and can get on splendidly without me.

> Affectionately,
> SUSAN B. ANTHONY

Susan sent her sister six hundred dollars during her illness, which was returned by her sister's husband at a future date. At the time,

however, it set her back in the payment of the *Revolution* debt.
The money was used by Hannah to finance a long Western sojourn, which began in Kansas and was continued in Colorado. She
spent four months in Colorado Springs, returning to Leavenworth
in September somewhat improved in health. It was thought she
might hold her gains if she continued to live in the West. Her husband sacrificed his business in Rochester and joined her with his
youngest son. A little house was rented. Daniel R. found some
employment for Mosher, even something for his son. Sister Mary
was taking care of the other Mosher children. Hannah undertook
to keep house.

Like so many families in the same situation, the clan rallied in
a heroic effort to accomplish the impossible. Every temporary improvement cemented them with hope; every setback united them
in grief. The aged mother was the only one who escaped the stress
and strain. When her second daughter threatened to follow the
example of her first, she quietly retired into a dreamland of her
own, apart from life. There she remained during Hannah's long
illness and indeed for the rest of her days.

The invalid made the bravest of fights for herself. Hannah had
a great deal of Susan's own spirit within her. She went to Colorado
quite alone, a housewife and mother who had never been away
from her family. Susan, always alone herself, grieved poignantly
over her sister's lonely state. But she could not go to her, for she
had to supply the money. Hannah kept up a brave front. "Letter
from sister Hannah, dated July 31st," notes the diary, "stating that
she is breathing easier and feeling full of hope and 'firm as a
rock.'"

But nothing could hide from Susan's experienced eyes the slow
and steady advance of the fatal disease.

III   Against this background of deep sorrow she put on a
second militant demonstration for suffrage. It was a sad coincidence in Susan's life that she had to stand trial for voting while
Guelma lay dying and stage her Philadelphia Centennial demonstration while Hannah was slowly passing away. To go forward
always, regardless of her personal feelings, was second nature to
Susan. In this she showed how truly Quaker-bred she was.

Preparations for the Philadelphia Centennial had been going on for a year, and the whole country was agog. The excitement began on January 1, rose to a climax on July 4, and continued throughout the summer. Even in the broken and shattered South, the Declaration of Independence had been restored to favor, and this Fourth of July was celebrated as a national holiday. Throughout the East and the West people planned to spend July 4, 1876, in Philadelphia, if they had to sell the last cow or a wedding ring to get there. The hundredth birthday of the Declaration of Independence wiped out all other events of the year.

The National Woman Suffrage Association took up the challenge early and began to prepare for their share in the show. Mrs. Stanton and Mrs. Gage shaped their plans early in the spring. After Susan returned from the West in May, she devoted her whole energies to organizing the demonstration. As a national organization, the suffragists boldly planned to enter the national celebration. They scarcely hoped to be cordially welcomed, but this did not deter them. Susan was made chairman of the Centennial Committee.

It had been decided to have a declaration of women's rights drawn up, to be entered on the record of the Centennial proceedings. Mrs. Stanton and Mrs. Gage, veterans of the pen and best brains of the movement, combined their wits to draft the document. They wrote with their usual force and vigor, adducing the injustices meted out to their sex and demanding the vote as a remedy. Without mincing words, they declared:

These articles of impeachment against our rulers we now submit to the impartial judgment of the people. To all these wrongs and oppressions woman has not submitted in silence and resignation. From the beginning of the century when Abigail Adams, the wife of one president and the mother of another, said: "We will not hold ourselves bound to obey laws in which we have no voice or representation," until now, woman's discontent has been steadily increasing, culminating nearly thirty years ago in a simultaneous movement among the women of the nation, demanding the right of suffrage. . . .

We ask of our rulers at this hour no special favors, no special privileges, no special legislation. We ask justice, we ask equality, we ask that all the civil and political rights that belong to citizens of the United States be guaranteed to us and our daughters forever.

Their intention was to present this document at the official July 4 proceedings. Mrs. Stanton, as president of the association, wrote a formal letter to the commissioner asking permission to do so, explaining that they did not wish to read the statement, only to present it. Permission was refused. Mrs. Stanton's next move was to request admission tickets for a suffragist delegation. These also were refused. Susan broke the jam by securing a reporter's pass to represent the Leavenworth *Times*. The commissioner then unbent sufficiently to issue four more tickets for the officers of the association. Mrs. Mott and Mrs. Stanton relinquished their tickets to younger women, considering themselves too old for the immediate work in hand. Susan and Mrs. Gage, both in their fifties, were not regarded as too old. They headed the delegation.

The Fourth of July turned out to be one of those broiling, humid days that so often afflict the seaboard in summer. It was exactly in such weather as this that Thomas Jefferson had sweated out the immortal lines of the Declaration one hundred years before. It seemed entirely fitting that a heat wave of the same intensity should descend upon the celebrants. Perspiring orators held forth in Independence Hall, crowded to the rafters, while the sun-baked, perspiring military ostentatiously surrounded it. President Grant, who should have presided, had followed his usual practice, where eloquence was demanded, of delegating the honor. The acting Vice-President, Senator Ferry, filled his place.

Mr. Ferry had long been a friend of woman suffrage, but today he did not see Susan and four representatives of the cause seated quietly in the audience. The women had decided that the proper time to present their own declaration would be immediately after the reading of Jefferson's Declaration. How they should manage, they did not know. They merely waited in breathless silence for their chance to come. As Mrs. Stanton described their feelings: "They would not, they dared not sacrifice the golden opportunity. . . . Their work was not for themselves alone, nor for the present generation, but for all women of all time. The hopes of posterity were in their hands and they determined to place on record for the daughters of 1976 the fact that their mothers of 1876 had asserted their equality of rights, and impeached the government . . . for its injustice toward women."

While Mrs. Stanton was biting her knuckles at home, the responsibility for action was in Susan's hands. Susan's sense of timing was, as usual, perfect. Circumstances, as they often do with people of her type, came to her aid. At the moment when the reading of the historic document was concluded, the brass band roared forth the Brazilian national anthem in honor of the Emperor, who was present. In further honor, the entire audience rose to its feet. Susan and her group rose with them. Their time had come.

Susan stepped forward, her companions close behind her, and gently wedged her way through the crowd until she stood directly in front of the Vice-President. With a few fitting words (no one seemed to know exactly what she said), she placed her rolled-up document in the vice-presidential hand. Ferry had just enough presence of mind to close his fingers upon it, so as not to let it drop, and to make a low bow to the ladies. The suffragists said that he turned very pale, which he may very well have done.

Their mission completed, the five invaders started for the door. As they proceeded, they took from their reticules printed copies of the parchment they had just delivered and handed them out to left and right. The people whom they could not reach scrambled over their neighbors to get a copy. A general good-humored tumult ensued; the Brazilian Emperor was forgotten. The gold-braided commissioner of the Centennial took over from Ferry, who had so lamentably mismanaged everything, and restored order.

Flushed with victory, the ladies saw their opportunity to hold an open-air meeting. Mounting the vacant bandstand out in front, they quickly turned the great milling crowd into an attentive audience. With the noonday sun pouring down on their heads, the people stood quietly and listened as Susan read, in her far-carrying voice, the Declaration of Women's Rights they had just presented. Faithful Mrs. Gage found an umbrella and held it over Susan's head while she read the long-drawn-out document.

The next stop of the flying wedge was the Unitarian church. A suffragist rally had been staged for the afternoon, to follow the (assumed) successful presentation of the morning. Lucretia Mott and Mrs. Stanton, who had been reserved for this meeting, spoke with renewed enthusiasm derived from the morning's triumph. Many leaders of the movement were present and all made speeches: Belva Lockwood, Lillie Devereux Blake, Sara Andrews Spencer, Phoebe Couzins, and Esther Morris, justice of the peace from

Wyoming. The speeches lasted five hours, and the audience seemed eager and ready for more when the meeting broke up.

The next day the newspapers proceeded to pronounce judgment. Not all of it was as unfavorable as might have been expected. But Mr. Whitelaw Reid, the editor of the *Tribune*, described the episode as ominous: "The demand of Miss Anthony and Mrs. Gage to be allowed to take part in a commemoration which many of their associates discouraged and denounced would have been a cool proceeding had it been made in advance. [It was.] Made, as it was, by a very discourteous interruption, it prefigures new forms of violence and disregard of order which may accompany the participation of women in active partisan politics." The protocol-minded young Reid little knew what a good prophet he was.

Having invaded the Philadelphia Centennial, the suffragists decided to make a thorough job of it. The National Association opened headquarters in Philadelphia for the summer. Mrs. Gage had started the enterprise while Susan was touring the West, paying off her debt. The scholarly and patriotic Mrs. Gage thought that Carpenters' Hall, where the first Continental Congress had convened, would furnish the right atmosphere. The Carpenter Corporation curtly refused. Susan, having now arrived on the scene, took over the quest. She found some pleasant rooms in Arch Street for one hundred dollars a month (Philadelphia rents had shot sky-high), signed a lease with the lady who owned the house, and directed Mrs. Gage to move in. Back in New York, she received the news that the lease was void. The husband of the lady refused to have suffragists in the house, and since he must ratify his wife's lease to make it legal, his decision was final. "What will Mrs. Gage do tonight when she leaves it?" was Susan's first thought in her diary.

At the next place, she looked more carefully into the law. This time it also operated against her. As the only *femme sole* on a committee composed otherwise of married ladies, she was the only one capable of making an independent contract. She therefore assumed financial responsibility for the lease. But of course she would have done this anyhow as the only Maecenas of the movement. The rooms she finally obtained were in Chestnut Street, comfortable and adequate in every way. Lucretia Mott, old as she was, took on the job of being hostess, and the rooms were kept open for two months. Visitors from all over the country dropped in, thousands of pamphlets and circulars were distributed, and the cost of the whole enterprise was seventeen hundred dollars. This was met by individual donations, collected by Susan, and the rooms closed without a deficit.

◄§ IV   Susan left Philadelphia late in July and went directly to Tenafly. She had planned to begin work with Mrs. Stanton on a history of woman suffrage. This was not seen at first as the monumental project which it turned out to be. Susan thought of it as a pamphlet to be completed in about four months. They figured that as they were no longer young, they should write the story of the suffrage movement as they had lived it, to serve as a stepping-stone for younger workers.

The weeks passed and nothing was done. The reason was that Mrs. Stanton worked only when Susan drove her, and Susan was so depressed that she could not drive herself. Her indifference and malaise increased as the time went by. "The boxes of old reports and papers for History from Rochester came. . . . Began looking over the old papers and letters today. It is sad work and yet very interesting. . . . Today have tried to get ahead with work. But my head is heavy, constant pressure through it from temple to temple that is not actually pain, but next-door neighbor to it. . . . My heart is heavy as if some great sorrow were pressing down upon me. The prospect of getting a *History* at all seems lessening. . . . Cold better today. The first day I have come to Tower since Sunday last. Have felt miserable enough. Just seems as if all of us were to follow dear Gula, and not very long after."

In January she took to the lecture field again. But lecturing did not relieve her mental depression nor improve her physical condition. She made her way painfully across Ohio and Illinois toward Hannah's Golgotha in Kansas. It was a sad pilgrimage, accompanied by the steady inflow of disheartening news. Susan's manager had piled up engagements for her and urged her to keep on the track. But at times her health threatened to break down. "I lay in bed until 11 o'clock, my cold settling down upon my lungs." She recovered and pressed on, but with failing energies. "Two postals from Slayton begging me to . . . go to first of May. I feel I ought to say no, on my own account as well as sister Hannah's, for I am getting dreadfully tired." She reached Leavenworth and her sister's bedside in April, having canceled a few of her last dates to get there at this time.

In May 1877, three and a half years after Guelma McLean, Hannah Mosher breathed her last. Only Susan, the in-between member of the trio, was left. From the time when, as little girls, they had played dolls in the attic on the Savoy Road, they had clung closer together than most grownup sisters do. Circumstances had not separated them, and the memory and influence of their father continued its enduring hold upon them. They were their father's daughters in a sense in which their younger sister Mary had never been. Mary was her mother's daughter.

To grief Susan had added a deep obsessive anxiety. Oppressed by the tragic coincidence of her sisters' fates, she was haunted by the fear that she too was marked for the same death. The fear had first attacked her while at Mrs. Stanton's, and each return of a cold was viewed as a premonitory symptom of the disease from which both her sisters had died. Her forebodings had arrested her work on the *History* and shadowed her path from that time onward. She needed help desperately and she had nowhere to turn for it. Besides, her trouble lay so deep that no remedy could be found outside of herself.

It so happened that a woman suffrage bill was up for action in Colorado. Within three weeks after Hannah's death Susan had written to the state committee and offered her services, as she said, "free gratis and for nothing." At one of the most successful periods of her lyceum career she was turning her back on its fruitful rewards. The Colorado people viewed her act as the height of generosity and self-sacrifice, which indeed it was. At the same time, it represented her shrewd Quaker sense of how to make the one hand wash the other. If she really had contracted Hannah's fatal disease, Colorado was the place to go.

Early in September she entered the state as planned. On the threshold of her work, before she had made a single speech, she had a strange dream. Dreams were important to Susan and she often recorded them. "This night at the State Hotel . . . I dreamed of seeing my father, fifteen years dead, a haggard-looking wreck from drinking. It was too horrible and haunted me all day."

She had had other dreams of her father after his death in which he had returned as the same noble and righteous parent he had always seemed to her in life. In this dream he had turned into something reprehensible.

Susan had lost so much through death and disappointment of late years. Through much suffering, her unconscious had been churned up from its depths. What it had produced in this dream was too horrible for her to contemplate, too unbelievably contrary to her whole life's experience. Yet it must have been there all the time, hidden away at the very bottom. It went back to the time when she was still a child and her father in his first phase as a temperance reformer. Susan pondered on this dream but could not explain it. For some time it haunted her day and night.

The writer questioned an expert on dreams about the incident. "Why did Susan choose to cast off her Oedipus complex at this particular time?" And the expert replied with fine irresponsibility, "Perhaps she was just tired of carrying it." So the writer has only this common-sense theory to offer in explanation of Susan's strangely unfilial fantasy. That it was important and significant to her is, however, a patent fact. Through its influence something had happened to her unconscious. From this point she was no longer pursued by the haunting fear that she must follow her two sisters into a tubercular decline. At least her diary, faithfully kept during her stay in Colorado, contained no more morbid thoughts on the subject. She had changed depression for composure almost overnight.

CHAPTER TWENTY-ONE

THE ROUNDING-OUT YEARS

◆§ I The Legislature of Colorado submitted the question of woman suffrage to a popular vote in 1877. The territory had blossomed into statehood in 1876, acquiring thereby the nickname of the Centennial State, still without much public interest in the question. Women had voted in the next-door territories of Wyoming and Utah for seven years without affecting the atmosphere of the mining commonwealth. However, a few enterprising spirits in the Legislature introduced a woman suffrage bill immediately after Colorado became a state.

Susan and Mrs. Stanton had paid a passing visit to Colorado in 1871. When Susan made her second visit in September 1877, it was still barren ground. "At one place," says Mrs. Harper's biography, "she spoke in the railroad station to about twenty-five men who could not understand what she wanted them to do." In many towns where she spoke woman suffrage had never been heard of before.

While Denver had grown into a city of forty thousand inhabitants, with a Brown Palace Hotel, tree-shaded lawns, and railroad and telegraph communications, and a few other cities were rising, most of the state remained a mountainous wilderness. Travel was mostly by stagecoach, buckboard, or horseback, and the roads were steep and dangerous. Bandits were common. At Lake City, where Susan paused to lecture, the stagecoach had come in only a few weeks before, stripped of about everything. "The coach," said the local newspaper, "was stopped near the Cheyenne River by road agents, who robbed the passengers of about $150. Twelve miles further on, they were stopped again by four bandits who took the passengers' arms and part of their blankets." Though Susan traveled the same roads, it so happened that she never met any bandits. In every other way, however, her courage was put to the test.

Starting out, she headed for a place called Ouray, one of the most inaccessible spots in Colorado. She never actually reached it, persuaded for once that the mountain trail leading thither was too dangerous. But on the way she traveled roads almost as bad to reach towns hung out at various altitudes in the Rockies. She lectured at Oro City, Leadville, Fair Play, Canon City, Del Norte, Lake City, Morrison, and the smaller settlements in between. Many of the miners were Mexicans who could not understand her language, much less her ideas. But in the new state they could all vote. The circumstance made Susan very bitter. Twenty years later, when woman suffrage came up again and had a good chance of winning, she still remembered it. Asked for aid, she replied tartly, "Are those Mexicans all dead?" But she did not refuse aid in spite of her tartness.

In 1877 she had to look after her own transportaton and find her own places to speak. There were no halls, no schools, no churches available. She spoke in saloons, railroad stations, hotel dining rooms, and general stores. One meeting she conducted from a dry-goods box on the courthouse steps. She was lucky if her audience could be seated. Sometimes the group was a handful; sometimes it was large. Often entering a town unannounced or, worse still, announced as by one local newspaper: "Anthony! A New Version! Suffrage! Free love!" she had to assemble her audience from unprepared or even hostile elements.

A comfortable night was not to be expected, and rarely found. A straw mattress and a separate room were luxuries. In one hotel she slept in a general room with a six-foot-high partition dividing male from female patrons. She saw few women along her way, and those she saw stood out. At Fort Sanderson her landlady informed her she did not want to vote. "A silly, weak woman and a wretched cook and housekeeper," Susan disposed of her. At the very next stop she stumbled upon "a beautiful, cultured woman, wants to vote, and everything neat and clean and well-cooked." Next to a good suffragist, what Susan valued most in life was a good house-keeper. In almost every town a few isolated intellectuals flocked to her support, but the bulk of her audiences consisted of home-less and ignorant miners.

At a town called Garland, a meeting place with seats had been unexpectedly provided and a large audience had gathered. This was due to one Mr. Alva Adams, a young merchant of the town and member of the State Legislature, later to be governor of the state. Mr. Adams writes in his reminiscences:

Her audience was good-natured, but not sympathetic. It was made up mostly of men—of freighters, prospectors, railroad work-ers, merchants, gamblers, and saloon men. It was a motley crowd. . . . However, there was the spirit of chivalry that pervades all frontier audiences.

During the argument a well-known travelling newspaper man attempted to show his drunken wit by interrupting with silly ques-tions. Miss Anthony figuratively hung his pelt upon the rafters, but the poor fool thought the crowd was laughing with him instead of at him, and persisted in his folly. Up rose half a dozen burly freighters and gamblers, who picked up the disturber, carried him out, and dropped him in Willow Creek.

At five the next morning Miss Anthony took the stage for Del Norte, nearly fourteen hours away. The only other passenger was the poor fool who interrupted the meeting the evening before. . . . His ducking had not cured him of his folly, and during that long and dreary ride he tried, whenever she would tolerate his talk, to convince her that woman suffrage was wrong.

Mr. Adams concluded his reminiscences by saying: "In punctur-ing the sophistry of the enemy, she was keen and merciless. . . . She was often sarcastic—and even bitter. . . . But as a rule, her speech kept to the high place of right, justice, and liberty. . . . In this Colorado campaign she made a splendid impression. She had the zeal of a prophet, the self-sacrificing spirit of a saint."

Though she traveled alone, Susan was not the only visiting cam-paigner. Several volunteers had come from a distance, including Lucy Stone and Mr. Blackwell from Boston. Apparently the Colo-rado women had not a speaker among them, as they were practically without funds to finance a campaign. The local newspapers (no town was so backward as to be without its printing press) were not always as courteous as they might have been. The Saguache *Chronicle* remarked: "The gray-haired champion, Mr. Blackwell, with Lucy Stone, and then Miss Anthony, have come some 2,000 miles to enlighten those whom they were surprised to find as intelligent, as patriotic, and as chivalrous as their Eastern friends of the average calibre." Whatever may be said about the truth of this assertion, it did not help the cause of woman suffrage.

As far as Susan was concerned, she did not expect the cause to win. She had undertaken the trip as a task in breaking ground. It was a strenuous experience but she enjoyed every moment of it. She had always loved mountains and rugged scenery. The immense ranges of the Rockies aroused her to rapture. A night drive through the mountains was described in her diary: "Took stage for Lake City at 7 P.M. And it was joy, joy all night long. At midnight at Wagon Wheel Gap I got cup and went down to the Rio Grande and drank at its clear icy waters. Scenery magnificent, by night equally so; bright moon." Trails that would have terrified most people exhilarated her. "Left Lake City at 6 A.M. Wound round the mountain side down the Gunnison River for 21 miles, a most rugged mountain grade." Twelve hours of this traveling would leave her without fatigue and ready to begin her evening lecture. "My ride through Turkey Creek Canon in the dark was most exciting" —it must have been that, and even more. She probably took the ride to make a lecture date. The other Eastern campaigners stuck to towns along the railroads.

The physical fearlessness native to her character throve on the mystery and grandeur of the scene. In a splendid upsurgence of well-being she forgot her fear of dying. Besides, her common sense told her that a sick woman could not have survived the hardships she encountered all along the way. Colorado had not cured her sister, but it had cured Susan; not of tuberculosis, which she did not have, but of her morbid fear of it—a state of mind which, unconquered, might have led to the disease itself.

In Denver, Susan found real rest and recuperation. A woman doctor who was going away lent her the use of her home. Susan also gave several profitable lectures in the city and one in Boulder, where the state university had just been opened. Thus she did not leave the state entirely out of pocket. While staying at Dr. Avery's, she wrote a lecture entitled "Homes of Single Women," in which she told the stories of Dr. Lozier, Dr. Avery, and the Mott sisters in Albany. It was not a popular success. Once after delivering it she wrote: "It is stale, flat, and unprofitable. I do not believe I shall ever be able to make but the one satisfactory speech and that is my Bread and the Ballot or Powers of the Ballot." It was true. She could give this lecture night after night, week after week, without tiring herself or her audience. It was a subject for which she could always muster fluency and fire.

~§ II   She spent the next two years of her life indefatigably lecturing. She had signed up again with the Slayton Bureau, and Slayton routed her mercilessly. He made capital of her reputation for keeping engagements, which was always a drawing card with the Westerners. She strove at all costs to live up to his circular. "Slayton's management thus far is simply fearful—breaking up my nights." As the climax of his drive, he prevented her from attending the national convention in Washington in January 1878. It was the second national convention Susan had missed in her whole life. On receiving letters from her friends telling how the convention, in spite of Mrs. Stanton's anti-clerical influence, had been turned into a prayer meeting, she resolved she would never miss another convention. And she never did.

Crisscrossing the same territory with her were Mary Livermore, Mrs. Stanton, Theodore Tilton, and Wendell Phillips. Sometimes they were very close—tantalizingly close—to her vicinity. Spending a solitary Christmas in Rochester, Minnesota, she noted: "Hear of Wendell Phillips lecturing all around, but nowhere that I can see and hear him. How I long to." Phillips had passed on from abolition and woman suffrage to promotion of the trade-union movement as a topic. In other respects also he had changed. He had learned to value Susan's work more highly since the days when he had preferred Anna Dickinson and Lucy Stone as allies. Stopping for a lecture in St. Louis, he told a reporter of the St. Louis *Post* that "of all the advocates of the woman's movement, Miss Anthony stands at the head."

The fame of one person whom she met on this year's tour was as yet unestablished. In Terre Haute, Indiana, a young man by the name of Eugene Victor Debs managed her meeting. Debs belonged to a literary club which had rejected Slayton's offer of Susan's lecture in favor of some other attraction. But Debs was interested and arranged for an independent engagement. Susan came to Terre Haute, and Debs afterward said in his memoirs that he was openly jeered at and scoffed at as he walked with her through the street. He was deeply impressed by her calmness under attack and became a convert to woman suffrage on the spot. On this same visit Susan also met for the first time Ida Husted Harper, the lone woman's rights apostle in Terre Haute, who afterward became so useful to Susan as her first biographer.

III   After the Centennial demonstration, the women were thrown back on the old right of petition as their only practical resource. To her dismay, Susan found that even in the Colorado campaign the speakers talked abstract woman's rights instead of doing campaign work for the Sixteenth Amendment. "So few of our speakers see the practical thing to be done and dwell entirely on the theoretical *right* instead of the *hour* to get it." The pressing need was to circulate petitions for a sixteenth amendment, to amass signatures by the thousands, to secure hearings before congressional committees, and to get the bill presented on the floor. This was the only program for activity in sight.

Even for this mild plan she received little support from Boston. As Boston had formerly urged that woman suffrage should wait upon the Negro, it now urged the Federal amendment should wait upon states' rights. Garrison wrote as discouragingly as he could, declaring that the Federal idea was "premature" and wholly valueless. Wendell Phillips, though beginning to think more highly of Susan's judgment, yielded to the Boston influence. "I still think the individual states must lead off," he wrote, "and that this reform must advance, state by state." Lucy Stone and Mr. Blackwell followed Garrison's lead as a matter of course. Later on they partially gave in and issued, as a supplement of the *Woman's Journal*, a blank petition form asking for a Federal amendment. "They have *always* believed in the Sixteenth Amendment," said Susan triumphantly. "Glad they are driven to make that avowal at last." But the *Journal* continued to advocate the state-by-state plan as the best.

≈§ IV The year 1880 brought two important changes that affected Susan's life. In that year her mother died and Mrs. Stanton
retired, once for all, from her career as a lyceum lecturer.

Susan herself was sixty. Tall, spare, and active, she showed few
marks of age beyond the loss of her own good teeth. She took this
loss seriously because it affected her lecturing. "So difficult to get
a plate that does not intercept full enunciation of my words," she
complained. So her dentist was obliged to keep at it until her flow
of words was perfect. Otherwise she was scarcely aware that the
years had touched her.

In April 1880 the long-expected death of Lucy Anthony occurred.
For several months before, Susan declined all lecture engagements
that would take her too far away, venturing only to nearby towns
and cities and returning home frequently. She conceived it her duty
to be with her loved ones at the end. So she was present when her
mother at last slipped out of her dreamland into eternity. For years
she had scarcely communed with Susan, but her death left a great
emptiness. As Susan described it, "Such constant watching and
care and anxiety for so many years all taken away from us." This
was the real loss. The faithful good mother and her lifetime of
service would have to be restored by an effort before this memory
too could be lost.

Her death brought another unexpected readjustment. Lucy Anthony had left a will by which the Madison Street house became
the sole property of her youngest daughter, Mary, in recognition
of Mary's faithful and devoted care for so many years. This must
have been a real shock for Susan, another unmarried daughter sharing her mother's roof. By her mother's will it had become Mary's
roof alone. A little later she began an entry in her diary: "Rochester, N.Y., Sister Mary S. Anthony's House and Home."

The circumstance recalls the time toward the end of the Civil
War when Lucy Anthony sold the farm, went with Mary to board
with the McLeans, and made no provision at all for Susan's home-
coming. Susan should have realized by now that her prolonged absences from home exposed her to the risk and the penalty of being
completely forgotten. The wanderer always told herself that she
would have preferred to stay at home and that her traveling was the

price she paid to achieve a better world. But the fact remained that she wandered.

Still, as matters turned out, Susan's mother showed shrewd foresight in leaving the house to Mary. Lucy Anthony had never forgotten the assignment of her Battenville home, together with all it contained, to her husband's creditors. She had also not forgotten the more recent business failure of Susan's *Revolution*. Susan was her father's daughter in more ways than one. If Lucy bequeathed the house exclusively to Mary, Mary would hold onto it to the end of her days and Susan would always have a home. By trusting everything to Mary, she assured the future of both daughters. Probably some such reasoning, rather than lack of affection for her elder daughter, guided the mother's act.

Susan would not allow herself to feel or to show resentment. Immediately after her mother's death she set forth on a lecture tour. From a Pennsylvania way station she wrote to her sister: "Of course I feel and know that your loss is far beyond mine; for never was there a child who so faithfully devoted herself to a mother . . . as did you. And I feel, too, that but for you I never could have done my public work." But a certain feeling of homelessness was left over in her mind.

With the summer came Mrs. Stanton's retirement from lecturing. Susan had not forgotten the history of woman suffrage they had set out to write. As Mrs. Stanton must do most of the actual writing Susan viewed her retirement as the signal for them to begin. She alone had the materials—circulars, pamphlets, newspaper clippings, letters—on which to base the work. She had saved everything, just as her father had once suggested in order that "her children" might read them. To digest that inchoate mass and compose an orderly history was the great task now at hand. Her trunks of materials had long been resting in Mrs. Stanton's "Tower" room. Susan followed them to Tenafly, to become again a member of the Stanton household as she had been during the Civil War. In this way she evaded the problem cast up by her mother's will.

This was no false beginning; this was the real thing. Mrs. Stanton could now give her whole time to writing, and Susan enjoyed nothing more than prodding that active brain to its highest productivity. She herself for the first time had leisure to give to the work— leisure and money. As the result of her last two lecture seasons she

had forty-five hundred dollars stowed away in the bank. (As her
mother might have foreseen, this would only stoke the fire.) To
these riches was added a thousand-dollar gift from a wealthy New
York suffragist whom she had interested in the project. And finally,
if funds began to run low, Susan, who could be better spared than
her collaborator, was prepared to dash forth to the lecture field to
replenish them. In October 1880 they set to work.

V Nothing was more characteristic of Susan than her trips to
New York in January 1877 to interview publishers. Not a line of
the *History* had then been written. With her usual optimism she
offered the finished work to one publisher after another. "The
times are too hard to undertake so expensive a job." . . . "Dreadfully sorry but still hope we may do it when the times get better."
In reality, no publisher wished to undertake the publication of a
work on such a controversial subject. Susan persevered until at last
she found a firm which proved co-operative.

The Fowler and Wells Company had been founded primarily to
publish the phrenological works of the Fowler family. Orson and
Lorenzo Fowler; Dr. Lydia Fowler, Lorenzo's wife; and Wells, husband of Charlotte Fowler, formed the partnership. They had made
a considerable profit out of publications on a controversial subject
and were less timid than most publishers in this respect. The
women of the family had been firm supporters of woman suffrage
for many years. Furthermore, the firm was known as a reputable
and reliable concern.

They seem to have made, on the whole, a fair bargain with Susan.
The authors were to pay for typesetting, printing, and engravings;
the publishers, for the paper, presswork, binding, and advertising.
The authors were to receive 12½ per cent royalty on the sales.
Everything depended on the sales. If the work achieved popularity,
the authors stood a chance of recovering their investment. If it
served only as propaganda, it seemed right that the suffrage promoters should pay the costs. In any case, the contract assured the
authors of actual publication and stimulated them, especially Mrs.
Stanton, to go promptly to work.

It is usually said that they spent ten years on the production of
the three volumes of the *History*. The project, from beginning to

end, occupied that much time, but the actual writing took much less. The speed with which they produced results, once they set to work, was truly amazing. Starting on Volume I in October 1880, they had it finished and ready for sale in May 1881. As was the practice of the time, each chapter was printed as soon as written, and all nine hundred pages were in type before the ink had dried on Mrs. Stanton's pen. The authors then took the summer off, resuming work on Volume II in the following November. The second tome, consisting of almost a thousand pages, was finished by the end of April 1882. In the various forms of collaboration undertaken by these two, this writing feat, accomplished in two successive winters, showed them at their best. They had much help from Mrs. Gage, whose prodigious knowledge of history came to their aid and whose name appears on the published work as one of the editors. But the bulk of the massive volumes was ground out by Susan and Mrs. Stanton in concert.

Their reactions to the grind were different. Mrs. Stanton, who enjoyed writing, was made doubly happy by a task that removed her from lecturing. "We are scratching from morning till night," she wrote. "We sit in the library surrounded with papers, our writing desk loaded with encyclopaedias, dictionaries, etc. I am so glad that I am not wandering on those Western prairies. It makes me shudder to think of my weary lecture tours from Maine to Texas during the last twelve years."

Susan, the foot-loose, was considerably less contented. She would have preferred the Western prairies to the present ordeal. The discipline struck to her very soul. "O, how I long to be in the midst of the fray," she wrote, "and here I am bound hand and foot. I shall feel like an uncaged lion when this book is off my hands." She felt like this more and more as time went on. "I feel like a lion champing the bars of his cage, shut up here, digging and delving among the records of the past when I long to be out doing the work of the present." These were not empty but real groans from the depths of her heart. She would gladly have exchanged her present job for a ride through a dark Colorado canyon. But she knew that no one else ever could, or would, preserve the history of the suffrage movement except herself and Mrs. Stanton. And Mrs. Stanton would not work without Susan by her side.

The research that was needed fell to Susan. While Mrs. Stanton sat like Buddha, driving her pen incessantly through reams of tall, thin, slanting script (a miracle that typesetters could ever read it), Susan would hie herself to the library to fill in the gaps. For a long time she turned up daily at the historic old Astor Library in Lafayette Place, which had cubicles with desks for research students. Mr. Frank Weitenkamp, the famous authority on prints, told the writer that he remembered Susan well, sitting at work in one of the cubicles. A page boy of sixteen at the time, he was already interested in all forms of art, including the popular cartoons of the day. He had seen caricatures of Susan in *Puck* and *Life*, and, although from them he could recognize her features, he was startled otherwise by the contrast. The tall, dignified lady, dressed most correctly in a costume of "two shades of brown" (he was ready to swear to the colors!) could not possibly be the strident female of the current cartoons. Yet this was unmistakably she. The impression of elegance and *savoir-faire* was so strong as to be preserved by the astonished youth for the rest of his days.

The publication of Volume I, bringing the suffrage movement to the outbreak of the Civil War, proved a mild literary sensation. The newspapers of all the large cities responded with complimentary notices. The critics had nothing but praise, agreeing that "we have long needed an authentic and exhaustive account of the movement for the enfranchisement of women." (Nobody except the Fowlers had previously seen the need.) The authors were praised handsomely and their book hailed as a welcome achievement. "The appearance of this book," said the Chicago *News*, "is not only an important literary occurrence but it is a remarkable event in the history of civilization." One might have thought that the authors were reformed characters. The aggressive sentiments expressed in their book seem to have been overlooked.

The fame of their work spread everywhere, even to Boston and overseas to England. This could not go on without a favorable effect upon sales. Still, it seems that the publication of Volume II left Susan with unpaid bills. The illustrations, consisting of signed steel engravings, had been most expensive; but Susan had insisted on this aspect of permanence. She had also begun the expensive practice of giving copies away; two thousand copies were thus promptly distributed. And so in spite of success and fame, Susan was still out of pocket.

The writing of Volume II was rushed through, and its publication followed exactly one year after that of Volume I. The production of the ponderous volume in six months had been a formidable task, accomplished only by excellent and concentrated teamwork. Mrs. Stanton, no longer able to restrain herself, departed precipitately for Europe with her daughter. She felt she needed a vacation, and the only way to get one was to put the Atlantic between herself and Susan. She left her collaborator to see Volume II through the press and to store away the materials for the remaining Volume III. They had brought the *History* only as far as 1876 and the Centennial demonstration. After writing two volumes under the pressure of fear that she might not live to finish them, Mrs. Stanton went cheerfully off to Europe, leaving the last volume to time and chance. Her life expectancy had been increased by an irrelevant stroke of good luck that had come to Susan.

~§ VI . Nothing succeeds like success. Susan had plunged into the *History* with limited funds, trusting as usual that "a way would open." Presumably the first volume had helped to pay for itself. She had reason to hope that the second volume would do as well. Anyway, she could trust to her earning and begging powers to carry on the work to the end. Her financial worries were practically over. It was the proper time for a windfall.

At last she had done something to impress her Boston friends— something the intellectuals rated higher than her Rochester march on the polls. (History might take a different view, but that was for the future to decide.) The success of her first literary adventure had gone far to redeem what she had lost, in Boston's opinion, through the deplorable *Revolution*. Her return to good behavior was to reap its reward.

Midway in her winter's work on Volume II at Tenafly, Susan received a letter from Wendell Phillips. It ran:

Dear Susan:
Our friend, Mrs. Eddy, Francis Jackson's daughter, died a week ago Thursday. At her request, I made her will some weeks before. Her man of business, devoted to her for twenty-five years, Mr. C. R. Ransom . . . is the executor. He and I were present and consulted, and we know all her intentions and wishes from long talks with her

in years gone by. After making various bequests, she ordered the remainder divided equally between you and Lucy Stone. There is no question whatever that your portion will be $25,000 or $28,000. I advised her, in order to avoid all lawyers, to give this sum to you outright, with no responsibility to any one or any court, only "requesting you to use it for the advancement of the Woman's Rights cause."

Faithfully yours,
WENDELL PHILLIPS

The arrival of this letter must have caused great excitement in the quiet "Tower." But Susan's reply was composed and dignified:

How worthy the daughter of Francis Jackson! . . . Never going to Boston during the past fifteen years, I had lost sight of her, though I had not forgotten her by any means. How little thought have I had all these years that she cherished that marvellous trust in me, and now I recognize in her munificent legacy your own faith in me, for such was her confidence in you that I feel sure she would not thus have willed if you had not fully endorsed her wish. So to you, my dear friend, as to her, my unspeakable gratitude goes out. May I prove worthy the care and disposal of whatever shall come into my hands. . . .

The history of the Jackson family, earlier referred to in this study, had taken a final interesting turn. Mrs. Eddy's father, Francis Jackson, was an heir of Patrick Tracy Jackson, one of the founders of the great New England cotton mills. The foundation of the family fortune was the low-paid labor of thousands of mill girls, whose lives and conditions have been so well reported in studies made by Edith Abbott and Hannah Josephson. In the columns of Susan's own *Revolution* can be found a letter from a girl worker describing the same conditions. Mrs. Eddy, as one of the last inheritors of the accumulated profits, had seen fit to return a portion of them to the cause of woman's rights. Phillips must have appreciated this fact if the aged Mrs. Eddy did not. Phillips had his own private sense of guilt to assuage. He had fostered the separation between Lucy Stone and the national suffragists and he had since seen the damage that had been done by the split. By dividing fifty thousand dollars equally between Susan and Lucy Stone he hoped to undo some of the harm.

According to Susan's diary, Mrs. Eddy's motives were of a more personal character. Her husband, James Eddy, had been something of a tyrant. Taking advantage of the father's sole guardianship rights under the Massachusetts law, he had carried his young daughters off to Europe without their mother's consent—"to the heartbreak of the dear mother," says Susan. "It was this act," she adds, "that moved Francis Jackson to place $5,000 in Wendell Phillips' hands for suffrage work [in 1858], and in turn caused Mrs. Eddy to will . . . to Lucy Stone and me, $24,000 each."

The announcement was followed by other news, deflating in character. One of Mrs. Eddy's daughters had died immediately after her mother. The husband now threatened to break his mother-in-law's will, declaring that Phillips had exercised undue influence on the aged lady, that she was of unsound mind, etc., etc. However, since the two surviving daughters stood firmly on his side, Phillips said he thought he could defend the will. The loyalty of Mrs. Eddy's remaining daughters must have been a deciding factor in the ensuing suit. But it was to drag along for quite a while. Phillips wrote a few months later:

Sept. 23, '82

Dear Susan:

I have the great pleasure of telling you that the suit against the will of Mrs. Eddy is withdrawn. . . . This result is mainly due to the Executor, Mr. Ransom, who has left no stone unturned and exercised wonderful ingenuity in securing this result (though we did employ Benjamin F. Butler as a big dog; he no doubt frightened them). There will be about $20,000 coming to you to use as you deem best for the W.R. cause. . . .

Yours with congratulations,
WENDELL PHILLIPS

If Susan thought this letter heralded the end, she had much to learn about the law and the legal settlement of estates. It was three years before the technicalities were all satisfied and she actually received her half of the bequest. In the meantime, she postponed the work on the suffrage history until the expected funds should come to hand. The long delay was not good for her enterprise, but with Mrs. Stanton a truant in Europe and the law taking its time, what else could she do?

The second volume was received as favorably as its predecessor. It concluded with a history of Lucy Stone's organization, the

American Woman Suffrage Association. This may have been an afterthought on the part of the authors, suggested by the view implied in Mrs. Eddy's will that Susan and Lucy were allies in the woman's rights cause. It might even have been already planned. In any case, the well-documented history of the American Association, as prepared by Mrs. Stanton's daughter Harriot, appeared in print through the efforts of Susan and Mrs. Stanton. Many years later Mrs. Stone's daughter remarked that the *History* was naturally "one-sided" because of the authors. It would have been even more one-sided had it included no account of the American group. What it contained was produced without help from the American Association and presented to the public at Susan's expense; that is, paid for out of her share of the Eddy inheritance. Susan and Mrs. Stanton had extremely high standards of their responsibility as historians. Thanks to them, and to them only, there exists at least a factual account of the American Woman Suffrage Association in the first years of its existence.

When finally completed with Volume III in 1886, the *History* brought the record of woman suffrage up to the year of publication. The authors had added much to the value of their work by including sections on the woman movement in England and Europe. They had brought up to date the history of a cause which was not yet won. All the arguments that had ever been used in its favor, and most of those used against it, were set forth in these volumes. The specimens of congressional oratory were about the same as those seen in the *Congressional Record* of today; but specimens of the women's oratory were far beyond anything accomplished by their successors of a later period.

The early suffragists spoke with the fire of revolutionaries. If Susan's deep-seated belief in the power of eloquence to move the legislative mind had been really justified, the women would have won hands down in those early years. She still hoped, by preserving these marvels of excellence, to influence the legislation of the future. Little did she realize how few latter-day suffragists, not to speak of legislators, would ever read them. But their historical worth, as reflecting the American past, has been increased rather than diminished by the passage of time.

Susan came out of the *History* a disciplined woman. She had been bound to a rigorous regime, new to her, and for the sake of an idea she had steadily endured it. In earlier years she had learned to brave mobs fearlessly. In her later years she learned to brave something almost as formidable—the composition of a ponderous history. Her work on this had endowed her with a profound and rounding-out experience.

CHAPTER TWENTY-TWO

THE GRAND TOUR

◦§ I It would be wrong to assume that the organization work of the National Woman Suffrage Association had lagged behind while Susan and Mrs. Stanton were absorbed in the *History*. When one considers the society's accomplishments in 1881 and '82, Susan's references to herself as a caged lion are hard to understand. If she was a lion at all she was a lion in the streets.

Both she and Mrs. Stanton attended the two annual conventions in Washington. The first of these conventions tried to get a "Standing Committee on Woman Suffrage" appointed in the Senate. Susan's old adversary, Roscoe Conkling, quietly defeated the plan. In 1882 they returned again to the scheme and, to their great joy and surprise, succeeded in accomplishing their aim. In the interim Conkling had resigned in a huff from the Senate, never—as it happened—to return. They had plenty of enemies among the other senators, but none as vigilant and expert as Conkling. The suffragists won their standing committee, and four of the seven members appointed were well-known friends of woman suffrage. Susan said in her diary: "If the best of worldly good has come to me personally, I could not feel more joyous and blest."

She was even happier when the committee, a few months later, issued a majority report in favor of the Federal amendment. It was the first time the suffragists had received a senatorial report in their favor. Susan, who was in Washington for this report, was elated.

In May 1881 the Seneca Falls anniversary was transferred from

New York to Boston, regarded by the National Association as the stronghold of the "conservatives." Perhaps Miss Rachel Foster of Philadelphia, who had lately become Susan's friend and lecture manager, had something to do with the change. A youthful recruit to woman suffrage, Miss Foster would scarcely have realized the depth of the estrangement between the National and American associations. Susan and Mrs. Stanton had little hope that the friendly gesture would do much good and did not take the occasion seriously. "Find out if there is any great speaker on Sunday whom we ought to go and hear," wrote Susan to Miss Foster. "What a luxury we shall have seeing and hearing the 'proper' people at the centre of 'aesthetic culture'!"

The Nationals were cordially received by the Boston papers and by a number of important (mostly masculine) persons. The governor and the mayor, the Republican boss, Francis Bird, and the head of the Jordan Marsh Company extended various courtesies. But noticeably absent from the programs and the receptions were the names of the Boston suffragists. One looks in vain for Caroline Dall, Lucy Stone, Mary Livermore, Julia Ward Howe, or even the Blackwells and Mr. Higginson, in the report of the proceedings. The dash into New England only served to bring out more clearly the separation within the cause. An observer reported that Susan seemed very sad and weary at the governor's official reception.

Still, that one Boston suffragist could be found to deliver the address of welcome was something. Braving the American taboo, Harriet Hanson Robinson stepped forth to do this honor for the visiting Nationals. They were so pleased that they at once elected Mrs. Robinson and her daughter to membership on their board. "They have certainly seemed very earnest in helping us to get everything right at the Hub," said Susan appreciatively. Harriet Robinson's support of the rival group can be partly explained by her past. As a child Mrs. Robinson had worked in the Lowell mills and at the age of eleven had participated in a strike. She had later married William S. Robinson, correspondent of the Springfield Republican and well known as a supporter of trade unionism. Very likely the leaders of the American Association had never cultivated Harriet Robinson nor invited her support. The Woman's Journal, when it took any notice of trade unions at all, was dead set against them. So Mrs. Robinson and her daughter were left to be garnered in as intelligent and able recruits by the New York wing.

Everywhere Susan went she gained recruits. It was this knowledge which kept her so constantly on the go. They varied greatly in importance and influence, from the anonymous woman who wrote her, "For the last ten years your name has been familiar to me through the newspapers, or rather through newspaper ridicule, and has always been associated with what was pretentious and wholly unamiable. Your lecture tonight has been a revelation to me. I wanted to come and touch your hand, but I felt too guilty. Henceforth I am the avowed defender of woman suffrage," to persons of influence and prominence, like Mrs. Robinson and her daughter, and even more strikingly to an adherent like Frances E. Willard.

For several years Susan had been wooing the president of the Woman's Christian Temperance Union. She recognized her as one of the ablest organizers of women in her day. She admired her success in this respect enormously. But she was firmly convinced that to promote a moral issue without striving for the political means to attain it was a lost cause in their generation. She refused to join the W.C.T.U., in line with her resolution to stick to her one great solution, but she insisted that Miss Willard adopt woman suffrage as an associated issue. For instance, she told a Chicago *Tribune* reporter in 1880: "Miss Willard is doing noble work, but I can not coincide with her views. . . . If women had votes the officials would no longer fear to enforce the law. . . . Miss Willard has a lever but she has no fulcrum on which to place it."

In 1881 Miss Willard invited her to attend the W.C.T.U. convention in Washington. That morning Susan wrote to Rachel Foster: "Today Miss Snowe and I go to hear Frances Willard's Suffrage Bomb-shell launched into the Christian W.T. Union camp." She knew then what was to happen. The president of the Union had been careful to ensure a majority for the suffrage resolution, but those who opposed it were intensely vocal. They identified suffrage with Susan B. Anthony, who did not present the proper Christian credentials. It was whispered about in the background that "she did not recognize God."

A general motion favoring woman suffrage was adopted and a department of suffrage was created. Miss Willard came near to losing her position as president in the melee, but the revolt, once conquered, stayed conquered. Like Constantine, who baptized his soldiers whether they wished it or not, Miss Willard endowed the suffrage movement with a host of new members. Susan, like all organizers, eager for numbers, wrote with much satisfaction in her diary: "So the Christian craft of that great organization has set sail on the wide sea of woman's enfranchisement."

While Mrs. Stanton was vacationing in Europe, Susan joined a campaign for woman suffrage in Nebraska. It was easier than usual for her. Though she traveled through half of the counties of the state, she was relieved of the management of details by Rachel Foster's outstanding ability at headquarters. Rachel also took care of the finances.

◄§ II The grand tour in Europe was imperative in those days for cultured young Americans. Growing up among plain people, Susan had not felt the urge at the proper time in her life. Mrs. Stanton had felt it very strongly. One suspects that she married Henry B. Stanton in 1840 partly for the sake of the European trip which the marriage offered. Returning with her daughter forty years later, she found, to her pleasant surprise, that she was received with high honors in her own right. Her fame as a suffrage leader and as co-author of the *History of Woman Suffrage* had preceded her and endowed her with some distinction. More than this, her partner in the production of that admirable work seemed also to have captured public attention. Susan was frequently inquired about.

This put the idea into Mrs. Stanton's head that Susan should also visit England. She began at once writing and urging her to follow. Nothing had ever been farther away from Susan's thoughts. It seemed right and proper to her that Mrs. Stanton, who gave her talents, her energies, and her peace of mind so unstintingly to suffrage, should spend her money on enjoying herself. Besides, she had the additional excuse of providing an educational trip for her daughter. They both considered that Susan, who had no children, could better afford to subsidize the suffrage movement financially. In her wildest dreams Susan could not conceive of using her own earnings for a European trip. But fortune, which was beginning to smile on her, suddenly dropped the trip in her lap.

Her young friend Rachel Foster casually offered it as a gift. Rachel had met Susan around 1879 and had immediately become a devoted friend, sharing in her personal as well as her public problems. Rachel had planned the Pennsylvania lecture tour when Susan could not go far from home on account of her mother's failing health. She had also planned and conducted in person the New England tour which had secured the adherence of Mrs. Robinson. She had run the Nebraska campaign. Assisted by her sister Julia, she had done some valuable research for the *History*, thus relieving Susan of much grinding work. Through all this co-operation the handsome and scholarly young suffragist had become the valued aid of her leader. For the first time Susan felt she could roll some of her burdens off upon younger shoulders. In the first throes of financing the *History*, long before she heard of the Eddy bequest, she wrote to Rachel and her sister:

Tenafly, N.J.
Feb. 25, 1881

My dear Girls—Rachel and Julia:

I am not going to accept your most generous proposition to sink $1,000 in the *History*. But I want to loan of you from time to time $1,000, and give you as security a 4 per cent $1,000 Government Bond, which I should send you now, only that it is at home, and I can not get it without my sister's knowing it, and I do not wish to give her the anxiety she would have, if she knew I were going to encroach upon my own money. I will give you notes from time to time if you decide to make the loan so that in case of my death before I get the Bond made over to you, you will have legal claim on my little estate left.

If you can thus help me to get this first volume out, without my letting any of my friends know that I am advancing money on it, you will do me a great favor, by saving me from troubling my one and only sister, who has care enough from me, without this added.

Sincerely yours,
SUSAN B. ANTHONY

Without knowing the outcome, it is a safe guess that the generous Foster sisters did not allow Susan to sacrifice her government bond, either with or without the knowledge of her sister Mary. Mary's whole lifetime of care and worry about Susan's methods can be deduced from this episode. The Foster sisters had not always been on hand to rescue Susan from her rashness.

Woman suffrage was an old cause in Philadelphia when Rachel Foster came along, and she grew up under its influence. Her father, J. Herron Foster, had been a pioneer citizen of the city of Pittsburgh, the founder and owner of the Pittsburgh *Dispatch*. A fearless supporter of Lincoln in a district that did not generally support him, he had on several occasions during the Civil War demonstrated great bravery. Dying in 1867, he had left his wife and young daughters extremely well provided for. The widow took up her residence in Philadelphia, where her daughters were educated in the best schools of the city. In the Philadelphia of that era there were many young women of the type so well depicted by Mark Twain as Ruth Bolton in *The Gilded Age*. Rachel and Julia Foster were among the restless ones. Of the two, Rachel was the more independent and aggressive, the inheritor of her father's spirit.

When Mrs. Stanton's letters urging Susan to visit England began to arrive, Rachel took them seriously. Perhaps she felt there was some injustice in a situation that sent Mrs. Stanton on a holiday while Susan continued to slave at home. Furthermore, as she had plans for a European trip on her own account, she conceived the idea that Susan should accompany her as chaperon and traveling companion. It was a not uncommon practice for the daughters of the wealthy to "see" Europe in this way. Louisa May Alcott had made the trip, which did so much to stimulate her literary activity, as the paid traveling companion of an invalid. Young ladies did not venture into the Old World alone. Even Martha Carey Thomas, the strong-minded niece of Mrs. Whitall Smith of Philadelphia, could go only when accompanied by a friend. Susan's function in the arrangement was a standardized service.

With Mrs. Eddy's bequest in prospect, she felt she could take a vacation with an easy mind. Rachel's invitation was well timed. She had never known a real vacation. While working on the *History*, she wrote in her diary: "O, these old letters! It makes me sad and tired . . . to see the terrible strain I was under every minute, then, have been ever since, am now, and shall be, I think, the rest of my life." She did not foresee how soon the spell would be broken by a year of real vacation and the privilege of foreign travel. Like Mrs. Stanton, she had driven herself mercilessly for fear she might not live to see the end; and now, like Mrs. Stanton, she found that she had plenty of time ahead. The success of the work had rejuvenated her.

Miss Anthony was now doing something else of which the newspapers could approve. After thirty years of unremitting labor she was going to take a long rest. The editorials praised her as a representative American woman whom the Europeans would delight to honor. The Kansas City *Journal* burst into a glowing tribute: "Susan B. Anthony . . . goes abroad a republican queen . . . uncrowned to be sure, but none the less of the blood royal." Presents flowed into the Foster home, where Susan was staying, the most practical being a handsome traveling bag from the Fosters themselves. An anonymous New Yorker sent her a gift of one hundred dollars to be used for the purchase of an India shawl. Letters and telegrams kept the Foster doorbell jingling. A farewell message, signed by eighty of Rochester's leading citizens, was officially forwarded. This touched Susan deeply, though she was even more touched by the thought of her old friend, Mrs. Lewia Smith, "trudging through the slush and rain to get those splendid names to that testimonial." She knew all too well what such a trudge meant.

A farewell reception held in the Philadelphia Unitarian church was crowded with friends and well-wishers. Testimonials were read, speeches delivered, prayers offered, and the prevailing atmosphere was that of a warm family gathering. At the close Susan said:

"I feel that I must speak, because if I should hear all these words of praise and remain silent, I should seem to assent to tributes which I do not wholly deserve. My kind friends have spoken almost as if I had done the work . . . alone, whereas I have been only one of many men and women who have labored side by side in this cause. . . . Alone I should have been a mere straw in the wind. . . .

"I have known nothing the last thirty years save the struggle for human rights on this continent. If it had been a class of men who were disfranchised and denied their legal rights, I believe I would have devoted my life precisely as I have done in behalf of my own sex. I hope while abroad that I shall do something to recommend our work here, so as to make them respect American women and their demand for political equality."

It was a cold, blustery day in February 1883 when Susan and Rachel embarked on the *British Prince* for Liverpool. The papers contained formal notices of their departure. The New York *Times* took note of what Susan wore. "Miss Anthony was attired in a black silk dress and wore a black velvet bonnet. A beaver-lined satin circular was drawn tightly about her form." Susan had made great progress from the days when she had been a derided old maid agitating for a ridiculous cause. She was going abroad as a celebrity. Miss Foster was mentioned only as accompanying Miss Anthony.

❧ III   Always faithful to her diary, Susan was never more so than during her strenuous tour. Her record shows how little the itinerary of those who "do" Europe has changed in recent years. Planned for a young lady's education, it suited Susan exactly, with a few important modifications of her own at the end. Her travel notes are models of correctness in spelling and historical allusions, which is fairly surprising in view of her rather limited formal education.

Foreign languages, of course, baffled her utterly and she gave up any and all attempts to grapple with them. Rachel Foster plunged bravely in, and by the aid of dictionaries and private lessons achieved some degree of communication. But this was the only way in which youth showed its advantage over age. When it came to all-night journeys, all-day sight-seeing, and impromptu excursions, Susan outdid Rachel. In the things that mattered Susan was never a drawback. She wrote in her diary at the start: "I am bound to get all the good possible, to body and soul, out of this trip—and as little harm as possible"; and she lived up to it. What harm could she have anticipated? It was simply hard for her to believe that a complete release from responsibility and strain could be an unmixed blessing.

The travelers pursued the usual hop-skip-and-jump journey across the Continent. They headed for Rome after a week in London, where Susan had several good visits with Mrs. Stanton. Arriving on Easter Sunday, Susan viewed the religious procession with a cold Quaker eye. Otherwise she showed the correct tourist spirit. "Tomorrow we go to Naples and Palermo and then return to finish Rome." Few finished Rome more thoroughly than did the two, with Rachel's education as the goal in mind. Susan's personal reaction was contained in a comment written to her brother: "One is simply dazed with the wealth of marble—not only statuary, but stairs, pillars, and massive buildings." This appears to have been her main aesthetic experience in the Eternal City.

A few extracts from her diary exhibit her energies:

Mar. 29.—In Naples. Rachel and self and Chain party went up to Vesuvius. . . . Had a splendid time. It was wonderful to see and hear the evidences of fire and commotion beneath our feet; and, booming up into the air, red-hot lava.

Apr. 2.—Rachel, the Adamses, and self explored the Sybils' Grotto. Carried on stout men's backs through two feet of water.

Apr. 21.—Landed in Zurich at 6 P.M. . . . After dinner Rachel and self took cab and called on Lizzie Sargent who is studying medicine here. She is very earnest and happy in her work.

Apr. 25.—Left Zurich. . . . Got in awful strait at 4 P.M., when car stopped. [Evidently got out for some purpose.] Frantically motioned and shouted, the car man shouting *No time.* But I persisted and finally, just as car started, he pushed me upon back platform, opened a door, and in I went and he banged it to. I rode then to the next station, downright mad at the Old World's R.R. accommodations. The total disregard for comforts and conveniences for women is outrageous!

Susan spent a happy week in Berlin with the Sargent family, who had been her traveling campanions through the snowbound Rockies in 1872. The California senator had been recently appointed by President Arthur as minister to Germany, and his family enjoyed all the comfort and luxury that Berlin afforded. Sargent's daughter Lizzie belonged to the first group of American women who invaded the Zurich University. Susan relaxed with the Sargents and saw the sights, while Rachel prepared herself for her presentation at the Court of St. James's. Susan was a bit staggered by Rachel's dress—"cream-white satin, low neck, *no sleeves at all,* and a four-yard train." When Rachel reported later, after the court event, that she had handled the train successfully, Susan replied: "I am glad to hear that you were not cheated out of teetering through the palace halls in front of the princess, and that you are not utterly prostrated by it."

❧ IV　Meantime the travelers had progressed—by way of Cologne, Worms, the Rhine trip, Heidelberg, and Strassburg—eventually to Paris. Almost the first thing Susan and Rachel did in Paris was to call on Martha Carey Thomas, whom Rachel Foster had known in Philadelphia. Miss Thomas had just achieved her Doctor of Philosophy, *magna cum laude*, in Zurich, a most awe-inspiring distinction for a young American woman. This paragon of learning, only twenty-six, was not as yet greatly interested in woman suffrage, but she was still much gratified that Susan B. Anthony took especial notice of her. The two women, so far apart in age and interests, had many things in common, including the same Quaker background. The call was one which both of them would have cause in later life to remember.

Paris did not do much for Susan. She ran into a slump of spirits in that stronghold of good cheer. Rachel had gone to London and left her stranded with a strange language. She had been invited to share the home of one Mme. de Barron, an obscure but hospitable friend of woman's rights. Like Susan, she was no linguist. Her greatest contribution to her guest's experience was to serve her breakfast in bed. "At quarter to eight the maid brought roll and coffee. So I for the first time positively ate my breakfast in bed. What my dear mother would pronounce most lazily."

Susan's sight-seeing took place under more favorable auspices. Mrs. Stanton's son Theodore, who lived in Paris as a New York *Tribune* correspondent, spared no pains in showing her everything. Still Susan did not relax under his guidance. "Everywhere here are the reminders of the ravages of war," she complained to Rachel, "the madness of ignorance and unreason. I want to get away from them and their saddening associations. You will think I am blue. So I am, from having lived a purposeless life, these three months. I don't know but the women of America, myself in particular, will be the greater and grander for it, but I can not yet see how this is to be." She left Paris with no wish to return.

❧ V　Returning to England was like coming home again. She was welcomed by real, live, breathing woman suffragists. The hope-

lessness about women that she had brought from the Continent
was promptly dispelled by the woman's rights advocates whom she
met on every hand. She was immediately immersed in a propaganda
world not unlike her own world at home. Here she had a lot to learn
and something to teach.

The past history of the English suffrage movement was of course
well known to her. As long as the *Revolution* existed, she had received regular newsletters from English correspondents. The English movement was almost as old as the American. After John
Stuart Mill introduced the first woman suffrage petition in Parliament in 1866 and Mrs. Peter Taylor formed the first suffrage committee to support it, the movement had never subsided for a moment. A second bill, drafted by Richard Marsden Pankhurst and
proposed in Parliament by Jacob Bright, had followed in 1870. Like
the first, it was defeated. The only bills allowed to pass were those
limited to specific aspects of woman suffrage. The municipal franchise had gone through in 1869 and a bill for women's property
rights in 1882. Susan arrived in England while the women were still
elated over this last victory.

The suffragists had moved forward and, though handicapped by
more splits than the American movement had ever dreamed of,
continued to gain momentum. Active headquarters had been established in London, Manchester, and Edinburgh and a program of
petitions and meetings (called "demonstrations" rather than "conventions") regularly carried on. The demonstrations were sometimes lively. Women appeared at the party conventions with a banner emblazoned "Women Claim Equal Rights with Men" held
high in the air. As early as 1880 a parade of women suffragists took
place in London, in which a group of workingwomen carried a
banner saying: "We're far too low to vote the tax. We're not too
low to pay it." From the very first the Englishwoman employed
lively methods.

When Mrs. Stanton arrived in England in 1882, the campaign
for the Married Women's Property Bill was in full swing. She took
part in the campaign and shared in the celebration that followed
its passage. She was associated with Mr. and Mrs. Jacob Bright and
Dr. and Mrs. Pankhurst, all of Manchester, who headed the successful movement. Mrs. Pankhurst, the former Emmeline Goulden,
was only twenty-four, but already an ardent worker, having in-

herited the cause, so to speak, from a suffragist mother. At that time she must have met Mrs. Stanton, the portly American lady with silvery curls, and later Miss Anthony, the tall, thin, straight-haired lady with spectacles, for Mrs. Jacob Bright brought them both to Manchester and introduced them to the Manchester suffragist circle. Though Mrs. Pankhurst's memoirs place her first meeting with Susan B. Anthony at a much later date, she must have met her as early as 1883.

The Jacob Brights, with their relatives and friends, promptly took charge of Susan on her return to England. The Bright family were Quakers, and all of them, except John Bright, the most famous, were suffragists adhering to the radical wing. John Bright followed Gladstone in opposing the cause. But even his daughter reverted to suffrage, making public speeches for the cause while her father opposed it. Jacob Bright, his brother, was a lifetime champion of the suffragists. The Brights passed Susan on from one pleasant home to another, in several of which her hosts were M.P.s and in all of which the womenfolk were advanced and intelligent. She enjoyed in 1883 the kind of social life that Mrs. Stanton had found so pleasant in 1840. One may assume that she gained in polish and poise and lost some of her brusquerie, though fortunately not all of it.

It is a bit surprising in view of her environment to find her voicing this criticism: "Nearly everyone here clings to the class and caste principle, thinks that the world can not exist if a portion of the people are not doomed to be servants, and that for the poor to have an ambition to rise and become something more than their parents makes them discontented." As she had visited only the most liberal English homes, she had apparently expected something different, something more like her own American attitude. The stubbornness of tradition in the Old World was a lesson hard to learn.

Mrs. Stanton and Susan were regarded in England as very important people. No sooner had the latter arrived than preparations were begun for big London meetings to be addressed by them. The National Women's Suffrage Society planned a special meeting in their honor, to be held in London on June 25. This was to be followed by a rally on July 5 in support of the current suffrage bill. The American suffragists were the featured speakers at both meetings.

Susan was in considerable trepidation about her appearance in "Princes' Hall" (thus Susan's diary; Mrs. Stanton's diary calls it "Princess Hall"). With Rachel's help she worked hard on her speech. Jacob Bright presided and the hall was filled to capacity. The meeting was a great success. "Rachel said I made a good statement," was the greatest self-praise she would permit herself, adding that "Mrs. Stanton gave them the rankest radical sentiments, but all so cushioned that they didn't hurt."

The Americans were called into conference by the English leaders. The pending suffrage bill proposed, by some obscure English reasoning, to extend the franchise to spinsters and widows, excluding married women. "I am expecting a great ferment in the meeting today," wrote Susan, "for those who agree with Mrs. Jacob Bright have asked Mrs. Stanton to confer with them about what they shall do now. She advises them to demand suffrage for all women, married or single; but I contend that it is not in good taste for either of us to counsel public opposition to the bill before Parliament." Susan usually had more regard for parliamentary politeness than her friend; and in this matter she chose to be correct. Besides, the English suffragists were themselves divided on the issue, and she was well aware of the mischief done by factions and tried to stand outside of them.

After her Princes' Hall speech (delivered in her old black silk) she was crowded with invitations and engagements. On June 26, says the diary: "Went out with Rachel in A.M. and P.M. and finally ordered a dark garnet velvet dress at Waterloo House." She said she had wanted to buy a black dress, but Rachel, her good angel, persuaded her to buy what she really wanted. Then there was that hundred-dollar gift to be spent on an India shawl. "Mrs. Wilson went out with me and bought India shawl. Paid $250, a tremendous sum to put in one wrap; but it is for the rest of my life-time and for nieces after me." In spite of its great price she never valued the India shawl as much as the garnet velvet dress. The garnet velvet remained for many years her garment for state occasions. The India shawl never attained real fame, like her red silk shawl of humbler origin. She wore the garnet velvet for the first time at an American Fourth of July reception.

At this point Rachel Foster left her to join her family on the Continent. Again Susan missed her young friend terribly, but she

was among the English-speaking and full of plans. She had resolved
not to return to America without Mrs. Stanton in tow. But Mrs.
Stanton's daughter had married in England and was expecting a
baby; her mother declined to leave her. So Susan was left with a
slice of time on her hands to spend as profitably as possible. Her
own tastes and interests were expressed in the journeys she chose.

Her first jaunt was to Edinburgh to visit the aged Mrs. Nichol,
one of the few survivors of the World Anti-Slavery Convention of
1840; also to visit Dr. Jex-Blake, the pioneer woman doctor whose
name was so revered by the English suffragists. After these visits she
started forth on her own again. She hunted up the home of
Thomas Clarkson, founder of the anti-slavery movement, and also
the home of George Fox, the founder of Quakerism. It cost her
some trouble to locate these shrines, for other tourists did not seem
to seek them out. She passed on through the Lake Country, visited
the home of Harriet Martineau, and eventually arrived in the village of Haworth. Susan, who never thought she could write, wrote
this paragraph about the Brontë sisters:

On Saturday, Mrs. Ford took me to Haworth, the home of the
Brontë sisters. It is a bleak enough place now, and must have been
even more so fifty years ago when these sensitive plants lived there.
A most sad day it was to me, as I looked into the little parlor, where
the sisters walked up and down with their arms around each other
and planned their novels, or sat before the fire-place and built air-
castles. Then there were the mouldering tomb-stones of the graveyard which lies in front and one side of the house, and the old
church pew, directly over the vault where lay their loved mother
and two sisters. And later, when Emily and Anne and their erring
brother Branwell had joined the others, poor Charlotte sat there
alone. The pew had to be removed every time the vault was opened
to receive another occupant. Think of those delicate women sitting
in the fireless mouldy church, listening to their father's dry, hard
theology, with their feet on the cold, carpetless stones which covered their loved dead. It was too horrible! Then I walked over the
single stone pathway through the fields toward the moor, opened
the same wooden gates, and was, and still continue to be, dipped
into the depths of their utter loneliness and sadness, born so out of
time and place. How much the world of literature has lost because
of their short and ill-environed lives, we can guess only from its
increased wealth, in spite of all their adverse conditions.

Susan's interest in the Brontë sisters went back to the time when she had feared she might follow her sisters Guelma and Hannah into the grave. She had read Mrs. Gaskell's *Life of Charlotte Brontë* and had preserved a haunting memory of the Brontës' tragedy. They were so much like her and her own sisters. Her identification with them had contributed to her fear that their fate might be repeated in her own doomed family. She had recovered from this fear, but the Brontës had remained living realities to her.

Her devotion to Charlotte's novels was the outgrowth of her personal sympathy. She who read so few novels gained her ideas of love and marriage from these romances. Many years later, when one of her nieces married, she recommended that the bride read *Shirley*, impulsively adding she would send her her own copy. She searched her bookshelves. "I found *Jane Eyre* and *Villette* but *Shirley* is gone. I'll get the book downtown this very P.M." And so she did. Her diary expense account shows that she bought a copy of *Shirley* that same afternoon.

⪜§ VI   Something more than mere sight-seeing drew Susan to Ireland. Her interest in the Irish had long-standing roots in the example of her old friend, George Francis Train. The waves of Irish immigration, bringing girls of appalling ignorance to cope with American conditions, had sustained her interest. She regarded these girls, most of them in domestic service, as a part of the American woman problem. She wanted to see at first hand the environment which had driven them forth into lives of such loneliness.

One of the first persons she met in Ireland was Michael Davitt, a leader of the Irish revolt. She called on Davitt in Dublin and recorded with great satisfaction that he was "deeply rooted in the principles of freedom and equality, and claiming all for woman that he does for man." In Belfast she was entertained by a leading temperance worker, who took her on a tour of the Belfast whiskey shops. "I could not urge them to vote down the whiskey shops, as these are licensed by a justice of the peace, appointed by the Lord Chancellor of Ireland, who receives his appointment from the Queen of England! . . . I do not see how they can submit thus voiceless as to their own home regulations."

She then set forth to see the country from the top of a stagecoach—her favorite mode of travel in the American West. It was September. She had often encountered rain on her American travels, but never anything like the floods that descended upon her here. On a fine day she would mount the stage hopefully, but— "Before I had gone ten miles my seat was a pool of water and it took all my skill to keep my umbrella right side up." (Susan and her umbrella were inseparable companions: her diary shows how often she had it mended; likewise her shoes; likewise her spectacles.) "When 20 miles had past [she continues], I dismounted at the poorest hovel where the driver changed horses, and the good woman wrung the water from ulster, dress, skirts, and drawers, and dried or warmed them on me before her peat-fire."

Travel in a third-class car was little better but varied the discomforts and brought her in closer touch with the people. Revolted as she was by the tobacco-smoking and whiskey-drinking around her, she could still observe with a clear eye the social conditions which brought on such habits. "Something surely must be wrong at the root to bear such fruit." Her discovery that women also drank in Ireland was registered without surprise. Their heartbreaking poverty and rags stood out to the exclusion of all other details.

In Killarney, the beautiful, she rose to the usual tourist rapture about the scenery. "Killarney is lovely!" But her mood was promptly shattered by another glimpse of reality—the worst, in fact, that she had yet been granted. Leaving her traveling companion in the hotel, she walked out to explore the village alone. The experience which followed she related in a letter to Rachel Foster:

Saturday I sauntered along the streets of Killarney, passed the market, and saw all sorts of poor humanity coming in with their cattle to sell or to buy. Many rode in two-wheeled carts without seat or spring, drawn by little donkeys, and nearly all the women were bare-headed and bare-footed. On the bridge I saw some boys looking down. I looked too and there was a spectacle—a ragged, bare-headed, bare-footed woman tossing a wee baby over her shoulders and trying to get her apron switched around to hold it fast on her back. I heard her say to herself, "I'll niver do it," so I said, "Boys, one of you run down there and help her." At that instant she succeeded in getting the baby adjusted, and to my horror took up a bundle from the grass and disclosed a second baby! Then I went down.

I learned that she had just come from the poor-house, where she had spent six weeks, and before going further had laid out her two three-weeks-old boys on the cold wet grass while she washed out their clothes in the stream. The clothing was the merest rags, all scrambled up in a damp bundle. She had heard her old mother was ill in Milltown and had "fretted" about her till she could bear it no longer, so had started to walk ten miles to her. I hailed a boy with a jaunting car—told her to wait and I would take her home—got my luncheon—fed the boy's horse, bought lunch for boy and woman—and off we went, she sitting on one side of the car with her two babies, wet bundle, two milk bottles and rubber append-ages, bare feet and flying hair, and I on the other, with the boy in front.

For a long while both babies cried; they were blue as pigeons, and had on nothing but little calico slips, no socks even. She had four children older than these—a husband who went to fairs selling papers and anything he could to support them all—and an aged father and mother who lived with them. She said if God had given her only one child, she could still help earn something to live on, but now he had given her two, she couldn't. When we reached Milltown I followed her home.

It was in a long row of one-room things with a door—but no window. Some peat was smouldering under a hole in the roof called a chimney, and the place was thick with smoke. On the floor in one corner was some straw with a blanket on it, which she said was her bed; in another were some boards fastened into bed-shape, with straw packed in, and this belonged to her father and mother. Where the four other children, with the chickens and the pig, found their places to sleep, I couldn't see.

I went to the home of another tenant, and there again was one room, and sitting around a pile of smoking hot potatoes on the cold, wet ground—not a board or even a flag-stone for a floor—were six ragged, dirty children. Not a knife, fork, spoon or platter was to be seen. The man was out working for a farmer, his wife said, and the evidences were that "God" was about to add a No. 7 to her flock. What a dreadful creature their God must be to keep sending hungry mouths while he withholds the bread to feed them! . . .

Susan had seen as much of Ireland as she could endure. By taking a solitary walk and yielding to a kind impulse she had penetrated more deeply into Irish conditions than she had ever dreamed of doing. "I had meant to make the tour of the western coast up to Londonderry," she told Rachel, "but my courage failed. It was to be the same soul-sickening sight all the way—only, I was assured, worse than anything yet seen." She had learned enough to know why the Irish girls left home to lead lives of lonely exile in American women's kitchens.

She returned to the fogs and darkness of London in October. "I saw smoky, foggy days here last March," she said, "but they could not compare with this." Still the English bore up under it with their immemorial stamina, and Susan felt ashamed to complain. She was whisked from one lecture to another and continued to meet the famous and the great. Mrs. Millicent Garrett Fawcett and Mrs. Peter Taylor gave receptions in her honor, and the Jacob Brights renewed their hospitality and solicitude. All this might have turned another woman's head—but Susan's was set on too firmly. Both she and Mrs. Stanton came through without a dint in their personalities. As Mrs. Stanton once said, they had been so tempered by the fires of persecution and blame that they were immune to praise and glory.

At last when Mrs. Stanton's grandchild came safely into the world, the two women began their preparations for going home. They engaged passage on a ship sailing from Liverpool on November 17, 1883.

Susan was leaving with something unfinished on her mind. All the while she had been in England she had been seeking for some way to unite the English and the American suffrage movements. The itch to organize tormented her. But how to propose an overseas union to these disunited and faction-ridden English suffragists baffled her ingenuity. They could not unite themselves.

She hesitated until she practically saw the Servia in sight. Then desperation gave her courage. The Liverpool suffragists were holding a farewell reception for the Americans. Mrs. McLaren and Mrs. Lucas, Jacob Bright's daughter and his sister, had come to Liverpool to see them off. So had Mrs. Alice Scatcherd, the Liberal lady from Leeds, and a Mrs. Margaret Parker from Scotland. With this handful of persons, and as always backed up in her daring deeds by Mrs. Stanton, Susan decided to launch her international movement. The little group was hastily formed into an international committee, and Susan boarded her ship with her conscience much relieved.

CHAPTER TWENTY-THREE

THE HARVEST

❧ I   Susan and Mrs. Stanton arrived in New York on November 27, to find that there was still no news from the Eddy bequest. Susan had hastened Mrs. Stanton's return quite needlessly, it seemed. It was discouraging.

Mrs. Stanton wandered off to Johnstown, her old upstate home, and settled there indefinitely. A year later Susan was writing, trying to extract her from her retreat, though not yet with the *History* as a reason. "Miss Booth and I talked over your duty to live in New York, and be at home to receive friends on certain afternoons and evenings. And thus help on; and Mrs. Phelps . . . said she stood ready to invite guests to meet you and that you should be at no expense. I am sure of one thing and that is that Johnstown is as good, or bad, as a *burial-place*. You are there lost to the work of pulling down the strongholds of prejudice against women either publicly or privately." Susan was determined to keep Mrs. Stanton at work if only as a social celebrity.

Her own reaction to the disappointment had been to proceed straight to Washington, without even going home, to see what could be done there. She arrived with the prestige of a successful European tour. The newspapers greeted her with flattering notices. Instinctively press-wise, Susan was ready for the reporters. Speaking for herself and Mrs. Stanton, she said, "I had no idea we were so well known in Great Britain or that there was such a cordial feeling toward us. Of course I met chiefly those known as Liberals and the sympathizers with our cause. Public sentiment there is rapidly growing in our favor."

Still nothing was heard from the Eddy case. But a faint breeze blowing out of Boston indicated some change. Returning to her hotel one afternoon, Susan found a caller waiting. It was Mrs. Caroline Dall, closely associated with the *Woman's Journal*. Mrs. Dall had been one of the earliest and most vocal among the Boston critics of the *Revolution*. "She had been a long time finding me," says the diary. "Said she had called twice before!!" (Punctuation Susan's.) There was no doubt that the chilly atmosphere of the Hub had moderated somewhat.

In February 1884 Wendell Phillips died suddenly. He had long been a sufferer from a weak heart, as he knew and as he had once confided to Susan. In January, just before she had left for Europe, she had seen him in connection with the Eddy business. At the time Phillips had handed her a copy of his Phi Beta Kappa oration before the Harvard alumni, saying, "Here is probably my last speech." Susan had replied, "Oh, no, you must not say so." But she had forgotten his warning. She took the oration with her to England and read it aloud on several occasions; once to the aged Ernestine Rose, whom she discovered in the last infirmities of old age without philosophy to bear them. She had not seen Phillips since her return, and now she would never see him again. The matchless voice was stilled. She attended his funeral in Boston and (as was the custom) gazed at the lifeless silent face which in former days had almost mystically enthralled her.

She did a brief span of work with Mrs. Stanton in Johnstown, whither she repaired, like Mohammed to the mountain, having first transported thither the cumbersome mass of materials from Tenafly. But neither of them was in her best form for work. Susan was breathlessly watching the fate of a suffrage bill in Oregon. When Mrs. Duniway's noble efforts ended in defeat, Susan was agonized. "I rushed to the bank and sent her $100," she said. Immediately after this the Liberal party in England dealt the woman suffrage bill in that country a stunning defeat. Susan's broadening sympathies had brought both Oregon and England close to her. She now had friends on all fronts.

There was nothing for her to do but return to her lecturing. The Slayton Bureau routed her on a difficult tour, extending from Illinois to Louisiana, with widely separated way stations. The seasoned traveler made her dates, as usual, along the tour mapped out. Passing through Iowa at the end of April, she received a summons from Boston. The courts had at last finished with all the legal complications connected with the Eddy will, and the legacy awaited her at the executor's office.

Susan's journey from Iowa to Boston was accomplished without a stop. She and Lucy Stone met for the first time in many years in the executor's office. The legacy of each, in stocks, bonds, and securities, all finally cleared in neat Boston fashion, amounted to $24,125. The famous Benjamin F. Butler, their counsel, had charged no fee for his services. Only the routine court fees and a few small legacies had been subtracted from the original amount.

Susan sewed all this wealth into a pocket of her petticoat. A lone woman, oppressed by the thought of the riches on her person, she went to sleep in her Pullman berth. This led to one of her dreams —a horrible nightmare. She thought that a woman stood at the head of her berth, strangling her, while a man cautiously slid his hand along the berth toward the bulging pockets of her petticoat. She gave a loud scream and awoke to explain it was only a dream. Everything was in order as she had left it. But she prudently decided not to go to sleep again, and completed the journey from Boston to Rochester wide awake and on guard. Susan had had several encounters with pickpockets in the course of her travels, so this dream was not wholly without a basis in experience.

Without waiting a single day after she reached home, she began work on Volume III. "On May 1st I had my books, boxes, and bundles all carried from cellar and wood-house of No. 7 into your dear Ma's front parlor," she wrote to Louise Mosher, "also two tables that were Aunt Gula's. . . . Then I put one of your Ma's bed-steads, filled an old feather tick with nice clean straw, and there I sleep and work." If she had expected to lure Mrs. Stanton to share this Spartan regime, she was doomed to disillusionment. But by a fortunate coincidence Mrs. Stanton regained possession of her Tenafly residence at about the same time. Once more the books, boxes, and bundles were on their way to New Jersey and the Tenafly Tower.

The authors resumed their old strenuous routine. Again the ladies toiled at record speed. Volume III was the hardest stretch of all, with its contributions from others and from the scattered states. One must consider that they had not the slightest secretarial aid, not even availing themselves of the typewriter. "Oh, what dreadful manuscripts some women do send us!" says Mrs. Stanton's diary. "It is enough to destroy our old eyes. It is astonishing what dry bones we receive from our collaborators." To decipher the manuscripts and to cover the dry bones were harder for Mrs. Stanton than to write the whole book. Susan plodded on faithfully, but she too found grounds for complaint. "Here Mrs. Stanton and I are, scratching, scratching every hour. . . . I can not get away from my ball and chain. . . . Now here is the publisher's screech for money. . . . O, to get out of this *History* prison!"

Like the other two volumes, Volume III was completed in six months of concentrated work. They had brought the American movement up to 1886, added historical chapters on England and France, and promised in the preface to supply pamphlets on future developments. It was a spirited history and almost, if not quite, as good as the first two volumes. A variety of contemporary subjects were dealt with and, though always with a polemical slant, the facts were reliable, and related moreover in most cases by eye-witnesses. As the authors had promised, it was history written by those who had lived it.

⚜ II   Was it the possession of a large legacy that reawakened Susan's desire to be a publisher? Or was she discontented with her present publishers? The following letter to Mrs. Stanton shows her at an early stage of Volume III scouting around to make a change:

[No date]

I talked with Mr. Putnam about taking our *History.* Said if I were now asking him he would probably take it, but he would not entertain the idea of taking hold of Volume III. Fowler and Wells will do it on the same terms as the other two volumes. I haven't decided whether to let them do it thus or to take it in hand myself; or in the name of the National Woman Suffrage Association, if that could be shortened. . . . Don't you think we had better thus place the *History* and leave it so that the National Association may have it as a source of income?

There is nothing to indicate that Fowler and Wells had not done well by them; nowhere is there any suggestion of unfairness on their part. Susan must have believed that they had found it a profitable venture or she would not have thought of bestowing the profits on the National Association. Her optimism was based on the success of Volumes I and II, promoted, incidentally, by Fowler and Wells. It was also based on her belief that she could publish for less money than the publishers were charging her. In short, with a little capital in hand, she at once thought of re-entering the publishing business on her own account.

Her daring reminds one of Mark Twain, who launched his unfortunate publishing business in that same year—1885. His act grew out of his chronic distrust of commercial publishers. Susan may have had a similar feeling, though she never said so. Twain's ultimate failure did not come soon enough to warn Susan. As usual, she moved quickly. No memory of her grand business scheme to raise silkworms in mulberryless Battenville came to stay her hand. She decided not only to publish Volume III herself but to take over the two previous volumes as well. She bought out the rights of Fowler and Wells and made a contract with a Rochester printer, an old personal friend, to print the forthcoming volume.

No sooner was the contract made than her troubles began. The printer was in Rochester, Mrs. Gage in Fayetteville, and Susan and Mrs. Stanton in New Jersey; all of them were immovable except Susan. She had to make the contacts, and even her high rate of speed was scarcely adequate. The appalling cost of the steel engravings continued unchanged. Mrs. Stanton decided that she was like Balzac and could not revise written copy, demanding proof sheets for the purpose. The cost was grueling for a publisher. Susan was visited by the absurdest of all fantasies for her. "It is the great drawback at every turn," she said, "that I have not the faculty to frame easy polished sentences. If I could but do this, I would finish up the *History* without asking aid of anyone." She had known from the inception of the idea that the project depended mainly on Mrs. Stanton's literary fluency for its success, not to mention the help of Mrs. Gage and other contributors.

For the first time Susan thought of the distribution end of the business. This she eased somewhat by sending the work as a gift to most of the libraries and colleges of the country. A thousand copies were disposed of in this way and another thousand were presented to legislators and distinguished friends of the cause. She did not intend to give all away but to sell as many as possible. But the psychological effect of her generosity was to undermine the market. Besides, even the business of packing and sending volumes without charge proved an onerous burden.

Mrs. Stanton and Mrs. Gage, with a healthy instinct for survival, demurred at Susan's freehandedness. They ended by withdrawing from the distribution part of the business. They settled their claims for future royalties with Susan, receiving lump sums of two thousand and one thousand dollars respectively. When Volume III was finished, she had paid out twenty thousand dollars on the work and her name appeared in the imprint as sole publisher. She alone was responsible for the sale of the entire History. She had come into the possession of a valuable property, whose true worth, however, depended on her own business activity. Charles Mann, the Rochester printer, had no interest in the sales. They were to be Susan's exclusive concern.

٭§ III   During the early 1880s, Susan saw little of her home in Rochester. Her European trip, writing the History, and congressional lobbying kept her occupied in far-distant places. The thought that it was Mary's house and home no doubt affected her subtly, though she had expressed herself as recognizing the justice of Mary's possession. During these years she spent more time in Mrs. Stanton's home than anywhere else.

In 1883, while Susan was in Europe, her sister retired from teaching. Mary had been principal of a public school three blocks from her house for fifteen years and a public-school teacher in Rochester for twenty-seven years. After her mother's death she had kept house for the two widowed brothers-in-law, looked after the education of two nieces, and managed two houses. At the age of fifty-six she decided to retire and did so without consulting Susan. She must have written the news to her sister in Europe, but the diary makes no mention of it. Susan was very far away from home at the time and the only thoughts she directed toward home were concerned with the education of her nieces.

Mary enjoyed the ownership of her house, which gave her a new dignity and status in the community. Every year when she paid her taxes she enclosed a formal protest. She did not, like the Smith sisters in Connecticut, allow her property to be sold rather than pay taxes to a government which denied her the vote, but every year she registered her protest again "taxation without representation." Often she registered it at considerable length. Occasionally her letter appeared in a local newspaper. This was her own private and special contribution to the cause of woman suffrage, one which even her sister, the famous suffrage leader, could not make.

The greatest change in the Rochester household came with Aaron McLean's withdrawal in 1886. This happened not through a second marriage, as Susan had once so bodefully anticipated, but through wholly unpredictable causes. McLean would gladly have remained for the rest of his life at 17 Madison Street, pursuing his daily round of business as long as strength remained, waiting for Mary to close his eyes at the end. But the California fever that he had escaped in his youth caught up with him in his old age.

The fever, long dormant, broke out in the second generation of his family. They had outlived the myth of gold, but the lure had been revived in another form. One of their descendants told the writer that his parents "went West to make a fortune out of growing grapes; but they did not make it." In 1886, however, the grape-growing project shone with bright prospects, and McLean's daughter and her husband George Baker set out for the Golden Fleece. The idea of separation from his grandson, the idol of his heart, almost his own child, was a thing that the aging McLean could not bear to contemplate. At seventy-four he retired from business and joined the highhearted adventurers headed for the West. What Susan had feared most for the stability of her home had come about through an agency that she could never have foreseen. Yet she might have realized from the start that the only rival from whom she had anything to fear was young Henry Baker.

Susan succumbed to an unusual depression on receiving the news. About to set forth from Mrs. Stanton's on a lecture tour, she wrote: "It never was harder for me to start. A heavy nothingness is upon head and heart." The end of this tour found her in Rochester. "Arrived home at 8 P.M. and found all well—the all consisting of sister Mary, the only one left." The home toward which she had always cherished such ambivalent emotions had reacted to her neglect by turning itself into a new and different place. The picture of her sister Mary as a lone woman touched her. It was probably then that she first began to feel reconciled to the thought of sharing the house with Mary.

◅§ IV   Another reason for Susan's prolonged absences from home had been her long stays in Washington. Starting in 1869 as a transient lobbyist, she had been able to lengthen her visits into long periods of residence. When Senator Sargent's family moved to the capital, she was invited to be their guest for as long as she wished or as the cause demanded. This was the beginning of a new life for Susan. On January 18, 1874, the diary says: "This afternoon Mr. and Mrs. Sargent and self rode all over Washington, my first ride over the city, though I have been here every winter the past six years." As long as Sargent remained in the Senate, finishing a term of six years, Susan had a Washington residence. Mrs. Sargent continued as her faithful and devoted friend and sturdy helper all this time. She served as treasurer of the National Association until obliged to resign by the end of her husband's tenure.

Providentially for Susan and the suffrage cause, Mrs. Sargent's hospitality was then replaced by that of Mrs. Jane Spofford, whose husband conducted the hotel known as the Riggs House. Mrs. Spofford provided not only a room but a suite of rooms for Susan whenever she cared to use them, and she did as much for Mrs. Stanton. During the twelve years that the Spoffords ran the Riggs House, the hotel was Susan's home and she was treated as any honored guest paying the highest rates. And Mrs. Spofford, like Mrs. Sargent, saw to it that she no longer made her weary pilgrimages on foot.

When Susan returned from Europe in the dreary last days of November, it was to the Riggs House that she turned instead of home. An unfriendly paper commented: "There must be money in being a reformer, for Miss Anthony lives at the Riggs House in good style, and expects to be there all winter, and this, after a summer in Europe, would be a severe drain on any but a long purse." The reporter must have known, or could easily have found out, that the generosity of Mrs. Spofford and Miss Foster made such things possible for Miss Anthony.

No one realized better than Susan that as long as men held the purse strings the donations of women must be made in services. She had run the suffrage movement mainly on such donations and was the first to acknowledge it. She once said fervently in a public speech: "Every woman presiding over her table in the homes where I have been has helped to sustain me, I wish they could know how much." So anxious was she to give them proper credit that she insisted on mentioning their names in her first biography. Though Mrs. Harper, the author, often protested and the literary effect was that of a very dull society column, Susan was obdurate. Her gratitude to Mrs. Spofford, who had contributed so much to her work in Washington, knew no bounds. As an old lady, Susan said, "What she did for me and the cause is beyond estimate." Still, one notes that she had carried on in the capital for six years without such help, showing how much she valued from the first her annual contacts with Congress.

⁂ V   It was no accident that the bright days of woman suffrage came along in the '80s while Susan, when not lecturing, sojourned in Washington. The congressmen knew that she was there. During a brief enforced absence she wrote Mrs. Spofford: "I shall return tomorrow night, if possible. I keep thinking of those men at the Capitol not doing what I want them to." For eight years after her return from Europe in 1883 she was able to keep the men at the Capitol well informed as to her wishes.

She never deviated from the belief that a Federal amendment was the primary solution of the suffrage question. At the first congressional hearing after her return from England she stated her position and her reasons in one of her best speeches. It ran in part:

"This is the fifteenth year we have appeared before Congress in person, and the nineteenth by petitions, asking national protection for women in the exercise of their right to vote. . . .

"But, you say, why do you not go to your several States to secure this right? I answer, because we have neither the women nor the money to make the canvasses of the thirty-eight States . . . to educate each individual man out of the old belief that woman was created to be his subject. . . . You know, gentlemen, if the negro had never had the ballot until the majority of white men . . . had

voted 'yes,' he would have gone without it until the crack of doom.
. . . We now appeal to you to lift the decision of our question
from the vote of the populace to that of the legislatures, that
thereby you may be as considerate and just to the women of this
nation as you were to the freedmen. . . .

"It takes all too many of us women from our homes and from
the works of charity and education in our respective localities, even
to come to Washington, session after session. . . . But when you
insist that we shall beg at the feet of each individual voter of every
one of the States . . . you doom us to incalculable hardships and
sacrifices, and to most exasperating insults and humiliations.

"Liberty for one's self is a natural instinct possessed alike by all
men, but to be willing to accord liberty to another is the result of
education, of self-discipline, of the practice of the golden rule. We
ask that the question of equality of rights to women shall be decided by the picked men of the nation in Congress, and the picked
men of the several States in their respective legislatures."

Devotion to the Federal amendment did not prevent her from
joining in practically every state crusade that came along. Through
lecturing and canvassing she was known in more states than any
other suffragist of her time, including the Bostonians who advocated state-by-state action. She had long recognized that the tide of
woman suffrage was rising in the West and would eventually roll
eastward. But with every Western area that she canvassed she became more convinced of the necessity for Federal action. She had
started out with the Garrisonian line and she never forsook it.

From 1884 the suffrage cause made good progress. In that year a
Senate committee submitted the first majority report in its favor
and a House committee produced a strong minority report. In 1887
the first floor vote on woman suffrage took place in the Senate.
This was an exciting occasion. Fifty women from all parts of the
country, headed by Susan, looked on breathlessly from the gallery.
They had not expected a floor vote in their favor, but their hopes
expanded in the heat of action to include all possibilities. They
were badly let down by the resulting vote—sixteen yeas to thirty-
four nays. The strongest opposition came naturally from the South,
where the legend, if not the practice, of chivalry still survived.
Oddly enough, the South was re-enforced by New England, whence
a pompous "remonstrance" signed by a small number of intellectuals and clericals had been sent to impress the voting congressmen.

Obviously the hopes of women for a Federal amendment lay in the West and Midwest.

Shortly preceding the senatorial vote, Kansas had granted municipal suffrage to women. Susan had participated in the campaign. For some unexplained reason the Kansas women woke up and the Kansas liquor interests went to sleep. The latter made no move to dispel a force which was sooner or later to bring on trouble for them. The campaign was the easiest—perhaps the only easy one—of Susan's whole career. She spoke only in the main towns of the state, but the country people flocked to hear her, driving thirty, forty, and fifty miles in their buggies and wagons. Twenty years before, she had ridden over trackless plains to reach them; now, with better roads, they came to her. When municipal suffrage won, a newspaper remarked: "It is seldom that the beginner of a great reform lives to see such fruitage of her labors."

Susan herself did not regard the fruitage as overwhelming. She had learned too much about municipal suffrage in England to hold it of vast account. But she could not fail to be gratified by the gain of half a loaf, attended as it was by so much demonstration of spirit. "We are holding . . . the most magnificent audiences—no church or hall holding them," she wrote. She saw this as no mere personal tribute but as the sign of a great advance in the popularity of her cause.

The run of good luck continued, culminating in the admission of Wyoming three years later as a full-blown, woman suffrage state. Women had voted in the territory since 1869. Now strong influences in Congress insisted that the practice be discontinued as a condition of statehood. The subject was once more agitated in Washington, and a Boston "remonstrance" was dusted off to overawe the congressmen. But the habit and practice of twenty years prevailed. The Wyoming Legislature simply declined to accept statehood except under its own conditions. Statehood was finally granted, though against a heavy vote in both Senate and House, with equal suffrage rights for both sexes. On July 4, 1890, the suffragists all over the country celebrated the birth of the first woman suffrage state.

✑§ VI Immediately after the municipal vote carried in Kansas, the Senate took up the Federal amendment. To the horrified surprise of the suffragists in the gallery, the senator from Kansas, Ingalls, was observed voting with the opposition. In their convention afterward, the women's indignation overflowed. Susan, who had never attacked a congressman in public, even the most inimical, yielded to an impulse and roundly denounced the senator. Contrary as it was to her usual form, this was news.

The senator was troubled. He wrote to Susan asking for an interview. Susan did not reply. He then called twice at her hotel and she was not in. Meeting her at last accidentally, he explained that he wished to propose a truce. Susan declined. Returning to Kansas later to canvass for the Federal amendment, she discovered that the senator had really been pinked. He had been making public speeches at home in defense of his stand. His arguments were the ancient ones and could have been applied to municipal suffrage, already a law in his state, as much as to the proposed Federal amendment. Susan used his speech for a text and took it apart in every town where she spoke. Ingalls was retired by his party at the end of his term. How much her speeches contributed to his downfall, one cannot say. She certainly did a great deal to show he was out of step with his party, which needed municipal as well as Federal offices in the state. Apparently the senator thought he had made a mistake. After his retirement he made a belated statement in favor of woman suffrage.

By her steadiness and persistence Susan had become a well-known and much-respected figure in Washington. From the first she had had powerful friends in Congress and had known how to use them. Among them were such men as Ben Wade of Ohio, Pomeroy of Kansas, Butler of Massachusetts, Palmer of Michigan, Reed of Maine, Dolph of Oregon, Sargent of California, Anthony of Rhode Island, Lapham of New York, Julian of Indiana, and Stanford of California. These men were not her converts, of course, but had been shaped by early environment and home influences to co-operate. So strong was the current of the woman movement in those days that the obscurest of housewives and mothers were often active promoters, exerting their anonymous influence sometimes on very prominent men.

A lobbyist without money, Susan had to ask many exceptional favors of her congressional friends. For one thing, she would have the suffrage hearings broadcast through a congressman's mailing list, under his franking privilege. The official reprints always gave both sides, but she was never against free speech. Even the *History* devoted pages to the adverse arguments. As long as the favorable arguments were heard, she cared not what accompanied them.

For some time Senator Blair of Maine figured as her closest aide. She "pressured" Blair mercilessly. "I thought just as likely as not you would come fussing round before I got your Amendment reported to the Senate. I wish you would go home," he wrote; "go home and get married." They planned and executed numerous small coups together. For instance, when Wyoming was admitted as a suffrage state, the English suffragists sent official congratulations. Susan wanted this promulgated and sought Blair's co-operation. "The memorial of congratulation which you sent me is not one which I could press for presentation as a matter of right," he reported, "but fortunately by a pious fraud I succeeded in reading it without interruption, so that it will appear, word for word, in the [Congressional] Record."

Susan had chosen a career which obliged her to depend upon men. While her principal fame rests on her influence over women, her actual work depended on her influence over men. Her whole effort and struggle required the co-operation and good will of the ruling sex. She knew perfectly well what "indirect influence" meant but was prohibited by nature and desire from using it. Her appeal was addressed to men's reason and fairness. A Tammany politician who presented a bill in Albany year after year for Susan and Mrs. Stanton and their friends was jokingly taken to task by his friends. "I respected those ladies," he replied, meaning that he unconsciously responded to their own self-respect.

Harriet Taylor Upton, a close friend of Susan's in her later years, has left this interesting comment: "Because of Miss Anthony's mental grasp of all affairs—both governmental and domestic—men were always attracted to her when she met them individually, for she could 'speak their language.' She could always understand their viewpoint. Because of this she formed close friendships with men whom she liked. This sometimes led to unkind remarks by others."

Mrs. Upton was the daughter of Representative Taylor of Ohio, friend of the suffragists and their sponsor in the House during the '80s. She lived in her father's home in Warren, Ohio, and Susan seldom failed to visit them when passing through the state. Mrs. Upton's opinion must have been her father's as well as her own. What she may have meant by unkind remarks about Susan's attitude toward men, she did not bother to explain. They probably sprang from the impression, common then as now, that Miss Anthony was uniformly and consistently prejudiced against the opposite sex.

In this connection, a legend, emanating from this time and originating with a close friend, has quietly persisted. Though the writer could find no direct substantiation, the story emerged in the following form: Susan was said to have received a proposal of marriage in her sixties from some man of consequence in her environment. Though she refused the proposal, she was said to have continued the alleged romance by correspondence for a long while. A friend who knew her well in later life made this comment on the story: "Miss Anthony could never have retired from her public work. I think it would have caused a frustration of either or both ways of life. And then, even so, there was Mary who was her alter ego." Considerations of the kind as well as her heart dictated a refusal, which was apparently not abrupt but friendly and did not terminate a cherished friendship. The story confirms Mrs. Upton's unexplained testimony—that she sometimes formed close friendships with men whom she liked.

The breadth of her outlook was that of maturity. It was she, among all the older suffragists, who saw and acted upon the necessity of recruiting younger women for their society. It was she who put Mrs. Stanton's daughter, Harriot Stanton Blatch, into the foreground of the national conventions. She valued Frances Willard, not only for her ability but for her comparative youth. To Rachel Foster she transferred many responsibilities, training her to grow up to them. Another young woman, May Wright Sewall, headmistress of an Indianapolis girls' school, was discovered and installed as a lieutenant. Other young adherents who came along were Clara B. Colby, who published a suffrage paper, and Harriet Taylor Upton.

Those who flocked about her were fine women. Susan estimated them by their efforts and their efficiency, never by their affection for herself, though this was usually a by-product. Her final yardstick for them, as for herself, was selfless devotion to the cause.

She was never condescending, even to the youngest, but treated them as fellow workers on her own level. When she spoke out of long experience her advice would run like this: "Your young shoulders will have to learn to bear the crotchets of all sorts of people and not bend or break under them. . . . Put the blame on me; they may abuse me but not you. . . . Vent all your ill-feelings on me but keep sweet as June roses to everybody else. . . . You will have to learn to let people pile injustice on you and then trust to time to right it all."

But up to the end of the '80s she had not found one who was willing to leave all and follow woman suffrage as she had done. This was not surprising. Even Mrs. Stanton often darted off to pursue false gods and had to be pulled back into line by her watchful friend. It was entirely possible that the movement might never cast up another single-minded, dedicated leader like herself. Susan squared her shoulders and resolved that she must live long enough to see the Federal amendment through.

≈§ VII The month of March 1888 brought the fulfillment of Susan's international dream. The small handful of women who, with herself and Mrs. Stanton, had formed an international committee on the eve of their sailing, was the small acorn from which the great oak grew. The others would have forgotten it, but Susan kept the idea alive by busy correspondence. In 1887 she induced the National Woman Suffrage Association to sponsor an International Council of Women. After five years of nurture the seed bore solid fruit.

Preparations for the council were carried on for a year. Rachel Foster and May Wright Sewall shared the preliminary labors, and Susan put in two solid months at the end. As the plan developed, it was decided that the council should include all phases of woman's work and that suffrage should be only a co-ordinate phase. Susan had seen too much of Europe to expect, from any but the English, a hearty response to a union based on suffrage alone. But she had also seen signs of an awakening on the Continent which she thought should be recognized.

At the same time she had no intention of soft-pedaling the suffrage idea for her own countrywomen. Her young lieutenants were somewhat confused and misled by her sudden broad-mindedness. "I have just received," says the diary, "proof of the 'Call' for the Council and struck out the paragraph saying, 'No one would be committed to suffrage who should attend.' I can't allow any such apologetic invitation as that! There is no need to say anything about it."

Her aim was to gather as many women as possible into the International Council; numbers were paramount. As expressed in the "Call," the council was to "give women a realizing sense of the power of combination." As long as the council was sponsored by the National Woman Suffrage Association and one of its purposes was to celebrate the fortieth anniversary of Seneca Falls, she thought enough had been said. By this compromise she showed how far she had developed in her feeling of security about the suffrage cause.

In the midst of the preparations she received a letter that pleased her more than she would allow herself to admit. The American Association accepted the invitation to take part in the event. She had let down the bars for the unconverted and the elect had rushed in. Susan hastily wrote the glad news to her friend, Mrs. Miller, at Peterboro:

Riggs House, Washington, D.C.
Jan. 26, 1888

My dear Mrs. Miller: . . . Everything looks bright as to the Council; very many conservative associations have appointed delegates—and Lucy Stone and Mrs. Caroline H. Dall have accepted the National's invitation to attend—apparently gladly!!

This she followed by a letter to Antoinette Blackwell, long estranged but never so much so as was Lucy Stone:

. . . So, my dear, I am very, very glad that you and Lucy are both to be on our platform, and we are to stand together again after these twenty years. But none of the past! Let us rejoice in the good of the present, and hope for more and more in the future.

The American Association came down in full force. Lucy Stone, Caroline Dall, Julia Ward Howe, Henry Blackwell, Edna D. Cheney, Mary Livermore, and still others took part in the council. All of them made speeches. They were accompanied by a

young minister, Dr. Anna Howard Shaw, whom they had recently
recruited into their organization. Dr. Shaw was a young forty-one,
full of enthusiasm for a cause she had embraced under the influence
of Lucy Stone and Mary Livermore. She preached a sermon at the
Sunday council meeting which, in spite of having St. Paul for its
text, was firmly slanted toward woman suffrage. As Susan listened,
she realized that Mrs. Stanton, with all her skill, had never been
able to make St. Paul speak for woman's rights. She also realized
with a burst of joy that in Anna Shaw the movement had acquired
another spontaneous and splendid orator.

This was enough for Susan. Staunch Mrs. Gage, with her wonderful mind and amazing scholarship, had never been able to make
an impression on the platform. Susan's young lieutenants did not
excel as orators. Yet here, matured and full-blown in a comparatively young woman, was the talent she craved for the cause. Anna
Shaw had previously heard little about Susan, and for reasons which
may be surmised that little had not been altogether to Susan's
credit. Reacting to unfavorable advance notices, Anna Shaw became, as one is likely to do in such cases, an ardent convert.

Susan and Anna Shaw had some confidential talks. The latter
says in her memoirs that at that time Susan persuaded her to drop
her temperance work, which had hitherto occupied a large part
of her time, and concentrate her energies on the suffrage cause.
Miss Shaw was entirely amenable. On returning to Boston she
wrote to Susan: "From my heart I pray I may always be worthy
of your love and confidence. To know you is a blessing; to be
trusted by you is worth far more than my efforts for our work have
cost me." A friendship was begun which was strong enough to last
them for the rest of their lives. Susan's judgment of people had
vastly matured since the days when she sponsored Victoria Woodhull and expected daring deeds of Anna Dickinson. Incidentally,
Anna had finally gone on the stage, definitely cutting herself off
from the field of social reform.

The International Council made a fine impression on the public.
Albaugh's, the largest opera house in Washington, was crowded
for eight afternoons and evenings. Forty-nine foreign nations and
fifty-three American organizations were represented. Flags of the
foreign nations and of the separate states were hung out, evergreens
and flowers were banked about the platform, and a large portrait

of Lucretia Mott hung over the president's chair. Elizabeth Cady Stanton delivered the opening and closing addresses of the convention.

That Mrs. Stanton was on hand to do this was wholly due to Susan's enterprise. As usual before each suffrage convention, Mrs. Stanton tried to back out. This time she had an excellent excuse, for she was staying with her daughter in England. When the familiar symptoms set in, Susan was terrified. In similar emergencies she had gone to Mrs. Stanton, wherever she was, and collected her bodily. This time she endured a great strain, as her diary records:

Feb. 1.—Received postal from Mrs. Stanton saying it was doubtful if she came to Council. Was too incensed to write, so waited.

Feb. 2.—Received Mrs. Stanton's letter to Rachel bidding her to get Susan ready to make the opening speech and get along without her. I was more on fire than ever.

Feb. 3.—At 9:30 this eve. mailed the most terrific letter to Mrs. Stanton in response to her postal to me and letter to Rachel Foster, saying she might not come to Council.

Feb. 14.—Wash., D.C. Riggs House.—Got cablegram from Mrs. Stanton this P.M. saying simply "Coming," showing that she had received mine of the 3rd. So my heart was relieved. Sent word immediately to Miss Foster and Mrs. Sewall, and ran downstairs to tell Mrs. Spofford.

Mrs. Stanton appeared in Washington a few days before the council opened. Susan's joy was partly quenched when she learned that her friend had not prepared a single speech, when two were expected, for the occasion. With Mrs. Spofford's aid she sentenced Mrs. Stanton to solitary confinement, in a hotel room well furnished with pens, ink, and paper, and she herself stood guard over the door. Her strong-arm methods worked. At the last moment Mrs. Stanton emerged with two excellent speeches. Susan opened the convention suavely and with the dramatic touch that she had planned: "I have the pleasure of introducing to you the woman who joined with Lucretia Mott in calling the first Woman's Rights Convention—Mrs. Elizabeth Cady Stanton."

The International Council was made permanent, with national councils assembling every three years and the international every five years. The idea of permanence originated with May Wright Sewall, who had worked too hard to see her efforts absorbed by a single occasion. Frances Willard was elected as the first president of the American National Council. She was Susan's selection for the office. At first Miss Willard took a prominent part in the affairs of the council but later on became immersed in American party politics. The council fell back into the care of Susan, Mrs. Sewall, and those who had first fostered it. It represented great things to Susan, being her first vision of a union of women transcending national boundaries. It was her first stumbling attempt to give her sex a concept of the world as one.

There was an aftermath of the council which upset Susan terribly. Rachel Foster's subsequent marriage to a man whom she had met at the International Council furnished the disturbing event. Susan had seen so many helpful young women drop out of the movement through marriage that she at once gave Rachel up for lost. She could not attend the wedding because she was busy lecturing far out in the West. But the fact that the Reverend Anna Howard Shaw performed the ceremony must have partly reassured her. Later when her lecture tour brought her to Illinois, Rachel came down from Chicago to Rockford to see her. The diary says, "She seemed happier than words can tell." In fact, Rachel was so happy that she wanted to make Susan happy also. She wanted to assure her that, as Mrs. Avery, she expected to do as much for suffrage in the future as she had done in the past. Even then young women were changing, and the change was taking place under Susan's eyes.

The International Council in Washington was the first place where Susan wore her traditional red shawl. She donned it for warmth at the council sessions—an ordinary red silk shawl with knotted fringe that a friend had given her. She continued to wear it at the Washington conventions until the reporters finally decided she had always worn it, from the beginning on. It was not that old, but it soon became fixed as a tradition. A Washington paper said, "Spring is not heralded in Washington by the approach of the robin red-breast but by the appearance of Miss Anthony's red shawl." The reporters loved it. At one convention, when she failed to wear it, a note came up from the press table: "No red shawl, no report." Susan laughed and sent a messenger to her hotel to fetch the missing garment. Henceforth it was a symbol. How long she kept up the custom we cannot say, but at least ten years after the council she was still wearing it.

CHAPTER TWENTY-FOUR

REUNION IN WOMAN'S RIGHTS

§ I   By the end of the '80s the suffrage movement had registered specific gains. The International Council had bestowed prestige, the adherence of the W.C.T.U. had expanded the membership, the municipal franchise in Kansas had been a political triumph, and Wyoming's equal franchise had come as a grand climax. But nothing indicated more progress than the final ending of the split between the two national suffrage bodies, which came about in 1890.

The reconciliation, so obviously suitable and desirable, had lingered for twenty years, while each organization had gone its own way. The Nationals, under the leadership of Mrs. Stanton and Susan, had forged ahead of the Americans, under Lucy Stone and her husband; but the Americans had also prospered. The public spectacle of the two organizations pursuing the same aim had long been detrimental to both. To justify it, differences of policy had been developed, which, of no importance at first, had acquired substance through time. The Americans stuck to their state-by-state program, while the Nationals focused on the Federal amendment. But both societies worked for both and there was (as yet) no practical conflict between their methods.

Step by step the reconciliation took place. Mrs. Eddy's legacy, announced in 1882, broke the ice. The slender olive branch extended by Susan and Mrs. Stanton in their *History*, in the form of a chronicle of the American Association, quickly followed.

Though the Americans did not value it as history, they were obliged to recognize it as a friendly gesture. Then all rapprochement stopped for a while.

When Susan was in London with Mrs. Stanton in 1883 she still had no expectation of any reconciliation. They called on William Henry Channing, their old ally of the '50s, who had gone to live in London and inherited the pulpit of James Martineau. Susan's diary notes: "At 3 P.M. Mrs. Stanton and self called on Rev. Wm. H. Channing and spent two hours. Told him of Lucy Stone's persistent persecutions through all these years since 1867. He expressed great surprise and sorrow and seemed fully to accept our word." They confided to Channing as to a father confessor, only to relieve their minds as they could not have done at home. They expected nothing from the interview, and nothing came of it. Channing had lost all interest in American affairs. He died soon afterward.

When the legacy was finally divided between Susan and Lucy, they embarked on similar careers with the proceeds—Susan with her History and Lucy with her Woman's Journal. They were both publishers of sorts. The new alignment established a new footing of equality between them. There was some alleviation of the defensiveness on both sides. Still Susan was not prepared for what followed.

At the annual meeting of the Americans in Philadelphia on October 31, 1887, a definitive step was taken. The following resolution was adopted: "Whereas . . . whereas . . . and whereas . . . Resolved, that Mrs. Lucy Stone be appointed as a committee of one from the American Woman Suffrage Association to confer with Miss Susan B. Anthony, of the National, and . . . that she be authorized . . . to appoint a committee of this association to meet a similar committee appointed by the National to consider a satisfactory basis of union. . . ."

Susan was touring Indiana when this resolution was passed. Speaking in one town after another in a swift canvass which covered the state, she never stopped for more than one or two days in the same place. "I have laid me down to sleep in a new bed every night of this entire time," says the diary. At some point on the road the notification reached her. To judge by her diary, she had paid no attention over the years to the Americans' conventions.

When Susan decided to forget, she did not pretend to forget; she forgot. To use her favorite word for such a surprise, she was simply "stunned" by the letter. She replied instantly to the message, saying that she would meet Lucy Stone in Philadelphia, whence the message came, within the next two weeks (leaving Indiana in the lurch); or she would meet her in Washington on December 9, when she was due to arrive there. Neither proposition suited Mrs. Stone, who had meanwhile returned to Boston. She pleaded ill-health and requested Susan to come to her.

A very small and exclusive group met just before Christmas in the Park Street offices of the *Woman's Journal*. The principals had decided to invite two other persons: Mrs. Stone brought her daughter, Alice Stone Blackwell, with her, and Susan brought Rachel Foster. The presence of the younger women was a tacit admission by both leaders that they had aged. It was likewise an easement of the emotional atmosphere. And, incidentally, it reveals the loyalty of Rachel Foster to Susan in sacrificing her home ties to suffrage business during the holiday season. As for Susan, Christmas had always been just another working day.

After their first conference Susan and Rachel repaired to a hotel to remain until the agreement could be set down in writing. The formal proposition, when it came, specified: that their respective committees should decide on a common name, a common constitution, and a common list of officers to be proposed first to their respective associations and then to a joint meeting. Susan replied promptly in the affirmative. Two days later Alice Stone Blackwell communicated the following suggestion in a note to Rachel Foster:

Since many members of the National Society regard Mrs. Stone as the cause of the division, and many members of the American regard Mrs. Stanton and Miss Anthony as the cause, Mrs. Stone suggests that it would greatly promote a harmonious union, for those three ladies to agree in advance that none of them will take the presidency of the united association.

This suggestion was a triumph of selfishness, for the superior numbers of the National made Mrs. Stone's chances of becoming president extremely remote. As an added ironical touch, it was handed to Susan on Christmas Day. She agreed, as she had agreed to everything, her one thought being to facilitate and hasten the reunion. But she and her companion then proceeded to depart, possibly to forestall any more of these complicating afterthoughts.

In Washington she quickly appointed her committee, with May Wright Sewall as chairman, Harriet Robinson Shattuck of Boston as a member, Rachel Foster as secretary, and a few others. The committee was afterward expanded to satisfy the demand of the Nationals. Susan herself proposed no conditions. She wrote to Rachel Foster:

I can not think of any stipulation I wish to make the basis of union save that we *unite*, and after that discuss all measures and ways and means, officers and newspapers, and cheerfully accept . . . the rule of the majority. . . . When united we must trust to the good sense of each, just as we have trusted during the . . . division. As Greeley said . . . *"the way to unite is to unite"* and trust the consequences.

◆§ II   But Susan was apparently the only one in a hurry. The negotiations dragged on. It was too much to expect that people so long frozen against each other should thaw, melt, and interflow all of a sudden. She could do nothing to hasten the amalgam. "I shall be glad when this frittering away of time on mere forms is past," she wrote to Rachel. Fortunately the International Council of Women followed in 1888, offering a chance for a rehearsal of the reconciliation.

The rest of the year was spent in bridging the gap. Slowly awakening to the idea, the membership of the National Association began to make trouble. Mrs. Stanton, for instance, had strong objections to the constitution as proposed by the Americans. She wrote:

In the matter of the union of our two national woman suffrage societies, I am urging simplicity in everything. I especially do not like [the article] which makes possible the election of a man to the presidency of the organization. I would never vote for a man to any office in our societies, not, however, that I am "down on" men *per se.* . . . Having men pray or preside for us at our meetings has always seemed to me a tacit admission that we haven't the brains to do these things for ourselves . . . On the whole I find the suggested constitution very wordy and obscure. It is a very mannish document. . . . I ask Susan what is the matter with our little old constitution, which we simple-minded women drew up back I do not know when.

Mrs. Stanton desired the reunion as much as Susan, but as usual she took the high ground, leaving her friend to negotiate and secure it for her. The American Association had at the moment a man for president, in keeping with its long-established policy. Except for the brief passage of Tilton, the National had held to the rule that no man was to be president. Mrs. Stanton would not willingly see herself replaced by a man, no matter how admirable he might be. However, this was all eventually worked out, for after all the National Association had the votes.

The Nationals in general did not welcome the Americans as warmly as had been anticipated. There was far more reluctance than Susan had expected. Objections rose from among the rank and file. They were going along all right as they were; why introduce a change? It would mean new personalities, new influences, new ideas, not necessarily congenial to National practice. Some of them said bitterly: "We shall be no more than an annex to the W.C.T.U. hereafter." Susan was kept busy reassuring the doubtful and persuading the recalcitrant. She saw the reunion as a providential chance to retrieve a historical error—such a chance as seldom comes around within a single lifetime. She was prepared to yield all, but her correspondents assured her that this could not be done.

When the word got around that Mrs. Stone, Mrs. Stanton, and Miss Anthony were all to refuse the presidency, the National's pot began really to boil. The membership almost as one woman declined the proposal. Susan soon saw that a vote for union could not be achieved unless the stipulation was abandoned. Either she or some associate persuaded the consulting committees to give it up.

All this took much time. Finally, on January 21, 1889, a committee from the National signed a basis of agreement with the American committee. It was a fairly simple agreement after all. The association would be called the National-American and the election of officers would be held at the first joint convention. There were a few other items, such as the one providing that the annual joint convention should be held in Washington, all of which were accepted without much discussion at the time.

The question of the presidency, once it had been opened up, created a minor whirlpool within the ranks of the National. Some of the members discovered that Mrs. Stanton not only had reached seventy-four but had lately shown a strong predilection for living in England. Moreover, she was perfectly willing to hand over the office to her bosom friend. Nothing could have displeased Susan more than to be forced into rivalry with Mrs. Stanton at this critical time. When she learned of the project, she was wroth beyond measure. Those who proposed it she viewed as dark conspirators against suffrage. Mrs. Gage, who had a hand in it, fell under her dire displeasure. Her anger was the measure of her fear that the promoters of the scheme might very well succeed. Aside from her personal devotion to Mrs. Stanton, she had reasons of principle for opposing the plan.

On the morning of February 17, 1890, the delegates of the two societies met in separate rooms at the Riggs House. "When 10 o'clock came," said Susan, "the Nationals packed the private dining-room to suffocation and the Americans looked lost in the great parlor. So I proposed to the Americans to exchange with the Nationals, which they did very cheerfully." The episode forecast the relative voting strength of the two bodies. Susan realized that all depended on the Nationals' producing a solid vote for Mrs. Stanton, as many of the Americans would probably vote for Susan. She gathered her energies for a supreme effort on behalf of her friend. Visibly much moved, she addressed the preliminary gathering of the National voters. Her voice was tremulous but her words were firm. She said:

"I appeal to every woman who has any affection for the old National or for me not to vote for Susan B. Anthony for president. I stand in a delicate position. I have letters which accuse me of having favored the union solely for personal and selfish considerations, and of trying to put Mrs. Stanton out. Now what I have to say is, don't vote for any human being but Mrs. Stanton. . . . When the division was made twenty years ago, it was because our platform was too broad; because Mrs. Stanton was too radical; a more conservative organization was wanted. . . . If you have any love for our old association, which . . . has stood like a rock in regard to creeds and politics, demanding that every woman should be allowed to come upon our platform to plead for her freedom— if you have any faith in that grand principle—vote for Mrs. Stanton.

"I want every one who claims to be a National to continue to stand for this principle. We have come now to another turning-point and, if it is necessary, I will fight forty years more to make our platform free for the Christian to stand upon whether she be a Catholic and count her beads, or a Protestant of the straightest orthodox creed, just as I have fought for the rights of the infidels the last forty years. These are the principles I want you to maintain, that our platform may be kept as broad as the universe, that upon it may stand the representatives of all creeds and no creeds—Jew or Christian, Protestant or Catholic, Gentile or Mormon, pagan or atheist."

Susan said not a word about the different political parties, which in 1890 were already beginning to affect the solidity of the suffrage ranks. She went back instead to the issues of the time when the Americans had originally rebelled and left the fold. She was resolved that in returning they should accept the broad-mindedness of herself and her friend as one of the policies of the future society. Her followers listened less to her words than to her strong feelings. Knowing her staunchness, they felt that she must be right.

At the meeting which followed, Mrs. Stanton was elected president. The most rigorous parliamentary rules were observed in the election. Susan received 90 votes and Mrs. Stanton 131. (Some of the large vote for Susan must have come from stubborn Nationals.) Susan was satisfied, though she would have preferred the Stanton vote to be unanimous. The continuity of the suffrage movement had been preserved and its descent from Seneca Falls fully established.

Lucy Stone was unanimously chosen chairman of the executive committee; Rachel Avery and Alice Stone Blackwell were made secretaries; and Jane Spofford remained treasurer. Susan retained her old position as vice-president-at-large. A lone man was tacked on at the end of the list as auditor. Anna Howard Shaw was appointed national lecturer.

After her eloquent and much-applauded acceptance speech, Mrs. Stanton hastily left just in time to board a vessel that was sailing for Europe. In fact, Susan had succeeded only by the most herculean efforts in holding onto Mrs. Stanton for her own election. Among other things, she had sent her her carfare to Washington and return. This was all right with both of them. Once Mrs. Stanton stood on the platform, giving utterance to the sentiments which Susan adored, the latter felt fully rewarded for her every effort. And Mrs. Stanton never disappointed her. She opened her acceptance speech by saying: "I consider it a greater honor to go to England as the president of this association than would be the case if I were sent as minister plenipotentiary to any court in Europe." When she rose to leave, the entire audience rose with her, cheering and waving a hearty farewell. Mrs. Stanton wrote in her diary that she was deeply touched by the demonstration. It never entered her thoughts, nor Susan's, that this wreath was laid at her feet chiefly by her admiring friend.

Susan took the chair, and as she did so a large bouquet of white lilies was handed to her. After all, the flowers had been reserved for Susan. A spirited session of speech-making followed, half of which was contributed by speakers from the Americans' side. The only missing note in the harmony was the absence of Lucy Stone, who had been detained at home by illness at the last moment and was represented by a letter. But her husband and her daughter took their turns on the platform. "Blackwell never spoke better," says Susan's diary.

The long separation was over; the hatchet was buried. That night Susan wrote: "Everything seems moving smoothly, though no doubt there is at heart some chagrin that Mrs. Stanton is the chosen standard-bearer." The chagrin, if any, remained well concealed. The diary continues, "All closed with seeming good feeling all round. . . . Mrs. Julia Ward Howe made most lovely word to me." The American Association had apparently come round to Susan's point of view—the way to unite was to unite. This way they were through with the burden of organizing. Henceforth that particular work would be rolled off onto the shoulders of the woman who had showed she could bear it.

At this point their co-operation ceased. In her first response to their overture, Susan had naïvely assumed that the union would somehow embrace the *Woman's Journal.* "Let us unite," she said; "all other questions including that of 'newspapers' can be settled afterwards." Her old dream of a single organ for the suffrage movement momentarily revived. For a time in the past Mrs. Gage's *National Citizen* had held out a slender hope. But in spite of all of Susan's efforts to preserve it, by gathering subscriptions after every speech she made, the *National Citizen* had gone out of existence.

Then the *Woman's Tribune*, founded in 1883 by Clara B. Colby in Beatrice, Nebraska, had come to take its place. Without benefit of trusteeship or incorporation, Mrs. Colby, a fine Western guerrilla type, had managed to keep her paper going up to now. After seven years in Nebraska she moved her enterprise to Washington, where it continued to prosper and to divide the field with the *Woman's Journal*. The *Tribune* came as near to being the organ of the National Association as Susan's and Mrs. Colby's co-operation could make it. But it continued to owe its existence to Mrs. Colby's sole management.

Susan had known Mrs. Colby since her first lyceum trips through the West, had campaigned with her in Nebraska in 1882, and had formed a strong friendship with her through the years. She promoted the *Tribune* as she had formerly promoted the *National Citizen*. At the first motion toward reunion she envisioned a combination of the *Tribune* and the *Woman's Journal*, issuing with double strength from a New York or Philadelphia office, and supported by the entire National-American membership. Her vision was quickly dispelled. The *Woman's Journal* was to remain, as it had always been, an independent journal, subject only to Mrs. Stone and her family and the corporation that controlled it.

This was more disappointing to Susan than to Mrs. Colby, who was quite content to pursue her precarious course alone. She did so quite successfully for many years. In fact, both papers went their ways contentedly. Susan alone deplored the waste of two suffrage papers in the field, and continued from time to time, but vainly, to try to persuade them to unite.

Obviously Susan and Lucy Stone found the reconciliation a trying ordeal. Though officially friends and officers of the same association, they still seemed fated to stay apart. On her side, Mrs. Stone missed the first united convention. Soon afterward she invited Susan to speak at the Massachusetts suffrage anniversary. Susan accepted cordially. She got as far as the Parker House in Boston, where her usual good health failed her and she succumbed to an attack of the grippe. Mrs. William Lloyd Garrison, Jr., took her at once to her Boston home and nursed her for a week. Lucy Stone did not call during her illness. She sent a note saying, "Everybody was disappointed that you could not be at the meeting so that they might at least see you." One of the best-known public figures

of the day, subject of cartoons and front-page news in most newspapers, Susan was a person still to be seen by the Boston suffragists.

The first time they faced the National-American convention
together was in 1891. Mrs. Stone said, "This is the first time I have
stood beside Miss Anthony at a suffrage convention in Washington,
but I have stood beside her on many a hard-fought battlefield before
most of those present were born." Lucy returned to Washington
again in 1892, and, together with Susan and Mrs. Stanton, appeared
before a congressional committee. She spoke well and vigorously.
On October 18 of the following year, she died. Susan's entry in her
diary that night ran: "Lucy Stone died this evening at her home
. . . aged 75. I can but wonder if the spirit now sees things as it
did 25 years ago." Her thoughts still went back to that old bitter
time instead of to their more recent happier relationship.

Whatever may have been at the bottom of the rift cannot be
discovered from the known facts of their lives. But it was too
fundamental to be easily wiped out. Susan, as a rule, was far more
able to forget and forgive than the average character. Her relationship with Lucy Stone stands out as exceptional in her life's pattern.
One cannot help observing, however, that the tenacity with which
she clung to Mrs. Stanton was equaled only by the tenacity with
which she rejected Mrs. Stone. Nothing could change or influence
her feelings for the two, slightly unreasonable as they were in both
instances. It seemed as if her friendship for the one and her hostility for the other were, in some way unknown to herself, interlinked
and for that reason could not ever be independently weighed.

⋙ III   Susan accepted the reunion philosophically. It was not
consistent with her Quaker habit to show great joy or sorrow. Regrets for wasted years she saw as useless; they only added to the
waste. She foresaw that out of the union must come new problems—as they did. The suffrage organization had acquired an influx
of new blood, a very important influx, one which would have to
be assimilated. One thing, apparent from the first, was that the
union had augmented the number of younger workers.

Frances Willard had long been detached from the American
Association and was now one of Susan's most dependable aides.
She bade fair to devote a long future to suffrage work. Alice Stone

Blackwell, a competent writer, speaker, and editor, came to the front as her mother's representative. Mrs. Harper's biography states emphatically that no other person contributed as much toward effecting the union of the two societies as did Alice Stone Blackwell. This was a prodigious feat for so young a woman (Miss Blackwell was thirty-three) and gave convincing evidence of her intelligence and executive ability. A daughter who can swing her own parents into line in a difficult situation must be credited with unusual talent.

Also out of the Boston wing came the natural-born orator, Anna Howard Shaw. Miss Shaw added a further attribute: she was footloose, like Susan. She once described the latter as "the founder of a modern school of women peripatetics, ready to grab their grips and start around the world at a moment's notice." Without hesitation Miss Shaw joined the peripatetics and soon piled up a record that rivaled that of the founder.

Still another addition from the Boston wing, though originally coming from the West, was Carrie Lane Chapman. Mrs. Chapman was a young widow from Iowa who had tragically lost her husband and turned her thoughts to woman suffrage. At thirty-one she had already achieved a reputation as lecturer and organizer in her native state. She appeared for the first time on the National suffrage platform at the reunion convention of 1890. Sharing the honors of the day with veterans like Mrs. Stanton, Mrs. Hooker, Henry Blackwell, and Julia Ward Howe, she did not attract much attention by her speech. (Susan's diary does not mention it.) But it was afterward to be remembered as a worthy contribution on her very first appearance.

In this group Susan gained what she had long been looking for, a younger generation of workers who could keep pace with herself. The American society did not bring strength in numbers, but it brought strength where it was needed—individuals with a talent for leadership. Mrs. Stone's slightly chaotic organization had perhaps been a better proving ground than Susan's well-disciplined ranks.

◂§ IV   On the eve of the final merger Susan rounded out her seventieth year. Her two devoted aides, May Wright Sewall and

Rachel Avery, conceived the idea that another birthday celebration was due, like the one she had had at fifty. Susan was at first delighted and then, on learning that the guests were to pay four dollars for the privilege, frightfully dismayed. Her old-fashioned sense of hospitality revolted. She told the young women that it could not go on: she would split the expenses with them. In the course of an excited correspondence she argued, "If it were to honor Mrs. Stanton, I would be willing to charge for tickets." It may be that this statement, once made, helped to bring her to her senses. If it was possible thus to honor Mrs. Stanton, it might be within the realm of possibility thus to honor herself. The younger women assured her that "it was done." She gave in finally, with the proviso that complimentary tickets should be issued to a long and formidable list. Mrs. Avery and Mrs. Sewall gladly accepted the list as a compromise.

The grand dining room of the Riggs House presented a festive scene on the night of February 15, 1890. The Washington *Star* began a notice of the affair by saying, "A company of the most remarkable women in the world were assembled." It was no exaggeration. Many women, distinguished in their own right, and some men, distinguished in the same way, graced the party. Senator Blair and Representative Pickler, whom the press sometimes referred to as "Susan B. Pickler," were among them. Seated to the right and left of Susan were the gray-haired pioneers of the cause: Mrs. Stanton, Mrs. Gage, Mrs. Hooker, and Miss Clara Barton. Among the younger women were Anna Shaw, Phoebe Couzins, Clara B. Colby, Ida Husted Harper, and Mrs. Stanton's two married daughters. Mrs. Avery, who had worked like a Trojan up to the last minute, was obliged to forgo the pleasurable rewards of her labors. According to the custom of the times, a pregnant woman was not supposed to show herself in society. Mrs. Sewall, beautifully gowned and unimpeachably slender of figure, presided over the dinner.

The guest of honor, tall, gray-haired, bespectacled, clad in her ageless garnet velvet adorned by point lace, sat quietly in her place, surveying the lively scene.

"She never looked better," said the New York *Sun* (violently anti-suffrage in policy), "never happier, and never so much like breaking down before her feelings. . . . Friends of her youth calling her 'Susan,' affectionate deference from everybody, and all saying she deserved a thousand such birthdays—young in heart, beautiful in spirit."

Letters and telegrams were read from Whittier, Senator Hoar, Senator Tom B. Reed, Frances Willard, Terence Powderly, Leonora Barry, and many others. The speech-making was of a high order. Mrs. Stanton, responding as usual to the inspiration of the occasion, delivered one of her best and most often quoted addresses. "The Friendships of Women," as she called it, concluded with this tribute to Susan:

"If there is one part of my life which gives me more intense satisfaction than another, it is my friendship of more than forty years standing with Susan B. Anthony. Ours has been a friendship of hard work and self-denial. . . . Emerson says, 'It is better to be a thorn in the side of your friend than his echo.' If this add weight and stability to friendship, then ours will endure forever, for we have indeed been thorns in the side of each other. . . . Dear friends, I have had no peace for forty years, since the day we started together on the suffrage expedition in search of woman's place in the National Constitution. . . . I have often wished that my untiring coadjutor might, like Elijah, be translated a few years before I was summoned, that I might spend the sunset of my life in some quiet chimney corner and lag superfluous on the stage no longer.

"After giving up all hopes of her sweet repose in Abraham's bosom, I sailed some years ago for Europe. With an ocean between us, I said, now I shall enjoy a course of light reading . . . and write no more calls, resolutions, or speeches for conventions—when, lo! one day I met Susan face to face in the streets of London with a new light in her eyes. Behold, there were more worlds to conquer. She had decided on an International Council in Washington, so I had to return with her to the scenes of our conflict. . . .

"Well, I prefer a tyrant of my own sex, so I shall not deny the patent fact of my subjection; for I do believe that I have developed into much more of a woman under her jurisdiction, fed on statute laws and constitutional amendments, than if left to myself reading novels in an easy chair, lost in sweet reveries of the golden age to come without any effort of my own."

Mrs. Stanton's speech was followed by many others, until at last Susan was obliged to rise and pay her acknowledgments. She expressed her thanks first to Mrs. Stanton, then to her own family, and then to the host of anonymous women throughout the country who had sustained her work. Her awareness of these absentees in such a crowded moment showed where her talent for leadership lay.

One feature of the celebration struck a more serious note. In honor of Susan's birthday Mrs. Colby issued a special edition of the *Woman's Tribune*, which contained a complete account of her 1873 trial for voting. While the minor events of Susan's life were being rehearsed in pleasant anecdotes, Mrs. Colby recalled to memory that grim and historic episode. It was a fitting reminder. The older people had forgotten it; the younger ones knew little about it. The *Woman's Tribune* called it back to life on this appropriate occasion.

The good cheer of the evening continued until a late hour. "I am ashamed to say," says Mrs. Stanton's diary, "that we kept up the festivities till after two o'clock. Those who were there will not soon forget February 15, 1890."

Susan, however, managed to forget it very promptly. The party took place on the eve of the great reunion. Early the next morning Susan was on hand to greet the Boston delegates to the first joint convention of the two societies. The convention was scarcely closed when her energies were again requisitioned without warning. A telegram from Rachel Avery informed her that Rachel's sister Julia had been taken seriously ill. Susan was in Philadelphia before Mrs. Avery had received the answer to her telegram. She accompanied the stricken Julia to a sanitarium and summoned her sister Mary from Rochester to stand by while she returned to Washington. Mary came at once (one of many instances when Mary responded without question to her sister's call for help), while Susan made a quick transition back to Washington, and from Washington out to South Dakota.

The outcome of this emergency reached Susan in the form of two telegrams, which overtook her at way stations in the West. The first, reaching her in June, announced that the Avery baby had arrived and all was well. The second, reaching her in November, brought the sad intelligence that Julia Foster had died. Susan was too far away when these telegrams came to do anything but send telegrams in return. When she returned in the spring she hastened to her friend and arrived in time to attend the baby's christening. Mrs. Avery, who had lost father, mother, and sister, had come to look on Susan as her nearest relative.

و§ V Preparing for the rigors of the South Dakota campaign, Susan complained, "The time draws near when I must start out compaigning and O, how I dread it!" Conditions in South Dakota proved to be worse than she had imagined. The pioneer cabins, the poor roads, the shabby hotels made traveling and stopping equally to be dreaded. The rawness of the country is seen by an entry in Susan's diary: "Elk Point. June 6, 1890. Guest of Mr. Smith. They have been here twenty years. Oldest settlers I have found."

She made her first rounds in the company of Mary Seymour Howell, whose healthy sense of humor helped to mitigate the hardships. Later on she was joined by Anna Howard Shaw, whose possession of the same quality was all that could be desired. Both of them left stories of their travels with Susan.

Miss Shaw relates how Susan was speaking on a hot afternoon under a canvas, when a baby immediately in front of her cried without ceasing. Susan finally said to the mother, "I think your baby is too warm. Take him out and give him a drink." The woman flaunted out, highly insulted, and spread the word that this was only what could be expected of an old maid suffragist. Susan and Miss Shaw were greatly alarmed. Miss Shaw, who was to speak the next day, resolved to redeem her friend's *faux pas* if possible. She soon had a chance. There were several babies in her audience, all crying at once. At last some of the men protested, saying, "Don't you want these children taken out?" "Oh no," she replied, "there is nothing that inspires me so much as the music of children's voices." She stood her ground, and the men had to bear it, however unwillingly.

Mrs. Howell recalled how she overheard their landlady exclaim, amid the clatter of dishwashing, "Well, I thought I couldn't live through having Susan B. Anthony here, but I'm getting along all right. You ought to hear her laugh; why, she laughs just like other people!" Susan's awesome reputation had preceded her, and one can judge from this good woman's remark what it had been like.

In Madison, South Dakota, on July 10, 1890, a more serious incident took place, according to Mrs. Howell:

That evening we spoke in the opera house in the city. While Miss Anthony was speaking a telegram for her was handed to me, and as I arose to make the closing address I gave it to her. I had just begun when she . . . put her hand on my arm and said, "Stop a moment, I want to read this telegram."

It was from Washington, saying that President Harrison had signed the bill admitting Wyoming into the Union with woman suffrage in its constitution. Before she could finish the great audience was on its feet, cheering and waving handkerchiefs and fans. . . .

Miss Anthony made a short but wonderful speech. The very tones of her voice changed; there were ringing notes of gladness and tender ones of thankfulness. It was the first great victory of her forty years of work. She spoke as one inspired, while the audience listened for every word, some cheering, others weeping. . . .

The gift for which Susan had so often prayed was vouchsafed to her for this obscure occasion. It was perhaps the highest flight of oratory in her career. What she would have given to be able to command this visitation of the spirit whenever she needed it, only she herself knew. Even this flight would have passed unnoticed but for Mrs. Howell's accidental witnessing of it.

Early in the summer Susan sent out letters asking for aid, most of them addressed to the new American allies. Mostly regrets and good wishes came back in response, but Henry B. Blackwell and Carrie Chapman Catt replied in the affirmative. Mr. Blackwell toured the state for six weeks at his own expense. Mrs. Chapman, who had become Mrs. Catt soon after her visit to the Washington convention, now lived in Seattle with her second husband. With this South Dakota tour Mrs. Catt initiated the formal agreement she had made with Mr. Catt, that marriage should not interfere with her work for woman suffrage. After only a few wedded months she left home for a long stretch of duty on the suffrage front.

It was Mrs. Catt's first experience in a frontier region. She rode on freight cars and handcars, ate the poor food, and spoke in the open, in barns, and in half-finished buildings. "When it got cold," says her biographer, "she bought some plaid flannel in a store and sewed it into a dress on Sunday and wore it on Monday." Her hardships were not lessened by any great hope of the outcome. A realistic observer, she wrote: "We have not a ghost of a show for success. . . . Ours is a cold, lonesome little movement, which will make our hearts ache about November 5th." Like Susan, she persevered throughout the hopeless campaign, never faltering or giving ground. The only difference between them was the very considerable one of age. Mrs. Catt was thirty-one and Susan was seventy.

It is an interesting side light on Susan that she failed to see at once in this vital young woman a new and driving force in the suffrage cause. She still nursed a certain distrust of the effect of marriage on ardent young suffragists, not realizing that a new and different generation had come along. She had overlooked Mrs. Catt's speech in Washington; it was too factual, too much like her own. In fact, Mrs. Catt had no wish to emulate the orotund style of the great pioneer, Mrs. Stanton. She had listened to Mrs. Stanton rather critically in Washington.

After her second marriage Mrs. Catt became Carrie Chapman Catt, retaining, for her own reasons, the name of her first husband. Susan privately criticized her for this, insisting that she should have kept her father's name instead. Susan had evidently forgotten that Paulina Wright Davis, the beautiful and brilliant suffragist who died in 1876, had done the same thing. Very likely Mrs. Catt was influenced by her example, and she could scarcely have chosen a better one. But Susan continued to refer to her in her diary and in her letters as "Mrs. Chapman" for years after her marriage to Mr. Catt.

Having little hope that the suffrage bill would pass, Susan withdrew her attention for once to observe the condition of the people. The newborn state was suffering from a prolonged drought. Susan's comment on the situation ran: "Why could not Congress have appropriated the money for artesian wells and helped these earnest, honest people, instead of voting $40,000 for a commission to come out here and investigate?" The settlers apparently agreed with her opinion. They joined the Farmers' Alliance and the Knights of Labor and waged a heated third-party campaign of their own. The intensity of the conflict left them little time for the women, who went from one convention to another trying to be heard. Mrs. Catt had said in her first prophecy: "Continuing as we are, we can't poll 20,000 votes." On election day they polled 23,000, or about one third of the total number of votes cast. In this, the most hopeless of their many state campaigns, the suffragists did not register a total defeat.

But the campaign had cost a great deal of money, all that the National-American could rake and scrape together, and a vast deal of energy. It had been uphill work, unrelieved by hope. Susan and Anna Shaw reached home in a state of complete physical exhaustion. Mary said of her sister that she realized for the first time that she was growing old. Mrs. Catt suffered the worst penalty of all. She had picked up a typhoid germ in her travels, which came very near then and there to ending her suffragist career.

CHAPTER TWENTY-FIVE

THE DULL NINETIES

⌐§ I   The so-called Gay Nineties of the American scene were rather the dull for Susan B. Anthony and her suffragist friends. As the result of the momentum gained in the previous decade, a few victories were chalked up; then the movement settled down to a long period of the doldrums. Still the effort for achievement was never once relaxed, and the moral ideal never for one moment lost its hold.

One must look into social and economic history for the chief cause of the slowdown, but there were incidents within the movement which contributed to its occurrence. One of these, without doubt, was Susan's withdrawal from the Washington scene in 1891. At the January convention of that year she announced her intention of retiring to housekeeping in Rochester. While the step was approved by her friends as appropriate to her age, her age was only one of the reasons that led her to take it. The chief reason was that the Spoffords, whose hospitality had made possible her long stays at the Riggs House, decided to retire and spend the rest of their days in their Maine country home. The Riggs House had provided Susan with a good lobbying base for twelve years. Accident had provided it and accident took it away.

Susan's announcement brought general rejoicing to her old friends. They had a wonderful time. Letters of approval poured in and presents began to arrive by the dozen. Furniture, linen, and silverware were sent to replace home belongings which were beginning to show wear. Susan's brother in Kansas, thoroughly enlisted in her scheme for once, presented her with sheets, bedspreads, tablecloths, and towels enough to last her the rest of her days. The Political Equality Club of Rochester, as a gesture of welcome, undertook a thorough refurnishing of the Madison Street house, including new curtains at the windows, new easy chairs in the rooms, new rugs on the floor, and a new table in the dining room. Rachel Avery and Mrs. Sewall sent a desk and office chair, and Rachel's husband, a set of new cutlery.

Everyone was overflowing with delight and good will. Chief of all, Mrs. Stanton wrote from England: "I rejoice that you are going to housekeeping. The mistake of my life was selling Tenafly. My advice to you, Susan, is to keep some spot you can call your own; where you can live and die in peace and be cremated in your own oven if you desire." Many wrote to express their joy that Susan was to have the rest and home life she had forgone for so many years. They were much like the children of an overworked mother who has long been urged to let go the helm; whereas, if she actually took them at their word, they would scarcely know what to do with themselves. While it lasted Susan's friends enjoyed a happy delusion.

Susan was happy because she had reached the solution of a personal problem. For many years she had evaded it, mainly by leaning hard on Mrs. Stanton's and Mrs. Spofford's hospitality, which she rightly considered as a donation to the cause rather than to herself. But at last she had settled it in her own practical way. She would become a rent-paying tenant in her sister Mary's house. It was agreed between them that Susan would pay twenty-five dollars a month (probably what former tenants, including McLean, had paid) and share the Madison Street house with Mary.

A further problem had come up in the meantime. After a long and thankless period of keeping house for relatives, Mary had grown thoroughly tired of the job and declined to resume it. She had been boarding with the tenants of the Mosher house next door, as Susan had also done during her occasional home visits. Susan proposed to take over the housekeeping entirely, while Mary was to become her boarder, paying a somewhat lesser amount for board than Susan paid for rent. It will be seen that Susan's new life represented a profound and practical readjustment. Henceforth she

would have a home of her own, supported by her own efforts—
something she had always sincerely longed for.

The agreement between the sisters, once made, was studiously
adhered to. Susan managed the house, hired the maid, bought the
coal, paid all the bills. On the first of every month she paid her rent
and Mary paid her board. The items were never balanced off but
actually paid, as the entries in Susan's diary show. They adhered to
the habit to the end of Susan's life. The last items entered by her
own hand in her diary read: "Pd. rent—$25. Rec'd MSA's board—
$20." This final entry might be interpreted as showing how impor-
tant the business arrangement had been to Susan all along.

Having her own home on these terms was undoubtedly one of
the main satisfactions of her later life. She wrote on January 1,
1892: "It was, it is, very pleasant, to have our very own New Year's
dinner at our very own table. And counting the cost for the six
months I have now run the house $500 covers it." She took pride
in her economical management. According to the diary, she succeeded, with some help from Mary, in combining her new responsibilities with lecturing and campaign work. Throughout her travels
she continued to keep her household accounts.

Her first reaction was an exuberant outburst of hospitality. Nothing exhibited her starved feeling for a home more than her great
delight in entertaining. Her diary abounds in such entries as these:

Anna Shaw and niece Lucy came today and we had five others
to dinner. A very pleasant thing to ask people to stop and dine. . . .
Brother D.R., sister Anna and niece Maud came today for a week.
It is so good to receive them in our own home. . . . Had Maria
Porter, Mr. and Mrs. Greenleaf and eleven altogether to tea this
evening. How I do enjoy it. . . . Who came this day? O, yes, Mrs.
Lydia Avery Coonley . . . her son and her mother. . . . It makes
me so happy to return some of the courtesies I have had in their
beautiful home. . . . Just before noon Mrs. Greenleaf popped in
. . . and we made her stay to dinner. The girl was washing and I
got the dinner alone: broiled steak, potatoes, sweet corn, tomatoes
and peach pudding, with a cup of tea. All said it was good and I
enjoyed it hugely. How I love to receive in my own home and at
my own table!

To add to her delight, Mrs. Stanton returned to America for
good that summer. She had finally decided to end her days in her

native land. The news of Susan's "retirement" had encouraged her
to believe she might be left in peace. She was promptly undeceived
on her arrival by a letter from Susan urging her to come to Rochester.

By your fastening yourself in New York I couldn't help you carry
out the dream of my life—which is that you should take all of your
speeches and articles . . . and put your best utterances on each
point into one essay or lecture . . . and then publish in a nice
volume, just as Phillips culled out his best. Your *Reminiscences*
give only light and incidental bits of your life—all good but not the
greatest of yourself.

   This is the first time since 1850 that I have anchored myself to
any particular spot, and in doing it my constant thought was that
you would come here . . . and stay for as long . . . as we should
be together to put your writings into systematic shape to go down
to posterity. . . .

   I can not help sending you this inner groan of my soul, lest you
are not going to make it possible that the thing shall be done first,
which seems most important to me. Then, too, I have never ceased
to hope that we would finish the *History of Woman Suffrage*, at
least to the end of the life of the dear old National.

   Susan would have done better to produce one project at a time.
It was too bad that Mrs. Stanton did not accept her help in collecting and arranging her writings. As a result, she is still known
only by her *Reminiscences*, which Susan very correctly estimated
as not her best. The final proposition of Susan's letter, that they
should resume work on the suffrage *History*, was a siren call from
which Mrs. Stanton had emancipated herself. No amount of determination on Susan's part would lure her into continuing that task.
She did what her friend begged her not to do—fastened herself
firmly in New York.

   Still, Susan's care for Mrs. Stanton's fame yielded one immediate good result. She invited her to spend the month of September
in Rochester, in order that a portrait bust might be made and
added to those already completed of Lucretia Mott and Susan B.
Anthony. During this month Susan's house was given over to the
project. Adelaide Johnson, the sculptor, and Mrs. Stanton lived
in the house. Between sittings, Susan and Mrs. Stanton improved

their nearness to Rochester University by inquiring of the president why girls were not admitted to the institution. He replied that the university could not afford it, and for the time being they let it rest at that.

When all was finished, Adelaide Johnson departed, with her three clay models, for Italy. There she would hew and chisel with her own hands the three marble images that would preserve and portray Lucretia Mott, Elizabeth Cady Stanton, and Susan B. Anthony for posterity. Her work came back in time to be exhibited at the Chicago World's Fair in 1893 and since that date has been transferred to the Capitol in Washington. Among the many sightseers who have from time to time paused to gaze upon it was one to whom it breathed its authentic and hitherto unuttered message. Edna St. Vincent Millay caught it and transfixed it in one of her most beautiful poems, preserved in her collection called *The Buck in the Snow*.

In addition to the old friends who welcomed Susan back to Rochester were these new friends, Mr. and Mrs. William C. Gannett. Mr. Gannett began his long and distinguished service as pastor of the Unitarian church coincidentally with Susan's return to her home town. Mrs. Gannett, who took an active part in her husband's work, was herself a Quaker, a suffragist, and a very advanced young woman for her times. For one thing, she rode a bicycle—something very new and revolutionary for her sex—so much so that Frances Willard felt called upon to write a whole book in its defense. Susan found Mr. Gannett's sermons interesting (she was a severe critic of sermons) and she quickly discovered a congenial spirit in his independent young wife. Her friendship with the Gannetts added much to her new life in Rochester.

&§ II   At the Washington convention of 1892 it became evident that Mrs. Stanton's health could no longer sustain the presidency. Though she presided as usual and read one of her best papers, entitled "The Solitude of Self," it could be seen that her wish for retirement was well justified. Susan reluctantly accepted the presidency in her stead, while Anna Shaw received the office Susan had vacated—that of vice-president-at-large.

Susan's grief at the moment found expression in a letter to Mrs. Elizabeth Miller:

Mrs. Stanton seemed so bright and splendid at Washington! And I think "The Solitude of Self" is her crowning speech—and so thought abler minds. Judge Taylor of Ohio . . . said it surpassed anything he ever heard. It made those ignorant and indifferent Southern men . . . wipe the tears that would moisten their eyes— as she sat and stood there alternately, and portrayed the soul's utter loneliness in all the deepest experiences of life. It is too cruel that such mental powers must be hampered with such a clumsy body. O, if we could but give her elasticity of limbs and locomotive powers! But we must be thankful that she still has her marvellous pen powers to push along our work for the redemption of the race from sex-slavery.

Except for the honor, Susan's elevation to the presidency meant little change in her life. She had long been the *de facto* president of the organization. One newspaper had said of her, apropos of her place in the movement, "Wherever Macgregor sits, there is the head of the table."

Her duties, however, were temporarily increased by the exigencies of the 1892 presidential campaign. In that hectic year Grover Cleveland came back to the presidency. The party conventions were extraordinarily heated, and the suffragists fluttered heroically into the partisan flame.

Susan made the rounds of all the party conventions. Her first step was the Republican convention in Minneapolis. She was alone, and the chairman of the platform committee had no time for vote-less speakers. Susan conceived a plot such as those she had some-times maneuvered with Senator Blair in Washington. She hunted up a friendly committee man who innocently offered to relieve the chair for a space. No sooner was he in the chair than he invited Miss Anthony to the platform, who then addressed the committee for a full half hour. The end result was a plank which really said nothing but which Susan decided to regard as mildly favorable.

Her next stop was the Democratic convention in Chicago, where she had Isabella Hooker for company. Both ladies were heard very briefly by the resolutions committee and politely bowed out. Mrs. Hooker had had hopes of addressing the entire convention. Susan's diary notes: "Mrs. Hooker remained in Democratic convention until 2 o'clock hoping to get a chance to speak before it!!" Susan had returned to her room at the Palmer House and gone to bed. She had not a single confederate among the Democratic hosts, which indicated the solidarity of the Democratic position. Their leader and ultimately triumphant standard-bearer, Cleveland, represented his party fully in this respect.

Then on to the Populist convention in Omaha sped Susan, accompanied by Anna Shaw. Here they were not allowed to speak, and the principle of woman suffrage, to which the party was partially committed, did not even receive mention in the platform. With new hopes of victory in sight, the Populists jettisoned the cause. Susan went to Kansas in the fall to help the Republicans, among whom she could at least count on some outspoken individual friends. To her vast surprise, Kansas went Populist that year without suffrage in the Populist platform.

A year spent on politics had yielded nothing at all. It was some consolation to Susan that the Chatauqua Assembly decided in the fall to open its platform to the woman suffrage question. At least it decided to stage a debate on the subject. Anna Shaw and some long-forgotten clergyman of the day were chosen to present the respective sides.

Susan had assembled a house party for the Chatauqua day. "We were called at 4:30 A.M., had breakfast and were in the carriage at 5:30 . . . Shaw, Foster, Avery, and self. . . . The great auditorium was packed. Geo. H. Vincent invited me, as a pioneer, to sit on stage, and he introduced Anna. She made the cleanest cut argument possible, while the audience cheered and buoyed her up—so that she fairly floated." The next day the counter-argument followed, while the three ladies had the satisfaction of noticing the great contrasting coldness with which the clergyman's talk was received.

The year 1892 had been indeed a strenuous one. What had become of the celebrated retirement? Apparently it had been quite forgotten by Susan as well as by her friends.

◄§ III   January 1893 found the usual annual convention assembled in Washington, presided over by Susan. She was unanimously re-elected, as were the other officers. Messages were read from Lucy

Stone and Mrs. Stanton, both honorary presidents and not able to be present. The question of taking part in the Chicago World's Fair was discussed, favorably decided, and turned over to a committee.

Then, to Susan's consternation, a strange motion was heard from the floor. It proceeded from Alice Stone Blackwell and proposed in effect that the annual convention should be removed from Washington. Susan was taken wholly by surprise, though she might have expected it and should have been prepared. The same motion had been made at the previous convention and voted down. Apparently Susan thought it had been finally disposed of. She should have realized that the proposition, representing the long-standing policy of the American Association, was likely to bob up again. The Americans had yielded almost everything else at the time of the reunion and they had decided, after three years of union, on retrieving a part of their loss.

If Susan had thought of it at all she had relied on the constitution to forfend such a course. In the old National document, dating from 1869, it was provided that the annual convention should be held in Washington. The provision had been incorporated in the agreement for reunion, which explicitly stated that the combined National-American should meet annually in Washington. It required determination to abrogate this agreement, but apparently the Blackwells possessed the determination. Besides the support of New England, they could rely on some new support from the growing Western contingent. A lady from Ohio argued: "It seems better to sow the seed of suffrage throughout the country by means of our national conventions," she said. It was the old refrain of the American Association, suddenly revived and advanced by a Midwestern supporter.

Susan had always regarded the Washington convention as the keystone of her work for a Federal amendment. She had mistakenly assumed that others could see the need as plainly as she could. It was appalling to find the policy of the Americans rising up at this late date to confront her, well supported, as it seemed, by Westerners who disliked the long and expensive journey to Washington. In her consternation she missed the sustaining presence of Mrs. Stanton. She had to face the crisis alone. Worst of all, she had to accomplish, if she could, at the last moment, what she should have been doing for the whole past year. She realized that while she was storming the political conventions this movement had been quietly going on. She left the chair and spoke from the floor:

"The sole object, it seems to me, of this national organization is to bring the combined influence of all the States upon Congress to secure national legislation. The very moment you change the purpose of this great body from National to State work you have defeated its object. It is the business of the States to do the district work; to create public sentiment; to make a national organization possible, and then to bring their united power to the capital and focus it on Congress. Our younger women naturally cannot appreciate the vast amount of work done here in Washington by the National Association in the last twenty-five years. . . .

"In the olden times the States were not fully organized—they had not money enough to pay their delegates' expenses. We begged and worked and saved the money, and the National Association paid the expenses of delegates from Oregon and California in order that they might come and bring the influence of their States to bear upon Congress.

"Last winter we had twenty-three States represented by delegates. Think of those twenty-three women going before a Senate committee . . . and convincing those Senators of the interest in all these States. We have educated at least a part of three or four hundred men and their wives and daughters every two years to return as missionaries to their respective localities. I shall feel it a grave mistake if you vote in favor of a movable convention. It will lessen our influence and our power. But come what may, I shall abide by the decision of the majority."

Susan had often done better than this in the defense of her own side. Knowing that she was right, she failed for some reason to defend the right with her accustomed energy. For instance, the last sentence of her speech was entirely unnecessary: it went without saying that she would accept the decision of the majority. Presumably she was hampered by her deep concern for the preservation of the newly formed union. She feared the least discord that might arise, and she dreaded the thought that she might be responsible for it.

She was acting without any strong personal support. Rachel Avery, who had been her agent in achieving the reunion, did not wholly back her up. Trained in the art of compromise—too well trained, perhaps—Mrs. Avery sprang into the breach by offering a substitute motion. She suggested that the convention should meet in Washington with every new Congress, and on the alternate years in some other city. This compromise, which satisfied nobody completely, was adopted. The vote was 37 to 28. A new regime was ushered in and the roving convention, abjured by the old National on principle, had been introduced.

Susan accepted the change with outward submission, as she had promised. She attributed the majority vote to the rising number of younger women in the ranks, who, she said, "did not comprehend the far-reaching importance of our hearings before Congress, the publication of the speeches by the Government, and the sending out of the speeches under the frank of the Members of Congress." As time went by she even grew concerned lest the one biennial meeting remaining in Washington should be sacrificed. Writing to Rachel Avery in 1899, she said: "I hope you will do all in your power to make our leaders, not only of our business committee but throughout all the States, understand its [the congressional contacts'] value. It is only by so doing that we shall save even the biennial meeting in Washington."

Any plan that took Susan out of Washington was a bad plan for suffrage. It was an unfortunate accident that deprived her of her free residence at the Riggs House, but it had to be accepted. The removal of the annual convention was an unnecessary misfortune, ignorantly invoked. The numerous state meetings, state campaigns, and state conventions would have carried the message to the grass roots as they had always done. Susan's influence as a lobbyist in Washington was something that had been carefully and laboriously built up and could not be replaced. The Washington *Star* said of her, "Miss Anthony is now at the capital, ready for the annual agitation before Congress of the proposed Sixteenth Amendment to the Constitution. She is one of the most remarkable women of the world." This was in 1890. Her annual agitation before Congress was kept up after her return to Rochester and would have been kept up as long as the annual convention met in Washington. It seems impossible that the Blackwells should not have known this (or did they?) and should have sponsored a plan that removed their best pleader from Washington.

In the *History of Woman Suffrage* (Vol. III, p. 12) there is a footnote that lists the favorable congressional reports on the Federal amendment from 1871 to 1892. Each is a committee report based on a committee hearing. Most are minority reports, but two Senate committees gave majority reports—one in 1884 and a second in 1892. A House committee adopted a favorable majority report in 1890. There were eleven favorable reports in all, of which the *History* says: "It is worthy of note that from 1879 to 1891, inclusive, Miss Susan B. Anthony was able to spend the Congressional season in Washington, and during this time nine of these eleven favorable reports were made." Up to the early '90s things were manifestly going better and better. For this reason some of the suffragists thought that Susan's presence in Washington could now be spared; whereas just the opposite course was indicated.

In the '90s it looked as if the states were beginning to move. Three more Rocky Mountain states were added to Wyoming: Colorado in 1893, Utah and Idaho in 1896. After this everything stopped. Federal and state actions were a mutual influence; when Federal action subsided, state action subsided also. Anna Shaw says in her memoirs, "The interval between the winning of Idaho and Utah in 1896 and that of Washington in 1910 seemed very long to lovers of the cause." It must have seemed long to Susan, who was doomed to spend the last ten years of her life without a single encouraging victory.

◄§ IV   After resuming her residence in Rochester, Susan could scarcely escape some involvement in local affairs. The Rochester State Industrial School fell under her scrutiny. The institution admitted girls, all right. But their reformation, along with that of the boys, was conducted by a board composed almost entirely of men. On the death of a member Susan wrote to the governor suggesting that another woman be added to the one already on the board to fill the vacant place. To her surprise, the governor responded by naming Miss Susan B. Anthony of Rochester for the office.

It was difficult for her to refuse. She had just been elected president of the National-American Association and she might have pleaded this as an excuse, but she feared if she declined a man might be put in the place. With some qualms she accepted.

Though she had supposedly retired, she was called away for suffrage work just as much as she had ever been. In her intervals at home she did the best she could for the girls. The diary records: "Feb. 28, 1893.—Spent entire day at the State Industrial School, getting the laundry girls, who had always washed for entire institution and ironed that old way, transferred to the boys' laundry room to use its machinery. . . . Girls, 12 of them, delighted." A simple thing, and it took the mind of the chief executive of the national suffrage movement to think of it. The next year she tried another reform. "Sept. 3, 1894.—The State Industrial School opened today and the experiment of having the primary boys, nearly 200 . . . put in with the younger girls has begun. I did not keep my promise to Sup't Peary to be present to see the coming together!" The reason she did not go was that Mrs. Catt had dropped in on that day to discuss suffrage business with her. She felt the strain of her conflicting obligations. Of course she should have been content to give the girls what she could, realizing how much her second-best meant to them. But it was not in her nature to extend half a loaf.

Early the next year her conflict came to a climax. After a long absence she returned home in March to find Mary in a high state of indignation over an item in the morning newspaper. It told how two Industrial School girls had been seen coming out of a questionable place with two boys, and how the girls had been arrested. The next day Susan and Mary both betook themselves downtown to the police court. The diary says: "Sister Mary and self went . . . to see the two bad girls tried by Judge Ernest. They were sentenced to prisons, Door of Hope and Albion. Their boy accomplices were not even arrested. Simply used as witnesses against the girls." If she went into this at all she would have to fight it out and she had vowed to give her life to suffrage. She went home and went to bed. "Just feel it is no use holding the place any longer." She wrote a letter to the governor resigning her position, giving as a reason her lack of time. She had grown wary of entering into public disputes which did not directly concern woman suffrage. If women had the vote, she told herself, such things would not happen.

◄§ V From the moment when she first heard that Chicago would hold a World's Fair, Susan was resolved that women should not receive the scant courtesy accorded by the Philadelphia Cen-

Susan B. Anthony at the age of 85.

tennial. She began early on her plans to prevent a repetition. A meeting of prominent ladies, mainly wives of senators and representatives, was called at the Riggs House in December 1889 to consider the need of placing women on the governing board. The idea was entirely Susan's; but she kept out of sight, functioning through Mrs. Upton, Mrs. Spofford, and a few trusted friends. The plan was for a women's group to resemble the International Council, the echoes of whose success had not yet subsided, and to be officially recognized. Susan continued to remain behind the scenes, busily drafting resolutions and petitions for others to adopt and present. "Ladies of the '93 celebration met in the Red Parlor," says the diary. Susan waited in her own room for Mrs. Spofford to appear and report on the results.

She had to act quickly, for the World's Fair Bill was well on its way. On January 13 she wrote: "Went to Senate and saw Mr. Platt present Women's Celebration Petition. It went to Fair Committee." With Mrs. Upton she went "calling on members' wives this P.M." and on another day "Mrs. Spofford drove me around to call on the wives of the members of the Cabinet." These attentions from the suffragist must have caused the "wives of" to suspect her interest, but it also showed her willingness to co-operate with ladies not dedicated to suffrage. Finally, in March 1890, her efforts were rewarded with the passage of a World's Fair bill incorporating a provision for a "Board of Lady Managers." As Mrs. Avery later stated in her report to the society, such action would not have been taken if Susan had not happened to be on the ground. It was one of the many achievements that were due to her residence with Mrs. Spofford.

Having taken so much trouble to give women a foothold in the World's Fair, Susan very naturally wished to be present and witness the results. She spent practically the whole summer in Chicago, staying first at the Palmer House and later at the homes of her Chicago friends, Mrs. Sewall and Mrs. Gross. From a figure in the background, she was promoted to the foreground as one of the most prominent and sought-after celebrities of the fair. The president of the Board of Lady Managers, Mrs. Bertha Honoré Palmer, paid her every possible honor, and few programs were considered complete without her presence. Wherever she went, she drew crowds, and often when she had finished she took the crowds with her. This was indeed a great change from the Philadelphia Centennial, when only by her courage had she succeeded in forcing an entrance. She was entitled to appreciate and enjoy the contrast. Without her lifelong work, the World's Congress of Representative Women, the Woman's Building, the prominence given women in general at the World's Fair would hardly have existed. The fair was a wonderful experience for her. On leaving she wrote in her diary: "This is my last sight of the White City in its full glory by night."

During her stay in Chicago, Susan had a memorable all-night session with Anna Shaw. Miss Shaw had just received an excellent reception by a huge audience before whom she had preached, and Susan was delighted. "Miss Anthony talked all night," says Miss Shaw, "sitting in a chair, wrapped in a blanket." As a result of this, Anna Shaw, who like Susan had to earn her living, was persuaded to cut down her lecturing to one third of her time and give the rest to suffrage. Henceforth Anna Shaw was dedicated. She liked to wear her hair cut short, but now she allowed it to grow long as a concession to public opinion. She reduced her bread-and-butter occupation to a minimum in order to serve the cause. From the time of this interview both she and Susan saw the future unfolding with Miss Shaw more and more coming to occupy the position in the movement now occupied by Susan.

Almost simultaneously other values besides oratory, Miss Shaw's special gift, were being demonstrated. While the World's Fair was going on, Colorado submitted a bill for woman suffrage to the voters. At first it was looked upon as a forlorn hope. But many circumstances favored it. The women of the state, chagrined by their defeat in 1877, rallied themselves for a supreme effort, formed suffrage clubs throughout the state, and called loudly on the East for campaigners to help. The National-American decided to send a full-time campaigner into the state and to pay her expenses. The chore fell to Carrie Chapman Catt. Mrs. Catt's herculean efforts, the energy of the women, the W.C.T.U. influence, the Populist support, and above all the stupefying belief on the part of the opponents that the amendment would be lost anyway—all these contributed to a rousing victory for woman suffrage when election day came around. At the next National-American convention, Mrs. Catt was appointed national organizer, an office she had created for herself by her successful work in Colorado.

A curious bit of history in Susan's career had its origin in the Chicago World's Fair. Frances Willard wished to have her represented in the gallery of famous women by a portrait bust made for that especial purpose. Miss Willard commissioned Lorado Taft, the famous Chicago sculptor, to do the work. When all was prepared for the first sitting, a small tempest broke out in the suffragists' ranks. They had already commissioned a bust for the fair, and Adelaide Johnson, then at work on it in Italy, would deliver it on time. They saw no need for another; but if another was indeed required, let it be done by a woman sculptor. Susan for a moment was staggered.

It took an incredible amount of correspondence to straighten this out. Miss Willard, who had contracted to pay for the bust, stood by her guns. "Please do not take counsel," she wrote, "of women who are so prejudiced that, as I once heard said, they would not allow a male grasshopper to chirp on their lawn." Lorado Taft, inclined at first to withdraw, decided on second thought to defend himself. "I can put myself in your place sufficiently," he wrote, "to appreciate in part the objections which you or your friends may feel toward having the work done by a man. My only regret is that I am not to be allowed to pay this tribute to one whom I was early taught to honor and revere [Taft's mother was an early suffragist]. . . . Come to think of it, I believe I am provoked after all. Sex is but an accident, and it seems to me that it has no more to do with art than has the artist's complexion or the political party he votes with." In the end Susan decided to accept the same point of view. Her diary for 1892 mentions a number of sittings that she gave to Mr. Taft.

This portrait of a famous American reformer made by a famous American artist would be an interesting memento for the afterworld to view. But since its exhibition at the World's Fair the bust has vanished. No one in the sculptor's family nor in Susan's knows what became of it. After an exhaustive search both in America and England this writer has been unable to locate the bust and forced to conclude that it no longer exists. Of the completed work, one only knows what Frances Willard wrote of it: "My beloved Susan, your statue is perfect. Lady Henry and I think that one man has seen your great benignant soul and shown it in permanent material."

~§ VI   The heart-warming cheers and plaudits of the Chicago crowds were quickly succeeded for Susan by a dose of disappointment and failure. Providence was certainly taking care that she did not become self-satisfied.

In 1894 she had two states on her hands—New York with a Constitutional Convention, and Kansas with a suffrage amendment. In both states the situation was urgent. Susan shuttled back and forth between them, making three trips to and from Kansas, not to mention her travels within the two states. In New York alone she spoke in every one of its sixty counties, traveling fifty to a hundred miles in a day. In 1894 she piled up one of the highest mileage records of her life.

Her home in Rochester served as headquarters for the New York state committee. The quiet rooms were transformed into busy offices, with Mrs. Jean Brooks Greenleaf of Rochester and Mary Anthony presiding over the workers. Young volunteers filled the house. Their business was to amass signatures for a giant petition, which, aiming at 100,000 names (Dana of the Sun had told Susan this number would be impressive), ended up with a total roll of 330,000. Meanwhile Susan, Miss Shaw, Mrs. Catt, and many others canvassed the cities and the countryside, lecturing, haranguing, explaining incessantly. All this cost the committee ten thousand dollars, exclusive of office rent, which they did not have to pay, and of any payment at all for Susan's and Mary's services. Susan was beginning to see that the cost of the movement was rising.

A similar group of workers was assembled in New York City under the leadership of Lillie Devereux Blake, author of the popular novel, Fettered for Life. This committee, most surprisingly, attracted many women of fashion who had hitherto regarded the cause as rather dowdy. They are referred to in Susan's diary as the "Sherry Group," as they maintained headquarters in the Sherry Restaurant. Unfortunately they stirred up ladies of similar position to take action in opposition to the cause. They founded a group called the "Antis," a mild imitation, in reverse, of the suffrage promoters. Susan never paid much attention to the Antis, except when she came in direct contact with them, as, for instance, at hearings. On one such occasion she helped the overawed members to find seats, incidentally requiring her good friend, Mrs. Harper, to give up her place to an Anti.

For some reason Susan had hopes of the New York Constitutional Convention. Perhaps she was encouraged by Colorado's example. As if the gentlemen of New York could be impressed by the action of a Rocky Mountain community! The officials of the Western suffrage states, when brought on for the purpose, spoke to politely deaf ears. When the vote was taken and suffrage lost by 98 to 58 (the suffragists, as usual, scoring their one third), Susan was more painfully disappointed than usual. But she rallied instantly. The women often told the story of how, as they trooped down the steps of the Capitol at midnight after the final vote, Susan began outlining the steps for another campaign.

She still had hopes for Kansas, the home of her brothers and heroic John Brown. Next to New York, she felt close to Kansas. She had already made two trips to the State and had written literally hundreds upon hundreds of letters of encouragement and advice. Still hoping, she returned once more in August.

In this campaign she had the assistance of Miss Shaw and Mrs. Catt. The National-American's three topmost representatives were at work besides lesser known but able co-workers. They were heartily aided by Mrs. Annie L. Diggs of the Populist party, then the dominant party of the state. Both the women and the Populists were confronted by a powerful Republican organization, carefully built up over the past two years to regain the party's lost control. The utmost exertions of the women could not induce the Republicans to endorse woman suffrage. This was serious politics; they had no time to waste on side issues like woman's rights. "We must redeem the State," they cried loudly as they quietly formed an alliance with the state liquor traffic. Their tactics won the election. The Republicans were returned to office and women suffrage was lost. This time it received, however, two fifths of the vote—slightly more than its usual one third.

When Susan arrived for her third visit to Kansas she saw at once that the cause was lost. The only hope for suffrage was for the Populists to come in. Early in the summer the Populists had put a suffrage plank in their platform. But even they had not yielded too easily. The delegates seemed at first opposed; but after Susan, Miss Shaw, and Mrs. Catt had labored with them in long speeches, they began to come around. The final persuasion was the work of Annie L. Diggs, who aroused sufficient enthusiasm to carry the plank—against the original intention of the majority.

A noisy demonstration broke out. The crowd cheered and whooped for the winners. Susan, Anna Shaw, and Annie Diggs were called forward to receive congratulations. Mrs. Catt's presence was apparently overlooked. Susan wrote to Mrs. Colby: "Mrs. Chapman Catt was not called out at the Populist Convention and compelled to say 'Thank you,' as were Misses Shaw and Anthony." But Susan and Miss Shaw shook hands with every delegate as he came along; so that, as one newspaper said, "Miss Anthony had to push up her sleeves as she warmed to her work." She was boisterously congratulated on having become a member of the Populist party.

In the East, where many people looked under their beds for a Populist at night, Susan's reported alliance brought her into sad disrepute. Mr. Blackwell wrote solemnly from Boston, urging her to remain non-partisan, as if he did not know that she had practically invented the policy and lived up to it religiously. She wrote in her diary: "One would think I had committed the unpardonable sin against the Holy Ghost in thanking the Populists . . . and saying I preferred them with justice to women, no matter what their financial folly, to the Republicans without justice to women, no matter what their financial wisdom." Susan had long since departed from the financial teachings of George Francis Train, which, as a matter of fact, she had never fully understood, and returned to those of William Lloyd Garrison, which she understood just as little.

So she decided to campaign for the Populist party. She wrote to Mrs. Miller, "The Republicans expect me to shout hallelujahs to them—and not say a thank you to the poor but honest old farmers of the Populist party for putting a plank in their platform. Well, I have not fallen so low as that yet." Having warned the party secretary and Mrs. Diggs that she would speak on woman suffrage only and on no other item of the platform, she campaigned with the Populists throughout. She had pursued the same course in campaigning for the Republicans when Grant was re-elected.

In Kansas a small cloud, no bigger than a man's hand, had appeared on Susan's personal horizon. A year ago it had not been there. Though the Kansas Populists had overlooked Mrs. Catt as a less famous figure than Miss Anthony and Miss Shaw, Susan was beginning to see Mrs. Catt plain. With all her experience in judging human material, Susan could not fail to be impressed. Though it must have cost her some pain to admit that Anna Shaw had a worthy rival, she forced herself to do so. She tried to be fair.

Two entries in her diary show what was going through her mind:

Leavenworth, Kan. May 7, 1894.—Mrs. Chapman came to Brother Dan's . . . and all were delighted with her. She spoke at the Leavenworth Co. mass meeting this evening; and "perfectly charming"—Mr. Page, brother, nephew D.R., and all. So all thought Miss Shaw could never equal her and hence the meeting had better adjourn with Mrs. C.'s splendid speech.

Leavenworth, Kan. May 8, 1894.—Miss Shaw, Chapman, and self all at Brother Dan's. . . . At evening the Chickering Hall jammed, and as Miss Shaw proceeded everyone was carried out of self. Dr. Page, Brother Dan and all felt she even climaxed Mrs. Chapman. It is splendid we have two such magnificent speakers. Each is best.

◦§ VII The time for the first national convention outside of Washington came around. To Susan, who viewed any place except the capital city as a mistake, it was a dismal prospect. If anything could have made her exile worse, it was the place chosen—Atlanta, Georgia. Susan's appreciation of the South had not improved much, if any, since her Abolitionist days. An avid reader of the newspapers, she kept up with the shrewd inventions of the South to keep the Negro from the polls, and she was naturally horrified by the record of lynchings. She knew little about the South except its treatment of the Negroes. Her imagination had expanded to embrace the West as far as the Pacific, and even to embrace to some extent the domain of England. But the South was still a foreign country to her. In obedience to the new policy of her society, she decided, since Atlanta was to be the objective, to make a tour of the entire South.

Frances Willard had broken ground in the South by her temperance crusades. Southern women had welcomed her as a "Western," not a "Northern," woman, and under her influence had made the first timid break from their homes to ally themselves with a public cause. This may have suggested to Susan the idea of inviting Mrs. Catt instead of Miss Shaw to accompany her. Though living in New York, Mrs. Catt was still regarded as a "Western" woman and as such she was described by most of the Southern newspapers during the subsequent tour. There was no device whatsoever by which Susan could escape the appellation of "Northern."

Mrs. Catt contributed much to the success of the tour, though Susan's fame was such as to overcome her handicap and attract large audiences everywhere. All went well from the first. Susan had been careful in her selection of material. She wrote to Mrs. Colby, whose print shop supplied it, "Do be careful to send only what might be called milk for babes. . . . Only words of cheer and encouragement must be said to these people; the rank and file have neither thought, read, or heard of our gospel, only the very few. . . . Especially, don't send any anti-Church things." Under her careful nurturing the tour progressed through Kentucky, Memphis, and New Orleans with success and even with social éclat.

At New Orleans the pilgrims turned eastward toward Atlanta. Their first stop was Jackson, Mississippi, where Susan had been invited to speak in the capitol. It was at this point that her assumption of cordiality broke down. Her diary tells the story. "Train was too late for me to speak at Jackson. Mrs. C.C. there and Miss Powers came to the train at 9:20, said Mrs. C.C. was holding a magnificent audience for my coming. But I had bought my ticket and checked baggage to Birmingham, and I was too oozed out to even be looked at, much less to try to speak in the Mississippi Hall of Representatives, packed with Southern chivalry." One infers that Susan was not yielding to the charm of the South. There is no other instance on record when she allowed a through ticket and a baggage check to keep her from addressing a group of lawmakers.

The trip was not improved by the blizzard which overtook them in Birmingham. A spell of bitter cold followed, such as occasionally overwhelms the South, smiting the orange groves, blasting the peach trees, and afflicting unprotected humans with frostbite. The cold wave continued for the rest of the trip. In that land of hospitality, Susan could not take advantage of the hospitality offered her. "Left my comfortable steam-heated room with misgivings, and found a real Southern home, cold; the little coal grates couldn't touch the cold. Shiver was the condition . . . so sent trunk back to Hotel and went back to my room after my lecture." In desperation she bought a whole ton of coal for $4.75—soft coal, which she loathed—to make one overnight stay endurable. On the last stretch of her journey, passing through Virginia, she encountered "a hard-coal fire in an old-fashioned Franklin stove." This was heaven.

Meantime, the Atlanta convention had taken place as scheduled. It proved to be a very normal convention. Delegates from twenty-eight states were present, though the average distance traveled by the delegates amounted to more than if they had gone to Washington. The city turned out en masse to swell the attendance, and the newspapers printed generous notices. Susan delivered the president's address and Anna Shaw (who met the travelers in Atlanta) delivered the sermon on Sunday. When Miss Shaw spoke, said the local paper, "There was not an empty chair in the house. So dense became the crowd that the doors were ordered closed before the services began."

The atmosphere may have convinced some of the visitors that they were making converts by the wholesale. Susan herself knew how quickly the waves would subside. The value of such sporadic efforts by comparison with a long-continued pressure upon a single strategic point was considered by her to be negligible. She was not happy about the whole thing. She wrote that night in her diary: "The National Convention for the first time moved out of Washington, D.C. since 1869 when dear Lucretia Mott was president."

At this convention Mrs. Catt received a well-deserved promotion. A standing National Organization Committee was created with Mrs. Catt as chairman. The chairman of a standing committee automatically became a member of the business committee, the main governing body of the society. Henceforward she ranked among the policy-making leaders of the movement.

Susan's tour of the South was scheduled to end in Washington on February 15, 1895. She reached the city on a pleasantly warm day. At the Ebbitt House she found Mrs. Sewall and Mrs. Avery waiting for her. A meeting of the National Council of Women was about to take place, and a birthday party in her honor was to be held that evening. It was her seventy-fifth birthday.

The feature of the party, to which she repaired cheerfully but with no great curiosity, was the presentation of a cash annuity to the guest of honor. Mrs. Avery made the formal presentation, explaining that two hundred friends had joined in raising five thousand dollars, that this had been invested with an insurance company, and that it would yield an annual income of eight hundred dollars for Susan's future years. "It was a great surprise to S.B.A.," says the diary; "probably every other one there knew but her." Mrs. Avery had arranged the matter so quietly and efficiently that no hint of the project had reached Susan's ears. She sat in stunned silence, saying nothing at all, passing up for once in her life an opportunity to make a speech on woman suffrage.

Mrs. Avery contributed a further great gift in the form of two hundred typewritten letters thanking the donors. All that Susan had to do was to sign them. They all said in conclusion, "Among them [the names of the donors] was yours, and I hasten to thank you for thus helping to lift me financially above the need of earning the necessary sum to meet my simple home expenses."

For this was the intention of the annuity. Susan's friends knew that she had reached the age of seventy-five without laying by anything for her old age. All she had earned or received as gifts had been immediately spent on the suffrage cause. Mrs. Avery had prudently tied up the gift, to be doled out in quarterly installments, so that Susan could use it only for her own current expenses. Modest as the income was, it would go far to maintain the simple life she shared with her sister in Rochester.

Susan was silent at the banquet, overcome with gratitude and also slightly surprised at the foresight exhibited on her behalf. What her prudent friends could not foresee, however, was that Susan, who had run the movement on a shoestring for forty years, could manage wonders on eight hundred dollars a year.

CHAPTER TWENTY-SIX

END OF AN ERA

◄§ I   The suffragists of Susan's era had not yet come out of the kitchen. They had furnished her house in Rochester for a home-body, which at seventy she was never likely to become. At the same time she possessed none of the conveniences of a business office. She wrote to a friend: "The other day a millionaire who wrote me 'wondered why I didn't have my letters type-written.' Why, bless him, I never, in all my fifty years of hard work with the pen, had a writing desk with pigeonholes and drawers until my seventieth birthday . . . and never had I even a dream of money enough for a stenographer and type-writer." The desk with pigeonholes and the office chair required especial treatment. It was installed in the front room on the second floor, and Susan for the first time had a study in the house. Mary had a similar office on the first floor.

At seventy-five Susan introduced other changes. With eight hundred dollars coming in every year, she felt as rich as the millionaire referred to in her letter. She soon employed a secretary and rented a typewriter for her use. It was several years before she felt rich enough to buy a typewriter of her own, at a cost of one hundred dollars, but even that day came. She drove a shrewd bargain, with-holding twenty-five dollars of the price for advertising the type-writer in Mrs. Colby's *Tribune*. On the same date she installed a telephone and bought a copy of Who's Who. Mrs. Avery's idea that she should spend the annuity on personal comforts was real-ized in the form of office equipment. Susan would still think twice before hiring a carriage to take her to the railroad station.

Her most ambitious undertaking consisted of adding an attic story to the house. Foreseeing a long dry spell for the Federal amendment, she determined to resume the suffrage history. The cellar, wood shed, and closets were bursting with her stores of documents. To assemble the hoard in a single space and to provide a workroom for the unknown scribe who was going to aid her, her imagination projected the attic. Susan and Mrs. Stanton were obsessed by the idea that literary talent could flourish only in an attic. Mrs. Stanton's house at Tenafly had boasted a "Tower," and Susan imitated the "Tower" in her own way.

She started the structure in the spring of 1895, immediately after receiving the annuity. In July she wrote to Mrs. Colby: "I have just come from my new and splendid garret, in the back room of which, the store-room, are tumbled in heaps all of my trunks, boxes, papers, pamphlets, etc., waiting for 'my double' and something more to come to the rescue." She was still seeking vainly for a collaborator to replace Mrs. Stanton. Mrs Colby would do excellently; but Mrs. Colby was tied to the *Woman's Tribune* in Washington, and no other rescuer was then in sight.

◄§ II   In the midst of this came Susan's second trip to California. In 1895 there was no pressing campaign business on hand, but she went anyhow. The only explanation is that no opportunity to visit the glamorous state could be resisted. An invitation to attend the California Woman's Congress, with all her expenses paid, furnished the opportunity. The following year would have seemed more appropriate, since a suffrage amendment was then to be submitted. However, she could help lay plans for the women to follow next year while she remained at home. When Anna Shaw, at her suggestion, was included in the invitation, her satisfaction with the arrangement was complete.

The journey with Miss Shaw proved much of a repetition of her journey with Mrs. Stanton in 1871. With no carking political crisis to contend with, Susan and her companion met only the applause and appreciation accorded to celebrities. They passed through Colorado, where women now voted, to the steady accompaniment of ringing ovations. In Cheyenne, Wyoming, the pioneers gathered in force to welcome them. In Salt Lake City, where women expected to receive the vote in November, they were honored by Mormons and Gentiles alike. Miss Shaw preached in the Mormon Tabernacle, and Susan addressed the Inter-Mountain Suffrage Society. After more ovations in Nevada, they reached Oakland, California, in the middle of May.

The Woman's Congress kept them busy in San Francisco for a week. They spoke at every meeting, and the crowds increased from day to day until the congress had to seek larger quarters. A local newspaper said: "Mere curiosity does not take the same people to nineteen consecutive sessions. . . . A year ago there were not more than a hundred women in San Francisco who could have been dragged to a suffrage meeting, but yesterday twenty-five times that number struggled and tore their clothing in their determination to hear Miss Anthony and Miss Shaw."

After the congress they were treated to a trip through the Yosemite Valley, as Susan and Mrs. Stanton had been twenty-four years before. They enjoyed the same adventurous rides on the donkeys and the same mountaintop views. A change was introduced in the form of a high honor to Susan. Some of the Mariposa big trees had been named after the presidents, and another tree was christened, to commemorate the visit, after Susan B. Anthony. On this trip Susan displayed almost the same sprightly energy as she had displayed almost a quarter of a century before.

From Yosemite they proceeded southward to Los Angeles and Riverside, where flowery and refreshment-laden receptions awaited them. The newspapers were flattering, and they spoke to packed audiences. Only one discordant note broke the harmony; this was when the suffragists proposed that Anna Shaw should deliver one of the patriotic orations on the Fourth of July. In view of the many political aspirants who wished to shine on this day, the committee did not consider they had time for her. But the suffragists, for once, showed fight, and the committee reluctantly granted their wish. Miss Shaw, who had felt the need of a little opposition, gave the most spirited oration of the day. It was cordially received and the audience called loudly for Susan also, so the suffragists had two women on the Fourth of July program.

The feature of the trip that personally meant most to Susan came near the end when they reached San Diego. Nearly ten years had elapsed since McLean's family had gone to California, and in the interval there had been but little communication. The young Bakers had not found the conditions as rosy as had been depicted and had naturally kept rather quiet about a bubble that had burst. But they had survived and become true Californians. Susan's grand-nephew, Henry Baker, had been educated as a doctor and was serving as a ship's surgeon on the Pacific. He happened to be at home on leave when Susan visited San Diego. They had some intimate talks about his future career. Susan reversed Greeley's advice to young men and urged Henry Baker to go East; which, in the sequel, he did.

Susan spent several days with these relatives who had once been such an intimate part of her life, but she must have been ill pre-pared for the change in Aaron McLean. She had last seen him as a well-preserved man in his seventies, still active in business. The effects of age, not to mention those of retirement and inactivity, must have been now apparent. He also showed signs of failing health. Her diary says nothing about her impressions, indeed not a word about seeing her brother-in-law again. It is filled with lec-tures, receptions, and public engagements, which crowded her stay in San Diego as everywhere else. If the reunion brought any par-ticular sorrow to her, she had no opportunity to feel it or express it.

On her way home she stopped as usual in Kansas. A Topeka suffragist waylaid her at the station and asked her to send a message to the Kansas women. Susan wrote: "Since 130,000 Kansas men declared themselves against woman suffrage at the last election and 74,000 showed their opposition by not voting, it is therefore the duty of every self-respecting woman in the State to fold her hands and refuse to help any religious, charitable, or moral reform or any political association, until the men shall strike the adjective 'male' from the suffrage clause of the constitution." The furor aroused by her message when reported by the newspapers can be easily imag-ined. A storm of editorial abuse broke forth such as she had not heard for a long while. The California portrait of a "sweet old lady" was changed to that of a wicked agitator. The suggestion of a strike of any kind was anathema to the press of those days; a strike by women, a monstrous idea.

Mrs. Harper's biography insists that Susan intended the message as a joke. It was a joke to the extent that she realized it would not be taken seriously. Otherwise, she meant it, and the press knew that she meant it. Perhaps she had had too much sweetness and light in her California sojourn and showed it by a sudden return to reality. She endured the abuse silently, but she wrote to Mrs. Colby: "What a howling the editors are making about my advice to the Kansas women to fold their hands and refuse to run the churches, charities, and reforms for the men; that is, let them run those institutions alone, as they have voted to run the government alone. I see nothing but Patrick Henryism in it—do you see it so spiteful?" As she knew it would if she held her tongue, the excitement quickly died down. She was careful, however, never to repeat the advice.

⤳§ III   Susan arrived home at three o'clock on the morning of July 17, 1895. "Got carriage for home and sat on door-steps and read morning newspapers until it was time for sister Mary to be astir." The carriage was an unusual concession to the lateness of the hour, for she was not conscious of feeling tired. They had done a lot of traveling, but Anna Shaw had borne the brunt of the speaking and the trip had been practically a vacation.

An incident in Chicago, where she had spent a day and night with Mrs. Gross, might have warned her that she was tired after all. Mrs. Gross had driven her to a photographer's studio, where after the sitting Susan had fainted dead away. She ascribed her weakness to the heat and said nothing about it. A Chicago paper of the same date said: "Miss Anthony has grown slightly thinner since she was in Chicago attending the World's Fair . . . thinner and more spiritual-looking. As she sat last night with her transparent hands grasping the arms of her chair, her thin, hatchet face and white hair, with only her keen eyes flashing light and fire, she looked like Pope Leo XIII. The whole physical being is as nearly submerged as possible in a great mentality." Between the lines of the notice one can read that Susan was looking unusually frail.

She spent her first days at home peacefully catching up with her household accounts and giving interviews to reporters. This was routine, including the interviews. It was interrupted by a message from Anna Shaw, saying that she had succumbed to typhoid fever and could not keep a Chatauqua engagement at Lakeside, Ohio, on

July 26. They both stood in great awe of Chatauqua opinion. Lakeside was no great distance from Rochester, and Miss Shaw felt that only Susan could adequately take her place. The only thing wrong was that Susan had not expected to take this journey or to be called on for this important speech. Still, she had no choice but to accept.

On July 26 she stood on the Lakeside platform and launched into her address before the Chatauqua audience. The diary relates what followed: "Spoke in great auditorium at 11 A.M. When speech was two-thirds done all turned black. Still, I managed to make a closing sentence and fell back to my seat. The next I knew there was a crowd around me, blanched and speechless." She said later, "If I had pinched myself right hard I would not have fainted." She was taken to the home of her hostess and a physician was summoned. The reporters present had assumed the worst of her public collapse and the Lakeside wires were soon humming with the news of Miss Anthony's demise. One reporter received from his paper this message: "5,000 words if still living, no limit if dead." His next morning's story was restrained to five thousand words.

As soon as she rallied, Susan insisted on returning home. She would have traveled alone, but fortunately Harriet Taylor Upton was in Lakeside and on her way to Rochester. Mrs. Upton was bound for a meeting of the business committee arranged to take place in Susan's home. They arrived to find the committee already assembled, and nothing could persuade Susan to take to her bed until this conference, which lasted for two days, had finished its business. She admitted afterward that she felt dull and unaware of what was going on. That the ladies did not immediately don their hats and go home is not to be understood; it is so hard for the family to believe that Mother can really break down.

It was four days after her original collapse when she finally went to bed; and it was not until fully a month later that she began to recover. "My first bath and dressing alone this A.M.," she wrote on August 30. She was under the constant care of a doctor and a nurse. Dr. Moore, the physician, diagnosed her case as nervous prostration. She had succumbed to an authentic nervous breakdown. She said in the diary that she felt all the while as helpless as a baby, receiving the nurse's attentions just as an infant accepts its mother's care. After a month of helplessness came a month of slow convalescence, and it was not until the middle of October that she first ventured to leave the house. During her convalescence a new bath-robe was given her by her friend, Mrs. Gross—"a dove-colored morning wrapper . . . trimmed with velvet of the same color and a Nile blue silk cord." She enjoyed this bathrobe excessively. The maternal ministrations received from the nurse had been trans-ferred to a somewhat higher level by Mrs. Gross's attentions.

While still in bed she dictated the following letter to Mrs. Colby:

It is awfully hard to have to be too lazy for anything. But don't magnify the lapse—it is just a month today since I simply collapsed, the whole of me coming to a sudden standstill like a clap of thun-der in a clear sky, without notice or warning. I have had nothing that might be called pain, simply inaction; and I tell my nurse that I expect to pass on to the beyond without knowing what excruci-ating pain is. But my temperature ran for days to 103 and 4; but no more. It seems a long, long time since that 26th of July, noon-day, at Riverside.

This slip, "Riverside" for "Lakeside," reminds us that Susan's usual phrase for dying was "crossing the river." She had rather ex-pected to die during her illness. Reason told her she could scarcely pass on without suffering, but she fancied hers might be a unique case. The suffering was going on all right, but at an unconscious level, and it might be true that, to some extent, it threatened her life. She must have received the right treatment to have recovered so well. This, added to her awakening common sense and her life-long habit of facing reality, must have effected the cure that slowly came about.

What caused her collapse, one does not know, but one can guess at it from our knowledge of her life history. Miss Shaw had re-turned from California with a real germ, but Susan had no germ (as far as we know). Her tour had been easy and pleasant. There had been one deep emotional experience, her reunion with her sister Guelma's family in San Diego. As she had several times demonstrated, she had a curiously prescient mind, and she may have divined that this was her last sight of Aaron McLean, even though she talked with him about coming back to visit Rochester. McLean died six months later. By going to California in 1895, Susan had realized her last chance of seeing him alive. Aside from

what he may have meant to her personally, he was tied up with all
the dearest memories of her life. The thought of the final parting
must have come as a painful shock.

It may be recalled that once before Susan had broken down under similar conditions. This was while lecturing in Indiana in 1873,
when she had also fainted in the midst of a speech. She had then
quickly rallied and returned after a few days to her work. She had
been oppressed at that time by her sister Guelma's approaching
death, only a few months away. Now once again she had been
shaken past all conscious endurance by the approach of the inevitable. Her second break was far more serious. Reconciliation with
reality seemed even harder to achieve. The threatened chords lay
deeper and their reverberations were more complex and more
deeply intertwined with her repressed emotional life. The conflict
was to be resolved only after a long and painful inner struggle, during which there were times when she thought she would rather go
than accept the coming blow.

When Guelma had died, Susan showed all her normal self-
control; and in the same way, when the news of McLean's death
reached her in Washington the following January, she received it
without signs of undue shock or disturbance. She merely wrote
sadly in her diary, "Jan. 18, 1896.—Found telegram from nephew
George L. Baker saying 'Grandfather died this noon.' . . . So all
is over. Brother Aaron was 83 on Dec. 31st . . . a ripe old age.
And yet I hoped he'd live to come back this side." She had already
outlived her grief and suffering on account of Aaron's death.

◄§ IV   One thing that stimulated Susan's recovery was her reali-
zation that Mrs. Stanton's eightieth birthday was to be celebrated.
She had determined that it was to be the grandest of all fetes. The
suffragists had already started their preparations; but Susan, rising
from her sickbed, declared they were not adequate. Mrs. Stanton, in
her opinion, belonged not only to the suffragists but to all women.
She wished therefore to place the celebration in the hands of the
National Council, composed of twenty different national societies,
in order that all the organized women of America should have a
share in it.

Susan insisted on remaining behind the scenes, helping with

raising funds, securing speakers, and sending out announcements. She worked hard, but the National Council, always good at making a display, also worked hard. They secured the New York Metropolitan Opera House, sold every seat in the house, and converted the vast platform into a bower of flowers. A throne of blossoms had been arranged for Mrs. Stanton, with Susan on one side and the president of the National Council on the other. When she entered she received an ovation from an audience of three thousand. The ovation would have seemed more arousing but for the so-called Chatauqua salute which had lately replaced hand-clapping with politely waving handkerchiefs. But Mrs. Stanton knew it for an ovation. "I have been affected to tears," she wrote, "during these days of triumph."

Susan had come down to New York in advance to hear Mrs. Stanton read her speech. As usual, Mrs. Stanton took a slap at the Church; and, as usual, Susan tried to persuade her to leave it out. "I tried to make her see," she wrote, "that the church had advanced as rapidly as the other departments but I did not succeed, and it is right that she should express her own ideas, not mine." So the offending sentiments came out resoundingly, mingling with the scent of flowers and the perfume of adulation, but not many handkerchiefs were waved in response.

Susan stayed that night at the Hotel Vendome, at the corner of Broadway and Forty-first Street. "The roar and thunder of cars and wagons kept me awake the whole night," says the diary. "It was fearful." The next day she went to Mrs. Stanton's apartment, where an Italian sculptor waited to make a cast of her hand clasped with that of Mrs. Stanton. The clasped hands commemorated almost half a century of friendship as well as this one rare day of fulfillment in both of their lives. It still survives in the possession of Mrs. Stanton's descendants.

⁣V   For some time before her birthday Mrs. Stanton had been engaged on the cherished project of her old age—the reform of the Church. "I can truly say," she says in her *Reminiscences*, "that all the cares and anxieties, the trials and disappointments of my whole life are slight when balanced by my sufferings in childhood . . . from the theological dogmas which I sincerely believed, and the

gloom connected with everything associated with the name of religion." Later on in life, fighting for woman's rights, she had encountered the hard-hitting St. Paul and other discriminating scrip-
tural authorities. As a result, she had built up an undying feud with
the Church and its symbol—the Bible. She decided that the Bible
ought to be revised in the light of modern reason and that her
revision should be called the *Woman's Bible*.

Seeking a committee to back up her enterprise, she wrote at once
to Susan. The latter replied, "No, I don't want my name to be on
that Bible committee. You fight that battle, and leave me to fight
the secular and political fellows. . . . I simply don't want the
enemy to be diverted from my practical ballot fight." Susan urged
her to forget St. Paul and do something about the Jim Crow laws
then emerging in the South. "Give your heartiest raps," she said,
"on the head of every Nabob, man or woman, who does injustice
to a human being for the crime of color or sex." But Mrs. Stanton
had left the world of current events and retired to the world of
books; also, to some degree, to the world of her childhood. In both
of these departments of her life the Bible filled a large place.

She got her committee together—a most respectable one, by the
way—and proceeded to write and publish, in pamphlet form, a
liberal commentary on the scriptures called the *Woman's Bible*.
Susan received one of the first copies. She talked it over with Mrs.
Miller and they agreed that it was not worthy of the author's
talent, that Mrs. Stanton was "letting down." The public did not
view the work from the literary angle; rather it was seen as an attempt to tear down the orthodox Christian teachings. There was
nothing Susan could do but keep silent and hope that the storm
would blow over.

The *Woman's Bible* appeared in December, immediately after
the birthday celebration and just before the suffrage convention.
With Susan in the chair, the convention did not dare to bring up
the *Bible*, although it was on the tip of everybody's tongue. The
younger element had introduced a policy of prudence into the
movement which had been unknown to the pioneers. They quietly
incorporated a statement in the annual report announcing that the
society had no connection with the *Woman's Bible*. When it was
read, Susan and her ally, Mrs. Colby, moved into quick action. By
a parliamentary ruse Mrs. Colby secured the elimination of the

offending statement. But the party of prudence was not thus to be defeated. They introduced the same statement in the report of the committee on resolutions: "This association is non-sectarian . . . and has no official connection with the so-called *Woman's Bible*, or any theological publication."

Mrs. Stanton was eighty, her fame had just been acknowledged by a vast demonstration, and her *Bible* was sponsored by an independent committee outside the association. The repudiation was gratuitous. Susan and her supporters tried to point this out. Some other leaven besides that of prudence must also have been working in the loaf.

The resolution did not pass so easily after all. There was an hour's debate. Among those speaking in its favor were Henry B. and Alice Stone Blackwell, Mrs. Avery, Mrs. Catt, Miss Shaw, and Mrs. Diggs. Among those speaking against it were Mrs. Colby, Mrs. Blake, Charlotte Perkins Stetson, and Susan. Susan left the chair to make an impassioned speech:

"The one distinct feature of our association has been the right of individual opinion for every member. We have been beset at each step with the cry that somebody was injuring the cause by the expression of sentiments which differed from those held by the majority. . . .

"Every new generation of converts threshes over the same old straw. The point is whether you will sit in judgment on one who questions the divine inspiration of certain passages in the Bible derogatory to women. . . . Many things have been said and done by our *orthodox* friends which I have felt to be extremely harmful to our cause; but I should no more consent to a resolution denouncing them than I shall consent to this.

"Who is to draw the line? Who can tell now whether these commentaries may not prove a great help to woman's emancipation from old superstitions which have barred its way? Lucretia Mott at first thought Mrs. Stanton had injured the cause of all woman's other rights by insisting on the demand for suffrage, but she had sense enough not to bring in a resolution against it. . . . I shall be pained beyond expression if the delegates here are so narrow and illiberal as to adopt this resolution. You would better not begin resolving against individual action or you will find no limit. This year it is Mrs. Stanton; next year it may be I or one of yourselves who will be the victim.

"If we do not inspire in woman a broad and catholic spirit, they will fail, when enfranchised, to constitute that powerful better government which we have always claimed for them. Ten women educated in the practice of liberal principles would be a stronger force than 10,000 organized on a platform of intolerance and bigotry. I pray you vote for religious liberty, without censorship or inquisition. This resolution adopted will be a vote of censure upon a woman who is without a peer in intellectual and statesmanlike ability; one who has stood for half a century the acknowledged leader of progressive thought and demand in regard to all matters pertaining to the absolute freedom of women."

The resolution was adopted by a vote of 53 to 41. Among those voting for it were some of Susan's nearest and dearest friends. They had gone over to the enemy; she had to face the heartbreaking fact. She presided over the rest of the session with stoical poise and dignity, restraining her emotions until she reached Mrs. Stanton's home. Here she gave way completely. Mrs. Stanton thought the only thing for them to do was to resign. At the moment Susan was inclined to agree with her. In her inward commotion she took a misguided step. She summoned Mrs. Catt, who had voted for the resolution, to Mrs. Stanton's residence to account for her act. Mrs. Catt came promptly and obediently.

What could be gained by such an interview? It is not mentioned in Susan's diary. But Mrs. Catt's biographer gives a brief account of the visit and makes an interesting statement about Mrs. Catt's reaction: "Her heart filled with pity for Miss Anthony and mingled exasperation and envy for Mrs. Stanton, who had apparently managed to live eighty years without repressing any desires." In this impression, of course, Mrs. Catt was very much mistaken. Nevertheless, it was by choice that Mrs. Stanton gave forth the aura so described, and if Mrs. Catt was convinced by it Mrs. Stanton should have been gratified. The main point is that Mrs. Catt was repelled by a quality which had a strong attraction for Susan.

Susan had scarcely reached home when the reporters were on her doorstep, asking about the *Woman's Bible*. She told them:

"No, I did not contribute to it, though I knew of its preparation. My own relations to or ideas of the Bible always have been peculiar, owing to my Quaker training. The Friends consider the book as historical, made up of traditions, but not as plenary inspiration. Of course people say these women are impious and presumptuous for daring to interpret the Scriptures as they understand them, but I think women have just as good a right to interpret and twist the Bible to their own advantage as men always have twisted and turned it to theirs. . . .

"In the same way the history of our Revolutionary War was written, in which very little is said of the noble deeds of women, though we know how they stood by and helped the great work; and it is the same with history all through."

It might be supposed that this explanation would have got her into as much trouble with the orthodox as Mrs. Stanton was having. But all it did was to reveal her as a faithful Quaker, and orthodoxy of any kind was what the public wanted. Unlike Mrs. Stanton, who had turned against the teachings of her childhood, Susan had stuck to hers, and the day had passed when Quakers were persecuted for their beliefs.

Once at home, Susan cooled off gradually under Mary's influence. The majority vote, though including her best-beloved, had not been overwhelming. Many of the silent ones in the convention had voted with her. "The rights of the minority are to be respected and protected by me," she wrote Mrs. Stanton, "as much as the action of the majority is to be resented." And to Mrs. Colby she wrote: "I think I will hang on this year for the sake of the forty, more or less, staunch and true women whose voices showed no lack of confidence in their leader." For the sake of these tried and true she resolved not only to hang on but with their help to bring the erring ones back into line. She did not resign, and neither did Mrs. Stanton.

Hardest of all for Susan to forgive was Rachel Avery. Susan traveled with Rachel by night boat from New York to Boston in December. "Rachel got into the berth with me and talked until almost morning, while the great machinery paddled us along." But Mrs. Avery was talking about her personal life and problems, for she always confided in Susan as a mother. She was not talking about the *Bible* episode. After it happened she had once told Susan she was sorry she had voted as she did and straightway forgot all about it. Not Susan; she found it hard to forget an injury to Mrs. Stanton, which was also an injury to civil rights. She scribbled in her diary: "Rachel is a wonderfully strong woman in many directions. If only she hadn't put that censure of Mrs. Stanton's *Bible* in her last year's report as corresponding secretary!—I should say in all directions. But that was caused by a weak or wicked spirit, I can not divine which, even at this distance."

On Christmas Day, Susan and her sister went over "to see the Mosher children's Christmas Tree." These were the grandchildren of her sister Hannah, whose son Frank had married and settled in Rochester. The green, candlelighted tree was a revelation to Susan, who had never in her own childhood known what it meant to have a Christmas tree or a Christmas toy in her home. For the first time in her life she gave Christmas presents that year, sending a pocket handkerchief to each of the Avery family, "to put on the Christmas Tree as from Aunt Susan." From that time onward she sent pocket handkerchiefs to her family and to the Averys at Christmas. In her late seventies she had discovered the joy of the Christmas spirit. Along with the typewriter and the telephone, Christmas had come into her life at a very late date.

§ VI As soon as the heat of the *Bible* controversy subsided, Susan installed herself in the new attic. Her plans had altered since she began building it. The project then envisioned, to add Volume IV to the *History*, had been changed to a history of her own life. After her illness in 1895, and probably because of it, she decided that it was time to leave her own testament to the world. Assisted by her cousin, Mrs. Sweet, whom she engaged as secretary, she unpacked her documents and began on the work. She soon found that Mrs. Sweet was what she had represented herself to be—a secretary —and nothing else. She was not a writer.

In her state of bafflement she welcomed a second call from California. The campaign for woman suffrage was on. She had not expected to take part in it; but when the drive actually started, the women began to call loudly for help from the National Association and from Susan personally. Making small progress in her attic, Susan heard the call with some relief. She had engaged her secretary for a year's work, however, assuming that she could complete her task in that length of time. Moreover, she could use Mrs. Sweet's services in California if she could once get her there. The committee had offered to pay her traveling expenses but not those of a secretary. Mr. and Mrs. Gannett of the Unitarian church, apprised of her problem, promptly raised the money for Mrs. Sweet's transportation. Susan was to continue paying the secretary's salary. Thus she contributed her own services and those of her secretary to the California campaign.

They left Rochester on February 27 and reached San Diego on March 10. Presumably Susan made this stop for the purpose of concluding arrangements for the transfer of Aaron McLean's body to Rochester, which had been contemplated for some time. Two months later Margaret Baker performed the last sad duty of transferring her father's remains to lie in Mount Hope Cemetery beside those of his wife. Susan's diary records: "May 16 [1896].—Letter from sister Mary saying . . . niece Maggie was expected Tuesday, A.M., the 12th, with her father's remains, to be placed in Mt. Hope." Susan could not be content until this ritual was accomplished.

It is pleasant to know that she enjoyed a comfortable home during the California campaign. Mrs. Sargent's residence at 1630 Folsom Street was converted into residential and official headquarters. Here Susan was joined by Anna Shaw and her niece, Lucy Anthony, and for eight months they lived in the lap of luxury whenever they had time to enjoy it. Woman suffrage had acquired some wealthy friends in the interim. Mrs. Phoebe Hearst contributed one thousand dollars to the campaign. Mrs. Leland Stanford provided enough free railroad transportation for the speakers and organizers to cover the whole state. Some others made contributions up to five hundred dollars. The bulk of the nineteen thousand dollars spent on the campaign, however, was raised by small donations from white-collar and other workingwomen, for the total cash provided by the wealthy came to less than three thousand dollars.

This California campaign ran head on into Mark Hanna's drive for the election of McKinley. In some ways the campaigns were similar; in others, strikingly different. Hanna is said to have spent, by a conservative estimate, three and a half million dollars on McKinley's election. Even allowing for the fact that Hanna's activities covered the nation, the nineteen thousand dollars spent by the women in California seems picayune by comparison. In the main, Hanna was not doing anything very different from what the women were doing. He spent the money (so he said) on printing and distributing campaign "literature," organization, and speakers. The suffragists spent their modest war chest on the same things. Hanna's famous "strategy," said to have elected McKinley, consisted of the traditional methods and devices and was distinguished only by the inflated sum of money spent on them. He invented nothing that the suffragists did not know and had not practiced, on a pin-money scale, for many years.

The suffragists' hopes rose high at first. They were cordially welcomed everywhere, in spite of the fact that one of the most heated presidential contests of history was going on. The crowd wanted to hear the women speak. As the crisis mounted, however, their welcome wore off. The political situation had become most confused and required close attention on the part of the leaders. The Populists and Democrats had been drawn closer together on the Free Silver issue, while the California state Republicans, having also declared for Free Silver, suddenly found themselves outside the national party and aligned with the opposition. Mr. Hanna's emissaries soon straightened this out; but the Republicans, having made one false step, were careful to avoid another. They discarded all extraneous issues, including woman suffrage. At the same time the Populists, the suffragists' best friends, fell silent for fear of offending their Democratic allies. Finally, the liquor interests sprang into action by organizing their own constituency. But it was not so much this old enemy that defeated woman suffrage as the exigencies of big politics which simply crowded them out.

The vote on the amendment was 110,000 for and 137,000 against. A switch of 13,500 votes in the state would have given women the franchise. Later Susan expressed this opinion of the outcome: "I have always felt that if we had stuck to it after the campaign of 1896, and Miss Shaw and I had stayed there through the winter and gone up to the Legislature . . . we should have succeeded in getting it re-submitted then." They did not do this. They stayed only for a lively rally immediately afterward, which filled a great San Francisco auditorium and strengthened the determination of the women for another try. Mrs. Harper, who was present, said that Susan spoke with as much inspiration at this meeting as at the beginning of the campaign.

Susan journeyed homeward with a lighter heart than the event justified. She had discovered in California the gold of her dreams—

the writer for her biography. As so often happened to her, help was found in the most unlikely of places. Trusting that "a way would open," she had made fumbling attempts on her own and had suspended the project in a discouraged mood.

Ida Husted Harper, a professional newspaperwoman whom Susan had met in Terre Haute when she first met Eugene Debs, was living in San Francisco. Susan discovered her on her arrival and suggested that she be made chairman of the campaign press committee. Formerly a staff writer on the Indianapolis *News*, Mrs. Harper had apparently been going to waste before Susan came. Together they visited the newspaper offices of the city to bespeak the respect and courtesy of the all-powerful editors. Susan became quickly aware that the new press secretary knew her trade and placed the campaign publicity entirely in her hands. Not without some skill and experience of her own in the field, Susan recognized in Mrs. Harper the trained newspaper hand.

The editors responded amiably to this competent pair. The press of San Francisco and of the state generally gave the campaign polite treatment and generous space. Mr. Hearst's *Examiner* made a special offer, proposing to publish free every Sunday a propaganda article from Susan B. Anthony's pen. Susan protested that she was no writer, but the *Examiner* would accept no substitute. After some parley she consented, and every Sunday for seven months the *Examiner* published an article of fifteen hundred words signed by Susan B. Anthony. Susan could never have done it without Mrs. Harper's skillful aid. There are numerous entries in the diary about "grinding out *Examiner* articles," so that they must have often worked together. It was like the grand old days when she had worked with Mrs. Stanton.

It was thus that Susan discovered who was to write her biography. How she persuaded Mrs. Harper to accept the task, she does not say, but it was probably by the same means she had used in persuading Mrs. Stanton. The new collaborator's only condition was that Susan should remain at home while the work was going on and give it her closest supervision and aid. Before Susan left California the date of Mrs. Harper's arrival in Rochester had been definitely fixed.

Very quietly, by comparison with California, the Idaho suffragists had been making a similar drive next door. On November

3, election day, the Idaho suffrage bill was passed. There were twice as many votes cast for the bill as were cast against it. Idaho was a poor state; it had no Hearsts, no Stanfords, no Goodriches to help out. The women raised and spent twenty-five hundred dollars in all. They did not appeal to the National Association for aid, probably for lack of funds to pay the speakers' traveling expenses. Mrs. Catt, as state organizer, was finally sent out with her expenses paid by the National.

As in Colorado, circumstances favored Mrs. Catt. All the political parties of the state gave their endorsement to the bill. Among the politicians the women counted some powerful friends, chief of whom was William E. Borah. Borah proved practical and helpful in getting the measure introduced, in having it passed, and finally in arguing it successfully before the State Supreme Court. But as in Colorado, the apple seemed to fall into Mrs. Catt's hand.

CHAPTER TWENTY-SEVEN

NEW TIMES, NEW DUTIES

◄§ I   Considering Mrs. Stanton's *Reminiscences* too casual and personal to serve as a history of the suffrage movement, Susan decided that her own life history should serve that purpose. She wanted it to be a documentary chronicle. Besides pamphlets, reports, calls, and masses of newspaper clippings, she had about twenty thousand handwritten letters on which to base the work. Mrs. Harper, who was to pour all into the hopper, arrived breezy and ready for a start in March 1897.

Mrs. Harper had made a few stipulations—some good, some not so good. She had exacted Susan's promise to stand by and share in the work, which Susan proceeded to fulfill with remarkable faithfulness. Mrs. Harper had also demanded a commercial publisher and had evidently herself secured such a one in Bowen and Merrill of Indianapolis, where she had formerly lived. A further stipulation, which Susan must have agreed to, was that all the original data, except the scrapbooks of news clippings, should be destroyed when the book was finished. Very early in the work—the book was scarcely started—Susan wrote to the editor of the *Century* in New York, offering condensed chapters to appear as a serial in the magazine and further stating: "When the biography is finished, I shall burn my correspondence and other documents, so that this will be the only *authentic* history of my life that ever can be written." The exclusive offer was courteously declined by the *Century* editor.

Beginning in March 1897, the work lasted, minus a couple of short interruptions, until Christmas 1898. Besides Mrs. Harper, Susan employed a secretary, Miss Genevieve Hawley, from Canajoharie. Mrs. Harper refused to handle the old letters until they could be ironed out, a duty which the secretary, Miss Hawley, found very amusing. Mrs. Sweet came in to take Susan's letters, and two or three extra typists were occasionally employed. "Three typewriters are this minute clicking in my ears," Susan wrote Mrs. Colby, "then the fourth girl is pasting things of 1895 into the . . . great scrap-book; then the girl in the kitchen with sister Mary and myself—all rushing around for dear life." While the actual writing went on in the garret, Mrs. Harper and Miss Hawley lived with the family. "I have got to feeling more wanted and at home here," Miss Hawley wrote her aunt, "and better acquainted. Miss Mary, especially, is very 'set' in her ways, and the household is very quiet indeed; but everything is nice and home-like and books are all about, and they want their guests to make themselves perfectly at home."

Susan was highly pleased with her garret crew. She wrote repeatedly to friends that Mrs. Harper was an indefatigable and painstaking author. At the same time, the impact of a professional writer on Susan's and Mary's household was not without its amusing aspects. To the sisters, no woman's life was complete without some domestic duties. The secretary, Miss Hawley, was expected to help with the dinner dishes. But Mrs. Harper declined all kitchen duty. She stayed in bed until it was time to begin work, nibbled a few crackers, and then fell to. In other ways Mrs. Harper maintained her own personality. "I am doing up some letters," wrote Miss Hawley, "while Mrs. Harper and Miss Anthony sit in the bay-window and look over old letters, from which interesting scraplets occasionally drift to me. Miss A. sits on one side of their table, straight in an old red tea-gown and a straight-backed chair, while Mrs. Harper, plump and cushiony, jogs back and forth in her rocker and nibbles pop-corn at intervals." The writing crew managed a life of perfect harmony in this Quaker household for a two-year period. Young and old, they were all united in single-minded devotion to the head of the production line.

Susan had great respect for Mrs. Harper's authority. Mrs. Harper testifies that her subject stayed at home more days in 1897 than in any of the previous fifty years of her life. But she made a few speaking trips and in November she broke away for a series of conventions in the Middle West. "I took train for home," she says, "Miss Hay and Mrs. Catt on the same train. I never heard more rollicking fun than this evening. Reached home . . . and found Mrs. Harper feeling I had put back the biography work fearfully. Well, it has been a rest to me, anyway." In the old days it was Susan who held Mrs. Stanton under her thumb; now the roles were reversed. Regarding some point of difference, Susan remarked, "There is no way but to do everything just as she wishes and let her find it out when she must."

Meantime Mrs. Stanton, who had judiciously declined to occupy the attic, offered herself to Susan as a vacation guest. In great distress Susan appealed to Mrs. Miller of Peterboro, who never failed her in a crisis. "I have to tell her," wrote Susan, "that our guest chamber is occupied by Mrs. Harper, the lady who is writing my biography. . . . Now that I have gone into the garret and made all plans to prosecute this work I cannot allow myself to be hindered from going ahead, for I hate the whole business so absolutely that I want to be done with it as soon as possible." Mrs. Miller not only invited Mrs. Stanton to Peterboro for the summer but also invited Susan and Mrs. Harper to pay her a visit there. One of the cherished memories of Mrs. Harper's sojourn in Rochester was her visit to the famous old Gerrit Smith mansion in Peterboro. Susan's visit with Mrs. Stanton was less satisfactory. She found her old friend engrossed in a new hobby. "Her craze now is educated suffrage," lamented Susan. She could not understand how Mrs. Stanton could deviate from the old Jeffersonian principles in which she herself had first initiated Susan and which the latter regarded as the foundation of democracy.

Susan was never in more vigorous physical and mental health than during the years spent on the biography. Mrs. Harper had no compunctions about driving her. She never mentioned Susan's health in her story except to extol it or to recall the great longevity of her ancestors, especially that of her grandfather, who lived to the age of ninety-seven. She never considered Susan's age, seventy-seven at the time, as an item of any consequence. The severe illness of two years ago had been outlived and forgotten.

∽§ II   From much dwelling on her childhood memories for the purpose of the biography, Susan probably got the idea of the Anthony family reunion. She had been invited to attend the annual meeting of the Berkshire Historical Society that year as a guest of honor. She decided to hold a meeting of the National Woman Suffrage Committee and a reunion of the Anthony family in Adams at one and the same time. This involved a great amount of preliminary correspondence, with which Mrs. Harper, who was to take part in the outing, was extremely sympathetic. She hoped the celebration would establish Adams as the cradle of woman suffrage.

Everyone was co-operative. The Berkshire Historical Society transferred its place of meeting to the old Anthony homestead. The far-flung Anthony connections, Reeds, Richardsons, Laphams, Dickinsons, came flocking in from great distances. About eighty of these relatives dined in Humphrey Anthony's old keeping room, where the famous local products, including the celebrated cheese, weighed down the tables. Susan's cousin, Mrs. Fannie Bates, occupying her grandfather's house, gave beds to as many as possible, other cousins did the same, and the rest went to the old Hotel Greylock in Adams. The Historical Society held meetings and the Suffrage Association held meetings, and the high-grade talent of the latter contributed its brilliant oratory to the success of both occasions.

Susan, Miss Shaw, and Mrs. Catt made their best suffrage speeches—to as little avail, I trow, as any they ever made in their lives. They passed on, and Adams, without turning over in its sleep, reverted to its Quaker memories on the one hand and its great industrial future on the other. That one soul had been saved there is good reason to doubt. Mrs. Harper's dream of stamping the Berkshire town as the cradle of woman suffrage vanished with the last trainload of departing suffragists. The town can still just manage to remember, when reminded by a monument erected and paid for by Susan's relatives, the Dickinsons of Chicago, that it was the cradle of Susan B. Anthony.

Accompanied by her brothers and her sister, Susan made a detour through Battenville and Centre Falls on her way home. The reunion had been a great joy to her, a renewal of the springs of her

deep clannishness. The graves of her ancestors in the Quaker cemetery, marked by headstones in 1897, formed impressive and imposing rows among the Quaker dead. To behold them was to know
the roots from which her life had sprung. Susan cherished her roots
as few individuals, historic or obscure, have ever done.

III   In 1898 the National-American convention returned to
Washington. Her friends spoke of Susan's return to "her beloved
Washington," as if the attachment was of a sentimental nature.
They seemed not to comprehend that Washington was synony-
mous in her mind with the Federal amendment. Now that the
congressional hearings could take place only every other year, she
tried to make the most of them. But this time her best speakers
struck no fire, few Congress members attended, and the hearings
were lifeless. She aroused herself to make an impassioned speech,
to which the gentlemen listened listlessly. Her important ties were
broken.

The convention, planned as a gala celebration of the fiftieth
anniversary of Seneca Falls, seemed doomed from the start. In the
first place, Mrs. Stanton sent a long paper on educated suffrage
(the voice of Seneca Falls had lost its pristine ring), which Susan
read loyally but without enthusiasm. On the second day the *Maine*
was blown up in Havana Harbor and the country was immediately
plunged into a war hysteria. Two days later Frances Willard died
at her hotel in New York. Much beloved by the suffragists, to
whom she had always remained loyal through long absences in
England and a long period of poor health, she was deeply mourned
by these friends. It was after this news came that Susan appeared
in the white shawl to which the reporters objected and which she
promptly exchanged for the red shawl demanded. All her life she
disapproved of wearing mourning in any form.

Susan spent the summer at home, helping Mrs. Harper cut the
biography down from 500,000 to 400,000 words. The Spanish-
American War absorbed public attention. Susan's thoughts ran
on the relation of women to the conflict. "My niece Maude's
husband . . . is on a ship bound for Cuba," she wrote; "Maude
is full of faith that her beloved will not be hit by a Spanish bullet.
Well, but for hope, the wives and mothers left at home would

surely perish!" Her friend, Mrs. Colby, contemplated some kind
of military enlistment, but changed her mind. "Well, I am glad
you have not flown off to Cuba. It is rough enough for our men
and boys to rush into the melee! Our women and girls had better
hold themselves aloof until they have a country that recognizes
them . . . that protects them in the right to a voice in saying
whether we shall settle our national difficulties by brute methods,
or by international tribunals." To another friend she observed: "It
does look as if the Spanish Cabinet must come to the conclusion
that they have cost enough suffering to their own people, to say
nothing about the Cubans or Americans, to make the best terms
possible with their sure-to-be-conquerors in the end. Our folks do
seem to have deadly guns, and to know exactly how to make them
take certain effect." And, holding onto the hope which seems to
die hardest in the human bosom, she wrote: "The death-dealing
inventions should make this the very last of the wicked barbarism."

On the whole she stood aloof from the war, maintaining a determined silence in regard to it. Only once, when an outbreak of
disease in the American camps called attention to their unsanitary
conditions, did she feel forced to speak out. In a public meeting
she denounced the government which took young men from their
homes without a "by your leave" to the parents, forced them to
occupy unsanitary camps, exposed them to the greed and graft of
those who provided them with food, and accepted with pious resignation the sickness and death which resulted. But many voices besides her own were raised in protest at the time, and she was not
duly noticed. But she could do little for suffrage. "It is philosophical," she said, "for us to lay on our oars and rest during this war."

Mrs. Harper's biography, in two volumes, was published at the
end of 1898. "It seems like getting out of a long nightmare agony,"
Susan said. The event did not receive as much attention as it might
have done had it not coincided with the conclusion of the Spanish-
American War. But the reviews were favorable and Susan's great
fear that she might leave somebody's name out of the book was
apparently not realized. The first unfavorable attack came about the
next year, and it came from within the ranks of the new consoli-
dated society, supposed to be moving along in full harmony. It was
Mr. Blackwell who shattered the harmony with a final blast from
the old suffrage division of 1869.

Susan and Mrs. Harper had been as noncommittal and discreet as possible on the subject, following the same line as the *History of Woman Suffrage*. When the *History* appeared, Lucy Stone had refrained from making any comment on the controversial subject. But now, said Mr. Blackwell, "I feel that I ought not to let this one-sided statement of the case be published a second time without comment." The one-sided statement, as summed up in Mr. Blackwell's words, ran: "Without saying so in express terms it implies throughout that [the split] was a causeless division, prompted chiefly by personal motives." Mr. Blackwell proceeded to mention the various causes, Mrs. Stanton's interest in divorce, her own and Susan's alliance with Train, Woodhull, etc. The danger of reviving an old quarrel did not deter him. In fact, he invited Susan to reply to his article in the columns of the *Journal*, in order to continue it. Nothing could have induced Susan to reply at this juncture, thirty years after the original altercation.

She kept a close rein on her tongue, her letters, and even her diary. Some errors of fact in Mr. Blackwell's statement she allowed to pass without correction. Her only expression of indignation is found in this letter to Mrs. Miller:

I do hope you and Nannie will read Mr. Blackwell's article of *nine columns* in the *Woman's Journal* of March 11 [1899]. So that when he and Alice are with you next month you will both know what he said in it; for he is sure to broach the subject with you. I know how disagreeable it is to you both, and it can be no less so to me, but all of us ought to be intelligent enough to know and tell him the truth when he falsifies the facts of those olden days. Of course I would not have either of you allude to his article on the old differences. Only I would have you well fortified if he opens the subject, which he is as sure to do as the leopard is to retain his spots.
P.S. Our State President . . . has just raised and sent to H.B.B. $100 with three hundred names for him to send his *Woman's Journal* throughout our State. Just to think of my sister Mary working thus to send his falsehoods thus broadcast—it makes me ache to the very centre of me.

Mrs. Miller, who held that a nice barrel of apples or a lovely spice cake could do no harm to hurt feelings, sent something of the kind post-haste to Rochester. She added a fine steamer wrap for Susan to wear on her forthcoming trip to England. For Susan was preparing to attend the meeting of the International Council of Women in London. At seventy-nine she had no intention of missing it. With such a pleasant prospect before her it was easy to put Mr. Blackwell's article out of her mind, and this she did successfully. Her talent for living in the present was splendidly surviving in spite of her years.

In London she spent a strenuous two weeks at the congress. The election of a new president, involving a slight contest, called out her skill. The American candidate, May Wright Sewall, was finally chosen, thanks to Susan's skillful but strictly constitutional management. She addressed many English audiences, gave long interviews to reporters, and attended many luncheons given in her honor. The International Council, after some maneuvering on Susan's part, was invited to Windsor to pay their respects to the Queen.

On her first visit to England, Susan had not seen Victoria. This time she saw her, though it was something of an ordeal. The members of the council, some of them titled English ladies, were kept waiting an hour outside the castle gate in the hot and glaring sun. Many of them, like Susan, were far from young. The Queen did nothing to shorten their vigil. When the regular time for her airing arrived, the gates were opened and the visitors were allowed to line up along the driveway to see the carriage pass. The Queen bowed to right and left as she drove along. The ladies were then invited into St. George's Hall and served with tea in the historic chamber by the Queen's retainers. "But a tired lot we were," says Susan.

Ida Husted Harper from Terre Haute, Indiana, observed all this with tongue in cheek. A trained newspaperwoman, Mrs. Harper kept a civil tongue in her head and Susan imitated her discretion. Their public utterances about the reception were without fault. After they were back in the States, *McClure's Magazine* sent Mrs. Harper to interview Susan on her impressions of the Queen. Between them they managed to turn some pleasant and well-deserved compliments but wound up with a just estimate of Victoria's scant services to her sex. "Either she has felt that popular sentiment would not sustain her or else she has lacked the philosophy to discern the relation between political power in the hands of women and . . . improved conditions of society. . . . I am inclined to think that she has failed in this perception rather than that she has desired to cater to the public."

The main feature of her London journey was the great vigor she showed in meeting all demands. When she had a little time to rest, she took a jaunt to Edinburgh to see Mrs. McLaren, Jacob Bright's sister, then eighty-four years old. She reached home at the end of August, ready to attend the State Federation of Women's Clubs and the American Federation of Labor convention. Any observer would have granted her another decade of activity.

◄§ IV　The fact remained that Susan would be eighty on her next birthday. As she stated to the association that year, she had decided in 1896 to resign the presidency of the society at eighty. She was probably prompted to her decision by the severe illness which attacked her in 1895 and which also induced her to turn to the writing of her biography. In pursuance of this design she announced at the convention of 1899 that she would resign at the next convention. The membership had a full year to deal with the problem of her successor.

The question had been agitated much longer. The rivalry between Miss Shaw and Mrs. Catt for the office had been quietly going on for some time. It was well known that Susan preferred Anna Shaw, but she had taken no part whatever in promoting her candidacy. She had long since decided on a hands-off policy regarding her successor. Mrs. Catt, it will be remembered, had originally entered the movement under the inspiration of Lucy Stone and her husband. Her candidacy was ardently promoted by the Blackwells through editorials in the *Woman's Journal*. Mrs. Catt had a party. Mr. Catt offered the utmost co-operation. It was obvious that she could better afford the position, which carried no salary, than Anna Shaw, who had to earn her living. Besides, Mrs. Catt had sterling claims, unrelated to her means, that placed her in the foreground. By the time of the election the outcome was so clearly foreseen that Miss Shaw declined to be nominated. Mrs. Catt, without a serious rival, was elected by a practically unanimous vote.

Anna Shaw says in her memoirs: "I will admit here for the first time that in urging Mrs. Catt's fitness for the office I made the greatest sacrifice of my life." But the sacrifice was made with complete outward amiability and poise. Susan also maintained her habitual composure, giving no sign of emotion except at one point by a certain tremor of the voice. This was quickly mastered. She introduced the new president in these hearty words: "Suffrage is no longer a theory, but an actual condition. New occasions bring new duties. These new duties, these changed conditions, demand stronger hands, younger heads, and fresher hearts. In Mrs. Catt you have my ideal leader. I present to you my successor." *New occasions bring new duties.* With this argument she had apparently been brought into line. Mrs. Catt offered the qualities of leadership required by the new times.

On being introduced, Mrs. Catt stood at first with downcast eyes, saying nothing. Most observers ascribed her attitude to a modesty becoming in a younger woman under the circumstances. But one suspects that something else was going on in Mrs. Catt's mind that prevented a direct and forthright approach to her new elevation. Whatever it was, she quickly mastered it and made a modest, tactful, and pleasing acceptance speech to the members.

The formal convention was followed by a birthday reception for Susan in the Corcoran Art Gallery. Susan sat on the stage, gowned in the historic garnet velvet trimmed with point lace. She looked very handsome, and Mrs. Harper, who was present, described her as seeming "at the very zenith of her powers." When she spoke, says Mrs. Harper, "her fine voice with its rich alto vibrations" rang out as convincingly as it ever had in her life. What a pity that the necessary mechanical inventions did not arrive in time to preserve the voice for us!

Susan's resignation was an emotional crisis for everyone. At many points of the conference, the speeches, and even the reception, the delegates freely gave way to tears. It devolved upon Susan, assisted ably by Anna Shaw, both of whom showed their usual self-control, to keep the affair going on a prosaic level. Miss Shaw could always produce amusing stories, and Susan, though not good at anecdote, could always quip wittily. Her farewell speech ran in part:

"I wish you could realize with what joy and relief I retire from the presidency. I want to say this to you while I am yet alive—and I am good for another decade—as long as my name stands at the head I am Yankee enough to feel that I must watch every potato which goes into the dinner pot. . . . I am now going to let go of the machinery but not of the spiritual part. I expect to do more work for woman suffrage in the next decade than ever before. I have not been for nearly fifty years in this movement without gaining a certain "notoriety" . . . and this enables me to get a hearing before the annual conventions of many great national bodies and to urge on them the passage of resolutions asking Congress to submit to the State Legislatures a Sixteenth Amendment to the Federal Constitution forbidding disfranchisement on account of sex."

She then announced that she would also raise a standing fund for the support of the movement. Suffrage could no longer survive on the pin money of wives and the small donations of self-supporting women. "I am going to raise the fund," she said, "so that you young women may have an assured income for the work and not have to spend the most of your time begging money as I have had to do." She planned to put on the biggest begging campaign of her life so that others after her might not have to beg. She hesitated about the amount but settled at last on a movable sum somewhere between $100,000 and $500,000. But she meant what she said and remained in Washington a week after the convention to take out incorporation papers for the standing fund.

She seemed oppressed by the poverty of the movement as never before. A slight note of bitterness appeared in a statement she gave out at this time. "Not one of our national officers ever has made a dollar of salary. I retire on full pay."

~§ V   In turning to her biography Susan had by no means given up the idea of adding Volume IV to the History. It was only deferred. All the while she was writing the biography Mrs. Harper had foreseen that she would be drafted for the work. She held out as firmly and as long as she could; said she could not stand another winter in the attic with the gas stove; "her hair had all fallen out." But Susan continued to broach the project at judicious intervals. She wrote to Mrs. Avery: "Mrs. Harper *almost promises* to come here through April and May . . . and help me get together Vol. IV of the History of W.S. Shan't I feel happy if the material gets all together for the rounding out of the work to the close of the

19th century, and the close of my *bossing the business.*" During the convention of 1900 Mrs. Harper finally broke down and bowed her head to the yoke. She wrote to Mrs. Stanton, "Providence or some other fellow seems to have decreed that I must go to Miss Anthony's assistance, now that you can no longer do these things for her."

In March the attic, with Mrs. Harper and Miss Hawley at the controls, was again going at full blast. Volume IV of the *History* was on the way. Susan had not a dollar in hand for the publication of the work. Her annual income of eight hundred dollars had been increased by Mrs. Avery's personal generosity by another four hundred dollars. Miraculously deployed by Susan, this took care of Mrs. Harper and Miss Hawley, but it would not take care of the high cost of publishing. Susan's career as a publisher had not been a paying experience; she had accumulated no profits. Most of the earlier sets had been given away, and the rest were in costly storage. Additionally, she had undertaken to raise a standing fund for woman suffrage. Mrs. Harper was deeply concerned about the financial problems, but Susan remained as serene as ever. She had never yet undertaken any great suffrage project with the money for it already in hand.

In May she left the *History* for a short trip to Boston. It was the first time she had gone to Boston since her visit in 1891, when she had fallen ill and failed to keep her appointment with Lucy Stone. This time she went straight to the *Woman's Journal* office and was invited to spend the night with Alice Stone Blackwell and her father in their Dorchester home. "There was a good deal of careful talk on the new President and the work before us," says the diary. No doubt Susan was just as careful. She spoke at a meeting in Faneuil Hall, where Miss Shaw and Mrs. Catt also spoke on the same program. "It was really quite like the old-time wide-awake meeting," she commented. She enjoyed it. She and Miss Shaw had buried once for all the old dream they had cherished together, that Miss Shaw would succeed her in the presidency. All was going ahead splendidly.

She had scarcely arrived at home when a telegram announcing the sudden death of her brother Merritt in Fort Scott, Kansas, came to hand. Miss Hawley described the event in a letter to her aunt:

The telegram came about 3 o'clock Friday morning and they were the only ones in the house who got up to meet it. Anna Dann was afraid it was about her father, who is ill in Canada, and so listened to their talking together till she found out what the matter was; and neither even cried, though she said 'there was a sob in Miss Susan's voice.' . . . Miss Anthony got no rest at all before taking the Empire Express in the afternoon. The day was very hot, too, and Mrs. Harper, Anna, and I were all anxious about her starting at eighty years alone on such a journey. . . . But she was determined to do it. Only in that way did she show her grief and excitement.

Merritt, the youngest member of the family, had dropped dead of heart failure while his wife was away visiting relatives. His death was so unexpected and shocking that Susan could not meet it with philosophy and calm. "It seemed impossible for me to do anything but weep," she wrote; "while I was in Ft. Scott I shed more tears than in years and years before. I thought I was done with tears, but no!"

Altogether it had been a hard year for Susan. Her resignation had not been easy; her successor had not been her choice; her brother's death without warning caused a hurt that reopened the other wounds she thought had been healed. She came home from the funeral deeply depressed. Though Mary urged her, she refused to call off the meeting of the Business Committee about to take place in her home. There were nine ladies on this committee, and they were to be entertained for a week. Susan, assisted by her sister, managed to bed and feed them graciously and hospitably. After three days, however, Mrs. Coonley Ward, who even at that early date wielded the famous hospitality of her Wyoming retreat, dropped in for a casual visit. A perceptive lady, she saw how things stood and immediately carried off the entire company to her house, including the hostess, distributing railroad tickets like Bagdad carpets for the journey. Mrs. Harper says she never saw Susan so happy as during this meeting. But it could still have been a great strain, following so closely upon her brother's death and other poignant experiences.

VI   Susan returned from Mrs. Coonley Ward's mansion admitting she was tired and saying she would rest. But business she

had left in the hands of others turned out to be most critically
unfinished.

The business in question concerned the admission of girls to
Rochester University. Originally proposed by Susan and Mrs. Stanton in concert, the request had not been allowed to die down. The
Political Club, with Mary Anthony and Mary Lewis Gannett as
active members, had kept up the agitation. The trustees had finally
announced that a fund of $100,000 would have to be raised to
meet the additional expense. A local committee, of which Susan
was a member, was formed to raise the money. Anna Shaw spent
a week in Rochester helping to stir up sentiment for the fund.
The trustees were at last induced to reduce the requirement to
$50,000, with a deadline placed at September 8, 1900. By this con-
cession the trustees were acting in opposition to a strong opinion
among the alumni of the institution, which resisted the admission
of girls on any terms. It was therefore important that the fund
should be raised and the question settled as speedily as possible.

She got home exactly four days before the critical date. On the
night before September 8 (not even two or three days beforehand), the chairman of the committee called her on the phone
and told her that eight thousand dollars were still lacking to complete the fund. Susan had supposed of course that the entire sum
was ready.

With only one day in which to raise eight thousand dollars,
Susan got up early the next morning and extracted two thousand
dollars from her sister before breakfast. She knew that Mary had
planned to leave two thousand dollars in her will to the university
in case it became coeducational in the meantime. Susan pointed
out to her that now was the time to achieve the desired result.
She then set forth in a carriage with the chairman of the Fund
Committee to collect the balance of the money. There was no
time to raise it anywhere except in Rochester, and Rochester was
milked dry. She was obliged to go to those who had already given.
Sarah Willis, an old Quaker friend, and the ever-helpful Gannetts
increased their donations by two thousand dollars each. She then
appealed to the aged Mr. Samuel Wilder, one of her oldest friends
in Rochester. But he felt he could give no more. Susan was struck
by a sudden thought; she could throw in her life insurance policy,

worth two thousand dollars. On second thought she decided to give it in Mr. Wilder's name. To this he consented.

Late that afternoon the Fund Committee appeared at the trustees' meeting. Having heard rumors that they were not ready, the trustees were somewhat surprised. As the diary says: "They had not expected it; they waited and queried." But all seemed to be in order, except possibly the final contributor. Mr. Wilder was very old and known to be ill; would his estate be responsible for his pledge? "I then told them the truth," says the diary, "that Mr. Wilder had given me permission to use his name, that I stood sponsor for the $2,000." She explained that her motive was to keep the coeducation question clear of any connection with woman suffrage; coeducation was not popular, but woman suffrage was even less so.

The trustees kept the committee waiting two days longer while they investigated the pledges. This imposed an added strain on Susan, who was intensely anxious about the outcome. On Monday, when the final answer was given, she wrote in her diary in a very quavering hand, "Well, they let the girls in. Said there was no alternative." So the gentlemen had none too graciously accepted the fund. Susan said in her diary that none of them had given anything, though some of them were millionaires. They took her insurance policy without a word of protest, but the ladies of the committee redeemed themselves for their early negligence by clearing the policy later and returning it to her.

◆§ VII   That evening the house in Madison Street was filled with girls who called to express their gratitude. Many of them expected to enter the university at once. In the midst of the gay celebration Susan disappeared. Mary, going to look for her, found her lying unconscious on her bed.

Susan continued very ill for a month and was ailing for long afterward. For a week she was unable to speak. Her physician, the same Dr. Moore who had attended her former illness, diagnosed her disease as a stroke. Apparently he did not inform her of this opinion during her illness but at some later time. The members of the household looked on her illness as a second nervous breakdown like her first.

Except for her inability to speak, which lasted for a week, no other symptoms of paralysis are noted by Mrs. Harper, who was living in her house and saw her daily. She seems to have suffered from no other form of helplessness. On the Sunday when she had anxiously awaited the decision of the trustees, she wrote in the diary: "Went to church today but had a sleepy time. . . . It seemed as if something was the matter with my tongue. . . . I had a feeling of strangeness—could not think what I wanted to say." The next morning, before the interview, Mary said "she would not talk." Mary thought she was saving herself for the appointment. Susan's thoughts centered around her speechlessness. After resuming the diary she wrote, "My last speech was made to the Executive Committee of the Board of Trustees," though her remarks then could scarcely have been called a speech. Still later she confided to Mrs. Harper that she would never again have confidence in her ability to speak in public. Of course she did speak again in public, many times, notably in Berlin and London in 1904, and on many other occasions, and always, as the papers reported, with the old ringing note in her voice. Only the lecture tours, with their two-hour-long performances, often night after night, were no longer possible.

In November, discouraged by her slow recovery, Susan paid a private visit to her doctor. "Had a nice talk with him," she wrote. "He said nothing could be done [italics hers]. Nature must do the remedy." The doctor repeated his diagnosis, telling her that she had suffered a slight lesion in the brain and that a second stroke might come at any time, though possibly not for years. He advised her to take care of herself, to avoid exhaustion and eschew crowds, though he might have saved his breath. It is of interest to note that Susan paid no attention to his advice, that she never had a recurrence of the stroke in the five and a half full years of life that remained to her, and that when she died it was not from apoplexy but from pneumonia.

Her first act on feeling slightly better was to summon Mrs. Harper, absent on vacation, back to work. "Of course you know," wrote Mrs. Harper to Miss Hawley, "she came very near going two weeks ago. I had a most pathetic letter from her yesterday. It looks as if you and Anna and I would have to stay with her now as long as she lives." Back at work, Mrs. Harper wrote to a friend: "Miss Anthony improves very slowly, and never yet has been able to examine a single chapter of the *History*. . . . In fact, her only interest in it seems to be that it shall be finished. She has exacted a promise from me that I will do it, whether she lives or not." For the first time in her life Susan began to show signs of worry about money. "The future seems so uncertain," she told Mrs. Harper. "Ask Genevieve to come at the rate of $10 per week, with the understanding that if anything happens to make it necessary she will give up the position on reasonable notice."

Without a definite future to count upon, she had undertaken a long-drawn-out project. At length Mrs. Harper, aided by Anna Shaw, persuaded her to use the three thousand dollars she had raised for the standing fund to publish Volume IV of the *History*. With the consent of the donors, this was arranged. As for the standing fund, that was an idea which would have to be abandoned indefinitely. "There are reasons why she does not wish to go on with the Standing Fund," wrote Mrs. Harper to a friend, "which probably you will divine. . . . Her struggles to regain her strength are perfectly heart-rending. She never has been accustomed to take care of herself, and when she feels a little better she does the most dreadful things, which counteract all that she has gained."

Even while this was being written, Susan was packing her bags to attend a Suffrage Bazaar in New York. The three octogenarians of the suffrage movement, Susan, Mrs. Stanton, and Julia Ward Howe had promised to attend the grand opening. Susan was the only one of the three who actually turned up. Miss Hawley wrote her aunt: "Miss Susan B. plucked up strength enough to go to the Suffrage Bazaar, and all we left behind are wondering how she will come back. It may do her lots of good and it may just absolutely finish her. She left Saturday morning . . . in a handsome 'new' made-over 'black silk' and in good spirits. . . . The cousins with whom she is to stay . . . are wealthy people, with a . . . carriage of their own, so that she will be independent of street-cars, and they will do all she will let them." It was a luxury for Susan to be independent of streetcars.

After a week in the Madison Square Garden crowds she came home none the worse for her experience. This was fortunate, for at home a crisis awaited her. Susan was always losing her good housemaids by urging and assisting them to seek a better employment. This had happened before and was about to happen again.

Miss Anna Dann, who had been her housekeeper for the past two years, had decided to enter a Rochester hospital to embark on nurse's training. The time for her novitiate was at hand. "There is trouble in the house of Anthony," wrote Miss Hawley, "even though Miss Mary, who is getting the worst of it, holds her peace with Quaker self-control. She has not got a girl yet." Miss Dann entered the hospital and at first seemed to be gone for good. But after three weeks she suddenly changed her mind and decided to take up stenography and typewriting instead of nursing. For the rest of the winter she gave her mornings to housework and her afternoons to business college. The solution was satisfactory to everybody, especially Susan, who had become closely attached to the young girl and who planned to employ her eventually in the capacity of a secretary. That she had surmounted the danger of losing Anna Dann from her household meant a great deal for her peace of mind. "Little Annie Dann," as she called her in her diary, kept her heart warm.

Another step taken at the time contributed to her well-being. She called in Dr. Sherman Ricker, a homeopathic physician and a close personal friend. She had cherished a lifelong leaning toward homeopathic medicine and she turned to it now. Dr. Ricker appears not to have confirmed the stroke theory of her predecessor. At any rate, she told Susan that she was simply suffering from overwork and that proper diet, rest, and sleep would ultimately restore her. While Susan was too realistic to dismiss her first physician's diagnosis, she was willing to entertain a less drastic view of her case. "My rest will prove whether there is something else at the bottom of it all," she said; but it was hard to benefit from rest while the threat of a stroke was hanging over her. At last, under Dr. Ricker's cheerful ministrations, the pall began to lift, and as time went on her mental outlook cleared more and more. Though her physical weakness remained, her normal attack on life returned and her native optimism reasserted itself.

✑§ VIII   Susan had planned to spend some time presenting the suffrage cause to the various national organizations of the country. These were organizations of men formed along religious, social, and industrial lines. Her relations with the trade-union movement were slight but sound. She had not much knowledge of the field, but she knew too much about workingwomen's problems to go far wrong on those of workingmen. Her attitude, contrasted with Frances Willard's and Lucy Stone's, for instance, was well balanced and sensible. Lucy Stone had expressed in her *Journal* the utmost abhorrence of trade unions as "a menace to business integrity and national prosperity." Frances Willard, on the other hand, plunged so deeply into labor politics as to confuse her relations with her own temperance cause. Susan never espoused the cause of labor; she only demanded that labor should espouse her cause.

She was a member of the Knights of Labor. Terence Powderly, storm center of the early labor movement, himself had initiated her at his home in Scranton. This was in the early eighties and before he initiated Frances Willard in the same way. As time went on, Powderly gave place to Samuel Gompers and the Knights of Labor to the American Federation of Labor. Susan watched the growing organization and coveted its support. In October 1899 she wrote to Gompers and requested permission to speak at the federation's annual convention. Gompers was friendly and granted her request. At Detroit, on December 12, she made her speech. To her great joy, the four hundred delegates adopted by a rising vote the resolution she proposed for a Federal amendment.

A month later she addressed the International Bricklayers and Masons in Rochester. On this occasion a stenographer was present and her speech ran in part:

"Your own interest demands that you should seek to make women your political equals, for then, instead of being, as now, a dead weight to drag down all working men, a stumbling block in their path, a hindrance to their efforts to secure better wages and more favorable legislation, the working women would be an added strength, politically, industrially, morally."

The bricklayers' union liked her views and published them in full in its organ, which, as Susan happily counted, reached sixty thousand persons.

In a letter to the *Voice of Labor*, a California paper, she elaborated this view:

The work of my life has been less to find out the causes of men's failure to successfully manage affairs, than to try to show them their one great failure in attempting to make a successful government without the help of women. It used to be said in anti-slavery days that a people who would tacitly consent to the enslavement of 4,000,000 human beings were incapable of being just to each other; and I believe the same rule holds with regard to the injustice practiced by men toward women. So long as all men conspire to rob women of their citizen's right to perfect equality in all the privileges and immunities of our so-called "free" government, we can not expect these same men to be capable of perfect justice to each other. On the contrary, the inevitable result must be trusts, monopolies, and all sorts of schemes to get an undue share of the proceeds of labor. There is money enough in this country today in the hands of the few, if justly distributed, to make "good times" for all.

Her staunchest friend in the labor movement was Eugene Victor Debs. After Debs had sponsored her appearance in Terre Haute in 1878, when both of them were nearly driven from the street by hoodlum mobs, his support never failed her. As fate contrived it, Susan, Debs, and Mrs. Harper met once again in Rochester during Susan's illness in 1900. Debs came to the city, campaigning for the presidency, at the beginning of November. Miss Hawley reported the sensational event to her aunt:

Eugene V. Debs, labor candidate for the presidency, spoke here Friday night. Mrs. Harper very much wanted to go and could get no company but me, so I went. He made a most eloquent speech, even though one could not say amen to all of his ideas; but it was two hours long, another man spoke . . . the band played . . . and we waited a good while. . . . Mrs. Harper was repaid however, for Debs saw her in the crowd and when he ended speaking and hundreds were wanting to shake hands with him, he came hurrying down to speak to her. . . . For it seems that they have known each other ever since she was a young bride and he was a boy at the High School. It was pretty to see how they both enoyed the meeting.

Susan was still too ill to go out, but she was able to receive callers. Debs visited her at her house and referred to the visit in an article he wrote many years later. "Almost twenty-five years passed after the meeting in Terre Haute in 1878 before I met Miss Anthony for the second and last time." He said she took his hand warmly in both of hers. "You remember me?" she said. "Remember you!"

said Debs. "How could anyone ever forget Susan B. Anthony?" He instantly noticed, he said, that "the years of trial, persecution, and incessant struggle had left their ruthless impress upon her noble features." The nobility and spirituality of her countenance were no doubt enhanced by the effects of her recent illness, but they were also permanently impressed there now for all time. Three years after this meeting Debs sent his warm birthday greetings by telegraph to Susan. He did not return to Rochester again for several years, when the woman he had once so admired and revered had vanished from the scene. Debs paid his last respects to her in her Mount Hope resting place, where, on a pouring, stormy day in 1910 he laid a rain-soaked wreath on her grave.

⚜ IX While Susan struggled slowly back to health, the garret crew forged onward under Mrs. Harper's direction. Mrs. Harper had returned to her servitude in April 1900 and stayed in the garret, with only two intermissions, until Christmas 1902. The first winter she rebelled against the gas stove and took off for Washington before Christmas, remaining there until March. Susan, reassured by Mrs. Harper's promise to finish the work no matter what happened, seemed quite willing to have her go. The next summer Mrs. Harper again took time off to work for *McClure's Magazine* in New York. She carried off with her Susan's favorite, Anna Dann, to act as her secretary and to see the sights of New York. Susan was much pleased with this arrangement, considering it as educational for her young protégée.

Miss Dann had been promoted to Mrs. Harper's working crew, though Mrs. Harper still had to compete with Miss Mary for her services. "Just as long as Anna stays here," Mrs. Harper grumbled, "she will have to do two or three hours work in the morning before she sits down to the type-writer." The professional writer resented every dish that Anna washed. But the youthful Miss Dann proved able to handle her own affairs better than Mrs. Harper could handle them for her. With the final arrival of a competent housekeeper, she asserted her independence. "I sit in my room and burn my lamp long after Miss Mary is in bed," she wrote a young friend. "I go out as many evenings as I like and stay out as long as I like, and I do not get up until breakfast is ready." And she added at the end of her letter: "Miss Susan is wonderfully well for her and I believe will be able to do a lot of good work." She was right. Susan assumed the active supervision of the proofreading and the other final details of the work.

How she financed the publishing after the first three thousand dollars had given out, one does not know. One does know, however, that she raked and scraped together the last penny of her own savings for the purpose. On March 9, 1904, she wrote in her diary: "Paid off the last penny for the printing and binding of Volumes I, II, III, IV; one thousand copies. It takes almost the last penny I have in the Bank. . . . I have come out a great deal better than I expected." She had expected to come out in debt. It is understandable that Mary, looking on, was sometimes moved to utter reproaches. Apropos of some such passage, Susan wrote in the diary: "I gave a hasty crisp retort to Sister Mary this A.M. . . . It does get so very wearing to be constantly rubbed on not being able to do a thing but *give away* all that I have." She felt guilty about her hasty retort to Mary but had no compunctions whatever about expending her all on suffrage.

The last stages of the *History* work were brightened by a love affair in the house. Along with her other youthful attractions, Miss Dann possessed a suitor. Indeed, it was more for his sake that she had given up her nurse's training than for any other reason, though she said little about that. Miss Dann was a philosopher. "I get very tired of the 'strenuous' life," she wrote, "the life that knows so much more than it can attain." She was engaged to be married from the time she left the hospital, but she told her fiancé that he would have to wait until the *History* was finished. In the spring of 1902, after a year of patient waiting, he was allowed to give her an engagement ring. As her diamond flashed above the typewriter keys, lighting up the dingy attic, Anna was about as happy as a girl with a clear conscience and an engagement ring could well be. The *History* was so far along that the wedding day could be set. It was fixed for October, when the leaves would be falling from the chestnut tree in front of the house and the last pages of Volume IV would be falling from Mrs. Harper's hands.

Everybody in the household was giving Anna advice. One day Susan overheard Mrs. Harper talking to the bride-to-be. To her horror, Mrs. Harper was advising her not to have any children.

Susan was aghast, but she also stood somewhat in awe of Mrs. Harper. She waited to corner the girl secretly but spoke as soon as she could. "I should be very sorry," she said, "to think you would never have children." Miss Dann, wise beyond her years, said nothing at all in the face of her conflicting advisers.

"I am to be married here in Miss Anthony's home," she wrote a friend, "by Miss Shaw, if possible. . . . Both Miss Anthony and Miss Mary asked me at separate times to make my plans to be married in the house." Miss Shaw would have canceled any engagement for the purpose, knowing how dear this young girl was to Susan. The house was beautifully decorated and an elegant wedding supper set forth. Susan joined with Mrs. Harper in giving the bride the latest model in sewing machines, and Susan added to her gift a check for fifty dollars. The young couple moved at once into their new home; but "our bride," as Miss Hawley called her, was always running in, "generally to get something she has packed away here." To Anna this house was home, and the tie of affection which bound her to Susan was to continue unbroken after her marriage.

As Mrs. Mason, Anna Dann closes her reminiscences: "I lived hard in that home in many ways, but I adored her." Lived hard— without doubt this was true. There were limited comforts, no luxuries, and incessant work in Susan's and Mary's home. They had started life under pioneer conditions, and the pioneer pattern they retained to the last. Any slightest increase in Susan's income meant a corresponding increase in her expenditures for suffrage. She sometimes used her money for practical necessities in her home but seldom for the purposes of additional refinement. She received many beautiful gifts for that purpose, but neither Susan nor Mary could sit down in their midst and fold their hands while they enjoyed them.

The writer once asked a descendant of Mrs. Stanton's why it was that Susan remained always "Susan" to Mrs. Stanton while the latter remained "Mrs. Stanton" to her. The writer had always assumed that this was Susan's unconscious acknowledgment of the superior social status of a matron as compared with that of a spinster. The answer, which came with a smile, contained something to the effect that Mrs. Stanton was a lady. Susan also was a lady, but no one would have thought of describing her by that term.

CHAPTER TWENTY-EIGHT

EBB TIDE

§ I   While Mrs. Harper and Miss Hawley were busily indexing the *History* (Mrs. Harper had said she would not do it, but she did), the news of Elizabeth Cady Stanton's death arrived, to turn the place into a house of mourning. On October 26, 1902, a telegram from Mrs. Stanton's daughter was handed to Susan. "Mother passed away at three o'clock." The life which had been Susan's guiding star for fifty years had come to an end for all time.

It was Sunday. The Sabbath calm was immediately broken by the rush of reporters to the door and the phone's incessant ringing. The press desired a statement at once from Susan B. Anthony. Miss Hawley's sympathetic pen kept up with the happenings:

It does seem as if they might have had consideration enough to telegraph to Miss Mary or Mrs. Harper, instead of letting that frail old lady of eighty-two open the quite commonplace telegram to be struck by the bald, brutal announcement. What it means to her one can guess; she keeps all the shock and loneliness and heartache to herself, and hardly says anything. . . .

We passed a lively time here till about midnight. First came Mrs. Hair, of the *Democrat and Chronicle*, and had a long interview with poor Miss Anthony, during which she sat silent and sad, and Mrs. Harper helped out by doing most of the talking. Then after Miss Mary and Miss Anthony had both gone to bed, the telephone bell rang-rang-rang, and lo! the representative of the New York *Sun* wanted Miss Anthony to come to the phone and be interviewed.

Mrs. Harper, in a very short black petticoat and a pink dressing-sack, standing on tip-toe to reach the phone, asserted herself with might. "I wouldn't call Miss Anthony out of bed tonight to give an interview to President Roosevelt," she said, as firmly as if in a tailor-made gown and a Paris bonnet. The unseen man at the other end of the phone meekly took the interview from Mrs. Harper.

Certainly there are penalties for fame as well as obscurity. To see poor Miss Anthony questioned over and over about her early times with her dead friend and climbing up to the attic to find a picture for the reporter, with her hands shaking so that she could hardly lift the cards, was a piteous thing. . . .

Early next morning Susan took the train for New York to attend the funeral. After entering the empty house she wrote to Mrs. Harper: "Oh, this awful hush! It seems impossible that voice is stilled which I have loved to hear for fifty years. . . . I am all at sea—but the laws of nature are still going on with no shadow of turning. . . . The papers, I believe, had good editorials—I have read them but I do not know, I can think of nothing. . . ."

It was true that the voice was gone, as Susan's was soon to be, never to be heard again except in memory. What might have assuaged Susan's grief was the fact that she had done more than anyone else to preserve the words and the spirit which went with the voice. One needs but to turn to the *History* to feel the flash and fire of Mrs. Stanton's great talent. A memorial of all the early women reformers, it is more than all else a memorial of Mrs. Stanton. One of the most vital and creative talents of her century, she would have scattered her writings to the winds had Susan not resolved in this way at least to preserve them. In the hour of her bereavement Susan could not find comfort in such thoughts. It was characteristic of her to prefer to think of nature still going on and on without a shadow of turning.

Her panacea for trouble of all kinds—hard work—was quickly offered. She found herself overwhelmed with requests for obituary articles. Mrs. Harper could not help her, for she was crowded by similar demands from other sources. All the leading American magazines clamored for articles at the earliest possible moment. Paced by the experienced Mrs. Harper, Susan made a good showing. She wrote an article for the *North American Review* which was ready for the December issue and filled eleven pages. Among other things, she wrote:

The title I claim for Mrs. Stanton is that of leader of women. They do not enjoy one privilege today beyond those possessed by their fore-mothers which was not demanded by her before the present generation was born. . . . In the light of the present it seems natural that she should have made those first demands for women; but at the time it was done the act was far more revolutionary than was the Declaration of Independence by the Colonial leaders. . . . Men from time immemorial had been accustomed to protest against injustice; but for women to take such action was without a precedent . . . in all history. . . . Women could neither fight nor vote; they were not sustained even by those of their own sex; and while they incurred no physical risk, they imperilled their reputation and subjected themselves to mental and spiritual crucifixion. . . . I hold that the calling of that first Woman's Rights Convention in 1848 by Mrs. Stanton, Lucretia Mott, and two or three other brave Quaker women was one of the most courageous acts on record. . . . She died in the full knowledge that the day of its full victory is clearly marked on the calendar of the near future.

Susan found relief for her loneliness in writing to Mrs. Miller. "How I do miss Mrs. Stanton," she wrote, "to talk to her about everything and everybody. . . . For me there are no letters coming from week to week, no messages! All is silent." To the very last, Mrs. Stanton, though feeble and nearly blind, had kept up her correspondence with Susan. For several years, however, their correspondence had been increasingly of a personal nature. Ever since the *Bible* affair, Mrs. Stanton had been well out from under Susan's thumb. When Susan had last visited her she had written in her diary: "She thinks the Church is now the enemy to fight and feels worried that I stay back with the children—as she says—instead of going ahead with her." That Mrs. Stanton would no longer take her to task about her tolerance of the Church was in itself a poignant grief.

Susan's practical comrade-in-arms was now Anna Shaw. Her name was more often associated with Miss Shaw's than with that of any other person. Susan comments on this in her diary: "It seems so strange to link with mine any other name than Mrs. Stanton's." But as long as she continued to live in the present instead of the past such changes were necessary.

The friendship between Susan and Anna Shaw, which had begun in 1888, been cemented by an all-night talk in Chicago in 1893, and continued by long and arduous suffrage pilgrimages together, had grown stronger with the years. Undisturbed by Anna Shaw's vote on the *Bible* resolution, undisturbed by the latter's failure to achieve the presidency, it had come to be the strongest tie of the present for both. Miss Shaw, twenty-seven years younger than Susan, called her "Aunt Susan," as Rachel Avery did. A thoroughly extroverted and warmhearted creature, Miss Shaw loved Susan with an expressiveness that her nature craved. Susan's own Quaker habit restrained her in such things. Anna Shaw's warmth, which required so little stimulus and in this respect resembled Mrs. Stanton's, replaced the old fond intimacy which was slowly fading out.

Susan and Anna Shaw understood each other perfectly. They had both come up the hard way. As a girl of twelve Anna Shaw had dug a well because there was no man on hand to dig it. Susan had washed and ironed and whitewashed in her early years. Neither of them had ever seen the inside of a college. Nothing had ever been made easy for them. Life for both had been an unceasing struggle for the means of existence, a long difficult road lighted only by the bright ideal that shone steadily for them at the end of the way.

Miss Shaw soon became a member of the Madison Street household. She braved any inconvenience, bad train connections, an overnight trip, a rush to fill a date, in order to drop in for a single day. Susan's diary is full of her entrances and exits, planned and unplanned. Witty and casual, she brought brightness and cheer to the whole household. The attic was allowed to suspend work on the *History* as soon as Anna Shaw appeared. At least once a month and sometimes oftener, she descended like Mercury alighting and kept the household *au courant* with events of the outside world. Best of all, Miss Shaw's discretion was absolute.

Anna Shaw's affection for Susan lived on after Susan's death. Years afterward, her heart still overflowing, she wrote in her memoirs: "It is of her I wish to write—of her bigness, her many-sidedness, her humor, her courage, her quickness, her sympathy, her understanding, her force, her supreme common sense, her selflessness; in short, of the rare beauty of her nature as I learned to know it."

◁§ II   Susan had reached eighty-three. Her diary is full of the piti-
ful frailties of old age alternating with entries about the business of
publishing. Doggedly she recorded from day to day the number of
Histories that came in from the printer and the number that went
out as gifts or sales.

"I had Dr. Ricker yesterday. She gave me . . . something for
my heart, which acts all the time as if I had been running at the
top of my speed. . . . It is very annoying in the night. I can't lay
on my left side with any comfort—indeed I hear the beating awake
or asleep." One day—"after a hard day's work, registering the books
that were sent out"—she had a fainting spell. "All worked like
Trojans," she said of the day's work, in which she had also done
her part.

Her joy in the completion of Volume IV rewarded her for everything. The reviews were good, notes Mrs. Harper, justifiably proud
of her own part in the achievement. The demand for the entire set
increased. "I want to tell you," Susan wrote Mrs. Miller, "that I
have received $2,500 toward the first cost. I never dreamed of sell-
ing so many books. . . . I think I shall find a place in eight hundred more of the best libraries in the country for them." Though
still distributing them gratis, she received orders from many libraries
accompanied by checks. For instance, Harvard University, which
had declined the first three volumes as a gift, sent an order for the
full set with the price. In the final accounting she sold enough
books to repay her for the actual cost of publishing. For her own
time and labor and that of her paid assistants she was never in any
way reimbursed. But she did not consider that she was actually out
of pocket. She had managed all that out of her savings and annuity.

The generous and well-conditioned Mrs. Miller bought sets
wholesale and presented them to the poorer libraries to prevent
Susan from giving them away. A single item will show how closely
Susan attended to her business. The express company once over-
charged Mrs. Miller to the extent of sixty cents. Susan phoned the
company and registered complaints tirelessly until the matter was
adjusted and the sixty cents returned to her best customer.

The handling, packaging, and dispatching of the volumes devolved entirely upon the publishing firm, "Susan B. Anthony, 17 Madison St., Rochester." This firm consisted of Susan, Sister Mary, the Misses Hawley and Dann, and Carrie Bahl, the new maid. Susan could not have foreseen that the publishing business required so much hard manual labor. Susan and Mary had need of all the muscle, bone, and grit inherited from a grandmother who had hauled water from a spring. Beyond the expressman who delivered and picked up the packages, they had no masculine aid whatever. The business formed a part of the household routine and remained a part as long as Susan lived. When she died and willed the enterprise to the National-American Suffrage Association, all this hard manual labor was transferred to strong-muscled warehouse men, who should have been doing it all along. But Susan loved the *History*, as she loved the *Revolution*, far too much to begrudge any effort that its distribution cost her.

⌐§ III   Mrs. Harper returned to Madison Street in midsummer 1903. She had returned for a sad duty, which in the view of the writer amounted almost to a funeral—the fulfillment of a clause in her original contract with Susan. "Did I tell you," wrote Miss Hawley to her aunt, "Miss Anthony is sifting out all the not-too-private autograph letters to send to the next suffrage fair to be sold for the cause? All the rest are to be burned when done with, except a few family letters." If any letters at all were ever sent to a suffrage fair, there is no account of it; not even to this extent was anything salvaged. As Mrs. Harper cheerfully remarked at the beginning: "After six months without criticism or corrections, it seemed safe to begin the work of destruction."

Susan sent her files of old anti-slavery journals and women's magazines, her scrapbooks, and many old books, out of print, to the Library of Congress. They were promptly accepted and installed with grateful acknowledgment to the donor. The files and files of old letters remained, which could also have been sent to the Library of Congress for further preservation. Perhaps Susan did not know this; or, if she did, she had already arranged with Mrs. Harper that they should not be preserved.

When the time came, her heart revolted at the sacrifice. "These are from So-and-so," she would say of certain letters. "They should not be thrown away." They would be reserved, until at last the reserved pile threatened to exceed the condemned. Brisk Mrs. Harper thereupon declared: "There is no use in wasting my time here if you are not going to allow this trash to be burned." Downcast and utterly miserable, unable to distinguish the wheat from the chaff—as who would not have been under the circumstances?—Susan finally withdrew from the whole heartbreaking performance. "The only thing for me is to wash my hands of the whole business," she said desperately, and fled.

Sister Mary took her place as a willing collaborator. As a result, the vital records of a whole century of history were swept into a pile by a couple of good housekeepers. The doomed archives, the "trash," was enormous. Mary tried burning it by installments in the cellar furnace, but the mass choked the draft. She then resorted to bonfires in the back yard, which for safety's sake had to be closely guarded. So she stood over the flaming pile with a shovel, while letters from William Lloyd Garrison, Wendell Phillips, Samuel May, Bronson Alcott, Beriah Green, Frederick Douglass, Robert Dale Owen, Ernestine Rose, Harriet Beecher Stowe, Ben Wade, Abigail Duniway, and Horace Greeley—to name only a few from the priceless hoard—floated into the neighbors' back yards in the form of black wisps. There was so much to be burned that the work of destruction lasted more than a month. Except for some letters from Mrs. Stanton and Lucy Stone, which were sent to their children, apparently nothing was saved. The holocaust was complete.

From Mary's enthusiastic share in this one may judge what the last six years had meant to her. Her house had never been intended for a workshop and warehouse as well as an overpopulated residence. It probably showed some signs of wear and tear from overuse. Her feeling was that nothing would restore it to the home it once had been but a thoroughgoing renovation. She had much of Sister Susan in her—no halfway measures for her. Carpenters, painters, and paper hangers were called in and took possession of the place. Everything outside and inside was repaired. In this happy and complete confusion Mary spent many exhausting days. When all was over and the house purified, cleansed, sweet, and homelike once more, Mary, at the age of seventy-six, was quite too worn out to enjoy it. She went to the Spoffords' home in Maine to rest for a while.

Quietly and meekly Susan had retreated at once from the renovation. Finding that she could not stand the fumes of paint, she said, she turned to the former Miss Anna Dann for refuge. Mrs. Mason, proud mistress of a new home, was only too happy to invite her for a visit. She lived comfortably in Anna's home for three weeks, washing dishes for the young couple if they wanted to go out in the evening and being much cosseted and privileged in return. She enjoyed a rest cure that she greatly needed.

When all was in readiness she returned home, while Mary departed. When Mr. Gannett and his wife came to call, to see for the first time the new and splendid improvements, they found Susan alone. Quite unabashed, Susan led them proudly through the house, accepting their admiration and congratulations as if they were her just due. If she seemed to take credit that did not belong to her, it was because in so many ways she had become identified with Mary. But it was probably one of many little things that led the Gannetts to take a strong line in their public and expressed appreciation of Susan's sister. It was the old story of Mary and Martha, oft repeated, in which presumably Martha also had her partisans, though the Master, it will be recalled, was not among them.

§ IV   The suffrage convention of 1904 turned out to be one of the happiest milestones in Susan's life. It took place in Washington, and she arrived in time for the meeting of the Business Committee. She wrote in her diary: "In Business Committee Session.— Mrs. Catt promised after due deliberation to take the Vice-Presidency if Miss Shaw would take the Presidency. So that question will be settled and not a break in appearance to the world." Miss Shaw had at last become president of the National-American Woman Suffrage Association. Susan had more reason than ever to believe in her program of patience.

As Susan's diary implies, the change had required some careful management. Mrs. Catt had fully vindicated her position as head of the organization. During her four years of tenure the membership of the society had increased by leaps and bounds and the cash in the treasury had grown to the unprecedented amount of twelve thousand dollars. It was true that all the advances achieved represented policies of the Boston suffragists and that little had been done to further the Federal amendment. But even Susan was impressed by the growth in membership and the improvement in finances. Had Mrs. Catt wished to continue in her office she might have done so indefinitely. For her own reasons she declined in 1904 to accept the presidency, and Anna Shaw, very reluctantly, accepted her place.

The honor which Miss Shaw had once so greatly coveted meant little to her now. When she renounced the presidency in 1900 she had meant it for all time. When first approached in 1904 she declined absolutely to succeed Mrs. Catt. It required all of Susan's powers of persuasion to induce her to change her mind. "I had lost my ambition to be president," says Miss Shaw in her memoirs. "At last, however, Miss Anthony actually commanded me to take the place, and there was nothing to do but obey her. . . . It was no time for me to rebel against her wishes; but I yielded with the heaviest heart I have ever carried, and after my election . . . I left the stage, went into a dark corner of the wings, and for the first time since my girlhood 'cried myself sick.'" She wept for a disappointment she had borne so well at the time but had never since forgotten.

Nothing had changed in Anna Shaw's situation since that election. The same reason that had prevailed against her election then prevailed now: financially, she could not afford the position. But the delegates were unanimous for her under the self-same conditions. It was a bitter pill for Miss Shaw to swallow. To receive the office as a gift from Mrs. Catt was not the same as receiving it at the hands of her adored leader. It was as fortunate for Miss Shaw as for the suffrage movement that Susan had lived long enough to smooth over the change. Miss Shaw had not yet lived long enough to become the political philosopher that she was to become, but she had the devotion to follow her leader.

It was Mrs. Catt's situation that had changed. The public was told that Mrs. Catt had resigned for reasons of poor health. Her real reason, however, was the decline of her husband's health. In explaining her resignation, she wrote to the Business Committee: "All I have done for suffrage during the last fifteen years I have been enabled to do by my husband's generosity. . . . But the heavy cares and responsibilities of his great business have worn his health,

until now, though he is still in his prime, he looks like an old man.
. . . My husband needs me now . . . and I will not leave him."

As a matter of fact, Mr. Catt had long been a sick man. As early
as January 1, 1899, Susan noted in her diary, while staying at his
house for a Business Committee meeting, that "Mr. Catt was too
ill to go to business," and that the day after "he was worse and
kept in bed all day." Apparently he continued subject to such attacks, short in duration, but recurrent. Mrs. Catt's chivalrous and
generous husband was suffering from the nemesis of the hard-
driving businessman—stomach complaint, which would nowadays
probably be called ulcers. It is easy to understand that his wife,
and probably he himself, did not pay too much attention to his
recurrent misery in its first stages. One's family grows accustomed
to some kinds of illnesses and does not grow alarmed until the case
is far advanced. When Mrs. Catt realized her husband's condition
it seems to have been with a sense of shock and self-reproach. She
resigned at once from the presidency of the suffrage association.

Mixed with her other feelings no doubt was some contrition on
Miss Shaw's account. Mrs. Catt was still a young woman, growing
with every experience. She must have blamed herself for having
accepted the presidency when she did, as it was at that time that
her husband's health began to fail. In passing on the high office to
Anna Shaw she was trying as well as she could to undo all the harm
that might have been done.

Two years later Mr. George Catt died, worn out, at the age of
forty-five, by the business of being a success. Of his death, the
newspapers said that "only a few days before he was in perfect
health." The explanation is that Mr. Catt insisted to the last on
disregarding his illness and behaving like a perfectly well man. It
was by his wish that Mrs. Catt attributed her resignation to her
own ill-health instead of his. He was sitting on a park bench with
his wife when seized by his last attack.

&§ V The International Council of Women held its meeting in
Berlin in the summer of 1904. When the first council had met in
Washington in 1888, a goodly number of French delegates ap-
peared along with one solitary German woman. Since that date the
German woman movement had effloresced and developed, until a

Bund deutscher Frauenvereine was now in flourishing existence. The Bund's interests centered around the welfare of women and children, making some radical demands in this field but paying slight attention to suffrage. The International Council, though originated by Susan and Mrs. Stanton, had never stressed suffrage as a principle. The German women, who among other things supported a couple of intelligent women's journals, were eminently qualified to form a national council, and they did so.

The previous International meeting had taken place in London. Soon afterward, very soon, the German women dispatched invitations for the next meeting to come to Berlin. Behind the invitation and the proffered hospitality lay a certain trend of history, since then well exposed. In 1904 Germany and England were actively competing for the favor of the United States. The race was about equal at the time. Even such a little thing as a visit of the Women's International Council (strictly of American invention) was a matter of rivalry. After London had welcomed the council, Berlin hastened to do the same. The German women were encouraged and assisted by some V.I.P.s in their own country, among others the head of the North German Lloyd Steamship Line, whose daughter happened to be prominent in the German woman's movement.

At first Susan thought she could not make the arduous journey. On leaving the London meeting she had declared: "Remember, you will have to manage the next Quinquennial without me." But when the time arrived, she could not resist the lure of a convention. The American leaders were all going. Even Mrs. Catt had consented to leave her husband for this important gathering. It was finally settled for Susan when Mary, who felt she had made her European trip and did not want to make another, broke down and consented to accompany her sister. An interesting side light on Susan's health is that during her subsequent three months' stay in Europe she was not ill for a single day.

As soon as Susan boarded the North German Lloyd liner, a telegram was handed her: "Susan B. Anthony and Comrades: Welcome under the German flag." As soon as she landed at Bremerhaven, another was handed her: "Welcome on German soil for you and all your friends." The note of national pride was sounded at this and all the subsequent international gatherings.

Two solid weeks of meetings and entertainment awaited the foreign visitors. The entertainment formed the more important part of the program. It would appear that every prominent government official in Berlin took time off to honor the women's conference. The wife of the Imperial Chancellor gave a garden party in the precincts sacred to the memory of Bismarck. The wife of the Minister of Internal Affairs entertained the whole council. The Bürgermeister of Berlin, together with its Board of Magistrates, staged a grand reception and banquet in the Rathaus. The whole of Berlin officialdom, clad in black ceremonial robes with heavy gold chains suspended from their necks, appeared to be on parade. They bowed from the waist and made pontifical speeches in their own language —speeches that meant nothing but awed the crowds of attentive women.

The Empress Augusta Victoria received the delegates in the Royal Palace with regal ceremonies. Gowned and beribboned in state, she passed down the line, personally shaking the hands of the ladies and making gracious remarks to them, often in their own languages. To Susan she paid especial attention, insisting that she should be seated and having a chair brought for the purpose. When Susan, who never lost a chance for propaganda, expressed to her the hope that the Emperor would soon see fit to grant equal rights to women, the Empress replied with surprising truthfulness accompanied by a slight smile, "The gentlemen are very slow to comprehend this movement." Without intending it, perhaps, she gave away her husband's show.

Mrs. Harper could not forbear a suspicious glance behind the scenes. "What is the influence," she wrote, "which has made it possible for this International Council to come into this most conservative city and hold the . . . most successful Congress in its history . . . ? Can any one doubt that back of it all is the shrewdest man who ever occupied a throne? . . . William II outwitted the women of the world who came to Berlin expecting to find womanhood oppressed, free speech curtailed, and public meetings frowned upon." The lady from Indiana did not exactly hit the nail on the head, but she made a wonderful pass at it.

Throughout the conference Susan was treated as the honored guest of the city. At the Rathaus banquet she sat on the right hand of the Bürgermeister; the Empress distinguished her with especial attention; Hedwig Heyl (North German Lloyd heiress) gave a grand breakfast at which even "the bonbons bore an excellent picture of Miss Anthony." Wherever Susan appeared, at concerts, museums, and council meetings, she received great public ovations. The newspapers hailed her as the "grand old woman of America" and as "Miss Anthony of the world."

It is not surprising to read in Miss Shaw's memoirs: "Miss Anthony told me in 1904 that she regarded her reception in Berlin, during the meeting of the International Council of Women that year, as the climax of her career." At least Susan was not more naïve than Theodore Roosevelt, who had recently preceded her in Berlin, had been photographed with the Kaiser, and then had put the picture in his reminiscences. When the Germans decided to honor an American guest in those pre-World War days, they did it with thorough Teutonic magnificence.

The meetings of the council brought one great surprise to Susan and her English friends. They were accustomed to think of themselves as superior orators—which they were. The discovery that the German women, in their own language, measured up to them and sometimes surpassed them seemed incredible. How had they been trained? Susan could only deduce that a strong and powerful woman's movement lay behind this. She was partially right. The German women were already well organized. They received further impetus through the International Council, and they prospered and grew stronger with the years, until, at the impact of World War I, their organizations were all wiped out. The gentlemen were slow to comprehend this movement.

There was only one flaw in Susan's happiness at this time. Though the council had previously eschewed woman suffrage as a plank in its platform, the American and English leaders decided in 1904 to form a collateral union for woman suffrage. Entirely outside of the council, though promoted by its members, the International Woman Suffrage Alliance was organized. Susan was made honorary president and Mrs. Catt, president. Other officers were chosen from Germany, England, and the Netherlands.

The step was naturally attended by some difficulties. The anti-suffrage, or non-suffrage, sentiment within the council grumbled audibly. The Americans proceeded very cautiously. Someone suggested it would be best if Miss Anthony's hand were not seen in the affair. Perhaps it was Mrs. Sewall or Mrs. Avery, whom Susan had pushed to the front in the original organization of the council, while she kept herself in the background. The idea was that Susan should absent herself from the first public meeting of the new suffrage alliance. Susan meekly complied, remaining alone in her hotel room, a sacrifice to the mealy-mouthed prudence of her over-trained friends.

Of course the meeting was more impressed by her absence than it would have been by her presence. At the first mention of her name a resounding demonstration broke forth, with the cheering and clapping lasting for ten minutes. At the conclusion Susan's friends rushed in a body to her room to describe the ovation. She listened and then broke into tears. She had missed the one meeting which, of them all, meant the most to her, and, as it seemed, quite need-lessly.

◄§ VI At eighty-four Susan still did a bit of sight-seeing in Eu-rope. With her sister she made a tour of the principal German cities, crossed into Switzerland, visited Alsace, and finally went to London. In London, Mary at last deserted her. Susan had been perfectly well all summer and Mary was worn out. Leaving Susan in the care of Miss Shaw, to spend another busy month in England, Mary went home.

As usual, Susan made her way to Mrs. Jacob Bright's group of suffragists in Manchester. They had invited her officially to be their guest. In Manchester she was joined by the venerable Mrs. Wol-stenholme Elmy, the aged but indomitable suffrage pioneer. They were guests of honor at luncheons, garden parties, and official meet-ings of the suffrage committee.

The Manchester newspapers gave much attention to the Ameri-can suffragist. One paper in particular published a long article on Susan's life, written by a talented young woman named Christabel Pankhurst. Miss Pankhurst's mother, Emmeline Pankhurst, a life-long friend and co-worker of the Jacob Brights who headed the more radical group of English suffragists, observed Susan with much interest. The Pankhursts, mother and daughter, met her at a Manchester meeting, and Christabel especially was deeply touched by the signs of her advancing age. They accentuated the

long, hard, uphill struggle, which Christabel had followed so intimately for the purposes of her article. Mrs. Pankhurst later wrote of
this visit:

In the summer of 1902—I think it was 1902 [1904 really]—Susan
B. Anthony paid a visit to Manchester, and the visit was one of the
contributory causes that led to the founding of our militant suffrage
organization, the Women's Social and Political Union. . . . After
her departure Christabel spoke often of her and always with sorrow and indignation that such a splendid worker for humanity was
destined to die without seeing the hopes of her life-time realized.
"It is unendurable," declared my daughter, "to think of another
generation of women wasting their lives begging for the vote. We
must not lose any more time. We must act."

Mrs. Pankhurst was forty-six at the time, a widow, earning a
meager living as registrar of births and deaths in Manchester. After
Susan's departure she and her daughter resolved to concentrate on
the suffrage cause. Mrs. Pankhurst's former friends and associates,
the Laborites, did all they could to discourage her. She was wasting
her time, they said, on "a barren issue of bourgeois politics." But
Mrs. Pankhurst refused to be discouraged or distracted. She formed
the Woman's Social and Political Union, which took for its slogan
"Votes for Women" and entered on a practical career for the
achievement of its aim.

Early the next year, while Susan was preparing for a "grass-roots"
convention in Oregon, a suffrage bill was again introduced in the
English Parliament and again by the time-honored English method
"talked out." As the opponents said, "That bill is for the future."
But Mrs. Pankhurst and her militants had decided that the future
was now. When the suffrage bill was talked out, they organized a
meeting of protest, headed by Mrs. Pankhurst and Mrs. Wolstenholme Elmy, and held it at the door of Parliament. The militant
suffrage movement had begun.

By the end of the year the suffragettes, as the English press had
dubbed them, were on their way to prison. They introduced the
hunger strike; the government retaliated with forcible feeding. The
suffragettes endured all and escaped to repeat their offenses. There
was no violence in their demonstrations. Their program was, rather,
what would nowadays be called a campaign of civil disobedience.

The government was at its wit's end but not at the end of its stubbornness. It passed one act after another in an ineffectual effort to stamp out the disorder.

Mrs. Pankhurst and her daughters went to jail repeatedly, were forcibly fed, and eventually released. It was the forcible feeding of Sylvia, Mrs. Pankhurst's second daughter, that led to the famous "cat-and-mouse" act, whereby the prisoner was released for a period and then rearrested. In 1913, the last year before the World War, Mrs. Pankhurst, aged fifty-five, was imprisoned and forcibly fed for ten days. Her battle for political rights was carried on unceasingly from the time of Susan's visit to Manchester in 1904 to the outbreak of World War I in 1914. At this time, having received tangible reassurance from the government that no future militancy would be necessary, she relaxed her campaign.

It seems one of the ironies of Susan's life that, coming from the farcical celebration in Berlin, she should have looked back on that event as the climax of her career. A far greater moment awaited her at a small gathering of the faithful in a dingy office in Manchester. She did not know it when she passed on the torch to other spirits like herself.

CHAPTER TWENTY-NINE

THE LAST CONVENTION

◄§ I Susan's popularity with the press was such that her sister and friends thought it best to conceal the date of her home-coming from Europe. Even so, when she reached Rochester, she found a New York *Times* reporter waiting at her door. "I gave him an account of my English and Scotland visits," she noted, modestly saying nothing about her personal triumphs in Berlin. She then took off her hat and went to bed for a month.

She had her favorite doctor in and the usual medication, but intense exhaustion was again the story. After a sweeping tour of Europe, long addresses to great crowds, and even a last-minute round trip to Edinburgh—all this without a day of illness—she came home to be a bedridden invalid. This was becoming more and more a routine with Susan. It must have driven Sister Mary wild with its frightful regularity.

Shortly before leaving England, Susan had received word from home that her brother Daniel R. was seriously ill. By the time she reached America his condition was reported as improved. But he continued to be feeble and expressed a strong desire to see his two sisters. He did not say "for the last time," but cheerfully proffered them the use of five empty bedrooms in his house which he said were going to waste since his children had married and left home. After her month in bed Susan girded herself for the journey, and, accompanied by Mary, set forth for Leavenworth.

Daniel Read Anthony was the successful member of the family.

A pioneer of the John Brown era, he had struck root in Kansas and grown up with the state. He became postmaster and mayor, member of the Legislature, trustee and director of several railroad corporations, and a holder of considerable property in the form of real estate. His chief claim to fame was his newspaper, the Leavenworth *Times*, which he had owned and edited for forty years and was now about to pass on to his son of the same name. His reputation was not national, but it covered a wide area of the Mississippi Valley, where his name was as well known as his sister's. The St. Louis *Globe-Democrat*, commenting on Susan's behavior in some crisis, said she "showed the great reserve power for which the Anthony family is noted." West of the Mississippi, Susan and her brother were lumped together as the Anthony family.

Yet Susan had carried on her career in complete independence of her brother's aid. At certain times D.R. sustained her public efforts; at other times he did not. He was heavily involved in politics on his own account and watched his step accordingly. She seldom appealed to him as she appealed to other public men to come out on her side. Her relations with D.R. were inherited from the cradle. He was her *brother*, and that described the relationship. There is no doubt that she had great respect and admiration for him. They were much alike in their persistency and steadiness of aim and in their unfailing devotion to all family ties.

As soon as Susan saw him, she realized now that the parting of the ways had come. "Found Brother D.R. at station to meet us, but, oh, so changed." She stayed in Leavenworth for two weeks and then went home with Mary, sadly to await the inevitable outcome. "Left Brother D.R. very weak. . . . He seems destined to go, but I hope against hope that he will recover." True to his character, D.R. fought stubbornly for life and stalled off death till the last possible moment. For four weeks his sufferings were acute and horrible. "We have looked every day for a telegram saying your father was gone," Susan wrote his daughter, "but he still clings to life. . . . I wrote your mother yesterday and begged her not to let the doctors administer another bit of nitro-glycerine, strychnine, digitalis, or anything just to make the heart go—that the vital spark had gone from his body—and just to keep up the muscular action only prolonged the misery for him and for her. What a tempestuous life he has had—and his death seems equally so. It is too bad that we have to suffer so to get out of the world."

When the expected telegram came, Susan and Mary returned to Leavenworth for the funeral. "It was indeed a great calm to see him so still," Susan said with a sense almost of relief.

The clerk of the Rochester Society of Friends opened his books once more to make an entry on Daniel Read Anthony. Received by the Rochester Yearly Meeting in 1853, he died according to the register in full membership on November 12, 1904. Looking over the records of the Rochester Quakers, the writer expressed surprise at this close attention to a man who had lived and died so far away from Rochester. "He had lived in Kansas for forty-five years," the writer remarked. "He never transferred his membership," said the clerk; "he always belonged to the Rochester Friends." The writer ventured further to comment: "And he was a man of violence." The clerk eyed the speaker quizzically. "And what about Susan?" he asked. After a moment of deep reflection, in which he seemed to peer down the vista of the years reflected in the Quaker histories around him, he added quietly, "It was a violent family."

◄§ II   In 1905 the roving National convention betook itself to Portland, Oregon. Susan announced early in the year her intention of attending it. "Each one knows her own limitations," she wrote to a friend; "I suppose if I paid much attention to mine I should stay at home altogether, but I feel it would be just as well if I reached the end on the cars or anywhere else as at home. It would make a little more trouble for others but I cannot give up going about my work through constant fear of that." She left home with Mary, who, fortunately, had never seen the Pacific Coast, and the two of them enjoyed without incident the long transcontinental trip. The comforts of railroad travel had increased greatly since Susan and Mrs. Stanton had first crossed the continent. They landed in Portland in good spirits and well rested and were installed in hotel rooms with a view of Mount Hood from the windows. Susan was always exhilarated by high peaks and tall mountains.

Anna Shaw, presiding, pushed Susan into the president's chair whenever possible. The Portland *Oregonian* said: "Reports have circulated around the country that Miss Anthony was feeble and no longer able to take an active part in suffrage affairs. But when she spoke her first words an astonished silence fell upon the house. Her voice is more vigorous than that of many women half her age and she speaks with fluency and ease."

The suffragists were in Portland for two purposes—to share in the Lewis and Clark Exposition then in progress and to open the campaign for a suffrage bill to be voted on the following year. A feature of the exposition was the dedication of a bronze statue of Sacajawea, the Indian woman who, with a papoose strapped to her back, guided Lewis and Clark safely to the Pacific and back. Susan was the main speaker at the Sacajawea dedication. "This is the first statue erected in this country," she said, "to a woman because of deeds of daring. . . . Next year the men of this proud state, made possible by a woman, will decide whether women shall at least have the rights in it which have been denied them so many years."

The convention transacted its usual business. There seemed little more to do until the next annual convention rolled around, which would, according to the present constitution, take place in Washington. Then Susan launched a weighty surprise.

She had never felt that the constitution was sacred since the American faction had tampered with it in 1893, substituting the roving convention for the annual Washington turnout. She had opposed the change with all her might but had failed to prevent it. At that time she was still naïve about Mr. Blackwell's methods, but since then she had learned. "You know as well as I," she had written to Mrs. Colby in 1898, "that H.B.B. will be there armed and equipped to voice the Association. . . . 'Nature abhors a vacuum,' and if you don't fill it, H.B.B. will! Now, burn this up, but resolve to fill the vacuum first." Her strategy on the present occasion was to create the vacuum first and then to fill it.

To the astonishment of all present, Susan rose and proposed that the by-law reading, "Every alternate Convention *must* be held in Washington," should be changed to read "*may* be held in Washington." As a corollary to this, she proposed that the next year's convention should be held, not in Washington, but in Baltimore, Maryland. This was carrying suffrage to the grass roots with a vengeance. Maryland had one of the most backward suffrage societies in existence. Besides, no one would have believed that Susan would ever of her own will and accord sacrifice a convention in Washington.

The motion threw the delegates into the utmost bewilderment and confusion. No one present, probably not even Anna Shaw, knew that Susan was going to broach this plan. Henry Blackwell, automatically heading the opposition, found himself in the singular position of defending Washington, which he had once desired to avoid altogether. The reversal of the traditional roles of their leaders was seen by the delegates as highly amusing. In the relaxed atmosphere the person with an intense purpose easily won. *This time* the person was Susan.

Susan had her own reasons for wishing to take the convention to Baltimore, and she felt that she could not afford the delay of as much as a single year. Otherwise she might have waited until Washington had had its turn. She must have felt that her sands were running out, and yet she possessed the hardihood and elasticity to dare and accomplish a successful political coup. In this as in so many instances she seemed to be guided by a strange prescience and seerlike quality of her own.

In great peace of mind Susan turned toward California. To visit the Pacific Coast and leave out California was unthinkable for her. Besides, Mary had never seen California. With her sister and Anna Shaw she was soon deeply immersed in scenery, fetes, receptions, and suffrage rallies from Mount Shasta to San Diego. Mary's faithful diary reported every step—the views, the vegetation, the temperature, the cost (the entire trip—out and back—cost each of the sisters two hundred dollars). To see rhododendrons, oleanders, and magnolias all in full bloom at the same time threw Mary into ecstasies. Susan never mentioned the flowers though she always mentioned the mountains.

In Los Angeles, Susan met Mrs. Rebecca Spring, the good friend of Margaret Fuller, aged ninety-five and still apparently hale and hearty in mind and body. Any conversation they might have had about Margaret Fuller is unfortunately lost to us, along with Susan's diary of this particular year. They were photographed together, and both of them spoke at a large suffrage rally. Margaret Fuller had been dead for fifty-five years. It must have given Susan a thrill to meet the friend who had been so close to her in her earthly life.

◆§ III   In the fall of the same year Susan paid her long-heralded visit to President Theodore Roosevelt. It was not a successful visit, suffering as it did from too much preparation and too much collaboration. Susan always did things better when she did them quickly and alone.

The plan dated back to the January convention of 1904 in Washington. Roosevelt had been three years in the White House and was running for President for the first time on his own. Susan was invited to a White House reception and received marked attentions from the Chief Executive. Governor Alva Adams of Colorado, who witnessed them, was deeply impressed:

My last glimpse of this noble woman was in the White House. I was at her side in the line that was being received by President and Mrs. Roosevelt. As we approached the President, he grasped Miss Anthony by the hand and arm, and with enthusiastic greeting pulled her to his side, there to remain during the reception. I passed on, and as I looked back upon these two dominant characters, there flashed into my mind the thought that, when this great woman and this great man are weighed in the scales of God, the woman will not be found to be the lesser figure.

Not only the President but his daughter showed especial courtesy to Susan. Miss Alice Roosevelt left a group of friends, saying, "I must speak to Miss Anthony, she is my father's special guest." Miss Roosevelt, aged twenty at the time, little realized how much she owed to this guest on her own account. It was largely due to Susan's lifelong fight against the conventions that hampered and crippled her sex that Alice Roosevelt was enabled to exhibit the social freedom and youthful self-expression that marked her White House years. What Susan had done toward freeing American women included the freeing of the President's daughter. At some time during that evening Susan said to Roosevelt, casually and pleasantly, "Now, Mr. President, we don't intend to trouble you during the campaign, but after you are elected, then look out for us."

But after the election in November Susan's brother was ill. His death, followed by a midwinter trip to Florida with Miss Shaw, postponed the execution of her promise. The Portland convention then intervened, overloading her with suggestions and directives, until by the time she was ready for the visit it had become a portentous interview. Attended by Mrs. Harper and Mrs. Upton, she arrived at the White House on November 15, 1905, fortified by a long memorandum. "Miss Anthony acted as spokesman," remarks Mrs. Harper somewhat naïvely. Susan began her interview by speaking from the notes in her hand. It was not an auspicious beginning, for she always spoke better without notes.

She worked slowly through her agendum, while the President responded coolly and noncommittally to each point as it came along. Then at last, with a burst of feeling, Susan became herself again. "Mr. Roosevelt," she said earnestly, "this is my principal request— it is almost the last request I shall ever make of anybody. Before you leave the Presidential chair, recommend Congress to submit to the Legislatures a Constitutional Amendment which will enfranchise women, and thus take your place in history with Lincoln, the great emancipator. I beg of you not to close your term of office without doing this."

Though startled into more attention, the President still refused to commit himself. But Susan, having resumed her own personality, continued to be spontaneous. "And I hope," she added, still earnestly, "you will not be a candidate for the office again." On this point, however, Roosevelt was ready to commit himself. "Miss Anthony, I have not the slightest intention of doing so," he said. She had come to ask for a Federal amendment, and all she had secured was the promise to adhere to an old Jeffersonian principle. It was too early in his second term for the President to make such an announcement, but apparently he trusted Susan completely. When she emerged from the audience, the reporters were waiting and gathered in a crowd around her. It was one of the few occasions in her life when she had nothing whatever to say to them.

She had not received one word of encouragement for her cause. Behind the official, immovable front, the Federal amendment seemed to recede and vanish into the far distance. Roosevelt's air of infinite leisure on this occasion, allowing the interview to take its own course, was a courtesy extended to an elderly lady whom he respected, not to be construed as interest in the cause. The arguments of the suffragists were familiar and stale, and the official resistance was fixed and gelatinized.

He had no idea—and neither had Susan—how quickly all this could change. A new generation was recharging the old clichés with renewed fire and spirit; words that had formerly seemed stereotyped and outworn were beginning to mean what they said. A suffrage revival was coming in America as it was coming in England. Even while President Roosevelt listened with such kindly boredom to Susan's phrases, two women were languishing in a Manchester jail for publicly saying no more than she had said. Even if Roosevelt and Susan had heard of this (and they probably had not), they did not realize the change that it portended.

◆§ IV Susan had ceased to dream that the cause of suffrage would be carried on by persons as penniless as herself. That people like the Pankhursts still existed, ready to give all and dare all for a principle, scarcely occurred to her any more. The child of her own America, she saw the suffrage movement as dependent on money for its continued survival. Events of the last decade had taught her that, more than all else, money was needed and would be needed, as far as she could judge, for an unforeseeable period. She no longer spoke of the standing fund, but this did not mean that she had not continuously thought about it.

Her contacts of late years had been increasingly intellectual. Many of the younger women flocking into the movement were college graduates. She herself had attained a certain literary standing as editor of the four-volume *History*. Though never counting herself as among the intellectuals, she welcomed the prestige they added to the suffrage movement. But even at a dollar a head they added little to the treasury. She had wealthy women friends, especially in California, but they were busily endowing California parks and universities; and Susan, who was infinitely tactful, encouraged their activities. Apparently she never once approached them on the subject of the standing fund.

Among the intelligentsia who had recently moved closer to woman suffrage were Miss M. Carey Thomas, president of Bryn Mawr College, and her friend, Miss Mary Garrett, both originally of Baltimore. Susan had met Carey Thomas first in 1883, when she had paid a formal call on the young Doctor of Philosophy in Paris. Immediately thereafter Miss Thomas had gone home to become a professor at Bryn Mawr. Ten years later she became its president. A single-minded reformer like Susan, she had spent the interim in making Bryn Mawr into a genuine instrument of higher learning for women. It was an uphill job. Though girls were going to college by the thousands, they were not expected to take it too seriously. To banish amateurishness among them was a task to which Miss Thomas proceeded to devote all her energies for a very considerable period.

Carey Thomas, like Susan, was born a Quaker. She never attended any but Quaker schools before she went to study in Europe. Her aunt was the famous Hannah Whitall Smith of Philadelphia, who championed woman suffrage in its pioneer days and in whose home Carey Thomas had partly grown up. Woman suffrage was an old story to Miss Thomas; but, as sometimes happens with inherited causes, she was inclined to take it very much for granted. It was not until Mary Garrett came into her life that she took an active interest in the cause. Miss Garrett, though an old Baltimore friend, first came to live at Bryn Mawr in the early 1900s. Miss Garrett was not a Quaker, but she was and always had been a live suffragist.

The heiress of a large fortune derived from the Baltimore & Ohio, the oldest railroad in America, Miss Garrett had become a very practical businesswoman. She realized the responsibilities as well as the advantages of possessing a large fortune and administered her estate with considerable discretion. For instance, she offered a large endowment to Bryn Mawr in 1894 if her friend, Miss Thomas, was made president. Miss Thomas was made president. The medical department of Johns Hopkins University was similarly endowed on condition that it be made coeducational. It was made coeducational.

It was probably Susan's efforts on behalf of coeducation at Rochester University that first attracted Miss Garrett's attention. In 1901 Miss Garrett commissioned the same sculptor who had memorialized Francis W. Child for Harvard University to memorialize Susan B. Anthony for Bryn Mawr. The bronze medallion portrait was presented to Bryn Mawr with appropriate ceremonies in April 1902. Susan was guest of honor and addressed the students for half an hour. She had practically risen from a sickbed to be there, but as usual she rose like a phoenix and delivered one of her most impressive and inspiring talks. The visit cemented her friendship with Miss Garrett and Miss Thomas.

In due time an invitation to hold the convention of 1906 in Baltimore, the home city of Miss Thomas and Miss Garrett, came through. As we have seen, Susan resolved to accept it though she had to revise the constitution of her society to do so. That she did not hesitate shows the high regard she attached to her new Bryn Mawr friends. If nothing else came of it, the prestige of being sponsored by these ladies was worth all the trouble. But Susan was far too practical-minded not to speculate on the possibility of other results. She was not at all frightened by wealth—and certainly not by intelligence. When the two were combined in one person, as they were in the case of Miss Garrett, anything might come of it.

Just before the convention Susan was invited to Bryn Mawr to inspect some new buildings and to make plans for the convention program. Miss Garrett told her of her intention to open the Garrett residence in Baltimore—long closed and unused—for the entertainment of Susan and the other suffrage officers. Miss Thomas undertook the preparation of a college woman's evening to feature the women professors of the East. Between them they proposed to stir up the old conservative Southern city to its very depths in honor of the visiting suffragists. The elite of every class were to be called out. But nothing beyond the approaching convention was talked about.

Returning from Bryn Mawr to Miss Shaw's home at Mount Airy, Susan fainted dead away. She lay in bed in a prostrated condition for two weeks. Miss Shaw's alarm was such that Mary was sent for. Again Susan rallied, suddenly as usual, and traveled home safely in Mary's company. "Glad to be here," she wrote Mrs. Miller, "and glad to be in my own bed again. Home is the best place after all." By January she was deeply involved with Mrs. Fullam, her favorite dressmaker, in the construction of a new crepe-de-chine dress for the Baltimore convention.

❧ V   During January, Susan's diary shows her about and active as usual. She started her January accounts: "For rent No. 17—$25; Board Sister M. $20; to Carrie Bahl (housekeeping) $20." An unexpected call from Dr. Henry Anthony Baker (Aaron's "little Harry") cheered her greatly. She had her stenographer in and wrote twenty letters in one day.

The Rochester winter closed in, blasty and cold. Though the weather was cruel the Political Equality Club could not forgo its demonstration on Susan's eighty-sixth birthday. This was moved up to February 2 in order to precede the Baltimore convention. The worst blizzard of the season raged through the streets that day and night. The guest of honor was taken to the party, and brought home, in a closed carriage. But still the exposure was too much for her. She awoke the next morning with a severe cold. This was the day scheduled for her departure for the South. Not even one day had been allowed for rest and recuperation after the birthday party.

During the long train journey Susan developed excruciating neuralgic pains in her head and on arriving at Miss Garrett's home was immediately put to bed. The best medical and nursing talent of Johns Hopkins University was called in, but nothing availed to relieve the patient's suffering.

Anna Shaw sent little notes from the front assuring her that all was going well. "I miss you as a body must miss its soul when it has gone out," she wrote; "and I long every moment to look at you and see if I am doing as you wish me to. I am putting just as much of your spirit into everything as I am able and I am so glad to tell you that everything is going beautifully."

No convention was ever attended by larger or more enthusiastic audiences. The veteran suffragists, Julia Ward Howe and Clara Barton, were given places of honor on the platform where Susan usually sat. They spoke with an eloquence of diction and sentiment which she could scarcely have equaled had she been there, but they provided no substitute for the great personality that was missed.

On the evening designated as College Evening, planned by Miss Thomas as a special tribute "to Susan B. Anthony and what she has accomplished for the higher education of women," the invalid put in an unexpected appearance. By a superhuman effort she rose from her sickbed, got herself arrayed in the new crepe-de-chine, and propelled herself with aid to the stage of the theater. All at once, there she was, seated in plain view on the platform. Thinking she had recovered, the audience went wild with surprise and enthusiasm. She sat through the long speeches of the evening to the very last, which was Miss Thomas's. In concluding, Miss Thomas, turning directly to Susan, said:

"To most women it is given to have returned to them in double measure the love of the children they have nurtured. To you, Miss Anthony, belongs by right, as to no other woman in the world's history, the love and gratitude of all women in every country of the civilized globe. We, your daughters of the spirit, rise up today and call you blessed. . . . Of such as you were the lines of the poet Yeats written:

> "They shall be remembered forever,
> They shall be alive forever,
> They shall be speaking forever,
> The people shall hear them forever."

As Susan rose to reply, the entire audience rose automatically with her. She could manage but a few words: "If any proof were needed of the progress of the cause for which I have worked, it is here tonight. The presence on the stage of these college women, and in the audience of all these college girls, who will some day be the nation's greatest strength, tell their own story to the world. They give the highest joy and encouragement to me.—I am not going to make a long speech, but only say thank you and good-night."

Again in bed under the anxious care of doctors and nurses, she paid the penalty in suffering. But a day later, when money was being raised for the Oregon campaign, she suddenly appeared on the stage again and started the collection by donating the eighty-six gold dollars just given her by Rochester friends as a birthday offering. Then, when the last evening came, she learned that Julia Ward Howe, who was to have made the principal address, had succumbed to an attack of tonsillitis. Her feeling for the disappointed audience drove her once again to make a supreme effort. She stood for an ovation that lasted ten minutes and then sat through the rest of the program. She then arose for what was to be her last speech before any suffrage convention:

"This is a magnificent sight before me, and these have been wonderful addresses and speeches I have listened to during the past week. Yet I have looked on many such audiences, and in my life time I have listened to many such speakers, all testifying to the righteousness, the justice, and the worthiness of the cause of woman suffrage. I never saw that great woman, Mary Wollstonecraft, but I have read her eloquent and unanswerable arguments in behalf of the liberty of womankind. I have met and have known most of the progressive women who came after her—Lucretia Mott, the Grimké sisters, Elizabeth Cady Stanton, Lucy Stone—a long galaxy of great women. I have heard them speak, saying in only slightly different phrases exactly what I have heard these newer advocates of the cause say at these meetings. Those older women have gone on, and most of these who worked with me in the early years have gone on. I am here for a little time only and then my place will be filled as theirs was filled. The fight must not cease; you must see that it does not stop."

It was not until after Susan had gone through this succession of ordeals that she attained her secret hopes. As she lay an invalid in Miss Garrett's house, Miss Thomas and her hostess formally asked her what she wished them to do for woman suffrage. Between her neuralgic pains she managed to make clear to these friends that what she wished them to do was to take over her pledge to raise a standing fund.

To their lasting credit, Miss Thomas and Miss Garrett acted promptly. Calling a meeting of the Business Committee, they proposed to form a committee, with Miss Garrett as chairman and Miss Thomas as treasurer, to raise a standing fund of $60,000, to be paid into the suffrage treasury in installments of $12,000 a year. It was not a staggering sum, but compared with Susan's dream of $100,000 in ten years, $60,000 in five years was rather better. The guarantee that stood behind it placed it practically in the society's possession. That the fund would be raised by those who loved, honored, and cherished herself and the suffrage cause was the final touch in Susan's happiness. In spite of her pain she felt a peace and contentment she had not known for years.

⊷§ VI   With a trained nurse in attendance and her friends in constant watchfulness, Susan went on to Washington for another birthday celebration. She sat on the platform and listened while speeches and complimentary tributes from senators and congressmen were delivered. Finally, when a message from President Roosevelt was read, so different from his cold reception of her last appeal for suffrage, her boredom exceeded her pain. Rising in her place, she exclaimed to the audience, "When will men do something besides extend congratulations? I would rather have President Roosevelt say one word to Congress in favor of amending the Constitution to give women the suffrage than to praise me endlessly!" At this unexpected sniff from the old war horse the suffragists broke into loud and joyful applause. But the end of the program found Susan very tired. She essayed a few words of appreciation and ended with these faltering phrases: "There have been others also just as true and devoted to the cause—I wish I could name every one—but with such women consecrating their lives—failure is impossible."

Waiting in her hotel room that evening for the train that would take her to Rochester, she went to the window for a last look at the Washington Monument, aglow at the moment in the light of the setting sun. "I think it is the most beautiful monument in the world," she said to Anna Shaw. "I prefer that of Bunker Hill," replied Miss Shaw. "Oh, no," said Susan, "this is much grander. Everyone who sees it must feel the love of freedom and justice and want to be true to the principles it stands for."

She was forced to travel home as quickly as possible and by-pass a birthday celebration planned in New York. She sent a telegram: "The word of a woman of eighty-six can not be relied upon like that of a girl of sixteen." The celebration took place without her. Mrs. Catt presided, Anna Shaw spoke on Susan's behalf, and Edwin Markham, known as the Socialist poet, read a long poem composed for the occasion, dedicated to Susan and entitled *To the Divine Mother*. Susan could scarcely have sat through the seventeen stanzas had she been present, for as she often declared, she was completely tone-deaf to poetry.

⤳ VII   Resting in her own bed, she seemed at first to improve. The neuralgia vanished and the Johns Hopkins nurse departed, leaving her in the care of her sister and Carrie Bahl, her excellent housekeeper. But she was profoundly and fundamentally exhausted. No one seemed to suspect the real danger, which neither thermometer nor stethoscope could probe. She had just rolled from her shoulders an unbearably heavy but life-giving burden. There was no other burden of equal importance to take its place.

She developed pneumonia; both lungs became involved. Once again, with the aid of her doctor and nurses, she passed out of danger. The lungs almost miraculously cleared up. Then something else happened; she could no longer retain her food. It seemed as if she were rejecting life each time it was re-offered her. In the early stages of her illness she expressed the belief that she would not recover, and throughout her illness she spoke of death with objectivity and calmness.

When Susan had left Washington, Mrs. Harper sat down in her hotel room and began to prepare biographical articles. She had promised Susan at the time of Mrs. Stanton's death that she would do this for her when the time came. As the daily reports from Rochester reached her, she continued to race her pen. Before the day when Susan's body was laid to rest in Mount Hope she had five long obituary articles ready for the press—articles which no other newspaper hand could have done so well or so wholly to the satisfaction of her deceased friend. In thus taking time by the forelock she was more faithful to Susan's spirit and memory than she could have been in any other way.

On Anna Shaw devolved the greatest responsibility of the hour. She kept the tone of the Baltimore convention and the New York celebration on a cheerful level despite her own heart-sinking dread. She then went home and busied herself with preparations for the Oregon campaign, almost upon her. But on the morning of March 7, she relates, she suddenly felt she must go to her friend. "I awoke with a feeling that Miss Anthony wanted me," she says. Though her feeling was mixed with a fear "that she might not be permitted to see her," being Anna Shaw, she took the first train for Rochester.

Arriving at the house at nine o'clock, she was greeted by absolute silence. There was a note on the door requesting that no one ring the doorbell, a jangling old-fashioned piece fixed in the side panel. She walked around the house and through a window saw Mary sitting in her accustomed place, reading or as motionless as if she were reading. She opened the kitchen door silently and was standing in front of Mary when the latter looked up. "Oh, Anna Shaw," she said, "we have been wanting you all day. Early this morning sister Susan said she must see you and talk with you. She insisted so much that I should write you that I finally did so and about an hour ago mailed the letter."

From this time on Anna Shaw remained in the house. The doctor decreed that her visits with Susan should be limited to four or five a day and should last no longer than fifteen minutes. Susan talked as fast and steadily as she could during these visits. First of all, she wanted her will changed. She had previously directed, in a will made just before her last trip to Europe, that her estate should be divided among her sister Mary, her niece Lucy, and her friend Anna Shaw. But now that the standing fund had been instituted, she wished to bequeath her all to that fund. The change was immediately made by the former beneficiaries. Later Miss Thomas and Miss Garrett made themselves responsible for the whole fund, and Susan's bequest was added independently to the suffrage cause.

Susan then took up another matter close to her heart. The old rivalry about the presidency had come back to bother her. She knew, says Miss Shaw, that "it had been hard for me to accept the presidency of the association and I did it only at [her] earnest and oft-repeated solicitation. Fearing that after she had passed away I might give it up, she besought me over and over again to promise her that I would devote all the remaining years of my life to this one cause." Miss Shaw gave her promise. Neither Susan nor Miss Shaw realized that Mrs. Catt would probably never again, in Miss Shaw's lifetime, willingly accept the presidency from her. Mrs. Catt was still outwardly the same reticent woman that she had always been, but inwardly she had changed greatly.

Much of the time Susan's mind seemed to dwell on the far-off days of campaigning in the West. "These have been wonderful years," she said. "How many happy, happy times we have travelled about together! Day and night, in stage-coaches, or freight-trains, over the mountains and across the prairies, hungry and tired, we have wandered. The work was sometimes hard and discouraging, but those were happy and useful years." . . . "She never complained," adds Miss Shaw, "but once, when the consciousness of approaching death seemed strongly to impress itself upon her, she said, holding up her hand and measuring a little space on one finger, 'Just think of it, I have been striving for over sixty years for a little bit of justice no bigger than that, and yet I must die without obtaining it. Oh, it seems so cruel!' " It was true that the outlook for woman suffrage seemed to be at its lowest ebb at the time of Susan's death. Like some other prophets of history, she was doomed to close her eyes without seeing the promised land.

As long as Miss Shaw remained by her, Susan showed improvement day by day. On the fourth day Miss Shaw thought it might be safe for her to go home. Susan protested at first but finally agreed on condition that she should return within a few days. When Miss Shaw left her that day, Susan said, "I'll sleep while you are gone and then we'll have a good visit, doctor or no doctor." These rebellious words were her last to her friend, for when Miss Shaw returned she could no longer speak, from pain. Her heart, weakened by pneumonia, had added a last fatal complication. Before her friend's anguished eyes she sank from a state of unbearable suffering into a state of unconsciousness.

For the rest of that day and the next Anna Shaw sat or knelt by her side, holding her hand. Mary sat on the other side of the bed, silent, suffering, unmoving. Very possibly she had not believed until now that her sister, who had made so many miraculous recoveries, was really going to die. On Tuesday morning, March 13, 1906, at twenty minutes before one, Susan breathed her last.

Her death was recorded in the Rochester Quaker Register as follows: "13th 3rd mo. 1906. Susan Brownell Anthony died this morning in the 87th year of her age at her home 17 Madison Street at 12:40 o'clock. Pneumonia the cause."

⌒§ VIII In accordance with Quaker custom, the house bore no symbols of mourning. No blinds were drawn and the room where the casket stood was flooded with sunlight. No crape was hung on the front door, as was then customary, but a wreath of violets was affixed to the old doorbell.

Mr. Gannett's church, which Susan regularly attended, was considered too small for the funeral, and the largest church in the city, the Central Presbyterian, was chosen instead. It was entirely in keeping with the liberal spirit of one who had spoken in churches of every denomination throughout the land. From ten o'clock to half-past one the body lay in state in the Presbyterian church. A guard of honor, consisting of young women gowned in white and drawn from the university and the Political Equality Club, stood, four at a time, in attendance on the casket. A continuous procession of people filed past the bier, their garments whitened from the heavy snowfall which had replaced the sunshine of the day before.

The ministers of the Unitarian and Presbyterian churches conducted the ceremonies. Memorial addresses were made by Anna Shaw, by Mrs. Catt, and others. It was also Miss Shaw who, as an ordained minister, spoke the last word at the grave. (Susan had requested this.) "Dear friend," she said, "thou hast tarried with us long; thou hast now gone to thy well-earned rest. We beseech the Infinite Spirit who has upheld thee to make us worthy to follow in thy steps and carry on the work. Hail and farewell!" Nothing was said about ashes to ashes and dust to dust.

Of the memorial addresses delivered by Miss Shaw and Mrs. Catt, that of Mrs. Catt, surprisingly enough, contained the most tender and arresting words. Less expressive as a rule than Miss Shaw, she seemed endowed at the moment with an angelic simplicity:

"We mourn for her today and every heart aches that we must let her go. We admire, we revere, and we honor her because she was great, but we mourn her because we loved her. Who can tell why we love? There was something in her one may not describe which won our hearts as well as our devotion. Perhaps it was her simplicity, her forgetfulness of self, her thoughtfulness of others, which made us love her. We have not lost a leader alone, but a dear, dear friend, whose place can never be filled. We shall never see her like again."

It was dark when the funeral party left the cemetery. The snow had been falling all day and now covered the ground, casting a pale light on the streets to light the homeward-bound. Mary Anthony's house and home in Madison Street was blanketed with snow when she reached it. The perfect interior, so recently renewed and redecorated, was beautifully clean and warm, thanks to Carrie Bahl's devoted service. But it seemed barren and cold to Mary. When her friends left her, she was desolate. Susan's interests and activities had overcrowded the house, sometimes to the point of arousing resentment in Mary. Now all seemed idle and lifeless, like a clock which has run down. Susan's continuing illnesses had made her Mary's child and Mary was like a mother bereft.

Anna Shaw and Lucy Anthony decided it was best to take her

along on the Oregon trip. It was a hotly contested campaign, filled with high hopes, and in the end lost. The suffragists turned homeward with feelings of disappointment and sadness which only Susan of old had been able to alleviate. She would have had the next campaign in view before the echoes of the former had died out. Mary was deeply depressed. She wrote in her diary: "It will be a lonely home when I return to it in June. O, she seemed too beautiful to be put away forever."

Immediately after her return she felt obliged to call in the doctor. Rather wistfully she tried to take up life again, working on the current scrapbooks day after day. But, though no one seemed to know it, she was already ill. She had begun to decline during Susan's illness, having then become subject to attacks of vertigo. Her low condition after Susan's death was attributed to grief and strain. During the summer after her Oregon trip she lost strength more and more. Her devoted friend, Mrs. Gannett, kept close watch over her and in January her niece, Lucy Anthony, came to stay with her. She died without great suffering, almost without a specific malady, February 5, 1907, less than a year after Susan's death.

Her loneliness must have been intense. In her last days she indulged herself in a pathetic fantasy of companionship. She begged Anna Shaw and Lucy to promise her that they would be buried in Mount Hope beside herself and Susan. They promised. The vision of a reunion after death seemed to comfort her.

Following her sister's example, Mary left practically all that she owned to suffrage. Susan's total estate amounted to about forty-five hundred dollars. This represented the entire fortune of Susan B. Anthony at the end of a long lifetime of unceasing labor. Like all of the money that she had ever possessed, this sum also went to woman suffrage. Mary Anthony, a comparatively obscure person, died a considerably richer woman than her sister. In addition to her house, which was sold for sixty-five hundred dollars, her personal assets, derived from thirty years of schoolteaching, amounted to thirteen thousand dollars. Of this, she left ten thousand dollars to be divided personally between Anna Shaw and Lucy Anthony, as an expression, she said, "of my appreciation of the devotion to the cause of woman suffrage on the part of these two women." Everything else was set aside as a suffrage fund to be used for local, state, and national work as the need arose. Between them, Susan and Mary bequeathed to suffrage the sum of twenty-four thousand dollars amassed by a lifetime of constant labor, ceaseless saving, and habitual self-denial. Compared with the gifts being made to suffrage at the time, it was a considerable endowment. And no one, before them or after them, ever gave out of so much self-sacrifice.

Standing in a room of the house where Susan had lived for forty years, the writer heard, in the compassionate voice of the woman guide, these words spoken beside her: "I don't know *how* she lived! I don't know *how* she lived!" It was her tribute to Susan's shoestring heroism, to the ineffable grace of an immortal ideal which sustained her without faltering through a long, hard pilgrimage. She was fed and clothed by the gift of faith. Better than any words can express it, her life expresses the power of faith as a practical endowment. She knew its potent secret and pure energy. She never attached it to the world beyond, for which most people of her generation reserved it. A woman of action, aggressive in many ways, she harnessed its powers to the things she thought good for this world. In her long battle for humanity it was her chief weapon. The outward and visible victories of her long crusade came from the same inner light which fed and clothed her.

BIBLIOGRAPHY

BOOKS and PAMPHLETS

Anthony, Charles L. *Genealogy of the Anthony Family; from 1495 to 1904.* Sterling, Ill.: Published by the author, 1904.

Anthony, Susan B. *An Account of the Proceedings of the Trial of Susan B. Anthony on the Charge of Illegal Voting at the Presidential Election in November, 1872.* Rochester: Daily Democrat and Chronicle Press, 1874. Pamphlet.

Anthony, Susan B., and Harper, Ida Husted. *The History of Woman Suffrage.* Vol. IV, 1883–1900. Rochester: Susan B. Anthony, 1902.

Anthony, Miss Susanna (collateral kinswoman of Susan B.). *Extracts from Her Writings and Brief Observations on Them.* Compiled and edited by Samuel Hopkins, D.D. Worcester, Mass.: Leonard, 1796.

Beard, Charles A. and Mary R. *The Rise of American Civilization.* New York: The Macmillan Company, 1939.

Biddle, Gertrude B., and Lowrie, Sarah (editors). *Notable Women of Pennsylvania.* (Article on Deborah Moulson.) Philadelphia: University of Pennsylvania Press, 1942.

Blackwell, Alice Stone. *Lucy Stone: Pioneer of Woman's Rights.* Boston: Little, Brown and Company, 1930.

Blackwell, Sarah Ellen. *A Military Genius: Life of Anna Ella Carroll, of Maryland.* Washington, D.C.: Judd and Detweiler, Printers, 1891.

Booth, Mary L. *History of the City of New York.* Illustrated by T. A. Emmet, M.D. New York: W. R. C. Clark, 1867.

Branch, E. Douglas. "The Lily and the Bloomer." In *The Colophon,* Part 12. New York: The Colophon, Ltd., 1932.

Brockett, L. P., and Vaughan, Mary C. *Woman's Work in the Civil War: With an Introduction by Henry W. Bellows, D.D., President U. S. Sanitary Commission.* Boston: R. H. Curran, 1867.

Bryan, Florence Horn. *Susan B. Anthony: Champion of Women's Rights.* New York: Julian Messner, Inc., 1947.

Bush, Harry. *History of Canajoharie, N.Y.* Canajoharie Library. Pamphlet.

Carmer, Carl. *Dark Trees to the Wind: A Cycle of New York Years.* New York: William Sloane Associates, 1949.

————. *Listen for a Lonesome Drum: A New York State Chronicle.* New York: William Sloane Associates, 1950.

Chester, Giraud. *Embattled Maiden: The Life of Anna Dickinson.* New York: G. P. Putnam's Sons, 1951.

Clemens, Samuel L. (Mark Twain), and Warner, Charles Dudley. *The Gilded Age: A Tale of To-day.* New York: Harper and Brothers, 1874.

Clemens, Samuel L. (Mark Twain). *The Love Letters of Mark Twain.* Edited, with an Introduction by Dixon Wecter. New York: Harper and Brothers, 1949.

Congress of Women. Held in the Woman's Building World's Columbian Exposition, Chicago, U.S.A., 1893. Published by the Board of Lady Managers. Edited by Mary K. O. Eagle. 1894.

Dartmouth, Mass. Vital Records to the year 1850. 2 vols. Boston: The New England Genealogical Society, Eddy Town Record Fund, 1929.

Dickinson, A. D., Kelley, Hon. Wm. D., and Douglass, Frederick. *Addresses at Mass Meeting, July 6, 1863, for the Promotion of Colored Enlistments.* Philadelphia. Pamphlet.

Dictionary of American Biography.

Dorr, Rheta Childe. *Susan B. Anthony: The Woman Who Changed the Mind of a Nation.* New York: Frederick A. Stokes Company, 1928.

Earhart, Mary. *Frances Willard: From Prayers to Politics.* Chicago: The University of Chicago Press, 1944.

Eddy, Sherwood, and Page, Kirby. *Makers of Freedom: Biographical Sketches in Social Progress* (chapter on Susan B. Anthony). New York: George H. Doran, 1926.

Ellet, Elizabeth L. *Domestic History of the American Revolution.* New York: Baker and Scribner, 1850.

Eminent Women of the Age: being Narratives of the Lives and Deeds of the Most Prominent Women of the Present Generation. By James Parton, Horace Greeley, et al. (article on Susan B. Anthony by E. C. Stanton). Hartford, Conn.: S. M. Betts and Company, 1868.

Finch, Edith. *Carey Thomas of Bryn Mawr.* New York: Harper and Brothers, 1947.

Foreman, Edward R. (editor). *Centennial History of Rochester, N.Y.* Rochester Public Library Publications, vol. III, 1933. Pamphlet.

Garrison, W. P. and F. J. *William Lloyd Garrison. 1805–1879. The Story of His Life Told by His Children.* 4 vols. Boston: Houghton Mifflin Company, 1894.

Genesee Country Scrapbook. Rochester: Rochester Historical Society, 1953. Pamphlet.

Gilbertson, Catherine. *Harriet Beecher Stowe.* New York: D. Appleton-Century Company, 1937.

Ginger, Ray. *The Bending Cross: A Biography of Eugene Victor Debs.* New Brunswick: Rutgers University Press, 1949.

Hale, William Harlan. *Horace Greeley: Voice of the People.* New York: Harper and Brothers, 1950.

Harper, Ida Husted. *The Life and Work of Susan B. Anthony: A Story of the Evolution in the Status of Woman.* 3 vols. Indianapolis: The Bowen-Merrill Company, 1898; Indianapolis: The Hollenbeck Press, 1908.

Hawthorne, Nathaniel. *The American Note-Books.* Based on the original manuscripts and edited by Randall Stewart. New Haven: Yale University Press, 1932.

Henry, Alice. *The Trade Union Woman.* New York: D. Appleton and Company, 1915.

Hibben, Paxton. *Henry Ward Beecher: An American Portrait.* New York: George H. Doran, 1927.

Higginson, Thomas Wentworth. *Common Sense about Women.* London: Swan Sonnenschein and Company, 1891.

Howe, Julia Ward. *Reminiscences. 1819–1899.* Boston: Houghton Mifflin Company, 1899.

Howe, M. A. De Wolfe. *Causes and Their Champions.* Boston: Little, Brown and Company, 1926.

Hudnut, James M. *Semi-Centennial History of the New York Life Insurance Company. 1845–1895.* New York: The New York Life Insurance Company, 1895.

Janney, Samuel M. *History of the Religious Society of Friends, from Its Rise to the Year 1828.* 4 vols. Philadelphia: T. Ellwood Zell, 1867.

Johnson, Oliver. *William Lloyd Garrison and His Times.* Boston: Houghton Mifflin Company, 1881.

Jones, Rufus, assisted by Isaac Sharpless and Amelia M. Gummere. *The Quakers in the American Colonies*. London: The Macmillan Company, Ltd., 1911.

Josephson, Hannah. *The Golden Threads: New England's Mill Girls and Magnates*. New York: Duell, Sloan and Pearce, 1949.

Josephson, Matthew. *The Robber Barons: The Great American Capitalists. 1861–1901*. New York: Harcourt, Brace and Company, 1934.

Livermore, Mary A. *My Story of the War: Four Years' Personal Experience in the Sanitary Service of the Rebellion*. Hartford, Conn.: A. D. Worthington and Company, 1888.

Lutz, Alma. *Created Equal: A Biography of Elizabeth Cady Stanton. 1815–1902*. New York: John Day Company, 1940.

Markham, Edwin. *To the Divine Mother*. Written for Susan B. Anthony's 86th birthday. Included in *Gates of Paradise*. New York: Doubleday, Page and Company, 1920.

McKelvey, Blake. *Susan B. Anthony*. Rochester Public Library Publications, April 1945. Pamphlet.

Mearns, David C. *The Lincoln Papers. Selections to July 4, 1861*. 2 vols. New York: Doubleday and Company, 1948.

Millay, Edna St. Vincent. *The Pioneer: Sonnet on the Unveiling of a Statue to Lucretia Mott, Susan B. Anthony, and Elizabeth Cady Stanton*. Included in *The Buck in the Snow and Other Poems*. New York: Harper and Brothers, 1928.

Pankhurst, Emmeline. *My Own Story*. New York: Hearst's International Library Company, 1914.

Pankhurst, E. Sylvia. *The Life of Emmeline Pankhurst*. Boston: Houghton Mifflin Company, 1936.

Parrington, Vernon Louis. *Main Currents in American Thought. An Interpretation of American Literature from the Beginning to 1920*. 3 vols. New York: Harcourt, Brace and Company, 1930.

Pease, Rev. C. S. *History of Cheshire, Mass.: Stafford Hill Settlement*. Pamphlet.

Peck, Mary Gray. *Carrie Chapman Catt: A Biography*. New York: H. W. Wilson Company, 1944.

Phillips, Wendell. *Speeches, Lectures, and Letters*. Boston: James Redpath, 1863.

Powderly, Terence. *The Path I Trod: Autobiography*. Edited by H. J. Carman, Henry Davis, P. N. Guthrie. New York: Columbia University Press, 1940.

Report of the International Council of Women. Assembled by the

National Woman Suffrage Ass'n, 1888. Washington, D.C.: Rufus H. Darby, Printer, 1888.

Reynolds, Helen Wilkinson. *Nine Partners Patent, Nine Partners Meeting, and Nine Partners School.* Dutchess County Historical Society Year Book. Vol. 20. Poughkeepsie, N.Y., 1835.

Riegel, Robert E. *Young America: 1830–1840.* Norman, Okla.: University of Oklahoma Press, 1949.

Rochester Historical Society Publications. *Quakers in Rochester and Monroe County,* by B. John Cox, Jr., and *Antislavery Days in Rochester,* by Percy E. Clapp. Vol. XIV, 1936. Pamphlet.

Ross, Ishbel. *Child of Destiny: The Life Story of the First Woman Doctor.* New York: Harper and Brothers, 1949.

Ross, Nancy Wilson. *Westward the Women.* New York: Alfred A. Knopf, 1944.

Rourke, Constance Mayfield. *Trumpets of Jubilee.* New York: Harcourt, Brace and Company, 1927.

Sachs, Emanie. *"The Terrible Siren": Victoria Woodhull (1838–1927).* New York: Harper and Brothers, 1928.

Schlesinger, Arthur M., Jr. *The Age of Jackson.* Boston: Little, Brown and Company, 1946.

Sears, Lorenzo. *Wendell Phillips: Orator and Agitator.* New York: Doubleday, Page and Company, 1909.

Seitz, Don C. *Uncommon Americans.* (Chapters on Susan B. Anthony and George Francis Train.) Indianapolis: Bobbs-Merrill Company, 1905.

Shaw, Anna Howard, with the collaboration of Elizabeth Jordan. *The Story of a Pioneer.* New York: Harper and Brothers, 1915.

Stanton, Elizabeth Cady, Anthony, Susan B., and Gage, Matilda Joslyn. *History of Woman Suffrage.* 3 vols. 1848–85. Rochester: Susan B. Anthony, 1889.

Stanton, Henry B. *Random Recollections.* New York: Harper and Brothers, 1887.

Stanton, Theodore, and Blatch, Harriot Stanton (editors). *Elizabeth Cady Stanton as Revealed in her Letters, Diary, and Reminiscences.* New York: Harper and Brothers, 1922.

Stein, Gertrude, and Thomson, Virgil. *The Mother of Us All: A Pageant.* New York: Music Press, Inc., 1947.

Stowe, Harriet Beecher (under pseud. Christopher Crowfield). *House and Home Papers.* Boston: Ticknor and Fields, 1865.

Thornton, Willis. *The Nine Lives of Citizen Train.* New York: Greenberg, 1948.

Train, George Francis. *The Great Epigram Campaign* of Kansas. Leavenworth, 1867. Pamphlet.

Whittier, John Greenleaf. *Leaves from Margaret Smith's Journal in the Province of Massachusetts Bay. 1678–9.* Boston: Ticknor, Reed and Fields, 1849.

Wood, James. *The Purchase Meeting.* Quaker Hill Series, No. XIV. New York: Quaker Hill Conference Ass'n, 1905. Pamphlet.

Woolf, Virginia. *A Room of One's Own.* New York: Harcourt, Brace and Company, 1929.

————. *Three Guineas.* New York: Harcourt, Brace and Company, 1938.

Young, James Harvey. "Anna E. Dickinson and the Civil War: For and Against Lincoln." In the *Mississippi Valley Historical Review,* June 1944.

MANUSCRIPT SOURCES

Ann Anthony Bacon Papers: Including Susan B. Anthony's diaries, personal reminiscences, letters, and speeches.

Library of Congress Manuscript Division: Susan B. Anthony Papers.
"   "   "   "   "   Anna E. Dickinson Papers.
"   "   "   "   "   Elizabeth Cady Stanton Papers.

Library of Congress Rare Book Room: Susan B. Anthony Scrap Books. 1838–1900.

Morgan Library: Rev. John Pierpont Morgan Papers. Collected 1907.

New York Public Library Manuscript Room: Susan B. Anthony Papers.
"   "   "   "   "   "   Horace Greeley Papers.
"   "   "   "   "   "   Elizabeth Smith Miller Papers.
"   "   "   "   "   "   Elizabeth Oakes Smith Papers.
"   "   "   "   "   "   Gerrit Smith Papers.
"   "   "   "   "   "   Elizabeth Cady Stanton Papers.
"   "   "   "   "   "   Robert Brewster Stanton Papers.
"   "   "   "   "   "   George Francis Train Papers.

Society of Friends: East Hoosac Monthly Meeting Records. Adams, Mass.

Society of Friends: Easton (N.Y.) Monthly Meeting Records. Greenwich, N.Y.

"   "   "   Genesee Yearly Meeting and Rochester Monthly Meeting Records, 1825–1915. Society of Friends, Records Committee, New York City.

Susan B. Anthony Memorial Collection. Los Angeles, Cal., Public Library (to be transferred to the Huntington Library, San Marino, Cal.).

Susan B. Anthony Memorial Collection. Susan B. Anthony Memorial House, 17 Madison Street, Rochester, N.Y.

JOURNALS

The *Agitator.* Owned and edited by Mary A. Livermore. 1869– Merged with the *Woman's Journal,* 1869.

The *Lily.* Devoted to the interests of women. Owned and edited by Amelia J. Bloomer. Seneca Falls, N.Y., 1849–54.

The *Revolution.* Edited by E. C. Stanton and Parker Pillsbury. Owned and published by S. B. Anthony. New York City, 1868–71.

The *Una.* A Paper Devoted to the Elevation of Woman. Owned and edited by Paulina Wright Davis. Providence, R.I., 1853– .

The *Woman's Journal.* Edited by M. A. Livermore, J. W. Howe, and Lucy Stone; later by A. S. Blackwell and H. B. Blackwell. Boston, 1869–1917. Merged with the *Woman Citizen,* 1917.

The *Woman's Tribune.* Owned and edited by Clara B. Colby. Beatrice, Neb., and Washington, D.C., 1890–1909.

INDEX